THE PAPERS OF
THOMAS JEFFERSON

BARBARA B. OBERG
GENERAL EDITOR

THE PAPERS OF
Thomas Jefferson

Volume 28
1 January 1794 to 29 February 1796

JOHN CATANZARITI, EDITOR

EUGENE R. SHERIDAN, SENIOR ASSOCIATE EDITOR

J. JEFFERSON LOONEY, JAMES P. McCLURE, AND
ELAINE WEBER PASCU, ASSOCIATE EDITORS

LINDA MONACO, EDITORIAL ASSISTANT

JOHN E. LITTLE, RESEARCH ASSOCIATE

PRINCETON AND OXFORD

PRINCETON UNIVERSITY PRESS

2000

Copyright © 2000 by Princeton University Press

Published by Princeton University Press, 41 William Street,

Princeton, New Jersey 08540

IN THE UNITED KINGDOM:

Princeton University Press, 3 Market Place,

Woodstock, Oxfordshire OX20 1SY

Library of Congress Cataloging-in-Publication

ISBN 0-691-04780-4

This book has been composed in Monticello

Princeton University Press books are printed on
acid-free paper and meet the guidelines for permanence
and durability of the Committee on Production
Guidelines for Book Longevity of the
Council on Library Resources

Printed in the United States of America

As INDICATED in the first volume, this edition was made possible by a grant of $200,000 from The New York Times Company to Princeton University. Since this initial subvention, its continuance has been assured by additional contributions from The New York Times Company and The New York Times Company Foundation; by grants of the Ford Foundation, the National Historical Publications and Records Commission, and the National Endowment for the Humanities; by grants of the Andrew W. Mellon Foundation, the Packard Humanities Institute, the Pew Charitable Trusts, the John Ben Snow Memorial Trust, and the L. J. Skaggs and Mary C. Skaggs Foundation to Founding Fathers Papers, Inc.; by benefactions from the Barkley Fund and the Lyn and Norman Lear Foundation through the National Trust for the Humanities, the Florence Gould Foundation, the Charlotte Palmer Phillips Foundation, Time Inc., the Dyson Foundation, and the Lucius N. Littauer Foundation; and by gifts from Robert C. Baron, James Russell Wiggins, David K. E. Bruce, and B. Batmanghelidj. In common with other editions of historical documents, THE PAPERS OF THOMAS JEFFERSON is a beneficiary of the good offices of the National Historical Publications and Records Commission, tendered in many useful forms through its officers and dedicated staff. For these and other indispensable aids generously given by librarians, archivists, scholars, and collectors of manuscripts, the Editors record their sincere gratitude.

FOREWORD

O^N 1 January 1794 President Washington accepted Thomas Jefferson's resignation as Secretary of State and Jefferson left Philadelphia to retire to private life at Monticello. His correspondence often reveals his desire to be free of public responsibilities and live the life of a farmer, spending his time tending to his estates. Turning his attention to the improvement of his farms and finances, Jefferson surveyed his fields, experimented with crop rotation, and established a nailery on Mulberry Row. He embarked upon an ambitious plan to renovate Monticello, a long-term task that would eventually transform his residence. Like many Virginia planters he had lingering debts from the tobacco trade, and he also faced lawsuits by British firms against his father-in-law's estate. While he tried to put Monticello on a sounder financial basis, to obtain ready cash he began to draw on the funds of William Short, whose business affairs he was handling in Short's absence.

Although Jefferson was distant from Philadelphia, the seat of the federal government, he was not as removed from the politics of the day as his expressions of disinterestedness might indicate. His friends, especially James Madison, with whom he exchanged almost sixty letters in the period covered by this volume, kept him fully informed about the efforts of Republicans in the press, Congress, the Virginia General Assembly, and county and town meetings to counter Federalist policies. Jefferson was well aware of the activities of an emerging Republican opposition that congealed in response to the Jay Treaty in 1795, and he was keenly interested in its progress. Although in June 1795 he claimed to have "proscribed newspapers" from Monticello, in fact he never entirely cut himself off from the world. At the end of that year he took pains to ensure that he would have two full sets of Benjamin Franklin Bache's *Aurora*, the influential Republican newspaper, one set to be held in Philadelphia for binding and one to be sent directly to Monticello.

Volume 28 reflects the efforts and talents of a number of people. We take this occasion to express our thanks to them and to record the changes that have taken place in the editorial staff since the publication of Volume 27.

It is with great sadness that we report the tragic death of Eugene R. Sheridan in an automobile accident on May 4, 1996. An outstanding historian of colonial and revolutionary America and a fine editor, Gene Sheridan was a thoughtful and productive scholar whose presence in the field will be missed. He authored several works in New Jersey

history, edited *The Papers of Lewis Morris, 1698-1746*, and partici-
pated in the editing of eleven volumes of the *Letters of Delegates to Congress, 1774-1789*. He joined the Jefferson Papers in 1981 and his name
appears on the title page of Volumes 21-24 as an Associate Editor and
of Volumes 25-28 as the project's Senior Associate Editor. He also left
his mark on the Second Series of *The Papers of Thomas Jefferson*, con-
tributing the historical introduction to *Jefferson's Extracts from the Gospels* (1983). The knowledge and wisdom that Gene Sheridan brought
to his editing of Jefferson's papers will be remembered by readers of
these volumes for many years to come.

J. Jefferson Looney, whose name has appeared on the title page of
five volumes previous to this one, left the project on 1 November 1996
to edit the *Dictionary of Virginia Biography*. We now welcome him back
into the Jefferson fold as the Editor of the retirement years of Jefferson's
correspondence, which is sponsored by the Thomas Jefferson Memorial Foundation and will be published by the Princeton University Press
as a part of *The Papers of Thomas Jefferson*.

John Catanzariti came to the *The Papers of Thomas Jefferson* in
1987. Five volumes bear his name as Editor, but they are only the beginning and most visible manifestation of his strong and lasting imprint
on the edition. In the Foreword to Volume 24 he reaffirmed with conviction and eloquence the editorial principles and standards set forth in
Julian P. Boyd's inaugural volume of this series. Volumes 24-28 stand
as splendid testimony to John Catanzariti's adherence to these principles. Under his strong and energetic leadership the staff has been rebuilt, the foundations for Jefferson's Vice Presidency set in place, and
the groundwork for the Presidential years begun. The Jefferson edition
will long be in his debt, and those of us who now inhabit the offices in
Firestone Library are ever mindful of his legacy. We offer our apprecia-
tion, honor, and affection.

BARBARA OBERG

1 October 1999

ACKNOWLEDGMENTS

IT IS the Editors' pleasant duty to record their gratitude to the many individuals who have assisted them in numerous ways as they prepared this volume for the press. Stuart Leibiger helped in its preparation and Stephanie Longo contributed greatly to the transcription of documents and entering of editorial corrections. Those who answered research queries or helped in other ways are Alfred L. Bush, Charles C. Gillispie, Anthony T. Grafton, Harold James, William C. Jordan, Princeton University; Karin A. Trainer, University Librarian, Mary George, Sooni K. Johnson, Rosemary Little, and Susanne McNatt of Firestone Library at Princeton University; Timothy Connelly, J. Dane Hartgrove, Michael T. Meier of the National Historical Publications and Records Commission; James H. Hutson and his staff at the Manuscript Division, especially Fred Bauman, Jeffrey Flannery, Gerard W. Gawalt, and Mary Wolfskill, and Rosemary Plakas of the Rare Book and Special Collections Division, the Library of Congress; Peter Drummey, Brenda M. Lawson, Virginia H. Smith, and the staff of the Massachusetts Historical Society; Zanne MacDonald, Lucia C. Stanton, Douglas L. Wilson, and Gaye Wilson of the Thomas Jefferson Memorial Foundation at Monticello; Michael Plunkett of the Special Collections Department and Pauline Page of the Copy Center at the University of Virginia Library; Scott M. Brown of Belle Grove Plantation, Middletown, Virginia; John S. Hopewell, Robert L. Scribner, and Minor T. Weisiger of the Library of Virginia; E. Lee Shepard of the Virginia Historical Society; Phillip S. Lapsansky of the Library Company of Philadelphia; Roy Goodman and Elizabeth Carroll-Horrocks at the American Philosophical Society; Paul Romaine of the Gilder Lehrman Collection; Margaret Heilbrun, Richard Fraser, and Megan M. Hahn of the New-York Historical Society; Melissa Malnati of the Bridgeman Art Library, New York; James R. Fleming of Colby College; David Shields of The Citadel; Chuck Hill of the Missouri Historical Society; James O. Sorrell of the North Carolina Department of Archives and History; Catherine Barnes of Philadelphia; our fellow editors of the Adams Papers at the Massachusetts Historical Society, the Papers of George Washington and the Papers of James Madison at the University of Virginia, the Papers of Benjamin Franklin at Yale University, the Papers of Robert Morris at Queens College of the City University of New York, the Papers of John Marshall at the College of William and Mary, and the Documentary History of the Supreme Court. To these and other colleagues the Editors tender their cordial thanks.

GUIDE TO EDITORIAL APPARATUS

1. TEXTUAL DEVICES

The following devices are employed throughout the work to clarify the presentation of the text.

[. . .], [. . . .]   One or two words missing and not conjecturable.

[. . .]¹, [. . . .]¹   More than two words missing and not conjecturable; subjoined footnote estimates number of words missing.

[   ]   Number or part of a number missing or illegible.

[roman]   Conjectural reading for missing or illegible matter. A question mark follows when the reading is doubtful.

[*italic*]   Editorial comment inserted in the text.

⟨*italic*⟩   Matter deleted in the MS but restored in our text.

2. DESCRIPTIVE SYMBOLS

The following symbols are employed throughout the work to describe the various kinds of manuscript originals. When a series of versions is recorded, *the first to be recorded is the version used for the printed text.*

Dft   draft (usually a composition or rough draft; later drafts, when identifiable as such, are designated "2d Dft," &c.)

Dupl   duplicate

MS   manuscript (arbitrarily applied to most documents other than letters)

N   note, notes (memoranda, fragments, &c.)

PoC   polygraph copy

PrC   press copy

RC   recipient's copy

SC   stylograph copy

Tripl   triplicate

All manuscripts of the above types are assumed to be in the hand of the author of the document to which the descriptive symbol pertains. If not, that fact is stated. On the other hand, the following types of manuscripts are assumed *not* to be in the hand of the author, and exceptions will be noted:

[xi]

FC   file copy (applied to all contemporary copies retained by the author or his agents)

Lb   letterbook (ordinarily used with FC and Tr to denote texts copied into bound volumes)

Tr   transcript (applied to all contemporary and later copies except file copies; period of transcription, unless clear by implication, will be given when known)

3. LOCATION SYMBOLS

The locations of documents printed in this edition from originals in private hands and from printed sources are recorded in self-explanatory form in the descriptive note following each document. The locations of documents printed from originals held by public and private institutions in the United States are recorded by means of the symbols used in the National Union Catalog in the Library of Congress; an explanation of how these symbols are formed is given in Vol. 1: xl. The symbols DLC and MHi by themselves stand for the collections of Jefferson Papers proper in these repositories; when texts are drawn from other collections held by these two institutions, the names of those collections will be added. Location symbols for documents held by institutions outside the United States are given in a subjoined list. The lists of symbols are limited to the institutions represented by documents printed or referred to in this volume.

CSmH	The Huntington Library, San Marino, California
CtHi	Connecticut Historical Society, Hartford
CtY	Yale University Library
DLC	Library of Congress
DNA	The National Archives, with identifications of series (preceded by record group number) as follows:

	CD	Consular Dispatches
	DCI	Diplomatic and Consular Instructions
	DCLB	District of Columbia Letter Book
	DL	Domestic Letters
	LPG	Letters sent by the Postmaster General
	MLR	Miscellaneous Letters Received
	NL	Notes from Legations

DNAL	National Agricultural Library, Beltsville, Maryland
GEpFAR	Federal Archives and Records Center, Atlanta Region, East Point, Georgia
ICN	Newberry Library, Chicago
ICU	University of Chicago Library
MHi	Massachusetts Historical Society, Boston

MdAN	United States Naval Academy Library, Annapolis, Maryland
Me	Maine State Archives, Augusta
MiU-C	William L. Clements Library, University of Michigan, Ann Arbor
MoSHi	Missouri Historical Society, St. Louis
N	New York State Library, Albany
NHi	New-York Historical Society, New York City
NN	New York Public Library
NNC	Columbia University Library
NNGr	Grolier Club, New York City
NNPM	Pierpont Morgan Library, New York City
Nc-Ar	North Carolina State Department of Archives and History, Raleigh
NhD	Dartmouth College Library, Hanover, New Hampshire
NjGbS	Glassboro State College, New Jersey
NjMoHP	Morristown National Historical Park, New Jersey
NjP	Princeton University Library
PHC	Haverford College Library, Pennsylvania
PHi	Historical Society of Pennsylvania, Philadelphia
PP	Free Library of Philadelphia
PPAmP	American Philosophical Society, Philadelphia
PPL	Library Company of Philadelphia
PWacD	David Library of the American Revolution, Washington Crossing, Pennsylvania
ScHi	South Carolina Historical Society, Charleston
Vi	Library of Virginia, Richmond, with identification of series as follows:
	USCC United States Circuit Court
ViHi	Virginia Historical Society, Richmond
ViU	University of Virginia Library, Charlottesville
ViW	College of William and Mary Library, Williamsburg, Virginia

The following symbols represent repositories located outside of the United States:

BPUG	Bibliothèque Publique et Universitaire de Genève, Switzerland
PRO	Public Record Office, London, with identification of series as follows:
	T Treasury
RuS	Russian National Library, St. Petersburg, Russia

4. OTHER SYMBOLS AND ABBREVIATIONS

The following symbols and abbreviations are commonly employed in the annotation throughout the work.

Second Series   The topical series to be published as part of this edition, comprising those materials which are best suited to a topical rather than a chronological arrangement (see Vol. 1: xv-xvi)

TJ   Thomas Jefferson

TJ Editorial Files   Photoduplicates and other editorial materials in the office of *The Papers of Thomas Jefferson*, Princeton University Library

TJ Papers   Jefferson Papers (applied to a collection of manuscripts when the precise location of an undated, misdated, or otherwise problematic document must be furnished, and always preceded by the symbol for the institutional repository; thus "DLC: TJ Papers, 4: 628-9" represents a document in the Library of Congress, Jefferson Papers, volume 4, pages 628 and 629. Citations to volumes and folio numbers of the Jefferson Papers at the Library of Congress refer to the collection as it was arranged at the time the first microfilm edition was made in 1944-45. Access to the microfilm edition of the collection as it was rearranged under the Library's Presidential Papers Program is provided by the *Index to the Thomas Jefferson Papers* [Washington, D.C., 1976])

RG   Record Group (used in designating the location of documents in the National Archives)

SJL   Jefferson's "Summary Journal of Letters" written and received for the period 11 Nov. 1783 to 25 June 1826 (in DLC: TJ Papers). This register, kept in Jefferson's hand, has been checked against the TJ Editorial Files. It is to be assumed that all outgoing letters are recorded in SJL unless there is a note to the contrary. When the date of receipt of an incoming letter is recorded in SJL, it is incorporated in the notes. Information and discrepancies revealed in SJL but not found in the letter itself are also noted. Missing letters recorded in SJL are, where possible, accounted for in the notes to documents mentioning them or in related documents. A more detailed discussion of this register and its use in this edition appears in Vol. 6: vii-x

SJPL   "Summary Journal of Public Letters," an incomplete list of letters and documents written by TJ from 16 Apr. 1784 to 31 Dec. 1793, with brief summaries, in an amanuensis's hand. This is supplemented by six pages in TJ's hand, compiled at a later date, listing private and confidential memorandums and notes as well as official reports and communications by and to him as Secretary of State, 11 Oct. 1789 to 31 Dec. 1793 (in DLC: TJ Papers, Epistolary Record, 514-59 and 209-11, respectively; see Vol. 22: ix-x). Since nearly all documents in the amanuensis's list are registered in SJL, while few in TJ's list are so recorded, it is to be assumed that all references to SJPL are to the list in TJ's hand unless there is a statement to the contrary

V   Ecu

ƒ   Florin

£   Pound sterling or livre, depending upon context (in doubtful cases, a clarifying note will be given)

s   Shilling or sou (also expressed as /)

d   Penny or denier

ₜₜ   Livre Tournois

℞   Per (occasionally used for pro, pre)

5. SHORT TITLES

The following list includes only those short titles of works cited frequently, and therefore in very abbreviated form, throughout this edition. Since it is impossible to anticipate all the works to be cited in very abbreviated form, the list is appropriately revised from volume to volume.

Adams, *Diary*   L. H. Butterfield and others, eds., *Diary and Autobiography of John Adams*, Cambridge, Mass., 1961, 4 vols.

Adams, *Works*   Charles Francis Adams, ed., *The Works of John Adams*, Boston, 1850-56, 10 vols.

Ammon, *Monroe*   Harry Ammon, *James Monroe: The Quest for National Identity*, New York, 1971

Annals   *Annals of the Congress of the United States: The Debates and Proceedings in the Congress of the United States . . . Compiled from Authentic Materials*, Washington, D.C., Gales & Seaton, 1834-56, 42 vols. All editions are undependable and pagination varies from one printing to another. The first two volumes of the set cited here have "Compiled . . . by Joseph Gales, Senior" on the title page and bear the caption "Gales & Seatons History" on verso and "of Debates in Congress" on recto pages. The remaining volumes bear the caption "History of Congress" on both recto and verso pages. Those using the first two volumes with the latter caption will need to employ the date of the debate or the indexes of debates and speakers.

APS   American Philosophical Society

Archives Parlementaires   *Archives Parlementaires de 1787 à 1860: Recueil Complet des Débats Législatifs & Politiques des Chambres Françaises*, Paris, 1862- , 222 vols.

ASP   *American State Papers: Documents, Legislative and Executive, of the Congress of the United States*, Washington, D.C., Gales & Seaton, 1832-61, 38 vols.

Bear, *Family Letters*   Edwin M. Betts and James A. Bear, Jr., eds., *Family Letters of Thomas Jefferson*, Columbia, Mo., 1966

Bemis, *Pinckney's Treaty*   Samuel Flagg Bemis, *Pinckney's Treaty: America's Advantage from Europe's Distress, 1783-1800*, rev. ed., New Haven, 1960

Betts, *Farm Book*   Edwin M. Betts, ed., *Thomas Jefferson's Farm Book*, Princeton, 1953

Betts, *Garden Book*   Edwin M. Betts, ed., *Thomas Jefferson's Garden Book, 1766-1824*, Philadelphia, 1944

Biog. Dir. Cong.   *Biographical Directory of the United States Congress, 1774-1989*, Washington, D.C., 1989

Bleiberg, *Diccionario*   Germán Bleiberg, ed., *Diccionario de Historia de España*, 2d ed., Madrid, 1968-69, 3 vols.

Brant, *Madison*   Irving Brant, *James Madison*, Indianapolis, 1941-61, 6 vols.

Brigham, *American Newspapers*   Clarence S. Brigham, *History and Bibliography of American Newspapers, 1690-1820*, Worcester, Mass., 1947, 2 vols.

Call, *Reports*   Daniel Call, *Reports of Cases Argued and Adjudged in the Court of Appeals of Virginia*, Richmond, 1801-33, 6 vols.

Childs, *French Refugee Life*   Frances S. Childs, *French Refugee Life in the United States, 1790-1800: An American Chapter of the French Revolution*, Baltimore, 1940

Cokayne, *Baronetage*   George E. Cokayne, ed., *Complete Baronetage*, Exeter, 1900-06, 5 vols.

Combs, *Jay Treaty*   Jerald A. Combs, *The Jay Treaty*, Berkeley, 1970

Cooke, *Coxe*   Jacob E. Cooke, *Tench Coxe and the Early Republic*, Chapel Hill, 1978

CVSP   William P. Palmer and others, eds., *Calendar of Virginia State Papers . . . Preserved in the Capitol at Richmond*, Richmond, 1875-93, 11 vols.

DAB   Allen Johnson and Dumas Malone, eds., *Dictionary of American Biography*, New York, 1928-36, 20 vols.

DeConde, *Entangling Alliance*   Alexander DeConde, *Entangling*

Alliance: Politics & Diplomacy under George Washington, Durham N.C., 1958

DHRC   Merrill Jensen, John P. Kaminski, Gaspare J. Saladino, and others, eds., *The Documentary History of the Ratification of the Constitution*, Madison, Wis., 1976- , 14 vols.

DHSC   Maeva Marcus and others, eds., *The Documentary History of the Supreme Court of the United States 1789-1800*, New York, 1985- , 6 vols.

Dictionnaire   *Dictionnaire de biographie française*, Paris, 1933- , 18 vols.

DNB   Leslie Stephen and Sidney Lee, eds., *Dictionary of National Biography*, 2d ed., New York, 1908-09, 22 vols.

DSB   Charles C. Gillispie, ed., *Dictionary of Scientific Biography*, New York, 1970-80, 16 vols.

EG   Dickinson W. Adams and Ruth W. Lester, eds., *Jefferson's Extracts from the Gospels*, Princeton, 1983, *The Papers of Thomas Jefferson*, Second Series

Ehrman, *Pitt*   John Ehrman, *The Younger Pitt: The Reluctant Transition*, London, 1983

Evans   Charles Evans, Clifford K. Shipton, and Roger P. Bristol, comps., *American Bibliography: A Chronological Dictionary of all Books, Pamphlets and Periodical Publications Printed in the United States of America from . . . 1639 . . . to . . . 1820*, Chicago and Worcester, Mass., 1903-59, 14 vols.

Fitzpatrick, *Writings*   John C. Fitzpatrick, ed., *The Writings of George Washington*, Washington, D.C., 1931-44, 39 vols.

Foner, *Paine*   Philip S. Foner, ed., *The Complete Writings of Thomas Paine*, New York, 1945, 2 vols.

Ford   Paul Leicester Ford, ed., *The Writings of Thomas Jefferson*, Letterpress Edition, New York, 1892-99, 10 vols.

Freeman, *Washington*   Douglas Southall Freeman, *George Washington*, New York, 1948-57, 7 vols.; 7th volume by J. A. Carroll and M. W. Ashworth

Gaines, *Randolph*   William H. Gaines, Jr., *Thomas Mann Randolph: Jefferson's Son-in-Law*, Baton Rouge, 1966

Goebel and Smith, *Law Practice of Hamilton*   Julius Goebel, Jr., and Joseph H. Smith, eds., *The Law Practice of Alexander Hamilton: Documents and Commentary*, New York, 1964-1981, 5 vols.

Harris, *Louisa County*   Malcolm H. Harris, *History of Louisa County, Virginia*, Richmond, 1936

HAW   Henry A. Washington, ed., *The Writings of Thomas Jefferson*, New York, 1853-54, 9 vols.

Heitman, *Dictionary*   Francis B. Heitman, comp., *Historical Register and Dictionary of the United States Army* . . . , Washington, D.C., 1903, 2 vols.

Heitman, *Register*   Francis B. Heitman, *Historical Register of Officers of the Continental Army during the War of the Revolution, April, 1775, to December, 1783*, new ed., Washington, D.C., 1914

Hening   William Waller Hening, ed., *The Statutes at Large; Being a Collection of All the Laws of Virginia*, Richmond, 1809-23, 13 vols.

Henry, *Henry*   William Wirt Henry, *Patrick Henry, Life, Correspondence and Speeches*, New York, 1891, 3 vols.

Hobson, "British Debts"   Charles F. Hobson, "The Recovery of British Debts in the Federal Circuit Court of Virginia, 1790-1797," VMHB, XCII (1984)

Hoefer, *Nouv. biog. générale*   J. C. F. Hoefer, *Nouvelle biographie générale depuis les temps les plus reculés jusqu'a nos jours*, Paris, 1855-66, 46 vols.

JAH   *Journal of American History*, 1964-

JCC   Worthington C. Ford and others, eds., *Journals of the Continental Congress, 1774-1789*, Washington, D.C., 1904-37, 34 vols.

Jefferson Correspondence, Bixby   Worthington C. Ford, ed., *Thomas Jefferson Correspondence Printed from the Originals in the Collections of William K. Bixby*, Boston, 1916

JEP   *Journal of the Executive Proceedings of the Senate of the United States . . . to the Termination of the Nineteenth Congress*, Washington, D.C., 1828

JHD   *Journal of the House of Delegates of the Commonwealth of Virginia* (cited by session and date of publication)

JHR   *Journal of the House of Representatives of the United States*, Washington, D.C., Gales & Seaton, 1826, 9 vols.

Johnston, *Memorials*   Frederick Johnston, comp., *Memorials of Old Virginia Clerks*, Lynchburg, 1888

JS   *Journal of the Senate of the United States*, Washington, D.C., Gales, 1820-21, 5 vols.

Karmin, *D'Ivernois*   Otto Karmin, *Sir Francis D'Ivernois, 1757-1842, Sa Vie, Son Œuvre et Son Temps*, Genève, 1920

L & B   Andrew A. Lipscomb and Albert E. Bergh, eds., *The Writings of Thomas Jefferson*, Washington, D.C., 1903-04, 20 vols.

LCB   Douglas L. Wilson, ed., *Jefferson's Literary Commonplace Book*, Princeton, 1989, *The Papers of Thomas Jefferson*, Second Series

Lefebvre, *Thermidorians*   Georges Lefebvre, *The Thermidorians &*

the Directory: Two Phases of the French Revolution, trans. Robert Baldick, New York, 1964

List of Patents   *A List of Patents granted by the United States from April 10, 1792, to December 31, 1836*, Washington, D.C., 1872

Madison, *Letters*   [William C. Rives and Philip R. Fendall, eds.], *Letters and Other Writings of James Madison . . . Published by Order of Congress*, Philadelphia, 1865, 4 vols.

Madison, *Papers*   William T. Hutchinson, Robert A. Rutland, J. C. A. Stagg, and others, eds., *The Papers of James Madison*, Chicago and Charlottesville, 1962- , 24 vols.

Malone, *Jefferson*   Dumas Malone, *Jefferson and his Time*, Boston, 1948-81, 6 vols.

Marshall, *Papers*   Herbert A. Johnson, Charles T. Cullen, Charles F. Hobson, and others, eds., *The Papers of John Marshall*, Chapel Hill, 1974- , 10 vols.

MB   James A. Bear, Jr., and Lucia C. Stanton, eds., *Jefferson's Memorandum Books: Accounts, with Legal Records and Miscellany, 1767-1826*, Princeton, 1997, *The Papers of Thomas Jefferson*, Second Series

Merrill, *Jefferson's Nephews*   Boynton Merrill, Jr., *Jefferson's Nephews: A Frontier Tragedy*, Princeton, 1976

Miller, *Treaties*   Hunter Miller, ed., *Treaties and other International Acts of the United States of America*, Washington, D.C., 1931-48, 8 vols.

Monroe, *Writings*   Stanislas Murray Hamilton, ed., *The Writings of James Monroe*, New York, 1898-1903, 7 vols.

National State Papers   Eileen D. Carzo, ed., *National State Papers of the United States, 1789-1817. Part II: Text of Documents. Administration of George Washington, 1789-1797*, Wilmington, 1985, 35 vols.

Notes, ed. Peden   Thomas Jefferson, *Notes on the State of Virginia*, ed. William Peden, Chapel Hill, 1955

OED   Sir James Murray and others, eds., *A New English Dictionary on Historical Principles*, Oxford, 1888-1933

Palmer, *Democratic Revolution*   R. R. Palmer, *The Age of the Democratic Revolution: A Political History of Europe and America, 1760-1800*, Princeton, 1959-64, 2 vols.

Peale, *Papers*   Lillian B. Miller and others, eds., *The Selected Papers of Charles Willson Peale and His Family*, New Haven, 1983-96, 4 vols. in 5

Peter, *Genève*   Marc Ernest Peter, *Genève et la Revolution*, Genève, 1921-50, 2 vols.

Peterson, *Jefferson*   Merrill D. Peterson, *Thomas Jefferson and the New Nation*, New York, 1970

PW   Wilbur S. Howell, ed., *Jefferson's Parliamentary Writings*, Princeton, 1988, *The Papers of Thomas Jefferson*, Second Series

Randall, *Life*   Henry S. Randall, *The Life of Thomas Jefferson*, New York, 1858, 3 vols.

Randolph, *Domestic Life*   Sarah N. Randolph, *The Domestic Life of Thomas Jefferson, Compiled from Family Letters and Reminiscences by His Great-Granddaughter*, 3d ed., Cambridge, Mass., 1939

Reardon, *Randolph*   John J. Reardon, *Edmund Randolph: A Biography*, New York, 1974

Ritcheson, *Aftermath of Revolution*   Charles R. Ritcheson, *Aftermath of Revolution: British Policy Toward the United States, 1783-1795*, Dallas, 1969

Scott and Rothaus, *Historical Dictionary*   Samuel F. Scott and Barry Rothaus, eds., *Historical Dictionary of the French Revolution, 1789-1799*, Westport, Conn., 1985, 2 vols.

Shackelford, *Jefferson's Adoptive Son*   George Green Shackelford, *Jefferson's Adoptive Son: The Life of William Short, 1759-1848*, Lexington, Ky., 1993

Shepherd, *Statutes*   Samuel Shepherd, ed., *The Statutes at Large of Virginia, from October Session 1792, to December Session 1806 . . .*, Richmond, 1835-36, 3 vols.

Slaughter, *Fry*   Philip Slaughter, *Memoir of Col. Joshua Fry . . .*, Richmond, 1880

Sowerby   E. Millicent Sowerby, comp., *Catalogue of the Library of Thomas Jefferson*, Washington, D.C., 1952-59, 5 vols.

Stewart, *French Revolution*   John A. Stewart, *A Documentary Survey of the French Revolution*, New York, 1951

Sutton, *Revolution to Secession*   Robert P. Sutton, *Revolution to Secession: Constitution Making in the Old Dominion*, Charlottesville, 1989

Swem and Williams, *Register*   Earl G. Swem and John W. Williams, *A Register of the General Assembly of Virginia 1776-1918 . . .*, Richmond, 1918

Syrett, *Hamilton*   Harold C. Syrett and others, eds., *The Papers of Alexander Hamilton*, New York, 1961-87, 27 vols.

TJR   Thomas Jefferson Randolph, ed., *Memoir, Correspondence, and Miscellanies, from the Papers of Thomas Jefferson*, Charlottesville, 1829, 4 vols.

TQHGM   L. G. Tyler, ed., *Tyler's Quarterly Historical and Genealogical Magazine*, Richmond, 1920-52, 34 vols. in 33

Tucker, *Life*   George Tucker, *The Life of Thomas Jefferson*, Philadelphia, 1837, 2 vols.

Turner, *CFM*   Frederick Jackson Turner, "Correspondence of French Ministers, 1791-1797," American Historical Association, *Annual Report*, 1903, II

U.S. Statutes at Large   Richard Peters, ed., *The Public Statutes at Large of the United States . . . 1789 to March 3, 1845*, Boston, 1855-56, 8 vols.

VMHB   *Virginia Magazine of History and Biography*, 1893-

White, *Federalists*   Leonard White, *The Federalists: A Study in Administrative History*, New York, 1948

WMQ   *William and Mary Quarterly*, 1892-

Woods, *Albemarle*   Edgar Woods, *Albemarle County in Virginia*, Charlottesville, 1901

Young, *Democratic Republicans*   Alfred F. Young, *The Democratic Republicans of New York: The Origins, 1763-1797*, Chapel Hill, 1967

CONTENTS

1794

CONTENTS

CONTENTS

CONTENTS

CONTENTS

1795

CONTENTS

CONTENTS

CONTENTS

CONTENTS

CONTENTS

CONTENTS

·◁⟨ **1796** ⟩▷·

CONTENTS

CONTENTS

ILLUSTRATIONS

Following page 336

GIUSEPPE CERACCHI'S BUST OF JEFFERSON

This rough pencil sketch, made by an unknown hand on the verso of a retained copy of a letter written by Jefferson's grandson Thomas Jefferson Randolph in December 1826, is the only extant image of a bust of Jefferson that Giuseppe Ceracchi modeled from life in Philadelphia sometime after 2 Mch. 1791. He intended to incorporate it, with other likenesses of prominent Americans, into a large monument that was never completed. In Florence during 1793 the artist transformed his original terra cotta study of Jefferson into a larger-than-life bust in marble, writing to Jefferson on 11 Mch. 1794 to report the work was finished. A year later Ceracchi, back in the United States, ordered the piece shipped to Monticello. There it became a distinctive feature of the entrance hall, where it faced a life-size bust, also by Ceracchi, of Alexander Hamilton. According to an expression attributed to Jefferson, the two old adversaries were thus symbolically "opposed in death as in life" (Randall, *Life*, III, 336; undated floor plan of Monticello by Cornelia Jefferson Randolph, in ViU).

This drawing shows the bust as Jefferson displayed it, atop a dark marble column and ornamented pedestal that Madame de Tessé had presented to him in 1789 (illustrated in Vol. 18). Although he hoped that after his death the sculpture and its stand might go to the University of Virginia, the Library of Congress acquired them instead, and in 1851 they perished by fire along with most of the great collection of books that Jefferson had sold to Congress in 1815. Architect William Thornton pronounced Ceracchi's representation of Jefferson in Roman attire "superb," William Wirt deemed it "exquisite," and Jefferson and his family praised it as a faithful likeness. One expert considers its loss "the most regrettable lacuna in Jefferson iconography." Ceracchi's terra cotta maquette and daguerreotypes that Robert Mills made of the marble bust have not been found (Alfred L. Bush, *The Life Portraits of Thomas Jefferson*, rev. ed. [Charlottesville, 1987], 15-17).
Courtesy of University of Virginia Library.

JAMES MADISON AND DOLLEY PAYNE MADISON

On 15 Sep. 1794 James Madison and Dolley Payne Todd were married at Harewood, in present day Jefferson County, West Virginia, the home of Dolley's sister Lucy Payne Washington, where their mother also resided. Illness kept the Madisons from returning to Montpelier after the wedding; instead they proceeded to Philadelphia in October, where they remained until early April 1795, shortly after the close of the Third Congress. In his first correspondence with Madison after the marriage, which would last more than forty years, Jefferson wished "a thousand respects to Mrs. Madison and joys perpetual to both." On 21 Sep. 1795 Jefferson urged Madison to keep his promise "to bring Mrs. Madison to see us, with whom we should all be glad to get acquainted." The couple obliged the request the following month, spending the first two weeks of October at Monticello. They probably sat for these pastel portraits in Philadelphia in 1796 or 1797. Although English portraitist James Sharples

[xxxvii]

often receives sole credit for the pastels of prominent individuals executed during his stays in the United States, his wife Ellen was also an accomplished artist who drew portraits herself, assisted her husband, and made exact copies of many of his works. Particularly in the case of this likeness of Dolley Madison, the work may have been by either James or Ellen Sharples, or perhaps by the two artists collaboratively (Madison, *Papers*, xv, xxix, 343n, 357-8n, xvi, xxvi; Katharine McCook Knox, *The Sharples: Their Portraits of George Washington and his Contemporaries* [New Haven, 1930], 13-16, 18, 46-7, 94, 99).

Courtesy of Independence National Historical Park.

FRANÇOIS D'IVERNOIS

From Great Britain, where he lived many years in exile from revolutionary upheavals in his home city of Geneva, François D'Ivernois wrote on 5 Sep. 1794 to renew an acquaintance with Jefferson. In a series of letters over the succeeding months, he sought Jefferson's aid (as well as that of John Adams and Albert Gallatin) in an unsuccessful effort to reconstitute in the United States the distinguished Academy of Geneva. D'Ivernois also wrote pamphlets and tracts lamenting the expansion of French revolutionary influences to Geneva. The silhouette was made in London, ca. 1800 (Lucien Cramer, *Correspondance Diplomatique de Pictet de Rochemont et de François D'Ivernois, Paris, Vienne, Turin 1814-1816*, 2 vols. [Geneva and Paris, 1914], I, facing p. 473).

Courtesy of Bibliothèque Publique et Universitaire, Geneva, Switzerland.

CHRISTOPH DANIEL EBELING

In this lithograph by Siegfried Bendixen, German author and librarian Christoph Daniel Ebeling appears with symbols of his prolific scholarly career. Appropriately, his pointing finger draws attention to a map of America. Immersed in writing a multivolume study of the United States and impressed by Jefferson's *Notes on the State of Virginia*, Ebeling on 30 July 1795 wrote from Hamburg about his research. Sometime after receiving that letter on 15 Oct. 1795 Jefferson set down on paper his thoughts in response, although it is not evident that he ever actually replied. A similar portrait in oil hangs in the Staats- und Universitätsbibliothek in Hamburg, the modern embodiment of the institution that Ebeling served as librarian. The lithograph was done in 1818, the year following his death (R. Arnim Winkler, *Die Frühzeit der deutschen Lithographie: Katalog der Bilddrucke von 1796–1821* [Munich, 1975], 35).

Courtesy of Harvard University Library.

PAGE OF JEFFERSON'S PRAYER BOOK

On this page of his *Book of Common Prayer* (Oxford, 1752), which he inherited from his father, Jefferson recorded the marriage of his older daughter Martha to Thomas Mann Randolph and the birth dates of their twelve children. He entered the information in at least two sittings, the first after 1803 but before 1806 and the second on or after 10 Mch. 1818. During the initial sitting Jefferson also recorded the death of the first Ellen Wayles Randolph, his only Randolph grandchild to die in infancy. The twelve pages containing Jefferson's

ILLUSTRATIONS

entries and notations are reproduced in *Thomas Jefferson's Prayer Book* (Charlottesville, 1952), with an introduction and bibliographical note by John Cook Wyllie. The prayer book survived the Shadwell fire in 1770 and is the only printed work known to have been purchased by Jefferson's family at the sale of his library in 1829, remaining with his descendants until 1951 when it was acquired by the Tracy W. McGregor Library at the University of Virginia.
Courtesy of University of Virginia Library.

DEED OF MANUMISSION FOR JAMES HEMINGS

This indenture in Jefferson's hand, signed and sealed by him, fulfilled his 15 Sep. 1793 agreement with James Hemings, by which he promised to free him after he had trained someone, perhaps his brother Peter Hemings, to take over his duties at Monticello. This is the second and last deed of manumission prepared by Jefferson, the first being for James's older brother, Robert, on 24 Dec. 1794.
Courtesy of University of Virginia Library.

JAMES HEMINGS'S INVENTORY OF KITCHEN UTENSILS

James Hemings accompanied Jefferson to Paris in 1784, where he received instruction in the art of French cooking and pastry making. He also took lessons in French grammar and learned to speak the language fluently. From the fall of 1787 until his manumission, Hemings served as Jefferson's *chef de cuisine* in Paris, Philadelphia, and Monticello. Hemings prepared this list of kitchen utensils, the only extant document in his hand, after his manumission, shortly before his departure from Monticello for Philadelphia.
Courtesy of the Library of Congress.

JEFFERSON'S NOTES ON EDMUND RANDOLPH'S *VINDICATION*

It is evident from Jefferson's letter of 31 Dec. 1795 to William Branch Giles that he devoted considerable attention to a careful reading of the pamphlet *Vindication* that Edmund Randolph wrote after his dismissal from the Cabinet. For Jefferson, the *Vindication* was unnecessary as an exoneration of Randolph but furnished "a great treat" in its bounty of information about decision making within the executive branch: "it is a continuation of that Cabinet history with the former part of which I was intimate." On a blank page in his own copy of the pamphlet, Jefferson made this key to the chronology of the events surrounding Randolph's dismissal.
Courtesy of the Library of Congress.

Volume 28

1 January 1794 to 29 February 1796

JEFFERSON CHRONOLOGY

1743 · 1826

1743	Born at Shadwell, 13 Apr. (New Style).
1760	Entered the College of William and Mary.
1762	"quitted college."
1762-1767	Self-education and preparation for law.
1769-1774	Albemarle delegate to House of Burgesses.
1772	Married Martha Wayles Skelton, 1 Jan.
1775-1776	In Continental Congress.
1776	Drafted Declaration of Independence.
1776-1779	In Virginia House of Delegates.
1779	Submitted Bill for Establishing Religious Freedom.
1779-1781	Governor of Virginia.
1782	His wife died, 6 Sep.
1783-1784	In Continental Congress.
1784-1789	In France as Minister Plenipotentiary to negotiate commercial treaties and as Minister Plenipotentiary resident at Versailles.
1790-1793	Secretary of State of the United States.
1797-1801	Vice President of the United States.
1801-1809	President of the United States.
1814-1826	Established the University of Virginia.
1826	Died at Monticello, 4 July.

VOLUME 28

1 January 1794 to 29 February 1796

1 Jan. 1794	Washington accepts his resignation as Secretary of State.
3 Jan.	Madison offers resolutions in House of Representatives to implement Jefferson's Report on Commerce.
5 Jan.	Leaves Philadelphia, arriving at Monticello 15-16 Jan.
21 May	Delivers first shipment from his nailery.
29 May-10 June	Travels to Chestnut Grove, Eppington, and Richmond.
7 Sep.	Declines offer of special mission to Spain.
23 Oct.	Calls Monticello in a state of renovation a "brick-kiln," but says he will recommence work on it in the summer.
24 Dec.	Signs deed of manumission for Robert Hemings.
26 Dec.	Authorizes J. P. P. Derieux and Thomas Mann Randolph to hire slaves for Monticello.
28 Dec.	Criticizes Washington's address defending use of federal troops to quell Whiskey Rebellion and denouncing the Democratic Societies.
29 Dec.	Explains his philosophy of crop rotation to John Taylor.
26 Mch. 1795	George Wythe suggests that Jefferson make available his collection of the laws of Virginia.
14-16 May	William Strickland visits.
21 July	Receives copy of Jay Treaty sent by Henry Tazewell.
26 July	Infant granddaughter Ellen Wayles Randolph buried at Monticello.
14 Aug.	Washington signs Jay Treaty, which Senate had ratified in June.
19 Aug.	Edmund Randolph resigns as Secretary of State.
ca. 1-15 Oct.	James and Dolley Payne Madison visit Monticello.
20-21 Nov.	Virginia General Assembly condemns Jay Treaty.
11 Dec.	Reports quality of his tobacco crop too poor to send to Philadelphia market.
18 Dec.	Publication of Edmund Randolph's *Vindication*.
12 Jan. 1796	Sends his printed collection of Virginia statutes to Richmond binder.
5 Feb.	Signs deed of manumission for James Hemings.

THE PAPERS OF
THOMAS JEFFERSON

·❧══════════❧·

From George Washington

DEAR SIR   Philadelphia January 1st. 1794

I yesterday received with sincere regret your resignation of the office of Secretary of State. Since it has been impossible to prevail upon you, to forego any longer the indulgence of your desire for private life; the event, however anxious I am to avert it, must be submitted to.

But I cannot suffer you to leave your Station, without assuring you, that the opinion, which I had formed, of your integrity and talents, and which dictated your original nomination, has been confirmed by the fullest experience; and that both have been eminently displayed in the discharge of your duties.

Let a conviction of my most earnest prayers for your happiness accompany you in your retirement; and while I accept with the warmest thanks your solicitude for my welfare, I beg you to believe, that I always am Dear Sir Your Sincere friend and Affecte. Hble Servant.

GO: WASHINGTON

RC (DLC); at foot of text: "Thomas Jefferson Esqr."; endorsed by TJ as received 1 Jan. 1793 but recorded in SJL as received 1 Jan. 1794. Dft (DNA: RG 59, MLR). FC (Lb in DLC: Washington Papers); with one minor variation.

To John Ross

Jan. 2. 1794.

Th: Jefferson presents his friendly respects to Mr. Ross: the sum which he finds his money-provisions fall short is about 450. Dollars; with which if Mr. Ross can have him furnished, he incloses him a substitution in due form to receive ₴ 390.62 at the bank of the US. on the 1st. day of April, and he will remit the balance at an earlier period. He considers himself as much indebted to Mr. Ross for his kind offer, and had before abundant motives to hold him in his particular esteem.

RC (Gilder Lehrman Collection, on deposit NNPM); addressed: "John Ross esquire"; endorsed by Ross as received and answered the same day; Ross also wrote at foot of text: "2d January 1794—Cash Supplied—450 Dollars." Not recorded in SJL.

A letter from Ross to TJ, recorded in SJL

as written and received on this date, has not been found. For TJ's arrangements to REMIT THE BALANCE, see his letter to Ross of 30 Apr. 1794.

ENCLOSURE

Power of Attorney

Know all men by these presents that I Thomas Jefferson named in a certain letter of Attorney from William Short of the state of Virginia Minister Resident of the US. at the Hague, to me bearing date the 2d. day of April 1793. and now lodged in the bank of the US. by virtue of the power and authority therein given me, do make substitute and appoint John Ross Esquire as well my own as the true and lawful attorney and substitute of the said Wm. Short named in the said letter of Attorney to receive from the Treasury or bank of the US. the interest which shall become due on the stock of different descriptions of the said William Short registered in the proper office of the US. at the seat of government in Philadelphia from this 1st. day of January 1794. to the 1st. day of April next ensuing, and becoming payable on the said 1st. day of April, amounting to three hundred and ninety dollars and sixty two cents: hereby ratifying and confirming the paiment of the said interest to the said John Ross, and the discharge which he shall give for the same, as done by virtue of the power of attorney aforesaid. In witness whereof I have hereunto set my hand and seal this 1st. day of January 1794.

sealed and delivered in the presence.   TH: JEFFERSON
THOMAS BIDDLE of Phila Clerk.
CLEMENT BIDDLE not pub

On this 2d. day of January 1794 Thomas Jefferson Esquire acknowledged the above letter of Attorney to be his Act and deed before me Notary at philadelphia   CLEMENT BIDDLE
                                                           Notary Pub

MS (PHC); in TJ's hand, signed by Thomas and Clement Biddle, with note at foot of text by Clement Biddle; endorsed by one clerk: "Power of Attorney Thomas Jefferson Esqr to Receive 390 $\frac{62}{100}$ Dollars due 1st. April *on Certificates. 1794*"; endorsed by another clerk in part as a "Power of Subsn."

To Certain Diplomats of the United States

DEAR SIR   Philadelphia Jan. 3 1794.

I have the honor to inform you that I have resigned the office of Secretary of state, and that Mr. Randolph late Attorney Genl. of the US. is appointed by the President and approved by the Senate as Secretary of state. He will be so good as to[1] acknolege the receipt of your several letters not yet acknoleged by me, and will answer in detail such parts of them as may require special answer.[2] I beg leave to conclude this last act of my public correspondence with you with very sincere assurances of the great esteem and respect with which I have the honor to be Dear Sir Your most obedt & most humble sevt   TH: JEFFERSON

RC (NjP: Andre deCoppet Collection); with date added; at foot of text: "Colo. Humphreys"; endorsed by David Humphreys. PrC (DLC); dated in ink: "Jan.   1794." RC (N); with date added; at foot of text: "Mr. Dumas"; with minor variation in last sentence; endorsed by C. W. F. Dumas as received 1 Dec. 1794. PrC (DLC); dated in ink: "Jan.   1794." RC (ICN); with date added; at foot of text: "Mr. Short"; endorsed by William Short as received 3 Apr. 1794. PrC (DLC); dated in ink: "Jan.   1794." PrC of another RC (DLC); at foot of text: "Mr. Morris"; dated in ink: "Jan.   1794"; contains slip of the pen. PrC of another RC (DLC); at foot of text: "Mr. Pinckney"; dated in ink: "Jan.   1794"; with variation (see note 1 below). PrC of another RC (DLC); at foot of text: "Mr. Carmichael"; dated in ink: "Jan.   1794"; with variation (see note 2 below; and note to William Carmichael to TJ, 19 Aug. 1791). Trs (DLC); 19th-century copies addressed to Dumas and Carmichael; both misdated "Jan. 1793." All recorded in SJL under January 1794 above 3 Jan. entry for the following letter.

The Senate APPROVED President Washington's nomination of Edmund Randolph as Secretary of State on 2 Jan. 1794 (JEP, I, 144). Randolph enclosed TJ's letters to William Carmichael and William Short in a dispatch to them of 10 Jan. 1794 in which he said that TJ's resignation "was accompanied with a general regret, founded on his acknowledged qualities for that Department, and the important services, rendered by his labours" (DNA: RG 59, DCI).

From the Ile de France on 15 Jan. 1794 William Macarty wrote a letter to TJ as Secretary of State that, as an official communication reporting on the detention of American merchant ships, TJ never saw (RC in DNA: RG 59, CD; printed in A. Toussaint, ed., *Early American Trade with Mauritius* [Port Louis, Mauritius, 1954], 24-5).

[1] Preceding five words omitted in PrC to Thomas Pinckney.
[2] Sentence omitted in PrC to William Carmichael.

To George Hammond

SIR   Philadelphia Jan. 3. 1794.

The bearer hereof, Mr. Louis Osmond, desires me to [convey?] to you the circumstances known to me relative to his emigration to America. Mr. Osmond, about three years ago, arrived in America from France, and brought me letters of recommendation from [several?] persons of rank and character there informing me that his fa[mily?] having from some circumstances lost their fortune there, [he had?] determined to come and settle in America, and ende[avor to] get into some business by which he might live. He [appearing?] to be under age at that time, some others as well as my[self in]terested ourselves and got him placed with [. . .] public. After doing business for some time, in that [. . .], [he] went into mercantile business and so continues. I [. . .] of the particular time when he executed the formal [. . .] himself an American citizen; but he certainly [. . .] with that intention. Having observed him to be [of extraordi]nary activity, diligence, and cleverness in whatever [. . .] to, it is with pleasure I perform this homage to [honor?] and to truth, and shall be sincerely happy if you think [this] information from me may authorize any act on your part which may prevent the wreck of his infant fortunes, which he seems to apprehend. I have the honor to be with great respect Sir Your most obedt & most humble servt.

TH: JEFFERSON

PrC (DLC); at foot of text: "Mr. Hammond"; right margin badly mutilated. For further information on LOUIS OSMOND (Osmont), see William Short to TJ, 7 Nov. 1790, and TJ to Osmont, 10 July 1791.

To Thomas Willing and Willink, Van Staphorst & Hubbard

SIR   Philadelphia Jan. 3 1794.

I have the honor to inform you that I have resigned the office of Secretary of state and that Mr. Randolph late attorney genl. of the US. is appointed by the President and approved by the Senate as Secretary of state. You will therefore be pleased to consider all authority heretofore held by me over any funds in the bank belonging to the department of state, as now transferred to him. I have the honor to be Sir Your most obedt. servt   TH: JEFFERSON

RC (Lee Gwynne Martin, New York City, 1963); with date added. PrC (DLC); at foot of text: "The President of the bank of the US."; dated in ink: "Jan.   1794." PrC (DLC); at foot of text: "Messrs. Willm. & Jan Willinck Nichs. & Jacob Van Staphorsts & Hubbard Bankers Amsterdam"; dated in ink: "Jan.   1794." Both letters recorded in SJL under January 1794 above 3 Jan. entry for the preceding letter.

From Horatio Gates

DEAR SIR   Rose Hill 5th: January 1793.[1] [i.e. 1794]

The Hermit of Rose Hill sees it confirmed by Yesterdays post, that you have actually Resign'd your Office! but his prophetic Soul, Augurs no Benefit to the State by such a Sacrafice; If the best Seamen abandon the Ship in a Storm, she must Founder; and if all Human means are neglected, Providence will[2] not Care for The Vessel; She must Perish! A Hermit, as He knows little of what passes in the World, cannot reason from Causes, to Conduct; He can only Lament your going to Monte

[6]

Celli, when you seem[3] so much wanted at philadelphia. Your Report to Congress upon the Trade of the US., Has Filled every Patriot Breast with Gratitude; and Admiration; You therefore Retreat covered with Glory; The Public Gratitude may one day[4] Force You from that Retreat, so make no rash Promises, lest like other great Men you should be Tempted to break them. If you go to Virginia, I request you will deliver the Letters, and Letter Book, which I had the pleasure to send you last Summer, to the Post Office.[5] If you come this Way the Hermits Cell is open to receive You. That Heaven may prosper You, wherever you go, is the prayer of Your Faithful[6] Humble Servant, HORATIO GATES

P.S. Mrs. Gates presents you her Compliments.

RC (DLC); misdated; endorsed by TJ as received 22 Jan. 1794 and so recorded in SJL. Dft (NHi: Gates Papers); lacks postscript; only the most important emendations and variations in wording are recorded below; at foot of text: "(Thos Jefferson Esq:)."

Gates sent TJ his LETTERS, AND LETTER BOOK, on 15 and 19 Apr. 1793, not LAST SUMMER (see also TJ to Gates, 12, 21 Mch. 1793).

[1] Corrected to "1794" in Dft.
[2] In Dft Gates here canceled "leave the Vessell to her fate."
[3] Dft: "are."
[4] In Dft Gates first wrote "and I trust, the Day will come when The public Gratitude will" and then altered the passage to read as above.
[5] Dft: "The Post," interlined in place of "Col. Wm. Smith, now at philadelphia, who will bring them to me."
[6] In Dft Gates here canceled "Friend &."

From Hauterive

Newyork Le 15 Janvier 1794
L'an 3e. de la Republique francaise, une et Indivisible

J'ai reçu, Monsieur, une lettre datée du 7. Septembre et Signée de vous; J'ai vu depuis, et après votre résignation du ministere, dans les papiers publics une déclaration qu'on vous attribüe sur les motifs qui vous ont Fait vous prêter aux différens actes de votre ministere qui étoient en opposition avec vos opinions. Des Considérations importantes et personelles me font vous demander, Monsieur, si cette déclaration a été insérée dans les papiers publics par votre ordre; et si la lettre que je viens de Citer, est du Nombre des actes qui étoient en opposition avec vos Sentimens. HAUTERIVE
consul de la republique francoise

RC (DLC); in a clerk's hand, signed by Hauterive; below dateline: "hauterive à Mr. Thomas Jefferson"; endorsed by TJ as received 2 Feb. 1794 and so recorded in SJL.

The DÉCLARATION in question was the following editorial commentary in the 6

Jan. 1794 issue of the Philadelphia *General Advertiser*: "It is not to be wondered at, a correspondent observes, that M. Jefferson should resign. The nature of the office he filled required of him to lend his name to measures which militated against his well known principles. As Secretary of State he was charged with certain correspondences founded on principles first settled in the Executive's council, where his influence was but trifling. To a man of his way of thinking and turn of mind it must have been a disagreeable task to give the sanction of his name to sentiments which his heart must disapprove."

Memorandum to Thomas Mann Randolph

[ca. 16-24 Jan. 1794]

The price of wheat [1] and whether it can be sold for the rise of the market? [2] The price of molasses. [3]

Whether my things from Philadelphia addressed to Colo. Gamble [4] are arrived?

If they are, send them up by Henderson's people of preference to the other things.

Send by them the sugar &c for which I wrote to Colo. Gamble. [5]

After the things last expected from Philadelphia I would wish to receive the tender articles, to wit, Nos. 2. 5. 10. 18. 19. 22. 25. 26. 27. 28. and next to these I wish for Nos. 45. [46.]

[*on verso:*]

Tell [6] Dr. Currie I expect by the first post to receive a letter from Mr. Ingersoll, which alone can enable me to give him information in his matter. [7]

MS (DLC: TJ Papers, 232: 42031); consists of a rough fragment written by TJ on both sides of an unidentified address cover, with notations by Randolph recorded in notes below; undated and unaddressed, being assigned on the basis of internal and other evidence (see below).

TJ evidently wrote this memorandum shortly after he returned to Monticello on 15 or 16 Jan. 1794, as Randolph prepared for a trip to Richmond. On 23 Dec. 1793, TJ had sent his books and furniture that remained in Philadelphia by sloop to Robert Gamble in Richmond. As Randolph indicated (see note 4 below), they had not yet arrived on 25 Jan. 1794. Already in March 1793, TJ had sent his first large shipment of furniture and belongings, which he numbered as boxes 1 through 66, to Richmond to be stored in a warehouse until he returned to Monticello. TJ's instructions to Ran-

dolph agree with an earlier notice he had given his daughter Martha when he wrote: "As I retained longest here the things most necessary, they are of course those I shall want soonest when I get home. Therefore I would wish them, after their arrival to be carried up in preference to the packages formerly sent" (MB, 30 Mch. 1793, 15-16 Jan. 1794; TJ to Thomas Mann Randolph, 28 July 1793; TJ to Caleb Lownes, 18 Dec. 1793; TJ to Gamble and TJ to Martha Jefferson Randolph, 22 Dec. 1793; TJ to Archibald Stuart, 26 Jan. 1794).

TJ's letter TO COLO. GAMBLE was probably that recorded in SJL of 17 Jan. 1794, which has not been found but may have been hand delivered to Gamble. For the TENDER ARTICLES, see TJ to Martha Jefferson Randolph, 12 May 1793.

TELL DR. CURRIE: since 1791, TJ had attempted to help Dr. James Currie collect a debt owed him by John Tayloe Griffin. In late 1793, TJ contacted Jared INGERSOLL to serve as Currie's attorney in his suit against Griffin (note to John Tayloe Griffin to TJ, 16 June 1793; TJ to James Currie, 8 Dec. 1793). A letter from Ingersoll to TJ of 15 Jan. 1794, recorded in SJL as received 2 Feb. 1794, has not been found. According to SJL, Ingersoll and TJ exchanged eight other letters between 2 Feb. 1794 and 4 Jan. 1796, all of which are missing.

[1] Beginning at this point, the following is interlined in Randolph's hand: "5/6 in Richd. at 30 days. 5/9 may be obtained at same credit in Petersg. it is said."
[2] Randolph here answered: "it cannot."
[3] Randolph here wrote: "3/4 by the Hhd."

[4] Randolph here interlined: "not arrived on Jan. 25."
[5] Randolph here wrote: "directed to be sent by 1st. waggon." He continued with the following interlineation: "and in consequence of the general inoculation it was impossible to get Porters."
[6] The following appears at the top of the fragment in Randolph's hand: "a box of the Encyclopedia sent round to — Mason in Richmond from Georgetown," Randolph adding, probably at a later date and in a smaller hand: "—directed to be lodged at Colo. Gambles to be taken thence by the first waggon."
[7] Following in Randolph's hand: "communicated by note."

From Harry Innes

DR SIR   Kentucky January 21st: 1794

Agreable to the promise contained in my last Letter I now inclose you the Remonstrance drawn and circulated by the Democratic society in this state. I shall only observe that it here meets with very general approbation.

I think I hinted in my Letter that foreign aid had been offered to Kentucky; it has been told me to day that Majr. Genl. Logan of the state Militia has resigned his state command and taken an Appointment of— I expect—a Brig. Genl. under the Repub. of France. Your old friend Clarke is first in command. It is also said that Colo. John Montgomery late of the Ileonoise Regiment has embodied 200 men in the Cumberland settlement and hath marched to the mouth of that River where he is now encamped and lately took several Boats loaded with provision destined for New Orleans.

These communications are made to you from report—yet I beleive are facts and are intended to inform you of the temper and opinions of the Western people on the subject of the Navigation of the Mississippi that Government may be watchful and take decissive measures in that business. You may rest assured that nothing has kept the people in this quarter quiet on that interesting subject but the furnishments made to the Army for two years past. I am with great regard Dr Sir your friend & Servt.   HARRY INNES

RC (DLC); at foot of text: "The Hon'ble Thos. Jefferson"; endorsed by TJ as received 31 Mch. 1794 and so recorded in SJL. Enclosure: Democratic Society of

Kentucky, *To the President and Congress of the United States of America. The Remonstrance of the Citizens West of the Allegany Mountains* (Lexington, 1793?), which warned that the people of Kentucky would take action to establish their economically vital right to navigate the Mississippi if federal efforts to secure Spanish recognition of this right continued to be unsuccessful (Evans, No. 46731).

MY LAST LETTER: Innes to TJ, 28 Dec. 1793. FOREIGN AID: a reference to an ultimately abortive plan by French minister Edmond Charles Genet for a joint attack on Louisiana by a French naval force and Kentucky volunteers (see notes to TJ to Isaac Shelby, 28 June 1793, and Notes of Cabinet Meeting and Conversations with Edmond Charles Genet, 5 July 1793).

From Robert Leslie

SIR   London January 22d 1794

I have Just receved your favour of December 12th. and return you my sincear thank for your good wishes, and shall do my best, to desarve them in future. I am sorry it is not in my power to alter the watch agreeable to your directions, as the numbers in wheels are not calculated for that pinion to make exactly one revolution in a minut, but if a delay of about two months will not be trespassing too much I hope to send you a watch that will answer much better for your own ware, for since the one intended for Miss Jefferson was begun, I have made som improvement on the gowing part of Watches, which had been examined by most of the best artists here, and has been acknowledged by all (tho aganst the intrest of several of them) to be the greatest improvement ever made in watches. It would requier a number of drawing &c to give you an Idea of them, and as I hope you will soon see one of the Watches I shall only mension, that one of the improvements, gives a perfect uniform motion to the Ballance, with out any of the wheels acting on it, the Ballance has a vibration of a whole circle, each way, and no friction whatever, but its own pivots, which in Dimond holes is very little. Four Watches of this kind, for the use of navigation, are now finished, and ware engaged by the first four Sea Captains that saw them, and a number of others are ordred. On the 13th. of December I obtained Patents for the above and fourteen other improvements in Clock and Watch work. I applyed for them early in the fall, but the business was retard by several Caveats being entred by different watchmakers, but when it came to the attorney genls office, they all withdrew reather than stand trial.

I am sorry to hear of your resignation, as I know it will be lamented by every American who is A lover of Liberty and his Country, but since it is your Choice, I wish you maney happy day in your Retierment, and if thare is any thing I can serve you in I hope you will at all times command your very humble Servent   ROBERT LESLIE

NB I am sorry you ware so unfortunate with the Clocks and whatever expence you ware at after I left Philada. for altering the large one, and the price of the small one, you will please to deduct from the bill of the Watch when, you recive it.   R Leslie

RC (MoSHi: Jefferson Collection); above postscript: "To Thos Jefferson Esqr"; endorsed by TJ as received 14 May 1794 and so recorded in SJL.

To Archibald Stuart

Dear Sir   Monticello Jan. 26. 1794.

Your favor of the 22d. has been duly received, and, in consequence of it, my manager Mr. Biddle now sets out for the sheep, as the approach of the yeaning season leaves no time to spare as to them. I could have wished to have made one trip serve for them and the potatoes: but I am advised that the latter would be in danger of freezing on the road. I must therefore, as to them wait for milder weather.

I arrived at home on the 15th. inst. When I left Philadelphia there was a great dearth of foreign news. Since my arrival here there are rumors favorable to France; but I know nothing particular. The Federal house of Representatives had given some pleasing expectations of their dispositions, by one or two leading votes. However, Mr. Madison's propositions, set for the 13th. inst. would be a better proof of the character of the majority. I think the next week's post may bring us some vote or votes on them which may indicate what we are to expect.—Now settled at home as a farmer I shall hope you will never pass without calling, and that you will make this your head quarters whenever you visit the neighborhood. Accept sincere assurances of my friendship & respect   Th: Jefferson

RC (ViHi); at foot of text: "Mr. Stuart."
PrC (DLC); left margin tattered.

Neither Stuart's favor of the 22d. re-
corded in SJL as received this day from Staunton, nor his reply of 30 Jan. 1794 recorded as received from Staunton a day later, has been found.

From Thomas Pinckney, with Jefferson's Note

My dear Sir   London 29 Jany. 1794

I have to acknowledge your private favor of the 12th. of December covering a bill for 13 st. which is duly honor'd. I wish the threshing machine may answer the purpose, I have no doubt that on a proper stream of water the effect of it would be astonishingly great and the principle being accurately described in the model may be applied to smaller machines for farmers whose strength of Cattle may not reach the power of this. Mr. Patersons Machine was worked by two strong horses at a time, the Diameter of his threshing wheel was greater than in your model being I think 8 feet and its velocity much less. The motion was given in a contrary direction whereby the grain instead of being thrown over the top of the wheel fell under it through a grating prepared for the purpose. Have you thought of the method used here occasionally of combing off the ears of the wheat? or of putting it as soon as threshed into cool subterraneous vaults, which I am told is the practice in Sicily? I am not without hopes that notwithstanding your former determination circumstances will have induced you to retain your situation beyond the time you had limited. I beg you to be assured, my dear Sir, that whether you continue in or retire from public office you possess the sincere attachment of Your affectionate & respectful Servt.

THOMAS PINCKNEY

[*Notes in TJ's hand:*]
Cogs &c of the wheels
$78 \div 17 = 4.6$
$59 \div 13 = 4.5$
$53 \div 11 = 4.8$
$4.6 \times 4.5 \times 4.8 = 99.36$
For every mile, by the hour, of the horse's motion the threshing wheel turns 100 times a minute.
Viz. if the horse goes

2 miles an hour, the wheel turns 100. times a minute	
$2\frac{1}{2}$	250
3.	300

RC (DLC); at foot of first page: "Mr. Jefferson"; at head of text: "(Private)"; with note by TJ at foot of text; endorsed by TJ as received 29 Apr. 1794 and so recorded in SJL. PrC (ScHi: Pinckney Family Papers).

From Ferdinando Fairfax

SIR   Shannon-hill, Berkeley, Janu. 31. 1794.

You have, no doubt, often received the congratulations of your countrymen upon your entrance into the several Public Offices and employments, to which your time and attention have been for so many years devoted. Permit me, now, to congratulate you upon your voluntary relinquishment of these employments, for that peaceful retirement, the proper relish and enjoyment of which constitutes the truest dignity of the human Character. This from me were indeed impertinence, if the title of American citizen, and, what I am much more ambitious of deserving, citizen of the World, cannot be considered as affording a sufficient excuse. Tho', in the former character, I cannot but join with the worthy part of the community in their hearty concern for your retreat from Public Life, whilst we remember with unfeigned gratitude the tenor and direction of your Public Services; yet, in the latter, I feel, with an interest that I cannot express, the influence which such an example must have—its encouragement to the persuits of calm Philosophy, Religion, and Virtue.

You, Sir, must have had the fullest opportunity of determining, experimentally, the true value of honors, preferment, distinction, public applause—upon which the hearts of the multitude are so warmly set; and when you can resign them all, and retreat to that serene and still life from whence you first set out, you add the greatest weight to the maxim, That happiness must consist in the disposition of the mind, that no external circumstances have power to confer it, and that it is not Station or Office which adds dignity to a Character, but vice versa.

It is much to be lamented that those who are most ambitious of distinction in Public Life, and especially those who express the warmest zeal for the Public Service, are generally the least deserving; and it is to be wished that good Men wou'd more generally undertake this Service: But, however some may doubt the existence of genuine Patriotism in the World, he must be a true Patriot indeed, who, having learnt justly to estimate the comparative advantages and value of the two situations, can be prevailed upon to give up the peaceful and heart felt pleasures of retired Life, for the hurry, fatigue, and not unfrequent vexation, incident to a Public station.

I cannot be suspected of any design in this address, because I can have no end to answer; and if it shou'd appear to be too much in the stile [of][1] the ancient Dedications, I can only offer in excuse the warmth of sincerity with which I am Sir, Your most respectful Humble servant

FERDNO: FAIRFAX

RC (DLC); at foot of text: "Thomas Jefferson Esqr."; endorsed by TJ as received 14 Feb. 1794 and so recorded in SJL.

[1] Word supplied.

To Horatio Gates

DEAR GENERAL   Monticello Feb. 3. 1794.

I left Philadelphia on the very day of the friendly letter you wrote me, and consequently it came to me at this place. The letter book with which you were so kind as to entrust me, came to my hands some little time before the infectious fever broke out at Philadelphia. I was just about putting it into confidential hands to extract the letters to or from myself, when that disorder obliged us to a precipitate flight, and I brought the book to this place where it is now safe. I have been arrived here but a short time. Within two months from this date a nephew comes to live with me whom I shall employ in making the extracts, and soon after that I will find some sure opportunity of conveying it to you. In the mean time have no anxieties about it, as it is sacredly safe here, and shall be most faithfully restored.

I receive with emotions of sincere pleasure your kind expressions of friendship, and invitations to Rose-hill, and make grateful acknolegements to Mrs. Gates and yourself, but the length of my tether is now fixed for life from Monticello to Richmond. My private business can never call me elsewhere, and certainly politics will not, which I have ever hated both in theory and practice. I thought myself conscientiously called from those studies which were my delight by the political crisis of my country and by those events quorum pars magna fuisti. In storms like those all hands must be aloft. But calm is now restored, and I leave the bark with joy to those who love the sea. I am but a landsman, forced from my element by accident, regaining it with transport, and wishing to recollect nothing of what I have seen, but my friendships. Some of these are indeed very dear to my heart. I shall cherish them in my thoughts, in my conversations and in my letters. But I think it more probable you should return to bask in the genial sunshine of this country, than that I should go to shiver under the frozen skies of the North. Adieu my dear General & friend and accept assurances of my constant affections & respect.   TH: JEFFERSON

RC (NHi: Gates Papers); addressed: "Majr. Genl. Gates New York"; endorsed by Gates. PrC (DLC).

LETTER YOU WROTE ME: Gates to TJ, 5 Jan. [1794].

QUORUM PARS MAGNA FUISTI: an adaptation of Virgil, *Aeneid*, 2.6, "quorum pars magna fui." TJ's change of the verb from the first person to the second credits Gates, not himself, with having played "no small part" in the "political crisis of my country" (see H. Rushton Fairclough, ed. and trans., *Virgil*, 2 vols. [Cambridge, Mass., rev. ed. 1934-35; repr. 1994], I, 294-5).

To James Innes

Dear Sir   Monticello Feb. 3. 1794.

Having occasion for information as to the practice [of the] Genl.
court in a particular matter, wherein it may probably be very different
from what it was when I was more familiar with it, I have no acquaintance at the bar to whom I would be more willingly indebted for it than
yourself. In settling a sterling debt and the paiments made on it, do they
convert them into currency? at the legal exchange? or at the exchange
current at market at the moment? If at the legal exchange, would it be
that which was so at the moment of contracting the debt, and of making
paiments, (if while the legal exchange was 25. pr. Cent) or at the present legal exchange of $33\frac{1}{3}$? Can you pardon this intrusion on you, as
well as the request for a line of answer by the return of post, as it respects
a case on which I am pressed to decide? I shall have the pleasure of
seeing you in Richmond as soon as it recommences business, and am at
all times with sincere esteem & respect Dear Sir Your friend & servt
                                              TH: JEFFERSON

PrC (DLC); left margin frayed; at foot of text: "Colo. Innes."

Innes's response of 16 Feb. 1794, re-corded in SJL as received from Richmond four days later, has not been found. SJL also records missing letters from TJ to Innes of 20 July 1794 and 9 July 1795.

To Edmund Randolph

Dear Sir   Monticello Feb. 3. 1794.

I have to thank you for the transmission of the letters from Genl.
Gates, La Motte, and Hauterive. I perceive by the latter that the partisans of the one or the other principle (perhaps of both) have thought my
name a convenient cover for declarations of their own sentiments. What
those are to which Hauterive alludes, I know not, having never seen a
newspaper since I left Philadelphia (except those of Richmond) and no
circumstances authorize him to expect that I should enquire into them,
or answer him. I think it is Montaigne who has said that ignorance is
the softest pillow on which a man can rest his head. I am sure it is true
as to every thing political, and shall endeavor to estrange myself to every
thing of that character. I indulge myself on one political topic only, that
is, in [dis]closing to my countrymen the shameless corruption of a
[por]tion of the representatives in the 1st. and 2d. Congresses and their
implicit devotion to the treasury. I think I do good in this, because it

may produce exertions to reform the evil on the success of which the form of the government is to depend.

I am [sorry] La Motte has put me to the expence of 140ᵗᵗ for a French translation of an English poem, as I make it a rule never to read translations where I can read the original. However the question now is how to get the book brought here, as well as the communications with Mr. Hammond which you are so kind as to promise me. I must pray you to deliver them to Mr. Madison or Colo. Monroe with a request that they will send them to Colo. Gamble by the first person coming in the stage to [Richmond], endorsing on the packet that they are to be put into the post office. As you are still interested in the agriculture of this country, I will mention to you that on James river the small grain never wore so dismal an appearance at this season. A snow of about 8. Inches fell five days ago, and is likely to lie so[me day]s longer. This will help it. At Richmond, our market, no property of any form, would command money even before the interruption of business by the small pox. Produce might be bartered at a low price for goods at a high one. One house alone bought wheat at all, and that on credit. I take this to be the habitual state of the markets on James river, to which shortlived exceptions have existed when some particular cash commission for purchases has been received from abroad. I know not how it is on the other rivers, and therefore say nothing as to them.

This is the first letter I have written to Philadelphia since my arrival at home, and yours the only ones I have received. Accept assurances of my sincere esteem and respect. Your's affectionately

Tʜ: Jᴇꜰꜰᴇʀꜱᴏɴ

PrC (DLC); torn and faded; unaddressed, but recipient identified from SJL and internal evidence.

Letters from Randolph to TJ of 14 and 19 Jan. 1794, recorded in SJL as received 2 Feb. 1794, have not been found. For the missing letter of 27 Oct. 1793 from ʟᴀ ᴍᴏᴛᴛᴇ, see note to TJ to Delamotte and Others, 5 Nov. 1793. For the publication of the ᴄᴏᴍᴍᴜɴɪᴄᴀᴛɪᴏɴꜱ between TJ and British minister George Hammond that the President had submitted to Congress on 5 Dec. 1793, see note to Edmond Charles Genet to TJ, 16 May 1793.

From O. A. Bertrand

Mᴏɴꜱᴇɪɢɴᴇᴜʀ   Londre ce 8 fev: 1794.

J'ai L'honneur de vous envoïer les pieces ci incluses; je crois, quelles vous feront plaisir, parcequ'il m'a paru, Lorsque j'ai eu L'honneur de vous voir chez le Sieur thouin en 1785, que vous preniez de l'intérêt à la digression, que je faisois Sur la fécondation végétale et artificielle; je vous prie Monseigneur de porter à la connoissance des Etats Unis, et que S'ils croyoient, qu'il Seroit util à L'Amerique de faire instruire quelques orphelins Americains dans la culture Belgique; que je m'empresserai de me Charger de cette bésogne Sans en exiger aucune récompense; ce Seroit avec le même empressement et le même désinteressement, que j'enverrois les graines, arbres, plantes, animaux, oiseaux, et tous les autres articles qui pourroient intéresser les Etats Unis; je croirois Monseigneur, que comme on établit Souvent des consuls dans des païs étrangers, qu'il Seroit avantageux aux états Unis d'établir au païs bas un consul agronomique; S'ils Suivoient mon opinion; je communiquerai volontier à ce consul mes idées Sur beaucoup de points d'agricultures; j'ai L'honneur d'être avec beaucoup de respect et en vous offrant mes Services aux païs bas Monseigneur votre très-humble et obéissant Serviteur

O: A: Bertrand
avocat et Cultivateur

P.S. Je Suppose Monseigneur que Le commencement de mes ouvrages, c'est à dire le guide du cultivateur et des annales demonstratives; que le sieur devaltravers S'ètoit Chargé de vous envoïer, vous sera parvenu: Si vous daigniez de m'ecrire, Les Sieurs Dubois Logés à Londre New Bassinghal Street; Se Sont chargés de me fair parvenir mes lettres.

RC (DNA: RG 59, MLR); endorsed by TJ as received 6 May 1794 and so recorded in SJL. Letter and enclosures enclosed in Tobias Lear to TJ, 12 Feb. 1794, George Washington to TJ, 24 Apr. 1794, and TJ to Edmund Randolph, 14 May 1794.

ENCLOSURES
I
List of Notes

L'avocat Bertrand a L'honneur d'offrir Au Seigneur Jefferson Secretaire d'Etats des Etats Unis d'Amerique des notes instructives sur les points suivans.

1

notes instructives sur les meilleurs moÿens de perfectioner L'agriculture et l'économie rurale.

2

notes instructives sur les meilleurs moÿens de perfectioner les arts et Sciences.

3

notes instructives sur les meilleurs moÿens de soulager les pauvres.

4

notes instructives sur les meilleurs moÿens de guerir et de prevenir beaucoup de maladies de L'homme et des animaux.

ces notes sont le fruit de vingt ans de recherches et de méditations; si vous daignez de les agréér j'aurai L'honneur de vous Les envoïer.

O: A: Bertrand

MS (DNA: RG 59, MLR); undated.

II
Agricultural Prospectus

> Description de quelques demonstrations expérimentales, que L'avocat Bertrand désireroit de faire par un de ses fils dans les environs de la ville de Washington, que les Etats Unis d'Amerique font batir.

> ### 1
> Demonstrations expérimentales sur les meilleurs procédés à Suivre pour constater la nature des sols et des terreins et pour les ameliorer.

> ### 2
> Demonstrations expérimentales sur les meilleurs procédés a Suivre pour déterminer la nature des végetaux. A

A Si on ne connoit pas exactement la nature des terreins et les moÿens de les ameliorer, Si on ne connoit pas exactement la nature des végetaux, qu'on cultive, il est impossible de poser des regles fixes et certaines pour perfectioner l'agriculture; il est donc util pour ne point dire nécessaire de faire les demonstrations expérimentales mentionés Sub N 1 et 2.

> ### 3
> Demonstrations expérimentales sur les meilleurs procédés à Suivre pour perfectioner les especes et variétés des vegetaux. B

B L'abondance et la perfection des récoltes dependant notoirement en grande partie de la perfection des especes et des variétés des végetaux, il est de la plus grande importance de déterminer expérimentalement les meilleurs procédés pour les perfectioner.

> ### 4
> Demonstrations expérimentales Sur des propriétés inconnues des [végétaux]. C

C La richesse et la prospérité des Nations dependent en partie des propriétés et avantages, qu'on peut tirer des végétaux; il est donc intéressant de les Connoître et de les Connoître expérimentalement, ceux Sur les quels je me propose de faire mes démonstrations expérimentales vaudroient des millions Aux Etats Unis.

> ### 5
> Demonstrations expérimentales Sur les meilleurs procédés à Suivre pour perfectioner la garance et les autres matieres Colorantes. D.

D Il est très-notoir, que la perfection des fabriques dépend en grande partie de la perfection de la teinture et que la teinture depend de la perfection des matieres colorantes; il est donc util de déterminer experimentalement les meilleurs procédés pour les perfectioner.

[18]

6

Demonstrations expérimentales Sur des procédés nouveaux de perfectioner la culture du Chanvre et du rouissage, item Sur des procédés nouveaux pour bassiner la filace et la blanchir. E

E La culture du chanvre occupe beaucoup de terrein, ses produits sont d'une Consideration majeure à plusieurs égards, il est donc très-nécessaire, que les demonstrations qui tendent à Sa perfection aient Lieu.

7

Demonstrations expérimentales Sur les meilleurs moÿens d'augmenter et de perfectioner les engrais, item Sur le moÿen de conduire autant d'engrais Sur une Charrette, qu'on conduit ordinairement Sur vingt et plus. F.

F Les terrein Steriles, qu'on a rendu au païs bas à l'agriculture, et la grande richesse, qu'on ÿ tire de la terre, prouvent à L'évidence que les engrais Sont pour ainsi dire L'ame et le Soutient de l'agriculture; augmenter les engrais, les perfectioner, diminuer les frais du Charriage, Sont donc des objets, qui méritent la plus grande attention; je m'en suis particulierement occupé, mes demonstrations le prouveront à L'évidence.

8

Demonstrations expérimentales sur des procédés nouveaux, et qui n'ont encore été emploiés par aucune nation pour défricher toutes les terres incultes, et pour lever les obstacles ordinaires le defaut de bras, d'argent, et d'engrais. H.

H L'utilité des defrichemens, est d'une notoriété si évidente, qu'elle n'a pas besoin d'être relevée; les recherches que j'ai faites Sur cet objet, et les résultats, que j'en ai eu me convainquent de la Supériorité de mes procédés Sur ceux, qu'on emploi ordinairement; les demonstrations espérimentales, que je desire de faire, ne laisseroient aucun doute de leur utilité.

Si Le seigneur Secretaire jugoit de L'utilité de ces demonstrations, comme J'en juge, je le Supplie de les presenter en mon nom aux Etats Unis, en observant, qu'il faudroit au moins mille acres de terre pour faire ces demonstrations convenablement et en grand, acres, que j'espererois d'obtenir en pleine propriété, attendu que les demonstrations vaudroient des millions aux Etats Unis.

O: A: Bertrand

MS (DNA: RG 59, MLR); undated; word in brackets supplied.

From Tobias Lear

Dear Sir   London Feby. 12, 1794.

The enclosed papers were put into my hands yesterday by M. Bertrand, whom I have met several times since I have been in this City. This gentleman is spoken of as a great Agriculturalist, and is much esteemed, as I am informed, by the Society of Agriculture in this Kingdom. His propositions, however, are not such as are likely to meet with encouragement in the United States and so I told him; but as he told me he had been known to you while you was in Europe, I could not decline taking charge of and forwarding his papers.

My passage from New York to Scotland was short, and I have met with every thing since I have been in this country that ought to make it personally agreeable to me; but sure I am that had I been ever so deeply impressed with a love of aristocracy before I came here, I have seen enough to have excited the utmost abhorrence of it. I have mixed with all ranks of society in this Kingdom, and excepting among a few of the higher class, I have found a strong expression of good will toward the U.S., and a high admiration of their government, with a full persuasion of the happiness of the people under it. My observations on these points are not very limited, for I have been in various parts of the Kingdom, and, as I observed before, among all ranks of men. At this critical juncture it will not be wise in me to detail opinions on the state of things. But I can venture to say from the best view I am able to take of matters, *that France will triumph*, and *that the cord is drawn so tight here that it must break, and that at no very distant period.* The prayer of good men here is that the U.S. may be kept at peace, and that the citizens thereof may be vigilent in guarding against those insidious advances of power which are so peculiarly dangerous to free governments.

I cannot but hope, my dear Sir, that you are still at Philadelphia and in the exercise of the office in which I left you. It is not my personal friendship for you that leads to this hope, but a conviction of the benefit which the U. S. must derive therefrom. With the most sincere wishes for your health and happiness, and with sentiments of pure respect and attachment, I am, Dear Sir, your obliged friend and Svt.

Tobias Lear

MS not found; reprinted from *Jefferson Correspondence*, *Bixby*, 61-2. Recorded in SJL as received 6 May 1794. Enclosure: O. A. Bertrand to TJ, 8 Feb. 1794, and enclosures. Letter and enclosures enclosed in George Washington to TJ, 24 Apr. 1794.

To Hartman Elliot

Sir   Monticello Feb. 15. 1794.

I received three days ago your favor of January 18. and am sorry to find by it that your driver has defrauded you of ten dollars. I was to pay you for your stage 5. dollars a day for seven days, and ferriages. I paid the ferriages and toll to Fredericksburg myself, exactly 2. dollars, and at Fredericksburg I paid your driver thirty five dollars for the stage, two dollars for his ferriages and toll [. . .], and 1. dollar gratuity. This I copy from my travelling memorandums, to which I have recurred. I also took his reciept in the following words. 'Recieved of Thomas Jefferson thirty five dollars for the hire of Mr. Hartman's carriage from Baltimore to Fredericksburg, and two dollars ferriages in full this 12th. day of January 1794. John + Williams.' And I now inclose you the original receipt. Besides this my memory serves to assure me there was no mistake in counting the money: for in the morning before my arrival at Fredericksburg I remember counting 30. dollars and placing them in the top of my portmanteau, where I could get at them easily; and as soon almost as I arrived at Fredericksburg I called him in, paid him the 30. dollars, added a 5. dollar Baltimore bank note which I had received from Mr. Brent and had in my waistcoat pocket, and two other dollars for the ferriages, the amount of which I did not know in the morning as I had still another river to cross. I went in the afternoon into the country, but returned between 9. and 10. the next morning, saw and spoke with your driver, and he had then an opportunity of mentioning any error in counting money, if there had been any. But I know there had been none, and so does he. I am Sir your humble servt   TH: JEFFERSON

PrC (MHi); torn; at foot of text: "Mr. Hartman Eliot"; erroneously endorsed in ink by TJ as a letter of 15 Feb. 1796.

Hartman Elliot (d. between 1817 and 1822) was a hack carriage keeper at 18 South Howard Street, Baltimore (William Thompson and James L. Walker, *The Baltimore Town and Fell's Point Directory . . .* [Baltimore, 1796], 24; *The Baltimore Directory, for 1817-18 . . .* [Baltimore, 1817], 58; Charles Keenan, *The Baltimore Directory, for 1822 & '23 . . .* [Baltimore, 1822], 89).

Elliot's missing FAVOR OF JANUARY 18. is recorded in SJL as received from Baltimore on 12 Feb. 1794. In his entries for that letter and this reply TJ recorded the surname as "Elart." In his account books TJ recorded paying Elliot's driver $33 of his own money and $5 he had received from William BRENT as the latter's share of the cost for traveling from Baltimore to Georgetown. The previous autumn TJ had paid Elliot $30 plus $3.18 for ferry expenses for bringing him from Baltimore to Germantown (MB, 1 Nov. 1793, 12 Jan. 1794, and note).

To James Madison

DEAR SIR   Monticello Feb. 15. 1794.

We are here in a state of great quiet, having no public news to agitate us. I have never seen a Philadelphia paper since I left that place, nor learnt any thing of later date except some successes of the French the account of which seemed to have come by our vessel from Havre. It was said yesterday at our court that Genet was to be recalled: however nobody could tell how the information came. We have been told that Mr. Smith's speech and your's also on your propositions have got into Davis's papers, but none of them have reached us. I could not have supposed, when at Philadelphia, that so little of what was passing there could be known even at Kentucky, as is the case here. Judging from this of the rest of the Union, it is evident to me that the people are not in a condition either to approve or disapprove of their government, nor consequently to influence it.—I have been[1] occupied closely with my own affairs, and have therefore never been from home since my arrival here. I hear nothing yet of the second person whom I had engaged as an overseer from the head of Elk, and the first I fear will prove a poor acquisition. Consequently I am likely to lose a year in the reformation of my plantations.—The winter has been remarkeably mild. No demand for produce of any kind, at any market of James river. Tobacco and wheat may be bartered at low prices for goods at high. But neither can be sold for cash. This was the state of things at Richmond when business was stopped by the smallpox. Here we can get tea at $2\frac{1}{2}$ Dollars, white sugar at 38 Cents, coffee @ 25. cents &c for wheat @ $66\frac{2}{3}$. Accept for yourself, Colo. & Mrs. Monroe my affectionate respects

Th: Jefferson

RC (DLC: Madison Papers); at foot of text: "Mr. Madison." PrC (DLC).

William Loughton SMITH'S SPEECH in the House of Representatives on 13 Jan. 1794 opened the Federalist attack on the PROPOSITIONS introduced by Madison ten days earlier to implement the proposals in TJ's Report on Commerce of December 1793. Madison replied in support of the resolutions on 14, 30, and 31 Jan. 1794. Beginning in late January, Smith's and Madison's addresses appeared in Augustine DAVIS's *Virginia Gazette, and General Advertiser* and in the *Virginia Gazette, and Richmond and Manchester Advertiser*, both Richmond newspapers. Davis took the reports from Andrew Brown's *Philadelphia Gazette*, which began coverage of the debates on 15 Jan. 1794. For TJ's reaction to the more extensive account of Smith's address, which appeared in the *Philadelphia Gazette* on 24 and 27 Jan. 1794, see TJ to Madison, 3 Apr. 1794. Madison prepared his key speeches for publication in Brown's paper, the first two appearing on 27 and 28 Feb. 1794 respectively, and the last running in the issues of 3-5 and 7 Mch. 1794. For the failure of Madison's resolutions, see Editorial Note on Report on Commerce, 16 Dec. 1793.

SECOND PERSON: Eli Alexander. POOR ACQUISITION: Samuel Biddle.

[1] TJ here canceled "immensely."

From Tench Coxe

Philada. Feby. 22d. 1794

I hope, Sir, that this letter will find [you][1] settled in your retreat at Monticello. It is the first which I have had the honor to address to you since your departure.

I congratulate you on the temperate conduct of the French Convention towards the U.S. in regard to the late Altercations of Mr. Genet with our Government and his conduct in general. I understood yesterday from the P. that Mr. Fauchet, their new Minister, on the occasion of his being received that day, had made the most satisfactory communications on those topics. This is in every view a happy circumstance. No less so for France than for the United States. It will disappoint a few persons, I am uncharitable enough to believe, who would not be dissatisfied to see a settled misunderstanding between the two Countries, and who do not like to see the Convention evince a sobriety and attachment towards those who wish them well, which it is often alleged they neither feel nor shew to any body. We are now in a good state with France, and I hope none among us will shew that the lashing of Mr. Genet proceeded from deeper and more important sources, than offence at his conduct.

The combined powers appear to be disposed to carry on the war, and are now trying to engage the Minor states of Europe with them. Genoa and Tuscany appear to be forced into the business. The Pressure on Denmark is seriously increased by the demand made upon their king, to furnish his Quota to the Germanic body as Duke of Holstein. I hope the french will be wise enough to consider this as no more in Substance, than the conduct of a power bound by treaty to furnish a specific supply of troops, or ships to their Enemies.

Toulon appears stronger on the land Side than was expected, and the gradual addition of force is such that if the french do not give the combined army a stroke in that quarter, there may be danger that some of the insurgents may be drawn into action in the South of France. The Sortie under the Commander in chief is a symptom however, of a pretty serious internal Situation. The check given to the Garrison on the occasion is therefore of real importance.

The month of November and the two first days of December appear to have exhibited the sharpest operations of the Campain, in the N.E. departments and on the borders of Germany. The severity of the climate and season will probably suspend the operations of the Germans in that quarter. Yet the state of things is so critical there that the French have the strongest impulses to further operations, and the allies have inducements no less powerful. To regain Weissembourg, or to possess Alsace for the winter must be important objects to the two sides.

The Armies of Flanders, and the North appear to be withdrawn from operation. The Germans will no doubt try hard to make their acquisitions in that quarter secure.

We do not find the insurgents around the Loire suppressed. The expedition under Lord Moira now reanimates them.

The french exhibit increasing prowess, but it appears to be all necessary for the task imposed upon them. I do not know what the coldness of the Dutch, the dissatisfactions in Britain, Ireland, and Poland, the exhausted state of the finances and Treasuries of the combined powers, and their own energies may do for them this winter, but at present it does not appear certain that any of their enemies will withdraw from another trial. The next campain, must be bloody (from the increased military abilities of the french, and the excessive acrimony on both sides) beyond all former examples. The struggle however does not appear to be less promising than in 1792 and 1793.

Our chances of peace, considering all circumstances seem to be as great as we could have expected. Unless a very triumphant success should attend the Enemies of France, it appears likely, that nothing like a formal war will be made upon us. But I expect to see disagreeable things in the Course of the summer. The bringing in and selling french prizes will prove a bone of Contention, I fear, particularly the latter. If the British succeed in the west Indies, we shall have their ships moving in those Seas, and no good can grow out of the freedom of our ports to ships of war, which are not under any check from a navy or from forts. We have seen how unpleasant these things may be in the Cases, which have occured this Season on the part of the French.

I do not think there is more moderation in our parties than when you left us. Personalities, which lessen the pleasures of Society, or prevent their being sought, have occured in private and at Tables. You will remember that I mentioned my opinion that one person would be greatly incommoded by the excessive Spirit of that kind, which was manifest and increasing. So it has happened. However, honest public views and principles give him the necessary firmness—and will continue to produce that effect, I trust. Nothing has occur'd, in the public eye or otherwise I beleive to abstract from the comforts of Mr. Randolph's Situation. Mr. Bradford's appointment was on the whole the best that could be made, in relation to his Ease and Satisfaction. I believe it will eventually serve and satisfy the public, even in these difficult times. [2]

I understand that Messrs. Priestlys and Cooper have decided upon the Banks of the Loyal Loch, 140 miles N.W. of Philada. in Pennsa. and that they have bought very largely. Another concern of the same description from Devonshire, seem determined upon Kentucky. The fate of the British Convention in Scotland will give extent to these Emigrations and Investments. I have the Honor to be with perfect respect, Sir, yr. most obedt. & mo. hble Servant   TENCH COXE

RC (DLC); endorsed by TJ as received 31 Mch. 1794 and so recorded in SJL.

CONDUCT OF THE FRENCH CONVENTION: a reference to the French government's acceptance of the American demand for Edmond Charles Genet's recall and its replacement of him by a four-member commission with instructions to redress some of the Washington administration's complaints about his behavior (DeConde, *Entangling Alliance*, 392-6). p.: the President. EXPEDITION UNDER LORD MOIRA: the British expeditionary force dispatched to Brittany in December 1793 under the command of Francis Rawdon Hastings, Earl of Moira, to aid rebellious royalists (DNB). MR. BRADFORD'S APPOINTMENT: William Bradford re-

ceived Senate confirmation on 27 Jan. 1794 as Edmund Randolph's successor as Attorney General of the United States (JEP, I, 147).

[1] Word supplied.
[2] Sentence added by Coxe.

From Tench Coxe

SIR   Philada. Feb. 27. 1794.

The inclosed accounts of the recapture of Toulon will give you satisfaction in a high degree. They are believed here by all parties. It is added that the Earl of Moira has returned without landing his Army in Britanny. This is the most important Advice we have received since the war, as I have the honor to mention to you *confidentially*, that Mr. P. writes from L. that Ld. Granville has finally answered in regard to the posts—that after so long and injurious a delay to perform the Treaty on our part the article relative to the posts could not be considered as binding! I wish this be carefully retained in your own bosom until or unless you have it from some other quarter, tho I have it not in official Confidence.

You will see in Fenno's Gazette an article extracted from an octavo volume of American papers I am republishing here, of which I shall have the honor to present you with a copy. I do not believe it will be completed before the rising of Congress. I have the honor to be in great haste yr. mo. respectful & mo. obedt. St.   TENCH COXE

Mr. Fauchet continues to hold the most satisfactory language.

Ld. G. acknowledged that Mr. Logie procured the Algerine truce, but said it was not to surprize us, but to leave the Portuguese fleet free to act on their views—confidential.

RC (DLC); dateline between first and second postscripts; endorsed by TJ as received 31 Mch. 1794 and so recorded in SJL.

MR. P. WRITES: on 24 Feb. 1794 President Washington had submitted to Congress a 25 Nov. 1793 letter from Thomas Pinckney to the Secretary of State describing an interview with Lord Grenville in which the British foreign secretary stated among other things that pending further negotiations

his country would continue to retain posts within the western borders of the United States in defiance of the Treaty of Paris and that, after nine years of failure by America to pay debts owed to British creditors as stipulated by the same treaty, England could justly retain them even if the United States now settled this outstanding British grievance (ASP, *Foreign Relations*, I, 327-8).

VOLUME OF AMERICAN PAPERS: see enclosure listed at Coxe to TJ, 20 Mch. 1795.

From James Madison

Philada. March 2d. 1794.

Your favor of the 15th. Ult: came to hand two days ago. It was not my intention that my first to you should have been procrastinated to the present date; but several causes have concurred in producing the effect. Among others I was in hopes every week to be able to furnish you with the proceedings on the subject grounded on your Commercial Report; and particularly with such of them as related to yourself. It has so happened that I never could find leisure to make out for the press, the share I had in them till very lately. The earlier part of my observations were sent to the Printer several weeks ago, but never made their appearance till thursday evening last. The latter part is following, as you will find, as fast as I can write it out, which from the extreme length of it, the brevity of my notes, and the time that has run since the observations were delivered, is a task equally tedious and laborious. The sequel will be forwarded to you as soon as it gets into print. As you are so little supplied with the current information it may be necessary to apprize you that after the general discussions on the measure proposed by me, had been closed, and the first general resolution agreed to by a majority of 5 or 6, several of the Eastern members friendly to the object insisted on a postponement till the first monday in March. It was necessary to gratify them, and the postponement was carried by a small majority against the efforts of the adverse party, who counted on the votes of the timid members if forced before they could learn the sense of their constituents. The Interval has produced vast exertions by the British party to mislead the people of the Eastern States. No means have been spared. The most artful and wicked calumnies have been propagated with all the zeal which malice and interest could invent. The blackest of these calumnies, as you may imagine have fallen to the lot of the mover of the Resolutions. The last Boston paper contains a string of charges framed for the purpose of making the Eastern people believe that he has been the counsellor and abettor of Genèt in all his extravagances, and a corrupt tool of France ever since the embassy of Gerard. It appears however that in spite of all these diabolical manoevres, the town of Boston has been so far awakened as to have a Meeting in the town house, and a pretty unanimous vote for a committee to consider the subject and report proper instructions for their members in Congress. The Committee consists of men of weight, and for the most part of men of the right sort. There are some however who will endeavor to give a wrong turn to the business. I see by a paper of last evening that even in N. York a meeting of the people has taken place at the instance of the Republican party, and that a committee is appointed for the like purpose. As far as I know the names, the majority is on the right side. One motive for postponing the question so long was the chance of hearing from England, and the probability that the intelligence would strengthen the arguments for retaliation. Letters from Pinkney have accordingly arrived. As yet they are under the seal of confidence but it is in universal conversation that they mark precisely and *more strongly* than ever the unjust and unfriendly features which have characterized the British policy towards the U. States. Soon after the arrival of the Packet, Mr. Randolph wrote to Hammond desiring to know whether an answer had been received to your letter of May 1792. His reply was simply that it had not.

The scheme of Frigates to block up the Mediterranean has been pushed slowly, but successfully to the stage of resolutions on which a Bill is to be reported. The majority has never exceeded two or three votes. Whether the scheme will finally take effect, is not certain. It probably will, unless accounts from Europe furnish hopes that Spain, or Portugal particularly the latter which is friendly and interested in our trade, may interpose.

Genèt has been superseded by Fauchèt, the Secretary to the Executive Council. The latter has not been here long eno' to develope his temper and character. He has the aspect of moderation. His account of things in France is very favorable on the whole. He takes particular pains to assure all who talk with him of the perseverance of France in her attachment to us, and her anxiety that nothing which may have taken place, may lessen it on our side. In his interview with the President, he held the same language; and I am told by E.R. that the P. not only declared explicitly his affectionate solicitude for the success of the Republic, but after he had done so with great emphasis, desired, in order to be as pointed as possible, that his expressions might be repeated, by E.R. who acted as Interpreter. Fauchet does not speak our language. La Forest comes over with the Minister as Consul General: And Petry, formerly Consul of S.C. as Consul for this place. The political characters of these gentlemen as heretofore understood, give some uneasiness to the Republican party; and the uneasiness has been increased by the homage paid by the leaders of the other party to the New Minister. They may probably aim at practising on him, by abusing the madness of Genèt and representing the Republicans as rather his partisans, than the friends of the French cause. But if he is not an uncommon fool, or a traytor, it is impossible he can play into their hands, because the Anglicism stamped on the aristocratic faction must warn him of its hostility to his objects. Genèt has not taken any decided step in relation to his future movements. He is said to be poor; and by some to meditate a return to France with a view to join the army, by others a settlement in this Country as a farmer. If he is prudent he will not venture to France in her present temper, with all the suspicions and follies with which he is loaded. You must have seen that Brissot and his party have been cut off by the Guillotine.

I am informed by an anonymous letter from N. York, that large purchases are making there, and in the Eastern States, for supplying the British armaments in the W. Indies; and that American Vessels are chartering for the conveyance of them. This is really horrible. Whilst we allow the British to stop our supplies to the French Dominions, we allow our citizens to carry supplies to hers, for the known purpose of aiding her in taking from France the Islands we have guaranteed to her; and transferring these valuable markets from friendly to unfriendly hands. What can be done. The letter writer suggests an Embargo. Perhaps the best step would be to declare that so long as G.B. will not allow the French to be supplied by us, we will not allow our supplies to go to her. It is not clear however that such a measure would stand the clamor of the merchants seconded by the interest of the farmers, and ship owners.

RC (DLC: Madison Papers); unsigned; endorsed by TJ as received 31 Mch. 1794 and so recorded in SJL.

For the debates GROUNDED on TJ's COMMERCIAL REPORT, see TJ to Madison, 15 Feb. 1794, and note.

The STRING OF CHARGES that Madison had long been a CORRUPT TOOL OF FRANCE and had been "the strenuous supporter of all Monsr. Genet's violent outrages" was leveled by "Fair Play" in the Boston *Columbian Centinel*, 19 Feb. 1794. Those attending the MEETING IN THE TOWN HOUSE at Boston on 13 Feb. 1794 selected a committee that drafted resolutions "recommending a discrimination against *Britain* and *Spain*, by imposing new duties on their vessels and goods," but these resolves were tabled indefinitely at a two-day gathering later that month (same, 12, 15, 26 Feb. 1794). The 20-man committee chosen by a MEETING OF THE PEOPLE of New York City on 27 Feb. 1794 prepared resolutions which attacked British infractions of the Treaty of Paris and violations of American neutrality but said

nothing of Madison's resolutions, calling only for the fortification of New York harbor. A second public meeting attended by 2,000 people unanimously approved these resolutions on 6 Mch. 1794 (New York *Daily Advertiser*, 28 Feb., 5-7 Mch. 1794).

In his message to Congress on 24 Feb. 1794, George Washington enclosed the 21 Feb. 1794 exchange of notes between Secretary of State Edmund RANDOLPH and British minister George HAMMOND relating to TJ's LETTER of 29 MAY 1792 to the latter (ASP, *Foreign Relations*, I, 328).

In response to a truce between Algiers and Portugal that unleashed Algerine corsairs on American shipping, resolutions calling for the establishment of an American navy were introduced in the House of Representatives on 2 Jan. 1794. Despite Republican objections, a bill authorizing the construction of six FRIGATES became law on 27 Mch. 1794 (note to David Humphreys to TJ, 6 Oct. 1793; *Annals*, IV, 154, 1426-8; Marshall Smelser, *The Congress Founds the Navy, 1787-1798* [Notre Dame, Ind., 1959], 48-63).

From James Monroe

Dear Sir   Phila. March 3. 1794.

The avidity with which I knew you sought retirement and peace, undisturbed by political occurrences, with the further consideration that no event of any importance had taken place since you left us, prevented my trespassing on you sooner. I am perfectly satisfied you will find in that retirement a contentment and tranquility not to be hoped for in publick life. And yours will be the greater, because you carry to it, notwithstanding the important and even turbulent scenes you have passed thro', not only the approbation of your own heart, and of your countrymen generally, but the silence and of course the constrained approbation of your enemies. I look forward with pleasure to the period, and it shall be no distant one, when I shall occupy as your neighbour the adjoining farm. To this end all my plans will hereafter have an undeviating reference, and I consider the death of Mrs. Monroe's father, an event lately taken place, lessening her attachment to this quarter of our country, as calculated to precipitate it.

You were aware of the motive in commencing the session by some act, connected with the present state of our affairs, founded on the publick sentiment, and which should at the same time vindicate our rights and interests, and likewise shun all possible pretext for war, on the part of the power it was meant to affect. And that the propositions introduc'd by Mr. Madison were thought best calculated to accomplish this object. Of their fate so far he says he will inform you, so that I need only add on that subject, that whether they succeed or not, they will certainly tend to open the eyes of the Eastern people respecting the conduct of their representatives as well as of the motive for it. Information is all they want: An opposition to our carrying trade by their own members, will affect them, in such a manner, they will all know the fact, and understand the motive. I therefore hope for the best effects from the discussion of these propositions, and think symtoms to the Eastward authorize the expectation it will be verified.

On friday last the Senate 14. to 12. declared that Mr. Gallatin had not been 9. years a citizen of the U. States when elected and that his seat was vacant. Upon this occasion Mr. H. of N. C. left us which prevented a division, and a decision from the chair; we have reason to beleive that decision would have been with us, from what has since transpired, upon the principle, his vote should not displace the sitting member. Morris had intimated in the beginning he should take no part in the question, but finding that Langdon was with us, and the question would probably depend on his vote[1] just before the vote was taken he rose and apologised for the necessity he was under from scruples of conscience (being convinc'd he had no right to his seat) to vote his colleague out. It appeared he had been near 14. years a resident, 3. years in Mass: where he was a professor of Harvard College, and where there is no citizen law, and inhabitance makes citizenship, by the constitution of that state. In opposition to which it was contended that the Englh. alien laws were in force there and that it was the practice of the State to pass special acts of naturalization for foreigners. That "inhabitant" means native or person so naturalized, and that the Confn. (4th. article) could not make an inhabitant tho' for 50 years in that state, not born nor naturalized there, a citizen in another imigrating there. The opposit of this doctrine was urged in both instances, and in particular in the first, that special acts of naturalization might be intended to dispense with residence, or as favors, and at best could not controul the constn. of the State which was paramount and a rule to us. He had not taken the oath of fidelity 9. years when elected nor when he took his seat.

About 3 weeks past a resolve passed the Senate by a majority of one for requesting the President to lay before the Senate the correspondence of Gr. Morris, with our Ex: and with that of France also. Two days past he laid before us a voluminous correspondence, stating "that he had omitted such parts as in his judgment ought not to be communicated." It has not yet been taken up. The opinion however of many is that his discretion should extend to time only—but this assumes the controul over the whole subject and in all respects. The removal of Mr. G., if it would have been proper in any event to discuss this point (considering the Senate a branch of the legislature) will I presume prevent it.

About a week past the question for opening the doors of the Senate was taken. By the 1st. vote it was rejected 14. to 13. Bradley of Verm: finding he could carry it moved to reconsider, which gained us immediately three others, and upon the final vote the opposition was reduc'd to 8. or 9. only: Ellsworth &ca voting for it, to take effect next session.

The Indian Treaty formed by Putnam after lengthy discussion was rejected. The arrival of Mr. Fauchet has removed Mr. Genet who is still here and I believe under some difficulty how to shape his course, on which head nothing final has transpired. Fauchet was received with the most profound attention by the party heretofore opposed to his country and her cause. Tis probable they might hope the fate of his predecessor would warn him to shun not only his errors but likewise the friends of France, upon the idea they were the friends of Mr. Genet. But this calculation cannot be verified. He must soon find that the republican party here are the only friends of that cause in his own country, and that it was owing to a zeal for that cause and a belief the man was honest, that his errors were in any degree tolerated by them. As yet the conduct of Fauchet appears to be reserved and prudent, and tis to be hoped he will finally take a course correspondent with what the interest of his country may require. We are well. Mrs. M. was called about three weeks past by the illness of Mr. Kortright to N. Yk. where she still is: I hope for her return in a few days. With great respect & esteem I am dear Sir sincerely yr. friend & servant   JAS. MONROE

RC (DLC); endorsed by TJ as received 31 Mch. 1794 and so recorded in SJL.

PROPOSITIONS INTRODUC'D BY MR. MADISON: see TJ to James Madison, 15 Feb. 1794, and note. For an analysis of the partisan vote by which the Senate on 28 Feb. 1794 vacated the election of the rising Pennsylvania Republican leader Albert GALLATIN, see Raymond Walters, Jr., *Albert Gallatin: Jeffersonian Financier and Diplomat* (New York, 1957), 59-63. MR. H.: Senator Benjamin Hawkins of North Carolina. The 4TH. ARTICLE of Confederation, which Gallatin had cited in defense of his qualifications to serve in the Senate, provided that the "free inhabitants of each of these states, paupers, vagabonds and fugitives from Justice excepted, shall be entitled to all privileges and immunities of free citizens in the several states" (DHRC, I, 87).

The 24 Jan. 1794 Senate resolution calling upon President Washington to submit the CORRESPONDENCE OF GR. MORRIS actually passed by a majority of two (JS, II, 25-6). The documents in question, which the Senate in fact received on 26 Feb. 1794, are in ASP, *Foreign Relations*, I, 329-78.

OPENING THE DOORS OF THE SENATE: although meetings of the Senate had been closed to the public since the establishment of the federal government, the upper house agreed on 11 Feb. 1794 to open its doors during discussions of Gallatin's disputed election. Then, on 19 Feb. 1794, the Senate first voted 14 to 13 in favor of a motion to postpone until the next session the question of allowing the public to attend all but its special secret meetings. Later in the day, with Stephen Bradley of Vermont, Theodore Foster of Rhode Island, John Langdon of New Hampshire, and Samuel Livermore of New Hampshire changing their votes, it voted 17 to 10 to open its doors to the public, except when secrecy was required, beginning with the next session of Congress (JS, II, 30, 32-3). See also Roy Swanstrom, *The United States Senate, 1787-1801* (Washington, D.C., 1985), 238-48.

By a vote of 21 to 4 the Senate on 9 Jan. 1794 rejected the treaty that General Rufus PUTNAM had negotiated with the Illinois and Wabash Indians in September 1792 because of its failure to secure preemptive rights of the United States to the lands of these tribes (JEP, I, 146). For the treaty itself, which Washington had submitted to the Senate in February 1793, see ASP, *Indian Affairs*, I, 338-40.

[1] Word canceled in MS.

From James Madison

DEAR SIR   Philada. March 9. 1794.

I send you the continuation promised in my last, which I believe makes up the whole. If there should be any chasm let me know, and I will supply it. I have some little doubt the paper of Tuesday March 4. may have been omitted, and would now add it, but can not get it conveniently in time.

The commercial propositions were postponed for one week longer, on the arrival of the appointed day. Tomorrow they will again come on, unless precluded by debates on other business, or again postponed. You will see by the inclosed in what manner the Meeting at Boston issued, and the course the subject is taking at N. York. There was a large Mercantile Meeting last night in this City, for obtaining a vote of remonstrance against the propositions. A paper was accordingly introduced by Fitzsimmons, Bingham &c. It was warmly and I am told ably attacked by Swanwick who explained and defended the propositions. He was clapped, and on the question, there were three or four nos for 1 aye to the paper. The minority had the arrogance notwithstanding to sign the paper individually, and will recruit all the names they can to day, among the Quaker's and others not present at the Meeting, in order to deliver in the paper with more effect tomorrow Morning. What the fate of the propositions will be is more uncertain than ever. Some of the friends of them, begin to say that more vigorous measures are rendered necessary by the progress of British outrages. The *additional* instruction of Novr. 6. which you will find in the inclosed papers, is so severely felt by the Merchants that some of them also, without relinquishing their opposition to what is proposed, talk of measures more congenial with the Crisis. An Embargo, on American vessels—on these and British also—and even on a seisure of British property, are in the mouths of some of them. The additional instruction is questioned by some as inauthentic; but it is infinitely probable that it is genuine. The doubt is founded on the earliness of its date compared with that of our last intelligence from Europe which is silent as to that matter. But it may have been decreed in the Cabinet and not put in force; or given into the hands of officers clandestinely, that the American prey might not escape. Our situation is certainly ripening to a most serious crisis. It does not appear however that in any event the commercial retaliation can be improper; but on the contrary that in every event it will be advantageous.

You will perceive that Fauchét is going on in the conciliatory plan of reversing the errors of his Predecessor.

The project of a squadron of frigates is pursued with unremitting ardor. In the course of the Bill the two 20 gun ships have been turned into 2 of 36 guns. So that the force is to consist of 6 in the whole, 4 of which will be of 40 guns. As the danger of a war has appeared to increase, every consideration rendering them at first unwise, now renders them absurd; yet the vague idea of protecting trade when it most needs it, misleads the interested who are weak, and the weak who are not interested.

I have this moment received a note informing me that there are letters from N.Y. containing definitive intelligence concerning Toulon. The British burnt sixteen French Sail of the Line in their escaping out of the Harbour. Many of the Toulonese were drowned in attempting to get on board the British Ships. All the remaining Inhabitants were drawn up in the public Square, and underwent military execution. The information comes by a Vessel from Carthagena. Adieu. Yrs. affy.

Js. MADISON JR

RC (DLC: Madison Papers); endorsed by TJ as received 31 Mch. 1794 and so recorded in SJL.

CONTINUATION PROMISED IN MY LAST: see Madison to TJ, 2 Mch. 1794. The Philadelphia MERCANTILE MEETING of 8 Mch. 1794 was followed three days later by another chaired by Stephen Girard which approved resolutions describing a policy of discrimination in tonnage duties based on the way nations treated American ships as "reasonable and just" and urged that American merchants who suffered losses from spoliations in violation of the law of nations be reimbursed with the proceeds from such increased imposts (*Philadelphia Gazette*, 5,

10, 12 Mch. 1794). The ADDITIONAL INSTRUCTION OF NOVR. 6. was an Order in Council authorizing British naval vessels to capture American ships trading with the French West Indies (printed in same, 7 Mch. 1794). French minister Jean Antoine Joseph Fauchet issued a proclamation on 6 Mch. 1794 REVERSING THE ERRORS of his predecessor Edmond Charles Genet by instructing French citizens to observe American neutrality and revoking and calling for the return of "All commissions or authorizations tending to infringe that neutrality" (same). Reports of the French recapture of TOULON appeared in same, 10 Mch. 1794.

From Giuseppe Ceracchi

DEAR SIR   Florence 11 Mz; 1794

With graet satisfaction I have recieved the honour of your first letter dated from Philodelphia the 14 of last Nov. in which I find explaned the case that retards the resolution on the intended Monument, which at any time that it will be resolved, I shall consider it as the most honorable commission coming to me throughof your inflonce with the United States, and the patronage you are plesed to grant me.

Your bust Sir is finished so far as my ability, and sentiments that I fil for the respectable Original coul'd permit me, I shall only aske your permission not to be defroded of the honnour of dedicating it to your Family. I must Kepe it with me few days more on request of several persons that having Know you in Urope will indolge them to see it.

You will never imagin Sir that I was exiled from Rome by the iniquos Priestes whom governed onder the influence of ignorance and superstition they feard of my principles of Liberty that I had certanly much moro improved in America but son time will show who shall be in the Wright.

Thinking upon the Idea I had the honour to exibited to the Congress concerning the Monument I find it susceptible of an impruvement therfor I am very eger with all my poetical immagination of brigning it to a perfection, and as son as I esstablished as I intend; shall comunicated to you. Accept assurances of my estime and sincere respect

Jo: CERACCHI

P.S. With your bust Sir I shall send you a profil executed in alabaster as large as the life of my friend Mr: Maddison. I bag you to accept it as a memory of so respectable man, and at same time afford me an occasion to show my sentiment of attachement to him. I trid to do it in marbre as rapresented with the bust I modeled but the block [torned?] with Spots and my situation in trables did'nt permit me to performe my proposition.

RC (DLC); endorsed by TJ as received 1 July 1794 and so recorded in SJL.

For the IDEA which Ceracchi presented to CONGRESS, see note to TJ to Robert R. Livingston, 6 Mch. 1792.

To James Monroe

DEAR SIR   Monticello Mar. 11. 1794.

The small pox at Richmond has cut off the communication by post to or through that place. I should have thought it Davies's duty to have removed his office a little way out of town, that the communication might not have been interrupted. Instead of that it is said the inhabitants of the country are to be prosecuted because they thought it better to refuse a passage to his post riders than take the small pox from them. Straggling travellers who have ventured into Richmd. now and then leave a newspaper with Colo. Bell. Two days ago we got that with the debates on the postponement of Mr. Madison's propositions. I have never received a letter from Philadelphia since I left it except a line or two once from E.R. There is much enquiry for the printed correspondence with Hammond, of which no copy had come to Richmond some days ago. We have heard of one at Staunton.

Our winter was mild till the middle of January. But since the 22d. of that month (when my observations begun) it has been 23. mornings out of 49. below the freezing point, and once as low as 14°. It has also been very wet. Once a snow of 6. I. which lay 5. days, and lately a snow of 4 I. which laid on the plains 4. days. There have been very few ploughing days since the middle of January, so that the farmers were never backwarder in their preparations. Wheat we are told is from 5/6 to 6/ at Richmond, but whether cash can be got for it I have not heard. At

Milton it is 4/6 payable in goods only at from 50. to 100. per cent above the Philadelphia prices, which renders the wheat worth in fact half a dollar. I do not believe that 1000 bushels of wheat could be sold at Milton and Charlottesville for 1/ a bushel cash. Such is the present scarcity of cash here, and the general wretched situation of commerce in this country. We are told that the market for wheat at Richmond will cease on the departure of the French fleet.

One of your people called on me the other day to speak about engrafting for you. The weather was then very severe, and I advised him to let it alone a few days. It is now fine, and I hope he will come soon. He seemed at a loss where to make his nursery. He said you had ordered it to be at your house, but that you had not then determined to sell it; and that since it's being advertised you had given no orders. I advised him to consider your offering the place for sale as a change of orders, and to go and prepare a place for his Nursery at Carter's. He took the proposition ad referendum.—We have often wondered together, when at Philadelphia, what our friends here could mean by saying they had nothing to write about. You now see that there is nothing but complaints for want of information—for want of commerce,—weather—crops and such things as you are too little of a farmer to take much interest in. My affectionate respects to Mrs. Monroe & Mr. Madison, and accept them yourself also.   TH: JEFFERSON

RC (Goodspeed's Bookshop, Boston, 1950); at foot of first page: "Colo Monroe." PrC (DLC).

From James Madison

DEAR SIR   Mar: 12. 1794.

The Merchants, particularly of N. England have had a terrible slam in the W. Indies. About a hundred vessels have been seized by the British for condemnation, on the pretext of enforcing the laws of the Monarchy with regard to the Colony trade. The partizans of England, considering a war as now probable are endeavoring to take the lead in defensive preparations, and to acquire merit with the people by anticipating their wishes. This new symtom of insolence and enmity in Britain, shews either that she meditates a formal war as soon as she shall have crippled our marine resources, or that she calculates on the pusillanimity of this country and the influence of her party, in a degree that will lead her into aggressions which our love of peace can no longer bear. The commercial propositions are in this State of things, not the precise remedy to be pressed as first in order; but they are in every view and in any event proper to make part of our standing Laws till the principle of reciprocity be established by mutual arrangements. Adieu

Js. MADISON JR

RC (DLC: Madison Papers); endorsed by TJ as received 31 Mch. 1794 and so recorded in SJL.

From Richard Peters

MY DEAR SIR   Philada. 13 March 1794

Permit me to present you with the Plan I send you for a State Society of Agriculture. I drew it up at the Request of our Philada. Society and have Hopes that I shall get it thro'. It is only the Beginning of a Plan I have in View in which, at some future Day, I will attempt embarking our Government. At present I keep it out of View. I wish every State would do something in this Way as the Agriculture of our Country is too generally bad. You can do much, if Leisure is allowed you, in these Plans; which are among the Arts of Peace. But I fear we shall have other Arts to practice, as our Situation seems very critical. You are like many of the good Things in this World of which the Value is not either known or properly estimated 'till it is lost. If we get into the Bustle of War, which I hope more than think we shall avoid, you will be drawn out of your Recesses. This is a shabby World for there are few in it that can do as they please. But as too many would please to do wrong I believe this is a good Arrangement, tho' it often disturbs honest Gentlemen who wish to be quiet. I am impatient for the Spring to open that I may have the Tranquillity and Enjoyments of my Farm. A small Portion of City Amusements is enough for me. Believe very sincerely yours

RICHARD PETERS

RC (DNAL); at foot of text: "T. Jefferson Esqr"; endorsed by TJ as received 24 May 1795 and so recorded in SJL. Enclosure: Philadelphia Society for Promoting Agriculture, *Outlines of a Plan, for establishing a State Society of Agriculture in Pennsylvania* (Philadelphia, 1794), presenting the report of a committee headed by John Beale Bordley urging the creation of a state agricultural society that would enjoy official recognition including incorporation, service of high state officials as Visitors, and eventual state contributions to a proposed program of endowed professorships of agriculture, a network of county agricultural societies and libraries, model farms, and sending agents to Europe to study farming techniques. See Sowerby, No. 715.

From Horatio Gates

DEAR SIR   Rose Hill, 14: March, 1794.

I had the satisfaction to receive your very Obliging Letter of the 3d. of Feb: from Monte Cello; it came to hand when I was Ill of a Fever, I am now thank God, quite recover'd; and have the pleasure to be able to acknowledge your kindness. I have never had the Smallest doubt, that if my letter book was in your hands but that it was as safe as in my Own; being satisfied of that, I am perfectly content; keep it as long as you see convenient. Neither Envy, nor persecution, can reap any benefit by calling my Conduct into Question; therefore I need no means of Defence; and for my own happyness, my conscience bids me be at peace. Happy that Fortune has placed me in circumstances, which I would not exchange for all the Honours, and Rewards, Fifteen Countries can Bestow—Though I should have done, as you have done; I do not approve your Fixed Resolve; Great Talents, Joind to Great Integrity, should not be always retired to Monte-Cello; Our rough Diamond wants polishing, which can only be well done by Masterly, and Faithfull Hands; therefore, be not too positive. Should you be called to take the Diamond in Hand, be ready to Obey the Voice of a great Nation. The News from Toulon must have reached You; I think the King of Sardinia must Tremble for his Capital, for there is but little to prevent the Sans Culottes from possessing not only that, but the whole of his Continental Dominions. Irritated by Disappointment, and Disgraced by Defeat; the Combined Princes will Exhaust all their Policy, and all the Sinews of War, to Subdue France the next Campaign; but it will be in Vain; Their Crowns will be Humbled to the Dust! and we may possibly live to see, France, England, and America; the three great Republics of the World, Bound together in one Grand Alliance, Offensive, and Defensive. Then The philosopher of Monte Cello, and his Disciple at Rose Hill, will Moralize on the Instability of Human Greatness, and Expand their Minds in Contemplating the Vast happyness they have assisted to Establish both in the old, and new World; From whence not only the present, but the Mighty Generations yet to come are made Free.

You seem to think the Climate of Virginia preferable to this, I tried one Winter at Williamsburg, It rained all February, and March; of consequence, The Damp was Excessive; here it is at times severely Cold; but then it is Dry, and not unwholesome; we had this year no Cold, to call severe, until February; it is now the 14th: of March. The Frost is out of the Ground, and Peas were yesterday sown in my Garden; If there is an Eldorado in the Territory's of the US., it must be on that rising Ground that Seperates The Waters of the Cherokee River; from

[37]

the Waters of the Mobile; when the Time comes, that we can remove there with Ease, and Safety, If I am able I will Joyfully attend You, where we will Spin out a Cheerfull Old Age, in that charming Climate, where I am assured, Vegetation never ceases. Mrs: Gates presents her Respects, and I beg you to believe me, most respectfully, your Faithfull and Obedeint Servant,   HORATIO GATES

P.S. I inclose this Mr. Maddison and request him to forward it to You.

RC (DLC); endorsed by TJ as received 16 Apr. 1794 and so recorded in SJL.

From James Madison

DEAR SIR   Philada. March 14. 1794.

The paper of yesterday inclosed, will give you a clue to the designs of the faction which has used Sedgwick for its organ. His immediate prompter will be seen both in his speech and in his propositions. Whether more be seriously aimed at than to embarrass the others which have been long depending, is by some doubted. Perhaps this may be one of the objects; but you understand the game behind the Curtain too well not to perceive the old trick of turning every contingency into a resource for accumulating force in the Government. It would seem however that less subtlety has prevailed in this than in some other instances. The ostensible reason for the provisional army is not only absurd; but remote from the present sensations of the public; and at the same time disarms the projectors of the cavil and calumny used with most success against the commercial propositions, towit, that they tended to provoke war by an unnecessary alarm and irritation to G. Britain. The commercial propositions were the subject of yesterday and will probably be resumed today. We admit that the change of appearances may require something further, but we contend that they ought to make part of our Code until the end be obtained; and that they will be proper whether we are to be at peace or war. In the former case they will have their intended operation: In the latter they will put our Extive. on the right ground for negocia[tion.]

RC (DLC: Madison Papers); unsigned; last word partly illegible; endorsed by TJ as received 31 Mch. 1794 and so recorded in SJL.

In the House of Representatives on 12 Mch. 1794 Theodore SEDGWICK, a Massachusetts Federalist, introduced and spoke on behalf of resolutions intended to deter further injuries from Great Britain by authorizing creation of an auxiliary army of 15,000 men and empowering the President to embargo ships in, and prohibit exports from, American harbors for up to forty days at a time (*Gazette of the United States*, 13 Mch. 1794; see also *Annals*, IV, 500-4).

From Tench Coxe

SIR   Philada. March 16. 1794.

Since I had the honor to write you last the inclosed have been delivered to me by a person, who received them from Europe. They were not accompanied by a letter, but were said to have come from the Editor.

Last Evenings post brought us the information from London under date of the 20th. Decemr. in Fenno's Gazette. It has added greatly to the former sensations on the Subject of the depredations on our commerce. The Merchants had entertained a wish, that a special mission to London might be adopted, to procure restitution and damages. But I find some damp has been thrown upon their hopes in that line. It is however among the ideas under consideration of the Government. The Secrecy which has been observed by the British Government in this Business is peculiarly exceptionable and shocking. Orders of the 6th. Novr. so material to our commercial harmony and peace not communicated to our Minister there on the 26th. of November, and most probably later— apparently first published on the 20th. December in London—and not known or communicated by their Minister here to this Hour present an example of the most injurious mode of executing the most injurious of measures. I am afraid this business will ruin many of our merchants unless indemnity be obtained from Britain, or unless it be taken from their property within our reach. The last is a dreadful idea, as a standing addition to the evils of war.

How happy is it that France has repelled the medley of Foes which possessed Toulon, and that the Expedition of the Earl of Moira is rendered abortive and disgraceful. You will observe the maltreatment of Britain appears to have been prior to the 20th. Decemr. and that the Affair of Toulon was of the 17th., 18 and 19th. and was known in London only on the 31st. Decemr.—and in Paris about the 24th. or 25th. The effect of this pill upon the people of Britain cannot be known in the smallest degree, but if they are not worse than senseless things, it must work them most severely. The Dutch people are becoming deeply anxious, comfortless and dissatisfied. The French are at this moment more than ever *en potence*. Military ardor, experience, political enthusiasm, confidence in themselves, the keenest animosity against their enemies, temper to their few friends, and, it is positively asserted, a full treasury are immense advantages. I hope, at the meeting of parliament there will be some more favorable circumstances on the french side, for between the 19th. of Decr. and the 11th. of January the Toulon army might act in grand divisions with the forces against Spain Italy, and the insurgents.

You will perceive we are taking some measures calculated for defence, and even for offensive operations. I am uneasy at our want of Sulphur and saltpetre. We shall be exceedingly restrained in our operations, if forced into a war, by the want of Gun powder. The times are serious and critical in the highest degree yet I trust the Successes of France, and the immense expences and numerous disappointments of her Enemies will give us advices of January promising peace. If we should go to war it will be with the utmost indignation against Britain, and I trust with an Unanimity and Energy that will make her weep and blush at the remembrance of follies and her crimes. I have the honor to be with perfect respect, Sir, your most obedt. Servant

TENCH COXE

It now appears, that the accounts from Guernsey were true in two particulars out of three—*the taking of Toulon* and *the fate of Moiras Expedition.* There was a third *the defeat and retreat of Wurmser on the 26th. or 28th. Decr.* The London paper of 1st. Jany. shews that the french were making continual and most serious attacks from the 16th. to the 20th. Decr. on Wurmser. I therefore give some faith to his being forced to retreat from Hageneau. By the 28th. he might know of the Affair of Toulon, and might expect it would give spirits and even reinforcements to the french force against him, and he might from prudence retreat. This, if confirmed will be a great matter.

I mention the Idea of a mission to London confidentially as it occured in a conference with Mr. Randolph, which he would of course not wish to be generally mentioned, tho he would doubtless avail himself of your Counsel on the subject, if you were near enough.

RC (DLC); dateline between signature and postscript; endorsed by TJ as received 31 Mch. 1794 and so recorded in SJL. For a general reference to one of the enclosures, see TJ to Coxe, 1 May 1794.

INFORMATION FROM LONDON: a reference to a letter "from an officer in Lord Howe's fleet, dated Torbay, Dec. 14, 1793," describing the fleet's failure while cruising in the West Indies in November 1793 to capture either the French West Indian convoy or a French naval squadron (*Gazette of the United States*, 15 Mch. 1794).

From James Monroe

DEAR SIR   Philadelphia March 16th. 94

Mr. Madisons propositions are yet depending and their fate incertain. The probability is they will pass in the H. of R. and be rejected in the Senate. The steady zeal with which any thing like a systematic operation on the British commerce, or indeed any branch of her interest is opposed, you have long witnessed and can of course readily conceive upon the present occasion. The opposition as you have seen commenc'd in the most open declarations in favor of G. Britain, justifying her in all her enormities; but latterly it has assumed a new tone passing into the opposit extreme. Mr. Sedgwick introduc'd the other day a proposition for raising 15,000 provisional troops founded upon the idea of providing for our defense against invasion, and the probability of such an event, considering the unfriendly conduct of G.B. towards us for sometime past. It is believed this was not only concluded by the leaders of the faction, but that all its members will support it. A change so extraordinary must have a serious object in view. At first I believed it was only to counteract by a new manuvre the propositions of Mr. M., shewing that the crisis was more urgent than they could remedy, and to remove at the same time the impression their partiality for B. had created among their constituents. But I am inclined to think that it contemplates some thing still further and is designed to lay the foundation of measures more destructive to the publick happiness. They are to be raised in no given quarter, and altho' they may be deem'd a kind of minute men in respect to their situation except in time of war, yet in every other respect they will be regulars. As such they will be officered by the general government, as such paid, and most of the officers will consider it as the commencement of a military establishment, embark in it with that view and use their utmost efforts to convert it into one. The order of Cincinati will be plac'd in the command of it, and being a part of the military establishment, one common chief will be at the head of the whole, as generalissimo, and immediately supercede Wayne. A particular character here is contemplated for this office, and two of our countrymen H. L. and C. are spoken of as persons deserving high rank in it. The influence of such an institution upon the measures of the government, in the patronage it gives &ca. you will readily conceive. Nor can it be doubted that if it should be so disposed as its leaders will be, it may even remodel and form it by the Englh. standard. It will likewise completely supercede the militia, who will afterwards become an useless and dormant body, scarcely retaining arms in their hands. Thus we see this faction in our councils seizing with avidity every incident that may possibly tend to promote the great object of a change in the government.

What course it will be proper for us to take in the present emergency becomes daily more difficult to decide. The aggressions of Britain have increased to a height to silence the voice of her friends, or nearly so. She regards no kind of form in the pursuit of our property, seizing whatever she can lay her hands on. Our vessels which remain are driven into harbour here and will I apprehend scarcely leave it again for the present. An embargo is proposed with the view of cutting off supplies from the Bh. west Indies, necessary in aid of her present operations there.

Urgent as the crisis is, the embarrassment increases still further from the consideration that not the least confidence can be reposed in our Executive council. To embark in a war when the whole force of the country will be in the hands of the enemy of the publick liberty a few characters only excepted[1] will be more dangerous than any now menac'd from B. and yet to take no step seems to evince a pusilanimity which will degrade us as a nation, and likewise suffer the ruin of our commerce and every other interest connected with it to take place.

Prior to the exclusion of Gallatin several votes had been taken and carried in the Senate which indicated a change in the general measures of that body. A particular one calling for the correspondence of G. Morris was more especially felt in a certain quarter. At that period R. informed us that a certain person began to doubt the views and principles of a certain faction and to think more favorably of others. And the members of that faction began to express similar doubts of him. But from the time of his removal we have heard nothing further of those doubts, on his part, and on theirs the antient spirit of confidence and affection has been revived. What will be the issue of our affairs time can only develope, but certain it is that at present the prospect is most wretched and gloomy. I had like to have omitted mentioning that as a remedy it was talked of by the fiscal party, to send an Envoy Extoy. to Engld. to complain of these injuries and seek redress, and that H. was spoken of for this mission. As the situation is in some measure a [parallel] one I should think it more suitable to employ John Dickinson, who I believe drew the last petition of Congress to the king, in the course of the late revolution. With great respect & esteem I am Dear Sir yr. affectionate friend & servt   JAS. MONROE

RC (DLC); endorsed by TJ as received 31 Mch. 1794 and so recorded in SJL.

A PARTICULAR CHARACTER: Alexander Hamilton (Ammon, *Monroe*, 109). H. L. AND C.: Henry Lee, the governor of Virginia, and Edward Carrington, the Super-visor of Revenue for the District of Virginia, two Federalists who had served in the Continental Army. R.: Edmund Randolph. H.: Alexander Hamilton.

[1] Preceding five words interlined.

From Diodati

Rolles en Suisse, pays de Vaud le 17. Mars 1794
Je Suis parti de Paris en May 1792, pour venir dans ce pays, Ou je Suis resté jusques a présent, et ou je resterai encore.

En conséquence et venant de lire dans plusieurs papiers publics, qui l'annonçent comme une chose positive que Vous Vous étes mon cher Monsieur, chargé d'une commission en France, Je m'empresse de Vous offrir mon appartement a Paris, Rue le Pelletier, Sur le Boulevard, Vis à Vis la Comédie Italienne lequel est tres bien Situé, tres agréable, Vaste et fort bien meublé, et dans le quel Vous Serez a tous égards convenablement. Il Sera doux a mon amitié de Vous Sentir logé chez moi, et je me flatte, Qu'il le Sera aussi a la Votre, ainsi, Vous ne refuserez point ma proposition que Vous me manderez avoir acceptée.

J'envoye cette lettre au Ministre des Etats unis en France, Monsieur Morrits, pour vous la faire parvenir, la Ou il Vous sçaura ou Supposera, Sans autres détaills, que je Supprime aussi icy, Sur toutes Sortes de Sujets. Je me borne donc a Vous dire, Qu'en toute occasion, Vous me trouverez empressé a Vous donner toutes les preuves qui dépendront de moi, du Souvenir, de tout l'attachement, que je Vous ay Voués et de la [consi]dération distinguée avec la quelle j'ay [l'honneu]r d'etre, Mon cher Monsieur, Votre tres Humble & tres obéissant Ser[viteur]

DIODATI

RC (DLC); last page partially torn; addressed: "Monsieur Monsieur Jefferson Ministre des Affaires Etrangères des Etats Unis de l'Amérique"; mistakenly endorsed by TJ as a letter of 5 May 1794 received 23 July 1794 and so recorded in SJL.

From James Madison

DEAR SIR   March 24th, 1794.

The past week has been spent chiefly on the question of an Embargo. It was negatived on Friday by 48 against 46, the former composed chiefly of Eastern, the latter of Southern members. The former are now for giving the power to the Executive, even during the session of Congress. In France, everything is in a state of vigor beyond what has been seen there. Fauchèt proceeds with great circumspection and prudence here.

MS not found; reprinted from Madison, *Letters*, II, 8. Recorded in SJL as received from Philadelphia on 16 Apr. 1794.

From James Madison

DEAR SIR   Mar: 26.[1] 1794

My last informed you that an embargo had been proposed and negatived. You will see by the inclosed that on a renewal of the proposition yesterday it went thro' the H. of Reps. by a very[2] large majority. The change took place among the Eastern members whose constituents were growing so clamorous under their losses in the W. Indies, as to alarm their representatives. The Senate will have the subject before them today, and will probably concur. It is said that some further measures are to be discussed in that House. The commercial propositions have not yet received a vote. The progress of the evils which they were to remedy, having called for more active medicine, it has not been deemed prudent to force them on the attention of the House during more critical discussions. They will however notwithstanding a change of circumstances, cooperate with other measures as an alternative system and will be pressed to a vote at the first favorable moment. Whether they can be carried into a law at the present Session is doubtful, on account of the lateness of the day, and the superior urgency of other questions. The point immediately depending is the discrimination between G.B. and other nations as to the proposed duties on manufactures. If this should succeed, the future parts will I think meet with little difficulty. The Enquiry into the Treasury is going on, tho' not very rapidly. I understand that it begins to pinch where we most expected— the authority for drawing the money from Europe into the Bank. H. endeavored to parry the difficulty by contesting the right of the Committee to call for the authority. This failing he talks of constructive written authority from the P. but relies on parol authority, which I think it impossible the P. can support him in. The old question of referring the origination of Taxes comes on today; and will in some degree test the present character of the House: I have written abundance of letters of late but fear they are stopped by the small pox at Richmond.

The people of Charlestown are taking a high tone. Their memorial, which is signed by Ramsay—the Gadzdens Young Rutlege and a very great number of respectable citizens marks the deliberate sense of the place.[3] The more violent has been ex[pres]sed by hanging and burning the effigies of Smith, Ames Arnold, Dumourier and the Devil en groupe.

RC (DLC: Madison Papers); unsigned; final paragraph written in left margin includes one partially illegible word; endorsed by TJ as received 16 Apr. 1794 and so recorded in SJL.

The enclosed newspaper described the passage of a resolution by the House of Representatives on 25 Mch. 1794 laying an EMBARGO on all ships in American ports for thirty days. The President approved the measure on 26 Mch. 1794 (*Philadelphia Gazette*, 26 Mch. 1794; JHR, II, 102, 104, 105). The 1794 congressional ENQUIRY INTO THE TREASURY begun at the request of Alexander Hamilton, who wished to refute Republican allegations of official misconduct as Secretary of the Treasury, is described in Editorial Note on Jefferson and the Giles resolutions, at 27 Feb. 1793. On 24 Mch. 1794 Congressman Andrew Pickens presented to the House of Representatives the 1 Mch. MEMORIAL by citizens of South Carolina requesting redress from British spoliations on American commerce and stating that they would even approve if

Congress voted "to suspend all commercial intercourse between Great-Britain and these States" (*Philadelphia Gazette*, 26, 31 Mch 1794). EFFIGIES of William Loughton SMITH, Fisher AMES, Benedict ARNOLD, William Pitt, and THE DEVIL were destroyed in Charleston on 15 Mch. 1794 (*Boston Gazette*, 14 Apr. 1794).

[1] Date reworked from what appears to be "25."
[2] Word interlined.
[3] Preceding three words interlined.

From James Monroe

DEAR SIR   Philadelphia March 26. 1794

Your favor of the 11th. reached me yesterday. We were mortified to find that our letters had not reached you, but hope the obstacle at Richmond is removed before this. As Mr. M. has written you I shall say nothing at present upon the subject of affairs here. I shall only commence with the inclosures of your correspondence with Hammond which after perusal by your family and any others whom you wish, shall thank you to send to my brother in Charlottesville. I sent Stuart at Staunton a copy—and we mean to transmit one with the one containing the correspondence with Mr. Genet to the Ex: for the legislature. I hope Peter has not failed to attend and pursue your advice respecting the fruit trees. We desire to be affectionately remembered to your family. I am sincerely yr. friend & servt   JAS. MONROE

RC (DLC); endorsed by TJ as received 11 Apr. 1794 and so recorded in SJL. Enclosure: the second separately paginated section of *A Message of the President of the United States to Congress Relative to France and Great-Britain. Delivered December 5, 1793.* . . . (Philadelphia, 1793). See Evans, No. 26334.

Six letters to TJ from Monroe's BROTHER IN CHARLOTTESVILLE, Joseph Jones Monroe, dated between 25 Mch. 1794 and 16 Aug. 1797, and three letters from TJ to him dated 18 Apr. 1795, 1 Feb. 1796, and 15 Feb. 1797 are recorded in SJL but have not been found. CORRESPONDENCE WITH MR. GENET: the first and the third separately paginated sections of the enclosure listed above.

From James Madison

DEAR SIR   Philada. Mar. 31. 1794.

I have written of late by almost every mail, that is, three times a week. From your letter to Monroe I fear the small pox has stopped them at Richmond. I shall continue however to inclose you the newspapers as often as they are worth it. It is impossible to say what will be the issue of the proposition discussed in those of today. I forgot to mention in my last that the question whether the ways and means should be referred to the Secy. of T. as heretofore, or to a Committee lately came on and decided the sense of the House to be regenerated on that point. The fiscal party, perceiving their danger, offered a sort of compromise which took in Mercer and with him sundry others in principle against them. Notwithstanding the success of the stratagem, the point was carried by 49 against 46. If the question had divided the House fairly there would have been a majority of ten or a dozen at least.

RC (DLC: Madison Papers); unsigned; endorsed by TJ as received 16 Apr. 1794 and so recorded in SJL.

Dunlap & Claypoole's American Daily Advertiser of this date printed congressional debate on Jonathan Dayton's 27 Mch. 1794 PROPOSITION that debts owed by American to British citizens be sequestered and held as a pledge to indemnify those who had suffered from spoliations on American commerce by Great Britain in violation of the law of nations. The House of Representatives' decision on 26 Mch. 1794 to appoint a fifteen-member committee on WAYS AND MEANS, including Madison, represented a decisive break from the precedent of referring to the judgment of the Secretary of the Treasury the question of how to raise revenue, a shift in legislative-executive relations that greatly vexed Alexander Hamilton. The SORT OF COMPROMISE evidently would have involved creating the committee but instructing it to call on Hamilton for advice (*Annals*, IV, 531-3; White, *Federalists*, 73).

From James Monroe

DEAR SIR   Phila. March 31. 1794.

The embargo passed two days since. [. . .][1] of some moment in the character [. . .] [. . .]ber of this city was discovered [. . .][2] had opposed the embargo on fr[iday an]d on monday introduced the proposition himself. It contained a proviso which implied a right that those vessels which had already obtained clearances should be exempt from the operation—but this was amended in the Senate. A vessel of his was caught near the capes by a french Frigate and sent up with a British passport which had cleared out on Saturday.

Propositions for sequestration and organizing the militia are dependant. An Envoy Extry. is spoken of for Britn.—and Hamilton, Jay, and King are those urged by that party. It will probably be one of them unless there should be found a vote for their rejection in the Senate which is not presumeable. Either will answer to bind the aristocracy of this country stronger and closer to that of the other. Yrs. affecy.

JAS. MONROE

RC (DLC); first five lines mutilated; endorsed by TJ as received 16 Apr. 1794 and so recorded in SJL.

The identity of the member who introduced the EMBARGO resolution in the House of Representatives on Tuesday, 25 Mch. 1794, is not known (JHR, II, 102; *Annals*, IV, 529-30). For the amendment that the SENATE made before passing this resolution on the following day, see JS, II, 55. In response to a message from the President,

Congress this day also approved a resolution clarifying certain ambiguities in the original embargo resolution (JHR, II, 106-8; JS, II, 58-9).

On this day the House passed resolutions on the organization of the MILITIA and the addition of an artillery and engineering corps to the United States Army that were enacted into law in May 1794 (JHR, II, 108; Annals, IV, 1444, 1445-6).

¹ Estimated three words missing.
² Estimated two or three words missing.

From James Monroe

DEAR SIR   Phila. April 2. 1794.

A committee of the H. of R. sits daily to provide funds for equiping the fleet and other measures connected with the exigency of the times. They have finally I believe agreed on nothing as yet, tho the fiscal party are for excises on tea &ca. The citizen party are for a land-tax, but seem backward on the subject in every view; regret that an occasion has been made for any great increase; this subject will take time. The fiscal party say to the other, you have taken the business from the Trsy. department, shew yourselves equal to it, and bring forward some system. The latter replies, the practice of reference has been condemned by the publick voice as other things will be when understood; the rejection of it is a triumph of the people and of the constitution over theirs and its abuse: but the provision of taxes is not the duty of those who have been more active in the rejection than of those who opposed it. If it is more the duty of one than the other side, it is particularly that of those who have made taxes necessary. The arrival by way of Hallifax of an account of some relaxation in [. . .] from the orders of the 8. of Jany. suspe[nds the?] proceeding on the sequestration of debts. [. . .] [Ross fr]om Washington is elected in the place of Gal[latin. He is?] perhaps not altogether the man whom the republicans would have chosen: but by them he was elected in opposition to one Coleman, from Lancaster county. Sincerely I am yr. friend & sevt.   JAS. MONROE

RC (DLC); parts of several lines torn and mutilated; addressed: "Thomas Jefferson [. . .]"; franked and postmarked; endorsed by TJ as received 16 Apr. 1794 and so recorded in SJL.

PRACTICE OF REFERENCE: for Republican opposition to the practice in the House of Representatives of making legislative references to the Secretary of the Treasury, see Memorandum on References by Congress to Heads of Departments, [10 Mch. 1792], and note. The House's recent rejection of a proposal for such a request is described in James Madison to TJ, 31 Mch. 1794, and note. The ACCOUNT OF SOME RELAXATION, which appeared in the Philadelphia Gazette of 28 Mch. 1794, was a text of the British order in council of 8 Jan. 1794 revoking that of 6 Nov. 1793 and promulgating new restrictions that allowed the United States to carry on noncontraband trade with the French West Indies directly, though not to participate in the trade between those islands and France. President Washington submitted a text to Congress on 4 Apr. 1794 (Ritcheson, Aftermath of Revolution, 302-5; ASP, Foreign Relations, I, 429, 431).

To Thomas Walker, Jr.

DEAR SIR   Monticello Apr. 2. 1794.

I send by the bearer three mares to be put to your Jack. I shall still be able to muster up four or five more but a view of the scarcity of money makes me fearful to enter into a money contract, which this number of mares would render considerable. If you can take wheat or flour of the growing crop delivered at Milton, I shall have no fear of engaging that, because I can be sure of it: and therefore ask the favor of an answer on that head by the bearer. One of the mares now sent, tho old, is as highblooded as any one in the state. I shall send another of the same blood and coloring and may hope a pair of mules from them fit to drive in my Phaeton. I have understood you sell sheep every year. I should like to purchase in the fall, payable in wheat or flour. I am with sincere esteem Dear Sir Your friend & servt   TH: JEFFERSON

PrC (DLC: Rives Papers); at foot of text: "T. Walker esquire."

Thomas Walker, Jr. (d. 1798), son of Dr. Thomas Walker, one of the executors of Peter Jefferson's estate, served as a captain in the Continental Army and lived at his Indian Fields plantation in Albemarle County (Woods, *Albemarle*, 334-6; Heitman, *Register*, 566).

To Benjamin Bankson

DEAR SIR   Monticello Apr. 3. 1794.

The suspension of our post during the inoculation at Richmond prevented my receiving your letter of Feb. 13. till three days ago. I hasten therefore by the first return of post to transmit you the testimony you desire. It will always be a gratification to me to bear witness to the merits of the gentlemen to whose diligence and fidelity I was so much indebted while I was in office, and feel the same sincere interest in their success as if they were members of my family. Be so good as to assure them of my constant wishes for their welfare, and to accept yourself the same from Dr. Sir Your most obedt. humble servt

TH: JEFFERSON

P.S. I rely with assurance that I shall receive the originals of my letters &c which I left to be entered as soon as the business of the office will permit.

PrC (DLC); at foot of text: "Mr. Benjamin Bankson." Enclosure: Certificate for Bankson, 3 Apr. 1794: "I hereby certify that Mr. Benjamin Bankson one of the clerks for the department of state, continued to do duty in the office of that department during the whole course of the malignant fever which prevailed in Philadelphia the last year, and that from about the middle of September to about the middle of November he had the sole charge of the office without the aid even of an office-keeper" (PrC in DLC; signed by TJ).

Bankson's letter of FEB. 13., recorded in SJL as received from Philadelphia 31 Mch. 1794, has not been found.

To James Madison

DEAR SIR   Monticello Apr. 3. 1794.

Our post having ceased to ride ever since the inoculation began in Richmond till now, I received three days ago, and all together your friendly favors of Mar. 2. 9. 12. 14. and Colo. Monroe's of Mar. 3. and 16. I have been particularly gratified by the receipt of the papers containing your's and Smith's discussion of your regulating propositions. These debates had not been seen here but in a very short and mutilated form. I am at no loss to ascribe Smith's speech to it's true father. Every tittle of it is Hamilton's except the introduction. There is scarcely any thing there which I have not heard from him in our various private tho' official discussions. The very turn of the arguments is the same, and others will see as well as myself that the style is Hamilton's. The sophistry is too fine, too ingenious even to have been comprehended by Smith, much less devised by him. His reply shews he did not understand his first speech: as it's general inferiority proves it's legitimacy as evidently as it does the bastardy of the original. You know we had understood that Hamilton had prepared a Counter-report, and that some of his humble servants in the Senate were to move a reference to him in order to produce it. But I suppose they thought it would have a better effect if fired off in the H. of Representatives. I find the Report however so fully justified that the anxieties with which I left it are perfectly quieted. In this quarter all espouse your propositions with ardour, and without a dissenting voice. The rumor of a declaration of war has given an opportunity of seeing that the people here, tho' attentive to the loss of value of their produce, in such an event, yet find in it a gratification of some other passions, and particularly of their antient hatred to Gr. Britain. Still I hope it will not come to that: but that the propositions will be carried, and justice be done ourselves in a peaceable way. As to the guarantee of the French islands, whatever doubts may be entertained of the moment at which we ought to interpose yet I have no doubt but that we ought to interpose at a proper time and declare both to England and France that these islands are to rest with France, and that we will make common cause with the latter for that object.—As to the naval armament, the land armament, and the Marine fortifications which are in question with you, I have no doubt they will all be carried. Not that the Monocrats and Papermen in Congress want war; but they want armies and debts: and tho' we may hope that the sound part of Congress is now so augmented as to ensure a majority in cases of general interest merely, yet I have always observed that in questions of expence, where members may hope either for offices or jobs for themselves or their friends, some few will be debauched, and that is sufficient to turn the decision where a majority is at most but small. I have never seen a Philadelphia paper since I left it, till those you inclosed me; and I feel myself so thoroughly weened from the interest I took in the proceedings there, while there, that I have never had a wish to see one, and believe that I never shall take another newspaper of any sort. I find my mind totally absorbed in my rural occupations. We are suffering much for want of rain. Tho' now at the 3d. of April, you cannot distinguish the wheat feilds of the neighborhood yet from hence. Fruit is hitherto safe. We have at this time some prospect of rain. Asparagus is just come to table. The Lilac in blossom, and the first Whip-poor-will heard last night. No Martins yet. I have some hopes Short has sent Cortez's letters for me by Blake. Pray ask E.R. if he has. My best affections to Colo. and Mrs. Monroe. The correspondence with Hammond has never yet come into this quarter. Accept sincere assurances of affection.   TH: JEFFERSON

RC (DLC: Madison Papers); at foot of first page: "Mr. Madison." PrC (DLC).

TJ's opinion that the Secretary of the Treasury was the TRUE FATHER of William Loughton Smith's speech of 13 Jan. 1794 on Madison's resolutions for the regulation of commerce is confirmed by a manuscript of Hamilton's containing some of the same language, although it is not certain whether Hamilton drafted all of Smith's speech or Smith drew on the extant Hamilton document to compose it himself. He made his major REPLY to Madison at the end of January (Annals, IV, 174-209, 401-10; Syrett, Hamilton, XIII, 406-36). For TJ's protracted efforts to obtain CORTEZ'S LETTERS, see his second letter to David Humphreys, 11 Apr. 1791. E.R.: Edmund Randolph.

From John Adams

DEAR SIR   Philadelphia April 4. 1794
    The inclosed Volume was lately sent in to me by a Servant. I have Since heard that the Author of it is in New York. The Book exhibits a curious Picture of the Government of Berne and is well worth reading.
    I congratulate you on the charming Opening of the Spring and heartily wish I was enjoying of it as you are upon a Plantation, out of the hearing of the Din of Politicks and the Rumours of War. This felicity will not fall to my Share I fear, before June. I am Sir with great Regard your humble Servant   JOHN ADAMS

RC (DLC); at foot of text: "Mr Jefferson"; endorsed by TJ as received 16 Apr. 1794 and so recorded in SJL. Enclosure: Jean Jacques Cart, *Lettres de Jean-Jacques*

Cart à Bernard Demuralt, Trésorier du Pays de Vaud, Sur le droit public de ce Pays, et sur les événemens actuels (Paris, 1793), which bears the following authorial inscription: "The Author to Mr. Jefferson by Mr. Adams's Chanal" (Sowerby, No. 2681).

From James Lyle

DEAR SIR   Manchester April 14. 1794

I have not had the pleasure of hearing from you for a long time. Mr. McCaul writes me complaining of short remitances, he says Colo. Jefferson will no doubt be punctual to his instalments. I have some time ago wrote the Company the reasons you gave me for your being behind, and that I expected this spring you woud make up what was due, which I hope it will be convenient for you to do.

Colo. J. Boling has not yet paid your order on him for R. Harvie. I will be glad to hear from you, and am with all due Respect & Esteem Your most hume sevt.   JAMES LYLE

RC (MHi); endorsed by TJ as received 23 Apr. 1794 and so recorded in SJL.

THE COMPANY: Henderson, McCaul & Company.

From James Madison

DEAR SIR   Philada. Apl. 14. 1794.

Having received one letter only from you, and that of very old date, I conclude that mine which have been numerous do not pass thro' the obstructions thrown in the way of the Mail by the small pox. I continue however to write, hoping that the channel will have been reopened by the time each letter may get to Richmond. I have also written a request to Mr. Dawson to have my letters to you taken out of the post office and forwarded from Richmond by private hands if necessary.

Three propositions levelled at G.B. have latterly occupied the H. of Reps. 1. to sequester British debts. 2. to establish a lien on British merchandize or the value of it, as it arrives. 3. to suspend imports from G.B. and Ireland till the spoliations be redressed and the Treaty of peace be executed. The last has taken the pas in discussion. A majority are apparently in favor. Delay is consequently one of the arts of opposition. It is uncertain therefore when a vote will be obtained. It is probable also that much will depend on the state of foreign intelligence which is hourly changing in some of its circumstances. The Executive is said to meditate an envoy Extraordy. to G.B. as preferring further negociation to any legislative operation of a coercive nature. Hamilton is talked of, is much pressed by those attached to his politics, and will probably be appointed unless overruled by an apprehension from the disgust to Republicanism and to France. His trial is not yet concluded. You will see the issue it will have in the inclosed papers. The letter from the P. is inexpressibly mortifying to his friends, and marks his situation to be precisely what you always described it to be. The committee on ways and means was unfortunately composed of a majority infected by the fiscal errors which threaten so ignominious and vexatious a system to our Country. A land tax will be reported; but along with it excises on articles imported, and manufactured at home, a stamp tax pervading almost all the transactions of life, and a tax on carriages as an *indirect* tax. The embargo will soon be a subject of deliberation again, as its continuance if proper ought to be decided some time before its expiration. Whether this will be the case cannot now be foretold. The French continue to triumph over their Enemies on the Rhine. We learn nothing from the W. Inds. except that Martinique had not surrendered on the 25th. Ult:

I put into the hands of your Cabinet workman here the Edition of Milton sent you from France. He was packing up things for you which afforded a commodious berth for it. Yrs. always & Affy

Js. MADISON JR.

Fauchet has informally intimated the distaste to Gour. M.[1] whose recall will follow of course.

RC (DLC: Madison Papers); endorsed by TJ as received 23 Apr. 1794 and so recorded in SJL.

During the first week in April 1794, Representative Abraham Clark of New Jersey introduced a resolution in the House TO SUSPEND IMPORTS from Great Britain until the SPOLIATIONS BE REDRESSED AND THE TREATY OF PEACE BE EXECUTED. On 21 Apr. the House passed the amended resolution forbidding commercial intercourse with the British and appointed a committee to bring in the bill. Clark reported the non-intercourse bill two days later and it passed the House on 25 Apr. 1794 by a vote of 58 to 34 (not by the 59 to 34 vote reported in Madison's letter to TJ of 28 Apr. 1794). For an analysis of the bill's defeat in the Sen-ate on 28 Apr. 1794, see James Monroe to TJ, 4 May 1794 (*Philadelphia Gazette*, 3 Apr. 1794; JHR, II, 114, 126-31; JS, II, 69-70).

George Washington to Alexander Hamilton, 8 Apr. 1794, was the letter so INEXPRESSIBLY MORTIFYING to the latter and HIS FRIENDS because of its lukewarm and qualified acknowledgment that the Secretary of the Treasury had had at least tacit presidential approval for his handling of foreign loans (printed broadside in DLC; Syrett, *Hamilton*, XVI, 249-53; Editorial Note on Jefferson and the Giles resolutions, at 27 Feb. 1793).

[1] Abbreviation later expanded to "Morris" by an unidentified hand.

To Edmund Randolph

TH: JEFFERSON TO E. RANDOLPH [17 Apr. 1794]

You are so kind as to ask what is to be done with the 4. drums of figs from Simpson. As his letter mentioned that two of them were for the Presidt. I hope you will have delivered them. Of the other two, acccept one for yourself and put the other on board any vessel bound for Richmond addressed to me to the care of Colo. Gamble.—Among the MSS. you had from hence were two 4to. vols. the one containing original reports of cases in the Genl. court, the other containing Wythe's and my discussions in the case of Bolling and Bolling. The volume of reports we have heard of in the hands of Mr. Wycombe who has been written to. Mr. Wilson Nicholas tells me he thinks he has seen that containing the case of Bolling and Bolling in the hands of Mr. John Nicholas. As he is at Phila. will you be so good as to enquire of him, and to give me any information you can relative to it: you will have heard that Mr. Wilson Nicholas is chosen one of our representatives in assembly. Adieu. Your's affectionately   TH:J.

PrC (DLC); undated, but recorded in SJL under this date.

A 12 Feb. 1794 letter from James SIMPSON to TJ, recorded in SJL as received 11 Apr. 1794 from Gibraltar, has not been found. The bound manuscript arguments in THE CASE OF BOLLING AND BOLLING are discussed at TJ to William Short, 1 June 1780

(Vol. 15: 586-7), and have been published as Bernard Schwartz, ed., with Barbara Wilcie Kern and R. B. Bernstein, *Thomas Jefferson and Bolling v. Bolling: Law and the Legal Profession in Pre-Revolutionary America* (San Marino, Calif., 1997). The letter from TJ to MR. WYCOMBE (probably John Wickham) has not been found.

To Charles Rose

DEAR SIR   Monticello Apr. 17. 1794.

In the case which is the subject of your letter of the 8th. Instant, the defendant cannot be sued in any federal court but of that district in which process is served on him. Nor can any notice of a motion to be made in Amherst court, served on him in Georgia, force him to answer in that court by the laws of Virginia, if they be the same in this particular as they were when I left the country 10. years ago. By these laws however as they then stood, if you could attach any article of his property, or any debt due to him, you might proceed against him in Chancery and obtain a decree. Upon the whole however I should expect it would be best to proceed against him in the federal court of Georgia.—A twenty years desuetude in matters of law, has produced a rust which will never be attempted to be rubbed off again. I rarely therefore permit myself to give opinions on the subject even in conversation. I have done it now to shew my desire of doing any thing which you desire; but the same wish to serve you obliges me to caution you against any dangerous degree of confidence in my opinion.—I have some expectations of a trip to Bedford, in which case I shall have the pleasure of seeing you either going or returning. I am with constant esteem Dr. Sir your sincere friend & servt   TH: JEFFERSON

PrC (DLC); at foot of text: "Charles Rose esq."

Charles Rose (1747-1802), an attorney and owner of the Bellevet plantation in Amherst County, Virginia, had during the American Revolution served as clerk of the county's revolutionary committee, deputy county attorney, and a colonel of the Virginia militia (Lenora H. Sweeny, *Amherst County, Virginia, in the Revolution* ... [Lynchburg, Va., 1951], 2n, 3, 35, 49, 75, 79, 82, 84). Rose's LETTER OF THE 8TH. INSTANT, recorded in SJL as received from "Ballivette" 10 Apr. 1794, has not been found. A 17 Mch. 1796 letter from Rose, recorded in SJL as received from "Bellivetti" on 19 Mch. 1796, and TJ's 19 Mch. 1796 reply are also missing.

To James Lyle

DEAR SIR   Monticello Apr. 24. 94.

Your favor of the 14th. inst. came to hand by the last post. I had intended to have been in Richmond and Manchester, with the first good weather of this month, but the small pox first, and then the embargo which suspended a considerable object of my journey occasioned me to postpone it. I shall be with you soon after the term fixed for the expiration of the embargo. In the mean time I had long ago made up in a packet for you, the bonds mentioned in my letter of April last. I shall deliver them to you myself, and they will overpay about £100. all mine due at this time, and consequently will go that far into the one to become due next July. One half of the bonds however will not be due till next winter. I shall see you so shortly that I shall add nothing farther than assurances of the esteem with which I am Dear Sir Your friend & servt

TH: JEFFERSON

PrC (MHi); at foot of text: "Mr. James Lyle"; endorsed in ink by TJ.

MY LETTER: TJ to Lyle, 15 Apr. 1793.

To James Monroe

Th: Jefferson to Colo. Monroe   Monticello Apr. 24. 94.

I wrote to Mr. Madison on the 3d. inst. Since that I have received his of Mar. 24. 26. 31. and Apr. 14. and yours of Mar. 26. 31. and Apr. 2. which had been accumulating in the post office of Richmond. The spirit of war has grown much stronger, in this part of the country, as I can judge of myself, and in other parts along the mountains from N.E. to S.W. as I have had opportunities of learning by enquiry. Some few very quiet people, not suffering themselves to be inflamed as others are by the kicks and cuffs Gr. Britain has been giving us, express a wish to remain in peace. But the mass of thinking men seem to be of opinion that we have borne so much as to invite eternal insults in future should not a very spirited conduct be now assumed. For myself, I wish for peace, if it can be preserved, salvâ fide et honore. I learn by your letters and Mr. Madison's that a special mission to England is meditated, and H. the missionary. A more degrading measure could not have been proposed: and why is Pinckney to be recalled? For it is impossible he should remain there after such a testimony that he is not confided in. I suppose they think him not thorough paced enough: I suspect too the mission, besides the object of¹ placing the aristocracy of this country under the patronage of that government, has in view that of withdrawing H. from the disgrace and the public execrations which sooner or later must fall on the man who partly by creating fictitious debt, partly by volunteering in the payment of the debts of others, who could have paid them so much more conveniently themselves, has alienated for ever all our ordinary and easy resources, and will oblige us hereafter to extraordinary ones for every little contingency out of the common line: and who has lately brought the P. forward with manifestations that the business of the treasury had got beyond the limits of his comprehension.—Let us turn to more pleasing themes. Young Mr. Lewis (Robert) has surveyed your land over the road. There are but 442. acres; occasioned by Carter's lower line making an elbow where it was thought to be straight, instead of running from A. to C. thus it turns off from B. towards D. deflecting 30°. So much the better however as he says, the land appearing to him to be thinner and more indifferent than he expected, and to have been bought too high. However, if the cream, tho' thin, be not suffered to be taken off with corn, and you cultivate it from the beginning in wheat, potatoes and clover, it will become thick, and perhaps preferable to what is by some thought better of. I rode to your plantation to day. Your wheat is better than your neighbors'. The two feilds on each side the road, are really good; that nearer the mountain as good as the seasons have admitted. We have had two glorious rains. The first about a fortnight ago, the effect of which was lessened by very cold weather. The last 4. days ago, followed by cloudy and some warm weather. The destruction of fruit in this part of the country, as far as I have yet learnt, is complete. Mine as usual has escaped without the loss of a single blossom. I am happy to tell you that yours also (at the new place) has escaped well. I examined many peach and cherry trees there to day, and they have as much fruit on them as they ought to have. This should encourage your timely attention to ex- tend orchards up into the mountain. Your man never called again for grafts. However I have had a good nursery prepared for myself, and will spare you some of every thing. Your overseer has got all his corn ground flushed and corn planted: his fences also nearly repaired, and is clearing up a swamp. He appears to be doing essentially well, tho' not over-nice as to matters of mere appearance.—Mr. Jones dined with me 4. or 5. days ago. I never saw him so low. The Staunton water had handled him very severely. He found himself something better however, and I hope he has continued to mend, for indeed his appearance was disquieting.— My best affections to Mrs. Monroe and Mr. Madison. Accept them yourself also.

RC (DLC: Monroe Papers). PrC (DLC).

SALVÂ ... HONORE: "Saving faith and honor."

[1] TJ here canceled "forming an alli."

From George Washington

DEAR SIR   Phila. 24th. April 1794.

The letter herewith enclosed, came under cover to me in a packet from Mr. Lear, accompanied with the following extract of a letter, dated—London February 12th. 1794.

"A Mr. Bartraud, a famous Agriculturalist belonging to Flanders, put into my hands a few days ago several papers for Mr. Jefferson on the subject of Manuring and vegitation, requesting that I would forward them to him by some vessel going to America; being uncertain whether Mr. Jefferson is in Philada. or Virginia, I have taken the liberty of put- ting them under cover to you."

Nothing, is more wanting in this Country, than a thorough knowl- edge of the first; by which the usual, and inadequate modes practiced by us may be aided. Let me hope then, if any striking improvements are communicated by Mr. Bartraud on the above important Subjects that you will suffer your friends to participate in the knowledge which is to be derived from his instructions.

We are going on in the old way "Slow" I hope events will justify me in adding "and sure" that the proverb may be fulfilled.—"Slow and Sure." With very great esteem and regard I am Dear Sir Yr. Obedt. & Affecte. Hble Servt.   GO: WASHINGTON

RC (DLC); at foot of text: "Mr. Jefferson"; endorsed by TJ as received 6 May 1794 and so recorded in SJL. Enclosures: (1) O. A. Bertrand to TJ, 8 Feb. 1794, and enclosures. (2) Tobias Lear to TJ, 12 Feb. 1794.

EXTRACT OF A LETTER: see Lear to Washington, 12 Feb. 1794, in DLC: Washington Papers.

To John Adams

DEAR SIR   Monticello Apr. 25. 1794.

I am to thank you for the book you were so good as to transmit me, as well as the letter covering it, and your felicitations on my present quiet. The difference of my present and past situation is such as to leave me nothing to regret but that my retirement has been postponed four years too long. The principles on which I calculate the value of life are entirely in favor of my present course. I return to farming with an ardour which I scarcely knew in my youth, and which has got the better entirely of my love of study. Instead of writing 10. or 12. letters a day, which I have been in the habit of doing as a thing of course, I put off answering my letters now, farmer-like, till a rainy day, and then find it sometimes postponed by other necessary occupations.—The case of the Pays de Vaud is new to me. The claims of both parties are on grounds which I fancy we have taught the world to set little store by. The rights of one generation will scarcely be considered hereafter as depending on the paper transactions of another.—My countrymen are groaning under the insults of Gr. Britain. I hope some means will turn up of reconciling our faith and honour with peace: for I confess to you I have seen enough of one war never to wish to see another. With wishes of every degree of happiness to you both public and private, and with my best respects to Mrs. Adams, I am Dear Sir your affectionate & humble servt.

TH: JEFFERSON

RC (MHi: Adams Papers); addressed: "The Vice-president of the US. Philadelphia"; franked; endorsed by Adams as answered 11 May 1794. PrC (DLC).

PAYS DE VAUD: a reference to the protests made by Jean Jacques Cart in the enclosure listed at Adams to TJ, 4 Apr. 1794, against the subjection of the French-speaking Pays de Vaud to the German-speaking canton and city of Bern in Switzerland.

To Ferdinando Fairfax

DEAR SIR   Monticello Apr. 25. 1794.

The interruption of the communication by post between Charlottes-ville and Richmond, by the prevalence of the small pox in the latter place has been the cause of this late acknolegement of your polite and friendly letter of Jan. 31. It is to the partial and indulgent views of yourself and others of my fellow-citizens that I am indebted for such acknolegements as you express, and not to any real service which would not have been rendered by others, had I not been employed. In taking my tour of duty, I have only done my duty, and acquired no merit. On the same principle, having performed my tour, I hope I retire without blame, and[1] the rather as I make room for younger and abler men to transact the affairs of my country.—I have returned to farming with an ardour which I scarcely knew in my youth, and which has entirely taken the lead of my love of study. I indulge it because I think it will be more productive of health, profit, and the happiness depending on these, and perhaps of some utility to my neighbors, by taking on myself the risk of a first experiment of that sort of reformation in our system of farming, which the progressive degradation of our lands calls for imperiously. Should you chance to pass this way again and honor me with your com-pany, you will find me more[2] willing to discuss the opinions of Home and Young, than my friend Genet did the worm-eaten aphorisms of Grotius and Vattel. In the mean time I have the honor to be with senti-ments of great esteem Dear Sir your most obedt. & most humble servt.

TH: JEFFERSON

PrC (DLC); at foot of text: "Ferdinando Fairfax esq. Shannon hill."

[1] Word altered by TJ from two illegible words.

[2] TJ here canceled "ready to."

To Madame Plumard de Bellanger

DEAR MADAM   Monticello in Virginia Apr. 25. 1794.

While I remained in public office, it was out of my power to ackno-lege the receipt of the letters with which you were pleased to honor me. My daily and necessary labours obliged me to deny myself the satisfac-tion of all private correspondence, which I rigorously did, and without a single exception but in the case of my children. I have now been able to disengage myself from public affairs, and to retire to the bosom of my family, my farm, my books and my neighbors. Among the pleasing cir-cumstances in which I find myself placed, a prominent one is the society of Mr. Derieux, your worthy relation, to whom I sincerely wish the partialities of fortune had been as great as are those of his neighbors and acquaintance, who join, one and all, in their esteem and good wishes towards him. But the casualties of fortune seem rarely to be in his favor. The handsome aid which you were so generous as to give him has been lessened in it's effect by singular circumstances. It found him engaged in a small commerce of West India goods in which he had found a profit which had aided to support his family. He ventured to remit a part of your gift to the islands for a new cargo. The revolution there occasioned it's total loss. He was living in a rented house at Charlottesville where he carried on his commerce. His landlord, having occasion for money, he lent him another part of your gift, for the rent of his house by way of interest, and it was a very high interest, and the landlord mortgaged the house to him as a security for repaiment. I fear he has lost this money, and that the house having in the meantime gone rapidly to decay, will replace but a small part of it. The legacy from his uncle was lessened greatly as you know by the depreciation of the assignats. The prudent measure you recommended of remitting the legacy in merchandize, not money, saved much of his loss, as he gained on the sale of a part of the merchandize, nearly what had been lost by the assignats on that part of the purchase. But still the loss was too much for his circumstances, and the net proceeds of that legacy have been in a degree absorbed by debts which he had been obliged to contract, living in Charlottesville without any means of support but his capital unemployed, and therefore yeilding no profit. I have thought this explanation of his affairs due to you in return for your goodness to him, and due to myself too, to shew you how the views which I laid before you for the employment of the money you gave, have failed. It is indeed one of the circumstances which makes me lament either that I was not here when your aid came to him, or that it had not been postponed till I came. Had either of these been the case, I may, from the confidence he is pleased to repose in me, venture to affirm, that the whole should have been invested in negroes and cattle, or in good land, not leaving a shilling of it to the risk of any casualty, and that with his prudence and turn for agriculture, he would have been placed out of the danger of want. In the present situation of things I confess I look forward for him with disquietude. With his wife and a fine family of children in Charlottesville, he must soon consume the rest of his capital, and tho' extremely anxious to go to a farm, he has not the means of doing it. The house there is all which remains to him, and I fear that is already become by decay a very small resource. Should the favor of his relations be directed towards him in future, and particularly if you should be so good as to give him any further help without incommoding yourself, I think I may pledge myself that it shall be every far-thing of it laid out in lands and negroes, which besides a present support bring a silent profit of from 5. to 10. per cent in this country by the increase in their value. I can assure you from my own knolege of Mr. Derieux that you cannot do favors to a more worthy relation, nor to one in more need of it. But this would be the effect of your own goodness only which is sufficiently marked by what you have already done for him.—I have filled my letter with his subject, as there is no other in this country interesting to you, and those of France are too much unknown to me to say any thing of them, avec connoissance de cause. This scrap of French reminds me that I ought to make an apology for not writing to you in your own language. But the little habit I had of explaining myself in that tongue, is entirely lost, and I have been forced to address you in English or to lose the benefit of doing it at all. I inclose you a letter from Mr. Derieux, and have the honor to be, with sentiments of the most perfect respect & attachment, Dear Madam, Your most obedi-ent & most humble servt   TH: JEFFERSON

PrC (DLC); at foot of first page: "Ma-dame Bellanger." Enclosure not found.

A 24 Sep. 1794 letter from Madame Plumard de Bellanger to TJ, recorded in SJL as received 25 Mch. 1795, and TJ's reply of 6 Sep. 1795, their last exchange, have not been found.

To John Garland Jefferson

DEAR SIR   Monticello Apr. 26. 1794.

A pressure of affairs of various kinds on my return home, prevented my going into a consideration of your letter of Dec. 8. for a considerable time, and on taking it up, I found the information, which your brother had been able to obtain, defective in so many particulars that I con-cluded to let it lie till I could see him in Richmond. Several circum-stances however having delayed and still delaying my journey thither I now think it best to write you on the subject, hypothetically, as you will be able to judge whether I have misconjectured any of the facts, and of the influence they might have in the conclusion. The question seems to be relative to two descriptions of lands. 1. a tract mortgaged by your father to Genl. Harrington, and the greater part of the mortgage money paid; (I call it a mortgage, because Chancery considers as [such] every conveyance, tho' apparently absolute, where a covenant to reconvey on the paiment of the money existed between the parties) of which tract Genl. Harrington made sale, and became himself the purchaser for

about one penny in the shilling of it's real value: but whether by authority of process from a court of justice, or without process, is not stated. If
without process, and the laws of N. Carolina be conformable to those of
England and Virginia in this particular, a bill lies against Genl. Harrington in a court of Chancery, which will consider his sale and purchase as a gross violation of his trust, and therefore merely null. The
object of the bill should be to call for a settlement of the mortgager's
accounts with him, on which he will have credit for the money unpaid
and interest, and he will be debited the profits of the land, and the balance will be decreed either way as it shall be found, and he to reconvey
the lands. If the sale were by process from a court, it will depend on the
laws of that state in what manner that may be overhauled. We[1] must
presume they give day to an infant after his arrival at age to shew cause
in some short way why the proceedings have been wrongful. Tho'
Genl. Harrington's having acted as an Executor for some time without
having qualified, made him an Executor de son tort, and would authorize a suit against him as executor jointly with the others, yet if no advantage would be gained by suing him as executor, I should think it best to
sue him as a mortgagee; because in that case the other executors may be
examined as witnesses to prove the circumstances of the estate, and their
depositions be used against him as evidence, which Chancery does not
allow their answers to be, if you make them co-defendants. 2. the second
description of lands in question seems to have been such as were sold for
the paiment of debts, under process of a court as I conjecture. On these
I can say nothing, because there is no information who sold, or bought,
under what sort of process, whether for bonâ fide debts, whether a day
of revision was or was not allowed for the infants to come in after age
and question the proceedings, and what the laws of N. Carolina are in
these particulars? As to all this you will undoubtedly procure information, and I feel the less reluctance at turning the matter over to your
enquiries, as I am sensible you will be a better judge of them than myself, with the rust of 20. years inhabitude in the law.—I know nothing
of the character of the judges and courts of N. Carolina as to science and
independance. You are entitled however, as the inhabitants of another
state, to bring your suit in the federal court of the district where your
process finds the defendant, and besides the greater degree of independence felt by the courts and officers of the federal government, and the
science and integrity which has generally procured their appointment,
you will have a sure opportunity of correcting any error by an appeal to
the supreme court of the union, where no influence can be feared.—I
inclose you the copy of your father's will, and your brother's letter, with
every wish for your success in this and all other matters interesting to

you; and hoping soon to hear that you are beginning to reap a good harvest from your past labours, I conclude with assurances of the esteem and attachment with which I am Dear Sir Your affectionate friend & kinsman   TH: JEFFERSON

PrC (MHi); faded; consists of first page only; at foot of page: "Mr. J. Garland Jefferson." PrC (ViU: Edgehill-Randolph Papers); consists of last two pages only. Tr (Nc-Ar; Orange County Land Records); 1797 copy certified by Waller Ford. Enclosures not found.

J. G. Jefferson's LETTER OF DEC. 8., recorded in SJL as written at Monticello and received there by TJ on 15 Jan. 1794, has not been found.

The TRACT MORTGAGED to Henry William HARRINGTON was situated on Browns Creek in Amherst County. Three years

later J. G. Jefferson, enclosing a copy of TJ's letter, sought to interest an acquaintance in buying his equity of redemption in this land or in recovering it for him in exchange for a share of the acreage, pleading his own financial inability to pursue the necessary litigation (J. G. Jefferson to an unidentified correspondent, 20 Feb. 1797, Nc-Ar: Orange County Land Records; Henry Gannett, *Gazetteer of Virginia*, U.S. House of Representatives, 58th Cong., 2d Sess., Vol. LXII, No. 727 [Washington, D.C., 1904], 30).

[1] MHi text ends here.

From James Madison

DEAR SIR   Phila. Apl. 28. 1794.

I have received yours of the 3d. instant. I have already informed you of my having forwarded you the French Edition of Milton received from E.R. Cortez's letters are not come to hand. It seems that Blake by whom you expected them is not the person thro' whom the Milton came, and that he is not yet arrived. The correspondence with Hammond has been forwarded in detachments by Col. Monroe.

The non-importation bill has passed the H. of Reps. by 59. against 34. It will probably miscarry in the Senate. It prohibits all articles of British or Irish production after the 1st. Novr. until the claims of the U.S. be adjusted and satisfied. The appointment of H. as envoy Extry. was likely to produce such a sensation that to his great mortification he was laid aside, and Jay named in his place. The appointment of the latter would have been difficult in the Senate, but for some adventitious causes. There were 10 votes against him in one form of the opposition and 8 on the direct question. As a resignation of his Judiciary character might, for any thing known to the Senate, have been intended to follow his acceptance of the Ex. trust, the ground of incompatibility could not support the objections, which, since it has appeared that such a resignation was no part of the arrangement, are beginning to be pressed in the Newspapers. If animadversions are undertaken by skilful hands, there is no measure of the Ex. administration perhaps that will be found more severely vulnerable.

The English prints breathe an unabated zeal for the war against France. The Minister carries every thing as usual in Parlt. notwithstanding the miscarriages at Toulon &c., and his force will be much increased by the taking of Martinique and the colouring it will give to the W. India prospects. Nothing further appears as to the views prevailing in relation to us. The latter accounts from the W. Inds. since the new Instruction of Jany. 8. are rather favorable to the Merchants and alleviate their resentments: so that G.B. seems to have derived from the excess of her aggressions a title to commit them in a less degree with impunity. The French arms continue to prosper, tho' no very capital event is brought by the latest arrivals.

RC (DLC: Madison Papers); unsigned; endorsed by TJ as received 6 May 1794 and so recorded in SJL.

For the vote on the NON-IMPORTATION BILL, see note to Madison to TJ, 14 Apr. 1794. On 16 Apr. 1794 President Washington submitted the nomination of John Jay as Envoy Extraordinary to Great Britain to the Senate, where three days later, after a series of intricate parliamentary maneuvers, the appointment was confirmed by a vote of 18 to 8, with Virginia Senators James Monroe and John Taylor among those voting in the negative (JEP, I, 150-2). THE MINISTER: William Pitt. For the English capture of MARTINIQUE, see *Philadelphia Gazette*, 17 Apr. 1794. NEW INSTRUCTION OF JANY. 8.: see note to James Monroe to TJ, 2 Apr. 1794.

To William Nelson, Jr.

DEAR SIR   Monticello Apr. 28. 1794.

I received a few days ago your favor of the 4th. instant. Having had occasion, while in my late office, to enquire into the situation of the boundary between our SouthWestern territory and Kentucky and to make a Report on it to the President to be laid before Congress, it became of course necessary for me to recur to the boundary between this state and Carolina, the extension of this being the true line I had to state. I happen to have preserved copies of the documents on which my report was founded, and among them that of which you enquire. It appears that the Governor of Virginia (probably in 1789. for this document happens to be without date) wrote to the government of N. Carolina, proposing the establishment of Walker's line, or if that should not be acceptable, that they would then appoint Commissioners on both sides to confer on the subject and to report to their legislatures. The assembly of N. Carolina referred this letter to a committee, who by Mr. Person their chairman reported that according to the best information they could obtain, Walker's was the true line, and recommended that a law should be passed, confirming it, with 'a reservation in favor of the oldest grants for either state, in deciding the rights of individual claimants in the tract between the two lines commonly called Walker's and Henderson's lines.' The assembly at their next session passed the following resolution. 'North Carolina, in the House of Commons 11th. of Dec. 1790. The Committee to whom the letter from the Governor of Virginia, on the boundary line between this and the state of Virginia was referred, report, that it is the opinion of your committee the boundary line between the state of N. Carola. and Virginia be confirmed agreeably to a report of a committee; concurred with by both houses last session of Assembly: and that a law be passed confirming the line commonly called Walker's line as the boundary between the states of N. Carolina and Virginia, reserving the rights of the eldest patents, grants or entries made in either of the states. All which is submitted. Thomas Person, Chairman. In the house of commons 11th. Dec. 1790. Read and concurred with S. Cabarrus C.H.C.—in Senate 11th. Dec. 1790. read and concurred with Wm. Lenoir. Spr. S. A copy from the journal of the H. of commons J. Hunt. Clk. Copies of original papers filed in the office of the clerk of the H. of Delegates of Virginia duly authenticated under the seal of the state of N. Carolina. Attest. Sam. Coleman. A. C.C.' Probably this joint resolution was intended to be final, and that no other act passed, and that this is the *official information* referred to in the act of the Virginia assembly of Dec. 7. 1791. and which was the foundation of that act.   This is all the information in my possession on the subject of your enquiries and I shall be happy if it fulfills your wishes, being with every sentiment of esteem Dr. Sir Your most obedt. & most humble servt   TH: JEFFERSON

RC (Edward McCague, Charlottesville, 1948); torn, with missing words on several lines supplied from PrC; addressed: "William Nelson esquire Atty at law. to the care of Benj. Harri[son] Rich[mond]"; endorsed. PrC (DLC).

William Nelson, Jr. (1754-1813), a Virginia attorney who had been a member of the House of Delegates in 1783 and of the Council of State from 1784 to 1786, served as a judge of the Virginia General Court from 1791 until his death (Marshall, *Papers*, I, 117n; Madison, *Papers*, VI, 500n; H. R. McIlwaine and others, eds., *Journals*

of the Council of the State of Virginia, 4 vols. [Richmond, 1931-67], III, 331, 444, 515).

Nelson's FAVOR OF THE 4TH. INSTANT, recorded in SJL as received from Charles City 23 Apr. 1794, has not been found. A REPORT ON IT: TJ's Report on Public Lands, 8 Nov. 1791. For the disputed BOUNDARY BETWEEN THIS STATE AND CAROLINA, see note to William Blount to TJ, 26 Dec. 1791. Except for the letter of the GOVERNOR OF VIRGINIA, Beverley Randolph, which has not been found, the other documents cited by TJ are listed as Enclosures Nos. 1 and 2 at Henry Lee to TJ, 24 Oct. 1792.

To John Ross

DEAR SIR   Monticello Apr. 30. 1794.

Your favor of the 7th. inst. has been duly received. Having occasion this day to order the shipment of some tobacco from Richmond (where nothing can be sold for cash) to Mr. Lownes of Philadelphia, for other purposes, I enable him on receipt of it to pay you the balance mentioned in your letter, for which and all other friendly attentions accept my renewed thanks. Among the recollections which I shall continue to cherish is that of the esteem I had entertained for yourself, and endeavored to cultivate whenever my harrassed condition would permit it. I am now enjoying in full draughts those rural scenes which you only sip at occasionally, and they are not the less relished by a great deal of active industry and exercise. With my best respects to Mrs. Ross, and every wish for your happiness, I am Dear Sir with sincere esteem & respect Your friend & Servt   TH: JEFFERSON

RC (PP: Historical Manuscripts); addressed: "John Ross esquire Mercht. Philadelphia"; stamped; endorsed by Ross as received 10 May 1794.

Ross's FAVOR OF THE 7TH. INST., recorded in SJL as received from Philadelphia on 16 Apr. 1794, has not been found. Also missing are a letter from Ross to TJ of 27 June 1797, recorded in SJL as received the same day, and TJ's reply recorded in SJL a day later. Both presumably dealt with the failure of Caleb LOWNES to settle the BALANCE of $59.38 due on the loan that Ross made to TJ on 2 Jan. 1794, and TJ's arrangement to have it paid by John Barnes (MB, 30 Apr. 1794, 28 June 1797).

Memorandum from Bowling Clark

List of Mr. Jefferson Stock Poplar Forest for 1794 april
at Hubbards quarter 9 cows 2 heffers 3 year old 1 Do. 2 year old 4 Do. 1 year old 3 stears 4 year old 2 Do. 3 year old 4 Do. 2 year old 3 Do. 1 year old 1 Bull 1 year old 2 work stears 4 calves the hold amount 35
46 grown hogs including the sows 30 pigs 4 months old 13 Do. of a smaller sise in the hold 89
at Morrices place 31 cows 5 Heffers 3 year old 10 Do. 2 year old 9 Do. 1 year old 5 stears 4 year old 3 Do. 3 year old 6 Do. 2 year old 7 Do. 1 year old 2 Bull 5 worke stears 21 calves in the hold 104
50 hogs above 8 month old including the sows 25 above 3 month old and under 8—30 pigs under 3 months old in the hold 105
the total amount of cattle at both places 139 of hogs 203.

NB sence the above list was drown of thare has 3 cattle died 1–2 year old heffer and 2 works

MS (ViU: Edgehill-Randolph Papers); entirely in Clark's hand.

Clark, TJ's overseer at Poplar Forest, may have enclosed this list in his letter to TJ of 24 Apr. 1794, recorded in SJL as received from Poplar Forest on 27 Apr. 1794 but not found. SJL also records eight other letters, now missing, exchanged by TJ and Clark between 22 Jan. 1793 and 27 Mch. 1794.

To Charles Carter

Dear Sir   Monticello May 1. 1794.

I have received your favor of Apr. 19. and supposing you would wish information as to the article of it relative to the concern of Carter & Trent, I take the liberty of mentioning that there was a balance due from me to that concern, which had been partly paid off before my return from Europe, and the residue was paid about two years ago as nearly as I can recollect. It was done by Lewis & Ware of Goochland on an order from Colo. Nich. Lewis while he took care of my affairs; which puts it out of my power to name the date or sum exactly, but I know it was about £[3. and?] was fully paid off. I should otherwise with great satisfaction have done any thing in my power to have aided you in lessening the enormous injuries which your father's estate ha[s?] suffered from that concern. I have the honor to be with sincere esteem Dear Sir Your friend & servt   Th: Jefferson

PrC (DLC); with faded words in right margin; at foot of text: "Charles Carter esq. Culpeper."

Carter's favor of apr. 19., recorded in SJL as received from Blenheim on 27 Apr. 1794, has not been found. The mercantile concern of his father, Edward carter, and Peterfield trent was dissolved on 1 Feb. 1774 (Virginia Gazette [Purdie & Dixon], 17 Feb. 1774; Woods, Albemarle, 163-4).

Letters from TJ to Carter recorded in SJL under 11 July 1794 and 9 Sep. 1795, and Carter's replies of 20 Aug. 1794 and 10 Sep. 1795, the first recorded in SJL as received 27 Aug. 1794 and the second erroneously recorded as received from Blenheim on 9 Sep. 1795, have not been found.

To Tench Coxe

Dear Sir   Monticello May 1. 1794.

Your several favors of Feb. 22. 27. and Mar. 16. which had been accumulating in Richmond during the prevalence of the small-pox in that place, were lately brought to me on the permission given the post to resume his communication. I am particularly to thank you for your favor in forwarding the Bee. Your letters give a comfortable view of French affairs, and later events seem to confirm it. Over the foreign powers I am convinced they will triumph completely, and I cannot but hope that that triumph and the consequent disgrace of the invading tyrants is destined in the order of events to kindle the wrath of the people of Europe against those who have dared to embroil them in such wickedness, and to bring at length kings, nobles and priests to the scaffolds which they have been so long deluging with human blood. I am still warm whenever I think of these scoundrels, tho' I do it as seldom as I can, preferring infinitely to contemplate the tranquil growth of my Lucerne and potatoes. I have so completely withdrawn myself from these spectacles of usurpation and mis-rule that I do not take a single newspaper, nor read one a month: and I feel myself infinitely the happier for it.—We are alarmed here with the apprehensions of war: and sincerely anxious that it might be avoided; but not at the expence either of our faith or honor. It seems much the general opinion here that the latter has been too much wounded not to require reparation, and to seek it even in war, if that be necessary. As to myself, I love peace, and I am anxious that we should give the world still another useful lesson, by shewing to them other modes of punishing injuries than by war, which is as much a punishment to the punisher as to the sufferer. I love therefore Mr. Clarke's proposition of cutting off all communication with the nation which has conducted itself so atrociously. This you will say may bring on war. If it does, we will meet it like men: but it may not bring on war, and then the experiment will have been a happy one. I believe this war would be vastly more unanimously approved, than any one we ever were engaged in; because the aggressions have been so wanton and barefaced, and so unquestionably against our desire.—I am sorry Mr. Cooper and Priestley did not take a more general survey of our country before they fixed themselves. I think they might have promoted their own advantage by it, and have aided the introduction of improvement where it is more wanting.—The prospect of wheat for the ensuing year is a bad one. This is all the sort of news you can expect from me. From you I shall be glad to hear all sorts of news, and particularly any improvements in the arts applicable to husbandry or houshold manufacture. I am with very sincere affection Dear Sir your friend & servt

TH: JEFFERSON

PrC (DLC); at foot of first page: "Mr. Coxe."

To John Taylor

DEAR SIR   Monticello May 1. 1794.

In my new occupation of a farmer I find a good drilling machine indispensably necessary. I remember your recommendation of one invented by one of your neighbors; and your recommendation suffices to satisfy me with it. I must therefore beg of you to desire one to be made for me, and if you will give me some idea of it's bulk, and whether it could travel here on it's own legs, I will decide whether to send express for it, or get it sent round by Richmond. Mention at the same time the price of it and I will have it put into your hands.—I remember I shewed you, for your advice, a plan of a rotation of crops which I had contemplated to introduce into my own lands. On a more minute examination of my lands than I had before been able to take since my return from Europe, I find their degradation by ill usage much beyond what I had expected, and at the same time much more open land than I had calculated on. One of these circumstances forces a milder course of cropping on me, and the other enables me to adopt it. I drop therefore two crops in my rotation, and instead of 5. crops in 8. years take 3. in 6. years, in the following order. 1. wheat. 2. corn and potatoes in the strongest moiety, potatoes alone or peas alone in the other moiety according to it's strength. 3. wheat or rye. 4. clover. 5. clover. 6. folding and buckwheat dressing. In such of my feilds as are too much worn for clover, I propose to try St. foin, which I know will grow in the poorest land, bring plentiful crops, and is a great ameliorater. It is for this chiefly I want the drilling machine as well as for Lucerne. My neighbors to whom I had distributed some seed of the Succory intybus, brought from France by Young, and sent to the President, are much pleased with it. I am trying a patch of it this year.—This drop from the tip of[1] Lazarus's finger to cool your tongue, I have thought even father Abraham would approve. He refused it to Dives in the common hell; but in yours he could not do it.—Pray let me have a copy of the pamphlet published on the subject of the bank. Not even the title of it has ever been seen by my neighbors. My best affections to the sound part of our representation in both houses, which I calculate to be $\frac{19}{21}$ths. Adieu. Your's affectionately

TH: JEFFERSON

RC (MHi: Washburn Collection); addressed: "John Taylor of the Senate of the US. Philadelphia"; franked. PrC (DLC).

John Taylor of Caroline (1753-1824), the Virginia lawyer, planter, legislator, and agrarian political economist, had been brought up by Edmund Pendleton after the death of his parents. After attending William and Mary for two years, he studied law with Pendleton and was admitted to the Caroline County bar in 1774. During the Revolutionary War Taylor served as a major in the Continental Army and as a lieutenant colonel in the Virginia militia, and was a member of the Virginia House of Delegates from 1779 to 1781 before deciding to devote himself fully to his legal practice the following year, when he sought TJ's opinion in a tangled case (see Vol. 27: 724-7). Taylor served again in the Virginia House of Delegates, 1783-85 and 1796-1800, and in the United States Senate, 1792-94, 1803, and 1822-24. In the 1790s he established himself as a leading agricultural reformer and political theorist, becoming a close political ally and regular correspondent of TJ's but exerting his greatest influence through his voluminous published writings, which from then until his death consistently warned of the perils posed to agrarian republicanism by the alliance between centralized government and a monied interest (DAB; Robert E. Shalhope, *John Taylor of Caroline: Pastoral Republican* [Columbia, S.C., 1980]).

After an initial and apparently unsuccessful experiment in 1774 with the plant, on 28 Apr. 1794 TJ sowed SUCCORY (*Cichorium intybus*) he had received from the President and thereafter kept it in continuous cultivation until at least 1818 to feed his livestock and for his own table (Betts, *Garden Book*, 47, 58, 210, 581; Betts, *Farm Book*, 245-6). PAMPHLET PUBLISHED ON . . . THE BANK: see first enclosure listed at Taylor to TJ, 1 June 1794.

[1] TJ here canceled "[my] finger."

From James Monroe

DEAR SIR   Phila. May 4. 1794.

Yours of April 24th. reached me yesterday. Since my last the proposition of Mr. Clarke for prohibiting the importation of British goods untill the posts shall be surrendered and compensation made for the depredation on our trade, was rejected in the Senate. Upon the question the first section which determined the fate of the bill, Jackson and Bradley withdraw which left us 11. only against 14.: in consequence of which every section was negatived, yet a question was notwithstanding taken whether the bill should be read a 3d. time and in favor of which these gentlemen voted, and Ross the successor of Gallatin taking into his head now to withdraw, the house was equally divided and the casting vote given by the V. President against it. Thus the bill was lost, the most mature and likely to succeed of all the propositions respecting G. Britn. which have been presented before the legislature during the session. Its fate may be ascribed to an executive maneuvre: for whilst it was depending in the Repe. branch and obviously a great majority in its favor, the nomination of Mr. Jay was introduc'd, as Envoy Extry. for the British court. From that moment it was manifest the measure would be lost, and altho' it passed the other branch and perhaps with greater vote than would have been the case, had not the sense of the Senate been clearly indicated by the approbation of the nomination, yet it was plain the prospect of success was desperate. An Extraordinary mission was a measure of conciliation, it was urged; prohibitory regulations were of a different character and would defeat its object. Thus you find nothing has been carried against that nation, but on the contrary the most submissive measure adopted that could be devised, to court her favor and degrade our character.

Tis said that the Envoy will be armed with extraordinary powers and that authority to form a commercial treaty will likewise be comprized in his instructions. Under a similar power upon a former occasion, granted too by implication only, this person had well nigh bartered away the Missisippi. What then may we not expect from him upon the present crisis, when the power is expressly granted and the fortune of the party whose agent he is, may be considered as hazarded in the success of his mission? After degrading our country by shewing to the world, that they were more willing to confide in retribution &ca from their justice and favor, than from the strength of our union and the decision of our councils, will this man return baffled in the enterprize, and seek to atone for himself and those who sent him, to the community, by owning his and their folly which had exposed us to such humiliation? And when it is considered that Britain contemplates the conquest of the French and perhaps afterwards of the Sph. Islands, and the downfal of the Sph. power in this region of the [world] a course of policy which will part her not only from Spn. but perhaps from the present combination of powers, is it not probable she will be disposed to seek an alliance here as well for the purpose of aiding her in these projects as detaching us from France? Some symtoms of discontent have already appeared in the Sph. cabinet, and these it is probable will be increased when the conquest of Britn. in the Islands is attended to, and her views become further developed. The circumstance of sending an envoy to negotiate with Engld. at the time that the minister of France, on the ground and cloathed with similar powers, is only amused with acts of civility, shews that a connection with the former power is the next object of the Executive.

The present French minister expressed lately the wish of his country that G. Morris should be recalled and in consequence arrangements are making for that purpose. Being forced to send a republican character the admn. was reduc'd to the dilemma of selecting from among its enemies or rather those of opposit principles, a person who would be acceptable to that nation. The offer of the station has been presented to Chr. Livingston as I hear in a letter written by the President. Tis thought he will accept it. Burr's name was mentioned to Randolph but with the success that was previously expected, indeed it was not urged in preference to the other, but only noted for consideration. I thank you for the intelligence respecting my farm near you. I think we shall adjourn in about 3. weeks after which I shall immediately proceed home. Mrs. M. joins in best wishes for your health and that of your family. Sincerely I am Dear Sir your friend & servant   JAS. MONROE

RC (DLC); words along margin partially covered by tape, with illegible word supplied in brackets from Monroe, *Writings*, I, 295; endorsed by TJ as received 14 May 1794 and so recorded in SJL.

UPON A FORMER OCCASION: a reference to the Jay-Gardoqui negotiations of 1785-86, in which Jay as Secretary for Foreign Affairs under the Articles of Confederation had been willing to relinquish a formal assertion of America's right to navigate the Mississippi for up to thirty years in return for a commercial treaty with Spain, an arrangement that Monroe had strongly opposed as a member of the Confederation Congress (Bemis, *Pinckney's Treaty*, 80-7). Washington first offered Chancellor Robert R. LIVINGSTON of New York the appointment as American minister to France in a letter of 29 Apr. 1794 and reiterated the offer in a letter of 14 May 1794, but Livingston declined to serve (Fitzpatrick, *Writings*, XXXIII, 346, 364).

From John Adams

DEAR SIR   Philadelphia May 11. 1794

Your favour of the 25th. of last month, came to my hands Yesterday and I am glad to find you so well pleased with your Retirement. I felt the Same delightful Satisfaction after my Return from Europe, and I feel Still every Summer upon my little farm all the Ardour, and more than all the Ardor of youth: to such a Degree that I cannot bear the thought of writing or reading, unless it be some trifle to fill up a vacant half hour.

The Case of the Pays de Vaud is curious enough. Dr. Cart the Writer of the Book I sent you is arrived at New York and Mr. Rosset whose Tryal and Sentence for high Treason, for dining at a civic feast and drinking two or three Patriotic Toasts, is mentioned in it, is here at Philadelphia. He has lent me in Manuscript a full account of his Tryal. As much as I have ever detested an Aristocratical Government, I did not believe that the Canton of Berne could have been So tyrannical, till I read this Manuscript.

I think nevertheless that "the Rights of one Generation of Men must Still depend, in Some degree, on the Paper Transactions of another." The Social Compact and the Laws must be reduced to Writing. Obedience to them becomes a national Habit and they cannot be changed but by Revolutions which are costly Things. Men will be too Œconomical of their Blood and Property to have Recourse to them, very frequently. This Country is becoming the Assylum of all the ardent Spirits in Europe. The Bp. of Autun and Mr. Beaumez, are arrived and Dr. Priestley is expected.

The President has Sent Mr. Jay to try if he can find any way to reconcile our honour with Peace. I have no great Faith in any very brilliant Success: but hope he may have enough to keep us out of a war. Another war would add two or three hundred Millions of Dollars to our Debt: rouse up a many headed and many bellied Monster of an Army to tyrannize over Us, totally dissadjust our present Government, and accellerate the Advent of Monarchy and Aristocracy, by at least fifty years.

Those who dread Monarchy and Aristocracy and at the Same time advocate war are the most inconsistent of all Men.

If I had your Plantation and your Labourers I should be tempted to follow your Example and get out of the Fumum et Opes Strepitumque Romæ which I abominate. I am Sir with much Esteem your Friend & Sert   JOHN ADAMS

RC (DLC); at foot of text: "Mr Jefferson"; endorsed by TJ as received 21 May 1794 and so recorded in SJL.

Ferdinand Antoine Louis ROSSET, a member of a distinguished Lausanne family, had been sentenced to twenty-five years imprisonment by the government of Bern for praising the French Revolution during a political banquet in his native city in July 1791 and had come to America after escaping from confinement with the help of friends (Charles Burnier, *La Vie vaudoise et la Révolution* [Lausanne, 1902], 222-38; Palmer, *Democratic Revolution*, II, 403).

BP. OF AUTUN AND MR. BEAUMEZ: Charles Maurice de Talleyrand-Périgord and his friend Bon Albert Briois de Beaumez or Beaumetz, a French nobleman from Artois who had served in the Constituent Assembly before fleeing to Germany and eventually joining Talleyrand in Great Britain, whence they sailed for the United States in the spring of 1794 (*Dictionnaire*, VII, 333; Childs, *French Refugee Life*, 26, 36-7, 113).

FUMUM . . . ROMÆ: "the smoke, wealth, and din of Rome."

From James Madison

DEAR SIR   Philada. May 11. 1794

Col. Monroe wrote you last week, and I refer to his letter for the state of things up to that date. The H. of Reps. has been Since employed chiefly on the new taxes. The Report of the Committee which was the work of a sub committee in understanding with the Fiscal Department, was filled with a variety of items copied as usual from the British Revenue laws. It particularly included, besides stamp-duties, excises on tobacco and sugar manufactured in the U.S. and a tax on carriages as an *indirect* tax. The aversion to direct taxes which appeared by a vote of seventy odd for rejecting them will saddle us with all these pernicious innovations,[1] without ultimately avoiding direct taxes in addition to them. All opposition to the new excises, tho' enforced by memorials from the manufacturers was vain. And the tax on carriages succeeded in spite of the Constitution by a majority of twenty, the advocates for the principle being reinforced by the adversaries to luxury. Six of the *N. Carolina* members were in the majority. This is another proof of the facility with which usurpation triumphs where there is a standing corps always on the watch for favorable conjunctures, and directed by the policy of dividing their honest but undiscerning adversaries. It is very possible however that the authors of these precedents may not be the last to lament them. Some of the motives which they decoyed to their support ought to premonish them of the danger. By breaking down the barriers of the constitution and giving sanction to the idea of sumptuary regulations, wealth may find a precarious defence in the sheild of justice. If luxury, *as such*, is to be taxed, the greatest of all luxuries, says Payne, is a great estate. Even on the present occasion, it has been found prudent to yield to a tax on transfers of stock in the funds, and in the Banks.

The appointment of Jay continues to undergo the animadversions of the Press. You will see that the Democratic Societies are beginning to open their batteries upon it. The measure however has had the effect of impeding all legislative measures for extorting redress from G.B. The non-importation bill which passed the H. of Reps. by a geat majority, was so instantly and peremptorily rejected in the Senate as an interference with the proposed Mission, that no further efforts of the same type have been seriously contemplated. Clarke did indeed move to insert among the new ways and means an additional duty of 10 perCt. on *British* Manufactures, but the symptoms of desertion soon induced him to withdraw it. A member from N. Carolina afterwards was incautious eno' to try a discriminating duty on British tonnage and by pushing it to a question with the yeas and nays, placed us in a very feeble minority. Notwithstanding this effect of the Executive measure, there is little serious confidence in its efficacy; and, as involving the appointment of Jay, is the most powerful blow ever suffered by the popularity of the President.

The embargo is Still in force. A member from Connecticut moved a few days ago to abridge its term a few days, as a notification that it would not be continued. A large majority was against taking up the proposition; but how far with a view to adhere to the embargo, I know not. Yesterday a motion was laid on the table by Smith (of S.C.) for continuing the embargo to June 25. The motion from that quarter excited surprize: and must be either a fetch at popularity, an insidious thing, or suggested by an idea that the balance of the effects of the embargo is in favor of G. Britain.

There are no late accounts of moment from Europe. Those from the W. Indies, as well with respect to the treatment of our vessels as the effects of the embargo, are so various and contradictory that it is impossible to make any thing of them. Yrs. Affecy.   Js. MADISON JR

RC (DLC: Madison Papers); endorsed by TJ as received 21 May 1794 and so recorded in SJL.

Despite Madison's objection that the TAX ON CARRIAGES was an unconstitutional direct tax, the House of Representatives approved it on 7 May and confirmed it in another roll-call vote on 29 May, the measure becoming law on 5 June 1794 (*Annals*, IV, 656-7, 729-30, 1452-4). Thomas Paine described THE GREATEST OF ALL LUXURIES as A GREAT ESTATE in 1792 in the second part of *Rights of Man* (Foner, *Paine*, I, 434). The Democratic Society of Pennsylvania passed resolutions attacking the APPOINTMENT OF JAY on 8 May 1794 (Philip S. Foner, ed., *The Democratic-Republican Societies, 1790-1800: A Documentary Sourcebook . . .* [Westport, Conn., 1976], 104-6). Congressman Abraham Clark of New Jersey made and withdrew his motion for an ADDITIONAL DUTY on British manufactures on 9 May 1794, the same day that a representative from N. CAROLINA forced a roll-call vote on an increased duty on foreign tonnage that placed the Republicans in a VERY FEEBLE MINORITY of 25 to 61. Consideration of the motion of Zephaniah Swift of CONNECTICUT to end the EMBARGO was deferred on 8 May 1794, but four days later both parties joined to defeat its continuation TO JUNE 25 (*Annals*, IV, 657-8, 668-71, 675-83).

[1] Remainder of sentence interlined.

To Edmund Randolph

DEAR SIR   Monticello May 14. 1794.

Tho Mr. Bertrand mentions having seen me at Paris, (of which I remember nothing) yet it is evident his letter was meant for me as Secretary of state, and not in my private capacity. The proposition to the government for an assignment of lands can only be answered by the government, if to be answered at all. I therefore inclose you his letter and papers. I also send back 6. packages destined also for the Secretary of state. I opened one of them at the end and saw that it's contents were the proceedings of the French convention, as I conjecture the other 5. to be, and to have been sent by Mr. Morris, or some of the Consuls, or perhaps some volunteer correspondent. I did not read a line in the one I opened for from all such reading good lord deliver me! Adieu. Yours affectionately   TH: JEFFERSON

RC (DNA: RG 59, MLR); at foot of text: "The Secretary of state"; endorsed by George Taylor, Jr. PrC (DLC). Enclosure: O. A. Bertrand to TJ, 8 Feb. 1794, and enclosures. Other enclosures not found.

To George Washington

DEAR SIR   Monticello May 14. 1794.

I am honored with your favor of Apr. 24. and received at the same time Mr. Bertrand's agricultural Prospectus. Tho' he mentions my having seen him at a particular place yet I remember nothing of it, and observing that he intimates an application for lands in America, I conceive his letter meant for me as Secretary of state, and therefore I now send it to the Secretary of state. He has given only the heads of his demonstrations, so that nothing can be conjectured of their details. Ld. Kaims once proposed an essence of dung, one pint of which should manure an acre. If he or Mr. Bertrand could have rendered it so portable I should have been one of those who would have been greatly obliged to them. I find on a more minute examination of my lands, than the short visits heretofore made to them permitted, that a 10. years abandonment of them to the unprincipled ravages of overseers, has brought on a degree of degradation far beyond what I had expected. As this obliges me to adopt a milder course of cropping, so I find that they have enabled me to do it by having opened a great deal of lands during my absence. I have therefore determined on a division of my farms into 6. fields to be put under this rotation. 1st. year. Wheat.—2d. corn, potatoes, peas.—3d. rye or wheat according to circumstances.—4th. and 5th. clover where the fields will bring it, and buckwheat dressings where they will not.—6th. folding, and buckwheat dressings. But it will take me from 3. to 6. years to get this plan under way. I am not yet satisfied that my acquisition of overseers from the head of Elk has been a happy one, or that much will be done this year towards rescuing my plantations from their wretched condition. Time, patience and perseverance must be the remedy: and the maxim of your letter 'slow and sure' is not less a good one in agriculture than in politics. I sincerely wish it may extricate us from the event of a war, if this can be done saving our faith and our rights. My opinion of the British government is that nothing will force them to do justice but the loud voice of their people, and that this can never be excited but by distressing their commerce. But I cherish tranquility too much to suffer political things to enter my mind at all.—I do not forget that I owe you a letter for Mr. Young, but I am waiting to get full information. With every wish for your health and happiness and my most friendly respects for Mrs. Washington, I have the honor to be Dear Sir your most obedt. & most humble servt   TH: JEFFERSON

RC (RuS); at foot of first page: "The President of the US."; endorsed by Washington. PrC (DLC).

A LETTER FOR MR. YOUNG: see Washington to TJ, 13 May 1793.

To James Madison

DEAR SIR   Monticello May 15. 1794.

I wrote you on the 3d. of April, and since that have received yours of Mar. 24. 26. 31. Apr. 14. and 28. and yesterday I received Colo. Monroe's of the 4th. inst. informing me of the failure of the non-importation bill in the Senate. This body was intended as a check on the will of the Representatives when too hasty. They are not only that but completely so on the will of the people also: and in my opinion are heaping coals of fire not only on their persons, but on their body as a branch of legislature. I have never known a measure more universally desired by the people than the passage of that bill. It is not from my own observation of the wishes of the people that I decide what they are, but from that of the gentlemen of the bar who mix much with them, and by their intercommunications with each other, have under their view a greater portion of the country than any other description of men. It seems that the opinion is fairly launched into public, that they should be placed under the controul of a more frequent recurrence to the will of their constituents. This seems requisite to compleat the experiment whether they do more harm or good?—I wrote lately to Mr. Taylor for the pamphlet on the bank. Since that I have seen the 'Definition of parties,' and must pray you to bring it for me. It is one of those things which merits to be preserved.—The safe arrival of my books at Richmond, and some of them at home, has relieved me from anxiety, and will not be indifferent to you.—It turns out that our fruit has not been as entirely killed as was at first apprehended. Some latter blossoms have yeilded a small supply of this precious refreshment.—I was so improvident as never to have examined at Philadelphia whether negro cotton and oznabrigs can be had there. If you do not already possess the information, pray obtain it before you come away. Our spring has on the whole been seasonable, and the wheat as much recovered as it's thinness would permit. But the crop must still be a miserable one. There would not have been seed made but for the extraordinary rains of the last month. Our highest heat as yet has been 83. This was on the 4th. inst.—That Blake should not have been arrived at the date of your letter, surprizes me. Pray enquire into the fact before you leave Philadelphia. According to Colo. Monroe's letter this will find you on the point of departure. I hope we shall see you here soon after your return. Remember me affectionately to Colo. and Mrs. Monroe, and accept the sincere esteem of Dear Sir your sincere friend & servt   TH: JEFFERSON

RC (DLC: Madison Papers); addressed: "James Madison junr. of the Virginia Representation in Congress. Philadelphia"; franked. PrC (DLC).

PAMPHLET ON THE BANK and DEFINITION OF PARTIES: see enclosures listed at John Taylor to TJ, 1 June 1794.

From Joseph L'Epine

Nouvelle York le 16 may 1794

Je suis des plus mortifiés, que L'Evénément de la mort de Mr. Joseph Dombey, soit la Premiere occasion, qui me procure l'honneur de vous Ecrire.

Mon Brig Le Boon Capne. Nel. Wm. Brown, partit en Janvier dernier, du havre de Grace pour se rendre icy; ayant pour Passager Mr. Jh. Dombey, qui fit signer audit Capne. des Connoissements de Ses Malles a vôtre adresse, et le 12 fevrier dernier, ce Brig Reçût un Coup de Vent si terrible, qu'il fit Voille (ayant une voye d'Eau) pour le premier port qu'il pouvoit trouver, et Il fit sa Relâche en détresse a la Guadeloupe, où Il fit réparer ledit Brig pour Continuer son Voy[age sans] son lest, Comme il étoit venu; et Mr. Dombey quoy [que] malade, se Rembarqua; mais Ils eurent le Malheur d'être Arêtés par Un Corsaire Anglois le 1er. avril dernier, qui les menat a Montserrat; et les Brigands dudit corsaire pillerent et traiterent Si mal Mr. Dombey, et Mr. Bacchus, qu'ils Contribüerent beaucoup a leur Mort: le Capne. dudit Corsaire avoit aussi Pillé des Effets et provisions de mondit Navire, et non Content de cela fit un Process au Captne. Brown, dans l'Espérance que Mr. Dombey avoit des Effets et argent dans Ses Malles; mais voyant les Connoissements a vôtre adresse, Ils n'y voulurent pas toucher; et apres avoir visité tout a bord, même Retourner le lest, l'on fit payer au Capne. Brown toute la Procédure, et l'on le Renvoya.

Je feray Remettre au Magazin Public les Malles de ce Mr., Jusqu'à ce qu'il vous plaise donner vos ordres a vos amis, pour les faire Retirer; et ledit Capne. Brown se flatte que vous le ferez Rembourser de Son Compte de Maladie, funérailles, [&c.] dudit Sr. Dombey. J'ay l'honneur d'être avec [mon pro]fond Respect Monsieur Votre tres humble & ob. serv.

Jh. L'Epine

RC (DLC); in a clerk's hand, signed by L'Epine; torn; at head of text: "Mr. de Jefferson Ecuyer Philadelphie"; endorsed by TJ as received 27 May 1794 and so recorded in SJL. Probably enclosed in a letter from Edmund Randolph to TJ of 19 May 1794, recorded in SJL as received 27 May 1794, which has not been found.

Joseph L'Epine was a merchant at 71 Stone Street in New York City (William Duncan, *The New-York Directory, and Register, for the Year 1794* [New York, 1794],

110). See also Joseph Dombey to TJ, 1 May 1793, and note.

In a letter to L'Epine of 19 May 1794, Edmund Randolph explained that he had opened L'Epine's letter above which was addressed to TJ as Secretary of State. He continued: "Being uncertain, how far anything could be done by me for your accommodation, I forwarded it to him by the mail. If it requires any service from me officially, you will be pleased to signify it to me. I have no document in the office, which speaks of Mr. Dombay" (Lb in DNA: RG 59, DL).

From William Short

Dear Sir   Aranjuez May 22. 1794

After writing my last letters of Nov. 7th. 11th. and 13th. I determined not to multiply my intrusions on your time and patience until I should have the satisfaction of once more hearing from you. The last private letter which I had then recieved from you was of the 11th. of July 1793. by Mr. Blake. The same silence continued until the 26th. ulto. when I recieved by the packet of the Spanish commissaries your private letter of Dec. 23. 1793. for which I beg you to accept my most grateful thanks. On the 3d. of April I had recieved the letter from the present Sec. of State, announcing to me his appointment and inclosing your last public, merely informing me of your resignation—and on the 5th. inst. Mr. Izard brought here from Lisbon your despatches of March 1793. for Mr. Carmichael and myself which have been detained there as you have been informed for want of a proper conveyance. In them were inclosed and recieved here at the same time your private letter of March 23. 1793. which inclosed also one from Mr. Mercer of the 2d. of the same month.

The curtain of public correspondence being now dropped I have at present to answer your two private letters of March 23. 1793 and Dec. 23d. of the same year. I will begin with the first though the last recieved.

The caution you are so good as to give me, my dear Sir, in your letter of March 23. I return you my most sincere thanks for, and shall not fail to guide myself by it in my future correspondence with that Gentleman. As in the instance there mentioned it was evidently his intention to sacrifice me to serve his favorite, or rather to make me the *plastron* for that favorite (in which I have no doubt he followed the intentions and wishes of his superior,) the least disagreeable mode to me he could have adopted was to give in the originals of my letters provided he gave in at the same time all my letters as well to himself as his favorite, and all the letters they wrote me—but this I apprehend he may have not done—and if he only selected such of our respective letters as suited his purpose, that may change the situation of things perhaps and enable him to present us all in a very different light from the true one. From the time I have had the irreparable misfortune of allowing myself to be employed by that department I have felt myself by instinct in an anxious and fatal situation. The cruel and unjust prolongation of my situation at Paris, and the still more cruel concealment of the Presidents intentions, as to the nomination to the place of Minister there is the true source of all my evils. Had I known what he knew, that he intended to keep me there only until his favorite could wind up his own business and that of the person whose Chargé des affaires he had been, and until he could find a proper moment for edging him into the place, I should not have remained to have been his *bouche trou*—and of course I should not have been thus put in the power of the Treasury to be delivered up during my absence and held out as a victim to answer the purpose of diverting public attention from that department and the President's favorite. Had I not concieved hopes that the execution of the important and confidential trust of the loans in Holland, would have probably procured me the less confidential post I desired of Minister at Paris, or had I not feared that my refusal to execute the one would have taken away my chance for the other I should not now have to regret having ever been employed in it. All the pain and anxiety I suffered in the discharge of that trust is indescribable—and I find it is not the intention of the Sec. of the treasury to lessen it—and if any thing could add to the cruelty and injustice of the conduct towards me, it is that it should be during my absence from my country, and on the business of my country in one with which all communication is cut off, so that I am for month after month and almost year after year without hearing of what is going on with respect to the business in which I am so nearly concerned.

Not only silence is observed towards me in this situation—but whenever it is interrupted it is to decieve me. On the 5th. of Feby. 1793. Mr. Hamilton wrote me a *private* letter the only one I ever recieved from him, in which mentioning the steps taken by Mr. Giles, and the resolves adopted by the house, he proceeded to say "An investigation intended to prejudice me is begun with respect to the circumstances attending the last payment on account of the French debt, which in its progress may draw your conduct into question. I think however you need be under no anxiety for the result. Your hesitations at a certain stage were so natural and your reasons so weighty for them that they will give little handle against you—besides the coincidence in opinion here about the expediency of a suspension of payment." On the 15th. of March 1793 in a public letter he wrote me, after treating of the business of the loans, he concluded by saying "the enclosed extracts from the minutes of the House of Representatives will inform you of the result of the affair about which I wrote to you not long since by way of England"—viz. in his letter abovementioned of the 5th. of Feby. He says not a word to me of his long report made on that subject to the House of Representatives, and certainly his letters abovementioned were calculated to leave me in the idea that if I were to be brought into the question it would be only incidentally. In honor and conscience he should have sent me his report and for greater security by different conveyances[1]—but I never even heard that he had made one notwithstanding 162. vessels came to Cadiz in the course of the last year—and should not have known it now if I had not by accident fallen on it among the gazettes which you sent me and which as you were informed were detained with your letters at Lisbon—they arrived here only on the 5th. inst. by Mr. Izard—so that a report made in March 1793. in which I am brought on the carpet and presented not[2] in a true light gets to my hands accidentally only in May 1794. I say represented not in a true light because as to the last payment to France, I am represented as the principal, and Mr. Morris as my agent employed only for a particular object by me whereas on my leaving Paris Mr. Morris became the principal and I his agent, as was shewn and mentioned in my letters to the Sec. of the Treasury. My letters to you will have shewn this also to have been the case from the nature of the thing. The rule of depreciation was to be settled before other payments could be made. On Mr. Morris's becoming Minister at Paris, he was of course and under the original instructions of the President to settle that depreciation. This was understood and agreed on between him and me when I left Paris for the Hague—as soon as it was done he was to communicate his orders to me that I might give them to the bankers, as they had formerly been directed to pay on my order. I was therefore only the chanel of M. Morris's orders—and a passive agent—until he settled the depreciation I could do nothing. On account of the particular circumstances when I recieved his orders, I did not fulfill them immediately because I was afraid the money would be lost for America. I proposed therefore that such a reciept should be given by the French bankers as I thought would secure the U.S. from loss—they took time to consider of it—and this occasioned a delay from the 17th. of August until the 4th. of Septr.—and that is all the delay that can be attributed to me. A further proof that I considered Mr. Morris as the principal in this business is that when I directed the payment on the 4th. of Sep. it was in obedience only to his opinion, and against my own—although the event has shewn that my opinion was erroneous. When therefore Mr. Hamilton stated me as the principal and Mr. Morris only as my agent, he stated what he knew was wrong. And he himself knew so well from the President's original instructions, Mr. Morris would be considered as having the direction of arranging the payments that he considered it necessary to write to me some time after my leaving Paris to inform me that the President had determined that they were to remain still under my control. Having then thought I suppose that it would be proper after sending his favorite to Paris, to take out of his hands this ticklish kind of business originally destined to the Minister of the U.S. at Paris—this letter was received by me after the King's suspension—not to hurt Mr. Morris's feelings I did not communicate it to him—but I wrote to the Sec. of the treasury and let him see in what light I considered this new apparent mark of preference.[3] As my letters to you will have explained these subjects in answer to yours of Jan. 3. 1793. I hope you will have put them in their true light—otherwise from the time of Mr. Hamilton's long report I should have appeared in a light which is not just and in which it was very ungenerous for him to have placed me, and which he would not have attempted if I had been on the spot instead of being absent in my country's service.

It was equally wrong for him when he brought me on the carpet to content himself with a general and vague declaration that he was convinced of the goodness of the motives which directed me. He should have gone further and stated clearly the things as they were, and not have left these motives to be looked for as scattered through my voluminous correspondence with him, which no member of the Senate I fear will have time or patience to read and compare throughout.

As to the question of political principles in general or as they affect France in particular I am willing that mine should be known to all the world—and that they should be compared and judged of with these of the favorite with whom it seems the Sec. of the treasury desired to contrast them to my disadvantage. I shall appeal to a different tribunal however than that of a person who has allowed himself to be deaf and blind to the words and deeds of the favorite, whilst he is all eyes and all ears as to me, where my enemies have tried to injure me for their own purposes. But after all, political principles had nothing to do with the short obstacle to the payment which proceeded from me—nor do I suppose they had any thing to do with Mr. Morris's opinion on the subject of the payment—the true state of the question is whether a person authorized to make a payment to A. has a right to make it to B. As things have turned out I am sorry to have interfered so as to have delayed this payment at all—but when I did interfere in proposing the form of the reciept to be given, the probability was that the Duke of Brunswic would arrive at Paris—and this was not only believed in Holland but at Paris also, and by those who composed the executive Council itself—now I could ask how under that idea I could have avoided taking on me the measure I did—and as M. Morris believed also in this arrival I might ask how he could during that belief consider the payment a proper one. For let us suppose either of the cases which might have existed on the arrival of the Duke of Brunswick—viz. the executive Council about to disperse at the moment of six millions of livres coming to their hands—

or the executive Council or some of them in intelligence with the Duke of Brunswick (which the national judgment has since decided to have been the case and which was then believed by many and suspected by more) I would ask how any agent of the U.S. could have answered the allowing this sum to have disappeared or to have been exposed to have disappeared as it would then have been. I shall ever be ready to meet any of my enemies on this ground. In fact what ought to have been done can admit of no question—and further the Sec. of the treasury of his own accord wrote to me to suspend all farther payments to France immediately on hearing of the 10th. of Aug. and followed this order a few days after by a confirmation of it from the President. I hope in producing our correspondence his candor will have induced him to have produced those letters also.

Had I recieved your private letter of March 23. 1793.—and the papers containing the report of the Sec. of the treasury on this business, in time to have sent an answer before the late meeting of Congress I would have gone into a more full developement and desired you to have laid it before them if any doubts existed—as I suppose the subject will have been again renewed during the session. At this distance I know not what step to take. I resolve therefore to wait until I shall learn what has been done during this session. I indulge myself in the hope that I shall soon learn the result from you—and not be as unfortunate as during the last year, viz. recieve the letters and papers 14. months after their date. It is impossible to have been more unfortunate than I have been—a malignant star seems to have presided over all the communications intended to have been made to me. The loss of the first papers respecting my mission to Spain, will have a most unhappy influence on all the rest of my life—and the detention of that at Lisbon with the papers containing Mr. Hamilton's report seems to have been arranged expressly by fortune for my mortification. If instead of the mistimed misarranged and unfortunate mission in Spain I had returned to America in the fall of 1792 (either by congé for which I asked, and to which no answer of any kind was given, or by any other means) I should have been on the spot to have met Mr. Hamilton and his report and to have placed what had been done in its true light. But such fortune is not for me—from the year 90. I have been condemned to an unsettled, uncertain and vagrant life, merely for the convenience of others—employed in a way which took away for two years past at least all chance of rendering service to the publick, and left me out of the way of defending or protecting myself against the active attacks or passive insinuations of my enemies. But I will put an end to this letter here, because I find myself plunged into that melancholy chapter which is inexhaustible in itself—and which at present can only serve to *ennui* others without at all saving Dear Sir, your unalterable friend & servant   W SHORT

P.S. I inclose a letter for M. Mercer not knowing his particular address which I ask the favor of you to give him being in answer to that you inclosed me from him.

A few days after the above was written an account came here that you had arrived in England, and this was followed by a letter from M. Pinckney informing me he had heard you had arrived in Paris—although this is not fully contradicted yet a letter from Cadiz gives me such reason to believe you are still in America that I determine to send my letter thither after having considerably detained it. The account was that you were gone to replace M. Morris, having been asked for by the committee of public safety.⁴ It would be much to be desired that you should be there. You may now have some idea why it was thought necessary to make the President believe that I had displeased the French government and would be disagreeable there. To the Prest. those who have exercised the Government successively will appear the same, but there is nothing more erroneous—those who had displeased the first executive Council would not be disagreeable to the present committee of public safety but on the contrary.

RC (DLC); at foot of first page: "Mr. Jefferson &c &c &c"; only the most important emendations are noted below; endorsed by TJ as received 17 Sep. 1794 and so recorded in SJL. PrC (PHi). Enclosure not found.

For the LAST PUBLIC letter from TJ to Short, see TJ to Certain Diplomats of the United States, 3 Jan. 1794, and note. THAT GENTLEMAN: Alexander Hamilton. HIS FAVORITE: Gouverneur Morris. HIS SUPERIOR: George Washington. PERSON WHOSE CHARGÉ DES AFFAIRES HE HAD BEEN: Robert Morris. RESOLVES ADOPTED BY THE HOUSE: the 23 Jan. 1793 resolves introduced by William Branch Giles that called upon Hamilton to provide the House of Representatives with a comprehensive account of his stewardship as Secretary of the Treasury (see Editorial Note on Jefferson and the Giles resolutions, at 27 Feb. 1793). HIS LONG REPORT: Hamilton's 13 Feb. 1793 report to the House of Representatives on foreign loans, which Short interpreted as an indictment of him for delaying a payment on the American debt to France after the fall of the Bourbon monarchy in August 1792 (Syrett, *Hamilton*, XIV, 17-26). See also TJ to Short, 3 Jan. 1793, and note.

¹ Preceding seven words interlined.
² Preceding three words interlined in place of "in a false light."
³ Word interlined in place of "confidence."
⁴ Short here canceled "God."

From James Madison

DEAR SIR   Philada. May 25. 1794.

Your favor of the 15th. Inst: came to hand yesterday. I will procure you the "definition of parties," and one or two other things from the press which merit a place in your archives. Osnabrigs can be had here. Negro cotton I am told can also be had; but of this I am not sure. I learn nothing yet of Blake. The inclosed paper will give you the correspondence of E.R. and Hammond on an occurrence particularly interresting. You will be as able to judge as we are of the calculations to be founded on it. The embargo expires today. A proposition some days ago for continuing it was negatived by a vast majority; all parties in the main concurring. The Republican was assured that the Embargo if continued would be considered by France as hostility: The other had probably an opposite motive. It now appears that through out the Continent the people were anxious for its continuance, and it is probable that its expiration will save the W. Inds. from famine, without affording any sensible aid to France. A motion was put on the table yesterday for re-enacting it. Measures of this sort are not the fashion. To supplicate for peace, and under the uncertainty of success, to prepare for war by taxes and troops is the policy which now triumphs under the patronage of the Executive. Every attack on G.B. thro' her commerce is at once discomfited; and all the taxes, that is to say excises, stamps, &c. are carried by decided majorities. The plan for a large army has failed several times in the H. of Reps. It is now to be sent from the Senate, and being recomended by the Message of the P. accompanying the intelligence from the Miami, will probably succeed. The influence of the Ex. on events, the use made of them, and the public confidence in the P. are an overmatch for all the efforts Republicanism can make. The party of that sentiment in the Senate is compleatly wrecked; and in the H. of Reps. in a much worse condition than at an earlier period of the Session.

RC (DLC: Madison Papers); unsigned; endorsed by TJ as received 10 June 1794 and so recorded in SJL.

The CORRESPONDENCE between Secretary of State Edmund Randolph and British minister George HAMMOND of 20-22 May 1794, promptly submitted to Congress by the President, concerned Lord Dorchester's provocative speech of 10 Feb. 1794 predicting to a delegation of the Western Indians that Great Britain would be at war with the United States within a year and would then enlist the assistance of Indian warriors, as well as a report received by Washington that Lieutenant Governor John Graves Simcoe and three companies of British regulars were on their way to build a fort at "the foot of the rapids of the Miami." In responding to these grievances with his own litany of complaints about American infringements on British forts on the frontier and infractions of neutrality on the coast, Hammond admitted that he could neither confirm nor deny the report, but he promised to seek clarification from British authorities in Canada and London (*Phila-delphia Gazette*, 26 Mch., 24 May 1794; ASP, *Foreign Relations*, I, 461-3; ASP, *Indian Affairs*, I, 477-82). The 24 May 1794 MO-TION for RE-ENACTING the embargo was withdrawn the same day by its author, Alexander Gillon of South Carolina, and easily defeated when he made the proposal again five days later (*Annals*, IV, 722, 731-4).

From James Monroe

DEAR SIR   Phila. May 26.[1] 1794.

The session begins to draw to a close. The 3d. of June is agreed on by both houses as the day on which it shall end, and I believe the agreement will be executed. The inclosed paper will shew you the state of things with Engld. This incursion into our country has no pretext to be calld or considered otherwise than an actual invasion, and as such presume it will be treated by the President whose powers are competent by the existing law to its repulsion. The Govr. of Pensyla. has a small force within 16. miles of Presque Isle, and intends taking possession of the latter post. Within a few days past however it has been notified to him by some Indians that it will be opposed, and in consequence thereof he has ordered out 1000 of the western militia to secure the lodgment. I suspect however these movements were dictated in Novr. last and should not be considered as an indication of the temper of the Englh. Ct. at present. They may even be disavowed if a change in circumstances requires it. The incident has been seized you will observe as a ground for pressing an increase of the military forces—in consequence of which a proposition was immediately introduced into the Senate for authorizing the President to raise 10,000 additional troops under provisions more popular than those rejected in the Reps. and of course more likely to succeed even there. In the Senate it will pass immediately, for the republican party is intirely broken in that branch. Thus it results that thro the influence of the Executive aided by the personal weight of the President, the republican party notwithstanding its systematic and laborious efforts has been able to accomplish nothing which might vindicate the honor or advance the prosperity of the country. I believe I intimated to you in my last that the President had offered to Mr. Livingston after the refusal of Mr. Madison[2] the legation to France in the place of Gr. Morris who would be recalled, that Colo. Burr had been a competitor. Since that time Livingston has declined and Burr has continued, under auspices very favorable to his success, sole candidate. Present appearances authorize the belief he will be appointed. Of course he goes as a republican, and I am inclined to think the President supposes he lays that party under obligations to him for the nomination, for I am persuaded in addition to other considerations he really surmounts some objections of a personal nature in making it. But when it is known that the Jersey members, Judge Patterson &ca, have promoted his interest our confidence in the steadiness of his political tenets will not be increased. We shall be with you as soon as possible after the adjournment. Sincerely I am yr. friend & servt   JAS. MONROE

As Mr. M. gives you the paper containing the correspondence referred to, and the others contain nothing I[3] send none.

RC (DLC); endorsed by TJ as received 10 June 1794 and so recorded in SJL.

INCURSION INTO OUR COUNTRY: see note to preceding document. For the controversy stemming from British and Indian opposition to the efforts of the Governor of Pennsylvania, Thomas Mifflin, to carry out an act of his state legislature providing for the establishment of a town at or near PRESQUE ISLE, see ASP, *Indian Affairs*, I, 503-7. The bill AUTHORIZING THE PRESIDENT TO RAISE 10,000 ADDITIONAL TROOPS, passed by the Senate on 29 May 1794, was defeated in the House the following day (JS, II, 92, 94; JHR, II, 187-8).

[1] Altered from "27."
[2] Preceding six words interlined.
[3] MS: "and."

From James Monroe

DEAR SIR   Phila. May 27. 1794.

Early yesterday morning and immediately after my last was written I was called on by Mr. R. to answer the question "whether I would accept the legation to France?" The proposition as you will readily conceive surprised me, for I really thought I was among the last men to whom it would be made, and so observed. He said the President was resolved to send a republican character to that nation; that Mr. Madison and Chr. Livingston had refused, that he would not appoint Colo. Burr, lest it should seem as if he sought persons from that state only, and probably it would not have been offered to L. but on account of his having been in the department of foreign affairs, and under these circumstances and considerations he was desired by the President to call on me and asartain whether I would act. As I had espoused B. I told Mr. R. I could not even think on the subject whilst there was a prospect of his success. He assured me he was out of the question, and if I declined, it would probably be offered to Govr. Paca of Maryld. or some person not yet thought of. That he would satisfy the friends of Colo. B. on this head. Before I would consult my friends I requested that this be done— and in consequence the above assurance was given some of them, and I presume they were satisfied. This point of delicacy being removed, I then desired Mr. Madison in conference with a few of our friends to determine what answer should be given to the proposition. The result was that I should accept upon the necessity of cultivating France, and the incertainty of the person upon whom it might otherwise fall. An answer was accordingly given last evening to the Presidt. to that effect, and the nomination sent in to day. I have not attended nor shall I till after that body shall be pleased to decide upon it. If approved it is wished that I embark immediately for France. I am however extremely anxious to visit albemarle before I sit out taking Mr. Jones in my way. But whether I shall be able to visit either of you is incertain, and will depend in a great measure upon the practicability of getting a vessel about to sail, in a term short of the time, it will take me to perform the journey. Upon this head however I can say nothing untill the nomination is decided on, nor can I say how the decision will be, for my services in the Senate have given me but little claim to the personal regards of the reigning party there. I suspect the nomination created as great a surprize in that house as the proposition to me did, yesterday morning. As yet I have not seen the President. I shall write you more fully in my next. With great respect & esteem I am yr. affectionate friend & servant

JAS. MONROE

Govr. Mifflins movment has been suspended by the President.

RC (DLC); endorsed by TJ as received 2 June 1794 and so recorded in SJL.

MR. R.: Edmund Randolph. For a discus-

sion of the President's nomination of Monroe as minister plenipotentiary to France, which the Senate promptly confirmed on 28 May 1794, see Ammon, *Monroe*, 112–14.

To John Garland Jefferson

DEAR SIR   Monticello May 28. 1794.

I recieved yesterday your favor of the 11th. inst. and imagine that soon after it's date you received mine of Apr. 26. on the subject of your lands. I am happy to learn that it is the opinion of a person learned in the laws of that state, that the lands may be recovered. As to the kind of process to be instituted, the lawyers of the state must be the best judges. Were I in your place, I would certainly join to Mr. Henderson the ablest lawyer of the same state practising where the suit must be brought. I return you the two letters.—I shall at all times be glad to hear from you, and particularly to learn that you meet with the success you merit: and I shall certainly with pleasure let you hear from me at times. I am however grown so lazy in writing that it is really an effort for me now to sit down to write a letter. My objects without doors are become so multiplied, and so interesting, that I scarcely read or write a sentence in a week: for even when in the house my meditations are on the things without. I have almost entirely withdrawn myself from all epistolary correspondence, and particularly as to political matters in which I am endeavoring to contract all the rust I can, by never reading a newspaper. I am however & shall be at all times Dear Sir Your affectionate friend & relation   TH: JEFFERSON

PrC (MHi); at foot of text: "Mr. J. Garland Jefferson"; endorsed in ink by TJ. Enclosures not found.

J. G. Jefferson's missing FAVOR OF THE 11TH. INST. was recorded in SJL as received from Amelia on 21 May 1794.

To Joseph L'Epine

SIR   Monticello May 28. 1794.

I have duly recieved your favor of the 19th. inst. and sincerely lament the loss of Mr. Dombay, whom, according to a letter I had received from him, I had expected for some time. He did not in that letter mention that he should address any packages to me, and therefore I imagine that those you mention as being so addressed, contain his own baggage, papers, and effects, on which he has placed such an address to protect them from capture, and I am happy to learn from you that it has had that effect. After declaring that I have no reason to believe myself interested in them, and, as far as depends on me, authorising any person legally empowered to act for Mr. Dombey, to open the packages, I take for granted the Consul of France at New York, who is authorised by the Consular convention for this purpose, will proceed to open and dispose of the packages, according to what he shall find to be their destination, from the nature of the objects they contain, and the written evidence which probably accompanies them. For this he has my warrant, as far as their address to me may be supposed to render that material. I have the honor to be Sir Your most obedt. humble servt   TH: JEFFERSON

PrC (DLC); at foot of text: "M. L'Epine." Enclosed in TJ to Edmund Randolph, 28 May 1794.

YOUR FAVOR OF THE 19TH: L'Epine to TJ, 16 May 1794. A LETTER I HAD RECEIVED: Joseph Dombey to TJ, 1 May 1793.

To Edmund Randolph

Th: Jefferson to
the Secretary of State Monticello May 28.[1] 1794.

I thank you for forwarding Mr. L'Epine's letter. Dombey was a man of sense and science, and had resided some years in Spanish America, with which he had made himself much acquainted. Should we have a war with Spain, he would have been a most valuable acquisition to us. I now think it probable that among his papers will be found a good deal of information as to that country, and particularly the best maps of it, notes of it's force, dispositions, resources &c. on which I found him well informed. If you can obtain these under the instrumentality of their being addressed to me, you are perfectly free to do so: for which purpose I inclose you my answer to L'Epine open.—Doubting whether you would enter into our feelings on the unpropitious seasons and prospects for our farms, and having nothing else worth notice to communicate, I shall only add assurances of my friendly respects, and attachment.

Th: Jefferson

RC (DNA: RG 59, MLR); addressed: "Edmund Randolph Secretary of State Philadelphia"; endorsed by George Taylor, Jr. PrC (DLC). Enclosure: TJ to Joseph L'Epine, 28 May 1794.

[1] Altered from "29."

From Tench Coxe

Dear Sir Philadelphia May 31st 1794

I had learned from Mr. Maddison and Mr. Monroe the delay of all letters to you before I had the honor to receive your acknowledgment of those I have written to you at Montecello.

Your agricultural pursuits must be a delightful recreation after the fatigue, vexations, and nonsense[1] of city life and public station. The subject is very captivating in the theory, and it is so peculiarly interesting to this country that I have it before me as a permanent topic of enquiry and consideration. To increase the productiveness of the United States, and to devise advantageous employment and consumption for the spontaneous gifts of Nature and the fruits of cultivation, are to give new vigor and the best direction to our most valuable energies and capacities. I am at present occupied with the strongest impressions in regard to the infinite importance of water in these views. Irrigation and water mills (for every purpose) appear to me to be of an intrinsic value of which to speak in figures not 10 ℔ cent is enjoyed, or even perceived. The latter is not the object of the farmer, but irrigation is more or less within the power of every land holder. I beg leave to recommend it to your examination, trial and consideration as superior in its facilities, in its certainties, and in its net advantages to the important, catalogue of manures. It is perfectly compatible with these, and indeed in detailing its good Effects, the increase of the precious compost of the Barnyard could not fail to occur.

I feel great comfort, Sir, in expressing to you an opinion that the contest between the great body of mankind, and the combined tenants of hereditary power, has taken a certain cast in favor of the former. The nation which must long be the first in the civilized world,[2] has so far frustrated and wounded the mighty combination against them as to change the hopes of foreign conquest into apprehensions for their own internal safety. The Master of the great military politician, who threatened with Destruction the Mass of the Inhabitants of Paris, and prescribed to all France the unqualified acceptance, through their late King, of a constitution to be virtually formed in the German diet, has declared that the scheme is impracticable. Whether collateral policy, real despair[3] or purchase has produced this change, or all three conjoined, is not material to France. Her revolution is as fixed, as her Territory.

Some extraordinary[4] discoveries are said to have been recently made in Europe. A letter[5] of respectability contains intimations, that measures conducing towards the Execution of the late King of France have been traced to Austrian influence. The policy is suggested to have been, to place subjugated france under the direction of the Queens party, during the long minority of her Son. It is added that after the Death of the King similar measures were instantly adopted by Prussia to procure the Execution of the Queen in order to frustrate the views of Austria. This comes, it is said, from a quarter not friendly to the French, and Dantons party is implicated in their suspicions, in the Prussian part of the Business. If true, it will steep the regal character in the blackest infamy.

It is agreed here by those[6] who have least approved the french Revolution in the later stages of it, that the Prussian defection has taken place, and that if that Court does not revert to its coalition with Austria and Britain the game is up. But should Prussia engage anew, nothing in my opinion can ever restore confidence among the combined Powers. The impression upon the neutral Nations cannot fail to be the most decided in favor of maintaining an united Neutrality. The confidence given to the[7] Whig interest of France, particularly the[8] great civil leaders, and the victorious military people of every description must be prodigious. The depression of the royalists and insurgents will be proportionate. The alarm to the unfriendly countries within the reach of the French Arms by Land and Sea, and to the Dutch, British, and Italian money lenders, must be as great as their dangers are real. Kings, Nobles and Priests appearing unsuccessful, will quickly be considered as impotent. The energies and success of the french People will enhance the Ideas of their own importance, and quicken the sense of their own wrongs among the deprived people of other nations. A greater and more expensive force will be required at home. The french will be thus relieved. Reasonably their Enemies should desire Peace, and they should consent to restore it upon proper terms. Their passions are at the height of human feeling against the British Government. Many of their people will desire to expel the privileged orders from the British System. The most moderate will probably insist on the restoration of every acquisition by the combined Powers—on a certain degree of protection to the Whig interest of the neighbouring countries, who have acted in their favor—and upon a settlement of the rights of neutral Nations, which will most painfully wound the British Spirit and, in their Judgment, trench upon their most important interests. Whether Peace will take place therefore, I have not a settled opinion. The french here are thoroughly well pleased, I believe, with the appointment of Mr. Monroe. Certainly he will, as far as his duty requires and permits, cherish[9] their representative government, and he will take no ungenerous[10] or dishonest advantages of them.

The latest accounts from London (of the fortnight preceding the 5th. of April) inform that their most cautious monied men are purchasing into the American funds and banks. Four or five Quaker Bankers and Merchants are among the number, and some of them persons generally supposed to be in habits of confidence with Mr. Pitt. Considering these proofs of public opinion, and other known facts indicative of it Mr. Hammonds last communication to our Government, proves him to be unfit for the management of their critical affairs with this Country. Lord Dorchester and Colonel Simcoes conduct and present situation must be very difficult of explanation to the people of reflexion in England. It will, however, serve us in our pending Negociation with Great Britain, that she is so fully understood from her own Conduct. It appears probable that things will stand very favorably, about the time of Mr. Jay's arrival. I am, with perfect respect, dear Sir, Your most obedient & humble Servant, TENCH COXE

June 4th. Since writing the above it appears that the King of Prussia has published his manifesto, that the attack upon Corsica is abandoned, and that Danton is said to be implicated with Hebert and his Associates. The articles relative Russia, Sweden, and the port merit attention. We suppose Doctor Priestly is arrived at N. York. Congress do not expect to rise to Morrow.

RC (DLC); in a clerk's hand, with several revisions, signature, and postscript by Coxe; endorsed by TJ as received 18 June 1794 and so recorded in SJL. Dft (PHi: Coxe Papers); lacks postscript; with numerous revisions, only the most important legible emendations being noted below.

MASTER OF THE GREAT MILITARY POLITICIAN: a reference to King Frederick William II of Prussia and the Duke of Brunswick. MR. HAMMONDS LAST COMMUNICATION: see James Madison to TJ, 25 May 1794, and note.

[1] Word interlined in Dft in place of "follies."
[2] In Dft Coxe first wrote "must be the first in [. . .] the two civilized quarters of

the globe" and then altered it to read as above.
[3] In Dft Coxe first wrote the sentence to this point "Whether policy, conviction."
[4] Altered in Dft from "Some very extraordinary and shocking."
[5] Altered in Dft from "Private letters of great."
[6] In Dft Coxe here canceled "of all Convictions."
[7] In Dft Coxe here interlined and canceled "triumphant."
[8] Remainder of sentence altered in Dft from "⟨bold⟩ great civil and military leaders must be very great."
[9] Altered in Dft from "duty permits, countenance."
[10] Word interlined in Dft in place of "little."

From James Madison

DEAR SIR   Philada. June 1. 1794.

The Stamp act was poisoned by the ingredient of the tax on transfers. The centinels of Stock uniting with the adversaries of the general plan formed a large majority. The carriage tax which only struck at the Constitution has passed the H. of Reps. and will be a delicious morsel to the Senate. The attempt of this Branch to give the P. power to raise an army of 10,000. if he should please, was strangled more easily in the H. of R. than I had expected. This is the 3d. or 4th. effort made in the course of the Session to get a powerful military establishment, under the pretext of public danger and under the auspices of the P.'s popularity. The bill for punishing certain crimes &c. including that of selling prizes has been unexpectedly called up at the last moment of the Session. It is pretended that our Citizens will arm under French Colors if not restrained. You will be at no loss for the real motive, especially as explained by the circumstances of the present crisis. The bill for complying with Fauchet's application for a million of dollars, passed the H. of R. by a large majority. The Senate will certainly reject it. Col. M. is busy in preparing for his embarkation. He is puzzled as to the mode of getting to France. He leans towards an American vessel which is to sail from Baltimore for Amsterdam. A direct passage to F. is scarcely to be had, and is incumbered with the risk of being captured and carried into England. It is not certain that Negro Cotton can be had here. German linens of all sorts can. Nothing of Blake. Tomorrow is the day of adjournment as fixt by the vote of the two Houses; but it will probably not take place till the last of the week. We have had 8 or 10 days of wet weather from the N.E., which seems at length to be breaking up. Yrs. Affy.   JAS. MADISON JR

RC (DLC: Madison Papers); endorsed by TJ as received 10 June 1794 and so recorded in SJL.

The STAMP ACT failed in the House of Representatives on 27 May 1794. The bill to RAISE AN ARMY of 10,000 was STRANGLED three days later (*Annals*, IV, 725-6, 735-9). For the background to the BILL FOR PUNISHING CERTAIN CRIMES, the so-called Neutrality Act of June 1794, see note to Memorial from Edmond Charles Genet, 27 May 1793. A section of this bill that banned SELLING PRIZES, a privilege denied by treaty to the enemies of France but still being exercised by that country, was deleted by the House on 2 June 1794 (*Annals*, IV, 747-57). Madison correctly predicted that the Senate would reject the APPLICATION by French minister Jean Antoine Joseph Fauchet FOR A MILLION OF DOLLARS in advance payment on the American debt to France (same, 129-30; Madison, *Papers*, XV, 336-7). COL. M.: James Monroe.

From John Taylor

DEAR SIR   Caroline June 1st. 1794

Your letter dated one month past, was delivered to me, as I was about to leave philadelphia, and this circumstance defered my answer hitherto.

It was my purpose previously to have seen Mr: Martin, who is the inventor of the drilling machine, the simplicity of which is its best recommendation; but a succession of heavy rains have swept off our mills and bridges, and left a gulf between Mr: Martin and myself, as impassable to flesh and blood, as that which incarcerated poor Dives, was to the spiritual benevolence of father Abraham.

I will with pleasure procure one for you, and forward it to Richmond, if you will let me know with whom it is to be lodged. This is the best mode of conveyance, and then also I can inform you of the price. I will endeavour to provide it in time for turnip sowing, the first object to which it can now be applied. Turnips are the panacea of sheep, and I understand it to be your special[1] intention to grow this kind of stock.

Permit me to suggest a doubt concerning the European system of a rotation of crops, as applicable to us. Their circle consists of six or Seven years at most, during which a plentiful dose of manure is invariably bestowed upon the land. If the improvement of their land, is chiefly owing to this article of the system, it is well worth considering, how far that system will suit this country.

Our labour is by no means commensurate to our land—we want the offal of cities—marl and lime are seldom used—chalk never—meadows are scarce—and pastures incompetent.

If a succedaneum for these deficiencies can be found, enabling us also to turn our surplus of land into an advantage, it would fit our case. And there must be some mortal malady in a system, which impoverishes land by croping, tho' land abounds and labour is scarce.

We have not the needful manure for the English system, nor have we the means of procuring it. If its basis was within our reach, we have not labour to manufacture and apply it in sufficient quantities.

To strike out a new system, or to abdicate nine tenths of our land, seems therefore an unavoidable alternative.

Inclosing, upon a principle directly opposite to the European reason, will I think fit our situation. Instead of sinking much labour in small inclosures for the purpose of pasturage, one, including all the arable land of a farm, would intirely exclude the lacerations of the hoof and teeth.

The atmosphere, that inexhaustible store of manure requires no labour to put on—an abundance of land enables us to avail ourselves of its fertilizing quality—and the immense portion of labour devoted by the English to manuring, might be chiefly converted by us to the extension of tillage.

Can any other system overspread with fertility our extensive fields?

The most judicious course of crops, without manure, and without rest, will presently destroy land. Pasturing is no rest.

From the trials I have made, land will bear two crops in four years, and no more. Even then, to improve, it must be sacredly inclosed. This can be effected, by having one half of the same inclosure, annually in culture.

Our extensive commons, and plenty of wet low lands for small grazing inclosures, are extreamly favourable to such a system. It is not however meant as the substitute, but as the auxiliary, of manure.

I seldom begin with wheat, unless by sowing it on a single furrow, above a clover stratum; and this can hardly be called a begining with wheat, as clover is admited to be a fallow crop. It would incommode my system of two crops in four years, whereas by making the wheat succeed a fallow crop, the land will rest two years and an half.

Buck wheat appears in my soil and climate, to be a great impoverisher. In several trials I have made of this plant, as well as of oats and rye, ploughed in green as a dressing, the improvement has been too trivial to reimburse the expense.

In a rival-ship upon a very small scale between clover and sainfoin, the former evidently has the preference. I shall continue and extend it. Wherever clover can be prevailed on to exist, it will improve the soil; but it will not live on poor land. I have reason for apprehending a similar disapointment, in this climate, from sainfoin. In the case of clover, I sustained so considerable a loss in seed, that my experiments of other grasses on poor land, are now very cautiously made.

In the case of grasses, even in England, the comparasons between drilling and broadcast, seem to preponderate in favour of the latter, owing to the expence of labour. A doubt there, removes all doubt here, and has decided me on the side of broadcast, both as to grasses and grains, on account of the dearness of our labour and the plenty of land. Drilling is invariably to be prefered in a garden.

Carrots and turnips, must be hoed if sown broadcast, therefore they had best be drilled, because that operation is performed more easily and cheaply by the horse than by the hand. A drill plough is useful for these crops and for peas.

I have never tried the succory. If you could furnish me with a spoonful of the seed, and a memorandum of its mode of culture, I will acknowledge the favour, by an assiduous attention to its effects. Pray is not this what Young calls Chickory?

I purpose to write to England for some Syberian melilot seed, highly recommended by Young.

Nor do I know why we have not tried in this country the English horse bean—the Vetches—and the tare—the two latter as dressings for wheat.

The Guinea grass, extravagantly commemorated, as an inhabitant of a botanical garden belonging to the late King of France, has not that I can learn, obtained a more honorable and useful station.

The avidity with which I lay hold of your drop of consolation, is conclusive evidence of good fortune, in my late escape, and of the hard usage of poor Dives, should he be still in durance.

Inclosed you will receive the bank pamphlet, and a shorter mischief which grew out of idleness.

Will it not be wiser at my age, to make the most of life, than to trifle longer with it? Some common good, and much individual quiet, is produced by my agrarian occupations; whereas my political opinions are seldom tried, and if they were tried, my expectations from them, would be regulated by a recollection of many errors commited in matters, which I much better understood. These opinions are either antediluvian, or barred by the act of limitations. Therefore for the sake of my own happiness I design rapidly to forget the things which I have seen heard or suspected within the last two years. Being regenerated to my former self,

I may possibly recover charity enough to coincide in your favourable opinion of the two houses of Congress. At present, as to that of which I am a member, the utmost stretch of my charity, is to allow that 15 are sound, 7 of one side, and 8 of the other. Be happy! With the utmost respect & esteem, I am Sir Yr: mo: obt: Sert.   JOHN TAYLOR

RC (DLC); endorsed by TJ as received 24 June 1794 and so recorded in SJL. Enclosures: (1) [John Taylor of Caroline], *An Enquiry into the Principles and Tendency of certain Public Measures* (Philadelphia, 1794). See Sowerby, No. 3175, and note to James Madison to TJ, 11 Aug. 1793. (2) [John Taylor of Caroline], *A Definition of Parties; or, The Political Effects of the Paper System Considered* (Philadelphia, 1794).

TJ used the seed DRILLING MACHINE constructed by Taylor's neighbor Thomas C. Martin until at least 1813. He regarded an improved version as "the most compleat machine in the world for sowing a single

row" (TJ to Taylor, 6 Apr. 1798; TJ to Isaac McPherson, 18 Sep. 1813; MB, 21 Dec. 1797). For favorable allusions by the English agriculturist Arthur YOUNG to chicory and Siberian melilot, see his *Travels, during The Years 1787, 1788, and 1789. Undertaken more particularly with a View of ascertaining the Cultivation, Wealth, Resources, and National Prosperity, of the Kingdom of France* (Bury Saint Edmunds, 1792), 109, 113. See Sowerby, No. 744. MY LATE ESCAPE: Taylor had resigned from the United States Senate on 11 May 1794 (*Biog. Dir. Cong.*).

[1] Word interlined.

From James Monroe

DEAR SIR   Phila. June 6. 1794.

Since my appointment I have been extremely occupied in a variety of respects. I had likewise flattered myself with the hope I should see you before my departure till within a day or two past—but of this I now begin to despair. I shall sail from Bal: for which place I sit out in 4. days hence. Tis possible the vessel may not be ready altho I am advised she is. I feel extremely anxious upon the subject of a cypher. Our former one is in a small writing desk at my house, can you get and send it after me in case I do not see you before I sail?

Danton has been executed, the charge the plunder of publick money—the King of Prussia withdrawn—and the British driven from Corsica. I will write by the several succeeding posts whilst I stay. I am yr. affectionate friend & servt   JAS. MONROE

RC (DLC); addressed: "Thomas [. . .]"; franked and postmarked; endorsed by TJ as received 18 June 1794 and so recorded in SJL.

From Thomas Pinckney

MY DEAR SIR   London 6 June 1794

Report says you are in France, if that report is founded, the interests of Madame Lafayette, on whose account your fellow citizens here are under the utmost anxiety, will of course be supported by your influence and exertions in manifesting the gratitude of our Country for the services we have received from her unfortunate Husband. I am happy to think that we may the more freely indulge this sentiment since the Virtues have been made the order of the day of the Republic; it is likewise pleasing to reflect that our gratitude on this occasion rests on grounds totally unconnected with the present politics of France.

I have only to add on this occasion my earnest wishes and those of such of my countrymen here as I have conversed with that this virtuous effusion may have on so interesting an occasion its most powerful influence and be attended with its merited success. I remain with sincere respect My dear Sir Your faithful & obedient Servant

THOMAS PINCKNEY

PrC (ScHi: Pinckney Family Papers); at foot of text: "Mr. Jefferson." Probably not received by TJ, being neither recorded in SJL nor acknowledged by him.

VIRTUES . . . THE ORDER OF THE DAY: a reference to the National Convention's 7 May 1794 decree on the Supreme Being, which among other things provided for annual festivals in honor of a long catalogue of virtues (Stewart, *French Revolution*, 526-7).

To James Brown

DEAR SIR   Eppington June 8. 1794.

Having seen in your hands the state of my account with Donald & Burton, I take the liberty of asking you to transmit me a copy of it by the Charlottesville post immediately as I wish to be able to form some idea of the general result of our accounts. I shall not omit to send you a statement of the monies I received from Clow & Co. I am with much esteem Dear Sir Your most obedt. servt   TH: JEFFERSON

RC (ViU).

This is the only extant letter of the five that TJ wrote during a brief trip to Richmond to deal with some of his financial affairs (see the following document, and note).

Earlier letters from Brown to TJ of 28 Jan. and 22 Apr. 1794, recorded in SJL as received from Richmond on 3 Feb. and 2 May 1794, respectively, have not been found.

List of Unretained Letters

[ca. 9 June 1794]

List of letters of which no copies have been retained.

Mr. Bolling's

1794. June 7. to Thos. Pleasants 4. mile creek, to engage Nanny Brewer to come to Monticello immediately after harvest to make 100,000 bricks, and to fix her wages. I to send a horse for her.

Eppington. June 8. to James Brown to send me a copy of Donald & Burton's account and promising to send him a statement of the money I recieved from Clow & Co.

do.　　　do.　　to Colo. Gamble to send my groceries left with Heath by a waggon to Charlottesville, and the fish by water by Colo. Lewis's boats.

do.　　June 9. to Colo. Skipwith. Apologising for not calling on him and informing him of the proceedings proposed against R. Randolph's representatives for indemnification to us against Bivins's judgment, and that Marshall thinks favorably on the question whether we shall be liable for the Guineaman.

MS (DLC: TJ Papers, 97: 16656); entirely in TJ's hand; undated.

This list documents four of the five letters TJ is known to have written during a brief trip to Richmond to attend to some of his financial affairs. Almost certainly setting out on 29 May—and going and returning by way of Chestnut Grove, the home of John Bolling, and Eppington, the seat of Francis Eppes—he arrived at the capital on 2 June and returned to Monticello on 10 June. This was the only extended journey TJ made during his present retirement from office (for his itinerary and business, see MB, 29 May-10 June 1794, and notes).

A reply from Thomas PLEASANTS, Jr., of 11 June 1794, recorded in SJL as received from Raleigh a week later, is missing, as are 10 other letters exchanged by TJ and Pleasants between 2 Apr. 1795 and 18 Sep. 1795. For the full text of TJ's letter to James BROWN, the only extant letter on the list, see the preceding document.

A reply from Robert GAMBLE of 10 June 1794, recorded in SJL as received from Richmond a day later, has not been found. SJL also records 26 letters that TJ exchanged with Gamble between 31 July 1794 and 22 May 1796, none of which have been found.

For the other missing letter written during the journey, see note to TJ to Thomas A. Taylor, 19 Feb. 1795.

BIVINS's JUDGMENT against the executors of John Wayles's estate concerned a suit for collection of a bond for £740 sterling which Richard Randolph gave to James Bivins, captain of *The Prince of Wales* out of Bristol, England, on 30 Dec. 1772, for which Wayles acted as security. (For a description of this bond, see note to Wayles to Bivins, 25 Jan. 1773, Document IX of a group of documents on the debt to Farell & Jones and the slave ship *The Prince of Wales*, printed in Vol. 15: 655.) The bond was still unpaid when Randolph died in 1786. Since the Virginia courts, for the most part, remained closed to British creditors seeking recovery of prewar debts prior to the implementation of the Jay Treaty, little could be done to collect the debt until 1790, when a recourse was offered by the establishment of United States circuit courts with jurisdiction over civil suits between foreigners and American citizens for claims over $500 (Hobson, "British Debts," 179-81).

On 14 Jan. 1791 James Bivins, Jr., heir of the Bivins estate, and Thomas Wigan, Jr., who succeeded his father as executor of the estate, both of Bristol, England, gave James Caton and John Nevison, merchants from Norfolk and Portsmouth, Virginia, respectively, the power to prosecute, if necessary, to obtain payment of the 1772 bond, with interest, from the estates of Randolph and Wayles "or any or either of them respectively" (Power of Attorney from James Bivins, Jr., and Thomas Wigan, Jr., to James Caton and John Nevison, 14 Jan. 1791, in Vi: USCC). The Virginia merchants hired John Wickham who immediately obtained a subpoena of Wayles's executors, initiated the case during the United States Circuit Court's 1791 fall term at Richmond, and filed a bill in chancery on behalf of Wigan and Bivins by April 1792. Although John Marshall is listed as attorney for Wayles's executors, it is unclear what action, if any, he took in behalf of the defendants (Rule Book No. 1, p. 51-2, 64-5, 78-9, in same).

In the undated bill in chancery, Wickham cited the bond given by Randolph to Bivins, noting that Wayles had not only served as security but that the bond had remained in his hands "for safe keeping." The letter from Wayles to Bivins of 25 Jan. 1773 and a copy of the original bond were annexed to the bill as evidence. Declaring that the plaintiffs would be unable to recover the debt from Randolph's heirs because they did not have the original bond and because "his whole Estate has been exhausted in the payment of other Debts so that they are wholly remediless," the bill requested that Wayles's executors, namely, TJ, Francis Eppes, and Henry and Anne Skipwith, be cited as defendants. Demanding "relief as is consistent with Equity and good Conscience," the plaintiffs requested a subpoena of the defendants (Tr in same, in clerk's hand; endorsed in same hand).

On 26 July 1791 a writ was issued directing the United States marshal to summon "Henry Skipwith and Ann Skipwith late Ann Wayles and Thomas Jefferson the executors of John Wayles deceased" to appear before the federal circuit court at Richmond on 27 Nov. 1791 to answer the bill in chancery exhibited against them by Wigan and Bivins. The summons was executed on the Skipwiths in Cumberland, Virginia on 24 Aug. 1791 (MS in same, printed form with emendations, being a writ for a subpoena, bearing seal, issued by William Marshall, clerk, endorsed by deputy marshal with notation, "Jefferson not found"; Rule Book No. 1, p. 51-2, in same).

Shortly after receiving the summons, Henry Skipwith reported the contents to TJ noting especially the omission of the Eppes family from the document. Acknowledging that the exclusion was significant, TJ sent queries to Francis Eppes about the suit and assured Skipwith that even if all were not named, each would be responsible for a third of the judgment (Skipwith to TJ, 4 Sep. 1791; TJ to Skipwith, 5 Oct. 1791; TJ to Eppes, 5 Oct. and 13 Nov. 1791).

On 11 Aug. 1792 the court issued a second writ requiring the Wayles executors to appear before the judges on 22 Nov. 1792 to answer the bill entered against them. Only Henry and Anne Skipwith were named in this document with TJ's name being written and canceled. Deputy marshal Paul I. Carrington served the summons on the Skipwiths on 24 Sep 1792 (MS in Vi: USCC, being a writ, bearing seal, issued by William Marshall, clerk, endorsed as an alias attachment, with additional note indicating that the writ was "For not answering a Bill of Complaint exhibited against them" by Wigan and Bivins, endorsed by Carrington, minuting his fees; Rule Book No. 1, 64-5, 78-9, in same).

On 7 June 1793 the court issued a decree in the case, noting that the failure of the defendants to file an answer to the bill, along with the exhibits and argument of counsel in behalf of the plaintiffs, caused the court to rule in favor of Wigan and Bivins. The court ordered Henry and Anne Skipwith, as executors of the Wayles estate, to pay £740 sterling ($3,288.89), with interest at 5 per cent from 30 Sep. 1773 and court costs, unless the defendants showed "cause to the contrary" during the term of court after which they were served with the decree. Wickham endorsed the decree noting that he had served the document on Henry Skipwith on 30 Nov. 1793 (Tr in same; certified by William Marshall, clerk; endorsed; proved in Henrico on 13 Nov. 1794 on the oath of John Harvie). As far as it can be ascertained, Wayles's executors made no attempt to answer this decree. They were already planning a suit against Richard Randolph's executors to collect this debt (see Bill in Chancery of Wayles's Executors against Heirs of Richard Randolph, [on or before 2 Mch. 1795], and note). In March 1796 TJ sent Wickham a partial payment for his portion of the Bivins debt (MB, 8 Mch. 1796, and note).

From James Monroe

DEAR SIR   Baltimore June 17. 1794.

The urgent pressure of the Executive for my immediate departure has deprived me of the pleasure of seeing you before I sailed. I sincerely regret this for many reasons but we cannot controul impossibilities. Will you forward me a cypher, and letters for your friends remaining in Paris to the care of Mr. R. as soon as possible. They may probably reach Paris as soon as I shall. I beg you to add whatever occurs which may be useful where I am going to the cause in which I am engaged, or to myself in advocating it. Being well acquainted with the theatre on which I am to act it will be much in your power to give me hints of that kind which may be serviceable.

As you will shortly see Mr. Madison who leaves this tomorrow or next day I decline saying any thing on the subject of the late proceedings in Phila. in either department of the government. Indeed you know so much of them already that I can add but little.

I shall place in the hands of James Maury of Liverpool a sum of money to answer my engagement to you. I have written to Colo. Lewis and Mr. Divers to intreat them to value Thena and her children and hope they will do it immediately. Let your draft be about Sepr. and payable at 60. days sight. Let it be accompanied with a letter of advice. The money shall certainly be deposited, unless you would prefer it in France of which you will advise me and draw on myself. I beg you not to omit this as the money will be idle in his hands in case you do not direct otherwise soon.

I shall confide to Mr. Madison yourself and Mr. Jones the fixing on a spot where my house shall be erected. The doubt will be between the hill to the left of the road as you approach towards Blenheim or the one where the barn stands. On which ever you place it I have given orders for an enclosure and the commencment of those improvments which are contemplated. Your advice on that head as well as the most suitable for the commencment of orchards of different kinds will be regarded.

We expect to imbark to morrow and to fall down the bay immediately. Accept my most affectionate wishes for your welfare and that of Mr. Randolph and your daughters and be pleased likewise to unite with them those of Mrs. Monroe. We contemplate a return in about 3. or 4. years at farthest—perhaps sooner. In the interim I wish every preparation for our final repose, I mean from active life, be in the farm adjoining yours. To this object my attention will be turned whilst abroad and I will indeavor to bring back what will contribute [to] its comforts. I wish you to command me in all respects wherein I can serve you. Perhaps you may wish things from the quarter I shall be in not obtainable so easily elsewhere. I am dear [Sir] with the sincerest regard yr. affectionate friend & servt   JAS. MONROE

RC (DLC); right margin on second page torn away; endorsed by TJ as received [24 June] 1794 and so recorded in SJL.

From Timothy Pickering

SIR   General Post Office June 30. 1794

Mr. Miller, the postmaster at Charlottesville, has signified his desire to resign his office; and waits only for the appointment of a Successor. Permit me to ask the favour of you to name a Suitable person, and who will accept the Office. Altho' the Commission of 20 per Cent may not be a motive with any one, perhaps the privilege of franking his own letters, not exceeding half an ounce in weight, may be an inducement with some gentleman who is in the practice of sending and receiving many letters. He will at the same time have the pleasure of affording a beneficial accommodation to his neighbours. I am &c   T. P.

FC (Lb in DNA: RG 28, LPG); at head of text: "Thomas Jefferson Esqr." Recorded in SJL as received 16 July 1794.

From Tench Coxe

DEAR SIR   Philada. July 7. 1794

Not knowing Mr. Madison's residence, but remembering that it is not far from you, I have the honor to inclose to you for him a pamphlet, which was left with me by a Mr. Callender. He observed that 25 Cents are the cost of it. You will find it amusing to read it. The British Judges and Juries do not hold, that unconstitutional acts of Parliament[1] are void or their constitution is miserably bad in regard to restraints upon the most pernicious corruptions of the commons house. When you send the pamphlet to Mr. M. be pleased to let my respects accompany it.

The King of Prussia you will find, has agreed to come into the war with 35,000 men, for a valuable consideration. He was obliged to supply about 27,000 from other and antecedent Engagements. These make his 62,000 men.

The loan in London to the Emperor appears to be a faithless measure. The subscribers to the British loan have taken *public* Notice of it, and, as it appears to me, may refuse in the hour of their own or of the public Need, to fullfil the violated contract. This step of Mr. Pitts appears to be the most inconsiderate, or the most seriously symptomatic of any, which he has taken. If he has really reflected it would seem to be a proof of the most alarming necessity.

I have long thought, that the stupendous mass of public debt in Europe must prove the mill stone of the prevalent form of Government in that quarter of the world. It will be probably one thousand Millions of Sterling money before the wars, now raging, shall be terminated.

It is said this morning, that two British Commissioners have arrived at Lisbon to settle a peace between Portugal and Algiers. They are to proceed from Lisbon to the Dey. Great Britain will take away the infamy of firing poisoned balls or will become herself an Object of execration.

It appears that France has really gained material advantages all round her confines, excepting the particular Vicinity of Valenciennes. There the conflict has been bloody and apparently unfavorable. She has escaped famine for 1794, and has checked insurgency and faction in the Convention. That is she has withstood what alone are serious to her, for I do not think the true character of her foreign war is now offensive on the part of her Enemies.

The Polish insurgents are bold men. They will certainly make a diversion favorable to France, and may have been among the influences upon the King of Prussia. I pray God they may be successful. They have been in a situation passing pity. I have not been able to think of their cruel situation without an aching breast.

Doctor Priestly is still here. I have seen him pretty often. He goes to Northumberland to Morrow. It is his opinion that the Conduct of the Government of Britain has rendered a revolution inevitable. I have the Honor to be dr. sir yr. mo. obedt. & hble servant   TENCH COXE

RC (DLC); endorsed by TJ as received 16 July 1794 and so recorded in SJL.

The enclosed PAMPHLET has not been identified, but may have been [James T.

Callender], *The Political Progress of Britain; or an Impartial Account of the Principal Abuses in the Government of this Country, from the Revolution in 1688. The Whole Tending to Prove the Ruinous Consequences of the Popular System of War and Conquest. Part First* (Edinburgh, 1792). A second, heavily revised, edition was published in Philadelphia in November 1794 under a slightly modified title (Evans, No. 26725). Neither edition is recorded in Sowerby, but

TJ later acquired two copies of Part 2, which was published in Philadelphia the following year (Michael Durey, *"With the Hammer of Truth": James Thomson Callender and America's Early National Heroes* [Charlottesville, 1990], 29, 44, 64, 212; Sowerby, Nos. 3184, 3519).

[1] Preceding three words interlined in place of "laws."

From John Leach

Ghent, 12 July 1794. A citizen of Boston, he left Massachusetts in February 1790 for the Isle of France and after his arrival sold his ship and cargo and was detained for a long time by a lawsuit. His business affairs settled, he took command of another American ship, sailed for Madras and then took passage for Bengal. Purchasing from an Englishman one half of an American built ship, he and the Englishman proceeded on a freighting voyage to Ostend, arriving in June 1793 and discharging the cargo and selling the ship. The Englishman severely mistreated him on the passage from Bengal, threatening his life and attempting mutiny, and for the safety of cargo and other lives he was obliged to put him in chains for about thirteen hours, after which the Englishman promised better behavior and he was released. Because he was not brought into port as a prisoner and turned over to authorities, the Englishman's friends thought that Leach was afraid and he was challenged to a duel. On the day it was to take place, the Englishman's friends persuaded him to prosecute the American instead. Arrested, cast into prison, and then released on bail to stand trial, he has been detained ever since (except for a fortnight in London), despite the promise of a trial month after month. Just as the trial was about to be finished, the French arrived and all business was suspended. For the last three months Leach has resided at Ghent, where he can live at less expense. The Englishman and his friends are doing everything they can to retard the trial. Upon the arrival of the French troops the American captain applied for a passport to travel to Ostend, where all his documents and belongings are. The only papers he has here are a receipt from Mr. Pinckney, ambassador in London, for the ship that was sold at the Isle of France and an introduction from General Lincoln to Colonel Fleury, who left prior to the American captain's arrival. The only other papers he has with him are insufficient to prove him an American and he is looked upon as "little better than an English spy." He requests a letter to the commandant at Ghent so that he may pass unmolested. Anyone from Massachusetts at Paris can attest to his identity, and he is known to Mr. Swan and Mr. Hichborn, who are said to be there. Now that the French are in possession of Flanders he knows that he will obtain the justice he deserves. Having been a staunch friend to that country, including French service in the last war, he finds it hard to be denied a passport when he can prove that he was born in Boston and sailed from that port seventeen years as a ship master. Taken for an Englishman, he fears he will be thrown into prison, which will surely cost him his life. He seeks relief from this truly disagreeable situation, and a letter can be directed to him through Monsieur Nobles, Ghent.

Dupl (DLC: James Monroe Papers); 3 p.; at head of text: "Copy"; at foot of text: "His Excellency—T. Jefferson—Ambassador from the United States of America at Paris"; endorsed by Monroe and a clerk. Enclosed in Leach to "The Representant from the United States of America with the french Republic," 6 Sep. 1794, which states that Leach concluded that his letter to TJ was waylaid or that TJ had left Paris, that Leach had managed to travel to Ostend since writing to TJ but found his property and papers had been taken to England, and that he needed a passport to Dunkirk (same). Recorded in SJL as received 25 Mch. 1795.

Sea captain John Leach (1752-1805) was the eldest son of a mariner of the same name who operated a navigation school in Boston before the American Revolution. The younger Leach, who in 1782 had commanded the privateer *St. Mary's Packet*, was a friend of attorney Benjamin Lincoln, Jr., a son of General Benjamin Lincoln (*New England Historical and Genealogical Register*, XIX [1865], 255; Gardner Weld Allen, *Massachusetts Privateers of the Revolution*, Massachusetts Historical Society, *Collections*, LXXVII [1927], 270; Leach to Benjamin Lincoln, Jr., 29 Mch. 1787, in MHi: Benjamin Lincoln Papers).

To Thomas Mann Randolph

DEAR SIR   Monticello July. 14. 1794.

It is possible that in the course of the voyages you are about to undertake for your health, you may sometimes be disappointed in the remittances provided to be made to you or your expences may exceed them. If therefore in any such event you should find it necessary to apply to other resources for money, and the addition of my name to your own would facilitate your obtaining it, I pray you to make use of it freely, as I freely add my responsibility to your own for any sums which may be furnished you during your absence. With the greatest concern for your health, and with the best affections I am Dear Sir Your's sincerely

TH: JEFFERSON

PrC (MHi); at foot of text: "Thomas Mann Randolph. esq."; endorsed in ink by TJ.

During the succeeding two years Randolph's VOYAGES to improve his health took him to Boston, New York, and western Virginia's mineral springs (Gaines, *Randolph*, 39).

To Timothy Pickering

SIR   Monticello July 23. [1794.]

I recieved your favor of June 30. [. . .] [the?] 16th. inst. and immediately attended to y[our?] [. . .] will doubtless ere this have informed [you?] [. . .] continue in the office, and as long [as?] [. . .] will execute it with more punctuality, [. . .] since the change of their rider, our letters [. . .] [I a]m with sentiments of great respect [. . .] your most [. . .]

Th[: Jefferson]

PrC (DLC); right side entirely faded and illegible, a third of each line being lost; at foot of text: "Colo. Pickering."

Pickering replied in a letter of 4 Aug. 1794, now missing, written from the General Post Office and recorded in SJL as received 12 Aug. 1794.

From William W. Hening

Sir   Charle. 24th of July 1794

Being about to submit to the tribunal of the public the work in which I have been so long engaged, I feel all that diffidence which is natural to an author, particularly to one of my age. Altho' I am conscious that neither pains nor expence have been spared to render the publication worthy of that patronage which, in every stage, it has experienced; yet I am sensible that no man can be a judge of his own performances—and that where the expences of the publication are partly sustained by the subscribers, they have a right to expect some better assurances of the merit of the performance than the author himself is able to give. It is from these impressions that I have never omitted an opportunity of laying it before gentlemen eminent for their literary talents—and with this conviction, I now, presume to trouble you with the revisal of a few sheets; requesting you would candidly point out the defects in the plan and execution. It will readily be perceived that, in quoting Hale, Hawkins, and other writers on Criminal law, I have not adopted their precise words, but in every instance have varied the expression, so as to suit the existing government and laws of this country. Whether this practice may be deemed justifiable or not, I am at a loss to determine; but of this I am certain, that it will be more generally pleasing to the people of America, and that the magistrates, in whose hands this book will principally fall, will thereby be less subject to error. I am very Respectfully yrs

Wm: W: Hening

RC (DLC); endorsed by TJ as received 25 July 1794 and so recorded in SJL. Enclosure not found.

William Waller Hening (1767-1828), the noted Virginia legal writer and lawyer who was currently practicing in Charlottesville, later served as representative for Albe-marle County in the House of Delegates, 1804-05, member of the Council of State, 1806-10, clerk of the Superior Court of Chancery for the Richmond District, 1810-28, and deputy adjutant general during the War of 1812. The work in which i have been so long engaged, *The New Virginia Justice, comprising the Office and Authority of a Justice of the Peace, in the Commonwealth of Virginia* (Richmond, 1795), to which TJ was one of the original subscribers, was the first in a series of writings that made Hening one of Virginia's leading legal scholars. After publishing a variety of other books on American and British law, Hening capped his career with his edition of *The Statutes at Large*, an indispensable source for the study of Virginia history that drew heavily on TJ's personal collection of Vir-

ginia legal records (DAB; Samuel M. Walker, Jr., "William Waller Hening," in W. Hamilton Bryson, ed., *The Virginia Law Reporters before 1880* [Charlottesville, 1977], 19-24; Sowerby, Nos. 1863, 1971).

According to SJL, Hening wrote letters to TJ on 16 and 30 Mch. 1800, received 29 Mch. and 7 Apr. 1800 respectively, the second from Richmond, and TJ wrote a letter to Hening on 7 Apr. 1800, none of which has been found.

To Richard Morris

DR. SIR   Monticello July 27. 1794.

I have waited for some time, since the receipt of your letter, with the samples of the cloth, in hopes a known opportunity might occur for sending you an answer: but am at length forced to write and let the letter take it's chance.

I think the rendering cloth waterproof, if it does not injure the quality, is a valuable discovery, even tho' the process should be somewhat costly; because it will inable many to guard themselves against the effects of wet: but it's importance will be truly great, if the process be so cheap as will admit it to be used for the laboring part of mankind. The rich have so many resources already for taking care of themselves, that an advantage the more, if confined to them, would not excite our interest: but if it can be introduced commonly for labourers, it then becomes valuable indeed. I have tried the samples you were so kind as to send me, and find them sufficiently water proof to answer every desireable purpose. The measures necessary for obtaining a patent are very minutely pointed out by the laws of Congress. They are nearly these. The inventor is to send a petition to the Secretary of state mentioning the nature of his discovery in general terms and praying a patent. He is also to send, what is called a specification of his discovery, that is, a minute description of his process, and a sample of the matter he composes, as well as of the cloth ready prepared, and he pays into the treasury of the US. 30. Dollars. The law requires an oath, the nature of which is pointed out. To this add some small fees (of 3. or 4. Dollars amount at the most) and every thing is done which is requisite for obtaining his patent. I have the honor to be with great esteem Dr. Sir Your most obedt. humble servt   TH: JEFFERSON

PrC (MHi); at foot of text: "Colo. Richard Morris."

Morris's LETTER of 27 May 1794, recorded in SJL as received from Charlotte on

12 June 1794, has not been found. Morris did not obtain a patent, and none was awarded for RENDERING CLOTH WATER-PROOF in the next five years (*List of Patents*, 8-20).

To Benjamin Carter Waller

SIR   Monticello July 27. 94.

Since my return to Virginia, it has not till lately been in my power to take a journey to that part of the country where Mr. Eppes resides, who has had the sole transaction of the business of Mr. Wayles's estate. I communicated to him the object of your letter on the subject of Mr. Welsh's account, and the purport of the answer I had written to you. The affairs of the estate being now too near a close to admit the interference of any other of the executors, Mr. Eppes undertakes to enter into arrangements with you relative to Mr. Welsh. Presuming that you must sometimes have business at Richmond or Petersburg, I cannot but hope you will find it convenient to call on Mr. Eppes, who is not far off the road between those two places: and that your powers are ample enough to meet him in such arrangements as will be just towards both parties. I shall chearfully approve whatever he does for the estate in general; or if, as was done by Farrel & Jones, our portions of the demand can be separated, I shall be ready to arrange with you my separate part. Referring therefore to the result of your communications with Mr. Eppes what is further to be done, and hoping to hear from you on that occasion, I am with great regard Sir Your most obedt. humble servt

TH: JEFFERSON

PrC (MHi); at foot of text: "Mr. Benj. Waller. Wmsburg."; endorsed in ink by TJ.

YOUR LETTER and TJ's ANSWER: see TJ to Benjamin Carter Waller, 21 Dec. 1793, and note.

From Benjamin Carter Waller

SIR   Wms.burg August 2d. 1794.

Your polite Letter I received many Months since—and should have answered, and proposed a plan for our Meeting, but Indisposition prevented. I am now again well. If the City of Richmond in the Month of October next about the 20th. will be agreeable to you, I can and will meet you with pleasure. Be assured there shall be no Difficulty on my part in the Accomodation, and the Terms you hint at in your Letter, will be allowed, as to my powers I trust they are unlimited. In short it is Mr. Welsh Wish to give you every Indulgence. Respectfully I remain Yr. most obt. Sert. BEN: WALLER

RC (MHi); endorsed by TJ as received 8 Sep. 1794 and so recorded in SJL.

To Christopher Clark

SIR   Monticello Aug. 5. 1794.

I inclose you the following bonds of persons residing in the counties wherein I understand you practice, to wit.

	penalty £ s	condition	time of paimt	date of bonds
James Branch William Minor Gabriel Minor	81– 5	40–12–6	1793. Dec.14.	1792. Dec.14.
John Clarke junr. John Clarke senr.	111–10	55–15–0		
Robert Hawkins Danl. B. Perrow Thomas Dillion	83–12	41–16		
Wm. Millner Simon Miller Wm. Miller	245–15	120– 7–6		
Danl. B. Perrow John Clarke senr. John Clarke junr.	41– 0	20–10.		

the whole payable to me. There was a condition subjoined that if they paid punctually at that day, the interest would be relinquished, not having done so it is to be required. Indeed I presume they had no intention of paying but at the end of a course of law, as I have never heard a word from any of them. Where you can apply for paiment without losing time, be pleased to do so; but to let no time be lost in bringing the suits and obtaining the money, this being the condition on which I am myself indulged with delay for the debt these bonds were destined to pay. Be pleased to pay the money when collected to James Lyle of Manchester or order. One article I must entreat you to attend to, that is, the payment of clerk's and sheriff's tickets yourself, so as that no one of them may ever be presented to me; it being impossible that I should know which are, or are not paid by you. I presume you may get money in time to pay these demands or make arrangements with the clerks and sheriffs, so as that the collection may answer it's own calls, and a clear account be rendered of the nett balance. I shall be glad to know at times how the collection goes on, but it is to Mr. James Lyle I would wish you to be most particular in giving information. Your fees you will of course take out of the proceeds of the collection. I am Sir Your very humble servt

TH: JEFFERSON

PrC (MHi); at foot of first page: "Mr. Clarke"; erroneously endorsed later in ink by TJ: "Clarke Wm." Enclosures not found.

Christopher Clark (1767-1828), a native of Albemarle County, was a Bedford County attorney who sat in the Virginia House of Delegates in 1790 and served parts of two terms as a Republican in the House of Representatives, 1804-06. TJ engaged him as an attorney again during a

land dispute in 1810, and five years later Clark suggested that TJ measure the altitude of the Peaks of Otter and extended him hospitality at his estate, Mount Prospect, during two ensuing field trips (*Biog. Dir. Cong.*; MB, 11 Apr. 1810, 19 Sep. and 12 Nov. 1815, and notes; Clark to TJ, 31 Aug. 1815).

Missing letters from Clark of 13 Sep. 1794 and 7 June 1796 are recorded in SJL as received 2 Dec. 1794 and 2 July 1796, respectively.

To Nicholas Davies

DEAR SIR   Monticello. Aug. 6. 1794.

I received by Mr. Poindexter your favor of July 21. with copies of your will and deed of trust. A twenty years abandonment of the practice and study of law, has really disqualified me from giving opinions on questions of law, which merit confidence. Nevertheless, to shew my desire to oblige you, I have given my best attentions to your papers.   Mr. Poindexter informs me that you wish by the deed, to convey not only the lands in Amherst, but those in Bedford also, to charitable uses. If so, I think the deed entirely defective in the descriptive clause, which is the first. The law is strict in the construction of deeds, and expressly requires that the lands meant to be conveyed shall be fully described in the descriptive clause, and will not suffer that clause to be enlarged by those which follow. If therefore you wish to convey the Bedford lands also by deed, I would advise you to add a description of them to that of the Amherst lands.

But the only effect of the deed is to put it out of your own power to change any thing relative to the trust yourself hereafter. The will is as fully competent to make any settlement you desire, as any deed can be. The death of some of the trustees named in the deed, or other circumstances, might induce you hereafter to wish to name others in the place of those dying, or to change them: this you will be able to do if you make the settlement by your will alone, but not if you execute the deed. I should therefore think it really more adviseable to cancel the deed, and perfect the will. If you do this it will be necessary in the clause of the 2d. page where you say 'as to all my other lands in Amherst and Bedford counties &c I leave to the management of my executors and trustees' &c it will be necessary I say to add words of inheritance, somewhat to this effect, to wit 'All my other lands in Amherst and Bedford &c I devise to my executors and trustees herein after named, to them and their heirs for ever, in trust for the several purposes expressed and to be expressed in this my will. All my lands now rented to my tenants'[1] &c as is now expressed in the will. When you come to the clause appointing executors say 'I hereby nominate and appoint my worthy friends Powhatan Bolling, John Dabney, and Thomas Logwood executors of this my last will, and jointly with James Poindexter of the county of Campbell, Charles Gwatkins of the county of Bedford, and Josiah Ellis senr. of the county of Amherst trustees for receiving the inheritance of my lands and for applying the same to the purposes before directed in this my will: and I hereby revoke all other wills' &c.

I observe an annuity of £10. in the will to Margaret Dyke, and that she is a witness to the will. If her attestation of the will should be necessary, it cannot be taken without her renouncing the legacy.

I learn with sincere pleasure that you still enjoy as good a degree of health as at your time of life may be expected. I earnestly wish it's continuance, and that of every circumstance which might contribute to make you happy. Persuaded that a reconciliation with your son, would tend much to the quiet of your mind, it would give me particular pleasure to learn that he could see the duty he is under of 'arising and going unto his father & saying, father I have sinned' &c and that you had fallen on his neck and kissed him. Wishing you every felicity of earth and heaven I am Dear Sir Your most obedt. humble servt

Th: Jefferson

PrC (DLC); at foot of first page: "Nicholas Davies esq."

Nicholas Davies, allegedly an immigrant from Wales, was a merchant who lived at one time or another in Henrico, Gloucester, and Cumberland counties before he obtained a land grant for 31,303 acres in Bedford and Amherst counties in 1771. He was a distant connection to TJ through his first marriage in 1733 to Judith Fleming Randolph, the great-grandmother of TJ's son-in-law Thomas Mann Randolph (TQHGM, VIII [1926], 140-1; VMHB, XXXII [1924], 392; Malone, *Jefferson*, I, 428; F. B. Kegley, *Kegley's Virginia Frontier . . .* [Roanoke, Va., 1938], 113).

Davies's FAVOR OF JULY 21 is recorded in SJL as received from Bedford on 5 Aug. 1794, but neither the letter nor the WILL AND DEED OF TRUST it enclosed has been found. Davies's SON by a second marriage was Henry Landon Davies.

[1] This and subsequent closing quotation marks conjecturally supplied.

To Thomas Mann Randolph

DEAR SIR   Monticello Aug. 7. 1794.

We received the day before yesterday your favor of July 28. from
Norfolk, and before that had recieved several from you written from
different parts of your road. It has been impossible to write to you in
return on account of the rapidity and incertainty of your movements.
The present is sent to New York tho' with little prospect of it's finding
you there, as it cannot be there till the 19th. which is near a week beyond your calculation. We are all here in perfect health. Jefferson has
had a little complaint in his bowels from the time you left us till lately.
But he seemed always to be superior to it, having been little affected in
his strength or spirits. We did nothing more than attend carefully to his
diet. He is still lazy in talking, that being the real reason of his back-
wardness, for he can say any thing he attempts. He tells us you are gone
to Bossum (Boston). Anne is in high health. Your matters at Edgehill
are well. One of your people from Varina tells us the crop there is most
extraordinary. I have not heard from Bedford since you left this; but
have just sent thither. We began to wish for rain to make our latter corn,
and yesterday there fell a very plentiful one, so that we shall scarcely
need another. The day before yesterday the mercury had got as high as
87°. This morning it was down at 59° a fall of 28.° in 36. hours.—We
have heard of an attack by the Indians at fort Recovery; but our information is too little to be depended on to hazard the particulars. We only
learn with some degree of certainty that both the sons of P. Marks were
killed in it.

We are sincerely anxious about the state of your health; and dread
almost as much the potent doses of Dr. Currie as the disease itself, whatever it may be. I wish it's form were more determinate, so that it's character should be precisely known. Still I hope the voyage to sea will have
proved advantageous, and if sensibly so, cannot but feel a wish you
would push the advantage as far as it shall be found practicable, as you
have gone through the greatest difficulty of the experiment, that of getting to sea from this inland place, and traversing the most bilious part of
our country and climate. Be assured we are all tenderly anxious for your
recovery and return. We are fully satisfied that the most solid of all
earthly happiness is of the domestic kind, in a well assorted family, all
the members of which set a just value on each other, and are disposed to
make the happiness of each other their first object. The void occasioned[1]
by your departure is sensible to us all; we are impatient to see it filled
again and hope it will be with a permanent restoration of your health.—
While at N. York, would it not be worth while to know on what terms

we can get supplied with our fall goods, and whether on a credit till our wheat and tobacco get to market? I think you will find N. York 10. or 15. per cent cheaper in goods than Philadelphia. With every wish for the recovery of your health and speedy return I am Dear Sir Your's affectionately   TH: JEFFERSON

P.S. Anne desires me to direct and inclose her letter to her Papa.

RC (DLC); at foot of first page: "Mr. Randolph"; endorsed by Randolph as received 24 Aug. 1794. PrC (MHi); lacks postscript. Enclosure not found.

SJL confirms the receipt of Randolph's missing FAVOR OF JULY 28. FROM NORFOLK on 5 Aug. 1794. His letters recorded in SJL as WRITTEN FROM "Hughes's" on 15 July 1794 and from Richmond a day later, received respectively on 22 and 23 July 1794,

are also unlocated, as is a letter written from New York on 5 Aug. 1794 and received 20 Aug. 1794. The SONS of Peter MARKS, Captain Hasting Marks and Lieutenant Peter S. Marks of the First Sublegion, United States Army, had not in fact been KILLED (Heitman, *Dictionary*, I, 689).

[1] Preceding two words interlined in place of "place left vacant."

From John Taylor

DR. SIR   Caroline August 15th 1794.

Some time past, I inclosed you the pamphlet you wrote for—accepted of your commission to procure the drill plow—and requested to know to whom at Richmond I should forward it. The plow has been ready for some time and delayed for want of an answer. Concluding at length, that my letter, or your reply has failed, I have forwarded it herewith to the care of Mr: John Harvie at Richmond, and requested him to receive it for you. Inclosed is an account of the cost and charges.

It is calculated to dril corn, peas, wheat, turnip seed, and any of similar sizes. Moreover by lessening the capacity of the cups with wax, it may be regulated to sow any grain less than corn, either thick or thin— and if the horse walks briskly, it will strew with great equality.

On one side of the plow are three screws, which will enable you so far to open that side, as to insert the bands to which the cups are affixed, and force them on the two cylinders on which they work.

The loose joint at the end of the wheel's axle, is of admirable use, as it enables the wheel to give way to clods and inequalities, and yet to perform its revolutions regularly; and as it bestows upon the driver a convenient mode of turning, without being incommoded by the wheel, or wasting the seed. This is effected by means of the staff with the crooked hook at the End, which hook is to be inserted with a screw to keep it fixed, into an iron aperture contrived for it at the end of a peice of wood, through which the axle passes near the nave of the wheel, for the purpose of keeping the wheel at right angles with the beam. This staff made fast, lies useless upon the handles, whilst the plow is at work, but when about to turn, the plow: man tucks it between the handles, or holds it tight, by which means he raises the wheel, and turns conveniently. There are two screws to raise one of the cylinders on which the cups play, to tighten the band if there should be occasion. There are three sets of cups.

Instead of the wooden heel, which is best to open a furrow for small seeds, you may substitute a plow for corn, or any thing else.

But I beg pardon for these remarks touching the mechanism of this plow, for you will very soon discover its principles.

I will however subjoin one convenience in its use respecting turnips. This is a vegitable of so delicate a constitution, as often to fail, if the season is not favorable to it, for a week or two after sowing. This plow enables us to take a double chance. You may sow early, and after the first horse or hand hoing, sow again between the rows. And as soon as it is ascertained which sowing succeeds best, we may destroy the other without any additional labour, in cultivating the crop. Seed is nothing. And a single man and horse, will drill six acres in a day at least, at three feet distance. I use twelve feet poles, and the land between is split three times by the Eye which brings it to three feet. Wheat sown about the first of October between the turnips will produce good crops. I am with great respect & esteem Sir Yr: mo: obt: Sert.   JOHN TAYLOR

RC (ViU); addressed: "Thomas Jefferson Esqr. Care of Colo. Harvie—Albemarle"; endorsed by TJ as received 30 Sep. 1794 and so recorded in SJL. Enclosure not found.

To James Steptoe

DEAR SIR   Monticello Aug. 16. 1794.

I received your favor by Mr. Clarke and thank you for your care of the great bone. If you will be so good as to deliver it to him, he will send it to me by some suitable opportunity. I shall certainly be in Bedford this fall. When last there (now 13. years ago) I was fully determined to have visited it once or twice a year. No body could then have imagined the series of circumstances which have so long prevented my doing it. This is the first year I have ever had it in my power, and shall not fail in the pleasure of seeing you there. I am with great esteem Dr. Sir Your most obedt. servt   TH: JEFFERSON

PrC (DLC); at foot of text: "Mr. Steptoe."

Years earlier TJ had designated James

Steptoe (1750-1826) as an intermediary to handle natural history specimens that might be sent to TJ from the frontier. Steptoe, who in 1771-72 acted as TJ's "agent at the

Secretary's office," served as clerk of the Bedford County Court from 1772 until his death. The two exchanged hospitality for many years during TJ's visits to Poplar Forest (Johnston, *Memorials*, 68-79; TJ to ——, 30 June 1771; TJ to Inglis and Long, 4 July [1772]; TJ to George Rogers Clark, 26 Nov. 1782).

Steptoe's FAVOR to TJ of 8 Aug. 1794, now missing, was recorded in SJL as received 13 Aug. 1794.

To Francis Eppes

DEAR SIR   Monticello Aug. 28. 1794.

I received yesterday your favor of Aug. 17. as I had before done that of July 15. This would have been sooner answered, but that Mr. Jones was expected here, to whom the custody of Monroe's papers had been confided. He has been here, and I got him to make a rigorous search for those we had delivered Monroe relative to R. Randolph's representatives; but they are not to be found. This however is of no other importance to us, than the expence of new copies; for the state of the two deeds to R. and D. Randolph was not exactly as you seem to think. R. Randolph's deed was *on good consideration* (viz. marriage) but *not recorded in time*. D. Randolph's deed was *recorded in time*, but *not on good consideration*, for it was for natural love. Of this I am certain, and I think it probable you have some memorandum or letter of mine, written at the time, which will shew it. The second post after my return [here I?] wrote to Wickam and inclosed him a paper of which I now send you a copy. This went from here July 17. and should have been received by him on the 20th. I answered the postage, that no obstacle might arise from that. In this paper you will perceive that I had stated to Wickam the defect of D. R's deed to be a want of *good consideration*, not a failure in it's being recorded. For fear he [should?] from any accident not have received my letter, it [might not be?] amiss for you to send him this paper, which suffices f[or b]ringing the suit. I had taken for granted the process had been taken out so as to be returneable to the next term. Nothing more was necessary from me to Wickam.—I have received from Marshall an answer to my letter inclosing my notes on the Guineaman. He expresses good confidence in the issue of that suit.

As to my attendance at the trial, I mentioned to Marshall and Innes that I would attend. My view was to add a motive the more for their attention to our cause. But my actual attendance is entirely unimportant: and I shall be obliged about that time to take a journey to Bedford to which place I have not had it in my power to go for fourteen years past. If therefore it were possible that I could know the precise day of the Federal court on which this case would come on, it would scarcely be probable that I could attend. My occupations at home and my aversion to leaving them have some influence also on the chance of my attendance.—You have not informed me to whom I must send the original receipt of which I sent you a copy in John Randolph's case.—I am sorry to hear of Mrs. Eppes's indisposition. But it appears of too transient a character to influence her movements thro' the year. We learnt through Co[l. C]ary's family that, at any rate, Jack and Betsy would visit us, [and?] that as soon as Jack's indisposition would permit. We hope that is over, and that we shall not be baulked in this part of our expectation. Mr. Randolph is returned, and is on the recovery. Our greatest alarm as to the nature of his complaint has [subsid]ed. Patsy is well as yet; but probably will be otherwise [. . . .] Every body else in good health and concurring in wishes [for the ha]ppiness of your family. My love to Mrs. Eppes and our young friends. I have no other channel to send the same to Mr. and Mrs. Skipwith and theirs, when you see them. Adieu. Yours affectionately

TH: JEFFERSON

RC (Thomas Jefferson Memorial Foundation, on deposit ViU); torn at folds; addressed: "Francis Eppes esquire at Eppington in Chesterfeild. to the care of mr Mc.Callum Ozborne's"; stamped.

Eppes's FAVOR OF AUG. 17. and THAT OF JULY 15., recorded in SJL as received from Eppington on 26 and 5 Aug. 1794 respectively, have not been found. SJL also records missing letters from Eppes to TJ of 20 May and 11 June 1794, respectively received from Richmond on 3 and 11 June 1794, and from TJ to Eppes of 27 July 1794.

Litigation by TJ and Eppes against R. RANDOLPH'S REPRESENTATIVES on the basis of TWO DEEDS formed a sequel to the Bivins case; see Bill in Chancery of Wayles's Executors against the Heirs of Richard Randolph, [on or before 2 Mch. 1795]. The letter that TJ wrote to John Wickham the SECOND POST AFTER MY RETURN from a June 1794 trip to Richmond is recorded in SJL under 18 June 1794, but neither that nor the PAPER OF WHICH I NOW SEND YOU A COPY has been found. SJL records no other correspondence between TJ and Wickham in 1794.

Both TJ's letter to John MARSHALL of 16 July 1794 and Marshall's ANSWER of 2 Aug. 1794, received from Richmond on 15 Aug. 1794, are recorded in SJL but have not been found. TJ's missing NOTES ON THE

GUINEAMAN related to litigation concerning the slave ship *Prince of Wales* (see Vol. 15: 643-8).

By referring to his ORIGINAL RECEIPT relating to JOHN RANDOLPH'S CASE, TJ very likely meant the State of Farell & Jones's Judgment against John Randolph, Document XXIII of a group of documents on the debt to Farell & Jones, printed above in this series at Vol. 15: 672. The case, one of several in which TJ was involved as an executor of the estate of John Wayles, concerned a bond of John Randolph, the former king's attorney for Virginia who from loyalist sympathies had emigrated to England in 1775 and died there in 1784 (DAB). Little is known about the bond itself except that Jerman Baker, the original holder, turned it over to Wayles, who acted as an attorney for Farell & Jones, in partial fulfillment of a debt to the Bristol firm. In 1768 the firm won a judgment against Randolph for £241.14.5 (Virginia) plus interest until paid, but was unable to collect. In December 1778, by which time interest had run the total to £364.12.2, TJ accepted £291.12 that had been recovered from Randolph. He immediately deposited the money in the state treasury to the credit of Farell & Jones under the 1777 Virginia sequestration law, which sanctioned such deposits as payment toward debts. However, after the war British creditors maintained that they were entitled, under the Treaty of

Paris, to full payment of debts in sterling money rather than the deposits of Virginia currency allowed by the sequestration act (MB, 19 Dec. 1778, and note; undated account of Baker's debt to Farell & Jones, in Vi: USCC; TJ to Eppes, 10 July 1788; Hobson, "British Debts," 176-8). Although Farell & Jones came to argue that before his death Wayles had assumed responsibility for payment of the bond, and that TJ's acceptance and deposit of the money in 1778 incurred an obligation on the part of Wayles's estate, in 1790 Richard Hanson, the agent of Farell & Jones in Virginia, wrote to the firm that "I observe you cannot find why you charged J. Randolph's Bond to J.W. The list of Securities you sent me is of no Use if I bring a Suit for it. Jerman Baker must clear it up." TJ and his fellow executors rejected the firm's claim and excluded Randolph's bond from the plan they negotiated with Hanson for the settlement of Wayles's debt to Farell & Jones (Hanson to Farell & Jones, 17 Nov. 1790, extract in PRO: T 79/30, claim of John Tyndale Warre; Memorandum of Agreement between Richard Hanson and Executors of John Wayles, [7 Feb. 1790], printed at Vol. 15: 674-6).

In 1792 the firm's surviving partner, William Jones, acting through Baker as his attorney, filed suit against Wayles's executors in the United States Circuit Court at Richmond (Rule Book No. 1, p. 68-9, in Vi: USCC). The complaint against TJ, Eppes, Henry Skipwith, and Anne Skipwith claimed that on 23 July 1771 Wayles was indebted to the firm for the sum of £241.14.3 sterling (see below) "for so much money, before that time, had and received," and that Wayles's and subsequently his executors' refusal to pay had resulted in damage to the plaintiff of £800 (MS in Vi: USCC; undated, but endorsed as filed July 1792 and so recorded in Rule Book No. 1, p. 68-9, in same; in Baker's hand, leaving multiple blanks). The defendants' arguments against that declaration have not survived. By the November 1793 term of the Circuit Court Jones was dead, and the firm's executor, John Tyndale Warre, whose name is often spelled "Ware" in the records of American courts, subsequently became the suit's plaintiff (Order Book No. 1, p. 241, in same; scire facias writ in same, 10 July 1794, con-

sisting of a printed form signed and with blanks filled by William Marshall, clerk of the court, endorsed by Marshall directing service on Eppes only, and endorsed by Eppes on 1 Sep. 1794 and by Deputy Marshal Samuel G. Adams to record service of the writ). After a series of continuations the case finally went to a jury in December 1797, and Hanson, smarting from defeat in the *Prince of Wales* case against Wayles's executors, reported to Warre that the jury had been unable to reach a verdict concerning the Randolph bond and that "in short it is idle to expect a Virginia Jury to find a Verdict against Mr. Jefferson" (Hanson to [Warre], 15 Dec. 1797, extract in PRO: T 79/30, Warre claim; clerks' endorsements, Jones v. Jefferson and others, in Vi: USCC). A second attempt in November 1798 again resulted in a hung jury, but that panel was discharged and a new one during the same term of court decided in the defendants' favor, declaring that John Wayles had not taken upon himself any debt originating with the old Randolph bond (Order Book No. 3, p. 116, 125, in same).

Several factors conspire to make the documentary record of the lawsuit confusing. The 1768 court judgment on the bond was for £241.14.5 in Virginia money, whereas the value cited in the Circuit Court filing was £241.14.3 sterling, a deceptively similar figure that actually included accrual of interest to July 1771 and accounted for conversion from Virginia currency to British sterling (undated Baker account in Vi: USCC). In the surviving papers and books of the Circuit Court it can be difficult to distinguish the Randolph bond case from the *Prince of Wales* suit, both being identified as actions by Jones against Wayles's executors. Moreover, early in the nineteenth century when Warre sought redress from British commissioners ruling on pre-Revolutionary American debts, he unwittingly or otherwise muddled the John Randolph bond with obligations incurred by a different John Randolph of Virginia, who died in 1775 with his own array of debts to British merchants (Warre claim in PRO: T 79/30; Jonathan Daniels, *The Randolphs of Virginia* [Garden City, New York, 1972], 71, 88, 119). Compounding the confusion about the suit, in the editorial note concerning the debt to Farell & Jones at Vol. 15:

648, the Editors mistakenly associated John Randolph's bond with a reference to "a loose and equivocal expression" by John Wayles, when in fact the "expression" was a key point only in the unrelated *Prince of Wales* case involving Wayles and Richard Randolph (see TJ to James Lyle, 12 May 1796). In addition, the Editors inferred that an oblique reference in a later letter (TJ to John Harvie, Jr., 22 Feb. 1796) meant the Randolph bond suit, when in fact it must have referred to the conclusion of the Bivins case—an error that led to an incorrect explanation at Vol. 15: 648 of the outcome of the litigation over John Randolph's bond.

From Edmund Randolph

DEAR SIR   Philadelphia August 28. 1794.

Notwithstanding you have fenced out from the purlieus of Monticello every thing, which assumes a political Shape, you must permit me to bring before you a subject, once extremely near to your heart, often the employement of your pen, and always a deep interest to the United States.

The delays, and evasions which you know to have been practised towards our Commissioners at Madrid, have at length terminated in an absolute stagnation, as you will discover from the enclosed letter of Mr. Jaudenes. I drew him from New York to explain; and the substance of our conference is contained in the copy, now sent, from the original, which was read to Mr. Jaudenes. Mr. Short had a little time before Mr. Jaudenes's communication represented the difficulty, which had been created, as to a supposed defect of powers; but we have not yet received the precise idea, which was stated to him, nor the particulars of the discussion, to which this unexpected stroke must have given birth.

The people of Kentucky, either contemning or ignorant of the consequences, are restrained from hostility by a packthread. They demand a conclusion of the negotiation, or a categorical answer from Spain. The tenor of the assurances, which have proceeded from you, has been repeated to them by me, with the addition of any subsequent events, which ought to be divulged. The President has lately determined to send a special Agent to develope the true situation of the business to the government of Kentucky; and we have reason to expect, that Colo. James Innes, of Virginia, will soon come on hither to acquire the information, necessary to be carried to that state.

But, prompted by the zeal, with which he has always pursued the free navigation of the Missisippi, he conceives it to be adviseable to adopt a further measure, which while it is due to the emergency, may subdue or at least hold in check the irritation of Kentucky, already arrived to an alarming height. He has therefore resolved to send to Madrid a special

Envoy, charged with powers, adequate to the occasion. Whether such a character, which has not yet existed in this negotiation, can be originated by him during the recess of the Senate, is not so clear; and therefore it is probable, that he will take the following course for the present: If the Gentleman appointed should be ready to sail (as it is hoped that he will) before the meeting of the Senate, he may either go with powers, as sole Commissioner plenipotentiary, or he may go without, relying that powers shall be forwarded to him, as envoy extraordinary. If it should happen, that he cannot be prepared for the voyage before the assembling of the Senate, he may commence it with a commission of Envoy extraordinary.

Motives, public and personal, induced the President to designate you for this distinction. He did indeed feel some hesitation in instructing me to offer it to you; as your ardor for retirement has predominated in all your late arrangements. But he yielded to this consideration: that from the declaration of Mr. Jaudenes, and the actual position of our affairs with Spain, your separation from home could not be of any considerable duration. Will you therefore suffer me to say to the President, that it would not be unacceptable to you, to undertake this important office? For myself, I see reasons to wish your acceptance, derived from very interesting sources. What if the government of Kentucky should force us either to support them in their hostilities against Spain, or to disavow and renounce them? War at this moment with Spain would not be war with Spain alone: the lopping off of Kentucky from the union is dreadful to contemplate, even if it should not attach itself to some other power. The people there ripen daily, I fear, for one or the other of these alternatives; and the progress of the mischief cannot be stopped but by a vigorous effort of our government thro' the medium of one, possessing their confidence.

I could extend the expressions of the President's desire for your acceptance to a degree, truly honorable to you, being sincere in him. I could add my own private anxiety to the same effect. But the present overture is from its nature a more satisfactory testimony of his esteem, than any language can make it; and my individual intreaty would not deserve to be counted in such a case.

I omit the mention of emoluments altho' they will undoubtedly be stamped with dignified propriety, because their rate would not be sought after in the forming of your resolution.

By the express, who will carry this letter from Richmond to Monticello, let me beg your answer. Should it be impossible to persuade you once more into the diplomatic field, I must request you to forward by the express the inclosed letter addressed to the Postmaster at Richmond. It contains another intended eventually for Mr. Patrick Henry with a similar object; and it is therefore unnecessary to hint that it would be agreeable to the President that this application to you, if unsuccessful, should rest with yourself. Should it meet your approbation, you will be so good, as to return the letter to the Postmaster under cover to me. I have the honor to be with great and constant esteem and respect yr. affectionate friend & serv.   EDM: RANDOLPH

RC (DLC); in a clerk's hand, with two minor corrections, complimentary close, and signature by Randolph; at foot of first page: "Thomas Jefferson Esqr."; endorsed by TJ as received 7 Sep. 1794 and so recorded in SJL. FC (Lb in DNA: RG 59, DL). Enclosure: Randolph to Patrick Henry, 28 Aug. 1794, asking him on behalf of the President to serve as "Envoy Extraordinary" to Madrid and requesting his reply by the express delivering this letter so that he can receive his instructions and leave for Spain as soon as possible; and briefly describing the course of negotiations with Spain conducted by John Jay, William Carmichael and William Short, and Short alone (FC in same). Enclosed letter to the Richmond postmaster not found. Other enclosures printed below.

The circumstances that had led the Spanish government in May 1794 to instruct its agents in Philadelphia to request the appointment of an envoy to supersede the American COMMISSIONERS AT MADRID, William Carmichael and William Short, in order to deal with the outstanding diplomatic differences between the two nations are discussed in Bemis, *Pinckney's Treaty*, 194-6, 208-9. Fearful that the federal government's failure thus far to win Spanish recognition of the American right to navigate the Mississippi would make the nation vulnerable to "the attempts of the British to seduce the inhabitants of the Western waters," the Washington administration had requested JAMES INNES, the attorney general of Virginia, to serve as a commissioner for the express purpose of officially informing the executive and legislature of Kentucky of American diplomatic efforts to vindicate this right (Randolph to Washington, 7 Aug. 1793, Randolph to Innes, 8, 22 Aug. 1794, and Randolph to Isaac Shelby, 15, 25 Aug. 1794, all in DNA: RG 59, DL).

TJ and Patrick Henry both refused to serve as SPECIAL ENVOY to Spain, and in November 1794 Washington appointed Thomas Pinckney (Bemis, *Pinckney's Treaty*, 208n, 235, 253-4; TJ to Randolph, 7 Sep. 1794; Henry to Randolph, 14 Sep. 1794, in Henry, *Henry*, II, 548-9).

ENCLOSURES

I

Josef de Jaudenes to Edmund Randolph

SIR   New York 16th. August 1794

With no small concern I see myself obliged to inform you, that no progress has been made in the negociation pending between the King my master and the United States on account of the reason I so often gave your predecessor, by writing and conversation, that His Majesty would enter into no Treaty if the powers delegated to the Ministers of the States were not ample or that they had private instructions that should have for their object the concluding a partial and not general treaty; and at least that the Ministers appointed for that purpose by the States should in every respect be such whose Characters, Conduct and Splendor would render them proper persons to reside near his Royal person;

which is required by the importance of the business to be treated on.

With this intent the King orders me to make known to the President of the U.S. "that Spain is ready to treat with the U.S. on whatever relates to the Limits, Indians, Commerce and whatever else may cement the strictest Amity between the two countries, but as the powers given Messrs. Carmichael and Short, the incompetency of the former being so notorious and the conduct of the latter having been also very close and circumspect, it is not possible to conclude such important matters with them—and in consideration of these reasons His Majesty hopes the US. will send another person or persons with full powers to settle the treaty, but such whose Characters and abilities will insure them a kind reception on the part of the King."

On this account I beg you Sir, to inform the President of the US. who I flatter myself will be willing to comply with His Majesty's request, and with all the brevity required for the interest of both countries; I beg you to inform me the result, that I may communicate it to His Majesty. I beg to repeat my assurances of respect, & am Sir, Your most obedient Servant   JOSEPH DE JAUDENES

Tr (MoSHi: Jefferson Collection); in a clerk's hand; at head of text: "Translation"; at foot of text: "Honble. Edmund Randolph"; certified and endorsed by George Taylor, Jr. RC (DNA: RG 59, NL); in Spanish; endorsed by Randolph as received 18 Aug. 1794. Tr (same); English translation.

II
Edmund Randolph's Memorandum of a Conference with Josef de Jaudenes

Substance of the Conference between Mr. Jaudenes, Commissioner of his Catholic majesty, and Edmund Randolph, Secretary of State, at the Office of the Department of State, on Monday the 25 day of August 1794; in consequence of the request of the said Secretary.

After expressing his regret at being obliged to draw Mr. Jaudenes from New York, Mr. Randolph stated the sensibility excited in the President, on being informed that the treaty between the United States and Spain was suspended for the causes expressed in his letter of the 16th. instant. Mr. Jaudenes observed, that he had at first meditated to make the communication orally; but he finally resolved to make it by letter, intending, if any explanations were necessary, to come to Philadelphia, should he be requested. He reciprocated the sentiments of regret at the situation, to which the Treaty was reduced.

Mr: Randolph then took up Mr. Jaudene's letter of the 16th. August, and desired to understand the nature of the objection, as to the powers of the Commissioners not being ample. Mr. J. entered into a detail of the transaction from its commencement in December 1791; as it appears from the memoranda of Mr. Jefferson, and the letters between the Spanish Commissioners and him; adding, that it appeared to be Mr. Jefferson's policy to negotiate for the Missisippi alone; whereas his Catholic Majesty would never treat, but upon *all* the subjects, unadjusted between him and the United States. Mr. J. observed, that he had indeed understood, that very comprehensive Powers had been afterwards given to the Commissioners; but the nature of them was not made known to him by Mr. Jefferson. As Mr. J. did not appear to have seen them, and he laid much stress upon an admonition, which he contends, he frequently gave Mr. Jefferson, that the Powers of the Commissioners should be as comprehensive, as those which Mr. Gardoqui formerly brought with him, Mr. R. shewed him the Powers of the American Commissioners. He considered them, as sufficiently comprehensive *upon the face of them.* Mr. R. remarked, that their comprehensiveness must have been known to the Spanish Ministry, at a very early period; as the exchange of powers precedes every act of Negotiation. This Mr. J. thought probable. Mr. R. expressed some degree of surprise, that after so much time spent in the negotiation, after repeated recognitions of its pendency as well by the Spanish Ministry, at Madrid, as the Spanish Commissioners here, the progress of it should be checked by an objection, which, if valid, ought to have been urged at the beginning, when it might have been immediately removed. To this J. replied, that he was not instructed in the reasons of his Court, farther than he had quoted to Mr. R. in his letter of the 16. August. But as the conference was free, he might conjecture, that they were governed by considerations like these: that the objection to powers was never too late, if as the business advanced, it was found, that they were narrowed by the instructions of the Commissioners, or by the obstinacy of their conduct, than they appeared to be on the face of the paper, which contained them: that his Catholic Majesty might be resolved to treat upon all the matters or none; being desirous of settling every controversy, and possibly seeing some connection between them: that Mr. J. had expressed his apprehension to his Court, that the Missisippi was the object, which the negotiation had principally in view: that this would naturally attract their attention, and induce them to sound and explore; and if they did not find perfect explicitness on the occasion, they might suspect, that the Union of all the subjects was not intended by the United States. Indeed Mr. J. dropped an Idea, that all the States were not solicitous for the Missisippi; that a majority of them were against it; and that the attempt to gain it, might perhaps be conceived, as set on foot, rather to pacify Kentucky, than really to obtain it.

This Idea, Mr. R. denied to have any foundation: but Mr. J. seemed to renew it in another form namely; that any concession, which might be necessary to adjust the dispute, tho' agreeable to some of the States would be disagreeable to the others, and that there was a kind of indisposition in the States for one of them to give up any of its own advantages for the accommodation of the others. To this Mr. R. answered, that there ought not to be a doubt for a moment, that what was stipulated by the United States in Treaty, would be faithfully fulfilled. But it was necessary to return to the supposition above mentioned, of secret instructions, or the particular conduct of the Commissioners restricting the powers to the Missisippi only.

This is the second part of Mr. Js. letter, requiring explanation.

Mr. R. inquired, whether the Commissioners had been interrogated upon their instructions, and had answered, that they were restricted? Whether they had declared that they would not proceed upon a new subject, until the Missisippi was definitively settled, without relation to any other matter? Mr. J. could afford no information; not being himself informed. He only observed, that the Spanish Nation being candid and sincere in its transactions would quickly receive disgust, if it should have appeared, that the Commissioners, deviated from Candor and sincerity on their part.

In the third place Mr. R. desired an explanation of what was meant by the requisition of a Minister, whose character, conduct and splendor, would render them proper &c. Mr. J. replied, that when the negotiation was first talked of, Mr. Jefferson asked him if Mr. Carmichael would be acceptable; to which Mr. J. answered with a reluctance, which nothing but a sense of duty could overcome, that there was a deficiency of decorum &c. &c. in Mr. Carmichael. Mr. Jefferson then said suppose we unite Mr. Short with him? Mr. J. replied, that he was not personally acquainted with Mr. Short; but he presumed that Mr. Jefferson would not contemplate an unfit person. Some time afterwards Mr. J. was about to say to Mr. Jefferson that Mr. Pinckney would be acceptable, and might probably touch at Madrid for that purpose; but he was told by Mr. Jefferson that the President had already nominated Messrs. Carmichael and Short. Upon hearing this, Mr. J. considered himself as being no longer at liberty to animadvert upon an appointment which was consummated. But Mr. J. still declaring his inability to assign any reasons, except those contained in his letter of August 16 which were the whole of what had been written by his Court, said, that he might conjecture it to be possible, that Mr. Short being as Chargé des affaires the author of the offensive Memorial which was addressed to Spain thro' the French Minister at Madrid had imbibed sentiments too violent and might have expressed them too vehemently. He might perhaps too have partaken too much of Mr. Carmichael's style of behaviour. Mr. J. then explained the words Character, conduct and Splendor thus. By character he meant a Diplomatic grade (no matter what) invested with full powers for all objects: by conduct, a proper attention to the Court and a proper behaviour in the management of the negotiation: by Splendor, *personal* dignity and self respect. Splendor as the effect of honorary birth, or proceeding from such Considerations was not included in his expression.

Mr. R. then asked Mr. J. if the negotiation was at a stand. He answered, that he presumed it was.

Mr. R. disclaiming all knowledge of what the President's ultimate opinion would be, but desirous of knowing whether if another character was to be sent to Spain, the old delays would be repeated, was assured by Mr. J. that in his Opinion, the business might be immediately settled, either by a treaty, signed and executed or by a statement of the terms, upon which a Treaty might be concluded.

EDM: RANDOLPH
August 26th. 1794

Tr (DLC); in the hand of George Taylor, Jr., and certified and endorsed by him. FC (Lb in DNA: RG 59, DL).

MEMORANDA OF MR. JEFFERSON, AND THE LETTERS: see Memorandum of Conversation with Jaudenes, 6, 27 Dec. 1791; TJ to Jaudenes and Viar, 25, 26 Jan., 23 Mch. 1792; and Jaudenes and Viar to TJ, 25, 27

Jan. 1792. OFFENSIVE MEMORIAL: William Short's 1 June 1791 letter to Montmorin, the French foreign minister, calling for Spanish recognition of the American right to navigate the Mississippi and the grant of a port of deposit under American jurisdiction near its mouth, which Montmorin forwarded to the Spanish government (Bemis, *Pinckney's Treaty*, 157).

From François D'Ivernois

L'interessante Geneve n'existe plus pour la liberté. Son Gouvernement qui étoit redevenu to[ut à] fait démocratique vient d'y etre renversé par u[ne] faction peu nombreuse, mais soutenue par un[e i]nfluence etrangere qui a enfin reussi à faire triompher sur la rui[ne d]es loix les plus libres la tyrannie populaire la plus effrayante. Une poignée de brigands y domine invinciblement la majorité de notre peuplade. Les confiscations les exils les imprisonments s'y comptent deja par centaines. Un Tribunal Révolutionaire a fait couler le sang de onze victimes. Cette fureur destructive n'a point respecté les anciens défenseurs de nos libertés parce qu'ils sont aussi les amis de l'ordre (1). Tous les Genevois qui avoient quelque avantage d'education ou de fortune sont dejà frappés ou menacés. Notre Religion sage et tolérante, ainsi que ses respectables Ministres, est devenue l'objet d'une persécution singeresse. Notre Académie, nos Colleges, nos institutions pour les arts subissent toute espèce de dégradation sous une populace qui regarde aussi les sciences et les lettres comme une branche d'aristocratie. Enfin cet affreux bouleversement de l'ordre social s'est opéré et consolidé dans Geneve à l'instigation des francois, pour ainsi dire sous leurs bannieres, et au nom de cette Révolution dont j'avois eu une fois la simplicité d'espérer le rajeunissement de l'ancien monde!

Mais le tableau historique que je joins ici (2), me dispense de m'etendre sur cette catastrophe.[1] Vous y verrez Monsieur, que la liberté de Geneve a été flétrie à jamais; que[2] l'élite de ses citoyens n'a plus à attendre qu'oppression et dépouillement; que leur unique espérance est de s'éloigner d'une ville pressée entre le crim[e,] la discorde la famine et l'indigence oiseuse et salariée. Vous y [ver]rez enfin que plusieurs d'entr'eux tournent deja leu[rs regards] et meme leurs pas vers vos Etats Unis. C'est pour les seconder, que j'ai conçu i[ci l'i]dée d'une entreprise grande noble et particulierement digne de vous avoir pour Protecteur. Ce seroit celle de transporter chez Vous Notre Académie, pour ainsi dire toute entiere, toute organisée, et avec elle tous les moyens d'instruc-

(1) A la tete de la liste des Proscriptions se trouve entr'autres Mr. *Du Roveray* qui a eu l'honneur d'etre connu de vous.

(2) Ce tableau où je ne fais aucune mention de mon plan, est destiné cependant à y préparer les Américains, et à les empécher de confondre nos emigrés avec des Aristocrates qui n'abandonneroient leur patrie, que pour y avoir perdu leurs privilèges exclusifs. Je l'ai donc écrit dans l'intention qu'il fut publié dans ceux de vos Papiers qui circulent davantage, et je l'ai adressé à cet effet en Pensylvanie. Mais dans la crainte qu'il n'y arrive point ou que la personne à qui il est addressé soit dans le fond de cette Province; je vous prie Monsieur, s'il n'est pas encore publié lorsque vous le reçevrez, de vouloir bien vous charger de ce soin.

tion qui avoient assuré à Geneve, si je puis m'exprimer ainsi, la branche la plus florissante de son commerce intérieur et extérieur, celle de l'éducation publique qui attiroit chez nous la jeunesse des Contrées les plus éloignées, et meme de la votre.

Vous le savez Monsieur, Geneve s'étoit acquise dans les lettres et dans les sciences une réputation qui avoit fait oublier sa petitesse, et qui sous ce rapport l'avoit placée de pair avec de Grands Etats; et vous savez aussi que ce brillant essor d'une Peuplade de 30,000 ames étoit le resultat de nos sages institutions pour l'éducation publique. Comme je n'ai l'honneur d'appartenir ni à notre Académie ni à notre College, il m'est permis de vous dire que c'étoit une des Corporations de ce genre la plus morale, [3] la plus modeste, la plus désinteressée, et que ses membres regardoient l'estime publique et les succés de l'Académie comme leur premiere récompense.

J'ai donné a S. E. Mr. S. Adams le 22 du mois passé, tous les détails qui lui sont rélatifs dans un long mémoire Anglois, que je l'ai particulierement prié de Vous communiquer ainsi qu'à S. E. le Géneral Washington. Vous y ve[rre]z Monsieur, qu'indépendamment de quelques [Maitr]es subalternes, cet établissement consiste en [envi]ron 26. Professeurs ou Instituteurs salariés par [l'Eta]t; qu'il n'en est pas un seul d'entr'eux qui ne se trouve aujourdhui dans la classe persécutée, et que le Glaive Révolutionaire se promène également sur leurs tetes, sur leurs propriétés, et sur l'établissement meme qu'ils honoroient. (3.) Voilà

(3) Sans parler ici des hommes distingués que notre Académie avoit formé à coté d'elle, mais qui n'appartenoient point précisément à son corps, et dont vous trouverez la liste p. 147. du premier des deux derniers volumes de mon *tableau des Revolutions de Geneve* que j'eus l'honneur de vous envoyer il y a quatre ans; je vous donnerai seulement un léger indice de ceux que je connois plus particulierement.

Le Principal soit le Président actuel de notre College est Mr. *Mouchon*, le meme qui avoit été choisi par les Encyclopédistes pour faire la table analytique de leur grand ouvrage, et qui par l'universalité de ses connoissances, ainsi que par son esprit methodique, en a fait un chef-d'oeuvre de précision de clarté et d'exactitude.

Mr. *Senebier* notre bibliothecaire profondément verse dans la science bibliographique, traducteur et commentateur distingué de *Spallanzani*, est connu par des ouvrages de phisique et de météorologie. Il est je crois le premier sur notre Continent qui ait fait un Almanach populaire, où il cherchoit à desabuser le peuple de ses prejugés, et à faire descendre la science du sommet des observatoires jusques dans les chaumieres.

La philosophie naturelle et rationelle est enseignée dans ce moment chez nous, par des hommes dont la réputation est deja faite en Europe par des ouvrages et meme par des découvertes importantes, tel que Mr. *Pictet*, que tous les étrangers qui ont assisté chez nous à ses cours, envisagent unanimement comme le Démonstrateur le plus clair et le plus habile en physique; Mr. *Prevost* de l'Académie des Sciences de Berlin et non moins distingué dans la littérature par ses traductions des Tragiques Grecs; et Mr. *Bertrand* le disciple le plus distingué d'Euler. Cette dernière chaire, si elle devenoit vacante, auroit plusieurs candidats, entr'autres Mr. *L'Huillier* qui fut appelé en Pologne par le College d'éducation Nationale pour les Mathématiques qu'au celebre La Grange.

Monsieur, la petite Colonie Académique à la quelle je viens vous solliciter de tendre le bras. Ouvrez lui en Amérique un azyle où ses membres puissent se retrouver ensemble, et continuer sous l'aile de la liberté leur commerce fraternel de lumieres et de services; et j'ose vous garantir que l'Académie de Geneve transportée sur un théatre aussi vaste que le sien étoit rétréci, et animée du besoin d'égaler les savans[4] que l'Amérique a deja formés,[5] prendra sous les auspices de votre gouvernement une émulation et un essor qui augmenteront la réputation dont elle jouit.

Mais vous comprenez Monsieur, qu'on ne peut ébranler un Corps pareil, et le transplanter [en] masse de l'autre coté des mers[6] qu'en donnant d'avance [à ses] membres la certitude d'une existence modeste sa[ns] doute, mais proportionée aux nouveaux devoirs qu'ils seroient apelés à y remplir. C'est dans ce but, que pour refonder notre Université dans quelqu'une de vos Provinces, je propose qu'on lui accorde et lui assure un Revenu annuel de 15,000 Dollars.

Quelque forte que soit cette somme, vous ne la trouverez point exorbitante Monsieur, quand vous considerez 1°. Que pour que la transplantation de nos Instituteurs ait lieu, il faut qu'elle puisse se faire en masse, c'est à dire, que celle des uns doit déterminer en grande partie celle des autres; et que pour cet effet, il seroit indispensable de donner à notre nouvelle Université dès sa renaissance toute l'extension dont elle est susceptible, et que nous pouvons lui assurer par nos propres ressources. 2°. Que dailleurs, il seroit question de fonder outre le salaire des Professeurs, celui des Maitres d'un College préparatoire aux études de l'Université, mais absolument séparé de cette derniere comme à Geneve, ainsi que d'un autre College dévoué exclusivement à la jeunesse qui ne se destineroit pas à l'étude des langues mortes et des sciences (4). Or pour ce dernier College sur tout, il seroit peut etre précieux que tout ce qui tiendroit aux secours d'instruction, y fut absolument gratuit, comme ce l'étoit chez nous.

[Je ne m]e dissimule pas Monsieur, que des diffi[cultés en gr]and nombre se présentent ici. J'espére ce[pendant qu]e je ne serai point apelé à combattre à leur [tete celle] que vous présentez vous meme avec tant de [force et] de sagesse, sur l'inconvenance pour l'Amérique [de hat]er une population, dont elle a sans doute dans son [propre] fond le germe le plus précieux et le plus assuré; [ainsi] que sur le danger d'ac-

(4) Il existe à Zurich, un institut public du meme genre pour l'éducation des enfans de l'autre sexe, et des résultats desquels j'ai entendu parler avec le plus grand éloge. Personne mieux que vous Monsieur, ne peut apprécier la praticabilité, et la convenance d'une pareille Institution en Amérique, l'avantage qu'on pourroit trouver à l'associer à l'autre, et la facilité qu'auroient les maitres de l'un des Colleges à vacquer aux instructions de celui ci.

corder des encouragemens [extra]ordinaires pour obtenir des immigrations d'étrangers [tous] neufs à la liberté tempérée, *who might infuse into your Provincial Legislations their spirit, warp and biass it's direction, and render it a heterogeneous incoherent and distracted mass.* Non Monsieur j'ose me flatter que vous serez le premier à faire sur cette doctrine profondement saine, une exception honorable en faveur d'une Colonie d'Européens Protestans et Républicains, de Republicains Démocrates, mais de Démocrates éclairés sur la liberté politique par de longues discussions, et par le spectacle[7] de ses prospérités de ses écarts et de ses revers; de Démocrates qui n'ont succombé avec elle, que par la foiblesse de leur peuplade, mais non sans avoir également lutté long temps contre les attentats du Despotisme Monarchique, et contre ceux de la licence populaire; enfin de Démocrates qui auront traversé l'Atlantique pour retrouver aupres de Vous, ce qu'ils prisoient le plus, une carrière honorable et laborieuse au sein de la liberté et de la paix.

Une difficulté plus grande mais purement locale, sera peut etre celle de déterminer l'une de vos Provinces à un sacrifice annuel aussi majeur, et cependant si indispensable pour une fondation de cette nature. En pareil cas, je ne désespérerois point de lever cet obstacle et je proposerois à cet effet, que la Province qui voudra accœuillir notre Université, au lieu de lui allouer un pareil revenu, lui appropriat des terres vacantes, pour une valeur dont le capital représentat le revenu que je demande. Des Genevois acheteroient eux memes ces terres dont ils deviendroient les propriétaires, et ils en payeroient le prix à cette Province qui y trouveroit immédiatement la dot de sa nouvelle Université.

Si cet expédient est, comme je le présume, plus facile et plus agréable à l'Amérique, il seroit également tres favorable à l'entreprise; car par ce moyen, notre Colonie Académique pourroit etre accompagnée d'une autre Colonie Agricole et industrieuse: Celle ci en fixant la premiere dans le centre de ses possessions (ce qui seroit sans doute la premiere condition d'un pareil achat) y trouveroit un grand encouragement à cette double Colonisation, puisqu'elles conspireroient au succès l'une de l'autre et en seroient mutuellement le Garant. Peut etre meme seroit ce le seul moyen de faire reussir avec quelqu'éclat la premiere entreprise, [puisque ce serait] un puissant attrait pour les familles attachées [à l'académie] de ne point se séparer des autres familles proprié[taires qui] ne lui appartiennent pas. Aussi est ce dans l'espéra[nce de voir] cette idée accœuillie, que je travaille deja à jetter ou à p[réparer] les fondemens d'une Compagnie d'actionaires qui ver[seroient un] fond de £100,000 St. valeur Angloise dont environ les [deux] tiers seroient appliqués à l'achat des terres, et le rest[e à] presser l'établissement agricole, à fonder les premieres manufactures dont il auroit besoin dans son

enfance, et à pourvoir aux autres avances nécessaires (5). Sans etre sur
d'y réussir, je suis loin d'en désespérer. Mais vous comprenez Monsieur,
que tout dépend ici de l'acquiescement préalable de l'une des Provinces
de l'Union à l'appropriation des terres dont le prix feroit le patrimoine
de l'Université; car les familles qui sont attachées à celle ci et qui font
l'élite de notre population, peuvent seules former le noyau de la Colonie
que j'ai en vue, elles seules peuvent y entrainer la transplantation de
celles des autres familles qui en feront les fonds et qu'il est le plus
précieux d'y associer tant pour l'agriculture que pour le commerce. Peut
etre meme les unes ne s'y determineroient elles point sans les autres,[8] ni
celles ci sans les premieres. Au reste sous ce second rapport, la proposition que j'adresse aux Americains peut leur présenter un double avantage, c'est à dire une double immigration et un double moyen de
prospérité pour la nouvelle Université.

Cependant le projet d'une appropriation de terres qui ouvriroit cette
double perspective ne laissera pas je le sens que de présenter des difficul-
tes de plus d'un genre. En effet, celle de vos Provinces qui ayant des
terres vacantes consentiroit à les appliquer à cet intéressant objet, en
possederoit-elle qui puissent reunir les convenances de situation tant
pour notre Colonie Académique que pour notre Colonie Agricole? Or
comme dans ce plan, ce seroit cette derniere qui feroit l'achat et par
conséquent les fonds, rien de plus essentiel que de combiner ses interets
avec ceux de l'Université, tant pour le choix de l'emplacement que pour
sa salubrité et pour les facilités du transport, comme aussi rélativement
à la fertilité des terres et à leur prix; car les actionaires desireront
naturellement que ce prix soit tel, qu'il leur permette l'acquisition d'un
district considerable, et leur assure un accroissement de valeur propor-
tioné aux sacrifices qu'ils y ajouteront pour hater le succes des deux
etablissemens. Enfin Monsieur, si cette Province ne possede plus de
terres d'une pareille description, mais qu'il y en existat qui y répondis-
sent, et qui apartiendroient à de simples particuliers; cette Province
pourra t-'elle et voudra t-'elle en faire l'échange avec ceux ci, contre
d'autres terres qui seroient encore à sa disposition?

Je ne puis avoir sur cette premiere difficulté que des apperceus bien
vagues, mais je crains bien plus que ce projet ne vous en présente d'une
autre nature et rélatives aux Genevois eux memes. Celle de la langue se
presentera peut etre à leur tête. Ici Monsieur, je vous ferois dabord ob-

(5) Ainsi par exemple en supposant un fond capital de 450,000 Dollars, les actionnaires en
réserveroient 150,000 pour l'avancement de l'entreprise, les premiers défrichemens
&c. &c. Sur les 300,000 qu'ils payeroient à la Province pour les terres, celle ci en appli-
quant 50,000 à l'erection des Colleges &c. &c. et en plaçant le Surplus dans le $\frac{3}{100}$ Congrès
y trouveroit précisément le revenu annuel des 15,000 Dollars, dont il est question.

server que huit de nos Professeurs donnent leurs lecons [9] en latin, or, il ne peut pas y avoir d'inconvenient à l'adapter aux études supérieures, du moins jusqu'à ce qu'ils puissent les donner dans la langue du pays, si on la jugeoit préférable. Quant à nos Professeurs en philosophie, ils entendent l'Anglois, et pourroient peut etre commencer immédiatement leurs Instructions dans cette langue. Au surplus, ce que je traite ici comme une objection pourroit bien etre considéré par vous Monsieur, comme un avantage, puisqu'en effet une Université où domineroit la langue francoise attireroit la jeunesse Américaine au moins pour y passer un an ou deux, et faire marcher de concert l'etude de cette langue avec celle des sciences. Vous remplirez ainsi par rapport au francois ce que Maupertuis avoit imaginé pour abréger l'étude du latin, c'est à dire la formation d'une ville latine. Il y a peu de vos jeunes gens qui apres une préparation et un séjour de quelques mois, ne fussent en état de suivre des cours en francois; et vû vos rapports avec l'Europe, j'imagine meme qu'il ne seroit pas indifférent que cette langue universelle du commerce s'entretint également dans les Colleges préparatoires, c'est à dire qu'une moitié des etudes s'y fit en francois et l'autre en anglois.

La différence de la marche actuelle de notre Académie et de celle de vos Universités, sera bien moins encore une objection, puisque la notre se conformeroit d'entrée au Règlement qui lui seroit prescrit par la Province. Cependant il me semble Monsieur, qu'il seroit vraiment digne d'une tête philosophique et législative comme la votre de préparer à ce sujet un travail où vous pourriez développer des vues toutes neuves, et offrir un second modele à l'Europe.

La difficulté de remplir les places vacantes de ceux de nos professeurs à qui leur grand age ou d'autres considérations interdiroient cette transplantation, ne seroit point non plus un obstacle à redouter; car comme la carriere de notre Académie étoit aussi honorable chez nous que celle de la magistrature, et plus recherchée comme moins orageuse; depuis environ vingt ans, la plus part des jeunes gens de fortune et d'éducation s'y vouoient par préférence, et il en étoit résulté que chaque place vacante etoit attendue et disputée par plusieurs candidats de mérite. En sorte qu'à la faveur de nos jeunes plantons de reserve, nous aurions non seulement de quoi rendre notre nouvel établissement complet, mais encore de quoi remplir honorablement des chaires aux quelles la pauvreté de notre [10] Etat l'avoit empêché d'attacher des salaires, telles que celles d'Astronomie, de Médecine, d'Anatomie, de Chimie, de Botanique, d'histoire, de droit des Nations &c. &c. En vous représentant nos sujets comme capables de les remplir, je sais bien Monsieur, que je m'adresse à un Juge éclairé, et que vis à vis d'un appréciateur tel que vous, mon premier intéret à moi meme est de rester au dessous du vrai plutot que de l'exagérer.

Encore moins seroit il possible d'élever en Amérique des doutes sur la ferme disposition des Genevois à profiter de l'azyle qui leur y seroit ouvert; et qui pourroit[11] entrainer à tout événement quelques travaux et quelques fraix préparatoires. Sans etre autorisé par aucun d'eux à prendre aucune espece d'engagemens rélatifs à cette negotiation puisque sa nature meme m'impose de leur en faire encore pour quelque tems un profond secret; ne me suffira-t-'il pas de vous observer Monsieur, que leurs bourreaux viennent d'entrer dans la carriere de tous les excès de la Révolution francoise, et qu'ils l'ont déja bien dépassée puisque la dixieme partie de notre population male a subi des jugemens plus ou moins severes. Leurs premieres dépouilles une fois partagées et dilapidées, il est impossible ni de calculer où pourra s'arrêter une populace qui pille pour etre soldée, et qui est soldée pour piller, ni d'esperer aucun remède à une Révolution dictée par les Francois, appuyée de la leur, et protegée au besoin de toute leur puissance. Aussi tous mes amis de Geneve m'écrivent'ils que leur patrie est perdue sans espoir de resurrection, et que quelqu'affreux que soit le présent, l'avenir est plus terrible encore. Leur unique et dernier espoir est fondé sur ce que la petitesse de notre territoire ne permettra point aux oppresseurs de retenir par force ceux des opprimés qui voudront fuir en abandonnant des propriétés foncieres qui ne sont deja plus à ceux memes à qui on ne les a point encore confisquées. J'en parle sans aucun ressentiment personel, contre les auteurs de cette Révolution, car ils ne m'ont encore placé sur aucune de leurs listes d'exils, de proscriptions ou de confiscations.[12]

Si donc l'Amérique accœuille mes propositions, la fidélité de ce tableau lui garantit suffisament le succès de cette entreprise si nouvelle dans les annales de l'histoire et de la liberté, et qui n'est pas moins digne ce me semble, d'etre encouragée par vos compatriotes que d'etre tentée et accomplie par les miens, puisque ce sera la liberté prospère et triomphante que tendra les bras à la liberté malheureuse et vaincue. Dailleurs, au milieu de la crise allarmante qui ne menace pas moins en Europe les lettres et les sciences que l'ordre social, il me semble Monsieur, qu'un Philosophe tel que Vous doit saisir avec empressement cette occasion unique peut etre pour planter dans l'Amérique libre ce nouvel étendart de ralliement, autour du quel tous les savans du Continent, menacés soit de la tyrannie des Despotes soit de celle des Révolutions, commenceroient à tourner dès à présent leurs regards avec complaisance, et seroient surs de pouvoir dans tous les tems trouver un refuge, et des occupations analogues à leurs talens.

En communiquant ce projet soit à notre compatriote Mr. Gallatin pour la Pensilvanie, soit à Mr. S. Adams pour la Nouvelle Angleterre, j'avois d'abord pensé que le climat du nord de l'Amérique pouvoit avoir plus de rapports avec le notre: Mais en cherchant à m'éclairer d'avantage et en relisant à cet effet, l'ouvrage précieux que je tiens de vous Monsieur, mes voeux se sont bientot étendus jusques vers le nord de la Virginie. J'ai meme pensé que s'il étoit encore possible de nous y fixer dans un certain degré de voisinage de la nouvelle ville fédérative, (6) ces deux établissemens naissans pourroient se marier admirablement l'un à l'autre; et conspirer à leurs succès réciproques. J'ai cru aussi que si votre Province n'a point encore réalisé toutes les Institutions d'éducation publique qu'elle avoit en contemplation en 1782, la notre pourroit y suppléer tres heureusement: J'ai cru que votre Province étant la plus peuplée de la confederation, et n'ayant point encore multiplié ses moyens d'instruction publique dans le meme rapport que la population qui en est l'objet, elle pourroit etre plus disposée qu'une autre à nous adopter. J'ai cru enfin que son opulence lui faciliteroit davantage le sacrifice nécessaire à cette adoption, et qu'elle y trouveroit plus particulierement qu'une autre de quoi suppléer à l'éducation étrangere et dispendieuse qu'une partie de sa jeunesse vient chercher sur ce Continent.

Mais ce n'est point au nom des intérets de votre patrie, c'est au nom de la mienne, au nom de la liberté vaincue et de l'humanité souffrante, que je viens vous conjurer Monsieur, de donner à ce projet toute l'attention qu'il mérite de votre part, et de le placer particulierement sous les auspices de votre respectable Président au quel je vous prie de le communiquer. J'ai deja invité Mr. Adams à ne point le laisser percer par le canal de vos papiers publics qui pourroient revenir jusqu'à Geneve, et y exciter nos tyrans à mettre de grandes gênes au depart des Professeurs qu'il concerne. C'est par l'extreme importance de ce secret, que je me suis déterminé à ne le confier jusqu'ici qu'à un seul de ces derniers, ce qui étoit d'autant plus nécessaire, qu'il m'annonce que plusieurs d'entr'eux portent leurs regards vers les Universités d'Allemagne qui les accœuilleront sans doute, puisque l'un de nos savans les plus distingués vient d'etre appellé à l'Académie des Sciences de Berlin. Or si cette dispersion avoit lieu, tout l'edifice de mon projet s'evanouiroit, puisque les Professeurs sont la clef de sa voute: Mais pour la prévenir, la personne à qui je me suis confié se bornera à leur déconseiller tout déplacement ou toute dispersion précipitée avant la fin de cette année. Cepen-

(6) S'il n'existoit plus de terres vacantes dans ce voisinage et qu'il y en eut dans le nord des Deux belles vallées qu'arrosent la Shenandoha et le Wapocomo, peut etre cette situation ne seroit elle pas trop eloignée pour notre Université, si elle reunissoit d'ailleurs pour elle tous les autres avantages qu'on doit avoir en vue.

dant ce tems leur paroitra d'autant plus long que leurs souffrances sont extremes, et vous comprendrez Monsieur, du premier coup d'oeil combien la célérité est précieuse dans toute entreprise pareille, dont le succès dépend principalement de l'accéleration, c'est à dire, du degré de rapidité avec le quel on peut la juger et y adhérer. Il faudra y renoncer si mes propositions ne sont pas adoptées dès qu'elles seront jugées avantageuses, et si l'on ne peut pas commencer l'entreprise dès qu'elles auront été adoptées. En un mot Monsieur, si vous l'approuvez, tout dépend évidemment de la possibilité que vous aurez de me donner en réponse non seulement des espérances vagues, mais des assurances positives et une certitude suffisante pour que je puisse tout à la fois, avec une pleine confiance dans notre résurection, l'annoncer à nos Professeurs Résidens dans Geneve à fin qu'ils puissent passer sur terres de Suisse, avant que le projet éclate; fonder la Compagnie des Actionaires pour qu'ils vous envoyent des agens qui mettent la derniere main au traité sur l'achat des terres, et sur leur choix; enfin pour que je puisse annoncer hautement alors à tous mes infortunés concitoyens, qu'une nouvelle Geneve se prépare pour eux dans l'Amérique libre, qu'une carriere nouvelle, et non moins laborieuse sans doute, mais plus brillante ou du moins plus sure, s'y ouvre au déployement de toutes leurs facultés; et qu'ils auront l'avantage inappréciable, d'y perpétuer cette meme Académie qui avoit constamment versé tant de prospérités sur leur ancienne patrie et sur ses enfans. J'ai l'honneur d'etre avec respect Monsieur, Votre tres humble & tres obeissant Serviteur

F D'IVERNOIS

P.S. Mon adresse est *chez Mr. Chauvet Kensington near London.* Veuillez Monsieur dans la réponse que j'attendrai de vous, avec tant d'impatience, me faire passer si vous adoptez ce projet, tous les éclaircissemens quelconques qui peuvent y avoir rapport; car vû la distance où nous sommes l'un de l'autre, il me sera impossible d'en obtenir de nouveaux avant d'etre appellé à mettre sérieusement la main à l'œuvre depuis le poste intermédiaire où je me trouve ici.

Si notre projet éprouvoit en Virginie des difficultés imprévues et insurmontables, et qu'elles fussent de nature à ne point se présenter également en Maryland, ne seroit il pas possible que cette Province nous adoptat aux conditions proposées? Dans cette double supposition, vous me permettrez sans doute Monsieur, de compter avec une égale confiance sur toute votre protection auprès de cette derniere Province où je ne connois personne.

Dupl (DLC); in a clerk's hand, signed and with corrections by D'Ivernois; par- tially torn, with missing words supplied in brackets from Dft; at head of text in D'Ivernois's hand: *"Duplicata du No 1r"*; at foot of first page: "A Monsieur Jefferson." Dft (BPUG: D'Ivernois Papers); in D'Ivernois's hand, with some revisions in an unidentified hand; undated and unsigned, with abbreviated complimentary close; containing numerous variations and emendations, only the most important being noted below; endorsed: "A Mr Jefferson No 1 le 5e 7bre 1794 partie le 9 pr Baltimore by the Indian Chief." Tr (NHi: Gallatin Papers); with variations, only the most important being noted below, and with those common to the Dft possibly reflecting readings in the missing RC; at head of text in D'Ivernois's hand: "Copie d'une lettre adressée à Mr Jefferson le 5 7bre 1794"; enclosed in D'Ivernois to Gallatin, 5 Sep. 1794 (same). Recorded in SJL as received 19 Nov. 1794. Dupl enclosed in D'Ivernois to TJ, 16 Sep. 1794; TJ probably forwarded it to Wilson Cary Nicholas, 23 Nov. 1794.

François (later Sir Francis) D'Ivernois (1757-1842), a Genevan printer, lawyer, historian, and propagandist against revolutionary France, appealed in this and subsequent letters to TJ, whom he had met in Paris seven years earlier, for support of his ambitious plan for transplanting the faculty of the Academy of Geneva to America in tandem with a small settlement of Genevan exiles. Aware of the hopes TJ had expressed in his *Notes on the State of Virginia* for transforming the state's educational system, D'Ivernois had conceived the scheme in London to rescue the best of Genevan culture from what he perceived as the catastrophic effects of the French-inspired revolution that shook the small city-state between 1792 and 1794. Born into a burgher family, which made him one of the small minority of citizens eligible to exercise full political rights in the city, D'Ivernois was educated at the College and Academy of Geneva, the venerable institution founded by John Calvin. In 1780 he journeyed to Paris seeking French support for the Burgher party's aspirations for political reform in Geneva; instead the French supported the 1782 aristocratic counterrevolution in Geneva, which deprived D'Ivernois of his citizenship, turned him against France, and drove him to take refuge in England. There he persuaded the Shelburne

ministry to support his plan for creating a Genevan settlement in Ireland, with the settlers to be recruited in large part from among the ranks of Geneva's celebrated clock and watchmakers, one of the inducements to settlement being the establishment of an Irish college along the lines of the Academy of Geneva. This plan was never realized, but it earned D'Ivernois a pension from the British government starting in 1789. During the 1780s D'Ivernois divided his time between England and the continent, working as a publicist, writing a history of Geneva's 18th-century revolutions, and serving as a tutor for prominent British families. In 1790, with the restoration of his citizenship during a period of political liberalization, D'Ivernois went back to Geneva, only to return to England in 1793 to begin 21 years of exile after the rise to power of a party of pro-French radical Genevan revolutionaries, who condemned him to death *in absentia* in September 1794 for abandoning his native city and engaging in counterrevolutionary activities against France and its Genevan allies. Convinced that the liberties of Europe would never be secure unless France was restricted to its prerevolutionary borders and the Bourbons were restored to the throne, D'Ivernois became one of the most influential English-based counterrevolutionary pamphleteers during the era of the French Revolution and Napoleon, unflagging in his support of the war policies of British ministries from Pitt to Liverpool and as an intermediary between the British government and various European powers. In gratitude for his efforts, George III made D'Ivernois a knight bachelor in 1796. After the collapse of the Napoleonic empire, D'Ivernois returned to Geneva for good in 1814, when he surrendered his pension, and served the city as a deputy to the Congress of Vienna as well as in other capacities (Karmin, *D'Ivernois*, passim).

As correspondence in this volume with D'Ivernois and others indicates, the Genevan's proposal to relocate the Academy of Geneva failed to attract any significant support beyond an initial positive response from TJ, who quickly recognized how well D'Ivernois's plan comported with his own preferences for educational reform in Virginia. His inquiry in the Virginia legislature failed to elicit any interest, however, and he so advised D'Ivernois in February 1795. The discouraging response he received from the President the following month convinced him of the futility of any further efforts on behalf of D'Ivernois's project, and he neither informed the Genevan exile of Washington's reaction nor corresponded with him again. D'Ivernois's simultaneous overtures to Albert Gallatin, his former Geneva schoolmate and future Republican leader and Secretary of the Treasury, and to Vice-President John Adams, whom he sometimes confused with Samuel Adams, yielded nothing beyond the publication in the United States of two of his letters condemning the recent upheaval in Geneva (*Notes*, ed. Peden, 146-9; D'Ivernois to John Adams, 22, 30 Aug., 4 Oct., 11 Nov. 1794, 24 Feb., 28 Mch. 1795, MHi: Adams Papers; D'Ivernois to Gallatin, 22 Aug., 5, 23 Sep., 4 Oct. 1794, 5, 12, 16 Mch. 1795, NHi: Gallatin Papers; and note to enclosure below).

s. ADAMS: that is, John Adams. UN LONG MÉMOIRE ANGLOIS: see Enclosure No. 2 listed at John Adams to TJ, 21 Nov. 1794. TABLEAU DES REVOLUTIONS DE GENEVE: D'Ivernois, *Tableau historique et politique des deux dernières révolutions de Genève*, 2 vols. (London, 1789). There is no evidence that TJ ever received this work. WHO MIGHT INFUSE: an almost verbatim quotation from *Notes*, ed. Peden, 85. INSTITUTIONS . . . EN CONTEMPLATION EN 1782: a reference to TJ's discussion of his 1779 Bill for the More General Diffusion of Knowledge in same, 146-9. As TJ explained in the preface, he finished writing this book in the winter of 1782. LA PERSONNE to whom D'Ivernois had confided his plan for transplanting the Academy of Geneva to America was Marc Auguste Pictet (Karmin, *D'Ivernois*, 278-9; Pictet to TJ, 1 Jan, 1795, and note). David CHAUVET was a former Burgher

party leader in Geneva who had been driven into exile in London by the aristocratic counterrevolution of 1782 (Karmin, *D'Ivernois*, 97n, 105, 166).

[1] In Dft and Tr the remainder of the sentence first read "dont les ennemis la liberté se saisissent deja comme d'un crime contr'elle."

[2] Remainder of this sentence and next sentence through "plusieurs" interlined in Dft in place of "pour la recouvrer il ne reste plus à ses sectateurs que de fuir un sejour qui la ferait presque haïr si elle pouvait l'etre; que pour en jouir de nouveau ⟨plusieurs⟩ l'élite de mes compatriotes ⟨fourn⟩ est apellée à de grands sacrifices, et que plusieurs." Tr has virtually identical revision.

[3] The Tr reads "la plus morale, la plus éclairée, la plus modeste, la plus unie."

[4] Word interlined in Tr in place of "⟨hommes celebres⟩ philosophes."

[5] Tr here adds "et de justifier la confiance qu'on lui auroit temoignée," which D'Ivernois interlined in Dft for insertion.

[6] Tr: "transporter si loin."

[7] Preceding two words interlined in Dft in place of "l'exemple." Tr reads "l'impression."

[8] Remainder of sentence canceled in Dft and omitted in Tr.

[9] Word interlined in different ink in Dft in place of "lectures," the word used in Tr.

[10] In Dft D'Ivernois here canceled "petit," but the word is retained in Tr.

[11] Dft and Tr here add "peut etre."

[12] Tr first read "Vous pouvez m'en croire, Monsieur, d'autant mieux sur le tableau que je vous Addresse de notre revolution, que par une espece de miracle, ses auteurs n'ont attenté ni à ma personne ni à mes biens" and was then altered to read as above except for one minor variation.

François D'Ivernois's First Letter
on the Genevan Revolution

Sir   Augt: 22d: [1794]

The interest you have taken in the history of the interesting Republic of Geneva has been such, that I should be wanting in not giving you the mournful recital of it's expiring convulsions. Such a detail will be void neither of interest nor utility to your prudent Countrymen: May they reflect on it with attention, and learn by the disastrous example of the most Democratic State that exists on the Continent of Europe, the extreme danger of foreign influence; and above all, how rapid and inevitable it is, to transgress the feeble interval which seperates the abuse of liberty from its ruin!

You know Sir, that after the long dissensions, which had chiefly related, 1st: To the extension of the right of election assigned to the body of the People, 2dly: To the degree of amovobility or right of removal to which its Magistrates were Subject, and 3dly: to the influence, which the engagement the three neighbouring Powers had entered into as guarantees, might have in our internal legislation, the popular party was at last overwhelmed at Geneva in 1782 by the irresistible power of the Count de Vergennes. Strange as it may appear to you, it is notorious that that Minister employed much greater pains and application, in the destruction of Liberty in Geneva, than he displayed at the same time to insure its triumph in America; and as all his secret intrigues failed in that pursuit, he did not obtain his end, but by openly marching against Geneva, some of those French battalions which had fought under America colours. His troops banished the principal Men who had defended the rights of the People and established on the ruins of our fundamental Constitution, not precisely an hereditary Aristocracy, but a Government armed with sufficient force to reign in opposition to the decided and well known will of the Majority of the Citizens of Geneva.

The existence of such a Government without doubt depended for its continuance on that of the despot who had imposed it. Scarce had the Count de Vergennes expired, when with one accord and in the midst of universal joy, all parties united to overthrow the edifice of Government which his dictates had erected. Our fundamental Constitution was reestablished on all its Republican basis; it's defenders were recalled and reinstated; and by an almost unanimous vote, every incident of the long litigation which had arisen for a century past betwixt the Assembly of the People and the Administrative bodies were definitively adjudged in favour of the former.

This happy resurrection of liberty commenced in 1789, and consolidated in 1791 presents the most prosperous and brilliant period of our Republic. Every heart was reconciled, a harmony of principles reigned amongst us, trade and our manufactures flourished, and our Academy, that admirable establishment of the celebrated Calvin, Our Academy, that nourishing vein of all our prosperity past and present, far from having interfered in, or suffered by the public dissensions, was solely devoted in directing the Genevese in their rapid advances towards the heights of science. So great have been its happy effects, that since the commencement of the present Century, our population has been doubled, the fortunes of individuals have increased in an inconceivable ratio, and foreigners never failed to visit and to admire the prodigies of liberty and public education in a small state of 30,000 Souls, in which the present generation had produced at once a greater number of men distinguished in the career of letters and of Science, than the three kingdoms of the North Europe taken together.

Scarcely can we seize the recollection of this period, so transient has it been; for scarcely had our liberties escaped the ravages of the despotic Boreas which had blown from France, and had for some years razed them to the ground, than a new destructive hurricane blowing from the same quarter, but at this time assuming the sacred name of Liberty, comes to tear them up by the roots for ever, and with them all religion, and every Republican virtue, which had so eminently distinguished Geneva.

Thus it was, that whilst the French Republic was preparing to attack Savoy, certain advices reached us from Paris, that its General had secret orders against Geneva. This was the period when the Brissotin party predominated in the Convention; which, as it is well known, had formed the project of encircling the French Republic with a line of Republics exactly modelled after its own government. Even Savoy was then to have been included in this vast plan.

We apprized the Swiss our Allies of the dangers which threatned us. They kept themselves ready to participate them, and there was no time to lose; for the day after Genl: Montesquiou had penetrated into Savoy, he advanced in force to declare war against us. His orders, the originals of which I have since seen, were to enter Geneva, *to take from thence 20,000 Muskets of which France stood in need, and to make that place one of its Bulwarks.*

The brave Helvetians arrived within our walls, at the same moment that the French General was at our gates. I was one of the Deputies, who were sent to demand of him the motives of the threatning warlike preparations which were displayed around us. He announced to us that we had committed an insult on the French Republic, by calling in the assistance of the Swiss; that we were, (perhaps without being aware of it,) in an actual coalition with the enemies of France, which besides accused our Government of ill will, and alledged as a proof of it, the passage and hospitality we had granted to some Emigrants.

We replied, that distrust was the sole safeguard of the weak against the strong; that with respect to the demand of assistance from the Swiss our Confederates, our little Republic had never neglected that measure from simple precaution whenever Savoy became the theatre of war; that we were even engaged to it by treaties guaranteed by France itself, and at which the despotic Louis XIV never took umbrage.

In proof of the perfect innocence of the intentions of our Government in relation to France, we observed to him 1st: That we were till then the first and only Independent State which had formerly recognized the French Republic. 2dly: That since its revolution, we had generously opened our corn granaries in favour of a neighbouring district of France threatned like ourselves with a famine. 3dly: That in pursuance of the pressing requisitions of the same district, exposed to a kind of Counter Revolution we had consented to open our arsenals and to lend it arms which it has not yet restored according to its promises and which on the contrary were then preparing to be turned against ourselves.

The evident justice of our cause, however would have no ways saved us, had it not been for the influence of the worthy General, before whom we pleaded it, and who strongly supported it to his Constituents by urging the extreme gratuitous and inevitable danger such a measure would incur of having all Switzerland in arms to contend with before so useless and dishonourable a quarrel of a Giant against a Dwarf could be terminated.

He got his orders of opening the trenches revoked, and obtained that of negotiating pacifically with us. The result was an honorable and equitable treaty, in which it was stipulated; that the misunderstandings on both sides having been happily removed by amicable explanations, the French Republic engaged to withdraw it's army from the neighbourhood of Geneva in consideration that the Genevese should dismiss their Swiss garrison. It promised amongst other things the full execution of our ancient treaties with the Kings of France. This treaty was reciprocally signed and concluded, after the French Plenipotentiary having on his part exhibited to us his full powers in due form.

We were hastening to execute it by beginning to send back the Swiss, when we learnt that the French Minister refused to ratify it, but on condition of inserting new clauses; for which purpose Mr. Genet* was sent to Geneva. What was our surprize when after having adhered to all these new clauses, we learnt that the Convention refused likewise to ratify this second treaty, and that in order to colour this violation of the laws of Nations, it launched a decree of accusation against Genl: Montesquiou who had negotiated and concluded it?

The convention imperiously exacted of us that we should forthwith send back the Swiss without conditions. In fact there was no longer time to obtain any; for on the faith of this treaty our faithful Allies had almost all quitted the Town. Geneva was no longer in a state of defence, and our obedience to this law from France being forced by the actual state of things it seemed that we had not at least any further dangers to apprehend from that quarter.

But Genl: Montesquiou, whom I had the happiness of saving from the daggers which awaited him at Paris, discovered a danger to us much more formidable even than the preceding one. The Convention said he, is resolved at all hazards to operate a political Revolution amongst you, after its own principles. It only remains for you to model yourselves to it by your own act, or to prepare to defend yourselves against it either by open war, or by internal intrigues by either of which you will infallibly be overwhelmed.

Nothing appeared more difficult than to conceive in what we could democratize ourselves more to please France, as by our Laws the Assembly of the people exercised collectively of itself all the Sovereign Powers which the French by their number had been obliged to intrust to their Representatives in Convention.

However the French Convention had discovered the only weak side, by which it could disorganize us; for having learnt that our Constitution admitted in the Sovereign Council only those Genevese who had acquired by themselves or their ancestors the title of *Citizens*, it loudly accused it of being a mere hereditary and aristocratical Council. This was so far from being the case, that it included more than two thirds of the Genevese heads of families, and that in order to attach and associate the rest to it, our late popular Laws had successively reduced the price of their admission to the moderate sum of about 27 Dollars to be applied to the Hospitals; a sum that seemed to be the lowest proof of personal independence, that can be required not only of an Elector, but of one born a member of a Sovereign legislative Council.

This last class called simply *Natives* had displayed in general the greatest alacrity and earnestness for the defence of the Republic. At the approach of the

* The same who has since been in America, and who if he still remains there, will no doubt testify the truth of the above relation.

French Army, all parties were united as by a stroke of Electricity, and, if we were to except about 50 Individuals citizens and natives, who had cowardly deserted our threatned ramparts, alledging that it was not permitted for the friends of liberty to fight against the French, Geneva at this moment of danger presented but one heart, one soul, one family. But as soon as the Class of Natives had learnt by the very debates of the French Convention that it no longer directed its views to the seizure of Geneva, but simply to extend to all its inhabitants the equality of the Rights of Man, they commenced openly to aspire to it, and found leading men amongst the citizens, who associated themselves to support this pretension, either with the view to act a conspicuous part, or carried away by the seducing effect of the intoxicating theory which the doctrine of extreme equality inspires. In a short time the French officers and Soldiers who were still at our gates, gave them open encouragement, and even offered them in secret their aid for the triumph of that Cause. Here Sir, commences, the first symptom of that Revolutionary crisis, which in less than two years has plunged Geneva first of all into the convulsions of anarchy, and finally into all the crimes which popular tyranny can invent. May I request you to lend all your attention, whilst I unravel this bloody clue.

Alarmed at the new peril, which inevitably threatned the Constitution of Geneva, or its Independence, Our administration could devise no other means to preserve itself from it but by proclaiming the admission of all the Genevese without distinction into the Sovereign legislative Body. But scarcely had the Great and Little councils adhered to the decree which was to be sanctioned a few days after by the Sovereign assembly of the Citizens, than some french emissaries represented to the Natives how unworthy it would be for them to receive as a favour the equality of political rights; that that equality was their birth right; and that it was a further outrage offered to it, in granting it to them through the medium of Constitutional forms.

The progress of this strange doctrine was such that the new faction refused indeed the favour which the assembly of the People was on the point of insuring to it for ever: at the same time, determined to carry it by force, they further demanded in order to assure their conquest: 1st: To fill up all the places of the Administration whatever with their partizans; 2dly: That there be forthwith an election of a National Convention with a view to finish the Democratizing of our constitution on this new principle.

Those who knew that this disorganizing party formed at that moment only the fourth part of our population, have severely blamed us for not having dissolved it by open force. Considerations however for our internal safety of the most imperious nature forbade it. The french Army still surrounded us, and waited but for the signal of the slightest disturbance to enter within our walls, where they had many an emissary and partizan.

In order to save our Independence from this imminent danger, the Majority had the Patriotism of yielding to the Minority. The little and great Councils voluntarily resigned all their places to the leading people of the opposite party, to those even who had fled during the siege, and whilst they thus gave up everything, they required no other promise but that of maintaining public order and not to deliver us up to France.* As there was no resistance, so neither was

---

* The latter placed so great a consideration on this that [one] of the chief men of the Convention addressed himself to the former in these terms "And if Geneva persists in not giving herself to us, we must beseech Geneva to permit us to give ourselves to her."

there any shock; and thus it was that in an instant, and only a few weeks after the arrival of the French army at our gates, the most lawful Constitution and Administration that Existed on this Continent was overthrown, without however this army having obtained the slightest pretext to introduce itself either by accord or by force within our walls.

Here commences the history of that first usurped administration, which lasted but about Twenty months, and which might in many respects be compared to the first party which triumphed after the French Revolution, since it appears certain that its intention in producing a Revolution by the Populace was founded in the hope of being able to stop it at its will and to interdict efficaciously at once any further excesses. It is to be allowed that the greater part of its members were men of some property, and of some education, and that they did what depended on them to maintain our Independence abroad and order within.

It is equally true that they have had to contend with three considerable obstacles, namely; 1st: Against the Successors of the Brissotins, who after having granted them the fraternal kiss, reproached them with having made but a half Revolution and created a multitude of impediments for the transportation of the articles of subsistence for our town:† whilst, instead of the good offices which the Genevese expected as having a right to them on the title of Revolutionists, they were even treated with much less consideration than the rest of Switzerland, who had made themselves respected by remaining solidly at the anchor of their ancient constitutions. 2dly: Against the ruin of trade and of private fortunes almost totally swallowed up in the funds of France; and against the annihilation of the public finances, rapidly exhausted by the enormous salaries which the new members of this government required, doubly as expensive as the former. 3dly: Against a new faction composed of the dregs of their own party, not numerous it is true, but who under the name of *Marseillois* and *Montagnards*, and having the French resident evidently at their head, desired nothing less than the downfall of all religion, preached the most extreme principles of the French, and seemed to aspire to imitate them in every thing or to deliver themselves up to them.

The vanquished party far from adding to these fatal obstacles recollecting that the new Administration had rallied all it's strength around our Independence, threw a veil over its past faults, and those which ignorance or the difficulties of the times made it commit. More than once they assisted it with their councils, and some of the deposed Magistrates consented to sit in the National Convention; which in order to please the French, was not able to invent any other means than to appropiate a part of the Executive power to the Legislative body of the People. In a word; the mass of citizens, without renouncing, it is true, their opinions on the political order, and without recognizing or contesting the legality of the title of this Government, shewed themselves ready on every occasion to stand by it with all their force to aid it in resisting with vigour the difficulties from without and the Agitators within. As these last appeared to be in the utmost poverty, with a view to shelter them from its consequences, and

† Thus for instance it was that the french, in opposition to the letter of the most positive treaties, and in order to add to the dreadful scarcity of articles of Subsistance the French Republic constantly refused under various pretexts the passage of the produce of our little territory invironed by that of France.

that of the state of idleness to which the sudden decline of our trade of watch making exposed them, the rich subscribed a considerable capital to support the prosecution of that manufacture untill some market was opened for its articles. Owing to such noble sacrifices both of passion and of interest Geneva seemed to navigate with tranquillity though so close to the French tempest, and still to be sheltered from the whirlwind, whose ravages she heard on every side. Even Switzerland astonished at this Revolutionary miracle of a first disorganization, which seemed to have been stopped in its source, Switzerland yielding at last to the generous sollicitations of the deposed Magistrates had just consented to resume its confederative relations, which had been suspended for 18 months, with the Government which had so violently dispossessed them. In short the latter seemed to gain both experience and strength from time and circumstances, and most of those citizens who had dreaded their excesses and had absented themselves, daily returned under the solemn promise of finding protection and security.

A security both perfidious and deceitful! The thunder of the French Revolution howled over Geneva without their doubting it. A Genevese Deputy at Paris, and one who by his mission was in the habit of assiduously seeing the most important leaders of the Jacobins, nourished in their bosom for more than a year, and from that time exercised in the profound theory of insurrections, had just returned to Geneva to put their lessons into practice, and to concert measures with the resident of France,* Counsellor Bousquet such is his name, proposed to himself five important points for his imitation. 1st: To deprive the administration, to which however he was associated, of the confidence of the populace, by accusing it of holding a secret connivance with the rich, or at least cowardly temporizing with them. 2dly: To suspend its powers as well as those of the assembly of the people, in order to invest a certain number of his armed partizans with them under the name of Revolutionary Government. 3dly: To cement this 2d: revolution by erecting a tribunal that should imbrue its hands in blood in the name of liberty, in order that thereby the breach should be irreparable, and that there should be no longer means for his associates to stop without danger in this new career. 4ly: To spread terror as the order of the Day, in every class of the people, that by this means the smaller number might domineer with impunity over the greater, and that the latter might esteem themselves happy to be able to purchase their lives at the price of their properties, which would furnish, a constant pay for the Revolutionists. 5thly. In short the destruction of religious worship.

This horrible edifice was erected in the course of one night. In order to succeed in such a Conspiracy, it was necessary to anticipate the period, when a proposition of new contributions on the rich was to be submitted to the assembly of the People, contributions which, were they accepted as was hardly doubted, might have removed every pretence of clamour against the rich, and restore that force to the Administration, which it risked to loose by the rapid annihilation of the public finances.

Then it was that Counsellor Bousquet began under hand to spread amongst the populace, that there were many other means of relieving the poor besides that of exempting them from all taxes; that for too long a time the rich had

---

* The Abbi Soulavie known since the Revolution by an obscene work entitled "The memoirs of the Duke of Richelieu."

devoured their subsistence or at least insulted their miseries by their enjoyments; and that in having destroyed the Aristocracy of Laws, it was but a childish exploit, unless they extirpated at the same time that of riches and morals. Then from fear that the acceptation of the new taxes might disconcert his plot, he chose the 18th: of July for its execution, the eve of the very day when they were to have been submitted to the decision of the assembly of the people and sanctioned by it. Every thing was organized for the insurrection, the parts allotted, the functions assigned, and the victims marked out; it was in the middle of the night that his brave associates flew to arms, made themselves masters of the Cannon, and proceeded to disarm in the midst of their slumbers, those citizens whose courage and despair they dreaded the most. In order at the same instant to confound the administration, they arrested the two principal Syndics leaders of the preceding Revolution and thus succeeded in preventing that Administration from taking any steps to ward off the blow that was meditated. They involved in it all the Magistrates deposed in 1792 and more particularly ransacked the houses of those who were supposed to have plate or money in their possession, and out of which they have since fixed a pay of about half a Dollar a day to each of the Janissaries of this expedition. Great care was taken at the same time to seize with these prisoners many obscure and poor citizens; for it was highly important at once to chill the courage of every one, and to strike consternation throughout every class. This plot, which was meditated in the profoundest secrecy, was thus openly executed in the course of a few hours and without resistance by a handful of villains, to whom their success associated immediately the morning after, the rest of the populace, every weak and cowardly spirit—and even a few persons of character who still flattered themselves with the hopes of stopping these crimes under the air of co-operating with them.

Counsellor Bousquet assembled them under arms, to honour them with the name of *Revolutionary Nation.* Then in the name of liberty and patriotism, he observed to them that it was to the salutary energy of the great measures of severity that the French owed their successes both abroad and at home: that the severity of these measures was constantly allied with justice and morality, and that it was highly expedient to commence the reign of virtue and of the Revolution by great examples. In consequence of which, the Administration was suspended, and provisionally reimplaced by a Revolutionary Tribunal, of which he got himself proclaimed President, and which was to judge those immediately who were imprisoned.

The number of these increased every moment, and at last amounted to between 5 and 600, thanks to the orders of the French Resident, who had those unfortunate Genevese delivered up, who had fled for refuge to the territory of France. Amongst these prisoners were the greater part of the Professors of our Academy whose moderate salaries are no doubt to be applied to their nefarious purposes; all the Masters of our College, and nearly without exception every one of our respectable Clergy, that Clergy on whom Geneva had so much right to pride itself as being of any protestant Clergy the most enlightened; the most tolerant,* the most united and the most religious of Europe. Fearful of letting a single one of these venerable ministers escape, the furious Revolutionists pur-

---

* It was neither it's luxury nor it's wealth, that could have excited the rage and envy of the Revolutionists.

sued them in arms into the very pulpits of the Churches, where in spite of all dangers, these heroes of religion had the intrepidity of attending to fulfill their appointed functions, in invoking the God of peace in behalf of their distracted country.

The Revolutionary Tribunal eager to enter on it's functions chose for its first victims, the ancient Syndic Caylar, who had displayed the greatest firmness in the defence of our fundamental laws, and my worthy friend the former Atty: General Prevost whose only crime in their sight was his having succeeded in negotiating with me the treaty which saved us two years ago from the first outrages of the arms of France. In two sittings held in the midst of howlings from the galleries, and without any direct accusation they were condemned as liberticides to death, with five others, by these new judges taken from the dregs of the people, who after having invoked the Supreme being, proceeded to deliver this sentence amidst the basest buffooneries.

The Revolutionary nation had however reserved to itself the right of appeal for every sentence of death, and consequently was convoked for that purpose. But although under the pretext of purifying it, half of the assembly of the People was excluded, a great majority of votes was for granting the lives to the chief of the devoted victims. The Conspirators, at the appearance of this first act of repentance and remorse, violently complained of false patriots having introduced themselves amongst them, and openly threatned to go and put to the sword every prisoner indistinctly, if their request of blood was not immediately acceded to. The Revolutionary Tribunal waited only this pretence to raise itself above the decision of the Majority of its own party,* and it instantly sent the seven victims to undergo their sentence, who had defended themselves with dignity, and died with all the courage that religion, innocence and virtue inspire.* The Swiss Governments chilled with horror at these transactions discontinued all communication with this second Nineveh; and those of their

---

*On the succeeding day, it stuck up a kind of an apology, which is nothing else than the manifesto of this new war, and which is a master piece of hypocrisy and falsehood. The Aristocrats that is to say the rich, are therein accused, of not having *renounced their pretensions nor abjured their ancient errors*, of not having *fraternized with the Revolutionists in their civic festivals, of longing after a French Counter Revolution, which necessarily would produce one at Geneva; of having made vows in favour of the rebels of Lyons*, and what is more of having entertained *an idea of rejecting the new taxes*. It therein discovers without disguise the thread of the conspiracy, by attributing the *unhappy prejudices* of the French against Geneva, to this *that the former had thought it right to distrust a people who boasted of having effected the triumph of the principles of liberty and equality and at the same time harboured a nest of incorrigible Aristocrats at peace in their very bosom*. In short this manifesto invoked the *fraternity* of the Revolutionary nation and conjured them *to be on their guard against the weakness of clemency, to put an end to the reign of impunity, to purify the atmosphere of their country of its perverse children, and to incapacitate them for ever from revolting against it. On its part the tribunal engaged, To Revolutionize both principals and morals, to regenerate the public mind; in short to proceed without delay to institute proper establishments to prevent the wants of the people, to form true citizens, and to prepare the happiness of all, &* !!!
* The only one amongst them who pronounced a few words was the Syndic Caylar. I should die *contented*, cried he, *did I believe that my Death would restore peace and liberty to my fellow citizens*. It was even Genevese of the faction of the Marseillois who disputed the honour of being their executioners, and of shooting them. It may be easily conceived that the effects of these unfortunate men were declared to be confiscated to the profit of the Revolution.

misled citizens, who had been worked upon by the same emissaries as ourselves, declared that they had received in time a lesson from which they knew how to profit.

However although the butcherers of Geneva have already set at liberty a hundred prisoners, whose great numbers embarrassed them they nevertheless continue in the career of their crimes; and as crimes lead on to crimes, and blood to blood, it is not to be doubted but more will be spilt for some time to come, since they have already prohibited the wearing of mourning. If they appear at this moment to stop the effusion of blood, it is only with a view to give the miserable inhabitants of Geneva time to accustom themselves to it; and the better to strip those who consent to save their lives by confessing the deposits of their effects. To the purpose of imitating the French, who began with confiscating the property of those emigrants who fought against their Country; they have begun their part with pronouncing the confiscation against those Genevese, who have succeeded in flying from their butchery. At the same time they have interdicted divine worship at least temporarily; and our churches are no longer open but for baptism.

Geneva is entirely another town, which stands on the same spot as the former: the spectacle it presents is that of crimes, pillage and desolation. Thus you see however, Sir, what the first step towards the Revolutionary Doctrine has been able to effect in so short a time, with a people, who in the midst of the most active civil dissensions had untill then always preserved as in a sacred deposit, a horror at the effusion of human blood, and a respect for property! In a word Geneva is lost beyond resource and without hope of being restored to liberty and morality. For supposing even that the majority of its inhabitants being disarmed should succeed by a noble effort of despair in delivering themselves from the yoke of these Cannibals, yet the french soldiery are still at our gates to protect and revenge them, and to devote us to the fate of Lyons.

It is true that the leaders of this ferocious faction still possess their determination of preserving Geneva independent of France. Undoubtedly it is more convenient for them to wage war against their disarmed countrymen, and to strip them of their property, than to go and fight battles on the Rhine or beyond the Pyrenees; but when they shall have plundered everything, and dilapidated their spoils, nothing will remain for them, but to sell themselves to France.

Happen what may Geneva no longer deserves liberty, it has been branded and dishonoured there; for the *present generation*, it can only be a residence of hatred and vengeance.

If this afflicting narration should appear long to you Sir, how much more so must it not have appeared to him who is a Genevese, and who has had the courage to trace it out to you? I know not even that I should have had the strength to have completed it, were it not for a pressing motive which animates me. I have just learnt that a number of my countrymen, have taken the courageous resolution of visiting America in quest of peace and liberty which have been banished from their native country; and considering the smallness of our territory, it will be impracticable to hinder those from flying, who dread not to abandon to the plunderers their landed property. Besides many of them possess a part of their fortunes in foreign trade, as in the funds of England and in those of America.

I come, Sir, in the name of suffering humanity and persecuted liberty, to conjure you to aid these unfortunate persons with your councils and support, and to recommend them to the generous hospitality of your fellow citizens. I dare guarantee to you that those of mine who are going to associate themselves to them, will carry with them in return for the asylum they shall receive, every thing that is valued as most estimable amongst you: Republican morals, the love of enlightened liberty, the sacred habits of equality in the sight of the Law, those of industry, respect for religion, and above all things the dreadful experience of the numerous evils which are involved by foreign influence and the first violation of the constitutional and fundamental laws of liberty. I am Sir yours &c

P.S. Letters from Geneva of the 3d: instant just inform us that the perpetration of these horrors is prolonged with impunity and with circumstances the most aggravating. About 20 Absent families of opulence have been condemned in the confiscation of their property, and also nearly an equal number of those who were imprisoned. Several of our most respectable Divines after having their houses pillaged, have been deposed from their functions, and condemned to imprisonments of greater or less duration. Many citizens have been banished. The two *Cramer* Professors have been sentenced to an imprisonment of one year in their own houses. But what is most alarming Two of the most respectable members of the ancient magistracy, M. M. Fatio and Naville Gallatin whom the Revolutionary Tribunal had condemned only to banishment and the confiscation of their estates, have been snatched from the prisons by its atrocious satellites, who conducted them to the place of execution, where they shot them!!! We have too much reason but to expect the most terrifying news.

Other letters from Geneva dated the 10th: Inst: inform us further that two fresh victims have been sacrificed to the sanguinary fury of the Revolutionists, and that some violent misunderstandings have already arisen between their leaders and the French Resident; The Reason of this is not as yet fully ascertained; but it is known that the former have gone so far as to address severe complaints against him to the committee of public safety at Paris.

Subsequent letters from the Pays de Vaud mention that a number of respectable citizens of Geneva daily arrive there, having been banished and previously plundered of every thing; that they are received with open arms; and that the unfortunate Genevese have no longer but one ray of hope remaining to them, that the example of the fall of Robespierre will force those who had aspired to follow his steps at Geneva on the very eve of his catastrophe at Paris to some serious reflections, and some retrieving measures.

The Government of Berne has just published the following Proclamation in all the Churches of its canton, which completes at the same time that it verifies the dreadful picture which I have endeavoured to describe.

"Public notoriety has informed you of the deplorable scenes, which have plunged the City of Geneva into the depths of affliction, that Republic, for whose welfare we have constantly been interested, resulting from the long and intimate relations as allies, and from the habitual connexions of a close neighbourhood, is now a prey to unheard of calamities, of which it is impossible to foresee either the extent, the duration or the consequences. At the moment when we were flattered with the hope of the return of peace and tranquillity by the new order of things, which the Government had just solemnly announced to us, and also to the Canton of Zurich, as the term of all dissensions, a set of lawless persons have attacked and overthrown by force of arms public liberty and private security; they have been seen breaking open dwelling houses, carrying away from thence a multitude of Individuals, arbitrarily arresting them, and dragging them to different prisons. These violences have been extended even to the ministers of Religion, in such a manner as indicates its approaching proscription, in a town which has long been one of its principal supports. In the midst of this general subversion, blood has been shed, several citizens have been sacrificed against even the Majority of the voters; new victims are marked out; further outrages on persons and properties are preparing and are put into execution in despite of the oaths the established forms and the laws of the state; and Geneva overwhelmed with consternation awaits in terror the fate preparing for her by these bloody Insurgents, who have usurped the right of disposing of the lives and fortunes of their fellow Citizens.

"We view with extreme grief the mournful destiny of a City, whose happiness and peace were at all times the object of our care, and whose situation so nearly interests the tranquillity of our state, and that of Switzerland; but the knowledge which we have acquired of the criminal participation of several individuals of our country in the horrible excesses which we have just related, aggravates more and more our grief and adds to our indignation. Our paternal sollicitude for the safety and honour of our Country does not permit us to tolerate on our territory those men stained with crimes; we ordain by the present publication, that entrance thereon be interdicted to them and it is our pleasure that all those of our Subjects who shall be known to have had a share in these atrocious scenes, be instantly denounced, and seized, reserving to ourselves to pronounce the just punishments which their guilty conduct in a city so long a time our Ally may have deserved.

"We doubt not, Dear and Liege, that participating with us the sentiments which animate us, you will redouble your activity and zeal in the execution of this present ordonnance; we take pleasure especially in the persuasion, that at the sight of the distressing events which so cruelly agitate this neighbouring Republic, you will the better appreciate the happiness of living under mild and equitable laws, which seconded by a beneficent religion, have for such a length of time afforded us the enjoyment of the inestimable blessings of peace and tranquillity, and of every kind of prosperity which God bestows on the people he loves. And that God, whose Almighty protection, we as well as our Fathers so sensibly experience, will not abandon us, if grateful for his benefits, and placing our confidence in him, we seek still to deserve his goodness and his favours by our virtues, and by our love for our Country."

Given in our Great Council
the 4th. Augt: 1794
Chancery of Berne

Dupl (MHi: Adams Papers); partially dated above postscript; in a clerk's hand, unsigned; slightly torn, with missing word supplied in brackets from pamphlet cited below; at head of text in D'Ivernois's hand: "No 1 Duplicata." Enclosed in D'Ivernois to Samuel [i.e. John] Adams, 22 Aug. 1794 (same), and Adams to TJ, 21 Nov. 1794.

This is the first of three manuscript letters on the Genevan Revolution of 1792-94 that D'Ivernois sent to TJ, Albert Gallatin, and

John Adams for publication in the United States (see also enclosures printed at D'Ivernois to TJ, 23 Sep. [first letter] and 4 Oct. 1794; D'Ivernois to Samuel [i.e. John] Adams, 22 Aug., and enclosure, 4 Oct. 1794, MHi: Adams Papers; D'Ivernois to Gallatin, 22 Aug., 23 Sep., 4 Oct. 1794, and enclosures, NHi: Gallatin Papers). The first two of these anti-French letters were printed, with minor stylistic variations and with the last six paragraphs of the postscript to the first omitted, in *Authentic History of* the *Origin and Progress of the Late Revolution in Geneva* (Philadelphia, 1794). See Evans, No. 27159. There is no evidence that TJ had a hand in their publication, and since the published text of the second letter is substantially shorter than the one Gallatin received, it seems most likely that Adams was responsible for the appearance of this

pamphlet, which bore the imprint of the Federalist printer John Fenno. D'Ivernois himself published rewritten and greatly expanded versions of the three letters in London in English and French editions (see enclosures listed at D'Ivernois to TJ, 11 Nov. 1794, 26 Feb. 1795).

From James Monroe

DEAR SIR   Paris Sepr. 7. 1794.

I have been here rather more than a month and so much engaged with the duties which devolved on me immediately that I have not yet been able [to]¹ send a single private letter to America. It happened that I took my station a few days after Robertspierre had left his in the Convention, by means of the guillitin, so that every thing was in commotion, as was natural upon such an event; but it was the agitation of universal joy occasioned by a deliverance from a terrible oppression and which had pervaded every part of the Republick. After encountering some serious difficulties growing out of the existing state of things, I was presented to the Convention and recognized in the manner the enclosed paper will shew you. Many incidents have since turned up to shew the pleasure with which the organized departments and the people generally have received a mission immediately from our republick to theirs, and I have every reason to believe that it will not only remove any previous existing solicitude, but tend to encrease permanently² the harmony between the two countries.

After Robertsperre's exit there seemed to be an end of divisions and altercations for sometime in the convention. Even those of his own party were most probably happy in the event, for in the progress of his power a connection with him had already been of little service, and it was to be apprehended that it would prove of less hereafter. It was not only necessary to be devoted to him, but to be unpopular with the community also. The list of his oppressions, and the acts of cruelty committed by means of his influence, in the convention and in consequence the revolutionary tribunal, would amaze you. He was believed by the people at large to be the foe to kings, nobles, Priests [. . .] the friend of republican government regardless of money and in fact devoted to their cause. Under this impression he perpetrated acts, which without perceiving the cause, had gradually spread a gloom over the whole republick. But as soon as they saw him in opposition to the Convention, the cause was known, his atrocities were understood, and the people abandoned him with demonstrations of joy rarely seen.

But it seemed improbable he should have been able to carry every thing in the Committee of p: safety and by means of it in the Convention &ca, without more associates than St. Just and Couthon who were executed with him or rather this was the opinion of others, for I can readily conceive that a man may gain an influence in society powerful enough to controul every one and every thing; as soon therefore as the preternatural³ calm subsided, which the Liberation from him had universally created, a spirit of inquiry began to shew itself, as to other accomplices. It terminated in the denunciation of Barrere Collot D Herbois, and some others. The Convention gave a hearing to the charges rejected them, and pass'd a censure upon the author as seeking to disturb the publick repose. Thus therefore that business rests, and I declare to you that I not only think hereafter they will be more free from parties of the turbulent kind heretofore known, but if they should not that I am persuaded their revolution rests perfectly secure in the unanimity and affections of the people. Greater proofs of patriotism and personal sacrifice were never seen in any country than are daily shewn in this, and in acts of heroism, they have thrown a shade over the antient and modern world. The spirit of the combination is absolutely broken. In the neighbourhood of Charleroy a decisive action was fought in July between Jourdan and Cob: and in which the former gained the victory with the loss of about 15000 men, and at the expence to the latter of about 10,000 slain on the feild. This has eventually driven the troops of the combined powers to Mastrecht and the neighbourhood of the Rhine, and of course out of all their possessions not only in France (including Condé and Valenciennes) but likewise their proper territory in the low countries. Tis thought they are about to hazard another great action, but they do it with hazard for they fight dispirited troops against those who are flushed with victory, superior numbers, and resolved to conquer, and sure in case of misfortune of immediate succour. If France succeeds and which I am led to believe from every thing I can hear and very dispassionately, the combination in the ordinary course of war will be at an end, and the several powers composing it entirely at the mercy of France, except the Islands in her neighbourhood whose safety will depend altogether on the superiority at sea, if preserved there. Tis said that these powers (the Islanders excepted and who probably prompted the others with a view of taking advantage in case of success) sounded this government last winter upon the subject of peace, but without effect: that on the contrary they were treated with the utmost contempt, and I have reason to believe they will never treat with them under the governments at present existing in each, [. . .] press the war till no force shews itself against them, and in case the people should rise in any one and organize themselves, treat such organiz'd body as the only legitimate government and aid it in crushing the antient one. If France succeeds in the battle contemplated this will soon be the state of things: indeed it must be so immediately after.

That Mr. Jay should easily obtain the object of his errand in Engld. will be readily inferred. The successful battles of France have plead our cause with great effect in the councils of that humane Cabinet. He will however arrogate to himself much merit for address in negotiation, and the concession of the court will be a theme for high panegeric to many in our country. They will deem it a proof of that sincere attachment to us which has always been shewn in that quarter.

The spirit of liberty begins to shew itself in other regions. Geneva has undergone a revolution—the people have taken the government into their hands, apprehended the aristocrats, and executed seven of the most wicked. And in Poland under the direction of   who acted with us in America, a formidable hand has been raised against Prussia and Russia. I have hopes that our trade, by mere regulation, will be plac'd on a very safe and good footing shortly: and that France will rescind the decree respecting the seizure of our vessels laden with provisions &ca as heretofore. Indeed I think she will go back to the ground of the commercial treaty. I have hinted the good effect such a measure would have in America, without positively requesting it to be done.

I rely upon yourself and Mr. Jones in planning many little tho' very important matters for me, about my farm—such as fixing the place for my house orchards and the like. It will not be very long before we join you. We are all well. Mrs. M. is with her child a pupil to a professor in the French language. They desire to be affectionately remembered to yourself and family taking it for granted you have Mr. R. and both your daughters with you. I am Dear Sir yr. affectionate friend & servant

JAS. MONROE

RC (DLC); edges torn; endorsed by TJ as received 16 Dec. 1794 and so recorded in SJL. Enclosure not found, but see note below.

The ENCLOSED PAPER has not been identified, but for an account of Monroe's enthusiastic reception by the National Convention on 14 Aug. 1794, see Ammon, *Monroe*, 119-21. A CENSURE UPON THE AUTHOR: on 30 Aug. 1794 the National Convention denounced as "fausses et calomnieuses" 26 articles presented to it on the previous day by one of its deputies, Laurent Lecointre, charging three members of the Committee of Public Safety and four members of the Committee of General Security with various acts of complicity in the Reign of Terror (*Archives Parlementaires*, 1st ser., XCVI, 78-9, 103-25). COB: Friedrich Josias, Prince of

Saxe-Coburg. UNDER THE DIRECTION OF: a reference to Tadeusz Kosciuszko. DECREE RESPECTING THE SEIZURE OF OUR VESSELS: see note to Gouverneur Morris to TJ, 20 May 1793.

[1] Word supplied.
[2] Word interlined.
[3] Word interlined.

To Edmund Randolph

DEAR SIR   Monticello Sep. 7. 94.

Your favor of Aug. 28. finds me in bed under a paroxysm of the Rheumatism, which has now kept me for ten days in constant torment and presents no hope of abatement. But the express and the nature of the case requiring immediate answer, I write to you under this situation. No circumstances my dear Sir will ever more tempt me to engage in any thing public: I thought myself perfectly fixed in this determination when I left Philadelphia,[1] but every day and hour since has added to it's inflexibility. It is a great pleasure to me to retain the esteem and approbation of the President, and forms the only ground of any reluctance at being unable to comply with every wish of his. Pray convey these sentiments and a thousand more to him which my situation does not permit me to go into.—But however suffering by the addition of every single word to this letter, I must add a solemn declaration that neither Mr. J. nor Mr.   ever mentioned to me one word of any want of decorum in Mr. Carmichael, nor any thing stronger or more special than stated in my notes of the conversation.—Excuse my brevity my dear Sir & accept assurances of the sincere esteem and respect with which I have the honor to be your affectionate friend & servt   TH: JEFFERSON

P.S. Your secret shall be inviolably kept. The express goes on to Davies.

RC (DNA: RG 59, MLR); at foot of text: "The Secretary of state." PrC (DLC); lacks postscript.

NEITHER MR. J. NOR MR.   : Josef de Jaudenes and Josef Ignacio de Viar, the Spanish government's agents in Philadelphia. NOTES OF THE CONVERSATION: Memorandum of Conversation with Jaudenes, 27 Dec. [1791].

[1] Preceding four words interlined.

Power of Attorney to Caleb Lownes

Know all men by these presents that I Thomas Jefferson named in a certain letter of Attorney from William Short of the state of Virginia, then Minister Resident of the United States at the Hague, to me, bearing date the 2d. day of April 1793. and now lodged in the bank of the

United States; by virtue of the power and authority therein given me, do make substitute and appoint Caleb Lownes of Philadelphia[1] as well my own as the true and lawful attorney and substitute of the said William Short named in the said letter of attorney, to receive from the Treasury or bank of the United States the interest which shall become due on the stock of different descriptions of the said William Short registered in the proper office of the US. at the seat of government in Philadelphia from the first day of July last past to the first day of October next ensuing, and becoming payable on the said first day of October, amounting to three hundred and ninety dollars and sixty two cents: hereby ratifying and confirming the paiment of the said interest to the said Caleb Lownes,[2] and the discharge which he shall give for the same, as done by virtue of the power of attorney aforesaid. In witness whereof I have hereunto set my hand and seal this 11th. day of September, 1794.

signed sealed and delivered   TH: JEFFERSON   (L.S.)
in the presence of
    J W EPPES

Virginia. Albemarle county to wit.
Before me Thomas Mann Randolph a justice of peace for the said county, appeared Thomas Jefferson named in the within power of attorney, and freely acknoleged and declared that the seal and signature thereto put, are truly his own seal and signature. Certified under my hand and seal this 11th. day of September 1794.

TH: M. RANDOLPH   (L.S.)

Albemarle county to wit
    I hereby certify that Thomas Mann Randolph whose seal and signature are placed above, is a justice of the peace for the (L.S.) said county, duly qualified, and that full faith and credence ought to be given to his acts. Certified under my hand, and the seal of the said county of Albemarle this 11th. day of Sep. 1794.

JOHN NICHOLAS C.A.C

MS (PHC); in TJ's hand except for signatures of Eppes, Randolph, and Nicholas; text partially obscured by Nicholas's seal.

TJ enclosed this document in his 17 Sep. 1794 letter to Lownes, recorded in SJL but not found. SJL also records a missing letter of 30 Apr. 1794 in which TJ sent Lownes a similar power of attorney, not found, authorizing him to receive an earlier interest payment of $390.62 when it became due to William Short on 1 July 1794. From the beginning of 1794 until the end of 1798 TJ loaned himself all of the interest payments he received on Short's behalf, applying them to the purchase of nailrod for the Monticello nailery and to sundry uses in Philadelphia, ultimately amassing a debt exceeding $9,000, plus interest. After casting his account with Short in 1800, TJ reported his astonishment at the size of the debt, and he did not finish repaying it until 1807 (MB, 1 Jan. 1794, and note, 30 Apr., 1 Oct. 1794; TJ to Short, 13 Apr. 1800).

The missing 2 Apr. 1793 LETTER OF ATTORNEY FROM WILLIAM SHORT was enclosed in Short's first letter to TJ of that date.

In addition to the letters noted above,

SJL records four letters from TJ to Lownes between 11 Mch. and 31 July 1794 and four from Lownes to TJ between 12 Apr. and 22 Aug. 1794, none of which has been found.

[1] Preceding four words inserted in space initially left blank.
[2] Preceding two words inserted in space initially left blank.

From François D'Ivernois

MONSIEUR   Londres ce 16 7bre 1794.

J'ai l'honneur de vous adresser le Duplicata de ma Dépeche No. 1r. expédiée *by the Indian Chief bound for Baltimore*. Je n'ai rien à ajouter à son contenu, si ce n'est de vous conjurer d'y donner toute l'attention qu'il me semble mériter pour votre Province et pour mes malheureux compatriotes.

Les dernieres lettres de Geneve sont de plus en plus affligeantes, mais elles me donnent aussi de plus en plus l'assurance qu'il ne tient qu'à la Virginie de réaliser le projet que je vous ai développé. Le sang coule de nouveau dans la malheureuse Geneve, et quoique ce soyent à la vérité les Révolutionaires eux-memes qui y sont maintenant aux prises les uns avec les autres; le terrible Tribunal y a repris ses fonctions de proscription et de dépouillement. Une foule de citoyens en ont reçu de nouveaux mandats d'arret, et tous les Genevois sensés et honnetes ne songent plus qu'à quitter à jamais et à tout prix ce séjour de crimes.

Deja quelques uns d'entr'eux ayant réussi à prix d'argent, à faire commuer leurs emprisonnemens Domestiques en un exil plus ou moins long, tournent directement leurs pas vers l'amérique. Et j'apprens qu'ils vont etre suivis à Hambourg par une seconde bande dans la quelle on désigne les deux meilleurs Régens de notre College. Il est vrai qu'ils paraissent tendre exclusivement leurs vues vers l'agriculture et vers le Nord de la Pensilvanie; mais dès que vous m'aurez mis à meme de leur communiquer mon projet, c'est à dire de leur en annoncer l'adoption de la part de la Virginie,[1] ce sera un signal heureux qui réunira en un meme instant tous les vœux, toutes les espérances, tous les cœurs et tous les interets.

Mais je ne saurais trop vous le répéter Monsieur, tout le succès de ce signal dépend de l'accélération avec la quelle vous serez à meme de me le faire passer, et de l'influence que vous aurez sur votre province pour lui faire sentir qu'une entreprise pareille dépend entierement de la confiance avec la quelle elle peut-etre adoptée, et de l'extreme rapidité de son exécution. Certes, quelque douteuse que la transplantation de notre Université puisse paraître à quelques Américains, non seulement plus je la médite, et plus je la crois possible, mais plus j'entrevois pour elle de ressources incalculables d'associations et de prospérités dans le résultat inévitable des convulsions croissantes de ce Continent, qui presque partout y ont dejà remplacé par des institutions purement guerrieres les institutions pour les sciences.

En effet Monsieur, voila tous les savans les plus distingués de la France en fuite, persécutés incarcérés ou cachés. Voila l'Université de Mayence dispersée depuis pres de deux ans, et toutes celles de Hollande ébranlées peut-etre jusques dans leurs fondemens. Ne Serait-il pas également utile pour l'amérique et digne d'elle, de leur présenter un port assuré en commençant par naturaliser chez elle l'académie de Geneve, cette Académie, contre la quelle dans tous mes voyages, je n'ai jamais entendu élever d'autre reproche si ce n'est que la jeunesse étrangere y contractait trop le gout de la liberté? Et sous ce rapport meme, ne vous paraitra-t-elle pas plus digne qu'une autre Monsieur, de former l'avant garde de cette honorable retraite des hommes de lettres de l'ancien monde vers le nouveau?

Plus je caresse cette grande idée, plus j'étudie les difficultés de son exécution, et plus je crois qu'elles se concentreront exclusivement sur les délais et sur les lenteurs que vos formes Républicaines apporteront peut-etre dans l'examen et dans l'adoption de mes propositions.

C'est pour ne rien négliger de mon coté de tout ce qui pourra hâter son accélération de la part des Genevois, que je prens la liberté de vous présenter ici d'avance une Série de questions, Sur les quelles il me sera précieux de pouvoir éclairer les émigrants de toutes les classes au moment meme où vous m'aurez mis à portée de leur annoncer mon projet et son adoption. En rédigeant ces questions, je suis parti de la Supposition que votre Province voterait le revenu annuel que je demande pour notre Université en nous autorisant à la fixer sur les terres que nous acheterions en Virginie. Et ce Serait en effet le moyen qui me paraitrait le plus sur de hâter l'entreprise, c'est à dire en d'autres termes de la faire réussir.

Aussi vais-je compter avec bien de l'impatience Monsieur, les semaines qui s'écouleront avant votre réponse. Puisse-t-elle etre complettement favorable, et m'apporter en meme tems tous les éclaircissemens nécessaires pour déterminer à la fois les émigrants de toutes les vocations! Car il est essentiel qu'ils puissent, tout en vous envoyant des agens, faire avec confiance leurs préparatifs pour partir avant d'avoir reçu des nouvelles de ces derniers, puisque l'obligation de les attendre pourrait différer leur départ jusqu'à l'automne ou meme jusqu'à l'hyver de l'année prochaine. J'ai l'honneur d'etre avec respect Monsieur, Votre tres humble & tres obéissant serviteur   F D'IVERNOIS

P.S. Les lettres de Geneve du 25 passé annoncent que les Révolutionaires ont cassé ou vont casser non seulement la Compagnie des Pasteurs, mais meme l'académie. Si cette derniere n'a pas encore éprouvé ce dernier coup, elle l'attend. Mais en supposant meme qu'elle y échappat; comment nos Professeurs pourraient-ils songer à continuer leurs fonctions dans une pareille Résidence? Heureusement le nombre des Genevois réfugiés en suisse est deja tres considérable, et s'y accroit chaque jour.

Il est une question sur la quelle je desirerais Monsieur, m'adresser exclusivement à vous. Je ne vous dissimulerai point que je redoute que les principes et les mœurs de la jeunesse envoyée à Notre Université ne pussent s'altérer au milieu d'esclaves des deux sexes: Et je désirerais savoir, si soit la Province, soit les établissements voisins du notre verraient avec quelque déplaisir que les Genevois se liassent entr'eux 1°. à ne point admettre d'esclaves dans leur Colonie, 2°. à soumettre leurs propres contestations pécuniaires à des arbitres choisis par les parties. Cette disposition presque universelle chez nous y avait absolument anéanti l'esprit processif, et peut-etre nous serait-elle plus précieuse encore dans un payz dont nous ne connaitrions pas dabord les loix particuliéres.[2]

RC (DLC); at head of text: "*No 2*"; at foot of first page: "A Monsieur Jefferson." Tr (NHi: Gallatin Papers); undated and unsigned, with abbreviated complimentary close; at head of text in D'Ivernois's hand: "*Copie*" and "Duplicata du No 2. A Mr Jefferson"; with minor variations, only the two most important being recorded below; enclosed in D'Ivernois to Albert Gallatin, 23 Sep. 1794 (same). Recorded in SJL as received 19 Nov. 1794. Enclosure: Dupl of D'Ivernois to TJ, 5 Sep. 1794. Other enclosure printed below.

[1] Preceding clause omitted in Tr.
[2] Tr: "pécuniares."

ENCLOSURE

Queries of François D'Ivernois

Queries
1st

Which are the largest tracts of uncultivated lands, contiguous together, to be sold in the Northern parts of the Province of Virginia? What is their quality and their price, as well as the price of the neighbouring lands either cultivated or uncultivated? What are their actual or future means of carriage by land or by water, and what is their distance from the next Settlements and from the Chief Towns?

2dly

Are there Settlements to be found in the neighbourhood of the most eligible of those tracts, where the emigrants might conveniently place at boarding for about six months their children and wives, in such a manner that they might learn the language and prepare themselves to their new avocations of farmers? And if so, what are supposed to be the terms of the best as well as of the cheapest boardings?

3ly.

Supposing the new Colony to consist in about one hundred families, half of which might arrive in the year 1795 and the other half in the year following; what class of Mechanics will it be proper for the first emigrants to take with them? What may be the advisable number of each of these to engage, such as carpenters, masons, joiners, smiths, tanners, shoe makers turners,[1] brewers, glaziers & &? And what is in Virginia the actual price of the labour of each of these workmen?

4thly

Amongst the Genevan Mechanics of all Kinds, which are those, who, without being useful to the settlement in its first infancy, would be sure to find employment in the Chief neighbouring Towns, such as book printers book binders, hatters, linen printers, tinmen, braziers, silversmiths, weavers &?

5thly

[As it] is likely that several emigrants and [especially] those who are in easy circumstances [will have] in their power to carry over with [them garden]ers, as well as family and farmer [servants, either] Genevans or swiss; what is [the best kind] of agreement to settle with [them before their] departure, and of which the Laws of the Province would, if necessary, enforce the faithfull execution? In the recompense agreed for their future services during a certain number of years, would it not be proper to stipulate the gift of lands at their arrival, for a sum specified, and the allowance of a fixed time of absence in the last year of their service to begin the clearing of them? The sending of the model of some contract of that Kind properly worded and reciprocally just and equitable would be very acceptable.

6ly.

Does there exist in Virginia the same Law as in the Province of New York, which does not allow an absent alien to possess or transmit landed properties, and which subjects him to the interference of an agent?

7ly.

In cases of *successions ab intestat*, how do the laws of Virginia divide the inheritance between the Widow and children?

8ly.

What are the actual wages of servants either white or black? And are they easily to be procured?

9ly.

Supposing that agents from the Academy and from the sharer's Company, should be able to arrive in Next March, and find the negociation in such a forwardness as to be able to conclude it and fix the place of settlement in April; would it be possible 1st. for the Province to have the Colleges back for the end of the year? 2dly. for the Company to find people who would undertake in the same space of time, to build a Church a tavern, a baking house, a saw mill, a corn mill, a public market as well as about 50 small but decent houses half of them in brick or stone, and to clear 200, or 300 acres of lands? If so, what would likely be the sum asked for this last undertaking?

10thly

Which is the most proper estimate to give to a family accustomed to easy circumstances, of the capital necessary at their arrival, to build a small but confortable brick or stone house, to furnish it, to begin a little farm, to buy the necessary utensils of husbandry, and stock of cattle, to clear out and cultivate 10 or 20 acres, and to support themselves in provisions with three children and 2 servants for the first year? What is also the least sum which such a family without servants[2] must provide for, before they undertake the same Kind of establishment in the most moderate way? In these calculations, the purchase of lands, which must vary according to the price of those upon which the settlement is to take place, is not to be included.

11ly.

Would the Company have any other more advantageous means of laying out their stocks than to deposite them in England, in order to have them remitted to America when wanted?

12ly

With regard to the private property which the individual emigrants may carry over with them, would this means also be the most advisable? Would it be better for them to carry it over in specie, or to purchase here American stocks, or even to take goods with them such as watches and jewels from Geneva, coarse muslins from Zurich, coarse and fine linen painted in Geneva, silk stuffs from france, french books & &.

13ly.

Would it be advisable for the Mechanics to carry over with them the instruments of their professions, and for the generality of the emigrants to transport a part of their furniture such as all their linens and even their Kitchin utensils, drawers, chairs, tables & &? For a [proper] answer to this quere, it must be [observed] that if it be still in their power [to go down] the Rhine in the next year [from Man]heim to Rotterdam, the price [of carriage] from Geneva to that seaport [would be about] three Dollars per hundred [weight].

14ly

What is the actual price of provisions in the North of Virginia and more particularly of meat, corn, butter, cheese and cyder?

15ly

What is in Virginia the legal interest of money?

16ly.

Will the Cloathes, books household furniture and implements of the emigrators be exempted from the import duty, if they are sent in different vessels from the one that carries the proprietors over?

17ly

If the civil Laws of the Province of Virginia and the regulations of the College of William and Mary are printed, a copy of them would be very acceptable as well as some map of the largest tracts of lands to be sold in the northern parts of Virginia.

MS (DLC: TJ Papers, 97: 16576-7); undated; in D'Ivernois's hand; words torn away supplied in brackets from Tr. Tr (NHi: Gallatin Papers); undated; with variations, only the most important being noted below; enclosed in D'Ivernois to Albert Gallatin, 23 Sep. 1794 (same).

[1] Tr here adds "weavers."
[2] Tr: "a servant."

To Joseph Mussi

Dear Sir   Monticello Sep. 17. 1794.

I have duly received your favors of Aug. 16. and 27. and will pray you to hold in your hands the balance of £7–9–3 as it will not be long before I may trouble you with a request of a supply of groceries similar to the last. I am glad you did not invest it, and particularly in oil at the price you mention. I had rather wait for yours, because I know it will be good and cheap. When it comes, I will take 10. gallons of it, as I would as lieve be out of bread as oil. Your repeated offers of your kind services, I receive with many thanks, and with the continuance of your permission I will avail myself of them from time to time.

Mr. Fleming, the merchant of my neighborhood who went to Philadelphia, has brought from thence a large supply of cotton, oznabrigs &c. which he offers me so reasonably that I conclude to take my wants from him, and not to trouble you for those articles.

I write the present under the pain of a severe attack of the rheumatism, under which I have now been for three weeks. This must apologize for my brevity, as it obliges me to conclude here with assurances of the sincere esteem of Dear Sir Your friend & servt

Th: Jefferson

PrC (DLC); at foot of text: "Mr. Joseph Mussi."

Mussi's FAVORS OF AUG. 16. AND 27., recorded in SJL as received from Philadelphia on 10 and 17 Sep. 1794 respectively, have not been found. SJL also records an additional eight letters exchanged by TJ and Mussi between 9 Jan. and 31 July 1794 that have not been found.

To Eliza House Trist

Dear Madam   Monticello Sep. 17. 1794.

The inclosed letter came under cover to me not long since and before I could forward it to you I was attacked with a rheumatism which has kept me ever since, and still keeps me in incessant torment. Since that I have learnt by a letter from Mr. Ciracchi that he is arrived with his family at Boston. I have felt the obligation therefore, notwithstanding the pain in which I write, to accompany the letter with this apology.— You have been long promising us a visit, but have avoided fixing dates. You will always find here a family every member of which will be happy to receive you. Patsy presented me about a fortnight ago with a third grand-child, a daughter. It will [. . .] for me to suppress my age, which in spight of my teeth [. . .] attested by these multiplied witnesses, as well as by the pangs of disease which oblige me to conclude here with assurances of the sincere esteem & respect of Dear Madam Your affectionate friend & servt   TH: JEFFERSON

PrC (MHi); mutilated. Enclosure not found.

TJ's THIRD GRAND-CHILD was Ellen Wayles Randolph I (1794-95), born 30 Aug., the only one of his Randolph grandchildren who did not survive infancy. See TJ to Thomas Mann Randolph and to Archibald Stuart, 26 July 1795.

From François D'Ivernois

MONSIEUR   Londres ce 23 7bre 1794.

J'ai eu l'honneur de vous adresser depuis quinze jours, by the Indian Chief bound for Baltimore, and by the two systers bound for James River, deux longues Dépeches qui contiennent 1°. un exposé historique de la Révolution qui vient de bouleverser la République de Geneve, et toutes ses institutions pour les sciences. 2°. Un projet que j'ai formé et sur le quel je vous consulte, de transplanter son Académie toute entiere en Amérique, et plus particulierement en Virginie, si votre Province veut lui ouvrir les bras. Je vous ai fait parvenir ces Dépéches par Duplicata, car rien n'est plus important au succès du projet qu'elles vous soumettent que de vous atteindre avec sureté et surtout avec promptitude.

L'exécution de ce grand projet tiendrait à un revenu annuel de 15,000 Dollars, que l'un des Etats-Unis accorderait à notre Université pour sa dot; en nous autorisant à la fixer sur des terres qu'y acheterait une Compagnie de Genevois, les quels y conduiraient une Colonie agricole et industrieuse.

Cette idée que j'avais dabord saisie pour mes malheureux compatriotes comme une planche dans leur naufrage, me devient de plus en plus chere à mesure que la ruine de notre petite et intéressante République devient plus complette et plus irrémédiable. Je vous adresse ici Monsieur, la Suite de l'historique de sa catastrophe. C'est pour vos papiers publics que j'ai destiné ce tableau, et il me parait ne devoir etre ni sans curiosité ni sans instruction, pour des Républicains qui mettent trop de prix à la liberté pour ne pas étudier avec intéret dans l'histoire les vertus par les quelles on mérite de la conserver, et les écarts qui exposent à la perdre sans retour. Cette seconde scène de notre Révolution vous mettra surtout à meme de juger Monsieur, combien est praticable et pressante la transplantation que je vous ai proposée.

J'apprens que la Province de Maryland a fait il y a quelques années pour un établissement Académique, un fond annuel bien plus considérable que celui que je sollicite en faveur du notre, et j'ignore les résultats de cette création: mais je me flatte que la dot que j'ai demandée suffira dabord pour donner une existence solide à notre Nouvelle Université; et si comme je n'en doute pas, elle réalise les espérances que la Virginie aurait fondées sur elle, je doute bien moins encore qu'une Législature aussi éclairée que la votre hézitat à lui donner dans la Suite tous les autres accroissemens et tous les encouragemens, dont elle se montrerait digne. Ne serait-il point possible Monsieur, d'en faire entr'autres dès à présent non seulement un séminaire pour les maitres de ces écoles primaires si utiles et si avantageuses que votre Province avait eues en contemplation il y a douze ans, mais encore *the General Grammar school* où elle se proposait d'envoyer à ses fraix les enfans qui se seraient distingués dans leurs ecoles de paroisse? Notre établissement offrirait en meme tems à l'émulation des plus méritans d'entr'eux la perspective d'etre introduits et soutenus de la meme maniere dans notre Académie. S'il est vrai Monsieur, que ce beau plan de votre Province, plan Si noble, Si vaste et Si utile, n'a été différé jusqu'à présent que par l'effet des circonstances, celle qui Se présente ne vous semblerait'elle pas singulierement favorable pour lui donner enfin l'existence en la rendant à notre Université qui pourrait tout à la fois fournir le germe d'un arbre aussi précieux en rassembler les rameaux, et en Soigner les fruits? Ressuscitée sous de pareils auspices en Amérique, elle y trouverait précisément les seuls avantages qui lui avaient manqué, [c'est] à dire un grand théatre et un puissant motif d'émulation dans l'assurance de pouvoir rendre avec usure à la Virginie ce qu'elle en aurait reçu. Qui sait meme si elle ne mériterait pas un jour dans sa nouvelle patrie l'éloge honorable que les savans suisses lui avaient accordé celui d'avoir fait de Geneve l'Athenes de l'helvétie?

Si la Providence l'apelle à de pareilles destinées en Virginie, et que votre Province adhére aux propositions que je lui ai soumises; il y aura Monsieur, un autre objet non moins essentiel au succès de notre résurection. J'entens par là tout ce qui aura rapport au choix de l'emplacement pour cette Geneve Académique, c'est à dire, l'achat des terres, leur étendue, leur prix, leur fertilité, la salubrité du district & &. Mais sous ce second point de vue comme sous le premier, je me permets encore de vous envisager d'avance Monsieur, comme notre Conseiller et notre fondateur. C'est surtout cet espoir encourageant qui m'anime; et si j'avais dans ce moment l'assurance que vous prendrez notre établissement sous votre Protection, je ne douterais deja ni de sa fondation ni de Ses prospérités futures, et je ne gémirais plus sur le sort de l'élite de mes compatriotes, puisqu'en transportant en Virginie leur Académie, c'est à dire leurs vrais Dieux Pénates, ils les placeraient enfin sous les ailes d'une Nation vraiment indépendante, deja puissante, et suffisamment à l'abri de l'influence étrangere qui a été la cause de tous les malheurs passés et présens des Genevois.

En vous adressant Monsieur, une proposition aussi nouvelle que celle que je vous soumets, je vous supplie de nouveau de me faire passer dès que vous l'aurez reçue vos premiers apperçus sur son succès: Car votre seule approbation me suffirait deja pour jetter les premiers fondemens de l'entreprise, en attendant que vous pussiez me mander la sanction définitive par la quelle votre Province me mettrait à portée d'annoncer à tous mes compatriotes une nouvelle patrie, et à tous nos Professeurs une nouvelle carrière. J'ai l'honneur d'etre avec respect Monsieur, Votre tres humble & tres obéissant serviteur   F. D'IVERNOIS

Mon adresse est chez *Mr. Chauvet Kensington near London.*

RC (DLC); with two words torn away supplied in brackets from Dupl; at foot of first page: "A Monsieur Jefferson." Recorded in SJL as received 19 Nov. 1794. Dupl (DLC); with several words omitted; at head of text: "No. 3" and "*Duplicata* dans l'original a été expedié by the Eliza bound for James River"; endorsed by TJ as received 10 Dec. 1794 but recorded in SJL as received the preceding day. Tr (NHi: Gallatin Papers); unsigned, with abbreviated complimentary close and no postscript; contains copying errors, some corrected by D'Ivernois; at head of text: "No. 3" and (with date in D'Ivernois's hand) "Copie à

Mr Jefferson ce 23 7bre 1794"; enclosed in D'Ivernois to Albert Gallatin, 23 Sep. 1794 (same). RC or Dupl possibly enclosed in TJ to Wilson Cary Nicholas, 12 Dec. 1794.

In May 1782 the General Assembly of MARYLAND passed an act providing that Kent Academy in Chestertown could become a college if it raised a private endowment of £5,000 sterling in five years—a goal that was reached in five months, leading to the formation of Washington College (George H. Callcott, *A History of the University of Maryland* [Baltimore, 1966], 10).

ENCLOSURE

François D'Ivernois's Second Letter on the Genevan Revolution

London Septr. 23d. [1794]

The troubles in Geneva seem to take a less violent turn. The people begin to feel the stings of remorse and even to confess it; but they never can recede from the Revolutionary career upon which they have entered; and although they already lament the innocent blood they have spilt, they are incapable of renouncing the pleasure of plundering, with which they have been once gratified: and the confiscations still continue. For the same reason that our modern philosophers have untill now found it easier to study the springs of liberty operating on so small a scale as that of Geneva, our readers will likewise be better able to judge from it of the action and effects of the new Revolutionary Doctrine, and a retrospective glance on its introduction and effects in Geneva will not perhaps be to them devoid of interest or utility.

In one point of view but only in this one, the Genevese Revolutionists have remained behind hand with the French, as of all the number of victims which include the 10th: part of what the males amount to, only one woman is to be found, who has been condemned to perpetual seclusion for having forwarded letters to some French Emigrants. Still it appears that this sentence, the only one which has affected her sex, was forced by the urgent influence employed by the French Resident.

But in every other point the Genevese in imitating the French have surpassed them. Thus it has been for instance that members of the Revolutionary Tribunal have themselves executed and shot the unfortunate Magistrates, whom they had just condemned. Thus it was that in the trial of Syndic *Caylas* they had the effrontery to place at the head of his accusations the charitable distributions he made by the hands of the Clergy during the rigorous winter of 1783, which amounted to 800£ Sterg: with the view as they imputed to him, of corrupting the minds of the poor. It is indeed but too true that he had ill applied his immense charities, as he had conferred them on the very set of people, who demanded his death, and obtained it. They reproach themselves at this day openly with it, but some extraordinary event alone could have forced them to this speedy recrimination.

It is to be remembered that the subversion of the Government of the 18th: of July was chiefly plotted and executed by the club of *Montagnards* half foreigners, half Genevese, to whom from terror, surprise, and cowardice half of the citizens joined themselves the following day. As such men as these Montagnards could only be the Grenadiers and not the Directors of so complete a Revolution, the instant the leaders of the preceding one were associated to them, they seized the reins from the Resident of France, who, in exciting the Montagnards, had flattered himself with the hopes of governing them, and of forcing by their means the little Republic to demand its reunion with France. And indeed as soon as this hope had failed him, he began an open rupture with the new leaders in which they treated him with so much the less discretion, as the fall of Robespierre, whose creature he was, gave them the prospect of overturning him,* of saving thereby the political independence of Geneva, and of preserving for themselves the fruits of the Revolution and its plunder.

---

* In answer to a violent note in which the French Resident accused the Revolutionary Government of being an Enemy to France, made mention of some pretended grievances and threatned to arm the neighbouring French districts against Geneva. The Syndics answered him by a very spirited letter, which will form an epoch in the new Diplomatic stile of Revolutions.

"Citizen Resident, replied they, the Syndics and Council of the Republic of Geneva, have never mistaken the nature of your dispositions in relation to the Republic and its government. A long time have they seen you follow without variation a plan which directly tends to implicate both with the Republic of France. From motives of peace, from respect for the public character with which you are invested, they have repressed the painful sentiments which they experienced, they have kept silent. But now that you yourself no longer respect this character at the same time that you throw aside every kind of respect towards the Magistrates of an independent people, they can no longer dissemble the sentiments which the extraordinary conduct you have held inspires them. They are bound to repel the truly hostile proceedings, of which they have been for some time past the object. We shall not undertake the enumeration of all the grievances, which we have to urge against you; the time will come when we shall specify them before those who are just and powerful enough to have justice rendered us; we shall confine ourselves to a few observations on your note of the 11th: Thermidore, and on the spirit which prevails throughout it. This note will suffice to prove how little you are scrupulous on the choice of the means, when you have in view to render the

Scarce had the daily pay of the Revolutionists ceased, which had been de-creed only for three weeks and which cost near £300 Sterg. a day to the State, than the Allies of the Resident, deprived of this resource, and forced to return to their work, began to demand a new pay and consequently a new Revolution to supply it. They loudly declaimed that the national vengeance had not been sufficiently satisfied, that the Aristocrats who had been spared should have their turn. They demanded in[1] short that the Revolutionary Tribunal should resume its functions, and proceed to execute justice on 5 to 600 other suspected citizens amongst whom they began to mark out a few Revolutionists who appeared the most attached to the independance of the Republic. At this last threat, their latter were roused up from their lethargy: They convoked all the Revolutionary Clubs on whom they made a deep impression by a speech which contains such unguarded confessions, and such remarkable insinuations against the french Resident as deserve to have some extracts presented here.

"I insist, said the speaker, that the proposal of erecting a new Revolutionary Tribunal, cannot be suggested but by the perfidy of an ennemy to our Independ-dance, and supported only by mislead persons or idle people, who now having the resolution of returning to their occupations, presume with reason the obliga-tion under which we should be placed of continuing the national pay, the instant every business should be stopped anew. For, who can still alledge without blushing at his ignorance or his intentions, any fear from Genevese Aristocracy? an ephemeric being crushed under the loss of his fortune, and under the im-mense rubbish of the french Monarchy, without means of force within, and without ressource from abroad. & &.

"France has placed justice as the order of the day, and can Geneva, which ought to offer to the world the sight of a city of brothers only, contain men, who

---

Genevese odious to the French. You mutilate facts, you misrepresent circumstances, what you seem to keep from the public appears to be worse than what you publish &c. And it is at the very time when the true friends of liberty and equality rise to destroy Aristocracy, that you attribute hostile views to the Genevese towards the French Republic! Where is a Citizen of Geneva to be found, if he be not a Traitor to his Country who can conceive any advantage to be derived from *fatiguing* as you say, the neighbouring people to *animate* and *arm* them against us? We tell you without feint, Citizen Resident, that these are insidious construc-tions, which you strive to give to events, and which are evidently made to *animate* the neigh-bouring people against us, and to commit us with them. Was it then for this purpose that you have been sent amongst us? The French Nation have made justice and probity the order of the day, and you who are it's representative, you falsify facts in order to impute wrongs to us! The French wish to fraternize with every free people, and *you* you make an abuse of the influ-ence attached to your situation to implicate with such a nation the only people who have adopted its principles! We know that the Committee of public safety will never refuse to lis-ten to us, that it will never judge a whole nation without hearing it: and that we shall have great truths to announce. Believe not therefore Citizen Resident, that your menaces avail. You have only opened to us a prospect of the arrival of the moment for which we so much long, that of these little intrigues of which we were to be victims. Citizen Resident we have held to you the language of free men; we have spoken hard truths: if our language offends you, your reiterated provocations will justify us before those, who have an esteem for frank-ness and firmness. We advise you Citizen Resident that we forward your note and our an-swer to the Committee of public safety at Paris. &c. &c."

Geneva the 5th: of August 3d year
of Genevese Equality. for the Syndics
& Council, signed *Didier*

are not yet satiated with victims, and who demand a second erection of a revolutionary Tribunal, which might judge arbitrarily, and wave its sword over every head? Are you not sensible citizens, of the dangers to which we shall be liable should the respectable Powers who border upon us, and on which we depend for our subsistance and trade, highly displeased with the repetition of scenes, which they have already marked with the testimony of their reprobation, should at last anathematize our country? Then Geneva the birth place of Rousseau, Geneva which had merited the esteem and consideration of all Europe, by the moderation which its citizens had ever displayed untill now in their intestine disputes; by their morals, their Religion, their instruction, and their abilities, Geneva will disappear for ever from the catalogue of free and independant Cities. Let us hasten to stop the consequences of such a revolution. & &"

This speech which was warmly applauded both by those who had commenced the Revolution, and by those who had associated themselves to it, though at the same time they detested it, was published by order of the Revolutionists, and restored courage and speech to those whom terror had petrified and untill then had carried along in the torrent of the montagnards. They resolved 1st. to arm, but not to receive any national pay. 2dly. to revive the Revolutionary tribunal to prosecute, no longer the pretended Aristocrats, but the real agitators, and amongst other things, to make a deep search into their conspiracy against the Independance of the state.

However the former Tribunal at the head of whom is *Bousquet*, seemed in resuming its formidable functions to wish to spare those montagnards who had served him as janissaries. He strived to divert the public vengeance from their heads by solliciting farther denunciations against the rich, who had escaped from the effects of the first Revolution, and to whom he still gave the appellation of *incorrigible ennemies*. But this time, the Revolutionists were no longer its dupes, for the very day after, (the 25 Augt.) irritated by its equivocal proceeding, and its hesitations, they presented the following address to it.

Citizens! 2139 Insurgents gave you order yesterday to erect yourselves into a Revolutionary Tribunal and to judge the criminals arrested in the morning. What have you done? Nothing . . . We are tired with so much inaction, and we now come to declare to you, that if at noon, you do not begin to try the arrested persons, you are responsible to us for the evils which may be the consequence. Let the first of your members who would disconcert your proceedings be instantly put in arrest: Let the montagnards be disarmed: Let the address found amongst their papers be communicated to all your fellow citizens: And let all the agitators be punished during the day. Signed Gerard secretary.

On seizing the registers of the Montagnards, they had indeed discovered the project of an address which tended no less than to plunge anew the little Republic into the most dreadful anarchy, in order to force it to throw itself into the arms of the great Republic of france. It is asserted that although the signatures had been effaced, they have been recovered by the means of a Chemical process, and that among others, that of the french Resident has appeared, who besides, finds himself named and strongly implicated in all the confessions of those montagnards who have yet been tried.

During these transactions, the Minister of the Republic of Geneva at Paris, a very able man, having had the address of availing himself of these discoveries, and of the fall of Robetspierre to interest the opposite faction in favour of Geneva, succeeded not only in obtaining from the french Committee the disavowal of the Resident *Soulavie* but likewise in having him recalled with public marks of disapprobation, and even procured a new recognition of the Independance of Geneva, by the french Convention, who granted that Minister the same honours as they had just conferred on the Minister of the United States of America.

Upon this news the Tribunal at Geneva no longer hezitated to execute justice on the montagnards, and several of them were conducted to condign punishment amidst the acclamations of that same populace who five weeks before had been the instruments of their destructive projects. Thus this little Drama presents even in its second scene a farther proof of that great truth advanced by a french orator, that every Revolution of this Kind is like saturne and devours its own offspring.

The oppressed Genevese are in hopes from this second scene will produce some amelioration of what they had been led to apprehend from the first; and particularly of enjoying some greater facility to quit this theatre of crimes; as some amongst them have already obtained by dint of money, the permission of commutting their year of Domestic emprisonment into perpetual bannishment without confiscation. And indeed, who can be surprized at any one's purchasing as a favour, a perpetual bannishment from a country polluted with the stain of innocent blood, from a city which is distracted with discord, famine and repentance, and where even those who lament the most the career of crimes on which they are entered, have not the possible means at command of quitting it? This frightful perspective is however so true, that in order to proceed against the montagnards who projected farther excesses, the best disposed among the Revolutionists have been in some measure forced to allow fresh ones to be committed; as the revived Tribunal with a view to give himself an air of impartiality, has confiscated the property of several absent persons who had escaped the avidity of its first researches: among these latter is one of the most distinguished Professors. It is not less in agitation than the speedy destitution of all nonrevolutionist persons charged with the care of public Instruction, so that every Class of them is to be abolished Clergy, Professors in every branch of sciences, public masters & &. But such of them as the public opinion mark out as being most indispensable for the present, will be put in a state of requisition as the plate & &.

Geneva is lost without ressource in respect to Religion, to morals, to the sciences, to the fine arts, to trade—to liberty, and above all to internal peace. Its convulsions can have no other term than that of those of france to the fate of which it has had the criminal inprudence irremissibly to attach itself, and of which it will suffer more or less all the shocks. For the fall of the Genevese montagnards is evidently nothing more than the rebounding blow of that of the partisans of Robetspierre in france. That power is now the only ally which remains to the feeble Geneva, and she would loose it and irritate it beyond the hope of reconciliation, should her citizens attempt, as already they desire it, to revert to the wise laws and the well tempered liberty which they have sacrificed for these two years past on the altar of the Revolutionary Doctrine.

facilis descensus Averni

sed revocare gradum, hoc opus, hic labor est.[2]

MS (DLC); in the hands of a clerk and D'Ivernois (see note 1 below), with note at head of text —"(Continuation for the american news papers)"—and corrections also in

D'Ivernois's hand; partially dated; ellipsis in original. Tr (NHi: Gallatin Papers); in two clerical hands, with note at head of text—"*Continuation*"—and two additional pages in D'Ivernois's hand (see note 2 below); with minor variations; enclosed in D'Ivernois to Albert Gallatin, 23 Sep. 1794 (same).

What appears to be a reference to the continuation quoted in note 2 below is contained in the first paragraph of D'Ivernois's second letter to TJ of 23 Sep. 1794, but there is no evidence that TJ ever obtained a copy of this addendum from John Adams or Albert Gallatin. FRENCH RESIDENT: Jean Louis Soulavie, the Jacobin French minister resident in Geneva from June 1793 until his recall in September 1794 (Peter, *Genève*, I, 156-7, II, 33). Salomon Reybaz had been the Genevan MINISTER . . . AT PARIS since 1793 (same, I, 52-3). FACILIS . . . EST: "The way to Avernus is easy but to retrace your steps, that is the task, the hard thing," an abbreviated rendering of Virgil, *Aeneid*, 4.126-9 (H. Rushton Fairclough, ed. and trans., *Virgil*, 2 vols. [Cambridge, Mass., rev. ed. 1934-35; repr. 1994], I, 514-15).

[1] Remainder of text in D'Ivernois's hand.
[2] The Tr contains two additional pages in D'Ivernois's hand:

"Continuation

"Other letters from Geneva dated the 10th. Instt. inform us farther that two fresh victims have been sacrificed to the sanguinary fury of the Revolutionists, and that some violent misunderstandings have already arisen between their leaders and the french Resident. The reason of this is not as yet fully ascertained; but it is Known that the former have gone so far as to address severe complaints against him to the Committee of public safety at Paris.

"Subsequent letters from the *pays de Vaud* mention that a number of respectable citizens of Geneva daily arrive there, having been bannished, and previously plundered of every thing: that they are received with open arms, and that the unfortunate Genevese have no longer but one ray of hope remaining them, that the example of the fall of Robetspierre will force those who had aspired to follow his steps at Geneva,

on the very eve of his catastrophe at Paris, to some serious reflexions and some retrieving measures.

"The Government of Berne has just published the following Proclamation, in all the Churches of its Canton, which completes at the same time that it verifies the dreadful picture which I have endeavoured to describe.

" 'Public notoriety has informed you of the deplorable scenes which have plunged the City of Geneva into the depths of affliction. That Republic for whose wellfare we have constantly been interested, resulting from the long and intimate relations as Allies, and from the habitual connections of a close neighbourhood, is now a prey to unheard of calamities, of which it is impossible to foresee either the extent, or the duration or the consequences. At the moment when we were flattered with the hope of the return of peace and tranquility by the new order of things, which the Government had just solemnly announced to us, and also to the Canton of Zurich as the term of all dissentions; a set of Lawless persons have attacked and overthrown by force of arms public liberty and private security: They have been seen breaking open dwelling houses, carrying away from thence a multitude of individuals, arbitrarily arresting them and dragging them to different prisons. These violences have been extended even to the Ministers of Religion, in such a manner as indicates its approaching proscription, in a city which long has been one of its principal supports. In the midst of this general subversion, blood has been spilt; several citizens have been sacrificed against even the majority of the voters; new victims are marked out, further outrages on persons and property are preparing, and are put into execution in despite of the oaths the established forms and the Laws of the state; and Geneva overwhelmed with consternation awaits in terror the fate preparing for her by these bloody Insurgents, who have usurped the right of disposing of the lives and fortunes of their fellow citizens.

" 'We view with extreme grief the mournful destiny of a City whose happiness and peace were at all times the object of our care, and whose situation so nearly interests the tranquility of our state and that of switzerland; but the Knowledge which we have acquired of the criminal participation of several individuals of our Country in the horrible excesses which we have just related, aggravates still our grief, and adds to our indignation. Our paternal sollicitude for the safety and honor of our Country does not permit us to tolerate on our territory those men stained with crimes: We ordain by the present publication, that entrance thereon be interdicted them, and it is our pleasure that all those of our subjects who shall be Known to have had a share in these atrocious scenes, be instantly denounced and seised, reserving to ourselves to pronounce the just punishments which their guilty conduct in a City so long a time our Ally may have deserved.

" 'We doubt not dear and Liege, that participating with us the sentiments which animate us, you will redouble your activity and zeal in the execution of this present Ordonnance. We take pleasure especially in the persuasion that at the sight of these distressing events, which so cruelly agitate this neighbouring Republic, you will the better appreciate the happiness of living under mild and equitable Laws, which, seconded by a beneficent Religion, have for such a length of time afforded us the enjoyment of the inestimable blessings of peace and tranquility, and of every Kind of prosperity which God bestows on the people he loves. And that God, whose almighty protection, we as well as our fathers so sensibly experience, will not abandon us, if grateful for his benefits, and placing our Confidence in him, we seek still to deserve his goodness and his favours by our virtues and by our love for our Country.'

"Given in our Great Council

"the 4th. of Augt. 1794

"Chancery of Berne"

From François D'Ivernois

MONSIEUR   Londres ce 23 7bre 1794

Vû la possibilité, que soit les affaires publiques soit vos affaires particulieres vous conduisent à Philadelphie à l'époque où arrivera en Virginie ma Dépeche No. 3, Je vous y en adresse le Duplicata. Je n'ai point le tems d'y joindre celui de la continuation de l'exposé historique de la Révolution de Geneve, mais MM. Adams ou Gallatin, aux quels je l'adresse aujourdhui, seront à meme de vous la communiquer si vous le désirez.

Je prens la liberté Monsieur, de vous présenter ici un léger apperçu bien incorrect sans doute de la premiere idée que je me fais de la masse des Instituteurs qui pourraient suffir dabord pour notre Université et pour ses écoles. Je ne doute pas que nos Professeurs de Geneve ne puissent proposer sur cette premiere esquisse des changemens convenables, et je doute bien moins encore Monsieur, que votre Province et vos lumieres personelles n'entrevoyent aisement ce qu'on pourrait en supprimer et ce qu'on devrait y ajouter: Aussi je vous répéte en vous la soumettant, que je ne la hazarde que comme un apperçu extremement vague et imparfait.

Je suppose donc qu'on pourrait diviser l'Université en 5 colleges, et qu'on entrerait comme chez nous dans l'un des trois derniers apres avoir passé successivement par les deux premiers.

1r. College
de
belles lettres
{ Un Professeur en langues et belles lettres Grecques et latines.
Un Prof. en langue & belles lettres francaises.
Un Prof. en langue & belles lettres anglaises.
Un Prof. en Géographie et en histoire.

N.B. Je présume qu'il serait convenable de joindre à ce College préliminaire, quelques tuteurs qui y seraient entretenus, mais qui reçevraient exclusivement leurs salaires des jeunes étudians aux quels ils seraient attachés.

2d. College
de
philosophie
{ Un Prof. en Mathematiques et en Astronomie.
Un Prof. en philosophie naturelle.
Un Prof. en philosophie rationelle.

N.B. Ce second College exigerait peut etre encore quelques Tuteurs.

college de
droit
{ un Prof. en loi commune
un Prof. en droit civil, en droit naturel et en droit des Nations

College de
Théologie
{ 2 Professeurs

College de Medecine
{ Un Prof. en Médecine
Un Prof. en Anatomie
un Prof. en Botanique, et en Chimie

Tous ces Colleges et toute l'Université seraient sous l'inspection et sous le controle d'un Président soit Vice Chancellier.

Ecoles

Il me semble qu'on pourrait les diviser en deux espèces, mais absolument séparées l'une de l'autre ainsi que de l'Université.

1re. Ecole *préparatoire* au Collège de belles lettres de l'Université, et où l'on enseignerait les langues mortes. On pourrait la diviser en trois classes dirigées par trois Régens et par trois sous Maitres. Ces derniers payés par les écoliers eux memes.

2de. Ecole soit *Ecole générale*, où l'on n'enseignerait point les élémens des langues mortes, et qu'on pourrait diviser également en trois Classes dirigées par trois Régens et par trois sous Maitres. Mais pour rendre cette école cy la plus gratuite possible, peut etre conviendrait-il que meme les sous Maitres en fussent salariés par l'Université.

Deux Maitres l'un d'écriture, l'autre d'histoire et de Géographie, salariés par l'Université, pourraient etre également attachés à ces deux écoles.

Ces deux écoles seraient sous l'inspection et le controle d'un Président qui pourrait peut etre faire en meme tems, du moins dans l'origine, les fonctions de bibliothécaire.

Dans un pareil plan, les maitres d'équitation, de dessein, d'armes, de langues vivantes, de musique, de danse, & & seraient payés exclusivement par les écoliers, ou ne reçevraient de l'Université qu'un salaire infiniment modique, mais suffisant pour les soumettre à son inspection annuelle et à son controle.

Je ne desespere point Monsieur, que le revenu que je sollicite ne put suffire à un établissement aussi vaste et aussi complet. A l'exception des Chaires en Loi commune et en belles lettres anglaises, j'ose me flatter que Geneve pourrait vous présenter pour toutes les autres des sujets dignes de votre adoption, et qu'à leur arrivée en Amérique, ils seront vivement animés par le desir d'égaler un jour la réputation de vos Professeurs of William & Mary, et de fraternizer et rivaliser avec eux en émulation et en services. J'ai l'honneur d'etre avec respect Monsieur Votre tres humble & tres obéissant serviteur   F D'IVERNOIS

RC (DLC); at head of text: "No 4"; at foot of first page: "A Monsieur Jefferson." Recorded in SJL as received 9 Dec. 1794. Probably enclosed in TJ to Wilson Cary Nicholas, 12 Dec. 1794.

CONTINUATION DE L'EXPOSÉ HISTORIQUE DE LA RÉVOLUTION DE GENEVE: see note to enclosure to preceding letter.

To Dabney Carr

DEAR DABNEY   Monticello Sep. 24. 1794.

As I think the learning French essential to the study of the law, I cannot help being anxious that you should do it, and that without loss of time, as for want of understanding it you must read every day is a disadvantage.[1] I think if you could come and stay here one month, applying yourself solely and constantly to that object, you would acquire it sufficiently to pursue it afterwards by yourself: and I wish it could be instantly, because tho myself and both my daughters can assist you in the learning it, yet it is my daughter Randolph who possesses the pronunciation the best, and who would most effectually aid you. She goes down the country in a few weeks, to stay the winter, which is the circumstance most urgent for your coming immediately. Another is that you will find here your mother, and Polly who are now here, and Mrs. Cary whom we expect every day.

I am in treaty for the sale of a considerable part of my law-books, and will therefore be obliged to you to embrace any safe opportunity which may occur of returning to me such of my books in your possession as you are done with. I am Dear Dabney, with my most respectful compliments to Mrs. Carr your grandmother. Your's affectionately

TH: JEFFERSON

PrC (ViU: Carr-Cary Papers); at foot of text: "Mr. Dabney Carr." Enclosed in TJ to Garrett Minor, 24 Sep. 1794.

A letter from TJ to Carr of 22 June 1795 and Carr's reply to TJ of 24 June 1795, received four days later, both recorded in SJL but not found, probably related to TJ's recovery of LAW-BOOKS for sale to Archibald Stuart (TJ to Stuart, 23 May, 30 June 1795; MB, 25 July 1795, and note). SJL also records missing letters from Carr to TJ of 21 Aug. 1795, received four days later from Bearcastle, and from TJ to Carr of 8 Nov. 1795.

¹ Thus in manuscript.

To Garrett Minor

DEAR SIR   Monticello Sep. 24. 1794.

I received a few days ago your friendly letter of the 8th. inst. as I had before recieved by my sister Carr the kind offer of three bushels of the May wheat. I am anxious to begin the culture of this wheat, and meant to avail myself of your offer. I had proposed ere this to have visited my antient tutor and friend Mr. Douglas: but I have been attacked by a rheumatism, which has confined me three weeks, and is as yet but a little abated in it's rigor. I therefore think it better to send the bearer for the wheat, as the season is wearing away. I reserve for it part of a good fallowed feild.—You are so near Mr. Douglas that I will trouble you with my affectionate respects to him, with an assurance that there is nothing I desire more than to see him once again, and that I will certainly do it if my health is restored in time before the roads become too bad. I will further trouble you with the inclosed letter to my nephew Dabney Carr, and with many thanks for the wheat I take the liberty of now sending for, I remain Dear Sir Your friend & servt

TH: JEFFERSON

RC (DLC: Garrett Minor Papers); addressed: "Colo. Garrett Minor Louisa"; endorsed by Minor. Enclosure: TJ to Dabney Carr, 24 Sep. 1794.

Garrett Minor (1743-99), the nephew of TJ's deceased brother-in-law Dabney Carr, was a Revolutionary War militia officer and local officeholder who represented Louisa County in the Virginia House of Delegates, 1792-93 (Harris, *Louisa County*, 23, 62, 65, 391; Swem and Williams, *Register*, 37, 40).

Minor's missing LETTER OF THE 8TH. INST. is recorded in SJL as received from Louisa on 21 Sep. 1794. SJL also records a letter from Minor of 1 Apr. 1798, received from Louisa on 24 Apr. 1798, and TJ's 3 May 1798 reply, neither of which has been found.

To Thomas Divers

Sir   Monticello Sep. 28. 94.

I was informed a few days ago that under the law of Congress our carriages were to be enlisted with a Mr. Rhodes. Being confined myself, I sent the tax-money for my Phaeton two or three different times by Mr. Randolph to Charlottesville on public days, but he could not meet with Mr. Rhodes or any body acting for him. Taking for granted that he is your deputy and that the entry and payment to you is sufficient I take the liberty of entering my phaeton, the only carriage I have in this county, and of inclosing you a guinea, 26/ the tax I believe being 24/. Should I be mistaken in supposing you the sufficient officer for receiving this, will you have the goodness to settle it with the proper officer for me, as I understand it must be done this month, and I have no prospect of being able to get on a horse my self for a month to come. I am with great regard Sir Your most obedt. humble servt   TH: JEFFERSON

PrC (MHi); at foot of text: "Mr. Thomas Divers"; endorsed in ink by TJ.

Thomas Divers, the brother of George Divers, owner of the Farmington estate near Charlottesville, was a former merchant in Charlottesville who in 1804 became a captain of an Albemarle troop of cavalry in the Virginia militia (George Gilmer to TJ, 11 June 1792; note to TJ to George Divers, 26 Nov. 1792; CVSP, IX, 405). Under the terms of the 5 June 1794 LAW OF CONGRESS "laying duties upon Carriages for the conveyance of persons," the owner of a PHAETON was obliged each September to pay a tax of six dollars (*Annals*, IV, 1452).

To Benjamin Franklin Bache

DEAR SIR   Monticello Sep. 29. 1794.

In a letter from Crosby, office keeper for the Secretary of state, he informs me you expressed some anxiety to receive the gong belonging to Mr. Franklin, the bringing of which here was the subject of a former apology to you. I have the promises of three several persons who went to China in different vessels in 1793. that they would bring me one each, and I presume I may count on their return the next summer. In the mean time Mr. Franklin's is used here as the bell for a chateau clock which I have. I take the liberty of assuring you it is in perfect safety, that whether I recieve one or not, the next summer, it shall be then most sacredly returned, and that in case of any accident to my self, I have given notice to my family that it is the property of Mr. Franklin and is to be safely returned. Still should you require it's immediate return, I will on receiving notice send it instantly to Richmond from whence there is a conveyance to Philadelphia every week. Retaining always the same sentiments of esteem & respect, I am Dear Sir Your most obedt. & most humble servt   TH: JEFFERSON

RC (PHi: Dreer Collection); at foot of text: "Mr. Bache."

The LETTER from Sampson CROSBY, dated 11 Sep. 1794 and recorded in SJL as received from Philadelphia on 24 Sep. 1794, has not been found. SJL also records a letter from Crosby to TJ of 14 Apr. 1794, received from Philadelphia on 29 Apr. 1794, and TJ's replies to these letters of 30 Apr. and 1 Oct. 1794, all of which are missing. For TJ's purchase of a replacement for the GONG BELONGING to Benjamin FRANKLIN, see MB, 30 Oct. 1794, 11 Dec. 1795.

To James Brown

DEAR SIR   Monticello Oct.[1] 1. 1794.

I now inclose you a draught on Mr. Lownes of Philadelphia for 108.58 D. to replace what you had paid for me to Mr. Moncrieff: and I have taken the liberty of desiring Messrs. Nicklin & Co. of Philadelphia to address to you for me a pipe and a quarter cask of wine, on which they will have paid the duties and all charges till put on board the vessel. The freight from Philadelphia to Richmond I must request you to answer. As soon as I know that this wine is arrived I will engage a couple of waggons to go down for the whole. I am in hopes you will have been so good as to transvase the wine of the injured pipe into a good one. Will you take the trouble of informing me what was the exchange on England on the 19th. of the last month?

I have examined my notes of money received from Clow & Co. on your account, and find you have omitted 200. Dollars, received Dec. 4. 1792. This added to the balance of your account and of Donald & Burton's makes a larger amount than I have any means of answering till the tobacco of the present year gets to market, which will not be till next spring. Then it shall be discharged.   I shall be obliged to you for the information asked relative to the exchange by the return of the post, as it concerns a case which is urgent. I am with great esteem Dear Sir Your friend & servt   TH: JEFFERSON

RC (CtY); at foot of text: "Mr. James Brown."

The enclosed DRAUGHT may have been the letter of this date to Caleb LOWNES, recorded in SJL but not found. SJL also records letters of 8 Sep. and 6 Nov. 1794 from Philip NICKLIN & CO. to TJ, received from Philadelphia on 17 Sep. and 18 Nov. respectively, and from TJ to Nicklin & Company of 17 Sep. and 20 Nov. 1794 and 27 May 1795, all of which are missing, although the subject matter of the last two can be inferred from MB, 19 Nov. 1794 and 27 May 1795.

[1] Word written over "Sep.," erased.

From François D'Ivernois

MONSIEUR Londres le 2. 8bre 1794

En vous adressant le Duplicata du No. 4 expédié par la voie de Philadelphie; les tristes nouvelles reçues de Geneve depuis cette epoque m'engagent à venir redoubler aupres de vous mes sollicitations en faveur du peuple le plus Malheureux qui existe. Le Tribunal révolutionaire y a prononce de nouveaux emprisonnements ou banissements contre 4. à 500 Citoyens, et pour se saisir des biens des absents, il en a encore condamné plusieurs à mort par contumace. Et vous devez comprendre que je suis loin d'être étonne de voir mon nom à la tête de ces derniers. Il est vrai que je ne suis pas sans espoir d'avoir reussi, ainsi que plusieurs de mes compatriotes, à sauver la meilleure partie des propriétés qui pouvoient me rester encore dans Geneve; Mais au surplus la perte des biens de la fortune, seroit le moindre des maux dans ce monde revolutionnaire, depuis que la qualité de propriétaire, y est devenue le premier des crimes. Le croiriez-vous Monsieur, les françois eux mêmes, les auteurs de toutes nos convulsions spoliatrices, affectent Aujourdhui d'en avoir pitié, et de blamer les excès de leurs imitateurs, auxquels ils ont ecrit pour les inviter à y mettre un terme? Ce dernier trait me paroit achever le tableau des Malheurs des Genevois.

Veuillez Monsr., je vous en conjure de nouveau venir à leur Secours, et leur preparer une 2de. patrie; Les nouveaux colons que je place sous vôtre protection spéciale, ne sont point des aventuriers, qui vont chercher au loin, une réputation, et une fortune perdues chez eux par leur faute. J'offre à la Virginie l'élite d'une petite peuplade Républicaine, frappée par le tonnere de la révolution françoise; d'une peuplade, que les Philosophes avoient comparée depuis longtems, à la ruche d'Abeilles, et qui en ce moment encore fixoit leurs regards par sa prodigieuse émulation, par l'œconomie laborieuse a la quelle tous ses individus opulents avoient dû leurs succes, et par l'extreme frugalité avec la quelle ils en jouissoient.

J'apprens qu'une 3e. petite bande de Genevois, vient de suivre à Hambourg ceux qui étoient alles s'embarquer pour L'Am. Sept. Et je gémis de l'inconvenance que je trouve, à leur communiquer en Europe, mon projet, avant qu'il ait atteint sa maturité en Amérique, c'est-à-dire avant d'apprendre qu'elle ait acceuilli mes propositions. Si cependant vous aviez Monsr. cette heureuse nouvelle à me faire passer, je vous prierais de la communiquer en même temps, à Mr. Duby jeune Ministre, qui doit s'être embarqué pour Philadelphie, et dont Mr. Gallatin pourra vous indiquer la résidence: Il est ainsi que Monsr. Salomon, son compagnon de Voyage, digne de toute votre confiance.

Je m'occupe toujours sans relache, à méditer, et à préparer tout ce qui sera nécessaire pour donner le branle, à cet etablissement, dès qu'il aura été adopté par la Virginie. Malgré la crainte de vous paroitre ridicule, en m'occupant des ornements de l'edifice avant d'en avoir jette les fondements; je vous dirai Monsr. qu'en pensant à la Nouv. Geneve il m'est venu l'idée, d'adopter pour ses batisses l'architecture rurale et simple des Toscans Modernes, à qui le climat assez semblable à celui de la Virginie, a fait adopter les portiques et les colonnades, qui environnent leurs petits domiciles, et qui en ajoutant aux agréments des formes, les mettent à l'abri de l'ardeur du soleil, et des injures de la pluie dont vous observez dans votre ouvrage, que la Virginie a une plus grande proportion que l'Europe. Tout ce qui pourroit réunir, à l'utilité réelle les graces de l'Architecture, me sembleroit ne devoir point être negligé, dans une cité Académique. Et si vous en pensiez comme moi, je n'hesiterois point à appeller, chacun de nos colons, à quelque leger[e dé]pense de plus, pour batir toutes leurs maisons, sur des plans réguliers, et fixés d'avance. J'ai pensé que pour la 1e. année, ils pourroient se contenter de batir soit en pierres, soit en bois, des Maisons simples, et à un étage d'environ 50 pieds de face sur 15 de profondeur, et 22 d'élevation, sous l'engagement de les doubler l'année suivante [sur le] devant de la rue en y ajoutant, pour l'usage du public, un portique ouvert de 15 pieds de largeur, formé par des Colonnes en bois, ou en briques, qui soutiendroient la face du premier étage,[1] la quelle serait aussi en briques. Vous comprenez Monsr. que je ne jette en avant cette 1re. idée, que parcequ'il m'importeroit de savoir à peu pres, ce que couteroient en Virginie, cette 1re. et cette 2de. construction.

J'aurois bien désiré Monsr. d'avoir pu, parmi nos Professeurs vous en offrir un d'Architecture, vers la quelle je présume bien que les Américains vont tourner leurs regards, de plus, en plus: Mais je suis forcé d'avouer, que les Genevois avoient trop négligé cet art non moins utile, qu'agreable: et que nos plus beaux monuments sont dûs à des Architectes étrangers, dont nous dépendions encore, quoiqu'il començat a se former chez nous quelques amateurs assez distingués. Ce seroit là un motif de plus pour s'en occuper d'avance, si jamais il doit être question de former une nouvelle Geneve.

J'entrevois de plus en plus Monsr. que cette Nouv. Geneve pourroit bien n'être en Amerique, que le précurseur de beaucoup d'établissements dûs à la même cause. L'Incendie Révolutionnaire de ce continent gagne et s'accroit avec une prodigieuse rapidité: sans prétendre rien préjuger ici des fruits que pourront en receuillir les générations futures; toujours me paroit-il certain que la génération présente, est condamnée à des calamites aussi longues, qu'incalculables, et que les débordements de ce Volcan, pousseront plus tôt, ou plus tard, une foule d'individus vers l'Amérique. La Lutte qui s'est élevée en Europe, entre les français, et les puissances Coalisées est à mes yeux plus loin que jamais d'être terminée, et à l'époque où elle le sera, tous les Rois de l'Europe, se trouveront inévitablement pour leurs finances, dans le même épuisement, et dans le même embarras, qui ont precipité la catastrophe de la Monarchie française. Nouvelle source de révolutions pour tous les peuples, que celle ci n'auroit pas encore atteinte. Heureux ceux qui apres y avoir passé, auront le bon esprit d'imiter les Américains, et de sentir qu'une 1re. revolution terminée a propos peut établir la liberté; Mais qu' alors toutes révolutions successives la détruisent d'autant plus irresistiblement, qu'elle en inspirent bientôt le dégout, et quelquefois même la Haine. Il n'est deja plus possible en ce moment, de calculer l'influence que va avoir sur le Nord de L'Europe, la révolution de Pologne, puisqu'il est tres certain, que le Roi de Prusse en voulant y étouffer à main armée l'esprit de liberté, lui a donné un ressort, qui s'étend dejà jusques sur ses propres états, et qui l'a forcé pour y accourir, à lever le siege de Varsovie. Je dois aux Anglois, de toutes les classes, et de tous les partis, la justice de dire que malgré le grand interêt qu'ils mettent à la coalition du R. de Prusse ils ont fait, et font encore hautement des voeux pour les succes des Polonais: Quelle cause en effet, fut plus digne d'interet que celle ci? Et Combien cet interet redoublera s'ils continuent à éviter les excès de tout genre[2] qui ont deshonoré le brillant dévouement avec le quel les français ont repoussé les armées étrangeres.

Ou je suis fort trompé, ou de toutes les contrées de L'Europe, la Gde. Bretagne sera la derniere, qu'atteindront les desorganisations révolutionnaires. Plus je vois l'Angleterre, et plus il me paroit averé ainsi qu'a Mr. Cooper, que la grande pluralité de la Nation, veut conserver sa constitution telle qu'elle est; et que la pluspart de ceux qui y désiroient des reformes partielles sentent qu'on ne pourroit point toucher aujourdhui, à la distribution intérieure de l'édifice, sans risquer de porter la sappe à ses fondements mêmes. Les proprietaires y sont nombreux, puissants, unis, armés, et suffisamment instruits des dangers qu'auroit pour eux l'introduction de la doctrine, de l'egalité des droits, sur la fortune des riches. Enfin la classe même qui avoit fait des voeux, pour les progrès de cette doctrine avant d'en connoitre les dernieres conséquences, commence réellement à la redouter, en voyant ces conséquences se développer, dans toute leur étendue, et se prolonger à l'infini. Mais surtout en jettant les yeux sur le sort de la plus part de ceux qui l'ont faite triompher en france, et sur la longue série de crimes, que se reprochent Mutuellement ceux d'entr'eux qui y ont survecu, et qui y dominent. Aussi le gouvernement de ce pays cy a-t'il toute la force nécessaire pour étouffer un premier germe d'insurrection, ainsi que pour la supprimer si elle venoit à éclater. Cependant quoique la prospérité y soit encore à l'ordre du jour, et que le Commerce, soit exterieur, soit intérieur, y paroisse presqu'aussi actif qu'avant la guerre; je ne m'aviserois point de calculer les évènements, et les embarras que pourra dans la suite susciter cette guerre, qu'on paroit tres detérminé à prolonger, et qui ne laisse gueres entrevoir pour l'avenir que de Nouveaux desastres, et de Nouvelles taxes.

Les autres puissances de L'Europe, plus allarmées encore sur un avenir qui leur paroit plus prochain, et plus menaçant pour elles, entreprennent dejà de grandes œconomies, qui portent principalement sur le luxe des cours. Les gouvernements suisses qui n'ont point de pareilles précautions à adopter; louvoyent avec adresse, se refusent toujours plus opiniatrement à prendre aucune part active dans cette guerre; qui soit qu'ils combatissent, pour ou contre la france, les exposeroit inévitablement, à des convulsions semblables aux siennes. Ils se bornent à redoubler de paternité, envers leurs peuples, aupres desquels les principes révolutionnaires qui dans l'origine avoient fait quelque progres, font évidemment aujourdhui des pas retrogrades, surtout depuis l'expérience des affreux Malheurs, que leur introduction a accumulés sur les Genevois.

De toutes parts, dans cet état universel d'allarmes, et a l'approche de tant de crises, les Européens timides, ou prévoyants, les vrais amis de la paix, et de la liberté sage, fixent leurs regards d'adoption, et leur espoir de refuge sur l'amerique libre. Et si elle persiste, et reussit à ne point jouer un rôle sur la scène de ce drame révolutionnaire, et guerrier, tout annonce qu'elle seule profitera des fautes de L'Europe, et que la providence l'apelle à servir de port à toutes les classes, que la persécution en chassera.

Il est vrai qu'on commence dejà à enlever ce dernier espoir aux Européens opprimés, ou allarmés, en leur annonçant, que L'Horizon politique, des Etats Unis, s'obscurcit, qu'il se charge même de Matieres inflammables, et qu'entr'autres, un parti dejà nombreux, cherche à entrainer son gouvernement vers la guerre avec L'Angleterre. S'il en étoit ainsi, il y auroit cette grande différence entre les deux païs; C'est que le gouvernement d'Amérique, redouteroit une guerre, que le peuple y desireroit, tandisque quoique les Américains accusent le Gouvernement Anglais de n'avoir pas craint de la provoquer, il n'en est pas moins tres certain, que l'universalité de la Nation, ne la désire point, et la verroit même avec une peine sensible. J'observe avec plaisir que les Horribles écarts de la revolution française ont fait peu à peu revenir les Anglois en arriere sur celle d'Amérique, et changent deja en applaudissements, les préjugés invétérés, qu'ils conservoient encore il y a peu d'années contre cette derniere. En un mot, je suis bien trompé si la Masse des Anglois, n'a pas repris pour les Américains, presque tous ses anciens sentiments fraternels, ce qui ne m'empecheroit cependant pas de craindre que s'ils envisageoient jamais leur gouvernement comme irresistiblement poussé, à une 2de. guerre, celle ci ne reprit tres promptement, et à bien des égards, le Caractere d'une guerre civile, et mutuellement tres destructive.

Voila Monsr. que sans y penser, je me suis prodigieusement écarté de l'objet qui m'avoit mis la plume à la main. Peut-être aussi cette petite digression politique y a-t-elle des rapports tres intimes, puisque si j'envisage comme mon 1r. devoir de chercher un port à mes compatriotes battus par la tempête des révolutions; le 2d. doit être de leur trouver une rade, ou ils soient parfaitement hors de l'atteinte des vents, qui ont entr'ouvert leur petit vaisseau. Helas il n'y a pas plus de deux ans que nous nous croions à l'abri de tout orage! Et ce qui nous a jetté en pleine mer, est précisemment, ce qui sembloit devoir nous fixer à l'ancre. J'entends par la l'extreme conformité de nôtre constitution démocratique, avec celle que venoient d'établir les françois.

Au surplus, je me repose avec confiance pour la paix, et le bonheur de l'Amérique, sur l'esprit sage, et éclairé de ses habitants, et sur l'immense intéret de ses propriétaires, qui heureusement y sont aux non propriétaires, dans l'inverse de la proportion qu'offre l'Europe. Je compte sur L'Heureuse dispersion de ses établissements agricoles, qui n'offrent point comme dans le vieux monde des Hommes refoulés les uns sur les autres, et des passions toujours pretes à s'allumer par le frottement journailler, de l'opulence, et de la Misère. Mais je compte surtout sur les sages Architectes, du bel édifice, qui s'y est élevé, et qu'ils ne laisseront sans doute point ébranler. En un mot malgré les pronostics de convulsions prochaines dont on commence à menacer ici les Américains, je ne pourrai jamais y croire, que lorsqu'elles auront éclaté, et jusques à cette époque, je ne me relacherai, sur aucun des travaux dont je m'occupe ici; et pour le succès définitif des quels mes espérances se concentrent toujours presqu' Exclusivement Monsr. sur votre protection speciale. J'ai L'Honneur d'être avec Respect Monsieur Votre tres humble & tres obéissant serviteur   F D'IVERNOIS

P.S Si la réponse que j'attendrai de vous Monsieur avec tant d'impatience, me donnoit des assurances de succès asses positives, pour que les Genevois n'hesitassent point à former immediatement leur compagnie d'Actionnaires, à en nommer les agents, et à les expédier en Amérique; il m'importeroit de savoir en même temps si quelque vaisseau de l'un des ports de la Virginie, seroit pret à mettre à la voile pour la Hollande, à peu pres à la même époque que partiroit vôtre réponse; qu'elle seroit l'époque probable de son retour, et s'il pourroit se charger d'un nombre assez considérable de passagers; car il me paroitroit convenable que la Compagnie des actionnaires engageat, et fit partir en même temps que ses agents, une Masse d'ouvriers propres à la construction de la Nouvelle ville: tels que Massons charpentiers, Maréchaux menuisiers serruriers charrons[3] &ca. et même quelques uns de nos meilleurs[4] jardiniers pour préparer des jardins, et planter les légumes d'automne, dont les suisses font une grande Consommation: Vous comprendrez sans doute Monsr. que quoique j'aye en contemplation une mesure provisionelle de cette importance; Elle ne pourroit être adoptée, qu'autant que vous seriez à même de me donner sur le succès de l'entreprise un degré de probabilité, qui ne nous laissat aucun doute, non seulement sur les intentions de la Législature de Virginie; Mais encore sur la promptitude, avec la quelle elles pourront se réaliser.

Dupl (DLC); in a clerk's hand, signed by D'Ivernois, with note at head of text in two different inks—"Duplicata du No 5 expédié par la Peggy"—dateline, part of complimentary close, and corrections and revisions by him, only the most important being noted below; faded in several places; at foot of first page: "A Monsieur Jef[fer]son."

[1] Remainder of sentence interlined by D'Ivernois in place of "à l'imitation de plusieurs petittes villes de suisse."
[2] Preceding three words interlined by D'Ivernois.
[3] Preceding three words interlined by D'Ivernois.
[4] Word interlined by D'Ivernois.

VOTRE OUVRAGE: TJ's work was *Notes on the State of Virginia*.

From François D'Ivernois

MONSIEUR   Londres ce 4. 8bre 1794

Au Duplicata du No. 5 que j'ai eu l'honneur de vous expédier by *the Peggy bound for Virginia*, je joins ici la continuation de la lamentable histoire des convulsions de Geneve. Sa lecture vous fera juger suffisamment combien est praticable et pressant l'établissement que j'ai proposé à la Virginie ou plutot que je sollicite d'elle en faveur des malheureux Genevois. Elle me justifiera en meme tems sur la multiplicité des lettres que je prens la liberté de vous adresser à cette occasion. J'ai l'honneur d'etre avec respect Monsieur, Votre tres humble & tres obéissant serviteur   F D'IVERNOIS

RC (DLC); at head of text: "No 6"; at foot of text: "À Mr Jefferson"; endorsed by TJ as received [8?] Dec. 1794 but recorded in SJL at 6 Dec. 1794.

François D'Ivernois's Third Letter
on the Genevan Revolution

London Octr. 4th.[1] [1794]

The Symptoms of mildness which the Revolution of Geneva seemed to assume, have soon given place to it's original character, viz that of pillage. Scarcely had the conspiracy of the Montagnards been discovered; Scarcely had the Revolutionary Tribunal been compelled to punish it's authors (who declared before they went to punishment, that they had done nothing which their very judges had not instigated, ordered and directed them to do). Scarcely indeed had this Tribunal got rid of that faction which alarmed them by threatning to make the fruits of the pillages of the Genevese Revolution pass into the hands of the French, than they began afresh these same pillages with an activity quite new, in directing them more particularly against the class of Merchants, whom they had lately denounced as being richer and more avaricious than the Aristocrats. It is true that in this third scene, the blood of innocent men has not been shed, and that three of them condemned to death for the purpose of seizing on their property have undergone this sentence only in effigy on account of their ,absence. But four or five hundred heads of families have not the less been included in a new list of confiscations, proscriptions and imprisonments.

Thus the scourge of this terrible revolution has already reached and struck about a thousand Citizens, that is to say more than the half of the general assembly of the people such as it was composed two years ago, when a thousand natives and nearly as many strangers were associated! In the mean time though the fourth part, and the worthiest of it's actual members, have been thus excluded, such are the fears of their oppressors on the true sentiments of the majority of the three thousand remaining members of that assembly, that they dare the less convoke it, as votes are given by a secret ballot. They have provisionally reimplaced it by 23 Revolutionary clubs, where the votes are given publicly, and where those alone for whom tranquillity is become a state of violence dare to give theirs, their boldness increasing there in proportion to the discouragement of the most honest.

These 23 little deliberating Republics meet every day, and make sometimes separately sometimes collectively the most contradictory proposals.

The fluctuation of this new democracy is inexpressible. Some times it permits those artists condemned to imprisonment in their own houses to go out three times a day to attend their avocations; and soon after recalls this permission. At other times wishing openly for the depopulation of Geneva it allows the inhabitants who have not been brought to trial to depart with their moveable effects; the next day, astonished at the croud of emigrants, and the quantity of goods which they had carried off the day before, it again forbids the departure of any inhabitant as well as of every kind of specie, merchandize &c.

The grand question which still divides their minds, is that of allowing the administration of the Republic either to the Revolutionary Tribunal, or to the Syndics and Council, which this Tribunal has lately dispossessed, just as the former had dispossessed the legitimate and constitutional administration in 1792.

To induce the Revolutionists to believe that although stigmatized by all their neighbours, they have still at a distance allies, and approvers of their enormities; The authors of these crimes have ordered for the 1st: of Septr: a civic festival, in which to take advantage of the compliment which the French Convention has lately payed to Geneva in placing it's colours beside those of the united states; They have displayed with pomp the American flag, for the purpose of lulling the Genevese in the sweet delusion that they are still worthy of being compared and associated to the Republic of the new world. It is true that at this show one could read in marked characters on the countenances of the Spectators, and assistants, shame and remorse. But what are we to expect from a people to whom no other virtue remains in appearance but that of discovering such remorse, and no other courage but that of surmounting it?

One Trait more will suffice to finish the picture of[2] their misfortunes: it is that the french the instigators of all these convulsions and plunder, dissatisfied either in not having been able to collect the fruits for themselves, or in having been so far surpassed in their Revolutionary career, pretend at this moment some compassion for the Genevese!(1) They have written to their disorganizers to persuade them to put an end to this scandalous and useless tragedy!

Whether these will persevere in prolonging it, or drop the curtain for a while; the fate of this little Republic is no longer doubtfull. If the Revolution of france is triumphant, Geneva already entirely surrounded by its territory is inevitably condemned to become a french city: Or if even by a miracle, it should escape that destiny, and its virtuous citizens should extricate themselves from their actual oppression, they would nevertheless be forced contrary to their inclinations, to let themselves roll in the orbit of the great Planet to the Revolutions of which Geneva has suffered herself to be attached as a satellite.

After these last consequences of a first step towards the Revolutionary doctrine, one may trace its source, its current and its overflowings from the moment when it announced itself with mildness by the modest and innocent tittle of *Citizen* which its partisans adopted among themselves; up to the period, when after having succeeded in proclaiming the *equality of rights*, they found out the art of extending that equality of rights, even *over the fortunes of those who did not think as they did*, and when after having disarmed them without resistance, they plundered banished and put them to death. Such are the late ravages which this Doctrine has introduced into Geneva!

There was not however in that small and interesting Republic, either abuses to correct or reforms to operate, nor even priviledged Classes to excite jealousy, since the Genevan Laws at no time acknowledged nobility, even among families the most ancient and the most opulent.(2) It must also be observed that the

(1) The french have among other things given orders or granted permission to print in the public papers of Paris, the eloquent Proclamation of the Great Council of Berne, which throws out a particular stigma against the Genevese Revolution: And the Deputy of the Convention who is lately arrived on the frontiers of swisserland expressed himself nearly on the same manner on this subject.

(2) One of the fundamental laws of the Constitution of Geneva runs so. *Let any member of this commonwealth be satisfied with the rank of Citizen without aspiring to any superiority or preeminence whatsoever above his fellow citizens except where public office entitles him and requires it.* Such was the base of the very first foreign Constitution against which the french have armed themselves: such was the Constitution, which under the imputation of aristocracy, they previously attacked with open force and afterwards by intrigues, and which they have at last overwhelmed in one common ruin with the people whose prosperity it had so much advanced.

ancient Government whose members have been so cruelly pursued and persecuted had always shown in the administration of justice and of the finances a
purity against which even the spirit of faction had never raised any doubts; and
that the exact public œconomy of the administrators could only be compared to
their personal disinterestedness. It was so much so in fact, that their successors
in seizing on their places, began to double and triple their salaries; and it seems
that they have not yet found them sufficient, since in the course of the last six
weeks there has been an expenditure of the public treasure or rather a dilapida-
tion of about £40,000 St.

Two great and important truths arise from this afflicting picture.

The 1st. That at all times, when this new Revolutionary Doctrine shall find
its way into a free state, it will make more havock than in any other, because
such a state will have nothing more to adopt of it than its excesses.

2dly. That a free people are nevertheless the most exposed to this dreadful
storm, since we are able to judge that *that* which has driven the Genevese into
the open sea, is precisely what ought to have fixed them at anchor, that is to say,
the conformity of their democratic Constitution with that which the french have
been establishing.

MS (DLC); in the hands of a clerk and
D'Ivernois (see note 2 below), with note at
head of text—"Continuation for the american News papers"—and several clerical corrections also in D'Ivernois's hand; partially
dated, with day altered by D'Ivernois (see
note 1 below); missing numbers in text ref-
erencing author's footnotes have been supplied by the Editors. Tr (NHi: Gallatin Papers); with minor variations; enclosed in
D'Ivernois to Albert Gallatin, 4 Oct. 1794
(same).

[1] Written by D'Ivernois over "2d."
[2] Remainder of text in D'Ivernois's hand.

From James Madison

DEAR SIR   Harewood Ocr. 5. 1794.

On my return to Orange I dropped you a few lines on the subject of
the deer. On my way into this part of the Country I passed Col. John
Thornton of Culpeper, who has a Park, and will spare you with pleasure two or three, if you can not be otherwise supplied. He thinks he
could by advertizing a premium of 10 or 12 dollars a head procure from
his neighbors as many fawns to be delivered at Monticello as you would
want. If you chuse to make use of his assistance, a line to the care of
Mr. Fontaine Maury at Fredg. would soon get to hand.

This will be handed to you by Mr. Bond who is to build a large
House for Mr. Hite my brother in law. On my suggestion He is to visit
Monticello not only to profit of examples before his eyes, but to ask the
favor of your advice on the plan of the House. Mr. Hite particularly
wishes it in what relates to the Bow-room and the Portico, as Mr: B.
will explain to you. In general, any hints which may occur to you for
improving the plan will be thankfully accepted. I beg pardon for being

the occasion of this trouble to you, but your goodness has always so readily answered such draughts on it, that I have been tempted to make this additional one.

I write at present from the seat of Mr. G. Washington of Berkeley, where, with a deduction of some visits, I have remained since the 15th. Ult: the epoch at which I had the happiness to accomplish the alliance which I intimated to you I had been sometime soliciting. We propose to set out in 8 or 10 days for Philada. where I shall always receive your commands with pleasure, and shall continue to drop you a line as occasions turn up. In the mean time I remain yrs. mo: affecy

Js. MADISON JR

RC (DLC: Madison Papers); with line drawing of bow room on verso; endorsed by TJ as received 31 Dec. 1794 and so recorded in SJL.

Madison's FEW LINES of 1 Sep. 1794, recorded in SJL as received from Orange on 18 Sep. 1794, have not been found. In his early landscaping plans for Monticello TJ had set aside part of the estate for a DEER park, which he began to stock as early as 1771 and where he evidently relished feeding ears of Indian corn to the animals by hand. The site of the park changed over the years, its location and size at this time being recorded in TJ's 1794 survey of the fields on the side of the mountain (MB, 20 Sep. 1769, cash accounts, 1771, miscellaneous memo-

randa, and notes; Betts, *Garden Book*, pl. XIII, facing 208).

Isaac HITE, the husband of Madison's sister Nelly, was constructing Belle Grove in Frederick County, Virginia. As an architect TJ favored the use of the BOW-ROOM, a chamber with a semicircular or octagonal bay, but no such feature was used at Belle Grove and the extent of his contribution to the house's final design is unclear (Frederick D. Nichols, "Belle Grove in the Developing Civilization of the Valley of Virginia," *Historic Preservation*, XX, nos. 3-4 [1968], 8, 18n). The ALLIANCE accomplished on 15 Sep. 1794 was Madison's marriage to Dolley Payne Todd (Brant, *Madison*, III, 410).

To John Barnes

SIR   Monticello Oct. 9. 1794.

My constant occupations while in Philadelphia prevented my renewing an acquaintance with you, which I recollect with pleasure to have had many years ago. I can now do it only by letter. Having occasion for about 20. ℔. of good tea annually, I think it best to rely for the choice of it on the good faith of some dealer in that article, both as to quality and price, and on no one do I rely more willingly than on yourself. I usually send to Philadelphia for my groceries once a quarter, and will on those occasions ask of you a quarter's supply of tea. At present I will beg the favor of you to pack for me *in a cannister* 5. ℔. of good tea. Young hyson we prefer both for flavor and strength, but if you have none good, let it be hyson of the antient kind. If, immediately on the receipt of this you will deliver it to Mr. Mussi, corner of 7th. and Market streets, he will pay your bill, and pack the tea with some other articles he will be sending me. Not doubting to recieve from you what will be good in quality and reasonable in price, I am with esteem Sir your most obedt. humble servt   TH: JEFFERSON

PrC (ViU: Edgehill-Randolph Papers); at foot of text: "Mr. Barnes."

John Barnes (ca. 1730-1826), a Philadelphia grocer and tea merchant, from 1795 to 1809 served as TJ's private banker, commission agent, and grocer. Born in England, Barnes moved first in 1760 to New York (where TJ initially met him in 1766), then in 1790 to Philadelphia, and finally in

1800 to Georgetown, of which TJ appointed him collector in 1806. He earned TJ's praise as the "most punctual and assiduous man in business I ever knew" (MB, 23 Apr. 1795, and note; TJ to John Peter Gabriel Muhlenberg, 10 Oct. 1802; Cordelia Jackson, "John Barnes, A Forgotten Philanthropist of Georgetown," *Records of the Columbia Historical Society*, VII [1904], 39-48).

To Benjamin Carter Waller

SIR   Monticello Oct. 9. 1794.

I recieved in due time your favor of Aug. 2. and proposed to have had the pleasure of meeting you in Richmond on the 20th. inst. according to your appointment. But about the beginning of September, I was attacked by a violent rheumatism, which after keeping me so long in constant agony, leaves me no prospect of release from my confinement within any given term of time. And were it now to leave me, I should not be able to undertake a journey by the time appointed. This however is of no consequence to the settlement of Mr. Welch's and Mr. Wayles's matter[1] as Mr. Eppes is the acting executor, and the only one who has any knowlege of Mr. Wayles's affairs, my continual absence having withdrawn me from them at a very early period. I therefore wrote to him in time for him to meet you, and notified to him, as I do now to you, my acquiescence in whatever he shall agree with you.   My anxiety for a friendly and reasonable arrangement induces me to express my extreme wish to you, that instead of meeting Mr. Eppes at Richmond, you could call on him[2] two or three days before the 20th. at his own house. I have always seen business done more easily and more amicably, where the parties have met in a friendly way and at a private house where they would have the leisure and the dispositions to explain and approximate their opinions, than in a public place, confined to a particular hour, and pressed and interrupted[3] by other business. I am sure you will find in Mr. Eppes the most just dispositions, and I have no doubt of your own, and it is to give fair play to these mutual dispositions, that I make to you this proposition, having informed Mr. Eppes that I would

do so, and therefore prepared him to expect you. I am with great esteem
Sir Your most obedt. servt.   TH: JEFFERSON

PrC (MHi); at foot of text: "Mr. Benjamin Waller"; endorsed in ink by TJ.

I THEREFORE WROTE TO HIM: SJL records
a letter from TJ to Francis Eppes, 25 Sep.
1794, which has not been found.

SJL also records a letter of 12 May 1796
from TJ to Waller which has not been
found.

[1] Preceding seven words interlined.
[2] TJ here canceled "a day or."
[3] Preceding two words interlined.

To George Wythe

TH: JEFFERSON TO G. WYTHE   [23 Oct. 1794]

I received a few days ago your friendly enquiries after my health. I
have had a painful and tedious rheumatic complaint. It has now nearly
left me.

I inclose for your perusal a little treatise by Kuster on the use of the
Middle voice in Greek. I never saw a copy of it till I met with this, nor
had ever heard of it. I presume therefore it may be new to you; and if it
gives you half the pleasure it did me, mine will be doubled still. His
position is that the middle voice is always intransitive, and is never confounded with either the active or passive in it's signification. According
to my own obervation, since his work suggested the idea, I have found
it almost always true, but I think not absolutely always.

I ever wish to have opportunities of enjoying your society. Knowing
your fondness for figs, I have daily wished you could have partaken of
ours this year. I never saw so great a crop, and they are still abundant.
Of three kinds which I brought from France, there is one, of which I
have a single bush, superior to any fig I ever tasted any where.—We are
now living in a brick-kiln, for my house, in it's present state, is nothing
better. I shall recommence my operations on it the next summer, and no
small part of the pleasure I promise myself in it's future accomodations,
is founded in the hope of possessing you here sometimes, and of gratifying your taste for books, by introducing you to a collection now certainly the best in America. Accept my most friendly & affectionate respects & Adieu.

PrC (DLC: TJ Papers, 98: 16749); undated, but recorded under this date in SJL.
Enclosure: Ludolf Kuster, *Lud. Kusterus de
vero usu Verborum Mediorum Eorumque
Differentia A Verbis Activis & Passivis. . .*,
3d ed. (London, 1750). See Sowerby, No.
4768.

Wythe made his FRIENDLY ENQUIRIES in a
missing letter of 5 Oct. 1794, recorded in
SJL as received from Richmond on 15 Oct.
1794.

To Thomas Mann Randolph

Th J. to mr Randolph   Monticello Oct. 27. 94.

The children are in high health and spirits. They have learnt to say 'Mama is gone.' Jefferson adds 'to Ichom' (Richmond). We had a most copious rain on Saturday and Sunday, and learn with concern that you passed those days at Mrs. Payne's.

It is important to me to know what was the exchange between Richmond and Liverpool on the 19th. of last month, for *ordinary* bills. (You know that bills of an *extraordinary* degree of credit command a higher price than ordinary ones, which is not what I want, but the value of bills of as good credit as the common run.) I wrote to James Brown to inform me, on the 1st. of this month: but his business has probably prevented an answer. In the mean time I am suffering for want of the information. Will you be so good as to ask of Mr. Brown what it was? He can answer it by only opening his book of bills.—Have you ever ascertained the price of wheat at Richmond before the arrival of the news of the embargo? My love to my dear Martha. We are anxious to know how Eleonor bore her journey. Adieu. Your's affectionately

RC (DLC); endorsed by Randolph. Not recorded in SJL.

To James Madison

Th:J. to J.M.   Monticello Oct. 30. 94.

In the moment of the departure of the post it occurs to me that you can, by the return of it, note to me the amount of Mazzei's claim against Dohrman, for the information of the Van Staphorsts. I will put off my answer to them for that purpose.—The day you left me I had a violent attack of the Rheumatism which has confined me ever since. Within these few days I have crept out a little on horseback, but am yet far from being well, or likely to be so soon. I wish much to see the speech, and to know how such an armament against people at their ploughs, will be represented, and an appeal to arms justified before that to the law had been tried and *proved* ineffectual, by the *fact*, not by the certified *opinion* of a magistrate paving the way to an embassy. Adieu. A thousand respects to Mrs. Madison and joys perpetual to both.

RC (DLC: Madison Papers).

DAY YOU LEFT ME: Madison visited Monticello ca. 20-25 Aug. 1794 (Madison, *Papers*, XV, xxix).

In his annual SPEECH to Congress on 19 Nov. 1794, George Washington justified dispatching an army of federal militia to quell the Whiskey Insurrection with, in part, the 4 Aug. 1794 CERTIFIED OPINION of

Supreme Court Justice James Wilson, already publicized in a presidential proclamation on 7 Aug. 1794, that in Pennsylvania's Washington and Allegheny counties those obstructing the execution of the federal excise laws had formed "combinations too powerful to be suppressed by the ordinary course of judicial proceedings, or by the powers vested in the marshal of the district" (Fitzpatrick, *Writings*, XXXIII, 460, XXXIV, 30).

To Henry Remsen

DEAR SIR   Monticello Oct. 30. 1794.

I received yesterday your friendly favor of the   inst. and have to thank you for your attention to the gongs. There being two of them did not merit apology: I am glad to get them, and can find use for both. Be so good as to tender to Mr. Gouverneur my particular thanks for his attention to this little commission. I inclose you an order for 25. Dollars[1] on Mr. Lownes of Philadelphia, which according to your statement will I presume pay for the gongs, the duty, and perhaps the box to pack them in. I will thank you to have them well packed, and sent by some vessel bound to Richmond (no other port) to the care of Colo. Robert Gamble merchant there.   I am so much immersed in farming and nail-making (for I have set up a Nailery) that politicks are entirely banished from my mind. I feel alive to nothing in that line but the success of the French revolution. I sincerely rejoice therefore in the successes you announce on their part against their combined enemies, and I cannot help hoping that the execution of Robespierre and his bloodthirsty satellites is a proof of their return to that moderation which their best friends had feared had not been always observed.—I thank you sincerely for the tender of your services. I have had too many proofs of your friendship to doubt it and can assure you it is sincerely reciprocated by Dear Sir your affectionate friend & servt

TH: JEFFERSON

RC (CtY); with a marginal notation by Remsen (see note 1 below); addressed: "Henry Remsen esquire New York"; stamped; endorsed by Remsen.

Remsen's FAVOR of 13 Oct. 1794, recorded in SJL as received from New York on 28 Oct. 1794, has not been found. The enclosed ORDER was probably the missing letter of this date to Caleb LOWNES recorded in SJL as concerning "Remsen's drt." SJL also records unlocated letters from Lownes to TJ of 6 Oct. 1794, received from Philadelphia on 21 Oct. 1794, and from TJ to Lownes of 9 Oct. 1794.

[1] Preceding five words underscored by Remsen, who wrote the following notation in the margin keyed to "order": "sent to Mr. Fisher of Philada."

To Archibald Stuart

Dear Sir   Monticello Oct. 30. 1794.

I recieved some time ago your favor on the subject of Mr. Dow-thwaite, and soon after that he called on me himself. I should have been glad to have served him for the double motive of wishing well to his enterprize, and for the interest you take in his success. But it seemed that he wished me to address the assembly either directly or indirectly on his behalf. This I could not do. A total retirement from all intermed-dling with publick affairs and public bodies is my object; besides that such an application to the assembly from me would have been as imper-tinent as ineffectual.—I have lodged with Colo. Bell two barrels of sweet potatoes for you. I think you told me they did not succeed well on your side the mountain. Hope therefore they may merit acceptance. I have been flattering myself that something might draw you downwards this season, and that I should have the pleasure of seeing you here. I still indulge the expectation, because, if eventually unfounded, it is in the mean while a pleasing one.—I am endeavoring to collect money to pur-chase two or three score of sheep. Should I succeed I propose to trouble you with the commission. Perhaps you can in the mean time have your eye on those which are for sale, not making any bargain however, as experience has taught me never to trust with certainty to the collection of money.—I congratulate yourself and all good republicans, on the complete success of the French this campaign. For, in this, *res nostra agitur*. My best respects to Mrs. Stewart, and am with sentiments of great esteem Dr. Sir your sincere friend & servt   Th: Jefferson

RC (ViHi); addressed: "Archibald Stew-art esquire Staunton." PrC (DLC).

Stuart's favor of 2 Oct. 1794, recorded in SJL as received from Staunton 16 Oct.

1794, has not been found. res nostra agi-tur: "It is our problem that is at issue here"; more colloquially, "you're fighting our fight."

From George Wythe

GW TJ salutem mittet   1 of november 1794

An apt begining to a letter containing a prescription.

Put on sheeps clothing. It will cure rheumatic pains, is comfortable in winter, after one summer not unpleasant in that season, less unpleas-ant than linen in all seasons, when we perspire freely. Probatum est.

You send Kuster for my perusal. I can peruse nothing but court papers. This employment by habit is become delectable. In it I regret only that I cannot participate the elegant entertainment to which Monticello invites. I return the book, supposing you to possess but one copy, lest by detaining it I should deprive you of a pleasure I am forbidden to enjoy; which, with Aesops leave, would be more than brutish.

Since I cannot taste of your figs at your house, send me some cuttings that I may endeavour to treat you with their fruit, when you come to my house.

RC (DLC); endorsed by TJ as received 19 Nov. 1794 and so recorded in SJL. Enclosure: see TJ to Wythe, [23 Oct. 1794].

SALUTEM MITTET: "sends greeting." PROBATUM EST: "it is proven."

From William Short

DEAR SIR .   Madrid Nov. 4. 1794

The object of the present letter is to satisfy a request made to me by Mr. Blake soon after his first arrival in this country and now repeated at the moment of his intended departure—namely that I would give him a letter recommendatory to you. Although you have now retired from public life, and will probably therefore have no occasion of seeing or serving Mr. Blake, and if you had would have no occasion of a letter from me for that purpose, as he is already known to you, yet I feel no difficulty in giving him this kind of certificate of his conduct during his long stay in this country, having been in every respect prudent and proper. As he has lived with Mr. Carmichael during the whole of that time he has been still more in the way of observing it, and he confirms this opinion of Mr. Blake's conduct, as he will mention in the letters he purposes writing to America on the subject. He will explain also to Government, if he has not already done it, the cause of Mr. Blake's detention here, so contrary to what I apprehend must have been their expectation. However this forms no part of the object of my letter, which as I have said above is destined merely for Mr. Blake, whom I with pleasure recommend to you, in the case you should have any opportunity of serving him, as he appears to me a young man of perfectly good dispositions, and of the strictest attachment to his adoptive country.

I shall send by him an edition of Don Quixote which I ask you to accept as a small token of my remembrance. It is the 8vo. edition of the academy and equally complete and correct with the 4to. edition, and more transportable, for which purpose I have chosen it, and send it unbound. If you have not previously had this edition, though I have some idea you have, I recommend particularly to you the Analysis at the beginning by Dr. Vincente de los Rios.

Mr. Carmichael has been fortunate enough to procure you the letters of Cortez—and will send them to you. It has been a long long time since I have had the pleasure of hearing from you, which is matter of much concern to your friend   W Short

PrC (DLC: Short Papers); at foot of text: "Mr Jefferson." Recorded in SJL as received 21 July 1795. Enclosed in James Blake to TJ, 6 June 1795.

For the mission to Spain undertaken by James BLAKE, see TJ to Blake, 12 July 1793, and note. EDITION OF DON QUIXOTE: see Sowerby, No. 4347. LETTERS OF CORTEZ: see TJ to Short, [ca. 12 July 1793], and note.

To James Madison

TH:J. TO J. MADISON   Monticello Nov. 6. 94.

A merchant neighbor of mine, sets out to-day for Philadelphia for his fall goods, and will return with them by water himself. This furnishes me a favorable opportunity of gleaning and getting the books I left in Philadelphia. But I must ask your friendly aid. Judge Wilson has Mably sur l'histoire de la France 4. v. 12mo. and Houard's Britton, Fleta, Glanville &c. 4. v. 4to. which he promised to deliver you. Pray press for them in my name.—E.R. has several, partly lent here during my absence, partly in Philadelphia. I write to him by this post to ask his lodging them with you. He will probably need being sent to for them.— After a very long drought which threatened to be fatal to our small grain, we have had two most abundant rains at an interval of a week, both followed by warm weather. The thermometer in the middle of the day from 55. to 69. It has been once only at the freezing point. Smart white frosts in the neighborhood, but none has extended yet to this place.—Fine beef 2d. Corn from the tub 8/, both cash. Wheat 5/ in goods @ $61\frac{1}{3}$ per cent on the Philadelphia price, which brings the wheat down to half a dollar at Philadelphia.—The Sheriffs, who are now going down with their money, declare that there never was so miserable a collection; men, hitherto the most punctual, having been obliged to ask indulgence, from the scarcity of cash. My best respects to Mrs. Madison. Adieu.

RC (DLC: Madison Papers). PrC (DLC).

MERCHANT NEIGHBOR: see TJ to Ed-

mund Randolph, 6 Nov. 1794. HOUARD: David Houard, *Traités sur les coutumes Anglo-Normandes, qui ont été publiées en Angleterre, depuis le onzième, jusqu'au qua-*

torzième siècle . . ., 4 vols. (Paris, 1776). See Sowerby, No. 1774. This work included medieval English legal writings by the author known as BRITTON (possibly John Le Breton) and by Ranulf de GLANVILLE, as well as the anonymous work entitled *Fleta*, all of which TJ also owned in separate editions (see Sowerby, Nos. 1769-70, 1772-3).

To Edmund Randolph

TH:J. TO E.R.   [6 Nov. 1794]

A merchant neighbor of mine (Mr. Fleming) going to Philadelphia for his fall goods, and being to return with them by water himself, offers me a good opportunity of collecting the remains of my books left in Philadelphia. In a memorandum kept here, during my absence, of books lent, I find the following set down to you.

Tacito del Davanzati. 2. v.

Tull's husbandry.

Da Costa's fossils

Crown circuit companion.

In my own memorandum kept at Philadelphia, I find the Treatise de la Morale et la bonheur set down to you, and I believe Mr. Thompson lodged with you for me a Nova Versio Graeca of some books of the bible. Such of these as you have I will thank you to deliver to Mr. Madison on whom Mr. Fleming will call for the others. I expect he will be in Philadelphia by the time you recieve this, and will stay only 3. or 4. days.—We hear that your land (Fry's) is sold to Mr. Champ Carter. This deprives us of the hope those lands had kept alive, of your ultimately fixing in our neighborhood.—I am still confined in a great measure by the remains of my rheumatism, being unable to go out, either on horseback or in a carriage, but in a walk, and small distances.—Mr. Short was to send me by Blake, Cortez's letters in Spanish. Is Blake returned and has he brought them? Adieu, with respects to Mrs. Randolph. Your's affectionately.

PrC (DLC); undated, but recorded under this date in SJL. Neither the first nor the second MEMORANDUM has been found.

From Samuel Blackden

MY DEAR SIR   Richmond Novemr. 9th. 1794

I have to lament being upon crutches as it deprives me of the pleasure of waiting on you and paying that Respect which I most sincerely feel for your character, your own goodness will on this account plead my excuse. Nothing but total inability could prevent my enjoying the happiness of seeing you.

The time which has elapsed since I left France puts it out of my power to give any information which you have not Received before, I shall only say that I beleave the Revolution is as firmly establish'd as the Rock of Gibralter; it matters not what party prevails for the Moment, nor what Numbers may fall in the contention for fame or Power, the People like water always find their level, they Rally and do Right.

I left France in May and after a few weeks stay at Lisbon arrived in Philadelphia the beginning of September, the ship in which I took passage was Danish—the Captain a Man of understanding, education, and fortune. He has been sent twice to Algiers with the usual Presents from the King of Denmark to the Dey, and has been treated by him with the most pointed marks of friendship and esteem. Having had frequent Opportunity of conversing with our worthy and Respectable countryman Colo. Humphreys, this Generous Dane offerd to go again to Algiers in order to facilitate the Release of the Captives, disclaiming at the same time every idea of Profit or Advantage. He proposed to take a Cargo on his own account to Alicant and having landed it, to cross to Algiers take them onboard and bring them to Lisbon without a Shilling expence.

When we arrived at Philadelphia being unable to wait upon the President at his country house, I inclosed and sent the letters I brought for him by express, and when he came to town made two Attempts to see him, but found his Garrison fortified with starch and buckram which my crutches could not remove, and therefore took the liberty of writing to him on the subject of the Captives. In seventeen days after I Received an answer from Mr. Randolph to whom I also brought letters saying that arrangements were taken for effecting this desirable object; from this answer I found that I had neglected the etiquette which is to be observed in applications to the President. However after two months attention to the Affair of our unfortunate countrymen, I was informed that every thing was setled for obtaining their Release.

How much have I to Regret your not being in Philadelphia, had that been the case I am confident the business would have been Accomplish'd in a few days.

> "Victims of pirates, on the insulted Main;
> Whose lot severe, these soothing lines complain.
> Lift up your heads; ye much enduring Men,
> In Western skies, the New Aurora Ken.
> Though long the Night, and angry lour'd the sky,
> Lift up your heads, for your Redemptions Nigh." (Humphreys) [1]

I have left Mrs. Blackden in Philadelphia, and Am Commission'd to convey in the most Respectful and Affectionate Manner her Regards to you Mrs. Randolph and Miss Polly. Mr. and Mrs. Barlow are at Hambourg where I hope he is doing well.

For my own part I cannot express the feelings of my heart for your goodness to me on all occasions but do most sincerely thank you, and ardently wish for the continuation of your health and happiness, with which I am Dear Sir your obliged hble Servant   S. BLACKDEN

RC (DLC); addressed: "Thomas Jefferson Esqr Monticello Albemarle County Honord by W. W. Henning Esqr"; endorsed by TJ as received 27 Nov. 1794 and so recorded in SJL.

The lines of poetry are from David HUM-PHREYS, *A Poem on Industry Addressed to the Citizens of the United States of America* (Philadelphia, 1794), p. 20. See Evans. No. 27145.

[1] Closing quotation mark and parenthesis supplied.

From François D'Ivernois

MONSIEUR   Londres ce 11e 9bre 1794.

J'ai l'honneur de vous addresser *le tableau de la Révolution françoise à Geneve* qu'on m'a fortement invité à faire imprimer dans ce payz cy, et où en rectifiant quelques erreurs legeres qui s'étaient glissées dans la premiere narration Anglaise, j'ai ajouté beaucoup de faits que j'ignorais encore lorsque je vous l'adressai. Je vois deja avec un vrai plaisir, que quoique ce petit écrit n'aborde aucune question de parti, et ne contienne aucune des déclamations du jour, il a fait, sur les personnes meme que je désirais surtout persuader, une impression plus profonde que je n'avais osé l'attendre, et que quelques Anglais l'ont deja jugé digne d'etre traduit. Dès qu'il le sera, j'aurai l'honneur de vous en envoyer un exemplaire, et si vous pensiez que la réimpression de cette traduction Anglaise en Amérique put y etre de quelqu'utilité, j'en serais d'autant plus flatté qu'apres le sentiment d'avoir rempli un devoir aussi sacré que pénible, rien ne saurait Monsieur, m'etre aussi précieux que votre suffrage.

Au surplus, je jouis deja du doux espoir, que la grande masse des Américains est trop éclairée sur la liberté et trop attachée aux devoirs qu'elle impose, pour avoir besoin des avertissemens terribles que présente notre histoire. La joye que j'ai éprouvée en apprenant que les Américains ne laissent point flétrir les principes d'ordre du nom d'Aristocratie, et qu'ils se sont levés en masse pour le maintien de leurs loix pures, ne pouvait presque etre égalée que par la vive douleur dont j'ai été en meme tems pénétré en apprenant par vos papiers publics, qu'un de mes compatriotes avait eu plus ou moins de part dans les égaremens auxquels se sont livrés quelques districts de Pensylvanie. Certes, je regrette presque d'avoir cédé au conseil que me donna Mr. Jay, d'écrire à Mr. Gallatin, et de lui confier mon plan. Puissent mes lettres lui avoir fait faire de sérieuses et salutaires réflexions! Puissent du moins la ruine de sa premiere patrie, l'assassinat de ses parens, et le desastre général de ses anciens amis, lui présenter avec fruit dans un cadre aussi resserré que Geneve le tableau de tous les crimes aux quels seront inévitablement entrainés et condamnés, tous les peuples qui chercheront la liberté et des réformes au flambeau de ce qu'on appele aujourdhui du nom de Révolution!

Je me hâte Monsieur, de reprendre l'objet si intéressant à mon coeur, et que j'ai eu le bonheur de pouvoir placer sous vos auspices, celui de Geneve Américaine. Je m'empresse de vous informer que j'ai enfin reçu de suisse les réponses les plus satisfaisantes à la communication que j'y avais donnée de toute ma correspondance avec l'amérique. Quoiqu'il n'y ait encore que trois personnes qui soyent dans le secret, savoir Mr. le Prof. Pictet, son frere, et Mr. le Prof. Prevost, ils s'accordent tous trois à penser que si les Américains adherent à mes propositions et protégent cette noble entreprise avec activité et surtout avec promptitude, elle pourra acquérir une consistence plus brillante encore que je n'avais osé l'espérer. Mon correspondant ajoute meme, *Qu'il ne doute point que Si la concession fondamentale s'obtient, on n'ait bientot les actionaires; et qu'on n'ait finalement peut etre plus d'embarras à repousser certaines personnes qui ne Conviendraient pas, qu'à attirer toutes celles qui conviendront.* Il me donne en meme tems par aperçu la liste de celles sur les quelles il croit qu'on pourra compter pour les trois établissemens Académique, Agricole, et commerçant; et j'y ai retrouvé avec une bien grande satisfaction toute l'élite de notre petite République. Mais ma satisfaction a redoublé en trouvant dans cette liste le nom du celebre *Mr. de Saussure*, qui pour se livrer exclusivement à l'achevement de ses beaux ouvrages, avait renoncé depuis quelques années à la chaire de philosophie en faveur de Mr. Pictet son digne Successeur. J'avoue que je le croyais indissolublement lié au malheureux sol de Geneve par la nature de ses propriétés toutes foncieres et meme par le voisinage des alpes. J'ai été bien agréablement détrompé en apprenant que nous pouvions compter sur lui et sur son fils, que le pere destinait à lui succéder un jour, et qui est déja un homme distingué dans la carriere de l'histoire naturelle où il a été introduit par un si grand maitre; et vous pouvez juger aussi bien que moi Monsieur, du lustre que donnerait Mr. *de Saussure* à la nouvelle Geneve Académique. Je retrouve également dans cette liste les noms de trois ou quatre de nos Médecins qui ont fait des études tres distinguées à Edimbourg, et qui seraient capables de remplir, meme avec éclat, les chaires d'anatomie et de Médecine théorique et pratique. Quant à l'établissement agricole et commercant, je me borne à vous dire Monsieur, que d'apres ce qu'on me mande, je ne doute plus que les cent Actions de £1000 Stg. chacune ne puissent se remplir, et se partager entre un égal nombre de familles ou environ. Or cette somme et ce nombre me paraissent également Suffisans pour le noyau d'une colonie ou le choix des membres me semble encore plus essentiel que leur multiplicité.

Ces assurances qu'on me fait passer sur le concours des Genevois à la colonisation Américaine sont fondées.

1°. Sur le nouveau *Décret* que j'ai l'honneur de vous adresser en original. Ce dernier acte du brigandage Révolutionnaire vous fera Suffisamment comprendre Monsieur, que ceux des propriétaires Genevois qui auraient pu etre tentés de rester sous le joug pour sauver leurs propriétés foncieres ne peuvent plus y etre retenus par cet espoir. Pres de onze cent personnes ont deja été frappées par ce nouveau Décret; et il est telle d'entr'elles qui s'est vue imposée à £16,000 Stg. On m'en nomme plusieurs, et entr'autres Mr. J. Tronchin, qui, plutot que d'entrer en marché avec les spoliateurs, et de leur livrer tout ce qui lui restait en propriétés personnelles afin de sauver ses campagnes et ses immeubles, a préféré leur abandonner volontairement toutes ces dernieres, estimées £500,000 Tournois; et a fui Geneve, en se réduisant aux propriétés qui lui restent dans l'étranger.

2°. Sur ce que l'émigration, loin d'etre jalousée et empêchée par les Révolutionnaires (comme je l'avais dabord craint) est au contraire ouvertement provoquée ou favorisée par eux et qu'elle est meme déja beaucoup plus nombreuse que nous n'en aurions besoin pour former partout ailleurs une petite Colonie prospere; que cette émigration est meme si rapide et si considérable que le Canton de Berne allarmé du renchérissement des subsistances, que l'arrivée de nos émigrés a causé dans le pays de Vaud, vient de se voir appelé à mettre des bornes aux facilités qu'il avait donné aux premiers venus, en sorte que ceux qui les suivent sont obligés de se disperser dans les différens districts de la suisse.

3°. Sur ce que la France loin de géner cette émigration, (comme je l'avais également craint,) n'y met aucune espece d'obstacles, et que la plupart des municipalités voisines la favorisent au contraire par simple esprit de justice et d'humanité; que c'est meme en se rendant sur le territoire français, que la plupart des Genevois qui émigrent trouvent toutes les facilités qu'ils desirent pour passer en suisse; et qu'enfin mon correspondant à qui j'avais indiqué la route du Rhin pour l'embarquement, ne pense qu'à celle de la france pour le Havre, route sur la quelle il ne prévoit aucun obstacle, et qui sera en effet plus courte et beaucoup moins dispendieuse.

4°. Sur ce que notre Académie a enfin reçu le coup de mort que je vous avais annoncé d'avance. Outre les emprisonnemens prononcés cy-devant contre divers Professeurs, cinq chaires viennent d'etre décidément supprimées, et le Professeur de Mathématiques qui ne l'était pas, insiste sur sa démission pour se retirer en Suisse. Il paraît que l'intention actuelle de nos Révolutionnaires est de borner l'étude des sciences à celle de la philosophie naturelle, la plus utile sans doute, mais qui n'en a pas moins besoin de tous les secours dont ces destructeurs aveugles prétendent la priver. Pour donner à cette branche d'instruction publique un nouveau lustre, ils comptent exclusivement sur Mr. Pictet que je crois vous avoir deja représenté comme l'ornement de notre Académie, et que sa réputation distinguée au dedans et au dehors a mis jusqu'à présent à l'abri de toutes vexations quelconques de la part des Révolutionnaires. Ils se flattent de le placer à la tete d'un *Museum national pour l'étude de la nature* qu'ils se proposent d'instituer à l'hotel de la Résidence, que le successeur de soulavie a trouvé trop magnifique pour l'accepter. Afin de tenter Mr. Pictet, ils offrent de lui acheter son superbe cabinet d'instrumens, qu'ils y placeraient en lui donnant à lui meme une habitation dans ce meme hotel, d'où sont sortis depuis si longtems tous les fléaux qui nous ont atteints et bouleversés. Au reste, quoiqu'ils ne négligent jusqu'ici aucune espece de caresses pour l'empêcher de porter ses vues ailleurs, et qu'ils lui fassent meme une espece de pont d'or pour l'en détourner, je connais mieux que personne ses vraies dispositions, puisqu'il est mon unique correspondant sur le projet américain, et que c'est lui qui me fait passer sur son succès les assurances que je viens de vous exposer. Il m'annonce meme expressement son acceptation de la place d'agent de la Colonie, ainsi que celle de son frere, homme non moins précieux que lui sous une foule de rapports. Ils parlent l'un et l'autre également bien l'anglois. Autorisé comme je le suis Monsieur, à vous annoncer leur adhésion, je n'ai pas besoin sans doute de vous prévenir de l'importance du secret dans tous les cas; mais je dois vous prévenir que ces deux Messieurs en se proposant de partir dès que nous aurions des réponses favorables d'amérique, ne s'y disposent cependant que pour le seul cas où elle réaliserait toutes nos espérances, c'est à dire où la Province qui nous adopterait se déterminerait à donner à cette noble entreprise tout le grand essor dont elle a besoin, pour exciter par la gloire de cette résurection l'émulation de tous ceux des Genevois qui sont les plus dignes d'y contribuer. Au reste, celle de vos Provinces qui embrassera une entreprise

si nouvelle comprendra aisement sans doute combien il est important de
ne point la tenter à demi, et de ne pas l'exposer ainsi au double risque de
causer le malheur ou le desappointement des immigrés sans produire
l'avantage du peuple généreux qui aura voulu leur tendre une planche
dans leur naufrage. Dailleurs M. Pictet sont l'un et l'autre peres de famille, et je ne pourrais les déterminer à une transplantation si lointaine,
qu'autant que les réponses que j'attends de vous Monsieur, oteraient
entierement à cette transplantation, tout ce que jusqu'alors elle parait
avoir d'hazardeux. Le Professeur, en la voyant placée sous vos auspices, y met cependant une telle confiance, et il épouse si chaudement la
belle perspective de pouvoir donner l'amérique pour patrie à ses enfans,
(perspective, qui offre en effet, me dit-il une seconde vie à recommencer
avec l'avantage de l'expérience qu'aura donné la premiere) qu'il m'a ex-
pressément chargé de faire arrêter provisoirement des démarches que
ses amis avaient entreprises dans ce pays cy pour lui procurer quelque
place assortie à ses talens: L'obtention de quelque place semblable lui
serait d'autant plus facile, qu'il a déja obtenu celle de membre de la
société Royale de Londres, à la suite d'un mémoire qu'il composa en
anglais, inséré dans les Transactions philosophiques de 1791 ou de
1792 sur la mesure d'un degré du Méridien et de deux du parallele de
latitude qui se coupent à l'observatoire de Geneve. C'est aussi lui qui a
levé les seules bonnes cartes que nous ayons de la Suisse française et de
la savoye. Enfin c'est un homme universel et dans toute la vigueur de
l'age. Je ne viens de m'étendre de nouveau sur son personel, que pour
vous faire juger Monsieur, du gage de succès que son association présen-
terait à notre Université Américaine, ainsi que du poids de son opinion
et de son exemple sur la disposition générale des Genevois. Au surplus,
il s'est bien gardé de leur communiquer le projet en lui meme, et s'est
borné à faire insinuer soit à Geneve soit en Suisse, à tous ceux des
Genevois que nous désirerions pour Colons, que la possibilité d'une
réunion en Corps sous un autre Ciel, doit leur faire suspendre, au moins
jusqu'au commencement de l'année prochaine tous projets définitifs de
dispersion.

Je ne dois pas négliger Monsieur, de vous transcrire ici quelques
fragments des lettres de Mr. Pictet en date des 3, 13, et 19 8bre. *Mon
frere et moi* me dit-il *nous savons deja notre Jefferson par cœur. J'ai
dévoré cet ouvrage où sous le titre modeste de notes on trouve tant d'information. Je vois dans ce pays, la mine la plus riche d'observations naturelles, et je sens que ma collection minéralogique et lithologique transportée là, y doublerait d'intéret, par les comparaisons à faire entre les
productions naturelles des deux hémispheres. Je picquai vivement la curiosité de Mr. de Saussure en lui parlant des observations géologiques de Mr.*

Jefferson dont il n'avait pas lu l'ouvrage, et je lui ouvris la perspective d'observations comparées de ce genre entre les montagnes des Alpes qu'il a si profondement étudiées et celles d'Amérique. Cette idée me parut le séduire fortement. Je dois aussi Monsieur, vous faire passer une observation de Mr. Pictet en réponse à mon projet de composition d'Académie dont je lui avais soumis la premiere idée avec la meme défiance qu'à vous. "Il me semble, dit-il, que dans un pays où la nature étale des richesses nouvelles, et où la plupart de ces richesses demeurent perdues pour l'homme qui ne les connait pas, les études et l'impulsion d'une Académie naissante doivent etre particulierement dirigées de ce coté. Tant de plantes et d'animaux utiles à connaitre, tant de minéraux à exploiter avec avantage, tant d'édifices publics et particuliers, de ponts, de chemins à construire, doivent commander l'attention et devenir les premiers objets d'un peuple placé dans ces circonstances. Je voudrais donc en admettant vos autres Chaires avoir un Prof. de *Botanique et d'histoire naturelle du regne végétal.* Un Prof. de *Chimie pratique, minéralogie, et métallurgie.* Un d'*architecture civile* et de la partie du *génie* qu'on nomme en france *ponts et chaussées.* La chimie théorique avec ses expériences fondamentales est du ressort du Professeur de phisique expérimentale. Je crois que cette division n'ajouterait au fond qu'un Professeur de plus à votre liste. Je pense encore que chez un peuple appelé à naviger autant que le sont les américains, un Prof. *d'hydrographie* et *pilotage* ne serait pas de trop. J'aurois un homme excellent pour le *génie,* et celui là nous procurerait peut etre quelqu'un pour cette derniere partie."

Ce qui vous étonnera peut etre Monsieur, c'est que le successeur de ce *soulavie* qui avait excité chez nous contre-nos savans et contre les Ministres de la Religion toutes les persécutions des Vandales aux'quelles ils ont été en proye, parait viser à recœuillir dans Geneve les débris du naufrage de nos sciences, et que la france adresse des offres considérables à tous ceux de nos gens de lettres qui seraient tentés d'aller remplir chez elle la place des victimes de sa révolution. Jusqu'ici on n'en a pu ébranler que deux, encore sont-ils d'une classe assez subalterne, et ont-ils promis de ne point se lier indissolublement avant le commencement de l'année prochaine. Je ne doute point que le nouveau Résident, que se trouve etre un Chimiste distingué, n'ait été spécialement chargé de faire surtout des offres tres brillantes à Mr. Pictet quoique ce dernier ne m'en fasse aucune mention. Mais je vous répons qu'aucune d'elles ne pourra le tenter. Je ne doute point non plus qu'avant six mois ou une année, tous les jugemens quelconques d'emprisonnement ou d'exil ne soyent révoqués, et que notre ouragan révolutionnaire n'ait perdu une grande partie de sa premiere fureur destructive. Mais quoiqu'il arrive, le sang innocent n'en aura pas moins coulé, le brigandage des spoliations n'en sera pas moins consommé et irréparable; la liberté et la moralité n'en auront pas moins été flétries pour longues années dans Geneve; et sans prétendre rien prévoir ici des destinées de la génération future, il est évident que pour la génération présente des Genevois hommes de bien, leur patrie est devenue un Séjour inhabitable, et que dès à présent la france elle meme en serait un préférable pour eux à tous égards, si l'amérique ne leur ouvre pas une nouvelle patrie.

Je viens Monsieur, de vous offrir enfin sur la haute probabilité de notre résurection en Amérique, des données positives sur les quelles je n'avais pu vous présenter dans mes premieres lettres que de simples apperçus. Si à l'époque où vous reçevrez cette dépeche, la Virginie a deja pleinement adhéré aux propositions que je vous ai prié de lui soumettre, vous pourrez lui apprendre qu'elle ne sera pas trompée dans les espérances qu'elle en aura conçues, et sans doute, que le succès de l'entreprise vous paraitra assez mur pour qu'on puisse dès à présent envoyer des agents à la recherche et à l'examen des terres qui nous seraient destinées, et pour le choix des quelles vous connaissez maintenant toutes nos convenances beaucoup mieux que nous memes. Si par malheur au contraire, votre Province avait été arrétée jusqu'ici par tout ce que le plan que je lui proposais pouvait avoir de vague à Ses yeux jusqu'à ce que je fusse à meme d'y ajouter la certitude que mes compatriotes y adhéraient, ou jusqu'à ce qu'elle put connaitre la tournure des derniers actes de notre Révolution; j'ose me flatter que ce ne sera point encore trop tard pour reprendre cette intéressante discussion, et la terminer par quelque vote qui ne puisse laisser aux Genevois aucun motif d'hésitation, et qui pourrait leur parvenir encore vers le primtems. C'est maintenant à votre Législature de voir, si cette entreprise est digne de toute la protection que j'implore également Monsieur, de vos lumieres, de votre influence, et ne me permettrez vous point meme d'ajouter de votre zele actif et éclairé pour les interets de l'amérique?

Si par hazard Monsieur, votre Législature pouvoit entretenir encore aucune espece de doutes, soit sur la disposition des Genevois à émigrer, soit sur les difficultés qu'ils pourront avoir à y réussir; je m'en référerai uniquement à l'extrait d'une brochure qu'un Révolutionnaire vient de publier à Geneve et que je joins ici: Vous y verrez qu'il a en quelque maniere déviné mon projet, et qu'il y avoue que les Genevois expatriés sont deja assez nombreux pour pouvoir fonder au besoin *une nouvelle Geneve*, qui rivaliserait et effacerait l'ancienne. C'est un morceau authentique et précieux à tous égards. Je vous laisse le juge Monsieur, s'il ne mériterait point d'etre traduit et inséré dans les papiers d'amérique; car lors meme qu'il ne lui démontrerait pas combien mon projet est praticable, et les divers avantages qu'elle pourra en retirer; c'est un avertisse-ment si terrible sur les remords tardifs, déchirans mais inutiles qui suivent les excès de la liberté qu'il est bien à désirer qu'il ne soit pas perdu pour les peuples qui ont le bonheur de ne l'avoir point encore flétrie.

Puisse la Virginie qui a donné la premiere au monde l'idée et l'exem-ple de la véritable tolérance, lui en donner un second, non moins digne peut etre d'ajouter à sa gloire, celui de la liberté pure vierge et triomphante tendant un bras protecteur à la liberté opprimée et persécutée! J'ai l'honneur d'etre avec respect Monsieur, Votre tres humble & tres obéissant serviteur   F D'IVERNOIS

P.S. Je ferai remettre au vaisseau le *Martin bound for Norfolk*, qui se charge de cette lettre six exemplaires du *tableau de la Révolution fran-caise à Geneve* à l'adresse de Mr. Jefferson.

Dupl (DLC); entirely in D'Ivernois's hand; at head of text: "*No 7*" and "*Duplicata dont l'original a été expédié à S. E. Mr Adams sous couvert de S. E. Mr Jay par le voye de New York pour faire passer à Mon-sieur Jefferson*"; at foot of first page: "A Monsieur T. Jefferson"; endorsed by TJ. RC (DLC); in a clerk's hand, with notes at head of text and foot of first page, dateline, two interlineations, part of complimentary close, and signature by D'Ivernois; at head of text: "*No 7*"; at foot of first page: "A Mon-sieur Th. Jefferson"; lacks postscript and contains minor variations in wording from Dupl; large portions of text illegible from bleeding of ink; endorsed by TJ as received 19 Feb. 1795 and so recorded in SJL. RC and enclosures enclosed in John Adams to TJ, 5 Feb. 1795. Enclosure: François D'Iv-ernois, *La Révolution françoise à Genève; Tableau historique et politique de la conduite de la France, envers les Genevois, depuis le mois d'Octobre 1792, au mois d'Octobre 1794* (London, 1794). See Sowerby, No. 298, for a 1795 edition acquired by TJ. Other enclo-sures printed below.

LES ÈGAREMENS . . . DE PENSYLVANIE: a reference to the Whiskey Rebellion. SON FRERE: Charles Pictet de Rochemont. Nicolas Theodore de Saussure, the FILS of Horace Bénédict de SAUSSURE, became a distinguished Swiss naturalist and chemist (DSB, XII, 123-4). SUCCESSEUR DE SOU-LAVIE: Pierre A. Adet, who succeeded Jean Louis Soulavie as French minister to Geneva in September 1794 (Peter, *Genève*, II, 33).

ENCLOSURES

I
Decree of the Geneva National Commission

Egalité, Liberté, indépendance.
Commission Nationale.
CITOYENS!

L'Etat de pénurie et d'inaction dans lequel se trouve dès longtems le Com-merce et l'industrie à Geneve, alloit plonger une foule de nos concitoyens, dans la plus éffrayante misère. Cette situation critique éxigeoit, pour en sortir, des moyens extraordinaires, prompts et efficaces. La Nation insurgée le sentit et les indiqua.

Elle chargea, entr'autres travaux, la Commission révolutionnaire de diriger ses vues sur la création d'institutions régénératrices, qui pussent guérir les maux dont nous sommes tourmentés, et ramener dans notre chere patrie, Non pas cet aspect d'un faste insultant, qui ne donne aux Etats que l'apparence mensongere de la prospérité, et fut toujours le précurseur certain de leur chute, ou l'indice de l'asservissement du peuple; Mais le vrai bonheur, celui de nos ancetres, celui des républicains, celui qui ne peut éxister sans la simplicité et sans la pureté des moeurs, Celui dont la vraie base est l'amour du travail et de l'égalité.

Ces établissemens sont difficiles et longs à former. La Commission révolutionnaire s'en occupa avec sollicitude dans tous les momens où elle ne fut pas détournée de cet objet par des interets urgens et provisoires, et par les circonstances qui forcèrent la Nation à l'ériger en tribunal révolutionnaire.

La Commission Nationale, elle même, n'a pu encore que préparer des matériaux et faire des essais. L'une et l'autre ont cherché à redonner de l'activité au Comptoir patriotique, et la commission Nationale s'occupa à le réorganiser. Elles ont établi un dépot ou les Citoyens peuvent recevoir des avances sur les produits de leur industrie, en en attendant l'écoulement; elles ont mis en train des fabriques de mouvemens bruts, elles méditent sur les moyens de procurer à chacun de l'ouvrage.

Mais pour donner à tous les établissemens projetés, la stabilité, l'extension et la perfection qu'ils doivent avoir pour le bonheur du peuple, il faut du tems, des expériences suivies, un grand travail, et surtout des fonds considérables. Or ces fonds, où les trouver?

Le peuple insurgé contre l'aristocratie, a des remboursemens légitimes à reclamer du parti qui provoqua ces dépenses énormes, suites funestes du régime despotique et militaire sous lequel gémirent plusieurs années les Citoyens depuis l'intervention des troupes étrangères en 1782; et les patriotes, qui sont dans l'aisance, sont assurément disposés à faire de grands sacrifices. Il a donc ordonné qu'il seroit prélevé, non seulement des indemnités, mais une contribution générale, *mesure extraordinaire*, qui seule peut sauver la république, justifiée par son indispensable nécessité, et dont la rigueur même est une base de sécurité future, qui doit rassurer sur la crainte d'un nouveau recours à de semblables moyens.

La Commission nationale, chargée par le peuple insurgé de ce pénible devoir, a cherché avec la plus scrupuleuse attention, le plan et le mode qui pourroit rendre ces indemnités et cette contribution suffisamment productives, sans énerver le commerce et l'industrie, qui sont nos plus précieuses ressources, et auxquelles son but essentiel est de rendre le ressort et l'activité qui leur manquent. La Commission nationale a aussi cherché à fixer avec justice, d'une maniere positive et génerale, les variations d'indemnités et de contributions dictées par les diverses situations des individus taxés, ainsi que par les diverses mesures de l'incivisme, de ceux qui se sont montrés les ennemis de l'égalité et de la liberté. Après avoir murement pesé toutes ces considérations, et s'être bien pénétrée de la nécessité de remplir l'attente du peuple, la Commission Nationale a pris l'arretté suivant.

article premier.

Les Citoyens patriotes ayant une proprieté audessous de £12000 ne sont point taxés, mais la Commission Nationale les invite, au nom de la Nation, à venir présenter l'offrande que leur suggérera leur patriotisme.

art. II.

Tous les Citoyens qui par des actes, par des propos, ou par leur égoïste inaction, se sont montrés contraires ou indifférens aux principes d'égalité et de liberté, qui ont été appelés par devant les tribunaux révolutionnaires, et qui ont une proprieté de £4000 et audessus jusqu'à £12000 exclusivement sont taxés comme suit: Ceux d'entr'eux qui se sont prononcés de manière à etre Classés comme aristocrates, payeront

sur £4000. $1\frac{2}{3}$ p% $\rbrace$ et ainsi de suite en augmentant de sur $\frac{5}{12}$ p% par
sur £5000. $2\frac{1}{12}$ p% $\rbrace$ chaque £1000 jusqu' à £12000 exclusivement.

Ceux qui seront classés comme englués ou égoïstes payeront comme tels.

sur £4000. 1 p% $\rbrace$ et ainsi de suite en augmentant d'un quart p% par
sur 5000 $1\frac{1}{4}$ p% $\rbrace$ chaque £1000 jusqu' à £12000 exclusivement.

art. III.

Tous les Citoyens patriotes, toutes les veuves et leurs enfans mineurs, toutes les filles majeures ayant une fortune indépendante, toutes les femmes séparées de corps et de biens, et ayant une propriété de £12000 et audessus, payeront une contribution définitivement réglée comme suit:

et ainsi de suite en augmentant progressivement d'un
sur £12000. 2 p% $\rbrace$ 6e. p% par chaque £1000 en sus. Le maximum net
£13000 $2\frac{1}{6}$ p% $\rbrace$ del la taxe de toutes les personnes désignées dans
£14000 $2\frac{1}{3}$ p% $\rbrace$ cet article, ne pourra, dans aucun cas, excéder 25
p% de la fortune du Contribuable.

art. IV.

L'indemnité due par les enlués, égoistes ou indifférens, qui ont une fortune de £12000 et audessus, sera d'une moitié en sus des personnes désignées dans l'article trois; en sorte que la ou la Contribution d'un patriote est de £400. celle de l'englué, égoïste ou indifférent sera de £600. et ainsi de suite pour tout le tableau comparatif. Le maximum de l'indemnité pour ces derniers, ne pourra dans aucun cas, excéder 30 p% de la fortune du taxé.

art. V.

L'indemnité due par les aristocrates sera de deux fois et demie la taxe des patriotes, en sorte que là ou le patriote paye £400. et l'englué £600. l'aristocrate payera £1000; c'est-à-dire autant que les deux ensemble, à fortunes égales, et ainsi de suite pour le tableau comparatif. Le maximum de l'indemnité due par l'aristocrate, ne pourra dans aucun cas, excéder 40 p% de la fortune du taxé.

art. VI.

La Contribution et l'indemnité seront levées sur les fortunes réunies du Mary, de la femme, de leurs enfans mineurs, et filles non mariées quoique majeures, d'ou qu'elles proviennent; sur celle du Pere veuf, de ses enfans mineurs et filles non mariées quoique majeures; sur celle de la Mère veuve, de ses enfans mineurs et filles non mariées quoique majeures, sur celle des freres et soeurs orphelins de Pere et de Mere. Dans tous ces cas la cumulation de ces fortunes aura lieu.

art. VII.

Sur toute Contribution ou indemnité exigée des gens mariés, il sera défalqué un 12eme. de cette contribution ou indemnité en faveur de la Femme, de chaque enfant mineur, et de chaque fille non mariée quoique majeure, et qui n'a pas une fortune indépendante; sur la taxe des veufs, des veuves et de [leu]rs enfans, il sera de même défalqué un 12e. pour chaque enfant mineur, et pour chaque fille non [marié]e, quoique majeure et qui n'a pas une fortune indépendante. Enfin sur la taxe des orphelins de Pere et de Mere, il sera défalqué un 10e. en faveur de Chaque pupille.

art. VIII.

Les Citoyens Célibataires, dans quelque Classe qu'ils se trouvent sur le tableau, depuis l'age de 35 ans et audessus, possédant une fortune de £12000 et plus, payeront un 10e. en sus de la contribution ou indemnité à laquelle ils seront taxés.

art. IX.

Les dons patriotiques faits dès le 19 Juillet dernier, la valeur de la Vaisselle mise en requisition, et celle des effets saisis, seront appliqués en déduction de la Contribution ou indemnité.

La Commission Nationale fera incessamment rentrer dans les coffres de la Nation, les indemnités et contributions cydessus. Elle se persuade qu'aucun individu ne la mettra dans le cas d'employer les moyens de Contrainte que la Nation à mis à sa disposition.

———

Citoyens! La Commission Nationale verra sans doute se réaliser les bons effets, de tout genre, que doit produire cette subvention extraordinaire, et c'est la plus douce récompense de ses travaux; mais il est de son devoir de déclarer à ses concitoyens, que pour assurer la prospérité publique, le repos de l'Etat, et le bonheur du peuple, il faut que cette mesure soit secondée par une disposition générale au travail. Une République bien organisée ou qui veut l'etre, flétrit la paresse, et voue tout oisif volontaire, au mépris ou à la proscription. Donné à Geneve le 28 7bre. 1794 l'an 3 de l'égalité.

Les Membres de la Commission sont

J. Bourdillon Disday	Jn. Dd. Cougnard	Dd. Jl. Matthey
Laurent Bernier	Jsc. Cornuaud	Theop. Martin
Alex. Bousquet	Frs. Gaillard	Matt. Nal.
Ant. Bideleux	And. Ces. Lagier	J. J. Odier Chevrier
Charles Cellier	Js. Malher	Frs. Romilly

LeComte Sécrétaire

Tr (DLC); in a clerk's hand; at head of text by D'Ivernois: "*Copie du Décret de la Commission Nationale de Geneve. N.B. Trois Livres Court de Geneve sont égales à cinq Livres de france*"; torn.

II

Extract from Etienne Pestre's Pamphlet

Extrait d'un pamphlet publié dans le milieu d'8bre. 1794 à Geneve, Signé par Ete. Pestre l'un des principaux révolutionnaires Genevois.

Après avoir prouvé par l'histoire ancienne et par celle de Geneve que les bannissemens ont toujours fait le mal des Etats qui ont admis cette peine, "Il me reste," dit l'auteur révolutionnaire, "à donner mon opinion sur le rappel des Exilés Genevois. Je vais le faire avec la franchise d'un ami né de la liberté et de l'égalité. La justice et l'humanité plaident en faveur de ce rappel. Nos arts, nos fabriques, notre Commerce ne le demandent pas avec moins d'instances. C'est dans ce rappel que nous trouverons le terme de nos maux. Je crois qu'il n'y a pas un Genevois qui ne verse des larmes de douleur, quand sa pensée s'arrête sur cette foule de Citoyens de toutes les Classes qu'un mouvement terrible à jettés sur une terre étrangère. Quel étoit leur crime? Ils avoient dit-on formé le complot de renverser la Constitution, cette meme constitution qu'ils venoient d'accepter librement. Cela est-il prouvé? Non. Car il n'en a pas même été question dans les interrogatoires qu'un petit nombre d'entreux à subi. Aussi ce prétendu Complot à-t-il été relégué avec celui de 1770. C'est avec éclat que cette conspiration avoit été annoncée, et c'est encore avec plus d'éclat qu'elle à été rendue publique. Mais c'est en vain que l'homme instruit cherche à en saisir les fils pour juger les dangers qu'il a courus. Partout ces fils lui échappent ainsi qu'à ceux qui ont voulu le dévoiler. *Heureusement que les Tribunaux n'ont eu pour base aucune règle quelconque, aucune loi particulière, aucune organisation*: car ils auroient été un peu embarrassés pour motiver leurs décisions. Cet aveu naïf est unique dans les fastes de la justice. Un reproche qui peut se faire aux exilés; c'est celui d'être attachés aux principes de l'aristocratie expirante. Mais une opinion ne peut etre soumise aux tribunaux sous le règne de la liberté et de l'égalité. Dailleurs ils partageoient ce prétendu crime avec *Rousseau* qui dit dans une de ses lettres. *Je préfére hautement l'aristocratie à tout autre gouvernement.* Les Loix ne doivent pas atteindre la pensée parce qu'elle est libre comme l'habitant des airs; les actions seules sont l'objet des loix répressives. Un despote confond l'un et l'autre pour arriver plus surement à son but. Quand je parcours la liste nombreuse des bannis à perpétuité par contumace &c. &c. je me demande si on à voulu transporter ailleurs notre industrie et notre commerce, car en rassemblant ces exilés on pourrait faire *une nouvelle Geneve*. Nous avons renversé dans le lac notre Patrie et des peuples plus sages la pêcheront. L'artiste naturalisera ses talens dans le lieu ou il se fixera. Les nouvelles fabriques achèveront la ruine des notres. Le commerçant dont le génie franchit tous les obstacles détournera au profit de sa patrie adoptive les canaux qui nous portoient l'abondance. Oh Geneve, oh malheureuse Geneve!"

Tr (DLC: TJ Papers, 97: 16705); endorsed by TJ: "D'Ivernois Oct.   94." Tr (DLC); with minor variations; slightly torn.

From Giuseppe Ceracchi

Philadelphia 13 Nov. 1794
Duelling house S: Street Sth No *213*

DEAR SIR

I postponed the anser to your Kind letter I received by Miss Trista because I couldnt give you any notice of the marbre bust which I find out lately in new York at the costum house under the care of Mr. Siton without any dictiones [i.e. directions], oing thus mistaken to my agent in Florens.

I fill my self relieved by the mortification I [. . .] thinkin of the disappointement of your Daughter in case it had been lost; This bust is belong to Her since I had the plaesor to beginn it therfor I must beg you Sir to obtane Her consent to Live it with me a little longer, been certain that the Eminent Subjet that it reppresents will produce a general satisfaction hear, and am flattered will reflect some honour upon the performance. Your congratulations upon my coming to America are very flattering my destiny as driven me again to this contry for I must Kindedly confesse whath ever was my inclination for it I never expect to returne in consideration of many difficulties, especting my theander Family. Now those difficulties are over I percive I can live happy in America. Mrs. Ceracchi as the honnour to eturne you her civilities che seems to be plaesed in general and whe are both glad that our Cildrens will recieve a Republican education instade of a pristly one. I am with perfect estim Your Most Ob [. . .] [servt]   J. CERACCHI

RC (MHi); several words illegible; endorsed by TJ as received 26 Nov. 1794 and so recorded in SJL.

Ceracchi wrote a letter to TJ on 17 Aug. 1794, recorded in SJL as received from

Boston 2 Sep. 1794, which has not been found. TJ's KIND LETTER of 17 Sep. 1794 in reply is also missing. SJL also records a letter from TJ to Ceracchi of 11 Jan. 1795 that is missing. SITON: William Seton.

From Maria Cosway

MY DEAR SIR   London 13 Novr. 1794

I am come home to England, and have the great pleasure to find I am not forgotten by Mr: Jefferson, t'is impossible to express my happiness, the less I say the better, and am Sure what I dont say will be added by a Heart who can conceive and interpatrate Sentiments of a feeling and greatfull heart. My Angelica has been the greatest joy on my return. She has flatterd me much by telling me my name was mentiond in most of the letters which come from America. Mr: Trumbull tells me the Same and offers to send a letter; Now I have Not time to make One, till now I did Not know how to send one, but hope that I shall in another find more to convince You how much I am your Most Affte.

MARIA COSWAY

RC (MHi); addressed: "Mr. Jefferson"; endorsed by TJ as received 17 Mch. 1795 and so recorded in SJL. Enclosed in John Trumbull to TJ, 20 Nov. 1794.

Maria Cosway, who last corresponded with TJ in 1790, had recently COME HOME TO ENGLAND from a four-year trip to Italy that she had undertaken to recover from a difficult pregnancy (Helen D. Bullock, *My*

Head and My Heart: A Little History of Thomas Jefferson and Maria Cosway [New York, 1945], 134-8; Cosway to TJ, 6 Apr. 1790; TJ to Cosway, 23 June 1790, and note). NOT FORGOTEN BY MR: JEFFERSON: an allusion to TJ's references to Mrs. Cosway in his letters to their mutual friend, ANGELICA Schuyler Church (TJ to Church, 7 June, 27 Nov. 1793).

From James Madison

Dear Sir   Philada. Novr. 16. 1794.

I have received your two favors of Ocr. 30 and Novr. 6, the former not in time to be answered on Monday last. Mazzei's claim on Dorhman is £2000 N.Y. Currency, with interest at 7 perCt. from Novr. 1788. It is secured by a Deed of Trust empowering me to sell a tract of land granted to Mr. D. by an Act of Congress of Octr. 1. 1787. (see Journals of that date). Mr. Randolph thinks that a Court of Equity would not interfere with a summary execution[1] of the trust. I hear nothing from Dorhman; nor can even say whether he is still in N. York. I have mentioned to Mr. R. the books and he has promised to let me have them. Judge Wilson is on the Southn. Circuit, and I suppose the volumes in his hands can not be got till he returns. I will however make the trial. The gentleman by whom they are to be sent to you has not yet made his appearance.

The Senate having not yet a Quorum I cannot send you the P.'s speech. You will have seen by the papers that the Western Scene is closed. H. is still with the army. You will perceive his colouring on all the documents which have been published[2] during his Mentorship to the commander in cheif. When I first arrived here the conversation ran high for a standing army to enforce the laws. It is said the Militia will all return with the same doctrine in their mouths. I have no doubt that such an innovation will be attempted in earnest during the Session, if circumstances should be favorable. It is probable however that the P. will not embark in the measure; and that the fear of alarming N. England will be another obstacle.

The elections for the next Congs. are generally over except in Virga. and N. Carola. and N. York. In N. Hampshire the choice is much the same. In Masshts. there has been a violent contest in most of the districts. All that will probably be gained is a spirit of enquiry and competition in that quarter. Ames is re-elected after the most unparalled exertions and calumnies in his favor, and according to report by the additional aid of bad votes. Dexter is to run a second heat but will probably succeed. Sedgwick's fate is not known. The chance is said to be in his favor; but it is agreed that he will be well sweated. As he has not yet appeared, he is probably nursing his declining popularity during the crisis. From N.Y. we are promised at least half of the new representatives for the republican scale. N. Jersey has lost old Clarke who will no doubt be replaced by a successor of other sentiments. In this State, the election, notwithstanding its inauspicious circumstances, is more republican than the last. Nine at least out of thirteen are counted on the right side; among them Swanwick in the room of Fitzimmons, a stunning change for the Aristocracy. Maryland pretty much as heretofore. I should have first noted that in Delaware Patten the Republican ex-member, is chosen by a large Majority. The representation of Maryland will vary little from the present. In S.C. Smith has been carried by the British Merchants in Charleston and their debtors in the Country, in spite of[3] the Rutledges and Pinkney's who set up against him Jno. Rutlege Jur. Tucker was also a candidate. Smith had a majority of all the votes. In general the changes also in that state will be for the worse. The death of Gillon has made way for Barnwell if he chuses to step in. Hunter also is out; but it is said his successor (a Mr. Harper) will be a valuable acquisition, being sound able and eloquent. The prospects for the Senate are—the reelection of Langdon for N.H. The election of Payne, an incognitum, in place of Bradley for Vermont who appears to have been out of favor with both parties—the reelection of King in N.Y. owing to the death of 2 Repubn. members of the State Legislature—the chance of a Republican successor to R. Morris, said to be a good one; a like chance in Delaware. In Maryland the Chance is bad, but nothing worse than the present delegation is to [be][4] apprehended. Potts has resigned, and Henry it is supposed will either withdraw or be rejected. The event in Virga. you will know. The information from N.C. is not decisive, but favorable; the same as to S.C. Izard has relinquished his pretensions. In Georgia the question lies between Gun and Telfair. The former it is thought will be rechosen.

I must refer to Newspapers which I suppose you occasionally see from Richd. for the posture of things in Europe. In general they are extremely favorable to F. and alarming to all the Sovereigns of Europe. England seems still bent notwithstanding, on the war. She is now to subsidize the Emperor as well as the K. of Prussia. According to the intelligence handed to the public it would seem that the humiliating memorial of Jay inspires less contempt, than the French victories do terror, and that the tone towards this Country will be much changed. It is even intimated[5] that satisfactory arrangements will be made on most, if not all the points in question. Not a line official or private from Monroe. His enthusiastic reception you will have seen.

Prices here are very different from those you mention—Wheat at 12/– Corn 6/6. Beef at 8d. and other things in proportion. House Rent 50 perCt. higher than last winter. Mrs. M. offers her best returns to you. Always & affecy. Yours   Js. MADISON

RC (DLC: Madison Papers); addressed: "Mr. Jefferson Monticello near Charlottesville, Virginia"; franked; endorsed by TJ as received 2 Dec. 1794 and so recorded in SJL.

Secretary of the Treasury Alexander Hamilton remained WITH THE ARMY sent to quell the Whiskey Insurrection after the President began his return to Philadelphia on 20 Oct. 1794, leaving Henry Lee as COM-

MANDER IN CHEIF (Thomas P. Slaughter, *The Whiskey Rebellion: Frontier Epilogue to the American Revolution* [New York, 1986], 216). In October 1794 American newspapers printed a 30 July 1794 MEMORIAL from John Jay to Lord Grenville requesting judicial or extrajudicial redress for Americans whose vessels or property had been improperly seized and condemned and for American seamen who had been impressed into the British navy (*Philadelphia Gazette*, 20 Oct. 1794). Republicans quickly condemned Jay's representation as

couched in terms of "the most humiliating, degrading, and nauseous flattery" (Philadelphia *Aurora*, 1 Nov. 1794).

[1] Madison first wrote "an execution" and then altered the phrase to read as above.

[2] Madison here canceled what appears to be "on the excise."

[3] Preceding two words interlined in place of "opposition not only to."

[4] Word supplied.

[5] Word interlined in place of "expected."

To John Barnes

SIR   Monticello Nov. 20. 1794.

I have to acknolege the receipt of your two favors of Oct. 19. and Nov. 5. It is possible I may trouble you in some of the various lines of business mentioned in the former, at some future day, and shall do it with entire confidence in you.   With respect to the bill of exchange for Messrs. Van Staphorst, I am too far from the scene of business to give any advice as to the rate of exchange which may be allowed. I can only say in general that the money is wanted for Mr. Mazzei, that I withold some other remittances to him, till I can receive this also and send all together, but that still great sacrifices in the rate of exchange ought not to be made, if there be a reasonable hope of a speedy and sensible fall. I can therefore only leave you to the exercise of your own good judgment and of Mr. Blair's directions in this matter.—Whenever you inclose the bill to me, would it be giving you too much trouble to quote to me the wholesale and retail prices of the articles below at Philadelphia, at that time? If not I should thank you for them. I am with great respect Sir Your most obedt. servt   TH: JEFFERSON

German oznabrigs.
British   do.
White plains or cottons such as we use for negroes.
striped blankets, for do. good.
plaid hose for do.

PrC (ViU: Edgehill-Randolph Papers); at foot of text: "Mr. John Barnes."

Barnes's FAVORS OF OCT. 19. AND NOV. 5., recorded in SJL as received from Philadelphia 12 and 18 Nov. 1794, respectively, have not been found. Barnes's 6 Dec. 1794 reply to this letter, recorded in SJL as received 16 Dec. 1794, is also missing.

To William Branch Giles

DEAR SIR   Monticello Nov. 20. 1794.

I have lately recieved from Donald & Burton their account crediting me for your bill of excha. £37–10 stirling, as also Mr. Brown's account, who by consigning my tobaccoes to another house on the failure of the former, placed my credits in his own account while the debets were with Donald & Burton, and thus saved you the £37–10 and me the rest of my tobacco. Not having been indebted to Donald & Burton at the time they credited your bill nor for long after, and consequently drawing no profit from the credit, I have given my bill but for the principal sum; the loss of interest you will place to account of the casualties which have happened in the whole of this business.

I remember you offered to return to me (in Philadelphia) some papers of mine respecting my demand against Bannister's estate. Was his promisory note among them? We cannot find it, and I am considerably embarrassed in another settlement for want of it. Pray inform me by return of post if you have it at all, and if with you, send it.

I do not know the present state of health of T. Shippen but if such as admits his being spoken to on business without uneasiness, and you should ever have an opportunity I will thank you to mention this demand to him. It is now somewhat upwards of £100. our money, and Mr. Dunbar being dead, I know not who to apply to for it. I am in real want of it. However if the state of his health would render such an intimation uneasy to him, say nothing about it.

We are here big with expectations of hearing that Detroit is attacked by Govr. Lee, as the declared purpose of that armament is hardly sufficient to be used as the ostensible one. It is presumed that the Executive must have serious information from Mr. Jay. We wish much also to see the speech: tho' that will hardly reveal the secret. We have no news to give you but of our cattle and crops: it is from you to us that news are expected. Adieu; believe me with sincere esteem Dear Sir Your friend & servt   TH: JEFFERSON

PrC (DLC); at foot of first page: "Mr. Giles."

RECIEVED FROM DONALD & BURTON: perhaps a reference to a 14 June 1794 letter from Alexander Donald, recorded in SJL as received from London 10 Sep. 1794, but not found. A letter of 15 Nov. 1794 from James BROWN, recorded in SJL as received from Richmond 19 Nov. 1794, is also missing. CREDITED YOUR BILL: see MB, 19 Nov. 1794.

For TJ's statement of the 3,173 livres and 19 sous that the ESTATE of John Banister, Jr., owed him with interest for the advances he had made to the young Virginian in Paris in 1787, see the account with Banister printed as enclosure to TJ to Francis Eppes, 11 Mch. 1792.

For the President's SPEECH, see Madison to TJ, 30 Nov. 1794, and note.

To James Maury

SIR   (Virginia) Monticello Nov. 20. 1794.

This serves to inform you that under the orders of James Munroe Min. Pleny. of the US. at Paris, whereof he has advised you, I have this day drawn on you in favor of William B. Giles for thirty seven pounds ten shillings sterling payable at thirty days sight which be pleased to honor. I am Sir Your very humble servt   TH: JEFFERSON

Dupl (PHi); opposite signature: "(Duplicate)"; at foot of text: "Mr. James Maury Mercht. Liverpool."

To Joseph Mussi

DEAR SIR   Monticello Nov. 20. 1794.

Your favor of Oct. 22. has come safely to hand, tho' not till the 12th. inst. I had not written on the subject of red clover seed, because I was not certain of the quantity I should want. That is now ascertained to be five bushels, which quantity I will therefore ask the favor of you to send me in a tight cask, by the first vessel for Richmond, noting to me by post it's cost, and the time of it's departure.

I thank you for your attention to my desire respecting the stone-cutter, and your assurance that his wages will be within my views. I am determined the ensuing summer to go on with both my house and my mill, so that I shall be glad to recieve him as soon as may be.   My rheumatism has been remarkeably obstinate not having yet entirely left me, tho' I am able to ride about my farm.   If clover seed of the present year can be got, it will be the best. However if that is not yet got out for market, I had rather recieve seed of the last year, than run the risk of your river's freezing up before it's departure. I am with sincere esteem Dear Sir Your friend & servt   TH: JEFFERSON

RC (DLC); addressed: "Mr. Joseph Mussi Philadelphia corner of Market & 7th. streets"; stamped; endorsed by Mussi.

Mussi's FAVOR OF OCT. 22. is recorded in SJL as recieved from Philadelphia on 12 Nov. 1794. SJL also records letters from Mussi to TJ of 27 Sep. and 7 and 17 Nov. 1794, received respectively on 9 Oct., 26 Nov., and 2 Dec. 1794, as well as a 9 Oct. 1794 letter from TJ to Mussi, none of which has been found.

From John Trumbull

DEAR SIR   London 20th. Novr. 1794.

I have the pleasure to enclose to you a line from our friend Mrs. Cosway, who arrived here a few days ago from Italy. She was to have written a longer letter, but I fear I shall not recieve it in time to go, with this.

Yesterday a Treaty was sign'd between Lord Grenville and Mr. Jay, whose Effect I hope will be not only to preserve peace but also to preserve a good understanding between G. Britain and America. Its objects are, first to do mutual Justice; and after to grant mutual conveniencies, reserving on our side in the most express manner all Rights and Stipulations contained in all former Treaties.

I understood some time ago that the Commissioners at Washington were dissatisfied with one of their principal Architects; and wrote to some of my friends recommending (if they wish'd to employ a Man of regular Education) Mr. George Hatfield, a Brother of Mrs. Cosway, who has just return'd from finishing his Studies in Italy, and is regarded here as the Man of the first Talents for his Years in the Country. The War occasions a Stagnation in the Arts, and He is of course not employ'd and would be glad to come out on reasonable terms. Should any opening of this kind offer, I am sure you will chearfully use your Influence in favor of the Brother of our friend when at the same time you are assured of rendering a service to our Country by introducing into it a man of Talents and Integrity. I beg my best Respects to Mrs. Randolph & Miss Jefferson—and Am Dr. sir Your most Obliged friend and faithful servant   JOHN TRUMBULL

RC (DLC); addressed: "The Honble. Thomas Jefferson Esquire Monticello Virginia"; franked by Edmund Randolph and postmarked; endorsed by TJ as received 17 Mch. 1795 and so recorded in SJL. Enclosure: Maria Cosway to TJ, 13 Nov. 1794.

From John Adams

DEAR SIR   Philadelphia Nov. 21. 1794

I am desired by our old Acquaintance Mr. D'Ivernois to transmit you the inclosed Papers for your inspection Opinion and Advice. The poor Fellow has been obliged to fly a Second time into Banishment. The first time, he was driven out as a Democrat: but it is now, Day about, as they Say, in Geneva, and he is compelled to run, as an Aristocrat.

Shall We print his History? What Shall We do with his Academy?

I have Spent my Summer So deliciously in farming that I return to the Old Story of Politicks with great Reluctance. The Earth is grateful. You find it so, I dare say. I wish We could both say the Same of its Inhabitants.

When will the Crisis of this fever in human Nature be over, and in what State of Health will it be left? Solitudinem faciunt, Libertatem[1] appellant.

Virginia I hope will send Us Some good Senators, We grow very thin. I begin to think the Senate Scarcely numerous enough for so large a People. But this is not a time for Changes: We must go on as well as we can. Make my Compliments, if you please to your Daughters, whom I had once the Pleasure to see, and for whom I retain much Esteem. I am, sir with great Regard, your most obedient   JOHN ADAMS

RC (DLC); at foot of text: "Mr Jefferson"; endorsed by TJ as received 2 Dec. 1794 and so recorded in SJL. Enclosures: (1) Enclosure printed at François D'Ivernois to TJ, 5 Sep. 1794. (2) D'Ivernois to Samuel [i.e. John] Adams, London, 22 Aug. 1794, soliciting Adams's support for and describing in great detail his plan for transplanting the faculty of the Academy of Geneva to America, requesting him to confer with President Washington, Secretary of State Edmund Randolph, and TJ about this proposal, and stressing the insurmountable obstacles to transplanting the Genevan "manufactory of watches" to America (Dupl in MHi: Adams Papers; in English in an unidentified hand and signed by D'Ivernois, who wrote at head of text "No 2" and "*Duplicata*").

SOLITUDINEM ... APPELLANT: "They make a solitude and call it liberty," Adams's adaptation of Tacitus.

[1] Word interlined in place of "Pacem."

To Wilson Cary Nicholas

DEAR SIR   Monticello Nov. 23. 1794.

I take the liberty of inclosing for your perusal and consideration a proposal from a Mr. D'Ivernois, a Genevan, of considerable distinction for science and patriotism, and that too of the republican kind, tho you will see that he does not carry it so far as our friends of the National assembly of France. While I was at Paris, I knew him as an exile for his democratic principles, the aristocracy having then the upper hand, in Geneva. He is now obnoxious to the Democratic party. The sum of his proposition is to translate the academy of Geneva in a body to this country. You know well that the colleges of Edinburgh and Geneva as seminaries of science, are considered as the two eyes of Europe: while Great Britain and America give the preference to the former, all other countries give it to the latter. I am fully sensible that two powerful obstacles are in the way of this proposition. 1st. the expence: 2dly. the communication of science in foreign languages, that is to say, in French or Latin: but I have been so long absent from my own country as to be an incompetent judge either of the force of the objections, or of the dispositions of those who are to decide on them. The respectability of Mr. D'Ivernois' character, and that too of the proposition, require an answer from me, and that it should be given on due enquiry. He desires secrecy to a certain degree for the reasons which he explains. What I have to request of you, my dear Sir, is that you will be so good as to consider his proposition, to consult on it's expediency and practicability with such gentlemen of the assembly as you think best, and take such other measures as you shall find eligible, to discover what would be the sense of that body were the proposition to be hazarded to them. If yourself and friends approve of it, and think there is hope that the assembly would do so, your zeal for the good of our country in general, and the promotion of science as an instrument towards that, will of course induce you and them to bring it forward in such way as you shall judge best. If on the contrary, you disapprove of it yourselves, or think it would be desperate with the assembly, be so good as to return it to me with such information as I may hand forward to Mr. D'Ivernois to put him out of suspence. Keep the matter by all means out of the public papers, and particularly if you please, do not couple my name with the proposition if brought forward, because it is much my wish to be in no wise implicated in public affairs.—It is necessary for me to appeal to all my titles for giving you this trouble, whether founded in representation, patriotism or friendship. The last, however as the broadest is that on which I wish to rely, being with sentiments of very cordial esteem Dear Sir your sincere friend & humble servt   TH: JEFFERSON

RC (Leslie H. Brown, Alexandria, Virginia, 1969); at foot of first page: "Wilson Nicholas. esq." PrC (DLC). Enclosure: see below.

Wilson Cary Nicholas was at this time one of Albemarle County's two representatives in the Virginia House of Delegates (DAB).

The enclosed PROPOSAL was probably François D'Ivernois to TJ, 5 Sep. 1794.

From Maria Cosway

SIR   London 24 Novr: 1794

I sent you a very short letter On My Arrival here, but promised Soon a longer One, here I am ready for it, from a great wish to converse a little with One whom ought to be my freind from a simpathy of Sentiments: You know this does not Mean that the reasons are the same, Mine may be raised by the Consciousness of your Merits, in that case I have nothing to pretend from you, but you May then return some acknowledgement built only on a sort of gratitude that will mingle the tenderness of freindship, forgit from what source it Comes, and be pure in its effect. Mr: Trumbull told me a few days ago he had an opportunity of sending a Letter, but was prevented from sending to him One. Last Night Mrs: Church told me she has another; sure t'is Opportunities coming with a reproach when they are felt with so much pleasure, and at the same time as a reward for what Seems a negligence not embracing the first without a fault, a second recompences the sensearly felt loss. Now this will Come accompanied by One from the Most charming of woman, My Angelica, I love her so much that I think and am persuaded she must be beloved by every One who know her, therefore give value to every thing which Comes from her Or she Notices with her regard. I will think she has Some attachment for me and I value it much. My great fear is that soon I shall loos her, I even thought I should not find her in England, but have been fortunate to meet this pleasure On my arrival, and certainly she was a great consolation to me. Could I but think it a lasting One, You know this Country, and believe you have heard My sentiments on it, My long stay in Italy and particularly the fine Climate and Most beautifull situation of Genova has Not alterd them but increased a surmontable Antipathy I feel, though the pleasure of the good society and amiable freinds Make in great Measure a recompence, t'is accompanied with a dampness of a gloomy cloud which withers the first blossom of the appearing charm, waits for some glimps of the raising sunn, and stops till t'is forgot in thought in Amazement, or indiference.

I often think of America, and every thing I hear of it pleases me and Makes me wish to come, why Can I not come? How Many thinks are like the Italians and Italy? There is a Comfort in freinds and their Society.

I have found a preaty little girl, I hope she will make some Comfort, she shows Natural Talent and a good, Soft disposition—painting and Musik for the present are forgoten by me, the long neglect has made me now give them up, and find no loss, better occupations will fill up My heavy hours.

Je vous fait Mon Compliment, et je vous suppose deja un *gran Papa*! May you have in every Circumstance of your life that happiness you so Much deserve, Much for the choise you Make of your happiness. Oh how few at this Moment! Where is there a smal spot unknown to Misery, trouble, and Confusion? You have retierd from it, but Much is the loss for those you Might have been of use to. Mr: Cosway desires his Compliments and joins with me in all I have said. He Might have wrote better English, but My wishes I will not give up to any body. Remember Me ever as one of your Most affte: freinds   MARIA COSWAY

RC (MHi); endorsed by TJ as received [5] May 1795 and so recorded in SJL.

A VERY SHORT LETTER: Cosway to TJ, 13 Nov. 1794. ACCOMPANIED BY ONE FROM . . . ANGELICA: there is no evidence that Angel-ica Schuyler Church wrote any letters to TJ during his retirement at Monticello from 1794 to 1796. A PREATY LITTLE GIRL: Louisa Paolina Angelica Cosway, Mrs. Cosway's daughter.

From Oliver Wolcott, Jr.

SIR   TD: C.O. 29th: Novemr. 1794.

I have received your favour of the 4th. instant and readily assure you of my assent and cooperation in effecting a transfer of Mr. Shorts stock under the power of Attorney of which you have transmitted a Copy. I have the honour to be with great respect Sir your most obedt. servt:

O W

Dft (CtHi: Wolcott Papers); at foot of text: "The Hon Thos Jefferson Esq Monticello." Recorded in SJL as received 9 Dec. 1794.

According to SJL, TJ did not write to Wolcott, the Comptroller of the Treasury, on THE 4TH. INSTANT, but did write a letter of 20 Nov. 1794 that has not been found.

From James Madison

DEAR SIR   Philada. Novr. 30. 94

Mr. Fleming has been here and set out on his return yesterday. I did not however know of his arrival till a very short time before his departure. Contrary to your expectation he returns by land, not with his goods. On this account added to the lateness of the Season, and my not being able to get all your books, I concluded it would be best to put off sending what I could get, till the Spring, when they can all be sent together, and perhaps be less exposed to accidents. The books in the hands of Wilson could not be obtained in his absence. And Mr. R. has not been able yet to find the Book on Mineralogy left with him. You will see by the inclosed that you are to receive a Sett of Chalmer's Treaties. I send you the letter to me accompanying it, for the sake of the references which if correct may deserve notice; tho' they issue from a Quarter not very learned one would suppose on such subjects. You will be so good as to return the letter, as I am yet to answer it.

The attack on the most[1] sacred principle of our Constitution and of

Republicanism, thro' the Democratic Societies, has given rise to much discussion in the H. of Reps. and has left us in a critical situation. You will have seen the P.'s Speech. The answer of the Senate was hurried thro', with the most full and emphatic eccho of the denunciation of these Societies. In the mean time the answer of the H. of Reps. tho' prepared and reported without any loss of time, was, contrary to usage, printed for consideration, and put off from Friday, till monday. On the intervening Saturday, the Senate presented theirs, which with the P's reply was immediately out in the Newspapers. I refer for both to the Richd. Newspapers which you will probably have seen. The answer of the H. of Reps. both as reported and as agreed to are inclosed. The Come. consisted of Sedgwick Scott and myself. The draught was made as strong as possible on all proper points, in order the better to get it thro', without the improper ones. This succeeded in the Come.; Scott concurring in the *expediency* of silence on that; tho' in the House he changed his ground. When the report was taken up on Monday Fitzimmons moved "to *reprobate* the self-created Societies &c. which tho' in strictness not *illegal*, contributed by their proceedings to mislead the weak and ignorant." This opened the debate which you will no doubt have an opportunity of reading in the Virga. papers if you chuse. It so happens that I can not send them by the mail. The arguments in favor of the motion fell with equal weight on the press and every mode of animadverting on public men and measures. After some time the proposition was new modelled, and in a less pointed shape underwent discussion for several days. On the first question which tried the sense of the House, the division was 47 against 45. for the usurped power. This was in a Committee of the whole. On a renewal of the same question in the House the decision was reversed by 47 in the affirmative and 45 in the negative. A motion was then made to limit the censure to the Societies within the scene of insurrection, which was carried by the casting vote of the Speaker. In this form the whole[2] proposition was abandoned. This was on thursday. On friday, it being foreseen that some evil accomodation would come from the other side and succeed, It was proposed by Mr. Nicholas to insert the sentence which distinguishes the first ¶ of the[3] Answer agreed to, from the Report. An attempt was made to add "and self created Societies," after "combinations," but it had so little prospect of success that it was withdrawn. The Answer was presented on saturday, and received the reply in the inclosed paper, which you will be at no loss to understand. The Republicans were considered by their opponents as rather victorious by the result in the House. The reply of the P. is claimed by the latter as a final triumph on their side; and it is probable that so it will prove. You will easily conceive my situation thro' this whole business. It was obvious that a most dangerous game was playing against Republicanism. The insurrection was universally and deservedly odious. The Democratic Societies were presented as in league with it. The Republican part of Congs. were to be drawn into an *ostensible*, patronage of these Societies, and into an ostensible opposition to the President. And by this artifice the delusion of N. Engld. was to be confirmed, and a chance afforded of some new turn in Virga. before the elections in the Spring. What the success of this game will really be, time must decide. If the people of America are so far degenerated already as not to see or to see with indifference, that the Citadel of their liberties is menaced by the precedent before their eyes, they require abler advocates than they now have, to save them from the consequences. Lengthy as the debate was, I took but little part in it; and that little is very erroneously as well as defectively stated in the Newspapers. No private letters from Monroe. An official one of Sepr. 15. speaks of the utmost prosperity at home—of the irresistable discipline and enthusiasm of their armies, and of the most unalterable affection to this Country. All that is given out from Jay's Negociation is in favor of some advantageous result. How is your Rheumatism—and Mr. Randolph's complaint?

RC (DLC: Madison Papers); unsigned; endorsed by TJ as received 16 Dec. 1794 and so recorded in SJL. Enclosure: George Joy to Madison, 56 Hatton Garden, London, 1 May 1794, in which he writes that he has found a copy of Chalmers's collection of treaties (see below) that he thinks will be of interest to TJ, with whom he is unacquainted, and is sending it under separate cover (RC in same; printed in Madison, *Papers*, xv, 317-20). For other enclosures, see note below.

BOOK ON MINERALOGY: see TJ to Edmund Randolph, 6 Nov. 1794. CHALMER'S TREATIES: George Chalmers, *A Collection of Treaties between Great Britain and other powers*, 2 vols. (London, 1790). See Sowerby, No. 1432. In his annual address to Congress on 19 Nov. 1794, George Washington reported the actions he had taken to suppress the Whiskey Insurrection and made an ATTACK on the democratic societies (Fitzpatrick, *Writings*, xxxiv, 29). The 21 Nov. 1794 ANSWER OF THE SENATE mimicked the address by attacking "certain self-created societies" for proceedings "founded in political error" and "calculated,

if not intended, to disorganize our government" (JS, II, 126). THE P's REPLY is in same, 127. Madison's 21 Nov. 1794 DRAUGHT of the response by the House of Representatives to the address condoled with the President on the painful prospect of civil bloodshed and expressed pleasure that the great body of Americans had rallied to support the will of the majority and republican government. After much debate his attempt to preserve SILENCE about the attack on the societies was modified by the addition of the following SENTENCE to the reply as adopted on 28 Nov. 1794: "And we learn with the greatest concern that any misrepresentations whatever of the Government and its proceedings, either by individuals or combinations of men, should have been made and so far credited as to foment the flagrant outrage which has been committed on the laws" (Madison, *Papers*, xv, 386-8; *National State Papers*, xxiv, 328-9; for House debate, see *Annals*, iv, 895-949). The REPLY OF THE P. a day later urged that "Every effort ought to be used to discountenance what has contributed to foment" the rebellion and that in future such "artful approaches" should be checked before military intervention became necessary (*National State Papers*, XXIV, 333). For James Monroe's OFFICIAL letter of 15 Sep. 1794 to Secretary of State Edmund Randolph, see ASP, *Foreign Relations*, I, 675-6.

[1] Word interlined.
[2] Word interlined.
[3] Preceding four words interlined.

To Archibald Stuart

MY DEAR SIR   Monticello Dec. 2. 1794.

I now place in the hands of Colo. Bell in Charlottesville fifty dollars to be forwarded to you, and have to ask the favor of you to purchase me sheep to that amount. The moment you notify me that they are ready, I will send off for them, so as to receive them from the seller, and not give you so much trouble with them as you had with the last purchase. Perhaps I may at the same time send a further sum, for a further purchase. But of this I am not sure, and therefore can only ask you to have your eye on a score more.—I am in the moment of the departure of the post, and therefore have only time to add assurances of the sincere esteem of Dear Sir Your affectionate friend & servt.   TH: JEFFERSON

RC (ViHi); addressed: "Archibald Stuart esq. Attorney at Law Staunton"; stamped. PrC (MHi); endorsed in ink by TJ. Recorded in SJL under 27 Nov. 1794 with following entry listed as 9 Dec. 1794.

TJ paid Thomas BELL the FIFTY DOLLARS a day later (MB, 3 Dec. 1794).

From William Branch Giles

DEAR SIR   Philadelphia December 7th 1794

I received your very friendly and polite letter three days ago, but had not an opportunity till yesterday of makeing the inquiry, you request respecting your demand upon the late Mr. Banister's estate. On yesterday I called on Mr. Shippen for that purpose, but was informed that he was too much indisposed to be seen on business. I intimated the thing however to Mrs. Shippen, who informed me that she had often heard from Mr. Dunbar and always conceived, that the demand had been satisfyed by him in his life time to Mr. Robert Pleasants, a gentleman who called himself your agent; that Mr. Dunbar's papers would probably furnish the evidence of the payment. But if the debt still remained unpaid Mr. Shippen was the proper person to receive the application for payment.

The papers respecting this business I have left in Virginia, and cannot charge my memory with certainty, whether the promisory note be amongst them or not. I am rather inclined to think it is.

I have to acknowledge the recipt of your Bill of exchange for £37.10, which is perfectly satisfactory to me, nor was any apology necessary for not includeing interest in the draft. I could never think of receiving interest from you in return for your goodness in rendering me a service.

Letters have been received here from our Friend Monroe, who seems to be in the most perfect confidence with the French nation, and who speaks of his situation as extremely eligible. Embarrassments of a delicate nature attended his first arrival at Paris, and I conceive the measures taken to relieve himself from them extremely judicious and decisive.

Great changes are about takeing place in the Cabinet here. Mr. Hamilton and Mr. Knox will go out of office at the end of January next, and possibly Mr. Cox and Mr. Wolcott. This latter circumstance will probably depend upon the manner of filling up the two first vacancies.

A greater degree of harmony is likely to characterise our legislative proceedings this session than formerly. The plan of denunciation produced considerable sensations at the opening of the session but they have in some measure subsided. It seems to be a source of general regret that the President should have been instrumental in these excitements.

Under the disguise of applause to our military agents, a way has been opened to a handsome exit for Mr. Hamilton, but it may yet be found hazardous to tread it. The maxim has been, that praise is the soldiers appropriate reward; but it will probably be appropriated to the heads of departments in the course of a month or two.

The news from Europe present the most pleasing continuation of French successes, and the increasing consternation of the combined Despots.

Two Newspapers will accompany this letter although I think you forbad me to forward any, the last time I had the pleasure of seeing you. If they should not amuse you perhaps they may some of your Neighbors.

Be pleased to accept my best wishes for your personal welfare and happiness and Believe me to be your sincere Friend &c

Wm B. Giles

RC (DLC); addressed: "Thomas Jefferson Esquire"; endorsed by TJ as received 16 Dec. 1794 and so recorded in SJL.

PLAN OF DENUNCIATION: see James Madison to TJ, 30 Nov. 1794, and note. AP-PLAUSE TO OUR MILITARY AGENTS: a reference to the House of Representatives's 4 Dec. 1794 resolution of thanks to the officers and soldiers who took part in the suppression of the Whiskey Rebellion (JHR, II, 252).

To James Madison

Th:J. to mr Madison Dec. 9. 94.

I write this merely as a way bill. The Orange post arrives at Charlottesville on Tuesday morning about 10. aclock and returns in half an hour. The Richmond post arrives in Charlottesville on Tuesday evening and returns on Friday morning. I wish to know the difference this makes in the conveyance of a letter to Philadelphia. I therefore write this by the Orange post, and will write such another by that of Richmond, and pray you to note to me the days on which you recieve both.—Your favor of Nov. 16. came to hand the 2d. inst. Our militia are returning it is said, without having been to Detroit. Where then have they been? The explanation of this phaenomenon is ardently wished here. Adieu. Yours affectionately.

PrC (DLC).

To Samuel Blackden

Dear Sir Monticello Dec. 11. 1794.

I received your favor from Richmond, and recieved it with great pleasure, as it assured me you were alive and well: but I should with more pleasure have recieved yourself here. You would have been obliged to give a history of things from the time I left France till you left it, that I might at length have learned the truths which have been floating undistinguished on the ocean of lies with which the English newspapers have deluged us. You would have found me in my farmer's coat, immersed soul and body in the culture of my fields, and alive to nothing abroad except the successes of the French revolution, and the welfare of my friends. But why on crutches? That you did not explain to me, nor had I heard of it. Not knowing how long your stay will be at Richmond, I send this there, to be forwarded to Philadelphia, if you are not at Richmond. I am happy to hear Mr. Barlow is well. Mrs. Blackden's health is also pleasing to us. My daughters join me in respects to both of you, and I am with great sincerity Dear Sir Your friend & servt

Th: Jefferson

PrC (DLC); at foot of text: "Colo. Blackden."

To James Madison

TH:J. TO J. MADISON   Friday morning. Dec. 12. 1794.

I wrote you a kind of way-bill by the Orange post, which arrived at, and left Charlottesville on Tuesday forenoon. I write this by the Richmond post which leaves Charlottesville on Friday Morning. The object is to know what difference there will be in the arrival of the two letters at Philadelphia.

We have nothing new for you; for it is not new that we have fine weather. It is, and has been delicious, with only two short intervals of cold. In one of them (about the 22d. of Nov.) it was extraordinarily cold, the mercury being at 19°. but it was only three mornings below freezing. In the other (Dec. 4.) it was one morning below the freezing point. But it has never once continued so thro the day. We have had fine rains at proper intervals, which is the only interruption our ploughs have had.—Corn has sold at 6/6 per barrel, half goods, half cash. It is now at 8/. Purchasers talk of that, sellers of 10/. Wheat 5/ in goods. Adieu. Yours affectionately.

PrC (DLC).

To Wilson Cary Nicholas

DEAR SIR   Monticello Dec. 12. 1794

I trouble you with another letter from Mr. D'Ivernois, containing a further development of his plan.

Since you were here, I have found the inclosed rough draught of a subscription paper for clearing our river, which may explain to you the views and wishes of the subscribers.

Nicholas and Jacob Van Staphorsts, wealthy bankers of Amsterdam, have for some time apprehended a storm in their country which might force them to seek a new habitation. Indeed Jacob Van Staphorst was long since driven from thence, having been at the head of the revolution attempted there about 1787. and 1788. I knew him in Paris as an exiled republican, and was acquainted with his brother in Amsterdam, both very worthy men. I then pressed on Jacob to come over and settle in Norfolk, pointing out to him the advantages of that position for a great capital in commerce. He was divided between that and New York, but prevented from coming at all by some circumstances. They now turn their eyes to the U.S. and particularly to this state, and wish to be made capable of holding lands here, that they may prepare for an event which the public papers seem to announce as close at hand. I wish a special act of assembly could be obtained enabling them to acquire a settlement here. They would be a most valuable acquisition, because they would determine the course of a considerable mass of capitalists in their own situation. I am with sincere esteem Dear Sir Your friend & servt.

Th: Jefferson

PrC (DLC); at foot of text: "W. C. Nicholas." Enclosure: Subscription for Extending the Navigation of the Rivanna, [before 8 Nov. 1790]. For other enclosure, see below.

TJ evidently enclosed one of the two letters from François d'Ivernois of 23 Sep.

1794. THEY NOW TURN THEIR EYES TO THE U.S.: see Willink, Van Staphorst & Hubbard to TJ, 10 Aug. 1793.

A letter from TJ to Nicholas of 4 Feb. 1795 is recorded in SJL but has not been found.

To James Lyle

Dear Sir   Monticello Dec. 14. 1794.

On this day my Bedford bonds of the 2d. instalment become due. Yet but one person has called on me. William Milliner called yesterday and paid me £72–8–8 which I now send you by Mr. Randolph to be applied to the discharge of my bonds in the order in which they are paiable. He promised me he would pay the balance £49–18–10 at the Bedford court of the present month to Mr. Clarke, who will of course remit it to you. I shall keep these second bonds in my hands till such time in the spring as will admit the debtors to sell their crops, and send you the money as fast as paid, and put the bonds unpaid into Clarke's hands then to be sued. I have further had them informed that they may pay to Mr. Clarke tho' the bonds remain with me. I remitted to Milliner the forfeiture of interest on condition his whole balance shall be paid at Bedford court. I am with great esteem Dear Sir Your friend & servt

Th: Jefferson

PrC (MHi); at foot of text: "Mr James Lyle"; endorsed in ink by TJ.

To William Branch Giles

Dear Sir   Monticello Dec. 17. 94.

I have made Mr. Bannister's affair the subject of a separate letter, containing a full explanation of it, because by giving in the letter, it will give you no more trouble. I will only add here, what would have been too urging if expressed there, that if any thing be said of early paiment,

I would rather be allowed to draw on any one there for the money than to have it sent here.

The attempt which has been made to restrain the liberty of our citizens meeting together, interchanging sentiments on what subjects they please, and stating these sentiments in the public papers, has come upon us, a full century earlier than I expected. To demand the censors of public measures to be given up for punishment is to renew the demand of the wolves in the fable that the sheep should give up their dogs as hostages of the peace and confidence established between them. The tide against our constitution is unquestionably strong but it will turn. Every thing tells me so, and every day verifies the prediction. Hold on then like a good and faithful seaman till our brother-sailors can rouse from their intoxication and right the vessel.—Make friends with the Trans-Alleganians. They are gone if you do not. Do not let false pride make a tea-act of your excise-laws. Adieu. Yours affectionately

TH: JEFFERSON

PrC (DLC); at foot of text: "Mr. Giles." TJ's SEPARATE LETTER of this date to Giles, recorded in SJL, has not been found.

To Richard Adams

DEAR SIR   Monticello Dec. 18. 94.

I received by the post of the day before yesterday a letter from Colo. Skipwith, covering one from you on the subject of a judgment recovered by Mr. Short against Dr. Griffin, and which you advise him may be recovered out of a debt due to Dr. Griffin at Baltimore. Being appointed by Mr. Short his Attorney in fact, and being totally uninformed of the ground on which this demand rests, I must ask your friendly information concerning it, with sufficient fulness to instruct his attorney at Baltimore to proceed on it. I shall chearfully co-operate with you in any thing which you may desire for facilitating the recovery of your own demand as well as Mr. Short's, which may consist with his interest. You will receive this probably on Saturday evening, and our post comes out early Monday morning; so that if you could have the goodness to write on Sunday the necessary information for me I shall receive it directly. I am with great esteem Dear Sir Your friend & servt

TH: JEFFERSON

PrC (DLC: William Short Papers); at foot of text: "Colo. Richd. Adams"; endorsed in ink by TJ.

Richard Adams (1726-1800), a Virginia merchant and planter who was reputedly Richmond's largest property owner, had represented New Kent and Henrico in the Virginia House of Burgesses before the American Revolution and had served as representative for Henrico in both houses of the General Assembly during the War for Independence (WMQ, 1st ser., V [1897], 161-2; Sutton, *Revolution to Secession*, 159-60).

LETTER FROM COLO. SKIPWITH, COVERING ONE FROM YOU: Henry Skipwith to TJ, 11 Dec. 1794, recorded in SJL as received 16 Dec. 1794, but not found; and Adams to Skipwith, 6 Nov. 1794, reporting that Skipwith has had a judgment of the Henrico County Court "as assignee of Short" against one Griffin (evidently John Tayloe Grif-

fin); that an execution has been served on Griffin, who released himself by providing a schedule of his estate and invoking the insolvency act; that he is involved as a security for Griffin in a debt due from a gentleman in Baltimore, and a judgment has gone against him for "a pretty Considerable sum," for which Griffin will give him a judgment; he is determined to try to get paid out of that debt, the "only and best Chance" Skipwith has of being reimbursed; and, if Skipwith agrees, requesting a power of attorney to receive his debt, without which nothing can be done, "as your debt is to be first paid" (Tr in DLC: William Short Papers; endorsed by TJ).

From James Madison

DEAR SIR   Philada. Decr. 21. 1794.

Your favor of the 9th. by the Orange post arrived here on the 18th. That of the 12 by the Richmond post, on the 20st. so that it appears the latter was one day less on the way. It is to be remarked however that as the Orange post leaves Charlottesville on tuesday, he might easily be in Fredericksburg on thursday, in time for the mail which passes thro' it on that day to Dumfries. If this despatch is not required of him it ought to be. It would make a difference of two days in the journey. Or at least the post might wait a day in Charlottesville and be in time for the saturday's mail at Fredericksburg.

Our weather here has been as fine as you describe yours. Yesterday there was a change. It was cold, cloudy, and inclined to snow. To day we have a bright day, and not very cold. Prices here are very different from yours. Wheat is at 13 or 14/. and flour in proportion. In general things are 50 PerCt. beyond the prices of last winter. The phenomenon you wish to have explained is as little understood here as with you; but it would be here quite unfashionable to suppose it needed explanation. It is impossible to give you an idea of the force with which the tide has set in a particular direction. It has been too violent not to be soon followed by a change. In fact I think a change has begun already. The danger will then be of as violent a reflux to the opposite extreme.

The attack made on the essential and constitutional right of the Citizen, in the blow levelled at the "self-created Societies" does not appear to have had the effect intended. It is and must be felt by every man who values liberty, whatever opinion he may have of the use or abuse of it by those institutions. You will see that the appeal is begun to the public sentiment, by the injured parties. The Republican Society of Baltimore set the example. That of Newark has advertised a meeting of its members. It is said that if Edwd. Livingston, as is generally believed, has outvoted Watts, for the H. of Reps. he is indebted for it to the invigorated exertions of the Democratic Society of that place, of which he is himself a member. In Boston the subject is well understood, and handled in the Newspaper on the republican side, with industry and address.

The Elections in Massts. have turned out rather better than was of late expected. The two republican members have stood their ground; in spite of the most unexampled operations against them. Ames is said to owe his success to the votes of negroes and British sailors smuggled under a very lax mode of conducting the election there. Sedgwick and Goodhue have *bare* majorities. Dexter is to run another heat, but will succeed; Gerry, his only considerable competitor and who would outvote him, refusing to be elected. There are several changes in the remainder of the Delegation, and some of them greatly for the better. In New York there will be at least half republicans; perhaps more. It has unluckily happened that in 2 districts two *republicans* set up against *one* Anti: The consequence is that a man is re-elected who would not otherwise have taken the feild: and there is some danger of a similar consequence in the other district. In N. Jersey, it is said that not more than one of the old members will be returned. The people all over the State[1] are signing with avidity a remonstrance against the high salaries of the Government.

Hamilton is to resign, according to his own notification the last of Feby. His object is not yet unfolded. Knox, as the shadow, follows the substance. Their successors are not yet designated by any circumstance that has escaped.

What think you of a project to disfranchise the insurgent Counties by a bill of exclusion against their Reps. in the State Legislature? The object is to pave the way for Bingham or Fitzimmons—as Senator—and to give an example for rejecting Galatine in the H. of Reps. at the next Congress—of which he is a member. The proposition has been laid on the table, and the event is uncertain. There is some probability the violence of the measure may defeat it; nor is it certain I am told that if carried thro', it would answer the purpose of its authors.

RC (DLC: Madison Papers); unsigned; endorsed by TJ as received 31 Dec. 1794 and so recorded in SJL.

A 9 Dec. 1794 address from the REPUBLICAN SOCIETY OF BALTIMORE "To the Government and People of the United States" maintained that that organization had consistently opposed the Whiskey Rebellion but stoutly defended its right to stand guard against "the intrigues and violence of ambitious men" (Philadelphia *Aurora*, 17 Dec.

1794). The NEWARK society met on 17 Dec. to consider "a question of considerable importance relative to the right of opinion" (same, 20 Dec. 1794). For letters in the NEWSPAPER ON THE REPUBLICAN SIDE in Boston defending the republican societies, see *Independent Chronicle*, 8, 11, 15 Dec. 1794. The petition and REMONSTRANCE to Congress AGAINST THE HIGH SALARIES of federal legislative and executive officials by certain New Jersey inhabitants alleged that discontent resulting from these expenses had been one of the causes of the Whiskey Rebellion and remarked on the huge disparity between the pay and travel allowances accorded Congressmen and the militia acting to quell the protests (Philadelphia *Aurora*, 20 Dec. 1794). On 1 Dec. 1794 Secretary of the Treasury Alexander HAMILTON had notified George Washington and the

House of Representatives that he would give up his post on 31 Jan. 1795, not FEBY., and duly resigned on that day. Secretary of War Henry KNOX left office on the last day of 1794 (Syrett, *Hamilton*, XVII, 405, 413, 570n, XVIII, 241). A motion in the Pennsylvania House of Representatives that the legislators from Westmoreland, Washington, Fayette, and Allegheny counties were "not duly qualified for said office—those counties having been, at the time of the election, in a state of insurrection"—was made on 16 Dec. 1794 and passed on 9 Jan. 1795, but most of the unseated members promptly sought and won reelection (Philadelphia *Aurora*, 20 Dec. 1794; Leland D. Baldwin, *Whiskey Rebels: The Story of a Frontier Uprising* [Pittsburgh, 1939], 262).

[1] Preceding four words interlined.

Deed of Manumission for Robert Hemings

This indenture witnesseth that I Thomas Jefferson of the county of Albemarle have manumitted and made free Robert Hemings, son of Betty Hemmings: so that in future he shall be free and of free condition, with all his goods and chattels and shall be discharged of all obligation of bondage or servitude whatsoever: and that neither myself, my heirs executors or administrators shall have any right to exact from him hereafter any services or duties whatsoever. In witness whereof I have put my seal to this present deed of manumission. Given in Albemarle this twenty fourth day of December one thousand seven hundred and ninety four.　　　　　　　　　　　　　　　　　　　　　TH: JEFFERSON

Signed, sealed and
delivered in presence of
D: Carr

MS (ViU); in TJ's hand, except for the signature of Dabney Carr, Jr.; indented, with TJ's seal affixed; words lost in frayed right margin supplied from PrC; notation on verso: "Charlottesville September District Court 1795. This Deed of manumission was produced into Court and acknowledged by Thomas Jefferson party thereto and ordered to be Recorded. Teste Jno.

Nicholas CCk"; endorsed in several hands: "Jefferson to Hemings } Deed of manumission" and "September 1795. Acknowledged & to be Recorded" and "Recorded." PrC (MHi); lacks Carr's signature.

Robert Hemings (1762-1819) was the first slave TJ actually released. TJ inherited him after the death in 1773 of his father-in-law John Wayles, who is now generally recognized to be Hemings's father. As TJ's personal attendant, Hemings went with him on his trips to serve in the Continental Congress in Philadelphia in 1775 and 1776 and in Annapolis in 1783 and 1784. In the latter city TJ paid for two-and-a-half months of barber's training for Hemings, who then accompanied him to Boston. He brought the horses back to Monticello from there when TJ took ship for France in July 1784. During TJ's absence in Europe and for most of his service as Secretary of State, Hemings was permitted to hire himself out to the master of his choosing, subject only to the requirement that he return to Monticello when TJ was in attendance. At some point during this period of comparative autonomy Hemings married and had a child with a Fredericksburg slave named Dolly. She subsequently moved to Richmond where her master, Dr. George Frederick Stras, agreed to pay TJ to free Hemings in exchange for Hemings's promise of repayment. TJ regarded the price of £60 set by arbitrators as inadequate and alleged that Stras had "debauched" Hemings from him, but he accepted the situation and the purchase price and turned over this deed to Stras to hold until Hemings repaid him, an event presumably marked by the recording

of the deed in the Albemarle County District Court in September 1795. Hemings subsequently operated a livery or hauling business in Richmond, first appearing on a Richmond tax list in 1799 and by 1802 owning a half-acre lot at the intersection of G and Seventh Streets. His death may have been related to a pistol accident in which he lost a hand (James A. Bear, Jr., "The Hemings Family of Monticello," *Virginia Cavalcade*, XXIX [1979], 80-1; "The Memoirs of Madison Hemings," in Annette Gordon-Reed, *Thomas Jefferson and Sally Hemings: An American Controversy* [Charlottesville, 1997], 245-8; MB, 21 June 1773, and note, 27 Oct. 1775, 7 June 1776, 3, 10, 13 Feb., 19 Apr., 30 June 1784, 24 Dec. 1794; TJ to Nicholas Lewis, 1 July 1784, 11 July, 16 Dec. 1788; TJ to William Fitzhugh, 21 July 1790; Thomas Mann Randolph, Jr., to TJ, 30 Apr. 1791; TJ to Daniel L. Hylton, 1 July 1792; TJ to Randolph, 26 Dec. 1794).

SJL records letters from Hemings to TJ of 28 Nov. 1794, 7 Jan. 1795, 29 July, 27 Oct., and 9 Nov. 1796, received respectively on 3 Dec. 1794, 6 Feb. 1795, 3 Aug., 30 Oct., and 11 Nov. 1796, and a letter of 21 Oct. 1796 from TJ to Hemings, none of which has been found.

To James Lyle

DEAR SIR   Monticello Dec. 24. 94.

A second debtor, Robert Hawkins, called on me yesterday and paid me his second bond £41–15. Having no immediate conveyance to Richmond for this money, I send to Mr. Randolph, who is on his way there, an order to recieve a like sum lying ready for me in Richmond and to pay it to you together with Milliner's £72–8–8 delivered him for you as mentioned in my former letter of which he is the bearer. Both to be placed to the credit of my bonds in the order in which they are payable. I am with great esteem Dear Sir Your friend & servt

TH: JEFFERSON

PrC (MHi); at foot of text: "Mr. Lyle"; endorsed in ink by TJ.

MY FORMER LETTER: TJ to Lyle, 14 Dec. 1794.

From Richard Adams

DEAR SIR   Richmd. Hill 26th Decr. 1794

I Received your Favor of the 18th. of this month and note the Contents. Upon Examining the Records, I find I was mistaken in the Information, I gave Mr. Skipworth in Respect to Mr. Shorts Judgment. Indeed at any Rate, I think the prospect I mentioned is so distant and uncertain, that I believe there is very little hope of obtaining any thing from that Quarter, I shall therefore decline it on my part. I am with the greatest Esteem & Regard Dr. Sr. yr mo Obdt. huml Sevt.

RICHD. ADAMS

RC (DLC); endorsed by TJ as received 31 Dec. 1794 and so recorded in SJL. PrC of Tr (DLC: William Short Papers); entirely in TJ's hand; at head of text: "Copy"; at foot of text: "To Th: Jefferson"; endorsed in ink by TJ: "Skipwith Henry." Enclosed in TJ to Henry Skipwith, 4 Jan. 1795.

Adams also wrote a letter to TJ on 20 Mch. 1798, which is recorded in SJL as received 27 Mch. 1798, but has not been found.

Authorization for J. P. P. Derieux

Having occasion to hire for the ensuing year four very able intelligent negro-men, I hereby authorize Mr. Peter Derieux to act for me therein, and oblige myself to pay whatever hire he may stipulate for me. And though I would not make it essential to have the hire payable in all the month of April after the year expired, yet as it is disadvantageous to be obliged to sell produce to raise money earlier than that, it influences the extent of the hire to which I have advised Mr. Derieux to engage me. I should be willing to pay interest from the end of the year to the day of paiment agreed on, which will sufficiently justify executors in agreeing to that delay.   TH: JEFFERSON

Dec. 26. 1794.

MS (privately owned, Philadelphia, 1999); entirely in TJ's hand.

The slaves TJ sought TO HIRE FOR THE ENSUING YEAR arrived at Monticello the fol-

lowing month. The four men—Essex, Isaac, Patrick, and Peter—were from the estate of Thomas Mann Randolph, Sr. (MB, 31 Jan. 1795).

To Thomas Mann Randolph

Dear Sir   Monticello Dec. 26. 94.

Your chariot was ready to have set off the day after Zachary arrived here; but an unlucky use of the permission you had given me respecting your waggon, has prevented it's departure. The post after you left us, I received information *from Philadelphia* that my nailrod had been lodged in Richmond before the last week in November, and could not be forwarded here for want of a conveyance. I immediately went to Colo. Bell to advise on the prospect of a conveyance from Richmond. He assured me it was desperate, as all the return waggons were engaged by the merchants. I was therefore obliged to avail myself of your kind permission to send your waggon, and having desired Robinson to get a load for her down, Billy set off with her for Richmond on Thursday, and expected to be back here on Thursday again, which was yesterday. I did not suppose however he could be back till to-day. Nor is he as yet arrived, but the moment he arrives, Zachary may set out. I would have sent one of my horses, if we could have made up another, but Zachary says that Billy is as essential as the horses.—Before the receipt of your letter, we had taken up our Asparagus bed, and after replanting had given the spare roots to a neighbor. We have however done our best to send Mrs. Fleming what more could be spared or collected. Patsy wrote for *Artichoke* roots. But I presume she meant *Asparagus*, as our artichokes are but newly planted, and are most of them of so indifferent a kind that, as soon as we can distinguish them, we mean to dig them up and throw them away.—If you can hire the four negromen for me at the hiring in Richmond Jan. 1. on advantageous terms, I shall be obliged to you, provided they are[1] from the country, and not of the town from whence I should not chuse any mixture with my own negroes. This would be so far adviseable as those of your father's estate may go too high. Otherwise I should have preferred these as they will think themselves still in the family and will be more contented and controuled by your presence.—You will find by the inclosed that Bob's business has been hastened into such a situation as to make it difficult for me to reject it. I had certainly thought it just that the person whom I suppose to have debauched him from me, as well as the special inconvenience of my letting him go for 2. or 3. years to come, and a total abandonment of his services for 11. or 12 years past should have been known and operated in estimating his value as a mulct on Mr. S. However all that has been kept out of view, and I have too much respect for the gentlemen who have valued him to have the subject revised. It remains therefore only to receive the money and deliver the deed, which you will find inclosed in the letter to Mr. Stras. I have made it to Bob himself, because Mr. Stras mentions it is for his freedom he is to advance the money, and his holding the deed will sufficiently secure the fulfilment of Bob's engagements to him. When you shall have received the money, be so good as to pay £41–16 currency of it to Mr. Lyle with the sum delivered you before, and hold up the balance, as I expect in 2. or 3 posts from Philadelphia to learn whether I owe it there or am to apply it to certain purposes here. Stras's letter and the valuation to be returned to me.[2]—Derieux removes to Wood's ordinary within a week. The children are and have been constantly well. I shall not close my letter till Billy arrives.[3]

Dec. 27. half after one. Billy arrived half an hour ago. I had told him that you would be at Richmond about the time of his being there. He mistook this for a direction to wait for you, and says he stayed two days there expecting you. I am endeavoring to get them off this afternoon if it be only for 8. or 10. miles as that will enable them to reach Rockcastle tomorrow. Billy has to go to Edgehill for clothes.—The old lady at Bearcastle is dead; by which the sons of Mr. D. Carr come into immediate possession of their lands, about 1500. as. $\frac{1}{3}$ of which are low grounds. There will be about 40 negroes to divide among the children of their grandfather and their representatives. I think Peter Carr will take the whole of his father's share, and of his uncle Sam Carr's. Tho as to this last it is more questionable, Mr. Wythe and Mr. Pendleton having differed in opinion. The question will lie between Peter and his uncles and aunts, and not between him and his brothers and sisters, who I think have no title under any hypothesis.

Billy has brought me 1500. ℔. of nailrod. The rest is at Manchester, and has been there above a month by Swan's own information to Lownes in Philadelphia, and communicated by Lownes to me. I shall endeavor to get the Milton boats to bring it up. If you were to fall in with any of them while you are in Richmond, be so good as to lend a hand to their getting it. But do not go out of your way to do it, as I shall be pretty sure of having it done.—We are all well and concerned for the impediments of your journey, and the state of your's and Patsy's health. My best affections attend you both always.

P.S. Pray lodge nine dollars of the money to be received of Stras in the hands of Colo. Harvie for J. Taylor to pay for the drill plough. I shall give Taylor notice that it is done. My groceries from Colo. Gamble's are come up.

RC (DLC); unsigned; addressed: "Thomas Mann Randolph Rockcastle"; second postscript written perpendicularly in the margin; endorsed by Randolph as received 30 Dec. 1794. PrC (ViU: Edgehill-Randolph Papers); lacks second page (see note 1 below). Enclosures: (1) George Frederick Stras to TJ, 21 Dec. 1794, not found but recorded in SJL as received 23 Dec. 1794; and an enclosed valuation, also not found, estimating the worth of Robert Hemings as £60 (MB, 24 Dec. 1794). (2) TJ to Stras, 24 Dec. 1794, not found but recorded under this date in SJL. (3) Deed of Manumission for Robert Hemings, 24 Dec. 1794.

YOUR LETTER: Randolph to TJ, 22 Dec. 1794, recorded in SJL as received 23 Dec. 1794 from Rockcastle but not found. SJL also records missing letters of 1 Nov. 1794 from Randolph to TJ, received from Richmond on 5 Nov. 1794, from TJ to Randolph of 18 Nov. 1794, and from Randolph to TJ of 28 Nov. 1794, received a day later. PATSY Jefferson Randolph's letter requesting ARTICHOKE ROOTS is not recorded in SJL and has not been found. Barbara Carr, the widow of John Carr and the mother of TJ's deceased brother-in-law Dabney Carr, Sr., was the OLD LADY AT BEARCASTLE, an estate in Louisa County (VMHB, II [1894], 221-3, V [1898], 441). John Swann, cabinetmaker and partner in the firm of Samuel & John Swann, was the Richmond agent of TJ's supplier of NAILROD, Caleb LOWNES of PHILADELPHIA (see TJ to Martha Jefferson Randolph, 14 Feb. 1796). SJL records missing letters from TJ to Samuel & John Swann of 23 Oct. and 18 Dec. 1794, and a reply from John Swann dated 23 Dec. 1794 and received five days later.

[1] Second page, consisting of remainder of paragraph, lacking from PrC.
[2] Preceding sentence interlined.
[3] Illegible sentence erased here.

To Thomas Walker, Jr.

DEAR SIR   Monticello Dec. 26. 94.

I did not take a memorandum in writing of the terms on which our mares went to the Jack, relying chiefly on Mr. Randolph's memory who happens to be now absent. If I recollect them rightly, it was 2 guineas a mare with the usual[1] deduction of 1. in 5. or one fifth, for those who sent over that number. If so my account stands thus.

7. mares @ [2 guineas?]	£19–12	
deduct one fifth	3–18– 5	
remains due to the Jack	15–13– 7	
add my debt to you for the mule	15–	
makes the whole sum of	30–13– 7.	accordingly I now send

£
by Mr. D. Carr   in gold 20–6–4
          34¼ Dollars   10–5–6 30–11–10
balance due for want of change   1– 9 which I will try to recollect at another time. But if I have mistaken the terms I pray you to charge it to my faithless memory, and not to a thought of injuring any mortal, and above all others, not Mrs. Barclay. In this case consider the money as paid on account only, and what is right shall be done as soon as I know it. If the Jack stands at the same place the next year, I will send the same mares and perhaps more to him on the same terms. Which I think you will find high enough, when we consider that the Connecticut supplies of mules, now regularly flowing in, fix the price of

a good mule at £15. two years old.   I am in hopes this money comes in time to fulfill my engagements, which having been to pay from the proceeds of produce, this could not be expected to be turned into money earlier than this, in this part of the country. I am with great esteem Dear Sir Your friend & servt   TH: JEFFERSON

RC (DLC: Rives Papers); worn at fold; addressed: "Thomas Walker esquire. Albemarle"; endorsed in part: "the jack (Don Carlos.)."

Letters from TJ to Walker of 15 Dec. 1794 and 23 May and 21 Nov. 1796 are recorded in SJL but have not been found.

[1] Preceding two words interlined in place of "a."

To James Madison

DEAR SIR   Monticello Dec. 28. 94.

I have kept Mr. Joy's letter a post or two, with an intention of considering attentively the observations it contains: but I have really now so little stomach for any thing of that kind that I have not resolution enough even to endeavor to understand the observations. I therefore return the letter, not to delay your answer to it, and beg you in answering for yourself, to assure him of my respects and thankful acceptance of Chalmer's treaties, which I do not possess: and if you possess yourself of the scope of his reasoning, make any answer to it you please for me. If it had been on the rotation of my crops, I would have answered myself, lengthily perhaps, but certainly *con gusto*.

The denunciation of the democratic societies is one of the extraordinary acts of boldness of which we have seen so many from the faction of Monocrats. It is wonderful indeed that the President should have permitted himself to be the organ of such an attack on the freedom of discussion, the freedom of writing, printing and publishing. It must be a matter of rare curiosity to get at the modifications of these rights proposed by them, and to see what line their ingenuity would draw between democratical societies, whose avowed object is the nourishment of the republican principles of our constitution, and the society of the Cincinnati, a *self-created* one, carving out for itself hereditary distinctions, lowering over our constitution eternally, meeting together in all parts of the Union periodically, with closed doors, accumulating a capital in their separate treasury, corresponding secretly and regularly, and of which society the very persons denouncing the democrats are themselves the fathers, founders or high officers. Their sight must be perfectly dazzled by the glittering of crowns and coronets, not to see the extravagance of the proposition to suppress the friends of general freedom, while those who wish to confine that freedom to the few, are permitted to go on in their principles and practices.—I here put out of sight the persons whose misbehavior has been taken advantage of to slander the friends of popular rights; and I am happy to observe that as far as the circle of my observation and information extends, every body has lost sight of them, and viewed the abstract attempt on their natural and constitutional rights in all it's nakedness. I have never heard, or heard of a single expression or opinion which did not condemn it as an inexcusable aggression.—And with respect to the transactions against the excise-law, it appears to me that you are all swept away in the torrent of governmental opinions, or that we do not know what these transactions have been. We know of none which according to the definitions of the law, have been any thing more than riotous. There was indeed a meeting to consult about a separation. But to consult on a question does not amount to a determination of that question in the affirmative, still less to the acting on such a determination: but we shall see I suppose what the court lawyers, and courtly judges and would-be Ambassadors will make of it.—The excise-law is an infernal one. The first error was to admit it by the constitution. The 2d. to act on that admission. The 3d. and last will be to make it the instrument of dismembering the Union, and setting us all afloat to chuse which part of it we will adhere to. The information of our militia returned from the Westward is uniform, that tho the people there let them pass quietly, they were objects of their laughter, not of their fear, that 100[1] men could have cut off their whole force in a thousand places of the Alleganey, that their detestation of the excise law is universal, and has now associated to it a detestation of the government, and that separation which perhaps was a very distant and problematical event, is now near, and certain and determined in the mind of every man. I expected to have seen some justification of arming one part of the society against another, of declaring a civil war the moment before the meeting of that body which has the sole right of declaring war, of being so patient of the kicks and scoffs of our enemies, and rising at a feather against our friends, of adding a million to the public debt and deriding us with recommendations to pay it if we can, &c &c. But the part of the speech which was to be taken as a justification of the armament reminded me of parson Saunders's demonstration why minus into minus makes plus. After a parcel of shreds of stuff from Aesop's fables and Tom Thumb, he jumps all at once into his Ergo, minus multiplied into minus makes plus. Just so the 15,000 men enter after the fables in the speech.—However the time is coming when we shall fetch up the lee-way of our vessel. The changes in your house I see are going on for the better, and even the Augean herd over your heads are slowly purging off their impurities. Hold on then, my dear friend, that we may not ship-wreck in the mean while. I do not see in the minds of those with whom I converse a greater affliction than the fear of your retirement; but this must not be, unless to a more splendid and a more efficacious post. There I should rejoice to see you: I hope I may say I shall rejoice to see you. I have long had much in my mind to say to you on that subject. But double delicacies have kept me silent. I ought perhaps to say, while I would not give up my own retirement for the empire of the Universe, how I can justify wishing one, whose happiness I have as much at heart as yours, to take the front of the battle which is fighting for my security. This would be easy enough to be done, but not at the heel of a lengthy epistle.—Let us quit this, and turn to the fine weather we are basking in. We have had one of our tropical winters. Once only a snow of 3. inches deep, which went off the next day, and never as much ice as would have cooled a bottle of wine. And we have now but a month to go through of winter weather. For February always gives us good samples of the spring of which it is the harbinger.—I recollect no small news interesting to you. You will have heard I suppose that Wilson Nicholas has bought Carr's lowground's and Harvey's barracks. I rejoice in the prosperity of a virtuous man, and hope his prosperity will not taint his virtue. Present me respectfully to Mrs. Madison, and pray her to keep you where you are for her own satisfaction and the public good, and accept the cordial affections of us all. Adieu.

RC (DLC: Madison Papers); unsigned. PrC (DLC); at foot of first page in ink: "Madison James." Enclosure: enclosure to Madison to TJ, 30 Nov. 1794.

[1] Figures written over partially erased "thous."

To John Taylor

DEAR SIR   Monticello Dec. 29. 1794.

I have long owed you a letter, for which my conscience would not have let me rest in quiet but on the consideration that the paiment would not be worth your acceptance. The debt is not merely for a letter the common traffic of a day, but for valuable ideas, which instructed me, which I have adopted, and am acting on them. I am sensible of the truth of your observations that the atmosphere is the great store house of matter for recruiting our lands, that tho' efficacious, it is slow in it's operation, and we must therefore give them time, instead of the loads of quicker manure given in other countries, that for this purpose we must avail ourselves of the great quantities of land we possess in proportion to our labour, and that while putting them to nurse with the atmosphere, we must protect them from the bite and tread of animals, which are nearly a counterpoise for the benefits of the atmosphere. As good things, as well as evil, go in a train, this relieves us from the labor and expence of cross fences, now very sensibly felt on account of the scarcity and distance of timber. I am accordingly now engaged in applying my cross fences to the repair of the outer ones[1] and substituting rows of Peach trees to preserve the boundaries of the fields. And though I observe your strictures on rotations of crops, yet it appears that in this I differ from you only in words. You keep half your lands in culture, the other half at nurse; so I propose to do. Your scheme indeed requires only four years and mine six; but the proportion of labour and rest is the same. My years of rest however are employed, two of them in producing clover, yours in volunteer herbage. But I still understand it to be your opinion that clover is best where lands will produce them. Indeed I think that the important improvement for which the world is indebted to Young, is the substitution of clover crops instead of unproductive fallows: and the demonstration that lands are more enriched by clover than by volunteer herbage or fallows: and the clover crops are highly valuable. That our red lands which are still in tolerable heart will produce fine clover I know from the experience of the last year, and indeed that of my neighbors had established the fact. And from observations on accidental plants in the feilds which have been considerably harrassed with corn, I believe that even these will produce clover fit for soiling of animals green. I think therefore I can count on the success of that improver. My third year of rest will be devoted to cowpenning, and to a trial of the buckwheat dressing. A further progress in surveying my open arable lands, has shewn me that I can have 7. fields in each of my farms where I expected only six: consequently that I can add more to the portion of rest and ameliorating crops. I have doubted on a question on which I am sure you can advise me well, whether I had better give this newly acquired year as an addition to the continuance of my clover, or throw it with some improving crop between two of my crops of grain as for instance between my corn and rye. I strongly incline to the latter, because I am not satisfied that one cleansing crop in seven years will be sufficient; and indeed I think it important to separate my exhausting crops by alternations of amelioraters. With this view I think to try an experiment of what judge Parker informs me he practises. That is, to turn in my wheat stubble the instant the grain is off, and sow turneps to be fed out by the sheep. But whether this will answer in our fields which are harrassed I do not know. We have been in the habit of sowing only our freshest[2] lands in turneps. Hence a presumption that wearied lands will not bring them. But Young's making turneps to be fed on by sheep the basis of his improvement of poor lands, affords evidence that tho they may not bring great crops, they will bring them in a sufficient degree to improve the lands. I will try that experiment however this year, as well as the one of buck wheat. I have also attended to another improver mentioned by you, the winter-vetch, and have taken measures to get the seed of it from England, as also of the Siberian vetch which Millar greatly commends, and being a biennial might perhaps take the place of clover in lands which do not suit that. The winter vetch I suspect may be advantageously thrown in between crops, as it gives a choice to use it as green feed in the spring if fodder be run short, or to turn it in as a green-dressing. My rotation, with these amendments is as follows.

1. Wheat, followed the same year by turneps to be fed on by the sheep.
2. Corn and potatoes mixed, and in autumn the Vetch to be used as fodder in the spring if wanted, or to be turned in as a dressing.
3. peas, or,[3] potatoes, or both according to the quality of the field.
4. Rye, and clover sown on it in the spring. Wheat may be substituted here for rye, when it shall be found that the 2d. 3d. 5th. and 6th. fields will subsist the farm.[4]
5. Clover.
6. Clover, and in autumn turn it in and sow the Vetch.
7. turn in the Vetch in the spring, then sow buckwheat and turn that in having hurdled off the poorest spots for cowpenning. In autumn sow wheat to begin the circle again.

I am for throwing the whole force of my husbandry on the wheat-field, because it is the only one which is to go to market to produce money. Perhaps the clover may bring in something in the form of stock. The other feilds are merely for the consumption of the farm. The Siberian Melilot, mentioned by you, I never heard of. The horse bean I tried this last year. It turned out nothing. The President has tried it without success. An old English farmer of the name of Spuryear, settled in Delaware, has tried it there with good success: but he told me it would not do without being well shaded, and I think he planted it among his corn for that reason. But he acknoleged our pea was as good an ameliorater and a more valuable pulse, as being food for man as well as horse. The Succory is what Young calls Chicoria Intubus. He sent some seed to the President, who gave me some, and I gave it to my neighbors to keep up till I should come home. One of them has cultivated it with great success, is very fond of it, and gave me some seed which I sowed last spring. Tho' the summer was favorable it came on slowly at first, but by autumn became large and strong. It did not seed that year, but will the next, and you shall be furnished with seed. I suspect it requires rich ground, and then produces a heavy crop for green feed, for horses and cattle. I had poor success with my potatoes last year, not having made more than 60. or 70. bushels to the acre. But my neighbors having made good crops, I am not disheartened. The first step towards the recovery of our lands is to find substitutes for corn and bacon. I count on potatoes, clover and sheep. The two former to feed[5] every animal on the farm except my negroes, and the latter to feed them, diversified with rations of salted fish and molasses, both of them wholesome, agreeable and cheap articles of food.   For pasture I rely on the forests, by day, and soiling in the evening. Why could we not have a moveable airy cow house, to be set up in the middle of the feild which is to be dunged, and soil our cattle in that thro' the summer as well as winter, keeping them constantly up and well littered? This, with me, would be in the clover feild of the 1st. year because during the 2d. year it would be rotting, and would be spread on it in fallow the beginning of the 3d. But such an effort would be far above the present tyro state of my farming. The grosser barbarisms in culture which I have to encounter, are more than enough for all my attentions at present. The dung-yard must be my last effort but one. The last would be irrigation.—It might be thought at first view, that the interposition of these ameliorations or dressings between my crops will be too laborious. But observe that the turneps and two dressings of vetch do not cost a single ploughing. The turning in the wheat-stubble for the turneps is the fallow for the corn of the succeeding year. The 1st. sowing of vetches is on the corn (as is now practised for wheat) and the turning it in, is the flush-ploughing for the crop of potatoes and peas. The 2d. sowing of the vetch is on the wheat fallow, and the turning it in is the ploughing necessary for sowing the buckwheat. These three ameliorations then will cost but a harrowing each.—On the subject of the drilled husbandry, I think experience has established it's preference for some plants, as the turnep, pea, bean, cabbage, corn &c and that of the broad cast for other plants as all the bread grains and grasses, except perhaps Lucerne and St. foin in soils and climates very productive of weeds. In dry soils and climates the broad cast is better for Lucerne and St. foin, as all the South of France can testify.—I have imagined and executed a mould-board which may be mathematically demonstrated to be perfect, as far as perfection depends on mathematical principles. And one great circumstance in it's favor is that it may be made by the most bungling carpenter, and cannot possibly vary a hair's breadth in it's form, but by gross negligence. You have seen the musical instrument called a sticcado. Suppose all it's sticks of equal length, hold the fore-end horizontally on the floor, to receive the turf which presents itself horizontally, and with the right hand twist the hind-end to the perpendicular, or rather as much beyond the perpendicular as will be necessary to cast over the turf completely. This gives an idea (tho not absolutely exact) of my mould-board. It is on the principle of two wedges combined at right angles, the first in the direct line of the furrow to raise the turf gradually, the other across the furrow to turn it over gradually. For both these purposes the wedge is the instrument of the least resistance. I will make a model of the mould-board and lodge it with Colo. Harvie in Richmond for you.—This brings me to my thanks for the drill plough lodged with him for me, which I now expect every hour to receive, and the price of which I have deposited in his hands to be called for when you please. A good instrument of this kind is almost the greatest desideratum in husbandry. I am anxious to conjecture before hand what may be expected from the sowing turneps in jaded ground, how much from the acre, and how large they will be? Will your experience enable you to give me a probable conjecture? Also what is the produce of potatoes, and what of peas in the same kind of ground?—It must now have been several pages since you began to cry out 'mercy.' In mercy then I will here finish with my affectionate remembrance to my old friend Mr. Pendleton, and respects to your fire side, & to yourself assurances of the sincere esteem of Dear Sir Your friend & servt   TH: JEFFERSON

RC (MHi: Washburn Collection); addressed: "John Taylor Caroline near the Bowling-green"; stamped; endorsed by Taylor. PrC (DLC); lacking two emendations, the more important of which is noted below.

MILLAR: Philip Miller, *The Gardeners Dictionary* . . . , 8th ed. (London, 1768). See Sowerby, No. 801. TJ had conceived his famous plow MOULD-BOARD of least resistance in 1788 and by 1790 had begun to share the design with other farmers (note to

Thomas Mann Randolph, Jr., to TJ, 23 Apr. 1790; TJ to Martha Jefferson Randolph, 8 Aug. 1790). For his fullest account of it, see TJ to John Sinclair, 23 Mch. 1798.

[1] Remainder of sentence interlined in RC in a darker ink and lacking in PrC.
[2] Word interlined in place of "richest."
[3] Word written over "and," erased.
[4] Preceding sentence inserted.
[5] Preceding two words interlined in place of "will allow me to make no more [corn] [. . .] enable me to support."

Memorandum from Eli Alexander

[ca. Dec. 1794?]

	Corn
A computation of the corn it will take for the stock from now till April 1 or for one Hundred days.	
6 plough Horses from this till April the first or for one Hundred days when ploughing aught to have 2 gallons a day Each, suppose 40 ploughing days, which	bushels
amounts to	60 corn
the same Horses when not in service one gallon of corn a day Each for 60 days is 45 bushil	45
4 breding mares one gallon a day Each which is 50 bush	50
2 plough horses to come fifty days a gallon & $\frac{1}{2}$ Each is	$18\frac{3}{4}$
8 Oxen when hauling to have 2 gallons Each suppose 40 days is 80 bushels of corn	80
Hogs $\frac{1}{2}$ bushel a day amount to 50 bushels.	50
3 Coults in the above menshined time 10 bushels	10
Milk cows 3 gallons a day is $30\frac{1}{2}$	$30\frac{1}{2}$
	$344\frac{1}{4}$

the consumsion of Shadwell will be 750 bushels of corn from this time till November next 25
theare is 320 barrels of corn measured but what theare is now I cant ascertain I suppose to be two hundred and sixty or seventy barrels.

MS (MHi); entirely in Alexander's hand; undated, but probably belonging to his term as overseer at Shadwell and Lego (see below); addressed: "Colo. Jefferson Monto cholo"; endorsed by TJ: "Corn for the winter Alexander's estimate."

Eli Alexander, a farmer at Elkton, Maryland, replaced Byrd Rogers as the overseer of TJ's Shadwell and Lego plantations early in 1794 and probably continued until the autumn of 1795, after which he remained in Albemarle County. In 1805 he obtained a seven-year lease of Shadwell and part of Lego, but TJ found him a difficult tenant, slow to pay his rent and posing arguments over the terms of the agreement so contentious that the dispute could only be resolved by arbitration. Nonetheless, in 1827 Alexander signed a petition urging the state of Virginia to buy Giuseppe Ceracchi's bust of TJ (TJ to Jacob Hollingsworth, 4 Dec. 1793; TJ to Thomas Mann Randolph, Jr., 8 Dec. 1793; TJ to James Madison, 15 Feb. 1794; Betts, Farm Book, 29, 47, 171-83; MB, 28 May 1794, 4, 7, 24 Nov. 1795, 20 July 1817, and note; TQHGM, VIII [1927], 244).

Memorandum from Eli Alexander

[1794-95?]

A Method for preparing buck wheat for table use first to fan it out from the chaff and then tak it and put it into a bag and tramp it well then Run it through the fan the second time then grind it Seperate from the Corne then put one forth Corne Meal and bolt it together and it is fit for use.

ELI ALEXANDER

MS (DLC: TJ Papers, 235: 42204); possibly in Alexander's hand; undated, but probably belonging to the period when he was overseer at Shadwell and Lego; endorsed by TJ: "Recipe Buck wheat."

For other advice from Alexander about BUCK WHEAT apparently also dating from his term as overseer of Shadwell, see Betts, *Farm Book*, 81.

Notes for Revising the Virginia Constitution

[1794 or later]

Notes for a Constitution

The legislature to provide for having periodical returns to them of the qualified electors of every county, to wit, every *man* of full age, who pays taxes to government, or is of militia.

The whole number of qualified electors in the state, an Unit of representation to be obtained, and every county to send a representative for every Unit or fraction exceeding an half Unit which actually votes at the election. If a county has not an half Unit, add it's votes to another.

The Unit to be so taken from time to time[4] that the legislature may consist of not less than 150, nor more than 300.

The legislature to be divided weekly by lot into 2. chambers, so that the representatives of every county may be as equally divided between the 2. chambers as integral[6] numbers will admit.

The two chambers to proceed as distinct branches of the legislature.

Every male citizen of the commonwealth liable to taxes or to militia duty in any county[1] shall have a right to vote for representatives for that county[2] to the legislature. The legislature shall provide that returns be made to themselves periodically of the qualified voters in every county, by their name and qualification,[3] and from the whole number of qualified voters in the commonwealth such an Unit of representation shall from time to time be taken as will keep the number of representatives within the limits of 150. and 300. allowing to every county a representative for every Unit and fraction of more than half an Unit it contains.

Every elector may vote for as many representatives as were apportioned[5] by the legislature to his county at the last establishment of the Unit.[7] But so many only shall be deemed elected as there are Units actually voting on that particular

[236]

election, adding one for any fraction of votes[8] exceeding the half Unit. Nor shall more be deemed elected than the number last apportioned.[9] If a county has not a half Unit of votes, the legislature shall incorporate it's votes with those of some adjoining county.

Older electors presenting themselves shall be recieved to vote before younger ones, and the legislature shall provide for the secure and convenient claim and exercise of this privilege of age.

The legislature shall consist of the representatives to be chosen as before provided. Their acts shall not be affected by any excess or defect of numbers taking place between two periodical settlements of the Unit.

The legislature shall form one house only for the verification of their credentials, or for what relates to their privileges. For all other business they shall be separated by lot into two chambers, which shall be called [a and w] on the first day of their session in every week; which separation shall be effected by presenting to the representatives from each county separately a number of lots equal to their own number if it be an even one, or to the next even number above, if their number be odd, one half of which lots shall be distinctively marked for the one chamber and the other half for the other: and each member shall be, for that week, of the chamber whose lot he draws. Members not present at the first drawing for the week, shall draw on their first attendance after.[10]

Each chamber shall appoint a speaker for the session, and it shall be weekly decided[11] by lot between the two speakers, of which chamber each shall be for the ensuing week; and the chamber to which he is allotted shall have one the less in the lots presented to his colleagues for that week.

[*on separate sheet:*]

Printing presses shall be free except as to false facts published maliciously either to injure the reputation of another, whether followed by pecuniary damage or not, or to expose him to the punishment of the law.

The legislature shall have power to establish by law the disqualifications of representatives or other officers

Dft (DLC: TJ Papers, 234: 41935-6); undated, consists of two sheets entirely in TJ's hand: the first bearing a 1794 watermark, with the right column being in the customary form for TJ's drafts and bearing extensive revisions recorded below, and the left being added in his smaller hand; the second (fol. 41936) containing two undated paragraphs in pencil in the form for drafts; brackets in original. MS (same, 41934); undated; consists of rough draft of one paragraph in TJ's hand (see note 10 below); endorsed: "plan of two houses."

The present undated notes stand in archival isolation, but in view of the watermark on the paper used for the main group, TJ very likely prepared them at various times in 1794 or after. While TJ had contributed significantly to the drafting of the Virginia constitution of 1776, he had long been critical of various features that found their way into the final version and was desirous of revising it, a task he had last attempted in 1783 before his mission to France. A convention to amend the Virginia constitution was not held until 1829-30 (Editorial Note on the Virginia Constitution, Vol. 1: 330; Editorial Note and documents on Jefferson's proposed revision of the Virginia Constitution, Vol. 6: 278-317; Sutton, *Revolution to Secession*, 60-1).

Two of TJ's suggestions made in the notes above reflected his long-standing concern that the Virginia constitution unduly restricted the size of the electorate and gave a disproportionate share of power in the legislature to the Tidewater. According to his own estimate, the extension of the franchise to EVERY MALE CITIZEN who was LIABLE TO TAXES OR TO MILITIA DUTY would have doubled the size of the Virginia electorate, and the establishment of a linkage between population and representation would have enhanced the legislative power of the Piedmont and the backcountry (*Notes*, ed. Peden, 118-19). On the other hand, his proposal to discontinue separate elections for senators and delegates and to have representatives rotate BY LOT . . . EVERY WEEK between the upper and lower houses of the legislature represented the abandonment of the efforts he had made in his draft state constitutions of 1776 and 1783 to find a mechanism for the indirect election of senators so as to ensure that men of wisdom served in the upper house (same, 119-20; Vol. 1: 341, 348, 358, 6: 296). As he later explained to a Greek patriot, the periodic rotation of members between each house would serve the public because it "would equally give the benefit of time and separate deliberation, guard against an absolute passage by acclamation, derange Cabals, intrigues, and the count of noses, disarm the ascendancy which a popular demagogue might at any time obtain over either house, and render impossible all disputes between the two houses, which often form such obstacles to business" (TJ to Adamantios Coray, 31 Oct. 1823; see also Frances Harrold, "The Upper House in Jeffersonian Political Theory," VMHB, LXXVIII [1970], 281-94).

[1] Preceding three words interlined.

[2] Preceding three words interlined.

[3] TJ first ended the sentence here and drafted the remainder of the text as two separate paragraphs:

"The legislature shall consist of not less than 150. nor more than 300. representatives, and from the whole number of qualified voters in the commonwealth such an Unit of representation shall be taken as will keep the number of representatives within those limits.

"Every county ⟨may⟩ shall send a representative for every Unit and fraction exceeding half an Unit as actually votes at the election, so as not to exceed the number of representatives last allowed to it by the legislature."

4 Preceding four words interlined.
5 Word interlined in place of "allowed."
6 Above this word TJ interlined "odd."
7 TJ here canceled "but ⟨so many representa⟩ no person actually recieving fewer votes than the Unit shall be deemed elected, except that where more than half and less than the whole Unit vote."
8 Preceding two words interlined.
9 Preceding sentence interlined.
10 MS: this rough version of the preceding paragraph reads:
"The legislature to consist of two houses, in each of which all laws shall pass ⟨through⟩ 3. several readings, ⟨by a⟩ on ⟨separate⟩ several days by the vote of a majority of ⟨those⟩ the members present ⟨on separate days⟩.

"The⟨se⟩ two houses shall be formed by a division of the representatives into two equal parts, or equal within an unit; which division shall be made by lot once in every week in manner following. ⟨Ballots marked with the name of each⟩ There shall be a ballot box ⟨prepared⟩ provided for each county, into which shall be put ballots equal in number to the representatives of the county and marked with the name of the one or the other house, as many of the one ⟨house⟩ as of the other or within unit⟨s⟩ as many ⟨an equal number of each or equal within a unit⟩, and every member when he shall first present himself in every week shall draw from the ballot-box of his county a ballot which shall decide ⟨in⟩ of which house he shall ⟨sit⟩ be for that week." The next to last cancellation is also an interlineation.

11 TJ first wrote "and the two speakers shall weekly decide" and then altered it to read as above.

From Marc Auguste Pictet

SIR   Paris January the 1st. 17[95]

Though personally unknown to you, I have some reasons to believe that my name has been mentioned to you by a friend who was endeavouring to shelter us against the Tempest which so [. . .] destroyed Geneva in July last. Circumstances have taken since a less severe turn and we are mostly indebted for our actual welfare to Mr. Adet who succeeded to Soulavie in the office of Resident at Geneva for the French Republick, and whom we are now most Sincerely regretting. The unrivalled Candour and rectitude of Judgement of this truly good Man will carry him clear through the most delicate missions and his well Stored head will procure him a favorable reception among the learned in your country. A common taste for the same branch of natural Sciences drove us towards one another and a moral affinity made us friends in a Short time; and when his new dignity tore him away from us to another hemisphere, not only myself, but every citizen of Geneva felt a most irreparable loss, and he was accompanied with the warmest thanks and vows of the whole people.

Particular circumstance has brought me here for a few days about the time that excellent man is Setting out for the united States. I begged of him the favor of taking this letter with him to have it carried Safely. I am still ignorant Sir, how far the ideas of my English friend will have been found executable and I can not but wish that they may be welcomed.

Our Situation is not however so desperate as it was at the time he wrote; no imminent danger is at the door, but a Slow consumption is to be feared; we must certainly die *for* our country in Some circumstances; we must perhaps in others accompany her to the grave but we are not bound to die *with* her, and we must think for our children. I have had a communication of my friends proposals and am approving of them so far as I am concerned in the affair. I am waiting with no Small anxiety for the answers, and indulging in the mean time the thought of Mineralogical and Geological excursions in a world entirely new to me and which brings on a number of instructive comparisons between analogous facts and natural phenomena. The reading of your precious Notes on Virginia Started many such comparisons and I can not but most ardently wish to be once enabled to realize them. I have the honor to be Sir Your most humble most obedt. Servt.   PICTET

Prof. of Philosophy at Geneva

RC (DLC); torn at corner; one word illegible; endorsed by TJ as received 22 Sep. 1795 and so recorded in SJL. Enclosed in Pierre Auguste Adet to TJ, 9 Sep. 1795.

Marc Auguste Pictet or Pictet-Turrettini (1752-1825), trained as a lawyer, was a distinguished Swiss natural scientist and professor of natural philosophy at the Academy of Geneva whose forced flight to France in the wake of the Genevan revolution of the previous year made him a strong supporter of the plan of his FRIEND François D'Ivernois for transplanting this institution of higher learning to America. In 1798 Pictet was one of the Swiss negotiators who helped to arrange the terms of the French annexation of Switzerland, and under Napoleon he served as a member of the Tribunate, 1802-07, and as an inspector general of the Imperial University, 1808-15. After the Emperor's fall from power Pictet returned to Switzerland and concentrated on his scientific studies for the remainder of his life (DSB; *Biographie universelle, ancienne et moderne*, new ed., 45 vols. [Paris, 1843-65], XXXIII, 208-10).

From William Branch Giles

DEAR SIR   Philadelphia *Jany 4th 1794* [i.e. 1795]

I Received your favors of the 17th Ultimo two days ago and thank you for their contents. I waited on Mr. Shippen last evening and mentioned your business to him. After remarking that he thought the estate of Mr. Banister's father should in strictness pay the debt, as he was travelling under his father's direction at the time it was contracted, Mr. Shippen promised to pay it himself, but not immediately. He wished to see the statement of it, which I had not with me at the time but am now about incloseing it to him. He is in extreme ill health, and I beleive beyond the possibility of recovering. I shall wait on him again after he shall have received the statement and will take pleasure in giveing you further information as to his determination.

Inclosed I send you two papers and think they will afford you some amusement. The debates are very incorrectly[1] taken, but they furnish the outline view of the proceedings. So much cunning and precaution were never before in such a dilemma. The post leaves town this moment. Accept my most affectionate regards &c.   Wm. B. Giles

RC (DLC); at foot of text: "Mr. Jefferson"; endorsed by TJ as a 1795 letter received 21 Jan. 1795 and so recorded in SJL.

SJL records letters from Thomas Lee Shippen to TJ of 8 Jan. 1795, received from Philadelphia on 20 Jan. 1795, and from TJ to Shippen of 21 Jan. 1795, neither of which has been found.

I send you two papers: probably the *Philadelphia Gazette* of 2 and 3 Jan. 1795, which carried a summary of the debates held in the House of Representatives on 1 and 2 Jan. on Giles's proposed amendment to the naturalization bill. See also James Madison to TJ, 11 Jan. 1794 [i.e. 1795], and note.

[1] Giles here canceled "and roughly."

To Henry Skipwith

Dear Sir   Monticello Jan. 4. 95.

Immediately on the receipt of your favor covering Mr. Adams' letter to you, I wrote to him for such further information as might enable me to instruct an attorney at Baltimore to proceed to recover Mr. Short's demand against Dr. Griffin. I inclose you his answer. Having Mr. Short's power of attorney, and this being my first and only information relative to this debt, I wish to proceed against the fund in Baltimore (which Mr. Adams has not pointed out to me) if I can find what and where it is, or any other fund of which you may have knolege. Will you be so good as to give me any information you can on the subject? And also to what office I may apply for a copy of Mr. Short's judgment, and to what office also for Dr. Griffin's schedule of his estate and debts? These being necessary for my proceeding to save Mr. Short. Perhaps you may have some means of finding out the Baltimore fund, if you do not already know it. Perhaps too the schedule may disclose it.—The state of Mrs. Skipwith's health renders us anxious about it. I shall hope to hear from you that it is getting better, and that yourself and family are well. I shall always be glad to hear from you, and to see yourself and family when you can make it convenient. Mr. and Mrs. Randolph are at present on a visit to Varina, so that Maria and myself are keeping house alone. My best love and hers to Mrs. Skipwith and family, and am with sincere affection Dear Sir your friend & servt   TH: JEFFERSON

PrC (DLC: William Short Papers); at foot of text: "Colo. Henry Skipwith." Enclosure: Richard Adams to TJ, 26 Dec. 1794.

For Skipwith's FAVOR, see note to TJ to Richard Adams, 18 Dec. 1794. Skipwith had been handling the business affairs of his nephew William Short in the United States before Short entrusted them to TJ (Shackelford, *Jefferson's Adoptive Son*, 135-6).

A letter from Skipwith to TJ of 13 Mch. 1795, recorded in SJL as received 17 Mch. 1795, has not been found.

To Thomas Mann Randolph

TH:J. TO MR. RANDOLPH   [8 Jan. 1795]

My letters of the last post inform me of Mussi's having sent on my clover seed; so that it is to him I must remit the 51 D.–67 c. balance of Stras's money, after taking out Mr. Lyle's and Taylor's. I must trouble you therefore to try and get a bill on Philadelphia for that sum paiable to Joseph Mussi, merchant Philadelphia, at the corner of 7th. and Market streets, and to inclose it to him. The clover seed was shipped in a cask marked TI. No. 1. by the sloop Samuel Capt. Brittle, addressed to Colo. Gamble, and sailed from Philadelphia Dec. 26. so that she is probably arrived. Pray get Colo. Gamble to forward it by the first safe waggon to Colo. Bell, as you know the importance of my receiving it in time. The cask contains 6. bushels.—I have tried two chances in this county and Louisa for hiring negroes, and failed in both: so that my only chance now to do it is through you. Mrs. Wood's able men hired for £20. here.—The children are constantly in good health. My sister, Polly Carr and Peter are with us. Dabney is returned to Louisa.—I believe your ploughing has gone on well. That kind of work has been stopped now for a few days, by light snows, which have not laid more than 24. hours each.—My love to dear Martha. If you do not return soon the children will have quite forgotten you. Adieu.

RC (DLC: TJ Papers, 106: 18164); undated, but conjecturally assigned on the basis of entry in MB, 8 Jan. 1795; endorsed by Randolph. Not recorded in SJL, but alternatively may be the missing letter to Randolph listed under 4 Jan. 1795.

Memorandum from Eli Alexander

January 10th 1795
Stock at Shadwell
6 work Horses
4 broodmares
2 colts 4 years old
1 colt 3 year old
1 2 year old do.
7 oxen
10 cows
1 bull 5 years old
2 male four years old
1 three years old do.
3 two years old do.
3 one year old do.
4 female three years old
2 two years old do.
2 one year old do.
4 calves and Tom shaklefoot's bull calf
Hogs
1 boar
7 sows
20 hogs for baken next year
35 young pigs
12 sheep
10 goats
some out laying hogs I have not a proper a count of

MS (MHi); in Alexander's hand; endorsed by TJ: "Stock. Shadwell Christmas 94";
notation on verso, by TJ: "delivd. 8 hides 171 ℔ soal," which refers to hides for shoe
leather (see Betts, *Farm Book*, 41).

To Archibald Stuart

DEAR SIR   Monticello Jan. 10. 95
I received your favor of the 26th. Dec. only two days ago, and tomorrow the bearer Mr. Petit, my overseer, will set out for them. The
weather for two days past would not admit of his moving, or they should
not have remained an unnecessary hour on your hands, as the trouble of
buying them is more than enough on you. You make me happy by the

prospect of seeing you here soon. I hope it will be to stay some time. I am Dr. Sir Your affectionate friend & servt   TH: JEFFERSON

PrC (MHi); at foot of text: "Mr. Stuart"; endorsed in ink by TJ.

Stuart's FAVOR OF THE 26TH. DEC., recorded in SJL as received from Staunton on 7 Jan. 1795, has not been found. TJ paid a total of £15.4.2 for 43 sheep acquired in two

purchases from Stuart (TJ to Stuart, 2 Dec. 1794, and note; MB, 11, 15 Jan. 1795). Hugh PETIT served as Monticello overseer from 18 Nov. 1794 to November 1796 (MB, 18 Nov. 1794, 12 Feb., 8 Aug. 1797; Betts, *Farm Book*, 54).

From James Madison

DEAR SIR   Phila. Jany. 11. 1794.[1] [i.e. 1795]

The last subject before the H. of Reps. was a Bill revising the Naturalization law, which from its defects and the progress of things in Europe was exposing us to very serious inconveniences. The Bill requires 1. A probationary residence of 5 instead of 2 years, with a formal declaration on oath of the intention 3 years at least prior to the admission. 2. an oath of *abjuration*, as well as of allegiance. 3. proof of good character, attachment to the principles of our Government, and of being well disposed to the good order and happiness of the U.S. 4. Where the candidate has borne any title or been of any order of Nobility, he is to renounce both on record. This last raised some dust. The Eastern members were weak eno' to oppose it; and Dexter as a set off moved a correspondent clog on emigrants attached to slave holding. Whether they will [be][2] able to throw the dust they have raised into the eyes of their Constituents I know not. It will not be easy I think to repair the blunder they have committed if it reaches the people. On the yeas and nays there [were][3] more than 60 for and little more than 30 against the clause. The Bill is gone to the Senate.[4] Our revenue from trade is so increased as to supply a fund for commencing the discharge of the public debt. The excises laid at the last Session will probably be left as they stand. The treasury bench have attempted to make them perpetual, and brought about a Report of a Committee to prolong them till the year 1801. Another Committee after conferring with the Sugar Bakers and Snuff Makers have agreed on a Counter Report which will probably defeat the project. The French gain victories faster than we can relate them. In Spain, Sardinia and Holland they are equally sweeping every thing before them. They were not in Amsterdam but expected in a few days. The patriotic party was openly[5] revived, and it was not doubted that the Stadholder would move off to England for his personal safety. The D. of York has been well drubbed again at Nimeguen. It was said to be agitated in the British Cabinet whether he should not with all his troops be withdrawn from the Continent. It is surmised that Prussia has actually treated with France, and that the Emperor is taking the same Course. It is indeed agreed that France can dictate peace to all her enemies, except England; and that she will probably do so in order to have a fair campaign with Engld. alone. Nothing final yet from Jay. It is expected here that he will accomplish much if not all he aims at. It will be scandalous, if we do not under present circumstances, get all that we have a right to demand. Not a word from Monroe. Knox is succeded by Pickering. The successor to H. not fixt, but likely to be Wolcot. H will probably go to N.Y. with the word *poverty* for his label. The Legislature of Pennsylva. have voted out the Western Members. It is said they will suspend important business till the seats can be refilled—but this will make little difference as the City party will still[6] be a majority. Bingham will be the Senator—Unless the Germans can be prevailed on to vote for Tench Coxe. They like neither the one nor the other; not Bingham because an Aristocrat—not Coxe on the old score of his being a Tory in the War.

RC (DLC: Madison Papers); misdated, with correction by TJ (see note 1 below); unsigned; endorsed by TJ as received 20 Jan. 1795 and so recorded in SJL.

During 31 Dec. 1794 debate on the NATURALIZATION bill, which retained the features described by Madison when it became law in late January, Representative William Branch Giles proposed requiring that new citizens RENOUNCE titles of nobility. Samuel DEXTER countered on 1 Jan. 1795 by proposing a CORRESPONDENT CLOG on slaveholding immigrants, admitting on the following day that he was motivated by Republican insistence on a roll-call vote on Giles's amendment and arguing that "You want to hold us up to the public as aristocrats. I, as a retaliation, will hold you up to the same public as dealers in slaves." The same day Dexter's amendment failed and

that of Giles passed by similarly lopsided majorities (*Annals*, IV, 1030-58, 1497-9). Later in the session a law was approved continuing most of the EXCISES LAID AT THE LAST SESSION until THE YEAR 1801, although the SNUFF MAKERS were mollifed with a measure replacing the duty on each pound of snuff with an annual tax on the machinery at snuff mills (same, 1511-15, 1526).

[1] Year canceled by TJ, who added: "for 95."

[2] Word supplied.

[3] Word supplied.

[4] Preceding two sentences interlined, with the first added after the second.

[5] Preceding two words interlined in place of "is."

[6] Word interlined.

To Henry Banks

SIR   Monticello Jan. 15. 95.

I have to acknolege the receipt of your favor on the subject of disposing of the Greenbrier lands mortgaged to me, in Philadelphia, and appointing some person there to receive the money for which they are mortgaged. It is certainly much my wish to have the money paid, but having delivered the bonds to Mr. Hanson to collect and apply the money to a particular credit, I can only refer you to him for such arrangements on the subject as may answer both your purposes. I have written to him thereon, and have expressed to him my opinion that if he has no agent there, the money might be deposited in his name, and to his credit, in either the bank of the United states or of North America; but leaving it entirely to himself to decide on. I am Sir Your very humble servt

TH: JEFFERSON

PrC (MHi); at foot of text: "Mr. Henry Banks"; endorsed in ink by TJ.

Henry Banks (1761-1836) was a Richmond merchant, lawyer, and land speculator who had supplied TJ with sundries in 1781 and had represented Greenbrier County in the Virginia House of Delegates in 1787 and 1788. Later in the present year, acting on behalf of the firm of Hunter, Banks & Company, he brought suit against TJ as former governor of Virginia to recover losses sustained during the British invasion of 1781. In 1806 Banks published essays enthusiastically supporting Napoleon and subsequently moved to Frankfort, Kentucky (TQHGM, XV [1933-34], 123, 237-8; Marshall, *Papers*, I, 348, V, 167, VI, 407;

MB, 7 Mch., 26 Apr. 1781; Swem and Williams, *Register*, 26, 28, 38; Joseph I. Shulim, "Henry Banks: A Contemporary Napoleonic Apologist in the Old Dominion," VMHB, LVIII [1950], 335-45; TJ to Robert Brooke, 24 May 1795, and note).

Banks's FAVOR of 25 Dec. 1794, recorded in SJL as received six days later, has not been found. The GREENBRIER lands had been MORTGAGED to TJ in connection with his sale of his Elk Hill plantation to Banks and Dr. Thomas A. Taylor (TJ to Richard Hanson, 20 Jan. 1793). A letter from Richard HANSON to TJ of 9 Jan. 1795, received from Richmond on 14 Jan. 1795, and the reply WRITTEN this day by TJ, both recorded in SJL, have not been found.

From Martha Jefferson Randolph

Varina Jan. 15 1795

We intended writing to my Dearest Father from Richmond but that care devolving upon me on account of Mr. Randolph's business it was as is often the case with me put off till the hurry of packing obliged me to neglect it entirely. Col. Blackden and W. C. Nicholas had both left Richmond before we arrived there the letter for the former was put in the post office imediately that to Mr. Nicholas Mr. Randolph thought better to keep untill a direct opportunity offered, of sending it as the post does not pass near Warren. I have the paper you desired me to get, it is not handsome but their was no choice their being only three pieces in Richmond that I could hear of except complete hangings for a room which they would not break in upon, borders were not to be had at any price.

I saw Bob frequently while in Richmond he expressed great uneasiness at having quitted you in the manner he did and repeatedly declared that he would never have left *you* to live with any person but his wife. He appeared to be so much affected at having *deserved* your anger that I could not refuse my intercession when so warmly solicited towards obtaining your forgiveness. The poor creature seems so deeply impressed with a sense of his ingratitude as to be rendered quite unhappy by it but he could not prevail upon himself to give up his wife and child. We found every thing here in such a ruinous condition that it is impossible to say what stay we shall be forced to make here. The monstrous crop of wheat which was represented to be 3000. bushels has dwindled away to 800 most of the corn out still at the mercy of thieves hogs birds &c. and in short every thing in such disorder that Mr. Randolph has been obliged to discharge the overseer and take the management of the plantation in to his own hands. We were quite happy at your having made use of the waggon as we were in no hurry at all for the horses indeed we did not leave Rock castle in several days after their arrival and then loitered away much of our time on the road. If you had any idea my dear Papa of the pleasure it gives us both for you to make use of any thing of ours you would never think of appologizing for it. Give my love to Maria and my two little angels and believe me my Dearest Father with constant tenderness your affectionate child   M. RANDOLPH

Mr. Randolph will write to you from Dover where the sale is to be he desired me to tell you that he has executed all your commissions.

RC (MHi); minimum punctuation supplied; endorsed by TJ as received 21 Jan. 1795 and so recorded in SJL.

BOB: Robert Hemings.

To Joseph Mussi

DEAR SIR   Monticello Jan. 21. 1795.

I have to acknolege the receipt of your favor of Dec. 27. announcing the shipment of the clover seed, and Colo. Gamble writes me on the 10th. inst. that he had received the bill of lading and would take care of the seed when it should arrive. Mr. Randolph my son in law being in the neighborhood of Richmond and to receive a balance of 51 D.–67 c. due me from a particular person in a bill on Philadelphia I desired him to take it payable to you and remit it by post. I have not heard from him, but hope it has been done. Having no account yet from Mr. Lownes, I can scarcely guess at the balance I had in his hands, and which you would recieve. Till I receive information of it from yourself or him, I shall be in the dark as to what I have still to remit you. Every thing came safe according to the invoice of the last shipment of groceries, except that instead of the box of oil which should have been T.I. No. 9. from Messrs. T. & P. Mackie there came a box of tallow candles 15. I. by 18 I. marked MI. or IW. At the top on one corner is C. ✖ and on the end T.13. I suspect that the C. denotes *Candles*, and the T. *tallow*. Supposing it possible the change of the boxes might have happened in Colo. Gamble's warehouse, I wrote to him. I have his answer of the 10th. inst. in these words. 'I can assure you the mistake of a box of candles, instead of a box of oil, did not take place with me. The articles were all put together in one apartment, where no other goods were, nor had I any candles in boxes.' I presume therefore that the error has been at the shop of Messrs. Mackies, in delivering one box for another. If the mark above described be of their shop, they will recognize it, and of course correct it by sending me a box of oil, and directing what shall be done with the candles, which may either be returned to them, or sold here on their account. If the error has not arisen with them, it will not be worth pursuing further, and I will ask the favor of you to send me another supply of oil by the first opportunity, as it is not the worth but the deprivation of the thing which has occasioned me to trouble you again about it.—We have had lately a spell of about 10. days of cold weather. The thermometer has once been as low as 10°. say 22°. below freezing by Farenheit's scale. This is among the greatest degrees of cold known in this country. But we have had no snow to lie 24. hours. The degree and duration of cold has been sufficient, as we hope, to destroy most of our weavil, so as that we may not be troubled with them for a year or two to come, which has generally been the effect of a cold a little greater than common.—The newspapers tell us France is beating the world into peace. The world will gain more by defeats leading to peace, than victories leading to war. God send us peace, and you health and happiness. Yours affectionately   TH: JEFFERSON

RC (DLC); addressed: "Mr. Joseph Mussi Mercht. Philadelphia corner of 7th. & Market streets"; postmarked; endorsed by Mussi as received 1 Feb. 1795.

Mussi's missing FAVOR OF DEC. 27. is recorded in SJL as received from Philadelphia on 6 Jan. 1795. Letters from Mussi to TJ of 27 Nov. and 3 Dec. 1794, received on 9 and 16 Dec. 1794 respectively, and from TJ to Mussi of 18 Dec. 1794, are recorded in SJL, as are the letter TJ WROTE TO Robert Gamble on 28 Dec. 1794 and Gamble's ANSWER OF THE 10TH. INST., received from Richmond on 20 Jan. 1795, none of which has been found. According to SJL, TJ and Mussi exchanged 15 additional letters between 2 Feb. 1795 and 10 May 1800, none of which has been found.

To Martha Jefferson Randolph

TH:J. TO HIS DEAR M.J. Monticello Jan. 22. 95.

I received yesterday yours and Mr. Randolph's letters from Varina of the 15th. and 16th. inst. I had been in hopes that you would have come up from the Dover sale, but am sorry to find that the affairs of Varina will claim Mr. Randolph's presence longer. In my last to him I asked the favor of him to remit the balance of Stras's money (after taking out Mr. Lyle's and Taylor's) to Mr. Mussi in Philadelphia. Mr. Watson's boats are bringing up the balance of my nailrod, and Snelson has undertaken for the Drillplough. Gamble promises the clover seed and gongs shall come by the first conveyance: so that from all these Mr. Randolph is relieved. There remain on his hands Martin and the Chariot. If the latter cannot be disposed of without better wheels I would be obliged to him to take the greater and larger diameters of the axle, and the length of the Nut of the wheel, as also the height of the fore and hind wheels, that I may have a set of good wheels made here, and sent down. Those now on the chariot will answer some purposes here.—We have little new in the neighborhood. Mrs. Wood and family are living at Milton. Derieux has begun to move, his family will go off this week. Mrs. Peter Marks is dead after a very long illness. Dr. Gilmer declining rapidly. We have had about 12. days of very cold weather; the thermometer has been once as low as 10°. and only once in the whole time as high as the thawing point, 32°. So much the better for our wheat, and for the destruction of the weavil.—But you are impatient to hear something of the children. They are both well, and have never had even a finger-ach since you left us. Jefferson is very robust. His hands are constantly like lumps of ice, yet he will not warm them. He has not worn his shoes an hour this winter. If put on him, he takes them off immediately and uses one to carry his nuts &c. in. Within these two days we have put both him and Anne into mockaseens, which being made of soft leather, fitting well and lacing up, they have never been able to take them off. So that I believe we may consider that as the only effectual shoe which can be made for them. They are inseparable in their sports. Anne's temper begins to develope itself advantageously. His tempests give her opportunities of shewing and exercising a placid disposition: and there is no doubt but that a little time will abate of his impatience as it has done hers. I called her in to ask what I should write for her to yourself and her papa. She says I must tell you that she loves you, and that you must come home. In both these sentiments we all join her. Maria gives all her love to you. We are alone at present; but are in hopes soon of a visit from my sister Anne. I shall address the next week's letter to Mr. Randolph.

In the mean while present me to him affectionately, and continue to love me yourself as I do you most tenderly. Adieu; come home as soon as you can, and make us happy in seeing you here, and Mr. Randolph in better health.

RC (NNPM); at foot of first page: "Mrs. Randolph"; endorsed by Mrs. Randolph. PrC (ViU: Edgehill-Randolph Papers); endorsed in ink by TJ.

The letter from Thomas Mann Randolph of the 16TH. INST., recorded in SJL as received from Varina on 21 Jan. 1795, has not been found. TJ's LAST TO HIM is printed under 8 Jan. 1795.

From James Madison

Dear Sir   Philada. Jany. 26. 95.

I have received your favor of Decr. 28. but [not]¹ till three weeks after the date of it. It was my purpose to have answered it particularly, but I have been robbed of the time reserved for the purpose. I must of consequence limit myself to a few lines and to my promise given to the Fresco Painter to forward you the enclosed letter. Nothing since my last from Jay or Monroe. The Newspapers as usual teem with French victories and rumors of peace. There seem to be very probable indications of a progress made to this event, except in relation to G.B. with whom a Duet Campaign is the cry of France. The Naturalization has not yet got back from the Senate. I understand however it will suffer no material change. They have the prudence not to touch the Nobility clause. The House of Reps. are on the Military establishment and the public debt. The difficulty and difference of opinion as to the former, produced a motion to request the P. to cause an estimate of the proper defence &c. It was in its real meaning, saying we do not know how many troops ought to be provided by our legislative duty, and ask your direction. It was opposed as opening the way for dragging in the weight of the Ex. for one scale, on all party questions—as extorting his opinion where he should reserve for his negative, and as exposing his unpopular² opinions to be extorted at any time by an unfriendly majority. The prerogative men chose to take the subject by the wrong handle, and being joined by the weak men, the resolution passed. I fancied³ the Cabinet are embarrassed on the subject. On the subject of the Debt, the Treasury faction is spouting on the policy of paying it off as a great evil; and laying hold of two or three little excises passed last session under the pretext of war, are claiming more merit for their zeal than⁴ they allow to the opponents of these puny resources. Hamilton has made a long Valedictory Report on the subject. It is not yet printed, and I have not read it. It is said to contain a number of improper things. He got it in, by informing the Speaker, he had one ready, predicated on the *actual* revenues, for the House whenever they should please to receive [it].[5] Budinot the ready agent for all sycophantic jobbs, had a motion cut and dry just at the moment of the adjournment, for informing him in the language applied to the P. on such occasions, that the House was ready to receive the Report when he pleased, which passed without opposition and almost without notice. H. gives out that he is going to N.Y. and does not mean to return into public life at all. N. Jersey has changed all her members except Dayton whose zeal against G.B. saved him. There are not more than 2 or 3 who are really on all points Repubns. Dexter is under another sweat in his district, and it is said to be perfectly uncertain whether he or his Repub: competitor will succeed. Adieu Yrs.

Js. M. Jr

RC (DLC: Madison Papers); endorsed by TJ as received 11 Feb. 1795 and so recorded in SJL. Enclosure: Ignatius Shnydore to TJ, 20 Jan. 1795 (recorded in SJL as received from Philadelphia on 11 Feb. 1795, but not found).

VALEDICTORY REPORT: Alexander Hamilton's Report on a Plan for the Further Support of Public Credit, 16 Jan. 1795, proposed a variety of measures for the sys-tematic reduction of the national debt (Syrett, *Hamilton*, xviii, 56-148).

[1] Word supplied.
[2] Word interlined in place of what appears to be "obnoxious."
[3] Word later reworked to "fancy" by an unidentified hand.
[4] MS: "that."
[5] Word supplied.

To Thomas Mann Randolph

Th:J. to mr Randolph   Monticello Jan. 29. 95.

I wrote to Martha last week. We all continue well. Jefferson's kunophobia appearing to increase so as to become troublesome, and almost a subject of uneasiness, we have determined to take a puppy into the house to cure him by forcing a familiarity to the form and safety of the animal. This is but the 2d. day of the experiment, so that we cannot yet judge of it's operation.—We have had no ploughing weather since Christmas. On the 24th. we had a snow 9.I. deep. Yesterday the South hill sides began to be bare enough for work. To-day we have a little rain and sleet which will end in rain probably and carry off the remains of the snow. Mr. Derieux brought me your note relative to the mares purchased and men hired. The latter are high: but I had rather have had them even higher than to have failed. I have been expecting them some days, but they are not arrived: which has been no loss as yet, the weather not admitting work.—By an accident we have failed getting our letters

yesterday from the post office. Should you have written, this circumstance will account for my not acknoleging the receipt of your letter.—
Could you take the trouble of knowing whether, if I find we have lost
the method of making bricks without treading the mortar, I can have
Mr. Pleasants' man, and on what terms? T. Pleasants, to whom I wrote
on the subject formerly, can give you the information. We all join in love
to our dear Martha and yourself, and in wishes to see you back as soon
as the situation of Varina will permit. Adieu affectionately.

RC (DLC); endorsed by Randolph as received 4 Feb. 1795.

From William Short

My dear Sir   Madrid Jan. 29. 1795

The last letter which I have had the pleasure of recieving from you
was of the 23. of Dec. 1793. It came to my hands on the 26th. of April.
1794. It acknowleged my letters private down to that of the 7th. of
October 1793. inclusive. This statement will give you some idea of the
great defalcation to be made in the pleasure I fondly anticipated in your
kind soothing and friendly correspondence after retiring from public
life. Few persons have ever had more need than I have constantly had,
of such relief from the time of my hard destiny having placed me in the
diplomatic career—and I myself have never had more need thereof than
since the moment of your return to Monticello and from which you have
discontinued your letters altogether. I always regretted their rarity—I
have now to regret their loss entire. But I beg you to be assured my dear
Sir that however painful these regrets may be to me, they can in no way
alter or diminish my invariable attachment to you, and my grateful
sense of the numberless marks of friendship which you have so long and
on so many occasions shewn me.

Posterior to my letter of Oct. 7. 1793. acknowleged by you as abovementioned I wrote to you Nov. 7th. 11th. and 13th. of the same year.
After such a rapid succession of letters I determined to wait without
troubling you again until I should be in some degree authorized thereto
by hearing from you. This determination was confirmed and continued
by the uncertainty in which I remained as to your continuance in or
retiring from, public life—and as to my own destination. I went on in
this way from day to day until I recieved the letter of your successor and
your own of the month of Jany. 1794—which was soon after followed
by your previous private of Dec. 23. abovementioned. And this again
was soon followed by a report which left me more than ever uncertain
as to the place or situation in which my letters would find you. That

report confirmed in a considerable degree by a letter from Mr. Pinckney as mentioned in the letter I wrote you on the 22. of May last, was that you were named to succeed Mr. Morris at Paris. This agreeable illusion continued for a long time. You may well judge of all the pain and mortification I experienced when this illusion was removed and when I learned what had been done in that respect—I felt more than ever—but contrary to my former usage I abstained from troubling you with my useless Jeremiades. I was sure however that if I allowed myself to write to you, my bosom would open itself however involuntarily and lay before you all I felt at seeing myself again passed over in the appointment for Paris (after I had so long resided there and been employed in the diplomatic career) by a person who was an utter stranger to the country—to the usages and even to the language there spoken and who had never been before in this career. I avoided therefore writing to you at all. As the *amour propre* of every one is ingenious and industrious in finding out cures for the wounds it receives mine suggested to me that this appointment was witheld from me, under the grounds which gave me a right to expect it, from the circumstance of my being supposed disagreeable to the French Government which I had reason to believe was admitted by our Government from what you had formerly written to me. Some reason there must be of that kind—for whatever may be the talents, virtues and abilities of the person appointed (and no body can have an higher idea of them than I have) yet the ignorance of the Country and of the language placed him necessarily in such a comparative situation with one acquainted with both, as could never have given a preference unless where there were some great and irremediable demerit and incapacity in the latter. After all, such things are merely relative—and had you been named as was reported, I should have been the last person in the world to have supposed that this argued any demerit in myself in the eyes of the President. To leave myself out of the question I will add only one word—and that is that in these times there is no Government in Europe which would have made such a *passe droit* in favor of any person who had never before been in the diplomatic line above all those employed by them and who had devoted themselves to an apprenticeship in that line. Formerly such things were done by these Governments in favor of rank or birth—at present it is only the Government of the U.S. that ventures to adopt such a system. An enquiry into what they have done in this line would form a *rapprochement* that would aid in the history of the progress of the human heart—I mean of the heart when at the head of governments—and would elucidate the following questions applied to the U.S.—which were some time ago proposed in the French convention as to France—d'ou venons nous? ou sommes nous? ou allons nous?

To return from this digression which I may perhaps be ere long in a situation and at leisure to examine and develope more fully—I recieved my nomination together with the information of that for Paris, under circumstances which did not admit of my refusing it, not withstanding all the pain and anxiety I had been previously condemned to—and not-withstanding all my health had suffered and was still suffering. One of the strongest inducements with me was the desire and determination to leave nothing untried to obtain for the inhabitants of Kentuckey in par-ticular and for the U.S. in general, those rights which they are entitled to, which I am sure they will never desist from and which time and circumstances inevitably insure them. If by my efforts I could have shortened that time or have rendered the means peaceable, I should have considered myself indemnified for all I had suffered—and thought this would in some degree wipe away that kind of imputation of demerit which could not fail to attach to me in the eyes of my countrymen from the manner in which the President has acted towards me in constantly giving others the preference to me, and employing me only in the lowest grades and least honorable manner. I have now recieved a letter from the Sec. of State of the 9th. of Nov. which fills up the measure which the President has determined on all occasions to deal out to me. I am there informed that he means on the meeting of the Senate to send Mr. Pinck-ney here as Env. Extr. to terminate the business hitherto in my hands— he mentions that you and Mr. P. Henry had both refused the mission. I infer from his letter that Mr. Pinckney is to be employed alone, that is to say that his name only is to appear, although he mentions to me that my corroboration will be asked &c. The Sec. of State pays me some compliments on one hand and thus humiliates me on the other. This however is the treatment I have been accustomed to for years back, and is not new to me—but what is new is to learn from him that such ex-traordinary missions are familiar in the diplomatic line. I know not where the Sec. of State has taken up this idea—but I pledge myself to shew in time and place if necessary that the annals of *diplomatie*, do not furnish an example of such an one, if as I suppose, I am after two years occupation thus excluded from it, and at the same time retained here— and if it be added that when I was sent here I was *joined* in a commission although the business was to be taken up *above*, where as now at the end of the labor, another is sent to enjoy the fruits of it *alone*. I forbear at present saying any thing more on this head. I have strived on all occa-sions by my zeal and activity to merit well of the President. I have met with repeated humiliation and constant slight. I blame my own stars. I am waiting the arrival of Mr. Pinkney to take my final decision or rather to execute it. I wish him most sincerely full success in his mission—and indeed that is already secured by existing circumstances—although similar to my usual fortune that at the very moment of attaining the goal I should be wrested from the race and another put in my place for the sole purpose of enjoying the fruit—although personally this cannot but be a painful circumstance to me, yet I never have as yet, and trust I never shall, allow any thing personal to weigh against the advantage of my country. Mr. Pinckney has therefore my best wishes—and if I can aid him, or at least if he should think so, he shall have my best efforts also—and this will be the last act of my public life, and I think not the least meritorious when it is considered in what an unexampled manner I am treated.

The Sec. of State tells me that the President had under consideration the diplomatick grade to be employed here. I have written often on this subject, because I felt that it interested much more essentially the U.S. than was considered by Government. The grade however never has had and will not now have any consideration with me.

Being certain the business would be terminated here during the winter one way or another, and my health suffering extremely here during the summer I wrote some months ago (long before I knew or suspected the President's intention of sending an Env. Extr. here) to ask for permission to go and pass the summer in France. I think it certain now I shall not be here to recieve any letter you may in future write to me, as I do not see that the public can suffer from my absence after Mr. Pinckney's arrival. Yet I fear to discourage you from writing—I beg you therefore to write to me and to address your letters to Mr. Yznardi the Consul at Cadiz—or Mr. Church, at Lisbon, or Mr. Donald in London, or our Agent there¹—who will know where I am to be found. Mr. Pinckney's stay here I take it for granted will be until he can recieve the ratification of the treaty he will sign, which of course will give the President the necessary time for chusing the proper permanent agent. I am waiting his arrival in order to announce to the President my final determination. I see and expect nothing that can prevent that determination being a retreat from publick life—which has been filled with thorns for me, whilst the roses have been distributed to the more favored. The most pleasing idea which now presents itself to me is that of ere long seeing and embracing my friends in my own Country. How happy would it have been for me if I had followed your former wise and friendly counsel in that respect.

I sent you by Mr. Blake who did not sail from Cadiz until the 21st. inst. the 8 vo. Academy edition of Dn. Quixote. Mr. Carmichael who is still here, sent on to Cadiz the edition of Cortez letters which he luckily obtained for you, and he has told me that he had authorized Mr. Blake to open the package and take this book out in order that it might sooner get to your hands.

In your kind letter of Dec. 23. 1793. you were so good as to inform me of the state in which my funds were—and to mention your ideas of vesting them in different ways. I have been waiting with much pleasure to learn the execution of your intentions. It would be a most agreeable circumstance to me—but I will not importune you respecting it—although I take it for granted you will have written to me on that subject. By an arrangement of the Sec. of State with Mr. Jaudenes I have been obliged to recieve this years salary and outfit in America. I desired him to pay the cash to you or to have it vested for me himself in our funds. His letter of Nov. 9. informs me he had begun that investment and would send me the account as soon as completed. I am in the mean time living on my own funds and credit. Should the Sec. of State turn these funds over to you I will thank you to manage them for me as you do those you have hitherto recieved.

I long most ardently and every day more and more to see my native land. I have forborne writing to you respecting the new federal city—I fear it is too late for criticism—but I lament most sincerely the great and irreparable defects which experience will shew in the plan. Your

W SHORT

RC (DLC); at foot of first page: "Mr. Jefferson. Monticello"; endorsed by TJ as received 12 May 1795 and so recorded in SJL. PrC (PHi).

AN UTTER STRANGER: James Monroe. MY NOMINATION: on 28 May 1794 the Senate had confirmed Washington's nomination of

Short as minister resident to Spain (JEP, I, 157). A letter from Joseph YZNARDI, Jr., to TJ, recorded in SJL as written on 14 July 1794 and received from Cadiz on 17 Sep. 1794, has not been found.

[1] Preceding nine words interlined.

Memorandum from Robert Bailey

[January 1795]

Seeds Saved 1794

Pease

Early Dwarf	Reid. Speckled Snap	Onions
Early Charlton	Golden Dwarf—	Strawsburgh
Hotspur	Sugar Bean	white Spanish
Marrow fat	Cabbage	corn Sallad
Pearl-eyed	Scotsh Cabbage	French Sorrel
Black eyed	York Cabbage	Hanover Turnip
white eyed	Colworts	Leaf Lettice
Small Green	Salsify	Green Do.

Black Indian	English Cress	Garlick
Beans	—Do. Turnip	Palm of christie
B. Windsor	Carrot	Pumpcons, kinds
Ey. Sesbon	Parsnip	Early cucumber
white Carolinia	Green Rape	watter mellon
white Snap	Spinage	musk Do.
Ground Snap	whit mustard	
Blue Speckled Snap		

[*on verso:*]

wanting—
$\frac{1}{2}$ oz Coly flower
$\frac{1}{2}$ oz Green Brocli
$\frac{1}{2}$ oz white Ditto
√ 1 oz[1] Solid cellery
⟨$\frac{1}{2}$ oz Currold Indive⟩
2 Broad leaved Do. endive[2]
1 ℔ English Scarlet Radis
⟨4 oz Turnip Radish⟩
$\frac{1}{4}$ peck of more, Broad windsor Beans

MS (MHi); written on a small sheet in Bailey's hand; with two lines deleted and emendations in a darker ink, possibly by TJ; undated; endorsed by TJ: "Garden seeds. Bailey's note. Jan. 95."

Robert Bailey (d. 1804), described by TJ in 1803 as "an old Scotch gardener of the neighborhood," lived at Monticello as TJ's gardener from February 1794 until around the end of 1796. He subsequently became a

gardener and nurseryman in Washington, D.C., where TJ used his services several times during his presidency (MB, 11 Feb. 1794, and note, 26 Dec. 1796; TJ to Madame de Tessé, 30 Jan. 1803; Betts, *Garden Book*, 279, 280, 287, 297).

[1] Check mark inserted; digit written over partially erased "$\frac{1}{2}$."
[2] Word inserted; digit in this line inserted in place of "$\frac{1}{2}$ oz."

From William Frederick Ast

SIR   Richmond 1. febr. 1795.

I do myself the honour to send You herewith a Copy of my Insurance Plan for Your perusal and beg to be so kind to make such Observations for Amendments as You think may be necessary.

As we do not begin till we have three Millions of Dollars in property subscribed which will take on an Average about 2000 houses then if each house Owner advances one Guinea will raise about 10000 Dollars, which will be a Sum sufficient to answer against the Accidents which we may reasonably suppose that might happen—and if each was to advance Ten Guineas will raise about one hundred Thousand Dollars a

Sum sufficient to pay all the Losses which have taken place since several Years in the *whole* State—then as no doubt we shall have a great deal more subscribed than two thousand houses there must very great Losses happen that each house Owners share would be Ten Guineas. Therefore by paying *once* the premiums which I have laid down and which are little more than what we pay annually in England at Baltimore or Phila. we stand a fair chance will insure our Buildings for *ever*. I have the honour to remain with great Esteem Sir Your most obt. humble Servant   WILLIAM F. AST

RC (MHi); addressed: "Thomas Jefferson Esqr. Montecello"; endorsed by TJ as received 20 Feb. 1795 and so recorded in SJL. Enclosure not found.

This year Ast founded the Mutual Assurance Society of Virginia, the first southern fire INSURANCE company, with which TJ began to insure Monticello in 1800 (MB, 17 Aug. 1800, and note).

Missing letters from Ast to TJ of 25 Oct. 1794 and 8 Jan. 1795, received from Richmond on 21 Oct. 1794 and 21 Jan. 1795 respectively, and from TJ to "Fred. W. Asp" of 4 Feb. 1795 are recorded in SJL. The first of these entries may be misrecorded.

From John Adams

DEAR SIR   Philadelphia Feb. 5. 1795

The inclosed Pamphlet and Papers I have received this Week from the Author, with his request to transmit them to you. I have before transmitted in the Course of this Winter, another Packet from the same Writer; but have as yet no answer from you: so that I am uncertain whether you have received it.

Mr. Jays Treaty with Britain is not yet arrived at the Secretary of States office, though there is some reason to Suppose it is arrived at New York.

You will see by the Changes in the Executive Department that the Feelings of officers are in a Way to introduce Rotations enough, which are not contemplated by the Constitution. Those Republicans who delight in Rotations will be gratified in all Probability, till all the Ablest Men in the Nation are roted out. To me these Things indicate something to be amiss somewhere. If Public offices are to be made Punishment, will a People be well served? Not long I trow. I am Sir with great Regard your most obedient   JOHN ADAMS

RC (DLC); at foot of text: "Mr Jefferson"; endorsed by TJ as received 19 Feb. 1795 and so recorded in SJL. Enclosure: François D'Ivernois to TJ, 11 Nov. 1794, and enclosures.

CHANGES IN THE EXECUTIVE DEPARTMENT: following the resignations of Henry Knox and Alexander Hamilton, the Senate had confirmed President Washington's nominations of Timothy Pickering,

Postmaster General, as Secretary of War and Oliver Wolcott, Jr., Comptroller of the Treasury, as Secretary of the Treasury on 2 Jan. and 3 Feb. 1795, respectively. Picker-ing's transfer resulted in the Senate's confirmation of Joseph Habersham as Postmaster General on 25 Feb. 1795 (JEP I, 168-9, 170, 171, 173, 174).

To James Madison

TH:J. TO J. MADISON   Monticello Feb. 5. 95.

Congress drawing to a close, I must trouble you with a bundle of little commissions

1. to procure for me a copy of the correspondence between Genet, Hammond and myself at large.

2. a pamphlet entitled 'Sketches on rotations of crops,' to be had I believe at Dobson's. The author in a note pa. 43. mentions some former publication of his, which I should be glad to have also; as I am sure it must be good. Who is the author? Is it Peters? I do not think it is Logan.

3. to procure for me from some of the seedsmen some of the seed of the Winter vetch (it is the Vicia sativa, semine albo of Millar). As it is cheap, you may be governed in the quantity by the convenience of bringing. I think it must be valuable for our fall-fallows.

4. to commission your barber to find for me such a seal as he let you have.

5. to enquire of J. Bringhurst whether Donath is returned from Hamburg, who was to bring me some glass? I know nobody who can give the information but Bringhurst, and I would not trouble you with it, could I have got a word from him otherwise. But I have written twice to him, and got no answer, and I have sent twice to Philadelphia by a neighbor of mine, whom he has put off by saying he would write to me. If I could only find out whether Donath is returned, and what is his address in Philadelphia, I could then enquire about my glass of himself by letter.

We have now had about 4. weeks of winter weather, rather hard for our climate—many little snows which did not lay 24. hours, and one 9. I. deep which remained several days. We have had few thawing days during the time.—It is generally feared here that your collegue F. Walker will be in great danger of losing his election. His competitor is indefatigable attending courts &c. and wherever he is, there is a general drunkenness observed, tho' we do not know that it proceeds from his purse.—Wilson Nicholas is attacked also in his election. The ground on which the attack is made is that he is a speculator. The explanations which this has produced, prove it a serious crime in the eyes of the people. But as far as I hear he is only investing the fruits of a first and only speculation.—Almost every carriage-owner has been taken in for a double tax: information through the newspapers not being actual, tho legal, in a country where they are little read. This circumstance has made almost every man, so taken in, a personal enemy to the tax. I escaped the penalty only by sending an express over the county to search out the officer the day before the forfeiture would have been incurred.—We presume you will return to Orange after the close of the session, and hope the pleasure of seeing Mrs. Madison and yourself here. I have past my winter almost alone, Mr. and Mrs. Randolph being at Varina. Present my best respects to Mrs. Madison, and accept them affectionately yourself. Adieu.

RC (DLC: Madison Papers). PrC (DLC).

COPY OF THE CORRESPONDENCE: *A Message of the President of the United States to Congress Relative to France and Great-Britain* . . . (Philadelphia, 1793). See note to Edmond Charles Genet to TJ, 16 May 1793. PAMPHLET: [John Beale Bordley], *Sketches on Rotations of Crops* (Philadelphia, 1792). See Sowerby, Nos. 707, 714, for later editions owned by TJ. In the NOTE on PA. 43 Bordley repeated that "treading the ground, in constant pasturing, is more injurious to soil than scraps of dung, dispersed and left exposed to the sun, are beneficial." The FORMER PUBLICATION making the same point was [Bordley], *Purport of a Letter on Sheep. Written in Maryland, March the 30th, 1789* [Philadelphia, 1789], 4. See Evans, No. 21699. TJ's letters to John BRINGHURST of 18 and 31 July and 30 Sep. 1794, recorded in SJL, have not been found. Samuel Jordan Cabell succeeded fellow Republican Francis WALKER in representing TJ's congressional district in 1795 and served until 1803 (*Biog. Dir. Cong.*).

To Martha Jefferson Randolph

TH:J. TO HIS DEAR MARTHA   Monticello Feb. 5. 95.

We are all well, and especially the children, who will forget you if you do not return soon. Jefferson is under daily discipline with our puppy. He mends a little of his fears, but very slowly. We have been all kept much within doors by a spell of very cold weather which has now lasted about 4. weeks. During this no ploughing done. The men Mr. Randolph hired for me arrived last Saturday with the 3. mares, all well. His having put Varina under Mr. Hughes, gives us hopes he will soon be relieved from his attendance there, and Jamey's being ordered down with horses has quickened our expectations. I inclose Mr. Randolph a letter from Clarke. I imagine it is as doleful as one I received from him, announcing a much shorter crop of tobacco than he had expected, as also the loss of horses. Our neighborhood offering nothing in the way of news, I have only to add my best affections to you both. Accept them tenderly and warmly. Adieu.

RC (NNPM); endorsed by Mrs. Randolph. PrC (ViU: Edgehill-Randolph Papers); endorsed in ink by TJ. Enclosure not found.

The DOLEFUL letter of 23 Jan. 1795 that

SJL records TJ received from Bowling Clark on 2 Feb. 1795 has not been found. SJL also records five letters from Clark to TJ between 5 June and 23 Dec. 1794, and a letter from TJ to Clark of 5 Aug. 1794, that have not been found.

To John Adams

DEAR SIR   Monticello Feb. 6. 1795.

The time which has intervened between the receipt of your favor, covering D'Ivernois' letter, and this answer, needs apology. But this will be found in the state of the case. I had received from him a letter similar to that you inclosed. As the adoption of his plan depended on our legislature, and it was then in session, I immediately inclosed it to a member with a request that he would sound well the opinions of the leading members, and if he found them disposed to enter into D'Ivernois' views, to make the proposition; but otherwise not to hazard it. It is only three days since I have received from him information of his proceedings. He found it could not prevail. The unprepared state of our youths to receive instruction thro' a foreign language, the expence of the institution, and it's disproportion to the moderate state of our population, were insuperable objections. I delayed myself the honor of acknoleging the receipt of your letter, till I might be able to give you at the same time the result of the proposition it forwarded. I have explained this to M. D'Ivernois in the inclosed letter, which my distance from any sea-port, and the convenience of your position will I hope excuse my committing to your care.—I have found so much tranquility of mind in a total abstraction from every thing political, that it was with some difficulty I could resolve to meddle even in the splendid project of transplanting the academy of Geneva, en masse, to Virginia; and I did it under the usual reserve of *sans tirer en consequence.* In truth I have so much occupation otherwise that I have not time for taking a part in any thing of a public kind, and I therefore leave such with pleasure to those who are to live longer and enjoy their benefits. Tranquility becomes daily more and more the object of my life; and of this I certainly find more in my present pursuits than in those of any other part of my life. I recall however with pleasure the memory of some of the acquaintances I have made in my progress through it, and retain strong wishes for their happiness. I pray you to accept with kindness those which I sincerely entertain for you, and to be assured of the high respect and esteem with which I am Dear Sir Your most obedt. & most humble servt

TH: JEFFERSON

RC (MHi: Adams Papers); at foot of first page: "The Vice President"; endorsed by Adams. PrC (DLC); badly faded. Enclosure: TJ to François D'Ivernois, 6 Feb. 1795.

YOUR FAVOR: Adams to TJ, 21 Nov. 1794. A LETTER SIMILAR: François D'Ivernois to TJ, 5 Sep. 1794. A MEMBER: Wilson Cary Nicholas.

To François D'Ivernois

DEAR SIR   Monticello in Virginia Feb. 6. 1795.

Your several favors on the affairs of Geneva found me here in the month of December last. It is now more than a year that I have withdrawn myself from public affairs, which I never liked in my life but was drawn into by emergencies which threatened our country with slavery but ended in establishing it free. I have returned with infinite appetite to the enjoyment of my farm, my family and my books, and had determined to meddle in nothing beyond their limits. Your proposition however for transplanting the college of Geneva to my own country was too analogous to all my attachments to science and freedom, the firstborn daughter of science, not to excite a lively interest in my mind, and the essays which were necessary to try it's practicability. This depended altogether on the opinions and dispositions of our state legislature which was then in session. I immediately communicated your papers to a member of the legislature whose abilities and zeal pointed him out as proper for it, urging him to sound as many of the leading members of the legislature as he could, and if he found their opinions favorable to bring forward the proposition; but if he should find it desperate, not to hazard it: because I thought it best not to commit the honour either of our state, or of your college, by an useless act of eclat. It is not till within these three days that I have had an interview with him and an account of his proceedings. He communicated the papers to a great number of the members, and discussed them maturely but privately with them. They were generally well disposed to the proposition and some of them warmly: however there was no difference of opinion in their conclusion that it could not be effected. The reasons which they thought would with certainty prevail against it were 1. that our youth, not familiarized but with their mother tongue, were not prepared to receive instructions in any other: 2. that the expence of the institution would excite uneasiness in their constituents and endanger it's permanence: and 3. that it's extent was disproportioned to the narrow state of population with us. Whatever might be urged on these several subjects, yet as the decision rested with others, there remained to us only to regret that circumstances were such, or were thought to be such, as to disappoint your and our wishes. I should have seen with peculiar satisfaction the establishment of such a mass of science in my country, and should probably have been tempted to approach myself to it, by procuring a residence in it's neighborhood, at those seasons of the year at least, when the operations of agriculture are less active and interesting. I sincerely lament the circumstances which have suggested this emigration. I had hoped that Geneva was familiarized to such a degree of liberty, that they might, without difficulty or danger, fill up the measure to it's maximum: a term, which though, in the insulated man, bounded only by his natural powers, must in society be so far restricted as to protect himself against the evil passions of his associates and consequently them against him. I suspect that the doctrine that small states alone are fitted to be republics will be exploded by experience with some other brilliant fallacies accredited by Montesquieu and other political writers. Perhaps it will be found that to obtain a just republic (and it is to secure our just rights that we resort to government at all) it must be so extensive as that local egoisms may never reach it's greater part, that on every particular question, a majority may be found in it's councils free from particular interests, and giving therefore an uniform prevalence to the principles of justice. The smaller the societies, the more violent and more convulsive their schisms. We have chanced to live in an age which will probably be distinguished in history for it's experiments in government on a larger scale than has yet taken place. But we shall not live to see the result. The grosser absurdities, such as hereditary magistracies we shall see exploded in our day, long experience having already pronounced condemnation against them. But what is to be the substitute? This our children or grandchildren will answer. We may be satisfied with the certain knowlege that none can ever be tried so stupid, so unrighteous, so oppressive, so destructive of every end for which honest men enter into government, as that which their forefathers had established, and their fathers alone venture to tumble headlong from the stations they have so long abused. It is unfortunate that the efforts of mankind to recover the freedom of which they have been so long deprived, will be accompanied with violence, with errors and even with crimes. But while we weep over the means, we must pray for the end.—But I have been insensibly led by the general complexion of the times, from the particular case of Geneva, to those to which it bears no similitude. Of that we hope good things. It's inhabitants must be too much enlightened, too well experienced in the blessings of freedom and undisturbed industry to tolerate long a contrary state of things. I shall be happy to hear that their government perfects itself, and leaves room for the honest, the industrious and wise, in which case your own talents, and those of the persons for whom you have interested yourself, will, I am sure, find welcome and distinction. My good wishes will always attend you as a consequence of the esteem and regard with which I am Dear Sir Your most obedt. & most humble servt   TH: JEFFERSON

RC (DLC); at foot of first page: "M. D'Ivernois"; endorsed by D'Ivernois. PrC (DLC); partially faded and overwritten in pencil by a later hand. Enclosed in preceding document.

A MEMBER OF THE LEGISLATURE: Wilson Cary Nicholas.

To Thomas Mann Randolph

TH:J. TO TMR.   Monticello Feb. 12. 95.

Your favor of the 1st. inst. came to hand on the 6th. We the next day strewed some clover seed on moistened cotton. This is the 6th. day, and the plate has been set on the hearth every night. They have not sprouted; but I think they are swelled. By the next post we may probably decide whether they will sprout or not. The weather continues cold, snowy, and unfriendly to the labors of the field. No ploughing since Christmas. All are well at Edgehill. I received my mule on the 6th. and for safe custody put her into the stable, from whence Jupiter let her escape on the 9th. If she should go to Varina, and any of your people should be coming up, be so good as to send her: if nobody should be coming, as soon as I know of her arrival there I will send Jupiter for her as a punishment for his carelessness. I inclose you a letter which came by the last post. Colo. Bell has had a serious illness. He has begun to mend. The children continue well as we are all. They would, if they knew how, join their expressions of affection with ours to our dear Martha and yourself, whom we shall hope to see as soon as the weather softens. Adieu

RC (DLC); endorsed by Randolph as received 20 Feb. 1795. PrC (ViU: Edgehill-Randolph Papers); badly faded. Enclosure not found.

Randolph's FAVOR OF THE 1ST. INST., recorded in SJL as received from "Presquisle," has not been found. Neither have his letters of 24 and 26 Jan. 1795, both recorded in SJL as received on 31 Jan. 1795 from "Hughes's" and "Watkins's," respectively.

From James Madison

Dear Sir   Philada. Feby. 15 1795

Your favor of the 5th. came to hand yesterday. I will attend to your several commissions. Mr. Hawkins tells me, that the seed of the Winter Vetch is not to be got here.

Altho' nearly three months have passed since the signing of the Treaty by Jay, the official account of it has not been received, and the public have no other knowledge of its articles than are to be gleaned from the imperfect scraps of private letters. From these it is inferred that the bargain is much less in our favor than might be expected from the circumstances which co-operated with the justice of our demands. It is even conjectured that on some points, particularly the Western posts, the arrangements will be inadmissible. I find that in N.Y. there are accounts which are credited, that the posts, after the surrender, are to be *thoroughfares*, for the traders and merchandize of both parties. The operation of this will strike you at once, and the sacrifice is the greater, if it be true as is stated, that the former regulation on this subject, secured to the U.S. the monopoly of the fur trade, it being impossible for the Canadian Traders to get to and from the markets, without using our portages, and our parts of the lakes. It is wrong however to prejudge, but I suspect that Jay has been betrayed by his anxiety to couple us with England, and to avoid returning with his finger in his mouth. It is apparent that those most likely to be in the secret of the affair, do not assume an air of triumph.

The elections in N. York give *six* republicans instead of the former *three*. E. Livingston had in the city 205 votes more than Watts the present member. In Massachts. the elections are in several instances, still to be repeated. Dexter is to run a *third* heat. In the last his rival outvoted him, but was disappointed by a few scattering votes, which prevented his having a majority of the whole. It is said that if nothing new turns up, Varnum will be sure to succeed on the next trial. The choice of Senators continues to run on the wrong side. In Delaware, where we were promised of late, a republican, it was contrived by a certain disposition of offices as some tell us, or according to others, occasioned by particular sicknesses, that Latimer of the H. of Reps. lately dropped by the people, has been appointed by the Legislature. N. Carolina has appointed Bloodworth whom you may recollect. His country men here do not augur favorably of his political course. Clinton has declined a reelection to the Govt. of N.Y. His party set up Yates and Floyd against Jay and Van-Ranslaer. Hamilton does not interfere with Jay. It is pompously announced in the Newspapers, that poverty drives him back to the Bar for a livelihood.

The Session has produced as yet, but few Acts of Consequence. Several important ones are depending, on the subjects of the Militia, of the military Establishment, and the discharge of the public debt. On the first little more will probably be done than to digest some regulations which will be left for public consideration till the next session. On the second, the present military Establishment will be continued and compleated; notwithstanding the late treaty with the Six Nations, the success of Wayne against the other tribes, and the disappearance of ominous[1] symtoms in the aspect of G. Britain. I am extremely sorry to remark a growing apathy to the evil and danger of standing armies. And, a vote passed two days ago, which is not only an evidence of that, but if not the effect of unpardonable inattention, indicates a temper still more alarming. In the Military Acts now in force, there are words, limiting the use of the army to the protection of the Frontiers. The Bill lately brought in revised the whole subject, and omitted this limitation. It was proposed to re-instate the words. This was rejected by a large majority. It was then proposed to substitute another phrase free from the little criticisms urged against the first proposition. The debate brought out an avowal that the Executive ought to be free to use the regular troops, as well as the Militia in support of the laws against our own Citizens. Notwithstanding this the amendment was lost by 8 votes. The House was very thin, and it is supposed, that the majority would have been in favor of the amendment, if all the members had been present. The mischeif however is irremediable, as the Senate will greedily swallow the Bill in its present form. This proceeding is the more extraordinary when the President's speech and the answer of the House of Reps. are recollected and compared with it. The third subject is the reduction of the public debt. Hamilton has in an arrogant valedictory Report presented a plan for the purpose. It will require about *30 years* of uninterrupted operation. The fund is to consist of the surpluses of impost and Excise, and the temporary taxes of the last Session which are to be prolonged till 1781.[2] You will judge of the chance of our ever being out of debt, if no other means are to be [used?]. It is to be lamented that the public are not yet better reconciled to direct taxes which alone can work down the debt faster than new emergences will probably add to it. Of this dislike the partizans of the Debt take advantage not only to perpetuate it, but to make a merit of the application of inadequate means to the discharge of it. The plan of Hamilton contained a number of new irredeemabilities, among the remodifications proposed by him. All these have been struck out.

Mr. Christie of the House of Reps. intends to visit England in the[3] interval between the present and next session. He is ambitious of a line from you introducing him to Mr. Pinkney, and has made me his solicitor for it. He is a man of good sense, and second to none in a decided and systematic devotion to Republicanism. Will you oblige us both by inclosing me such a letter. You need not fear its reaching me, as I shall be detained here some time after the adjournment. Adieu

RC (DLC: Madison Papers); unsigned; addressed: "Thomas Jefferson Charlottesville Virginia"; franked, stamped, and postmarked; endorsed by TJ as received 3 Mch. 1795 and so recorded in SJL.

Two of the three MILITARY ACTS NOW IN FORCE alluded to the PROTECTION OF THE FRONTIERS as the purpose of the regular army. Despite Madison's attempts on 13 Feb. 1795 to retain this restriction, the statute which replaced these laws lacked such language. The PRESIDENT'S SPEECH to Congress on 19 Nov. 1794 had stressed the importance of the militia in enforcing laws and suppressing insurrections, and the ANSWER OF THE HOUSE OF REPS. of 28 Nov. 1794 had agreed on its vital role (Annals, II, 2284, 2415-18, III, 1344, 1345, IV, 948, 1221-3, 1515-19; Fitzpatrick, Writings, XXXIV, 35).

[1] Word interlined in place of canceled and illegible word.
[2] Above this date "1817" is interlined by a later hand (see Madison, Papers, XV, 475n). The correct date was 1801 (Syrett, Hamilton, XVIII, 91).
[3] Madison here canceled "Spring."

To Robert Morris

DEAR SIR   Monticello Feb. 19. 95.

I have never lost sight of the present of your Spanish sheep, nor lessened in my conviction of it's importance. But during the latter part of my stay in Philadelphia no safe opportunity occurred for sending them to Virginia, and in the beginnings of my operations here too many other things pressed upon me more indispensably. I am now prepared to send for them in the spring and to have them brought by land. I think neither the trouble nor expence disproportioned to the value of the object: to others, I mean: because as to myself, my houshold manufactures will never extend but to the coarsest cloths, to which our own wool is adequate. But I shall think the Spanish sheep an acquisition to this state, because the similarity of climate will probably prevent it's degeneracy. Further North I have no doubt it's wool would[1] immediately become coarser, as it is agreeable to the usual economy of nature to change the constitution of animals with their change of climate. Should you be disposed to try the experiment with you, you will of course be so good as to send me only such as are not wanted for yourself. Or if you would rather defer your trial to a later time, I shall always be ready to deliver you a stock to begin with either at Richmond or Fredericksburg from which places vessels go every week to Philadelphia. I will thank you for a line by post informing me whether any thing has occurred which would render my mission fruitless.

I have not been disappointed in the satisfaction I expected from the society of my family and occupations of my farms. The latter have engrossed my attentions beyond what I thought possible, and as I advance in the execution of my plans, I find myself more and more engaged by them, and new ones opening upon me. Master of my own time, my own operations and actions, secured by their innocence towards the world against the censures of the world, and against newspaper denunciations, I look back with wonder and regret over my useless waste of time in other employments. I am *told* it is in the newspapers, (for I make a point to read none of them) that you also are retiring. I congratulate you on the sensations you will experience; though I doubt whether you can enjoy them fully, residing as you do at the very fountain-head of torment and associating as you must daily with those who are broiling on the public gridiron, you cannot avoid participating of their pains. You have the comfort however that you can retire from them when you please. I shall always be happy to hear that you are so, and to assure you of those sentiments of personal esteem and respect with which I am very sincerely Dear Sir Your most obedient & most humble servt

TH: JEFFERSON

RC (MdAN); addressed: "The honble Robert Morris Philadelphia"; endorsed by Morris. PrC (DLC); with one variation (see note 1 below).

For a discussion of the ram TJ later received from Morris and TJ's interest in raising the merino breed of SPANISH SHEEP to which this animal was related, see Barbara McEwan, *Thomas Jefferson: Farmer* (Jefferson, N.C., 1991), 122-8. YOU ALSO ARE RETIRING: Morris retired as a United States Senator from Pennsylvania in 1795 (DAB).

[1] TJ first wrote "it would" and then altered it to read as above, a revision not in PrC.

Notes on Letters from François D'Ivernois

[19-23 Feb. 1795]

D'Ivernois.
No. 7. Nov. 11. 94.
      100. actions of £1000.
          divided among 100. families
          Pictet
          his brother

Prevost
De Saussure
his son.

add Botany. and Natl. history in the Vegetable department
Chemistry practical, mineralogy and metallurgy.
Civil Architecture
Hydrography and Pilotage.

No. 1. pa. 3. 26. professors in Coll. Geneva having public salaries.

Mouchon. Presidt. appointed by Encyclopedists to make
Analytical table that work
Senebier. libraria. commentaries on Spalanzani.
works in Nat. Phil. and Meteorology.
translator of the Greek tragedians
Pictet. Natl. philos.
Prevost.
(a) Bertrand &c.

requires annual revenue of 15,000 D.
this is not only for the professors of the university
but for masters of a preparatory college for the studies of
the University
and of another, of common education, gratuitous.

(a) Bertrand ⎤
　　L'Huillier ⎦ mathematics, inferior to none but La Grange.

instead of the revenue, he proposes
that lands shall be appropriated = the capital represented by 15,000.D.
Genevans agricoles will buy the lands and deposit the
money.
the University to be in the center of the lands.
he is preparing to obtain actionnaires for 100,000.£.
sterl. = 450,000 D.
of which 300,000.D. to be paid for the lands.
150,000. to be reserved by the actionnaires
pour defrichemens &c.
the professorships, at Geneva, of Astronomy, medicine, anat-
omy, chemistry, botany, history, law of nations &c. were
not salaried by public

MS (DLC: TJ Papers, 98: 16725); entirely in TJ's hand; undated.

TJ undoubtedly prepared these notes on
François D'Ivernois's letters to him of 5 Sep.
and 11 Nov. 1794, the latter of which he received on 19 Feb. 1795, in preparation for
his letter to George Washington of 23 Feb.
1795.

To Thomas Mann Randolph

Th:J. to mr Randolph   Monticello Feb. 19. 95.

James arrived yesterday with your favor of the 14th. the book, and the Cole seed. Your clover seed put on the moistened cotton has not yet sprouted. Perhaps this is owing to the severity of the weather. This has indeed been very unusual, and I fear fatal to a great proportion of our wheat. The morning cold for these 10. days past has been from 11. to 33. The afternoon from 25. to 37°. No ploughing could be done, and very little of any other work: so that to those who, like my overseers, lost the fall, very little time will have been furnished by the winter to regain their loss: and for our wheat of the next year, we shall have only a spring fallow instead of a fall one. When at Richmond will you be so good as to pay Mr. John Brown clerk of the General court 63. cents for me? I am in want of some black lead for cleaning our stoves, which we have set up much to our comfort and the economy of wood; for I think we have double the heat with half the wood. I have some idea of having seen black lead advertized for sale in Richmond by the quantity. If not to be had there, I think, while you are at Mr. Eppes's, you could know whether he could get me some from Winterham, which I believe is on the road between Eppington and his Angola plantations. For the present a peck would do, but if to be had merely for the getting, a larger quantity would not be amiss, as I believe I shall adopt the general use of the stove against the next winter. The children have both had colds. Jefferson's produced only a little hoarseness, and is nearly gone off. Anne's has affected her eyes for these 2. or 3. mornings, which have mattered a little. Both were delighted with their presents by James. Jefferson's lasted him, as a gun, near 3. hours. When the barrel was broke off, he used it as his candle to light in the fire. Tender love from Maria and myself to our beloved Martha. Adieu affectionately.

RC (DLC); endorsed by Randolph as received 9 Mch. 1795.

Randolph's FAVOR OF THE 14TH., recorded in SJL as received 18 Feb. 1795, has not been found. SJL records a letter from TJ to JOHN BROWN of 4 Feb. 1795 and Brown's reply of 11 Feb. 1795 from Richmond received on 18 Feb. 1795, neither of which has been found.

To Archibald Stuart

Dear Sir   Monticello Feb. 19. 95.

Your favor of the 17th. is duly received, with the turneps and rape. There is quite enough of both to answer my purpose; and indeed of the latter I have obtained an additional supply. I concur readily in your proposition respecting the Spanish sheep, and have this day written to Mr. Morris to know if any circumstance has occurred which might disappoint us of getting them. I may expect his answer in a month, and you shall then hear from me. I inclose you my notes on the subject of potash, and am persuaded that your contemplation of the subject will end in your adopting the business, and be a means of introducing it among us.—We have had a hard winter since you left us. I am afraid we shall lose a great deal of our wheat by the frosts.—I need not write news to you who read the public papers so much more than I do. I am with great affection Dr Sir Your sincere friend & servt   Th: Jefferson

RC (ViHi: Stuart Papers); addressed: "Archibald Stuart esq. Staunton." PrC (MHi). Stuart's favor of the 17th. Feb. 1795, recorded in SJL as received a day later, has not been found.

E N C L O S U R E

Notes on Potash and Pearl Ash

Notes on Pot and Pearlash.

a man will cut and burn $2\frac{1}{2}$ cords of wood a day.
a cord of wood yeilds 2. bushels of ashes. [neither pine nor chesnut will do]
a bushel of ashes sells for 9. cents.
it will make 6. ℔ of brown salts, which make 3 ℔ to 5 ℔ pearl ash in the common way and 5. ℔ of pearlash in Hopkins's way.

for a small work, 2 kettles suffice to boil the lie into brown salts
    and 1. to melt up the brown salts.
$\frac{1}{4}$ cord of wood a day maintains one fire, which will do for 5. kettles.
to keep 3. kettles a going will require the attendance of a man and boy.
there should be 15. or 16. tubs of 100. bushels each.
3. kettles will turn out 1000 ℔ of pearl ash a week.
consequently will require 100. cords of wood a week and 7. cutters to keep them constantly at work.
each kettle costs 24. Doll.
Potash is worth in England   the ton, and in America $114\frac{2}{3}$ D.
Pearlash is worth in England £40. sterl. and in America £40. lawful.

An estimate of the profit and expence of such a work at 3. ℔ pearl-ash to the bushel of ashes, which is 100. ℔ pearlash a day. And counting 5. days to the week, which would give only 500 ℔. of pearl ash a week, instead of 1000. ℔ the common calculation.

£

500 ℔ of pearl ash a week, is 13. tons a year, @ £40. Virga. currcy.   520– 0–0

	£	s	d
7. cutters hired @ £12. a year, adding maintenance and clothing	128–	16–	0
a manager for his hire and provisions	50–	0–	0
a boy	10–	0–	0
implements annually	10–	0–	0
a waggon, team, and driver, all expences included	111–	15–	0
	310–	11–	0
Clear profit in cash	209–	9–	0
	520–	0–	0

[@ 4 ℔ pearlash to the bushel, (a very moderate calculation) it would add 5 ton a year, worth 200£. @ 5. ℔ to the bushel £400.]¹

add to this the clearing 150. acres of land a year, whatever it is worth.

Note. I was told by Hopkins that ashes burnt in the open field cannot be made into pearl ash in the common way: but answer well for that in his way. This, if certain, is a very important circumstance in Virginia.

MS (ViHi: Stuart Papers); entirely in TJ's hand; undated; brackets in original. PrC (MHi); endorsed in ink by TJ.

These notes follow closely a similar calculation in TJ's Farm Book (Betts, *Farm*

Book, 117). For HOPKINS's WAY of making potash and pearl ash, see Samuel Hopkins to TJ, 27 June 1791, and note.

¹ Bracketed text inserted by TJ.

To Thomas A. Taylor

SIR   Monticello Feb. 19. 95

Your favor of Dec. 27. came to my hands only yesterday. I had before received one from Mr. Banks on the same subject, and one from Mr. Hanson, informing me the proposition had been made to him for disposing of the mortgaged lands in Philadelphia, and paying the mortgage debt to any person appointed there. The money being destined to pay a debt to Mr. Hanson, and the bonds put into his hands to collect, on conditions too convenient to me to risk their forfeiture by any intermeddling of mine, I referred Mr. Banks to Mr. Hanson altogether, inclosing my answer to him to Mr. Hanson, open, to be forwarded. In that to Mr. Hanson, I also left it to himself to do as he pleased only expressing my *opinion*, that I saw no danger in acceding to the proposition if he should require the money to be lodged in his (Hanson's) name in any of the banks of Philadelphia. I should with great chearfulness give my consent to any measure which would ease you, and not deprive me of the benefit of my stipulations with Mr. Hanson. I hope my answers to him and Mr. Banks will ere this have produced some concert on the subject, my anxiety being that the money should be paid as early as possible. I am with great respect Sir Your most obedt. servt

TH: JEFFERSON

PrC (MHi); at foot of text: "Dr. T. A. Taylor"; endorsed in ink by TJ.

Dr. Thomas Augustus Taylor (1744-1822) represented Chesterfield County in the Virginia House of Delegates as a Republican for six terms, 1794-95 and 1797-1801. He agreed to purchase Elk Hill from TJ in partnership with Henry Banks in 1793, but ultimately bought it in his own right when the transaction was finalized in 1799 (Marshall, *Papers*, III, 71; Swem and Williams, *Register*, 41, 43, 48, 50, 52, 55; note to TJ to Daniel L. Hylton, 3 June 1792).

SJL records an earlier letter from Taylor of 20 Mch. 1794 as well as his FAVOR OF DEC. 27., which were received from "Ozborne's" on 21 May 1794 and 18 Feb. 1795, respectively. According to SJL, TJ's 1 June 1794 reply to the former was written at "Mr Bolling's" during his trip to Richmond (see note to List of Unretained Letters, [ca. 9 June 1794]). None of these letters has been found. For TJ's letters from Henry BANKS and Richard HANSON, see note to TJ to Banks, 15 Jan. 1795.

To Richard Claiborne

DR SIR   Monticello Feb. 21. 95.

I have recieved with great pleasure your favor of Jan. 8. informing me of your return to America, and of the measures you have taken for adding useful arts and inhabitants to our country. The machines which perform the labours of man are peculiarly valuable in a country where there is more to do than men to do it. Perhaps we may not be entirely mature for all the articles of your catalogue, but we are so for most of them, and a little time will shew which of them it may be most advantageous to pursue or to abandon. I wish every possible success to them all, as well as to your college. I have myself withdrawn my attentions within the limits of my farm, absolutely tired out with public affairs, and giving place to those who have longer to live and to feel the benefits or evils which are to result from the management of them. I retain however my good wishes for the worthy characters which I have had occasion to know in my course of public life: and I beg you to accept particularly your share in them, and the sentiments of esteem with which I have the honor to be Dear Sir Your most obedt. & most humble servt

TH: JEFFERSON

PrC (DLC); at foot of text: "Colo. Richard Claiborne."

Claiborne's FAVOR OF JAN. 8, recorded in SJL as received from Philadelphia on 27 Jan. 1795, has not been found.

YOUR COLLEGE: on 29 Dec. 1794 Claiborne, an amateur artist and friend of Charles Willson Peale, was elected secretary of "The Columbianum," an association established in Philadelphia for the "protection and encouragement of the Fine Arts" in

America. For committee minutes signed by Claiborne and other documents pertaining to the short-lived organization which proposed to support artists by founding an Academy of Architecture, Sculpture, and Painting within the United States, see Peale, *Papers*, II, pt. 1, 101-13. For the controversy which divided and destroyed the organization, see Charles Coleman Sellers, *Charles Willson Peale*, 2 vols. (Philadelphia, 1947), II, 65-75.

From Robert Pollard

SIR   Richmond February 22d. 1795

Mr. Ross has just offered me Twenty shares in the James River Company at Eighteen shillings ⅌ pound provided the money can be paid him by the first of April next or sooner. This is the only chance I know of to purchace any number of shares together, but the time of payment being shorter than you contemplated, I did not choose to make a positive agreement with him untill I heard from you.

If you approve of his offer please write me by return of post. I am Sir Your most Obd.   ROBERT POLLARD

RC (DLC: William Short Papers); endorsed by TJ as received 25 Feb. 1795 and so recorded in SJL.

Robert Pollard (1755-1842), a Richmond merchant and brother-in-law of Edmund Pendleton, was a member of the mercantile firm of Pickett, Pollard & Johnston (WMQ, 1st ser., X [1902], 198, 202).

According to SJL, TJ wrote a missing reply to Pollard on 25 Feb. 1795, which evidently instructed him to acquire the TWENTY SHARES IN THE JAMES RIVER COMPANY for William Short (see Pollard to TJ, 1 May 1795). Pollard's 8 Mch. response, recorded in SJL as received 17 Mch. 1795, has also not been found. In addition, SJL lists earlier missing letters from TJ to Pollard of 9 Oct., 12, 17 Dec. 1794, 22 Jan., and 4 Feb. 1795, and from Pollard to TJ of 11, 20 Oct., 1 Nov., 23 Dec. 1794, and 25 Jan. 1795.

To James Madison

TH:J. TO J.M.   Feb. 23. 95.

I inclose two letters to the President and Secretary of state open for your perusal and consideration. I pray you to bestow thought on the subject, and if you disapprove it, return me my letters, undelivered, by next post. If you approve of them, stick a wafer in them and have them delivered. I also put under your cover a letter to the Fresco painter from whom you inclosed me one. His not having furnished me with his address obliges me to give you this trouble. Nothing new. Adieu affectionately.

RC (DLC: Madison Papers). PrC (DLC). Enclosures: (1) TJ to George Washington, 23 Feb 1795. (2) TJ to Edmund Randolph, 23 Feb 1795. Enclosed in TJ to David Rittenhouse, 24 Feb. 1795.

TJ's 21 Feb. 1795 LETTER TO THE FRESCO PAINTER Ignatius Shnydore is recorded in SJL but has not been found.

To Edmund Randolph

DEAR SIR   Monticello Feb. 23. 95.

I have received from a Mr. D'Ivernois, a Genevan now in London (author of the history of Geneva I once put into your hands) several letters informing me of the suppression of the college of Geneva by the late revolution there, and proposing it's transplantation to this country. The desire of the President to apply his shares in the canals of Patowmack and James river to some public purpose,[1] has occasioned me to communicate D'Ivernois' information and proposition in a letter which goes by this post. As this will of course be communicated to you I shall not repeat here what I have said there. You know the celebrity of that college, and the degree in which several of it's professors stand in the republic of letters. D'Ivernois is not of the college himself, nor meaning to be of it. He was known to Mr. Adams and myself as an exile from Geneva for too much republicanism in 1785. He is now an exile for having too little. Should his proposition be approved, the favor I must ask of you is *dispatch*. Otherwise a letter which I have written him may put the thing out of our reach. In the same case, as some negociation will be requisite there I should suppose it might be well confided either to Pinckney or Monroe to settle such points as must of necessity be settled as preliminaries to their embarcation. I am with sincere esteem Dear Sir Your friend & servt   TH: JEFFERSON

PrC (DLC); at foot of text: "The Secretary of state." Enclosed in TJ to James Madison, 23 Feb. 1795.

HISTORY OF GENEVA: François D'Ivernois, *Tableau Historique et Politique des Révolutions de Geneve dans le Dix-Huitième Siècle* (Geneva, 1782). See Sowerby, No. 297. A LETTER WHICH GOES: TJ to George Washington, 23 Feb. 1795. LETTER . . . WRITTEN HIM: TJ to D'Ivernois, 6 Feb. 1795.

A letter from Randolph to TJ of 16 Feb. 1795, recorded in SJL as received 25 Feb. 1795, has not been found.

[1] Preceding four words interlined.

To George Washington

DEAR SIR   Monticello Feb. 23. 1795.

You were formerly deliberating on the purpose to which you should apply the shares in the Patowmack and James river companies presented you by our assembly; and you did me the honor of asking me to think on the subject. As well as I remember, some academical institution was thought to offer the best application of the money. Should you have finally decided in favor of this, a circumstance has taken place which would render the present moment the most advantageous to carry it into execution, by giving to it in the outset such an eclat, and such solid advantages, as would ensure a very general concourse to it of the youths from all our states and probably from the other parts of America which are free enough to adopt it. The revolution which has taken place at Geneva has demolished the college of that place, which was in a great measure supported by the former government. The colleges of Geneva and Edinburgh were considered as the two eyes of Europe in matters of science, insomuch that no other pretended to any rivalship with either. Edinburgh has been the most famous in medecine during the life of Cullen; but Geneva most so in the other branches of science, and much the most resorted to from the continent of Europe because the French language was that which was used. A Mr. D'Ivernois, a Genevan, and man of science, known as the author of a history of that republic, has proposed the transplanting that college in a body to America. He has written to me on the subject, as he has also done to Mr. Adams, as he was formerly known to us both, giving us the details of his views for effecting it. Probably these have been communicated to you by Mr. Adams, as D'Ivernois desired should be done; but lest they should not have been communicated I will take the liberty of doing it. His plan I think would go to about ten or twelve professorships. He names to me the following professors as likely if not certain to embrace the plan.

Mouchon, the present President, who wrote the Analytical table for the Encyclopedists, and which sufficiently proves his comprehensive science.

Pictet, known from his admeasurement of a degree, and other works, professor of Natural philosophy.

his brother, said by M. D'Ivernois to be also great.

Senebier, author of commentaries on Spallanzani, and of other works in Natural philosophy and Meteorology; also the translator of the Greek tragedians.

Bertrand ⎫ both mathematicians, and said to be inferior to nobody
L'Huillier ⎭ in that line, except La Grange, who is without an equal.

Prevost, highly spoken of by D'Ivernois.

De Saussure and his son, formerly a professor, but who left the college to have more leisure to pursue his geological researches into the Alps, by which work he is very advantageously known.

Most of these are said to speak our language well. [1] Of these persons, the names of Mousson, Pictet, de Saussure and Senebier, are well known to me, as standing foremost among the literati of Europe. Secrecy having been necessary, this plan had as yet been concerted only with Pictet, his brother, and Prevost, who knew however, from circumstances that the others would join them: and I think it very possible that the revolution in France may have put it in our power to associate La Grange with them whose modest and diffident character will probably have kept him in the rear of the revolutionary principles, which has been the ground on which the revolutionists of Geneva have discarded their professors. Most of these are men, having families, and therefore M. D'Ivernois observes they cannot come over but on sure grounds. He proposes a revenue of 15,000.D. for the whole institution, and supposing lands could be appropriated to this object, he says that an hundred Genevan families can readily be found who will purchase and settle on the lands, and deposit for them the capital of which 15,000 D. would be the interest. In this revenue he means to comprehend a college of languages preparatory to the principal one of sciences; and also a third college for the gratuitous teaching of the poor reading and writing.

It could not be expected that any propositions from strangers unacquainted with our means, and our wants, could jump at once into a perfect accomodation with these. But those presented to us would serve to treat on, and are capable of modifications reconcileable perhaps to the views of both parties.

1. We can well dispense with his 2d. and 3d. colleges, the last being too partial for an extensive country, and the 2d. sufficiently and better provided for already by our public and private grammar schools. I should conjecture that this would reduce one third of his demand of revenue, and that 10,000.D. would then probably answer their remaining views, which are the only important ones to us.

2. We are not to count on raising the money from lands, and consequently we must give up the proposal of the colony of Genevan farmers. But, the wealth of Geneva in money being notorious, and the class of monied men being that which the new government are trying to get rid off, it is probable that a capital sum could be borrowed on the credit of the funds under consideration, sufficient to meet the first expences of the transplantation and establishment, and to supply also the deficiency of revenue till the profits of the shares shall become sufficiently superior to the annual support of the college to repay the sums borrowed.

3. The composition of the academy cannot be settled there. It must be adapted to our circumstances, and can therefore only be fixed between them and persons here acquainted with those circumstances, and conferring for the purpose after their arrival here. For a country so marked for agriculture as ours, I should think no professorship so important as one not mentioned by them, a professor of agriculture, who, before the students should leave college, should carry them through a course of lectures on the principles and practice of agriculture; and that this professor should come from no country but England. Indeed I should mark

Young as the man to be obtained. These however are modifications to be left till their arrival here.

Mr. D'Ivernois observes that the Professors keep themselves disengaged till the ensuing spring, attending an answer. As he had desired his proposition to be made to our legislature, I accordingly got a member to sound as many of his brethren on the subject as he could, desiring if he found it would be desperate, that he would not commit the honor either of that body or of the college of Geneva by forcing an open act of rejection. I received his information only a fortnight ago, that the thing was evidently impracticable. I immediately forwarded that information to D'Ivernois, not giving him an idea that there was any other resource. Thinking however that if you should conclude to apply the revenues of the canal shares to any institution of this kind, so fortunate an outset could never again be obtained, I have supposed it my duty both to you and them, to submit the circumstances to your consideration.

A question would arise as to the place of the establishment. As far as I can learn, it is thought just that the state which gives the revenue should be most considered in the uses to which it is appropriated. But I suppose that their expectations would be satisfied by a location within their limits, and that this might be so far from the federal city as moral considerations would recommend, and yet near enough to it to be viewed as an appendage of that, and that the splendour of the two objects would reflect usefully on each other.

Circumstances have already consumed much of the time allowed us. Should you think the proposition can be brought at all within your views, your determination, as soon as more important occupations will admit of it, would require to be conveyed as early as possible to Mr. D'Ivernois now in London, lest my last letter should throw the parties into other engagements. I will not trespass on your time and attention by adding to this lengthy letter any thing further than assurances of the high esteem and respect, with which I have the honour to be, Dear Sir, Your sincere friend & humble servt   TH: JEFFERSON

RC (DLC: Washington Papers); addressed: "The President of the US. Philadelphia"; endorsed by Washington as received 7 Mch. 1795. PrC (DLC); at foot of first page in ink: "President Washington"; faded. Enclosed in TJ to James Madison, 23 Feb. 1795.

For the SHARES in question, see Washington to TJ, 25 Feb. 1785. A MEMBER: Wilson Cary Nicholas. MY LAST LETTER: TJ to François D'Ivernois, 6 Feb. 1795.

[1] Sentence interlined.

To David Rittenhouse

DEAR SIR   Monticello Feb. 24. 1795.

The inclosed letter to Mr. Madison covers two to the President and secretary of state, which were left open to be perused and then delivered by him. But as he may have left Philadelphia before they got there, and it is important they should be delivered without delay I take the liberty of putting the whole under cover to you, and open for your perusal as the subject will interest you. If Mr. Madison be not gone be so good as to stick a wafer in his cover and have it delivered. If he be gone, throw his cover into the fire, stick wafers into the letters to the President and Secretary of state, and *when dry* have them delivered. You will perceive that the subject of the letter has been desired to be kept secret as much as it's nature will permit.

I am here immersed in the concerns of a farmer, and more interested and engrossed by them, than I had ever concieved possible. They in a great degree render me indifferent to my books, so that I read little and ride much, and I regret greatly the time I have suffered myself to waste from home. To this indeed is added another kind of regret for the loss of society with the worthy characters with which I became acquainted in the course of my wanderings from home. If I had but Fortunatus's wishing cap to seat myself sometimes by your fireside, and to pay a visit to Dr. Priestly, I would be contented. His writings evince that he must be a fund of instruction in conversation, and his character an object of attachment and veneration. Be so good as to present my best respects to Mrs. Rittenhouse, and to accept yourself assurances of the high esteem of Dear Sir your sincere friend & humble servt   TH: JEFFERSON

PrC (DLC); badly faded; at foot of text: "David Rittenhouse." Recorded in SJL under 23 Feb. 1795. Enclosure: TJ to James Madison, 23 Feb. 1795, and enclosures.

To John Barnes

SIR   Monticello Feb. 25. 1795

As attorney in fact for Mr. William Short one of the ministers in Europe for the US. I inclose you two 6. per cent certificates of his amounting to three thousand eight hundred ninety three dollars eighty nine cents, to be sold to the best advantage you can for his account, as also to receive three hundred and ninety dollars sixty two cents due on his stock of different descriptions, (including these two certificates) due at the Treasury of the US. the 1st. day of April next, the said interest and the proceeds of the sale of the said certificates to be applied to the paiment of any bills Mr. Robert Pollard of Richmond may draw on you not exceeding in the whole three thousand six hundred dollars payable on the said 1st. day of April next, and the balance which may remain in your hands after their paiment, to be reserved subject to my order or that of Mr. Short. I pray you to use your best endeavors to obtain the highest price you can for the said certificates, for which purpose I have left you time for their disposal till the 1st. of April, counting that you will receive the present within ten days or a fortnight from it's date. I am Sir Your very humble servt   TH: JEFFERSON

PrC (CSmH); at foot of text: "Mr. John Barnes. Philadelphia"; endorsed in ink by TJ. Enclosures not found.

A 10 Mch. 1795 letter from Barnes to TJ, recorded in SJL as received 25 Mch. 1795, and letters from TJ to Barnes of 11 and 26 Mch. 1795 have not been found.

From François D'Ivernois

MONSIEUR   [26 Feb. 1795]

Limpatience avec la quelle j'attens encore une 1re réponse aux diverses lettres que j'ai eu l'honneur de vous adresser est journellement accrue par celle que prouvent a ce sujet en suisse mes malheureux compatriotes dont toutes les esperances et tous les projets se trouvent Suspendus jusqu'à cette epoque. Japprens que l'un d'entr'eux dont je crois vous avoir indiqué le nom soccupe avec activité a achever un ouvrage tiré de Morse de Cooper et des notes Sur la Virginie destiné a servir d'instruction à tous les infortunés de ce Continent qui ainsi que les Genevois tournent leurs yeux du Coté de celui de l'amérique libre et nentendent pas la langue Anglaise. J'apprens d'un autre coté que quelques Genevois deja arrivés en Amérique y ont deja formé un projet assez informe de la fondation d'une nouvelle Geneve, mais comme ils ne connaissent encore ni les esperances que nous fondons sur votre protection ni les ressources que je cherche à rassembler d'ici, je ne doute pas que lorsqu'ils en seront instruits ils ne soyent tres disposés à faire de leur projet une branche du notre.

Jai lhonneur Mr. de vous adresser mon ecrit en Anglais qui poursuit le tableau de nos malheurs à une epoque plus recente que lEdition francaise. Ce pamphlet a eu ici un succès infiniment plus grand que je n'avais osé m'y attendre quoiquil vienne d'en paraitre un autre sur le meme sujet, où l'on me reproche quelques opinions trop democratiques et entr'autres d'avoir pensé that I pronounced the Eulogy of Mr. Reybaz the Genevese Minister to the french Repub. by saying that Mr. Reybaz is much considered and respected at Paris when we all know what kind of persons they are who form and direct the public opinion in that city.

Javoue que si mon tableau est lu en Amerique et j'en envoye a cet effet a Phil. 200 exemplaires de la 1re Edition Anglaise, je craindrai plutot qu'on ne lui fit un reproche d'un autre genre.[1] Et cependant si j'en juge par limpression qu'il a produit sur les amis les plus chauds de la liberté il me semble que j'ai rempli mon but. Mais ce que jenvisagerais à cet egard comme la veritable pierre de touche de ce but et de mon ouvrage ce serait assurement le suffrage de lauteur distingué des notes sur la Virginie.

Permettez moi Mr. de vous adresser mes félicitations les plus Sinceres sur la maniere noble eclatante et prompte avec la quelle les Américains se Sont levés en masse pour faire triompher leurs loix pour soutenir leur Gouvernement legitime et pour sauver la liberté du plus grand coup quelle aurait encore reçu si ses ennemis avaient pu jamais dire que la liberté Americaine navait servi qu'à preter des forces à la licence et a fournir des armes pour renverser votre beau systeme politique que ses admirateurs envisageaient comme le plus favorable a lespece humaine. Jai lhonneur d etre

Dft (BPUG: D'Ivernois Papers); in D'Ivernois's hand, heavily emended; undated and unsigned; at head of text: "A Mr Jefferson No 9 ce 26 fevr 1795." Not recorded in SJL or acknowledged with a reply, and possibly not sent by D'Ivernois. Enclosure: François D'Ivernois, *A Short Account of the Late Revolution in Geneva; and of the Conduct of France towards that Republic, from October 1792, to October 1794. In a Series of Letters to an American, by Francis D'Ivernois, esq.* . . . (London, 1795).

UN OUVRAGE: Charles Pictet de Rochemont, *Tableau de la Situation Actuelle des États-Unis d'Amérique, d'après Jedidiah Morse et les Meilleurs Auteurs Américains*, 2 vols. in one (Paris, 1795). See Sowerby, No. 3965. POUR FAIRE TRIOMPHER LEURS LOIX: a reference to the suppression of the Whiskey Rebellion.

[1] D'Ivernois here canceled "Et certes dans les circonstances presentes, ce n'est pas un des moindres écœuils qu'un Ecrivain politique ait a rencontrer que celui de publier."

To Thomas Mann Randolph

TH:J. TO TMR.   Monticello Feb. 26. 95.

I recieved yesterday your favor of Feb. 20. and am truly concerned and alarmed at the crisis respecting Varina, and the more so as I apprehend the mode of procrastination proposed by you cannot be made use of. It was in a letter I wrote you from Germantown, if you recollect, after I had written to LeRoy, that I mentioned the possibility of a cross bill brought by myself &c. the object of which should be to pray the Chancellor to subject the Dover estate in the first place to the payment of the debt, on the supposition that both tracts were comprehended in the same mortgage, and to secure the same debt. In this case there cannot be a single doubt but that the Chancellor would have done it, but I observed in that letter that if the two tracts were separately mortgaged for separate parts of the debt, it would entirely change the case: and this I think I have since learnt to be the fact. Varina being alone mortgaged for a particular portion of the debt, Dover is no more liable to exonerate it than any other part of the estate. In this case the Creditor is left free to act on his mortgaged subject, and you come in as a creditor against the estate for reimbursement, distinguished indeed very advantageously from the others, as being the executor, and authorised to repay yourself your whole debt out of the first money coming to your hands: unless there be creditors of higher degree sufficient to absorb the whole, which I apprehend to be impossible as the debt to you is founded on the deed which is a specialty.—But the anchor of my hope had been in the bill of exchange which I thought was sufficient to discharge the mortgage on Varina, if applied to that. The indulgences given by LeRoy to Ross, would in any case have charged him with the debt, and have made it a discharge of Colo. Randolph's estate, and more especially in the case which has happened of Ross's failure in the mean time: for tho' we have no act of bankruptcy ascertaining the acts and moment of bankruptcy, yet a merchant permitting himself to be carried to prison for a debt, and conveying his whole estate for the paiment of debts, are evidences of failure which need no act of the legislature to declare them such. Were indeed Mr. LeRoy, acknoleging himself obliged to consider the bill of exchange as so much paid, to say he would not credit it to the Varina mortgage, but to that of Dover, there indeed would be ground for application to the Chancellor, and no doubt that he would order it to the credit of Varina, in protection of the marriage settlement. Whether this is to be done in the settlement before the Master in Chancery, or by a new bill, depends on changes in the practice made during my absence from the country with which I am not acquainted. If by a new bill, and my becoming a party will be of avail, and proper, you are free to have such bill brought in my name, and a previous communication of it to me will be unnecessary. But I rather expect it may be insisted on before the Master in Chancery, and that on his refusing to apply the bill to the credit of the lands under marriage settlement, there might be an appeal to the Chancellor.—If a bill however be necessary, and in my name, the following are the facts material for the information of your counsel.— Colo. Randolph in a letter of Jan. 30. 90. written in contemplation of your marriage says 'I shall put my son Thomas immediately in possession of my estate at Varina, where there is, or may be at a small expence made a very convenient dwelling house and other houses.' This I received on the 4th. of Feb. and on the same day wrote him in answer that I was contented with the provision proposed for you, and would myself convey 1000. acres of my Poplar forest lands and 25. negroes, but I insisted that both his provision and mine should be by deed of conveyance expressed to be in consideration of the marriage proposed, and executed before the marriage. He accordingly executed the deed, and wrote to me Feb. 15. then for the first time mentioning the mortgage on Varina: but says 'the sum of money for which it is encumbered is only £1200. sterlg. Mr. David Ross is now under a promise to pay £600. and the money as I am told by his nephew is now ready for the payment, but Mr. Ross having been at his iron works for some weeks past prevents my seeing him. The other payment of £600. will not become due till the 1st. day of next February.' On the reciept of this letter, I executed my deed, Feb. 21. in which yourself, Martha, and your father are all named as parties, and the considerations expressed in the deed are 1. the marriage proposed to be had, 2. the advancement of my daughter, and 3. the conveyance by Colo. R., for the same purposes, of Varina and 40. negroes. This is recorded in the General court. [By the bye have you examined the record of the mortgage to see whether that was in time? This is always worth attention.] Upon this state of the case your counsel will judge whether I can be introduced as a party in a new bill either for myself or as the prochein amy of my daughter, and whether it be necessary in order to effect delay or any other useful purpose. They will advise you also whether appeal or contumacy may not be made a means of delay. The former is a ruinous one, but would fall on the estate, not on you.[1] In the case of contumacy or resistance, you should be very clear that the money can be produced before the compulsions of the Chancery can be displayed.—It may be of some consequence to mention to you the following fact. I authorised Pollard to buy for Mr. Short 20. shares in the James river co. Yesterday's post brought me his information that Ross would sell 20. on condition of payment by the 1st. of April. This post conveys 3600.D. worth of stock to Pollard, to be forwarded to Philada. for sale, liable to his draughts on John Barnes payable Apr. 1. Perhaps Ross may have had you in view in this; or perhaps you can prevail on him to give you the benefit of it.—Would it not be worth your while to employ Washington in this case? With equal natural abilities, greater reading in the law, he has the reputation of being all attention to his business and that of his client. A little want of attention may lose you some advantage never more to be recovered, and in the scale against which the fee of another counsel would be as nothing.—This being a letter of business, I shall add nothing more but that we are all well, and wishing to see you and our dear Martha, not forgetting Eleonor. Adieu affectionately.

RC (DLC); consists of four pages, with dateline at foot of text; brackets in original; endorsed by Randolph as received 9 Mch. 1795. PrC (ViU: Edgehill-Randolph Papers); consists of first and third pages only; badly faded. PrC (MHi); consists of second page only.

Randolph's FAVOR OF FEB. 20., recorded in SJL as received from "Chesnut grove" on

25 Feb. 1795, has not been found. TJ's letter FROM GERMANTOWN was dated 17 Nov. 1793. He HAD WRITTEN to Herman LeRoy on 11 Nov. 1793. The letter of FEB. 15. 1790 from Thomas Mann Randolph, Sr., is printed in Vol. 27: 776-7.

[1] TJ here canceled: "Also whether the non service of the process on."

From James Madison

[ca. February-March 1795]

Bringhurst says he has written to you and will write again. Donath is in Philada. He was disappointed in the importation of his glass, by the Protest of Bills occasioned by the Yellow fever in Philada. If you still want the Glass, it will be proper to renew your orders to Donath. Letters addressed to him to the care of Jno' Bringhurst, or without that precaution will be pretty sure to get to him.

RC (MHi); unsigned and possibly fragmentary text written on a small scrap; undated and not recorded in SJL, but clearly a further response to TJ to Madison, 5 Feb. 1795, to which Madison first replied on 15 Feb. 1795.

The letter John Bringhurst claimed to have WRITTEN TO YOU is not recorded in SJL and has not been found. He did not WRITE AGAIN for nearly a year (Madison to TJ, 31 Jan. 1796, and note).

From Dugald Stewart

DEAR SIR   Edinburgh 1 March 1795

The Gentleman who will have the Honour of presenting this letter to you (Mr. John Millar) has been long a particular friend of mine, and I can with great confidence recommend him to your acquaintance, as a man of worth, learning, and talents. I shall leave to himself the detail of the circumstances which have suggested to him the plan of settling in America, and shall content myself with assuring you in general that they are such as could not fail to add to your estimation of his character. I need not inform you that *our* modes of thinking on political subjects are not altogether the same with *yours*.

Mr. Millar was bred to the Law, under the particular inspection of his Father, Professor Millar of Glasgow, with whose excellent works *On the Distinction of Ranks*, and on *The English Constitution* I presume you are acquainted. Should an opening occur in any of your literary establishments, I am persuaded you would find him a valuable acquisition as a Professor; and the variety of his attainments leave him a considerable latitude in his choice of a situation. I should suppose that General [1] Jurisprudence or some of the branches more immediately connected with it would be most agreeable to his wishes; but as he has received a very liberal Education, there are few branches of Academical Instruction which he could not undertake with a fair prospect of success.

Altho' Mr. Millar has been strongly recommended to Mr. Jay by Lord Landsdowne and others, I could not think of his setting out for America, without availing myself of the Honour of your acquaintance, in expressing my warmest wishes to you for his comfortable establishment. Allow me likewise to recommend to your civilities *Mrs.* Millar, who is a Daughter of our late celebrated Professor of Medicine Dr. Cullen, and who inherits a large portion of her Father's genius.

I felt myself highly flattered in being associated with the very distinguished names in the American philosophical society, and beg to return you my grateful acknowledgements for an honour to which I could have no claim but thro' your Recommendation. I am Dear Sir Your most Obedt. & faithful Servant   DUGALD STEWART

RC (DLC); addressed: "Honble Mr. Jefferson"; endorsed by TJ as received 21 July 1795 and so recorded in SJL. Enclosed in John Craig Millar to TJ, 10 July 1795.

EXCELLENT WORKS: John Millar, *Observations Concerning the Distinction of Ranks*

in Society (London, 1771), and later editions; and same, *An Historical View of the English Government, from the Settlement of the Saxons in Britain to the Accession of the House of Stewart* (London, 1787).

[1] Word interlined.

Bill in Chancery of Wayles's Executors against the Heirs of Richard Randolph

[on or before 2 Mch. 1795]

To the honorable George Wythe esquire Judge of the honorable the high Court of Chancery, humbly complaining, shew unto your honor, your orators Francis Eppes and Thomas Jefferson executors of the last will and testament of John Wayles deceased; that on the 13th. day of December 1772, Richard Randolph esquire of Curles being indebted to

James Bivins of the City of Bristol, in the sum of £740. sterling, executed a bond to the said Bivins, binding himself, his heirs &c. in the penalty of £1480. like money; to the payment of the said sum of £740. with interest from the 30th. September then next following, within twelve months from the date; the said bond was also executed by the testator of your orator as security to the said Randolph. That the said Bivins shortly after departed from this Country and left the bond aforesaid in the care and custody of your orators' testator, taking a copy and a receipt for the original. That some few years after this, your orators' testator departed this life, being then in possession of the said bond, no part of the principal or interest of which had been paid off by the said Randolph, so far as they know or believe. That in the year 17   a suit in Chancery was instituted by the representatives of the said James Bivins, in the Federal circuit court for this state, against Henry Skipwith and Anne his wife, late Anne Wayles executrix of the said John Wayles, for the recovery of the principal and interest due on the said bond, and at the May Session 1793, a decree nisi was entered for the sum of £740. sterling, of the value of 3288 dollars and eighty nine cents, with interest at five per cent per annum from the 13th. day of September 1773, till payment, and the costs. That neither the said Skipwith and his wife, nor your orators being able to shew any just cause against the decree, the same remains absolute. All which will more fully appear, reference being had to the said original bond now in the possession of your orators, and ready to be produced, and by the records of the said Federal circuit Court. That your orators having the management of the estate of their testator, have thought it belonged to them to pay, out of the assetts in their hands, the said debt, though they are not named in the decree; they have accordingly made considerable payments and are going on to make more; an account of all which will in due time be laid before this honorable Court. They further beg leave to shew unto your honor, that the said Richard Randolph, on the 21st. day of March 1786, made and duly published his last will and testament and thereby gave the residue of his estate after several devises and bequests to be equally divided between his four sons Richard Randolph, David Meade Randolph, Brett Randolph and Ryland Randolph, and he appointed his said four sons his executors. That shortly afterwards, he departed this life, and the said will was duly proved and admitted to record in the County Court of Henrico, as will more fully appear reference being had to a true copy of the said will, and to the certificate of the probate thereof, which are hereto annexed. That the said Richard Randolph deceased, died largely indebted, and the said executors give out in speeches that they have already sold all the slaves and the personal estate of their testator and applied the proceeds to the discharge of his debts so far as the same would extend, and that there are many debts to a large amount still due from the estate. Whether this be so or not, your orators are at present unable to say certainly, but they believe they have yet assetts in their hands. They further shew unto your honor, that on the 11th. day of October 1780, the said Richard Randolph being indebted on the bond and otherwise, to an amount equal to, if not exceeding, the whole of his estate, and being seized of a tract of land in Bermuda hundred in the County of Chesterfield, and possessed of a large number of slaves, did seal and execute a deed conveying the said tract of land and all the stocks of horses, cattle, sheep and hogs, and all the plantation utensils on the said land, together with nineteen slaves named in the said deed, unto the said David M. Randolph, his son, his heirs and assigns forever, for and in consideration of his natural love and affection for his said son, and for his advancement in life, as will more fully appear, reference being had to a true copy of the said deed which is hereto annexed (marked B.) That the said Richard Randolph deceased, being indebted as aforesaid, and being seized of a large and valuable estate in the said County of Henrico called Curles, did, on the 20th. day of September 1785, execute a deed conveying the same to his son Richard Randolph, above named, his heirs and assigns forever, after the death of him, the said Richard Randolph deceased, and Ann his wife; the consideration expressed in the said deed, being a marriage shortly to be had and solemnized between the said Richard, the son, and Miss Maria Beverley, the daughter of Robert Beverley, but the said Maria was not a party to the said deed. That the same was not proved until the third day of July 1786, as will more fully appear, reference being had to a true copy of the said deed, and to the certificate of the proof thereof in the County Court of Henrico, which are hereto annexed (marked C). That the said Richard Randolph deceased, was at the time of making his said will, and at his death, seized in fee simple of two considerable tracts of land in the Counties of Cumberland and Prince Edward, the one called Sandy Ford, the other Clover Forest; as also a valuable mill and   acres of land adjoining, also in the said County of Prince Edward; he was also seized as aforesaid of a tract of land containing about 130 acres, lying in the County of Chesterfield, and another tract of about the same extent lying in the last mentioned County, known by the name of Elams. That by the said will he devised the tract called Sandy Ford to his said son Brett Randolph and his heirs forever; the land known by the name of Clover Forest and the tract opposite to Curles, he devised to his said son Ryland and his heirs forever. The mill and 50 acres adjoining, he gave to his sons Ryland and Brett, in fee simple, as tenants in common, and the tract called Elams he devised to his son David M. Randolph and his heirs forever, as will more fully and at large appear, reference being had to the said will. That the said devisees entered upon and were seized of the said tracts of land respectively and are now seized of them as aforesaid. That the said Richard Randolph the younger is the eldest son and heir at law of Richard Randolph deceased. That the aforesaid deeds executed by the said Richard Randolph deceased, were made by him when he well knew that his estate in possession was insufficient to pay his debts, and with intent to defraud his just creditors and that as your orators are advised, they are void as to the creditors not only for this reason but because the conveyance to David M. Randolph was not made on consideration good in law against creditors, and the conveyance to Richard Randolph was not recorded in due time according to the act of assembly in that case made and provided. That they are entitled, as they are advised, to a discovery of the personal estate and slaves that have come to the hands of the said executors, and an account of the manner in which they have been disposed of, and if any should now remain in their hands to have them applied to the discharge of the debt aforesaid, or to a reimbursement of what monies your orators may have paid in discharge of the same. That if the said assetts should prove insufficient, they are entitled to a like satisfaction out of all the said lands, or any other real estate of the said Richard Randolph deceased, they being entitled in equity as they humbly conceive in respect to the real estate of the said Richard Randolph deceased, to stand in the place of the original creditor on the bond aforesaid, and of any other creditors by specialty who have been paid their debts out of the assetts in the hands of the said executors. That they have in a friendly manner represented their just claims to the said executors and requested them to pay off the balance due on the said decree, and to reimburse them for such payments as they have made in discharge of the same. Your orators further charge that the said Richard Randolph, the son, hath conveyed the said estate called Curles to Anthony Singleton by way of mortgage, and the said Singleton is since dead, and William Fenwick and William Berkeley are his executors; the said Richard Randolph hath also conveyed the same estate by way of mortgage to William Heath, who, together with the said William Fenwick and William Berkeley, are prayed to be made defendants hereto. But now so it is, that the said Richard Randolph, David M. Randolph, Ryland Randolph and Brett Randolph, altogether refuse so to do. In tender consideration whereof, and for as much as your orators are only relievable in equity; To the end therefore that the said Richard Randolph, David M. Randolph, Brett Randolph, and Ryland

Randolph, who they pray may be made defendants to this their bill, may on their corporal oaths make full, true and perfect answer to all and singular the premises, and that as if the same were herein again set forth and they thereto interrogated. That they may make a true discovery of the assetts that have come to their hands of the estate of the said Richard Randolph, and make up a full and compleat account of their administration; that the demand of your orators may if the personal estate is insufficient, be satisfied out of the real estate of the said Richard Randolph and that as well the lands and other property mentioned in the deeds aforesaid as those devised may be made liable thereto, and that your orators may have such other relief as is consistent with equity; may it please your honor to grant a writ of Subpœna, commanding the said Richard Randolph, David M. Randolph, Ryland Randolph and Brett Randolph &c. and your orator &c.

Tr (PRO: T 79/19); in claim of James Buchanan & Co.; exhibited in Virginia High Court of Chancery on 2 Mch. 1795; in hand of John Brown, clerk of Virginia Court of Appeals; consists of part of record of case of Eppes v. Randolphs, in 48 numbered pages sealed by Brown on 29 Dec. 1804 and certified by Governor John Page, 31 Dec. 1804. Enclosures: (1) Last will and testament of Richard Randolph, 21 Mch. 1786, specifying distribution of his estate and appointing his sons Richard Randolph, David Meade Randolph, Brett Randolph, and Ryland Randolph as executors and his friends David Meade, Richard Kidder Meade, Edmund Randolph, and Jerman Baker as guardians of his children, witnessed by Jerman Baker, James Currie, Henry Randolph, and Thomas Blodget, with attestation of Clerk of Court Adam Craig that the will was proved in a monthly court of Henrico County on 3 July 1786 by the oaths of James Currie and Henry Randolph (Tr in same, in hand of John Brown). (2) Deed, 11 Oct. 1780, Richard Randolph the elder conveying to David Meade Randolph an estimated 900 acres in Bermuda Hundred, Chesterfield County, with all its buildings and appurtenances, utensils, livestock, and 19 slaves, recorded at General Court in Richmond, 11 Oct. 1780, as attested by Clerk of Court John May (Tr in same, in hand of John Brown). (3) Deed, 20 Sep. 1785, Richard Randolph the elder conveying to Richard Randolph the younger

the tract known as Curles in the parish and county of Henrico, with adjoining tracts and appurtenances, witnessed by Brett Randolph, Wilson Cary, and Thomas Nelson, Jr., also witnessed on 21 Mch. 1786 by James Currie, Jerman Baker, Henry Randolph, and David Meade Randolph, proved in Henrico County court on 3 July 1786 on the oaths of Currie, Henry Randolph, and David Meade Randolph as attested by Clerk of Court Adam Craig, with certification by Currie on 25 Mch. 1794 as to the dates of witnesses' signatures (Tr in same, in hand of John Brown).

The lawsuit that commenced with this bill in chancery arose from an issue that had its origins in 1772, when the Bristol firm of Farell & Jones acted as broker for the consignment to Richard Randolph and John Wayles, TJ's father-in-law, of a cargo of African slaves for sale in Virginia. Probably due to a copying error in the case record, in the above complaint an incorrect date, THE 13TH. DAY OF DECEMBER 1772, is attributed to the BOND that Randolph and Wayles gave to James Bivins, the captain of the ship The Prince of Wales, on 30 Dec. 1772. The COPY of the bond with Wayles's RECEIPT is described in the note to Wayles's letter to Bivins of 25 Jan. 1773 (printed in Vol. 15: 655 as Document IX of a group of documents on the debt to Farell & Jones and the slave ship The Prince of Wales). Since this bond did not involve Farell & Jones, it was not part of the agreement negotiated in February 1790 between Richard Hanson, the firm's agent in Virginia, and Wayles's executors—TJ, Francis Eppes, and Henry Skipwith (see Memorandum of Agreement between Richard Hanson and Executors of John Wayles, [7 Feb. 1790], printed in Vol. 15: 674-6). In 1791 Bivins's executors had instituted chancery proceedings in FEDERAL CIRCUIT COURT, which in a decree in 1793 held Wayles's executors liable for the payment of the bond (see List of Unretained Letters, [ca. 9 June 1794], and note).

The above bill in equity set the matter on a new course. Wayles had only been security for the bond to Bivins, with Randolph its principal. TJ and Eppes, therefore, sought to make the estate of Randolph, who had died in June 1786, responsible for payment. That was a formidable task, since any assets of the heavily indebted Randolph were presumed to be long gone and inaccessible to creditors—"they are making away with the Estate," Hanson said of the heirs in 1791. Although the Richmond attorney John Wickham may have drawn up the bill of complaint printed above, it was TJ who contrived the key strategem: to challenge the disposition of the estate's assets by probing, through technicalities, the legitimacy of two major conveyances of land from Randolph to his sons (Hanson to Farell & Jones, 17 Mch. 1790, 14 May 1791, extracts in Farell & Jones claim, PRO: T 79/30; TJ to Eppes, 28 Aug. 1794; TJ to Wickham, 20 Jan. 1797).

Since multiple court judgments already encumbered lands that had devised upon two of Randolph's four sons, Brett and Ryland, by their father's will, the suit hinged on whether or not their brothers, David Meade Randolph and Richard Randolph the younger, were "fair purchasers" of tracts their father had transferred to them by deed during his lifetime. If they were not, those lands would be liable to claims by creditors. The deed of THE 11TH. DAY OF OCTOBER 1780 for Bermuda Hundred, if based solely on Richard Randolph's paternal affection for David Meade Randolph, lacked sufficient CONSIDERATION to constitute a fair purchase under the law. The deed of THE 20TH. DAY OF SEPTEMBER 1785 could not be challenged on the same basis, for its conveyance of the Curles plantation to the

younger Richard Randolph, made in consideration of his pending marriage, was adequate for a fair purchase. The Curles deed, however, might be vulnerable on the simple question of its date, for it was not proved in court until 3 July 1786. Under an ACT OF ASSEMBLY passed in 1748 "for settling the Titles and Bounds of Lands," a deed had to be recorded within eight months of its "sealing and delivery," a requirement found also in an act—part of the revisal of the laws—that was passed in 1785 to take effect in 1787 (Hening, V, 409, XII, 154, 158; Call, *Reports*, II, 125-90; above in this series, Vol. 2: 405-9).

On the filing of Eppes's and TJ's complaint, the judge of the High Court of Chancery, TJ's old law mentor George Wythe, granted the requested process of subpoena. David Meade Randolph submitted an answer as acting executor of his father's estate and for himself personally on 6 June 1795, and his brothers filed individual answers on 12 Mch. 1796. In reply to the critical points about the two deeds, the Randolphs presented evidence that the Bermuda Hundred indenture, although it did not say so on its face, was "in consideration of the marriage," part of a prenuptial bargain between David's father and his prospective father-in-law, Thomas Mann Randolph, Sr., and they contended that the Curles deed dated not from 20 Sep. 1785 but from 21 Mch. 1786, when it was newly witnessed (Virginia Court of Appeals record, in claim of James Buchanan & Co., PRO: T 79/19; Call, *Reports*, II, 127-32).

In the spring of 1797, after depositions had been taken regarding the deeds' technical points, other creditors of the Randolph estate, all of whom had old unpaid judgments for debt against Richard Randolph the elder, joined Wayles's executors as plaintiffs in the suit. The new parties to the case were: John Lloyd, executor of the English firm of Capel Hanbury and Osgood Hanbury; Thomas Main, executor of John Hyndman, who was the surviving partner of James Buchanan & Co., another British firm; Thomas Pleasants of Virginia, the executor of Robert Pleasants, Jr.; and Charles Carter, as a trustee for William Byrd. The entry of new complainants required the filing of their bills of complaint and answers by the defendants, and introduced the question of whether the earlier court judgments constituted liens on the Randolph lands. On 25 May 1797, Wythe ordered Commissioner Andrew Dunscomb to submit an account of the properties of the deceased Richard Randolph beginning 16 July 1770, the date of the earliest of the prior judgments for debt (Call, *Reports*, II, 132-5).

Wythe issued his opinion in the case on 5 Oct. 1797. He held that the 1780 conveyance to David Meade Randolph was legitimately in consideration of marriage and could not be challenged, but he ordered that the lands of the younger Richard Randolph be sold to pay creditors, on the basis that too much time had expired between the writing of the deed in September 1785 and its recording the following July. Richard appealed the decision to the Virginia Court of Appeals, which simultaneously heard a suit initiated by his father-in-law, Robert Beverley, who had bestowed considerable property on his daughter as part of the marriage arrangement with the Randolphs and sought confirmation of Richard's title. For eighteen months the Court of Appeals was delayed by the recusal of three of its five members who considered "themselves interested in the event of this suit, or otherwise disqualified to sit therein" (Virginia Court of Appeals record, PRO: T 79/19; Marshall, *Papers*, v, 148n). By the time replacements were found and the panel heard the case in November 1799, Richard Randolph the younger had died. It took three days to argue the suit, with Daniel Call, William DuVal, John Warden, John Marshall, and Edmund Randolph representing the appellants—the Randolphs and Beverley—and George Hay and John Wickham arguing for the creditors (Virginia Court of Appeals record, PRO: T 79/19; Call, *Reports*, II, 137-83).

In a decree read on 9 Nov. 1799 by Edmund Pendleton, the presiding judge, the Court of Appeals ruled in the Randolph heirs' behalf. The court held that the deed to Curles was sealed and delivered on 21 Mch. 1786 and so had been properly recorded within the required eight-month period. The appeals court also affirmed that the conveyance to David Meade Randolph had been in consideration of marriage, and held that any liens deriving from the old judgments against the elder Richard Randolph had expired (Call, *Reports*, II, 183-9). Conceding one point, the court did agree that Wayles's executors should "be considered as bond creditors, standing in the place of" the original bondholder, Bivins (same, 188). That ruling entitled them to seek redress against the estate's real property, in effect granting them higher standing in the long queue of demands against Randolph's estate than they would have had as simple contract creditors (Marshall, *Papers*, v, 156n). But since no Randolph property was ruled liable to seizure by creditors, that designation had no practical effect, and TJ, Eppes, and Skipwith were left with the obligation to pay the 1772 Randolph-Wayles bond (TJ to William Short, 13 Apr. 1800).

The records of the High Court of Chancery are no longer extant. Some documents from the Buchanan & Co. claim (PRO: T 79/19) and Call's *Reports* are printed with notes in Marshall, *Papers*, v, 117-60.

To James Madison

TH:J. TO MR. MADISON   Monticello Mar. 5. 95.

Your favor of Feb. 15. is duly recieved and I now inclose the letter for Mr. Christie,[1] which you will be so kind as to deliver to him open or sealed as you think best, and apologize to him for my availing myself of the opportunity of getting the vetch from England which you say is not to be had in Philadelphia. The universal culture of this plant in Europe establishes it's value in a farm, and I find two intervals in my rotation where I can have crops of it without it's costing me a single ploughing.

My main object is to turn it in as a green dressing in the spring of the year, having sowed it on the fall fallow. In the mean time, should a short crop of fodder or hard winter call for it as fodder, it is a most abundant and valuable green fodder through the whole winter.—We are in despair here for F. Walker. The low practices of his competitor though seen with indignation by every thinking man, are but too succesful with the unthinking who merchandize their votes for grog. He is said to be a good republican: but I am[2] told this is the only favorable[3] trait in his character. Adieu affectionately.

RC (DLC: Madison Papers); addressed: "James Madison Congress Philadelphia"; franked. PrC (DLC). Enclosure: TJ to Thomas Pinckney, 5 Mch. 1795.

COMPETITOR: Samuel Jordan Cabell.

[1] Word written over "Pinckney," erased.
[2] Word written over "believe," erased.
[3] Word reworked from "tolerable."

To Thomas Pinckney

DEAR SIR   Monticello Mar. 5. 1795.

The bearer hereof, Mr. Christie, a member of Congress for Maryland, proposing to visit London, I take the liberty of introducing him to you. The confidence of his country, evidenced in their election of him to take care of their federal interests, would sufficiently testify his merit to you. To this permit me to add that of my friends who serve with him in Congress, who enable me to assure you that the worthiness of his character will do full justice to whatever attentions and civilities you may be kind enough to shew him. It will not lessen his value in your eye to be assured that he is entirely orthodox in his republicanism, a distinction of value here where there is some leaning towards a British constitution.

To save you the trouble of another letter, I take the liberty with Mr. Christie as well as yourself, of solliciting you to procure me some seed of the winter vetch or tare, so much cultivated in the English farms, and which, unknown here as yet, will fill with considerable value some intervals of time and space in our farms, both as fodder for animals, and manure for the lands. I specify below the two kinds which I shall be glad to recieve, in the terms in which any seedsman will find them distinguished in Millar's Gardener's dictionary. There are always ships bound from London to Richmond which will furnish a conveyance to me. This being a common produce of the farms, the cost of the little necessary to put me in seed, will not merit an apology to you. I have the honor to be with great & sincere esteem & respect Dear Sir Your friend & servt   TH: JEFFERSON

Vicia biennis, from Siberia. The 4th. Species enumberated by Millar. Vicia Sativa, his 5th. species. I should be glad of the variety with white seeds.

PrC (DLC); with subjoined directions written perpendicularly in the margin; at foot of text: "H. E. M[r.] Pinckney." Enclosed in TJ to James Madison, 5 Mch. 1795.

To Thomas Mann Randolph

Th:J. to TMR.   Monticello Mar. 5 95.

We are all well here, except that the children have little colds, which however are going off. As you will be out of the post-road, I shall not write again, which I mention, that my silence may give no uneasiness. We have now fine weather for work. As your clover seed did not sprout, I have advised the leaving it unsowed till you come. I shall not sow mine till the last week in March. I had your bags of clover seed emptied to search for the radish seed, but no such thing was in them. There was a paper of clover seed found in one of them, which I suppose has been put in by mistake for the other. If this finds you in Richmond, pray get me some of the scarlet radish seed, as it is not [to][1] be had in this neighborhood, and is I think the only kind worth cultivating. Maria joins me in love to our Dear Martha. Adieu affectionately.

RC (DLC); endorsed by Randolph as received 8 Mch. 1795.

SJL as received two days later but not found.

Randolph replied to this letter in one of 8 Mch. 1795 from "Windsor," recorded in

[1] Word supplied.

From John Taylor

Dear Sir   Caroline March 5. 1795

There is a spice of fanaticism in my nature upon two subjects—agriculture and republicanism, which all who set it in motion, are sure to suffer by. Tho' there is no comfort, there is a warning in the confession, enabling you at this moment to escape from its effect.

For I am about to go farther into the means which I have practised for the recovery of worn out lands, the experiments I have made, and the conjectures I have resulted from them; with the design of defending two leading features in mine, and contesting the propriety of their absence, in your system.

The basis of my system is, that as labour is scarce and dear, it ought to be so employed as to be comparatively profitable—otherwise it is bad economy to employ it at all.

No proffit, or but a trivial proffit can be made by tilling poor land; it is an interment of labour, of which there is never a resurrection.

Its cultivation, for the object of improvement by a course of ameliorating crops alone, is making a loan, for the sake of repayment in the next world.

If I am not mistaken, no such idea is to be found in the books of husbandry, and Young, the most strenuous advocate for including ameliorating crops in his course, never fails to include also an ameliorating coat of manure.

Therefore I absolutely exclude the idea of relying upon a rotation of crops, as the chief means for recruiting lands, tho' I admit it to be extreamly useful for their preservation, when once in heart.

To recruit them, a combination of efforts, within reach of our circumstances, must take place. To omit any one, is diverting a stream, which with several others, is but barely sufficient to supply a reservoir.

There are three cardinal means within our reach.

1. enclosing.
2. manuring.
3. clearing fresh lands.

The first is the most easily practised, because it is both a saving of labour in the article of fencing, and a reference to nature, in that of fertilization.

The labour thus happily saved by the first article of the system, seems naturally to devolve upon the other two.

Clearing is a comfortable exercise during winter, and in summer, chasms of liesure occur for removing manure.

The best mode of raising manure in our present circumstances, may be asserted perhaps, to be the best system of practicable agriculture. Manure can only come of great offals, and great offals, only of great crops. These great crops, and great offals then, are the desiderium.

No man could have commenced agriculture, with a stronger theoretical prejudice against indian corn, than myself. To this prejudice I yielded for some years. To myself, I appear to have been gradually beaten out of it by experience. And now as my last letter stated, it occupies the chief place in my system. In my defence, I will briefly consider corn, with a reference to this desiderium.

Indian corn produces, bread—hay—offal—and housing, all in abundance—turnips and potatoes, bread for beasts only—peas, bread and straw, both scantily.

Corn is almost a certain crop in strong land—turnips—potatoes—

and peas are precarious. More ground can be prepared for wheat by using corn as a fallow crop, than by resorting to any other. Potatoes require vastly more labour—turnip ground must be in garden culture before sowing, and allows not sufficient time for seeding large fields in wheat; including thining, turnips require more labour—and peas are more troublesome to plant.

Wheat may be sown among corn in great quantities in proper time—it is the reverse with its three rivals. Two of them must be previously taken from the ground; and it would destroy the turnips to sow wheat early among them.

Corn is superior to all crops in durability—even peas are very liable to worms and weavel.

Corn is food compleat for man and beast—the others not. Young in his tour through France, bestows high encomiums on maize. The line of its cultivation he says, is invariably the mark between plenty and poverty. Plenty attending maize, and poverty all other crops.

In corn there is a prodigious saving of seed—the contrary is severely felt in the articles of peas and potatoes.

But, above all, corn is a profitable, the others a losing fallow crop. Young seldom or never makes his turnips or potatoes repay the expence of their cultivation, and all the proffit arises out of the following wheat crop. Now I have experienced that my crop of corn is usually worth three times as much as my crop of wheat in unmanured ground. Wheat invariably occupies all the ground occupied by this its predecessor, and besides I throw in all the potatoe, turnip—pea—cotton and clover lay ground. Yet I often sell one third of my corn for as much as the wheat, exclusive of seed, is worth, and the remaining two thirds chiefly subsist the estate.

If turnips and potatoes are losing crops in England, will they not be such here, as less adapted to our climate. Now corn is a native.

We seek after a vegitable proper for poor ground—it is found in corn; and if it succeeds in poor, how will it thrive in rich?

If 50 load of manure (unrotted) to the acre, is put on for corn and wheat, as for turnips or potatoes and wheat, 40 bushells of corn and 20 of wheat may be expected. Sixty bushells exceeds the European average. For I take the fodder, tops shucks, stalks, and husks of the corn, to ballance a fallow crop of turnips.

Corn if cultivated without hills, exhibits a fine plane for sowing wheat. And so it should be cultivated, because its roots form an intire web under the surface of the ground; by withdrawing earth from some, and piling it up on others, all are placed in an unnatural position. Besides, hills by precipitating water into currents, cause gullies, and they also throw off the grain into the lower and worst ground. This web as it decays becomes pabulum for the wheat.

The stalks of corn will make much more manure, than the straw of wheat, growing on the same fields. There is no loss of stubble. Cut and strewed twice a day on the farm pen, they are good food, are greedily gleaned, and presently secure a dry footing for the cattle in any weather. Before January they have much sap—straw has but little.

With the tops and rails is constructed an annual and itinerant cow-house in the shape of this figure—⌊⌋—open only to the south, contiguous to the place designed to be manured to save carriage, and having a lane of stakes and rails, leading to water.

In this farm pen are consumed the potatoes, turnips, hay, shucks, chaff, straw and stalks of the farm. The straw, by strewing it on the stalks, after they are trim'd—the other articles, in racks and troughs within the figure, under cover. Lastly, the covering of the house itself is greedily eaten, after the first of April, when it is no longer necessary.

About one acre is manured for every labourer male and female above 16 years old. In the same proportion fresh land is cleared, meadow ground excepted, of which only half as much can be achieved. And these two means combined with inclosing, bestow fertility so rapidly, that labour need not long be lost on exhausted ground. This is left to grow up in cedar and pine, and it does so with such haste, that it regenerates woodland, much faster than I have been able to open it. With you, locust, mulberry and briars would be more improving.

Corn has been considered as an impoverisher. The three shift system which is yet general, was the first improvement upon the old execrable no system. The perpetual rotation of this is, 1st. corn. 2d. wheat. 3d. pasture. The pasture commencing the moment the wheat is off, and being always surcharged. For above a century our lands have born this or a worse system without any manuring, and yet their impoverishment is attributed to corn. Something like it was lately general in Scotland in their outfield and infield. The latter received all the manure. The former is stated in a voluminous georgical work published in Scotland about 1772, to be sown in oats once in seven years—the product 5 to 8 bushells an acre. And corn did not cause this impoverishment.

But our climate is more genial. In the corn and wheat system, which I am endeavouring to defend, a good crop is taken one year in two, or two in four, instead of a bad one every seventh year; and yet I have experienced a great improvement in the soil, if inclosed, without manure. Young does not appear to have contemplated the possibility of such an event.

By resting the field two years and an half successively, the seeds of annuals sprout and perish, and do not infest the field when in culture—such as crab grass for instance. It becomes set with perennials—such as white clover and goose grass if the land is in heart, the roots and straw of which keep the land from washing whilst in fallow under corn.

If then land improves in this system without manure—if the system from its plentiful offal, is the best by which to raise manure—if the crops are the most valuable—if the worst land will give existence to new forests without planting or culture—and if labour and timber to a vast amount is saved, by excluding crop fences, is there not a happy coincidence of agricultural objects?

It is admited that your lands are better for wheat, and perhaps worse for corn than ours. This fact may weaken some of the foregoing observations, but is not I think strong enough to overturn my corn and wheat system.

It may perhaps be asked, why I do not manure for corn? The reply is, that the manure of the previous winter is not ready for removal at the time we must be preparing our corn ground. 'Tis not all made.

But there are other reasons. All manure according to my hypothesis, ought to be put on before it is roted. Vegitables by some hidden laboratory, convert the atmosphere into a solid form. They have a tendency to restore what they have absorbed. Should they rot in an exposed situation, they yield to this tendency by evaporation. Hence the virtue, as well as the bulk of manure, is greatly diminished. Yet fermentation will add to their virtue. By manuring potatoes in a large drill, in the spring, with my farm yard litter, and covering it with earth, the contiguity of the manure remains, so that fermentation goes on, and putrefaction ensues whilst the crop is growing; and the coat of earth imbibes those particles, which would otherwise evaporate; whereas by intermingling the long litter with the earth, the fermentation is destroyed, and putrefaction greatly delayed. To this cause I have attributed the superior improvement of ground manured for potatoes, in this way, which an accurate experiment upon a large scale, has clearly evinced.

My land where I live is hilly. By runing my potatoe drills across the face of the declivity, with a trowel hoed plow, and two mould boards, at three feet distance—placing the slips at bottom—and treading in the manure by covering it backwards, they serve as so many covered drains, and effectually prevent washing.

The disadvantages attending potatoes, are 1st., the great quantity of seed requis[ite—]ten bushells per acre is as little as ought to be planted. 2ly. the great labour of [. . .] planting the slips at four inches distance. 3ly. The time expended in the slow process of diging or plowing them up—by the latter mode there is a great loss. 4ly. They make no litter.

My crop last year was 105 bushells to the acre; the land exceeding poor, but aided by 48 load of the long manure to each acre.

My sheep will hardly eat the potatoes. Hogs will die upon them. They are good food for horses, but for cattle excellent. Where I live only 7 acres were grown. Seventeen old cattle were fed upon the potatoes and timothy hay. Eight were killed, some fine beef, the others good, without any change of food—and the rest were fed three weeks longer on turnips and potatoes alternately. 150 bushells yet remain. In this way I shall constantly use them.

But I shall extend my turnip culture, until that vegitable has a full trial, not as a rival to corn, but to potatoes. The saving of seed and of labour in planting is immense, but the food is extreamly bulky, and the least nutritive. An ox will eat his weight in 48 hours. The crop is less precarious than the potatoe crop, because it depends chiefly upon sowing at the lucky moment, for I have experienced no fall that will not make good turnips, sown at some season or other. About the 20th. of July succeedes oftenest. Now as seed is nothing, the dril husbandry enables an attentive man to hit the right season. He ought to sow the same land three times over, at three different periods, most proper in his judgment—these drills may be twelve inches—let him thin the most flourishing, and cut up either two or one at the first hand hoeing. I grow turnips three feet by nine inches, if the ground is strong; otherwise nearer.

In poor land I could never succeed. One year I sowed 20 acres in natural ground not poor, broadcast, for sheep pasturage—it failed, from the small size of the turnips only.

The last year I drilled two acres of good land in cotton—at its last hoeing turnips were drilled between the cotton—when the cotton was gathered, barley was sown between the turnips. The two first crops succeeded well—if the last does, three good crops will be gathered from the same ground within nine months. Clover will be sown on the barley this spring. With you a small white bean, which has no vine, might be substituted for the cotton.

Last year six acres of turnips were grown where I live, and the crop is good. Once only I have had a finer, one acre of which being measured, produced 1200 bushells.

The ground is always laid down in grain between the drills, for which, that cow pen'd after the farm pens are broken up, is best prepared by this crop. The sowing is the last working for the turnips.

My future purpose is, to erect the wandering farm pen within my corn field, where I design to manure. It will be convenient for collecting the fodder and stalks. So soon as the wheat following the corn is off, I will put on the manure, plow in that and the stubble together, and prepare the ground for turnips. Between the drills I will sow barley or wheat late, and I will feed off the turnips by pening sheep upon what they can eat in twelve hours. The grain being young will hardly be regarded by them as food, and it will not be trodden to death in 12 hours. A double dressing of manure will ensure a fine crop of grain, and noble crops of clover. But this is projecting—and I confess that I very often fail in my agricultural projects. An object in this project, will be, to avoid the loss of manure from its long exposure, and from crumbling it among the earth, so as to destroy its fermentation, and delay its putrefaction. Upon this point turnips must yield to potatoes, nor can the same quantity of manure invigorate as much land, in the culture of the former as of the latter.

To diminish the loss, I leave the manure undisturbed upon the farm yard, 'til it is to be removed—it is removed—spread—and plowed in as quickly as possible. Being trodden throughout the winter, it lies hard and compact between one and two feet thick. Hence it will ferment and putrify more rapidly, and is less pervious to the rays of the sun. To save it further, I cover it over very snugly with bushes, so as to shade it compleatly. This had a most happy affect last summer—but it is to be remarked, that the summer was singularly wet. The practice of the English farmers, not rejected even by Young, of diging over and over their manure, is in my way of thinking founded upon no principle. At every turning an immense stench and dense smoke arises. What are these but the finer particles of the manure—and does it not enrich the atmosphere for an universal, instead of the earth, for a particular benefit.

Permit me to express my doubts, whether sheep are to be prefered to cattle for feeding your negroes, or upon any other score. My observations hitherto upon sheep and cattle are as follow:

Sheep	Cattle
Of a dog like constitution liable to many fatal distempers	The most healthy domestic animal.
delicate—hard to fatten—pining on separation.	Hearty—consume the coarse food of a farm—easy to fatten—contented.
four will eat as much as a cow—fleece at 2/ each worth 8/ —	One produces more meat and tallow than 4 sheep—Skin worth raw 15/—but we cannot skin her annually.
Not proper for the farm pen, or to convert coarse litter into manure.	Will persevere throughout the winter in rearing manure, and two will furnish the means of enriching a whole acre.

Yield no milk cheese or butter.

A cow yields her value annually in manure—and also her value in milk, cheese and butter.

Yet I purpose to try sheep as a means of turning turnips into manure, and if it succeeds to extend that species of stock, but by no means to the diminution of my cattle; the flesh milk and butter of which constitute the principal food of my family.

Clover ought to be sown upon every spot which will produce it, but our lands will not produce it, without manure. All crops succeed after it. A fallow upon a clover lay, is the best chance for fine wheat that I have ever tried. The best, and I think the cheapest fallow of a clover lay, is to hill up the earth—deep—and hills large, at 3 feet 4 inches distance as if for tobacco—to let them lie 'til sowing time—to level the hills, and plough the wheat in deep without mould boards, smoothing the ground with a harrow.

After five years accurate trials of rye, the facts resulting in our soil and climate, are, 1st. That it never produces more than wheat to the acre. 2ly. Often less. 3ly. That it is a greater impoverisher. Wheat is more valuable.

In ameliorating crops without manure or rest, I have no confidence, and therefore if the clover remained tolerable, I believe that your land will be more [ben]efited by bestowing your seventh year upon that, than by any crop. It is my custom neither to cut or feed it the last year.

Nor have I any confidence of great benefit from plowing in green vegitables, having tried oats—rye—and buck wheat, without obtaining an improvement adequate to the expence.

I have tried a summer farm pen. The cattle were confined to as much cut clover as they could eat. The quantity was immense and the labour great. They were protected by arbours from the sun, and had free access to water; no litter except the wasted clover. They did not thrive, nor did I manure as fast as by the cow-pen. Because in the latter mode I move the pen every 7 or 10 days, and immediately turn the manure in, to save it from the depredations of the sun and air—in the former it was necessarily exposed for a much longer period—and the treading aided its evaporation. The litter of a farm may be advantageously exhausted in winter—And besides it is unsafe to keep wheat straw or chaff 'til the spring, if as I believe, the weevel is nurtured by the grains it retains.

Will not combined agricultural efforts be more efficacious, than successive? Several thousand men might have tug'd to this day in attempting to raise a column at Rome, had not a peasant cried out "wet the ropes."

Irrigation alone frightens me, and yet I cannot think of it, without being thrown into a fever. I have a farm of 1340 acres, to at least 1300 of which water might by proper cuts, be conducted. But the labour—the labour. If however my health regains any permanency, a part of the canvass at least, shall not remain long without some character of the kind.

Your mould board is at present the impliment I need most—for that and the succory seed, I shall not wait very patiently. I am trying what is called the white bent grass. Its appearance last summer promises much for hay and pasture—if it succeeds, you shall be furnished with the seed.

I am delighted with your idea of marking out your fields by peach trees. Fences of earth wood or stone, have been thought becoming. But lines, equally strong adorned with the ravishing plumage of spring, or teeming with the delicious fruits of summer, will interest even a clod, far beyond those unsentimental, because inanimate, circumvallations. If we had but time? Slower growing trees might be introduced, and the scenery greatly diversified. Your thought converts the weary tread of hard labour, into a long range for pleasure, and a delicious and abundant repast for the most innocent of human appetites. It does not even lose sight of considerable proffit.

In several instances I have very freely differed from your system, without fealing a disagreeable sensation, because of my conviction that you are in this, and in all other cases, abstractedly in search of truth. And therefore to you Sir I shall make no apology for it.

But the reciprocation of ideas, by which I must be the gainer, is a benefit, which I meant to recognize by a hope, that out of the abundance of matter something retributory might be gleaned. Such is my motive for the length of this letter. It is not intended as a draft upon you for future favors; for altho' I acknowledge the pleasure and edification which I derive from a communication of your ideas, yet such a gratification occasionally is all the spoil which my utmost vanity would lead me to commit, upon time, in which mankind are so deeply interested. With the greatest respect & esteem, I am, Your friend   JOHN TAYLOR

RC (DLC); margin frayed; endorsed by TJ as received 21 Mch. 1795 and so recorded in SJL.

Arthur YOUNG had bestowed HIGH ENCOMIUMS ON MAIZE in his *Travels, during The Years 1787, 1788, and 1789. Undertaken more particularly with a View of ascertaining the Cultivation, Wealth, Resources, and National Prosperity of the Kingdom of France* (Bury Saint Edmunds, 1792), 301. See also Sowerby, No. 744.

To Joshua Fry

DEAR SIR   Monticello Mar. 8. 95

Your favor of Feb. 25. came to hand ten days ago. I mentioned, if you recollect, that Hopkins would come here if [three] persons would take each of them a patent licence (at £50.) [each?] or if one would undertake the business on partnership account. The former was what I should have undertaken, as I meditated to have the whole benefit proceeding from my own timber. Since you were here, Mr. [Stewart] was with me, and being in a similar situation with yourself, is about determining to engage in the same business, if a third can be found. I will then immediately write to Hopkins to come at the time they shall chuse. I have had some conversation with Mr. Wilson Nicholas on the subject, who is in your situation also, having much land to clear. The idea was new to him but he seemed to like it. Should a third offer here, I will let you know it. Should you find a third, let me know it, and I will write immediately. I am with great esteem Dr. Sir Your friend & servt   TH: JEFFERSON

PrC (MHi); badly blurred and faded; at foot of text: "Joshua Fry esq."

Joshua Fry (b. ca. 1760), the grandson and namesake of the surveyor and College of William and Mary professor who collaborated with TJ's father in preparing the 1751 Fry-Jefferson map of Virginia, was a teacher and Revolutionary War veteran who represented Albemarle County for one term in the House of Delegates, 1785-86, and moved shortly thereafter to Kentucky (Slaughter, *Fry*, 42; WMQ, 1st ser., X [1902], 259; Swem and Williams, *Register*, 21; Charles Kerr, William E. Connelley, and E. M. Coulter, *History of Kentucky*, 5 vols. [Chicago, 1922], I, 306).

Fry's FAVOR OF FEB. 25., recorded in SJL as received two days later, has not been found.

From Giuseppe Ceracchi

SIR   Philadelphia 9 March 1795

Agriculture been the support of every action; I should be sorry to occasion any waste of your time at the expence of the rular occupation. The bust is ordered to be shipped to Richmond directed to Mr. Gramble Merchant, which shall forward it to Monticello; I hope it will be find caracteristick of what it is maent, and be tolerated in what it may be want, the elevation of it should be upon a stending 4 feet high, and covered the lower part of the windows, for to obtaine some effect.

I am no doubtedly happy in this country because I dont fear persecution for my principles but in other respects I find some inconviniences; house kiping excessive dear, the Laws in favour of servants have deprived me of three of them that I brought over, which disconcerted my family very much. America is good for Merchants, farmers, and for those that have nothing to posses; I am out of thises articles; To exstablishing my self in the Federal City; permit me Sir to expose with the usual ingenuity that it would be contrary to the profession I follow, and here I shall make a digression.

Artists must live where there imagination can be costantely at work in composing the Vast Nature of whose beutys there are to be the translators; I dont restraine my self in the mere beuty of regular forms but comprehende Stile, Caracter, and expression, of every age of the both Sexes. Therfore an artist Living in a depopulated place would deprive his imagination of the nourishments, and resurces to set at work the springs of the soul and genius, let us consider the lifes of ancients and modern Artist, whe will find them always in the must brillant Cities, where there speculative mind observing and studing every class of people in publicks spectacles, games and exercises, relived there self in the solitude of there atterlier to discorge there pregnant mind and impresses with there chissel the purest exst[acy?] upon the blocks of marbre.

But you will find Sir that I agree with you in respect of adorning the Federal City with Magnificent Monument of the plan of which you will be better informed by your Friends. The Subjet I exibit is the most purest and sublime which I imagined in the moment of prosecution; then my exile from my Mother Contry was necessary for to fixe the glorious Statue of Liberty. I reppresent this Goddess Standing on her car darting through a volume of clouds; in her wright hand brandiches a flaming dart dispelling the mist of Error, her left calling upon the People of America, her head covered with the Pileus, and adorned with long flotting hear, the bent brow expressing the energy of her caracter, and from her lips partely open burst the echoes of her awful voice through the vault of heaven in favor of the rights of Man.

I glorify with this idea because as been approuved and find it grand by every man of wit, in Urope as well as in America. If the project now in motion scould succeede, Paris must be the place of its execution, in America would cost twoice as much, and considering only the [. . .] it will prove impossible, for want of graet number of different articles wich would stop the performance at every moment. I shall be happy if you find some reason in what I have expressed, and can give farther explanations, when I shall have the honour to come and see you at Monticello. May this Spot alrady renowned unite the Celebration of those of Cincinnatus, Cicero, and Oratius. With sentiments of full veneration and respect, I am Your Most Obe Serv and Fr'd   J. CERACCHI

RC (DLC); with one word illegible and another partially obscured by tape; addressed: "The Honble. Tomas Jefferson Esqr Monticello"; franked and postmarked; endorsed by TJ as received 25 Mch. 1795, with date of letter mistakenly interpreted by TJ as 4 Mch. 1795 and thus entered in SJL.

Ceracchi's PLAN for a monument to the American Revolution is contained in *A Description of the Monument Consecrated to Liberty* (DLC: Washington Papers; being one page of a three-page broadside printed on verso of a letter from Washington and sixty others, including members of Congress and present and former members of the Cabinet, to Secretary of State Edmund Randolph, 14 Feb. 1795, asking him to organize the subscription for the proposed monument in his private capacity and enclosing the third page consisting of "Articles of Subscription" of the same date signed by Washington and five others, including the four members of the Cabinet).

To John Mason

DEAR SIR   Monticello Mar. 11. 95.

So long ago as June 29. of the last year I inclosed you a draught on Caleb Lownes of Philadelphia for 92 D–80 c the amount of my balance to Mason & Fenwick, and desired Mr. Lownes to answer it out of monies placed in his hands. I was surprised yesterday, on receiving an account from him to find that the money still lies in his hands uncalled for. Apprehending my letter must have miscarried, tho' sent to you at George-town by post, I take the liberty of repeating the information to you that the money is and has been constantly at your order in the hands of Caleb Lownes. I shall be sorry if any miscarriage of my letter shall have left me in the mean time under the imputation of having neglected the paiment of this balance. I am with great esteem Dr. Sir Your most obedt. servt   TH: JEFFERSON

RC (NjMoHP: Lloyd W. Smith Collection); addressed: "Mr. John Mason Mercht. Georgetown on Patowmac"; endorsed by Mason as answered 23 Mch. 1795.

TJ's letter of JUNE 29. OF THE LAST YEAR to Fenwick, Mason & Company, recorded in SJL but not found, was a reply to a missing letter from the firm of 9 Apr. 1794, recorded in SJL as received from Georgetown on 6 May 1794. Mason's missing 23 Mch. 1795 response to the present letter is recorded in SJL as received from Georgetown on 31 Mch. 1795. Letters from Mason to TJ of 24 May 1796, 2 Dec. 1796, and 17 Mch. 1797, received on 3 June 1796, 10 Dec. 1796, and 3 Apr. 1797, respectively (the first and third from Georgetown), and from TJ to Mason of 5 June 1796, 11 Mch. 1797, and 23 Apr. 1800 (the last "by Mr. Barnes"), are all recorded in SJL but have not been found.

To Henry Remsen

DEAR SIR   Monticello Mar. 11. 1795.

I have duly recieved your favor of Feb. 3. and have to acknolege the safe receipt of the gongs, and thank you for your care of them. The threshing machine was also safely received very long ago, and I thought I had acknoleged it.—I am engaged in a nail manufactory, which I carry on altogether with my own boys, and am enlarging it as more and more of these grow up. I have 9 now at work, and in the course of the year shall have 16. under the care of a smith of my own, so that I have not a single hired hand. My proper object then you will observe is to confine myself to those branches of the nail business, which being beyond the performance of the cutting machine, has no competition but from human labor. In this the cheapness of my means gives me the advantage of others. Possibly I may hereafter proceed to employ my grown smiths in the cutting process. If I should propose to do it, perhaps I may trouble you for further information on the subject. Indeed I would be glad to know the cost of the cutting and heading machines, and of the right to use them if under a patent. I could employ a cutter and 3. headers of my own conveniently enough.—I remember you once told me you had a purpose of going into some branch of commerce. Did you do it, and what branch? It might happen that I might at some times send or carry grist to the mill, which it would give me very great pleasure to do, or to serve you in any other way in my power. I am with great esteem Dr. Sir Your sincere friend & servt   Th: Jefferson

P.S. The prices current at your market, and particularly of nail rod, and castings will always be an acceptable post-script to your letters.

RC (NjP: Andre DeCoppet Collection); at foot of text: "Mr. Remsen"; with postscript written lengthwise in left margin.

Remsen's letter of FEB. 3, recorded in SJL as received 25 Feb. 1795, has not been found. NAIL MANUFACTORY: see note to TJ to Caleb Lownes, 18 Dec. 1793.

To William Champe Carter

Dear Sir   Monticello Mar. 15. 95.

Having understood that you were disposed to sell the lands between Colo. Monroe's and the Blenheim tract, and being desired to purchase a tract for a friend of mine, I took the liberty of going to examine them. I need say nothing to you of the condition of those cleared, or the quality of the uncleared, of which you are doubtless well apprised. On a full examination of them, I think they will but justify me in giving the price which Colo. Monroe gave for his, that is to say 23/ per acre, this being more than such lands in this neighborhood had before sold at. I should pay three thousand dollars cash, on the presumption that there is as much land within the limits pointed out to me, as would amount to that. The surplus, if on actual survey, there should be found more, should be paid on very short notice after the survey. When I speak of cash however, I must explain myself. The means of paiment put into my hands are public stock. I should in the instant of confirming the bargain send as much of this as would raise 3000. Dollars to a broker in Philadelphia, and give you at the same time a draught on him at six weeks sight, or as much earlier as he should find it advantageous to sell the stock, that term being taken to prevent the necessity of selling were there to be a momentary depression of the price of stock. Should this offer meet your approbation, I will thank you for a definitive answer by the first or second post, as I learn that I might purchase a convenient tract in another quarter. With compliments to Mrs. Carter and esteem to yourself I am Dear Sir your most obedt. servt.   TH: JEFFERSON

P.S. I beg leave to observe that good draughts on Philadelphia, under 60. days date, command cash at Richmond, at par, and that Mr. Pollard, broker of that place, as being already acquainted with the grounds of the draught I propose, would satisfy any purchaser of its solidity.

PrC (DLC: William Short Papers); badly faded and extensively overwritten in ink by TJ; postscript written perpendicularly in left margin; at foot of text: "Champe Carter esq."; endorsed in ink by TJ.

William Champe Carter, the great-grandson of Robert "King" Carter and the son of Edward Carter, a prominent planter, public official, and proprietor of Blenheim in Albemarle County before his death in 1792, was himself the owner of the Dicks and Wheelers plantations in TJ's native county (VMHB, XLIV, [1936], 352-3; Woods, Albemarle, 163-4). For the LANDS that TJ purchased from Carter for his FRIEND William Short, see TJ to Short, 25 May 1795.

From George Washington

DEAR SIR   Philadelphia March 15th 1795.

I received your letter of the 23d. ulto.; but not at so early a period as might have been expected from the date of it.

My mind has always been more disposed to apply the shares in the inland navigations of Potomac and James River (which were left to my disposal by the legislature of Virginia) towards the endowment of a *University* in the U States, than to any other object it had contemplated. In pursuance of this idea, and understanding that other means were in embryo, for establishing so useful a seminary in the federal city; I did, on the 20th.[1] of Jany. last, announce to the Commrs. thereof, my intention of vesting, in perpetuity, the fifty shares I hold under that act in the navigation of Potomac; as an additional mean of carrying the plan into effect; provided, it should be adopted upon a scale so liberal, and so extensive, as to embrace a *compleat* system of education.

I had but little hesitation in giving the federal dist. a preferrence of all other places for this Institution, and[2] for the following reasons 1st. on account of its being the permanent seat of the government of this Union, and where the laws and policy of it must be better understood than in any local part thereof. 2d, because of its centrality. 3d, because one half (or near it) of the district of Columbia, is within the Commonwealth of Virginia; and the whole of the state not inconvenient thereto. 4th, because as *part* of the endowment, it would be useful; but *alone*, would be inadequate to the end. 5th, because many advantages, I conceive, would result from the Jurisdiction which the general government will have over it, which no other spot would possess. And lastly, as this Seminary is contemplated for the *completion* of education, and study of the sciences (not for boys in their rudiments) it will afford the Students an opportunity of attending the debates in Congress, and thereby becoming more liberally, and better acquainted with the principles of law, and government.

My judgment and my wishes point equally strong to the application of the James River shares to the same object, at the same place; but considering the source from whence they were derived, I have, in a letter I am writing to the Executive of Virginia on this subject, left the application of them to a Seminary, *within the state*, to be located by the Legislature.

Hence you will perceive that I have, in a degree, anticipated your proposition. I was restrained from going the whole length of the suggestion, by the following considerations: 1st, I did not know to what extent, or when any plan would be so matured for the establishment of an University, as would enable any assurance to be given to the application of Mr. D'Ivernois. 2d, the propriety of transplanting the Professors in a *body*, might be questioned for several reasons; among others, because they might not be all good characters; nor all sufficiently acquainted with our language; and again, having been at varience with the levelling party of their own country, the measure might be considered as an aristocratical movement by more than those who, without any just cause that I have been able to discover, are continually sounding the alarm [3] bell of aristocracy. And 3d, because it might preclude some of the first Professors in other countries from a participation; among whom some of the most celebrated characters in Scotland, in this line, I am told [4] might be obtained.

Something, but of what nature I am unable to inform you, has been written by Mr. Adams to Mr. D'Ivernois. Never having viewed my intended donation as more than a part of the means, that was to set this establishment afloat; I did not incline to go too far in the incouragement of Professors before the plan should assume a more formal [5] shape—much less to induce an entire College to migrate. The enclosed is the answer I have received from the Commissioners: from which, and the ideas I have here expressed, you will be enabled to decide on the best communication to be made to Mr. D'Ivernois.

My letter to the Commissioners has bound me to the fulfilment of what is therein engaged; and if the legislature of Virginia, in considering the subject, should view it in the same light I do, the James River shares will be added thereto; for I think one good Institution of this sort, is to be preferred[6] to two imperfect ones; which, without other aids than the shares in *both* navigations, is more likely to fall through, than to succeed upon the plan I contemplate. Which, in a few words, is to supercede the necessity of sending the youth of this country abroad, for the purpose of education (where too often principles and habits not friendly to a republican government[7] are imbibed, which are not easily discarded) by instituting such an one of our own, as will answer the end; and by associating them in the same seminary, contribute to wear off those prejudices, and unreasonable jealouses, which prevent or[8] weaken friendships, and impair the harmony of the Union. With very great esteem & regard I am—Dear Sir Your Obedt. & Affectionate

GO: WASHINGTON

PS. Mr. Adams laid before me the communications of Mr. D'Ivernois; but I said nothing to him of my intended donation towards the establishment of a University in the Federal District. My wishes would be to fix this on the Virga. side of the Potomac, therein;[9] but this would not embrace—or accord with those other means which are proposed for this establishment.

RC (DLC); at foot of first page: "Thomas Jefferson Esqr."; endorsed by TJ as received 7 Apr. 1795 and so recorded in SJL. PrC (DLC: Washington Papers). FC (Lb in same); with variations, only the most important being noted below. Enclosure: Commissioners of the Federal District to Washington, Washington, 18 Feb. 1795, stating that they agree with the need for a national university expressed in his 28 Jan. 1795 letter; that they hope he will personally inspect and approve the site they have chosen for one; that some donations for the national university have been subscribed and more can be expected when his support for it becomes known to the public; that they have received partial plans for the national university, but no general plan has been forthcoming, although they learned some time ago that William Thornton had long been contemplating one for submission to the Executive and had made some progress in it; that they will solicit and receive donations for the national university, despite their lack of authorization from Congress and the Maryland legislature; that the Maryland legislature will pass the requisite legislation when necessary because of the national university's obvious utility to the state; that they hope their efforts will be considered as part of "a work in which United America are equally concerned until Sufficient Sums are collected to erect the necessary buildings and insure success to the object"; and that they will discuss their ideas more fully when they meet with Washington during his expected visit in March (RC in same, in a clerk's hand, signed by Daniel Carroll, Gustavus Scott, and William Thornton; FC in DNA: RG 42, DCLB).

Washington's letter to the Commissioners of the Federal District of 28 JANY. LAST (see note 1 below) is in Fitzpatrick, *Writ-*

ings, XXXIV, 106-8. His letter of 16 Mch. 1795 to the EXECUTIVE OF VIRGINIA is in same, 149-51. See also Freeman, *Washington*, VII, 231-2n.

[1] FC: "28th."—the correct date.
[2] Preceding four words interlined.

[3] Word, omitted in FC, interlined.
[4] Preceding three words omitted in FC.
[5] Preceding two words interlined.
[6] Washington here canceled "much."
[7] Preceding six words interlined.
[8] Preceding two words interlined.
[9] FC: "river."

From William Champe Carter

DEAR SIR   Williamsburg 19th. March [1795]

I have received your favour of the 15th. instant and immediately replied. From the offer you have made I think it almost certain we shall bargain. I will take for a part of the land between Colo. Monroe's and the Blenheim tract 24/ per acre, the line of division to begin on the top of the mountain, thence runing paralel with Monroe's to the back line. Permit me to observe that the quality of this land is generally supposed superior to Monroe's and that its price exceeds what he gave only by six pence in the acre. If you are disposed to accept these terms I shall be ready to confirm the contract on the first of next month at which time I intend visiting Albemarle. With respects to the family at Monticello—I remain Dr. Sir yr. ob Servant   WILLIAM CHAMPE CARTER

RC (DLC: William Short Papers); endorsed by TJ as received 31 Mch. 1795 and so recorded in SJL.

From Tench Coxe

DEAR SIR   Philadelphia March 20th. 1795

I take the opportunity by Mr. Madison to transmit to you a copy of a collection of papers which one of our printers has lately published and of which I request you will do me the honor to accept. They may assist to shew foreigners, our young people, and those, who have been out of the way of seeing for themselves, some of the considerable facts, which have affected the political and private affairs of this country, since the year 1786.

You may add to the public Documents, that the 4th. year of exports, ending on the 30th. September 1794, have run up (by the returns now actually received) to a little more than thirty *three* millions of Dollars. If this be partly owing to the depreciation of money, it is felt much in the prices of produce, and of land, and will therefore, tend to relieve the indebted parts of the United States if they shall be prudent.

I am very anxious to hear the Event of the final [Collection] of the combined forces in the Province of Guelders or Utrecht about the beginning of this Year. I wish the french may have been prepared for such an Event, and I hope the people of the United Netherlands will be active in making good that revolution to which they are impelled by every solid consideration.

The unfortunate Poles have been thrown back in the course of freedom, in part, I fear, from the fatal error of attempting a Revolution, by any other means than the aggregate powers of the people.

I do not find that Great Britain has been very lavish in solid tokens of friendship, from any thing I can learn of the treaty, nor has she been precipitate in her Manner of bringing them forward. Whether she has bestowed liberal favors, or only a part of Justice has been obtained, there appears to me dispositions to procrastinate, to temporize, and if possible to pass from her the unpleasant cup. I have not however any regular information. The form of obtaining reimbursement, the West India Tonnage, and time of giving up the posts are so uniformly spoken of, that I consider the public as probably possessed of the greater part of the truth on those points. It is asserted too, that the treaty extends to 12 years, for the European, and four for the West India Dominions of Great Britain.

I am apprehensive that the french, perceiving how all [impor]tant to the British our trade now is, and sensible of the convenience which the British exports to the United States would afford them, will follow the example of England in carrying in our Vessels to and from British ports. Such a stroke would produce great disorder in England, Ireland and Scotland now that the french, flemish, Spanish, Germans and Dutch commerce are lost to them, or much deranged. It would also produce most serious consequences here. I hope it will not occur. I have the honor to be, with great respect, dear Sir, Your most obedient and humble Servant,

TENCH COXE

RC (DLC); in a clerk's hand, with emendations and signature by Coxe; words torn away supplied in brackets from Dft. Dft (PHi: Coxe Papers). Recorded in SJL as received 24 May 1795. Enclosure: Tench Coxe, *A View of the United States of America, in a Series of Papers, Written at Various Times, between the Years 1787 and 1794* (Philadelphia, 1794). See Sowerby, No. 3632.

From François D'Ivernois

MONSIEUR   Londres ce 21e Mars 1795

Il y a deja précisement six mois que j'ai eu l'honneur de m'adresser à vous en faveur de mes malheureux compatriotes,[1] et l'impatience avec la quelle j'attens encore, tant de vous Monsieur, que de Mr. Adams, une premiere réponse à mes lettres n'est pour ainsi dire calmée[2] que par l'espérance légitime dont je me nourris,[3] que vous etes l'un et l'autre occupés des moyens d'accœuillir la transplantation de notre Université; car j'ai droit de croire, que si vous aviez envisagé d'entrée cette transplantation comme impraticable ou douteuse, vous vous seriez empressés de m'en faire part, et de détruire une illusion qui tient mes compatriotes dans une suspension[4] dont il me presse d'etre à meme de les tirer.

Mr. Jay, à qui j'ai representé hier tout ce que cette suspension avait de pénible, n'a pas hézité à me conseiller d'inviter mes compatriotes à se former immédiatement en Compagnie d'Actionaires, la quelle nommerait des Commissaires qui partiraient sans délai pour l'Amérique, où ils mettraient la premiere main à notre établissement s'il y est deja-adopté, donneraient sur les lieux les éclaircissemens qu'on peut désirer pour cette adoption définitive, ou finalement y renonceraient s'il leur était prouvé qu'aucune Province d'Amérique n'est disposée à faire les sacrifices nécessaires pour la transplantation en masse de notre Université.

Je viens de faire passer cet avis à mes correspondans en joignant à cet égard mes instances à celles de Mr. Jay. J'ai lieu de croire qu'ils y adhéreront, sans se laisser retenir par ce qu'une pareille mission semblerait avoir d'hazardeux, et S'ils suivent mes conseils, ils nommeront des Commissaires qui se mettront immédiatement en route. Mais quelqu'accéléré que puisse etre leur départ; il ne pourra gueres avoir lieu que vers la fin de May, et s'ils n'arrivent en Amérique que vers la fin de Juillet, ils y trouveront le Congrès deja levé ainsi que toutes les Législatures Provinciales, et des lors toute négociation prompte leur serait encore fermée, à moins que soit le Congrès, soit votre Législature n'eussent deja adopté mes propositions ou nommé quelque Comité pour les examiner, et pour procéder aux mesures nécessaires pour les mettre en exécution.

Dans la double supposition que quelque résolution de ce genre n'eut pas encore été prise, et que la Législature de Virginie mit cependant quelque prix à l'acquisition de notre Université; je viens Monsieur, vous prier de l'engager à ne point se lever, sans avoir nommé quelque Comité chargé des pouvoirs suffisans pour s'occuper de cette affaire dès l'arrivée de nos Commissaires, et meme pour prendre vis à vis d'eux soit des engagemens positifs, soit des engagemens qui n'auraient besoin que de la ratification de votre Législature.

Je vous prie encore de vouloir bien addresser de ma part la meme priere à Mr. Adams pour ce qui concerne le Congrès; car je ne puis quelquefois m'empécher de croire qu'il est dans les probabilités politiques, que la Législature de Virginie pourra s'associer avec le Gvt.

fœdératif pour placer notre Université dans les environs de la ville Fœderative, et pour concourir à lui former la dot nécessaire à sa fondation et à ses succès.

En effet Monsieur, plus j'étudie la Situation Géographique qui pourrait le mieux convenir à notre Université pour nous et par cela meme pour l'Amérique; et plus je suis tenté de fixer mes regards vers les environs de la Ville Fœderative, c'est à dire vers le Nord de la Virginie, où votre Province n'a point d'établissement pareil, et qui offrirait en meme tems une espèce de situation centrale tant pour les deux Carolines qui en manquent, que pour la plupart des autres Provinces des Etats Unis. A ce grand avantage géographique, me sembleraient se réunir ici d'autres avantages moraux et politiques qui n'échapperont sans doute ni à votre pénétration ni à votre patriotisme. L'Amérique libre a fondé une Ville fœdérative: Pourquoi ne fonderait-elle pas en meme tems une Université Fœdérative? S'il était possible qu'elle eut deja quelques légers symptomes de la grande maladie de tous les Corps politiques, c'est à dire des petites jalousies de Provinces à Provinces, des rivalités secretes d'Etat à Etat, si ses philosophes redoutent que ces rivalités ne prennent de nouvelles racines dans la disposition qu'ont les habitans de chaque province à élever leurs enfans dans les Académies qui sont dans l'enceinte de leur Province; ne serait-il pas digne de l'attention du Gouvernement fœdératif qui leur appartient à toutes également,[5] de leur donner un nouveau lien par la fondation d'une nouvelle Université, la quelle n'appartenant précisement à aucune d'elles, mais au centre de toutes, attirerait des plus riches[6] d'entr'elles cette partie de la jeunesse Américaine capable des sacrifices nécessaires pour achever son éducation, et où cette jeunesse, plus particulierement destinée aux affaires publiques par son éducation et par sa fortune, aurait l'avantage de briser les préjugés provinciaux, de former dès l'age le plus tendre ces liaisons vraiment patriotiques, qui attachent le Sud au Nord, et qui se prolongeraient pendant toute la durée de leur carriere politique? L'avantage immense et durable de ces intimes rélations d'enfance entre tous les membres épars d'un vaste Corps politique, est bien digne ce me semble de fixer les regards d'une République naissante, et en effet Monsieur, si vous jettez votre œil scrutateur sur la réunion prolongée de l'Irlande à l'Angleterre, et sur l'extreme fragilité des liens artificiels qui les ont unies jusqu'ici, vous donnerez un grand poid sans doute à une observation que j'ai souvent entendu faire; c'est que l'éducation que les jeunes Irlandais de fortune, et apelés à influer chez eux, viennent depuis longtems recevoir à Oxford et à Cambridge, les affilie bien plus intimement à la Grande Bretagne que toutes les autres mesures qu'a adopté celle ci, sans avoir peut etre jamais songé à celle à la quelle je l'attribue.

Sous ce rapport encore Monsieur, notre titre d'*Université Etrangere* loin d'etre une objection serait plutot un avantage, puisqu'il nous mettrait d'autant mieux dès notre fondation à l'abri du reproche de préférence que les Universités des différentes Provinces pourraient etre tentées d'élever, si on accordait à l'une d'entrelles plus qu'aux autres; tandis que d'un autre coté par la facilité qu'aurait la jeunesse des Etats Unis, d'acquérir les langues vivantes dans notre Université, plutot Américaine que Provinciale, celle ci[7] offrirait un attrait aux jeunes gens qui en quittant les autres Universités pourraient venir s'établir chez nous au moins une année, et y contracter ensembles de nouvelles rélations dans l'age où le cœur est le plus ouvert aux affections de l'amitié.

Si ces considérations, non moins politiques que morales, frappaient également le Congrès et votre Province, serait-il donc impossible Monsieur, que ce premier nous assignat quelque position convenable et salubre à une distance plus ou moins grande de la ville Fœderative, qu'il fit en quelque maniere de notre Université, l'Université Fœdérative de l'amérique, et qu'enfin chacune de ses Provinces vit avec un égal plaisir les secours que lui tendrait le Congrès, et aux quels la Virginie concourrait sans doute, puisqu'alors, sans lui appartenir exclusivement, nous serions du moins dans son enceinte, et nous regarderions sa jeunesse comme nous appartenant?

Si une pareille idée pouvait etre adoptée, j'y mettrais un tel prix que je n'heziterais pas en pareil cas, à conseiller à mes compatriotes de se borner à une acquisition de 10, à 30,000 acres dans une position salubre et sur les bords d'une riviere navigable;[8] dussent-ils appliquer (mais comme simple placement d'argent) le reste de leurs Capitaux à l'achat d'autres terres éloignées que le Congrès pourrait leur vendre, et où il trouverait une partie du Capital dont les interets seraient destinés à la dot de l'Université Fœdérative. Mais encore, pour l'exécution meme de cette idée, qui faciliterait singulierement celle de la totalité du plan,[9] il est tres important qu'il autorise avant la levée de sa séance actuelle ( ) quelques uns de ses membres[10] pour procéder soit vis à vis de nos Commissaires à une pareille vente, soit avec le Comité de votre Législature pour déterminer la quotepart pour la quelle la Virginie devrait contribuer à la fondation d'un pareil établissement.

Vous me trouverez Monsieur, en quelque maniere dévancé dans ces idées dans la lettre incluse que je prens le parti de vous envoyer en

( ) C'est en considération de l'extrème importance de la nomination d'un pareil Comité, (s'il n'est pas deja appointé par le Congrès) que je prens la liberte Monsieur, de vous prier de donner incessamment communication de cette lettre à Mr. Adams, vû que la *Becky* qui la prend part ce soir, et qu'il ne partira de quelque tems aucun vaisseau soit pour Philadelphie soit pour New York.

original. Elle est de l'un de nos anciens Magistrats frere de Mr. le Prof. Pictet, presque non moins distingué que lui dans la carriere des sciences, et qui jouit chez nous d'une confiance si universelle et si méritée, que si, comme je l'espere, il consent à etre nommé l'un des Commissaires, il ne me restera rien à désirer pour un pareil choix. Vous y verrez aussi par la maniere dont il s'applique et réussit à écrire l'Anglais, que la difficulté de cette langue ne sera pas longtems un obstacle insurmontable pour notre petite Colonie.

Vous y verrez aussi Monsieur, que mes amis tiennent encore un peu à l'idée de placer leur établissement agricole au centre de quelque District considérable de terres à eux appartenant et reculé sur les derrieres. Mais à cette idée que j'avais concouru moi meme à leur donner, j'ai bientot préféré celle d'acquérir en commun des terres pareilles mais non pour les habiter, et de nous fixer sur d'autres plus couteuses peut etre, mais[11] que nous acquererions dans quelque situation plus rapprochée de la mer ou du moins des rivieres qui y conduisent: et je ne doute pas que les considérations que je leur ai présentées à ce sujet, et qui portent également sur l'avantage de notre Université comme sur l'importance de ne point nous en détacher, n'ayent quelque poid sur eux.

Le Prof. Pictet[12] m'écrit aussi qu'il a remis à Mr. Adet, le nouveau Ministre de France en Amérique[13] une lettre pour vous Monsieur, et que ce Ministre, sans etre dans notre secret, lui a cependant promis de lui faire passer des renseignemens sur l'Amérique. Il est assez bizarre que tandis que les Machinations de soulavie Nous ont arraché à notre ancienne patrie, la commisération de son Successeur le pousse à nous en ouvrir une nouvelle. Au reste, tout ce qui me fait plaisir dans cette disposition de sa part, c'est qu'elle prouve évidemment que la France ne mettra aucune opposition à notre départ et à nous laisser traverser son territoire. J'ai l'honneur d'etre avec respect Monsieur, Votre tres humble & tres obéissant serviteur   F D'IVERNOIS

RC (MHi: Adams Papers); at foot of first page: "A Monsieur Jefferson." Dupl (same); in a clerk's hand, with "*Duplicata*" at head of text, complimentary close, and signature by D'Ivernois; endorsed by John Adams; contains numerous variations, only the most important being recorded below. FC (BPUG: D'Ivernois Papers); undated, unsigned, and unaddressed; only the most important variations are recorded below. The Dupl and FC have a symbol within the parentheses indicating the author's note. Recorded in SJL as received 26 May 1795. Enclosure not found. RC presumably enclosed in TJ to Adams, 27 May 1795; Dupl presumably enclosed in D'Ivernois to Adams, 28 Mch. 1795 (MHi: Adams Papers).

FRERE DE MR. LE PROF. PICTET: Charles Pictet de Rochement, brother of Marc Auguste Pictet, whose LETTRE POUR VOUS is printed above at 1 Jan. 1795 (Karmin, *D'Ivernois*, 278n).

[1] Dupl here adds "fugitifs."
[2] Preceding six words interlined.
[3] Dupl here adds "que ce délai même est une preuve."
[4] D'Ivernois here canceled "pénible."
[5] Word omitted in Dupl and FC.

[6] Preceding two words interlined in place of "de la plupart."

[7] Clause from the semicolon to this point in Dupl and FC: "et que par la facilité d'y acquérir les langues vivantes elle."

[8] Dupl and FC here add "dût cette acquisition etre plus couteuse qu'une Situation plus éloignee et moins centrale, et."

[9] Dupl and FC here add "S'il est vrai que le Congrès ait Suspendu la vente de ses terres."

[10] Dupl and FC here add "à entrer en négociation."

[11] Preceding five words omitted in Dupl and FC.

[12] Dupl: "Le frere de M. Pictet." FC: "Le frere de M.   ."

[13] Preceding seven words omitted in FC.

From James Madison

DEAR SIR   Philada. Mar. 23. 1795

Your two last favors contained, one of them the letter for Mr. Christie, which has been sent to him; the other accompanied the letters to the President and Mr. Randolph. The two latter were duly delivered also. The President touched on the subject the other day in conversation with me, and has no doubt written to you on it. There are difficulties I perceive in the way of your suggestion, besides the general one arising from the composition of the scientific body, *wholly* out of foreign materials. Notwithstanding the advantages which might weigh in the present case, against this objection, I own that I feel its importance. It was not sufficient however to induce me to withold your remarks from the P. as your letter would have authorised me to do.[1] Whilst I am acknowledging your favors, I am reminded of a passage in a former one, which I had proposed to have answered at some length. Perhaps it will be best, at least for the present to say in brief, that reasons of *every* kind, and some of them, of the most *insuperable* as well as *obvious* kind, shut my mind against[2] the admission of any idea such as you seem to glance at. I forbear to say more, because I can have no more to say with respect to myself; and because the great deal that may and ought to be said beyond that restriction will be best reserved for some other occasion, perhaps for the latitude of a free conversation. You ought to be preparing yourself however to hear truths, which no inflexibility will be able to withstand.

I have already told you of my failure to get from E.R. one of your books which has slipped out of his memory as well as his hands. I have since after repeated applications got from Wilson Houdon's Fleta Bracton &c. Mably, he says, he lent to Gallitine with your permission. This was not mentioned however till very lately; and Gallatine is at present in N.Y. As soon as he returns I will renew my efforts. I have procured for you "The Sketches on rotations,"[3] which I find to be truly a good thing. It was written by Mr. Boardly. The other publications referred to in p. 43. are not to be had at the Booksellers. I propose, if an opportunity offers, to get them thro' some friend who can carry the enquiry to the author himself. I have also procured you the correspondences with Hammond &c. All these with some other things deemed worth your possessing, I shall pack up for a conveyance by water to Richd. addressing them to the Merchant there from Staunton, whose name I cannot at this moment recollect.

The Treaty with England arrived soon after the adjournment. It is kept an impenetrable secret by the Executive. The Senate are Summoned to meet it the 8th. of June. I wish it may not be of a nature to bring us into some delicacies with France, without obtaining fully our objects from G.B. The French it is said are latterly much less respectful than heretofore to our rights on the seas. We have no late private letters from Monroe. His last public ones were no later than Novr. 20. They contained a History of the Jacobin clubs, in the form of an apology for the Convention. Extracts on that subject were immediately put into the Newspapers, and are applied to party purposes generally, particularly in N.Y. where the election of Govr. is on the anvil. Yates and Jay are the candidates. The last accounts from Amsterdam foretell in the next the capture of that place by the French. The inclosed speeches of Pitt and Fox will give you the English politics, and a general view of the crisis in Europe.

I have been detained here by a sick family; and am so at present, by the state of the roads, which are kept bad by the rains and the frosts. I am extremely anxious to be on the journey and shall set out as soon as I can prudently venture. Yrs. always & mo: affectly.

Js. MADISON JR

RC (DLC: Madison Papers); endorsed by TJ as received 7 Apr. 1795 and so recorded in SJL. Tr (DLC: Nicholas P. Trist Papers); extract made in January 1828 by Nicholas P. Trist (see note 1 below); conjoined to extracts of Madison to TJ, 14 June 1795, 5 Dec. 1796.

YOUR TWO LAST FAVORS: TJ to Madison, 23 Feb., 5 Mch. 1795. For the PASSAGE IN A FORMER letter, see TJ to Madison, 28 Dec. 1794. HOUDON'S FLETA BRACTON &C.: for the work in question, which was actually edited by David Houard and included Britton's condensation of Henry de Bracton's *de Legibus et Consuetudinibus Angliæ*, see TJ to Madison, 6 Nov. 1794. See also Sowerby, No. 1771.

[1] Tr begins here and continues to end of paragraph.
[2] Madison here canceled "any idea."
[3] Closing quotation mark supplied.

From Jean Antoine Gautier

MONSIEUR   Paris ce 24e. Mars 1795 Vieux Style

J'ai eu l'honneur de vous écrire diverses lettres au Sujet de la Commission dont vous m'aviés chargé pour Mr. Romilly et de quelques ouvrages et brochures que j'ai pris la liberté de vous addresser par divers voyageurs. J'ai aujourdhui celui de vous communiquer, Monsieur, la perte que nous avons faite l'Eté dernier de Mr. Grand Père, notre ancien et digne chef. Depuis la mort de Son Epouse l'année précédente, il n'avoit fait que languir et à terminé Sa carrière en Suisse Sa patrie, où Son fils est maintenant établi et retiré des affaires de Commerce, pour s'occuper principalement du Soin de Sa famille et d'Agriculture.

Il me charge, Monsieur, de vous présenter ses respects et l'assurance de Son dévouement. Le Buste dont vous aviés décoré le Sallon de Passy, et qui est cher à toute la famille, sera placé dans le Sallon de Sa nouvelle demeure près de Lausanne et toutes les occasions de vous témoigner, Monsieur, le Sentiment que nous conservons de vos bontés, lui seront, comme à moi, véritablement précieuses.

Veuillés recevoir mes félicitations Sur la prospérité croissante et le bonheur dont jouit votre Patrie et mes vœux pour Sa continuation. Madame Helvetius vit toujours à Auteuil et la Dame de qui vous teniés une demi colomne qui ornoit votre cabinet, avec des Inscriptions Sur la Révolution d'Amérique, vit en Suisse, où elle avoit acquis un domaine qu'elle vient de revendre. J'ai l'honneur d'être avec un veritable respect Monsieur Votre très humble & très obeissant Serviteur

J ANT GAUTIER

RC (DLC); at foot of first page: "Monsieur Thomas Jefferson à Monticello en Virginie"; endorsed by TJ as received 15 Aug. 1795 and so recorded in SJL.

LE BUSTE: probably one of the plaster busts of TJ by Jean Antoine Houdon (Vol. 15: xxxvi-vii; Alfred L. Bush, *The Life Portraits of Thomas Jefferson*, rev. ed. [Charlottesville, 1987], 11, 13). LA DAME: Adrienne Catherine de Noailles, the Comtesse de Tessé, who in 1789 had given TJ a truncated column of marble that commemorated American liberty in its inscription and later served as a pedestal for Giuseppe Ceracchi's bust of TJ (TJ to Madame de Tessé, 27 Aug. 1789; Vol. 18: xxxiii-iv).

From Grand & Cie.

MONSIEUR   Paris le 24 mars 1795

Nous prenons la liberté de nous référer à la Copie cy dessus de nôtre lettre du 25 may 1793. a la quelle nous n'avons pas été honnorés de votre réponse. M. Short a qui nous avions[1] reiteré notre priere de vouloir bien disposer du depot qu'il nous avoit remis ne put alors nous en donner,[2] mais par une lettre qu'il nous a fait depuis[3] l'honneur de nous écrire le 16. decembre dernier et qui a eté retardée il nous mandoit que d'après les nouvelles prieres que nous lui avions faites il avoit l'honneur de vous entretenir de l'objet de notre demande et qu'il ne doutoit pas que vous n'eussiez la bonté d'y pourvoir que quand à lui cela ne lui étoit pas possible pour le présent. Permettez que nous prenions la liberté de vous rappeller cet objet et de Solliciter vos bontés pour que ce depot nous Soit retiré. Nous vous demandons la même grace au Sujet du Solde que nous Restons devoir aux Etats Unis Suivant le Compte que nous avons eu l'honneur de vous addresser ainsi qu'a Monsieur Hamilton.

Nous avons celui de joindre ici deux Circulaires auxquelles nous prenons la liberté de nous référer. Vous trouverez comme nous que le changement qu'elles vous annoncent dans nôtre Société presente une Convenance de plus pour que les objets dont nous venons, Monsieur, de vous entretenir Soient liquidés et retirés le plutot possible. Nous avons l'honneur d'être avec Respect, Monsieur, Vos tres humbles et très obeissants Serviteurs   Grand & Co

Dupl (DLC: TJ Papers, 86: 14952); in a clerk's hand, signed by Jean Antoine Gautier for the firm; at head of text: "Duplicat"; endorsed by TJ as received 11 Aug. 1795 and so recorded in SJL. RC (same, 14949-50); in Gautier's hand; with variations, only the most important being noted below; subjoined to Tr of Enclosure No. 1; endorsed by TJ as received 15 Aug. 1795 and so recorded in SJL. Tr (same, 99: 16923); lacks salutation, complimentary close, and signature; with other important variations noted below; at head of text: "Copie de la Lettre Ecrite a Monsieur Jefferson, Sécrétaire au département des affaires Etrangeres Le 24 Mars 1795"; enclosed with Grand & Cie. to TJ, 11 Sep. 1795. Enclosures: (1) Grand & Cie. to TJ, 25 May 1793 (second letter). (2) Grand & Cie. and Gautier & Cie. to TJ, 24 Mch. 1795 (see following document).

[1] RC here adds "à la même époque."
[2] RC here adds "Ses dispositions." Tr: "ses ordres."
[3] Word omitted in RC and Tr.

From Grand & Cie. and Gautier & Cie.

Paris, 24 Mch. 1795. Grand & Cie., announcing that the company has come to an end and will continue only to liquidate itself, requests TJ to carry on his business with its successor firm. J. A. Gautier & Cie. announces its formation, to pursue business under the attached signatures of Jean Antoine Gautier and Pierre Claude Etienne Corsange, and solicits TJ's continued confidence in their diligent attention to his interests. P.S., Paris, 24 Mch. 1795. They had the misfortune of losing the elder Grand in his native Switzerland, where he had retired after the death of Madame Grand. They will always consider themselves happy to have opportunities of proving their devotion.

RC (DLC); 2 p.; in French; consisting of two circulars printed on a sheet folded to make four pages, the circulars appearing on the first and third pages; signed by Jean François Paul Grand and Jean Antoine Gautier for Grand & Cie., and by Gautier and Pierre Claude Etienne Corsange for Gautier & Cie.; with date, salutations, blank spaces, minor corrections in text, and postscript completed in ink by Gautier; at foot of text: "L'Honorable Mr Thomas Jefferson A Monticelle en Virginie"; endorsed by TJ as received 11 Aug. 1795 and recorded in SJL as individual letters from the two firms received on that date. Enclosed in preceding document.

From George Wythe

G WYTHE TO T JEFFERSON   26 of march, 1795.

Can you contrive that people who want, may obtain, copies of the acts of general assembly, now to be found in your collection only, without trouble to yourself, and without danger of loss or detriment to the books? Farewell.

RC (DLC); endorsed by TJ and recorded in SJL as received 7 Apr. 1795.

This letter and TJ's 18 Apr. 1795 response began the protracted but successful effort to provide public access to the collection of manuscript and printed ACTS OF GENERAL ASSEMBLY of the colony and state of Virginia that TJ had spent many years gathering in order to preserve it for posterity. Later this year Chancellor Wythe headed a committee appointed by the state legislature to publish Virginia laws relating to lands. For TJ's endorsement of the project and call for its extension to encompass all Virginia statutes, which initially faltered but ultimately came to fruition in William W. Hening's edition of *The Statutes at Large*, see Wythe to TJ, 1 Jan. and 27 July 1796, 1 Feb. 1797, and notes; TJ to Wythe, 12 Jan., 16 Jan. (two letters), 8 Aug. 1796, 22 Jan. 1797, and notes; Sowerby, No. 1863; and Hening, I, vii-xi.

From Jean Nicolas Démeunier

MONSIEUR   philadelphie Le 30 Mars 1795.

En arrivant dans vos heureuses contrées, J'eprouve un Vif regret que Monticelo Soit Aussi eloigné des Lieux ou Je retrouve des amis dont Je ne puis encore me Separer. J'aimerois a vous dire de Vive voix Le Tendre et respectueux attachement que vous m'avés inspiré. Ma vie politique, J'ose Le dire, a eté Si pure, et La récompense de mon Zele et de mes Services est Si cruel que Je ne crains pas de compter encore Sur votre estime et Sur votre bienveillance.

Il est rare que Les peuples aient de La reconnoissance des Services publics, et Je n'en demande pas à mes Concitoyens. Pour achever Les revolutions il est assés commun de voir ecraser, Ruiner et Sacrifier Ceux qui y ont eu Le plus de part; La Calomnie S'acharne principalement Sur Les gens de bien; Linstinct Avertit Les intriguans et Les Scelerats qu'ils doivent poursuivre Surtout Ceux qui Sont honnêtes et qui ont quelques Lumieres: Je n'ai pas attendu La revolution de france pour Savoir tout Cela, et Je ne murmure point de mon Sort. S'il me restoit d'Autres Sacrifices a faire a La Liberté et Au bonheur de mon pays, Je Les ferois avec plaisir. Que Les portes de La france Se rouvrent pour moi, et que Je puisse y rentrer d'une maniere Convenable, Je Suis bien decidé a y porter Le dernier Tribute qui Soit en mon pouvoir, celui d'un Reste de Vie qui n'a eté remplie que de devouement et d'intentions Genereuses. Mais vous voyés, Monsieur, La position de nos affaires, et malgré La moderation des dernieres mesures, il est difficile de croire à La fin prochaine des injustes persecutions. On me rendra Justice après ma mort, Je n'en doute pas; Je Suis convaincu qu'aucun des personnages influens Aujourdhui n'a de moi une mauvaise opinion; mais dans La Situation où ils Se Sont placés que Leur importe Le Sort d'un individu? Le Tems des reparations envers plusieurs d'entre nous n'est pas arrivé; Je pense qu'il ne Sera operé que par d'Autres hommes doués de plus de Courage Sur ces Sortes d'objets, et qu'il pourroit bien Avoir Lieu, Lorsque Je n'en Aurai plus besoin. Je dois donc Calculer Tout Au pis, agir en consequence, et voir ce que Je pourrois faire parmi vous Si Je dois y finir ma destinée. S'il m'avoit eté permis d'apporter des capitaux dans cet exil, quelques fussent mes regrets Sur Les affections que J'ai Laissées dans ma patrie, Je me consolerois de vivre dans un pays que J'ai Tant Aimé, et qui par Sa position, Son Gouvernement et Ses Lois me convient Sous Tous Les Rapports. Mais on ne m'a pas Laissé Cette espêce de bonheur.

Dans cette position, Je ne crains pas de vous importuner, Monsieur, en vous priant de m'éclairer de vos Conseils Sur Le Genre de Travail qui pourroit offrir des Ressources à Celui qu'on a dépouillé de Tout.

J'ai eu L'honneur, Monsieur, de vous écrire d'Angleterre une Lettre ou j'ai pris La Liberté de vous donner de plus Longs details Sur ma vie publique et Sur Les circonstances qui à La fin m'ont obligé a quitter La france. J'apprens ici qu'elle doit vous être parvenue, mais à L'epoque a peu près, ou Je me Suis embarqué pour Les etats unis. Je Les ai Tant cheris, Je me suis occupé Si Longtems Avec vous de Tout Ce qui pouvoit fonder Leur prospérité et Leur Bonheur Sur Les vraies bases de La Liberté que c'est pour moi une bien agreable distraction de voir de près La consideration si Generale et Si meritée qu'on vous porte, et L'heureux effet de Tant d'institutions que nos patriotiques voeux appelloient Si cordialement.

Je Loge ici Avec M. Talleyrand et M. Beaumetz qui vont S'établir à New York au commencement de May et ou je Les Accompagneray. Puis je esperer, Monsieur, que vous prendrés La peine de m'ecrire quelques mots? Vous pourriés Les adresser Union Street No. 16—ou

chez M. Robert Morris. Je Suis Avec Le plus Sincere et Le plus respectueux attachement Monsieur Votre Très humble et Très obeissant
Serviteur   J. DÉMEUNIER

RC (DLC: TJ Papers, 83: 14428-9); endorsed by TJ as received 14 Apr. 1795 and
so recorded in SJL, which identifies
Démeunier as "the Encyclopedist."

Démeunier, a former member of the Estates General and president of the Constituent Assembly who had received assistance
from TJ in 1786 for an article on the United
States in the *Encyclopédie Méthodique*, had
left France in November 1793 and gone to

England, before coming to America in
March 1795 and returning to his native land
the following November (Vol. 10: 3-11;
Kenneth Roberts and Anna M. Roberts,
eds. and trans., *Moreau de St. Méry's American Journey [1793-1798]* [Garden City,
N.Y., 1947], 180, 205, 207-8). There is no
evidence that TJ ever received the letter
that Démeunier wrote to him while in AN-
GLETERRE.

From George Washington

DEAR SIR   Philadelphia 30th Mar: 1795
    A short time since I wrote to you, and hope the letter got safe to your
hands. If this should reach them, it is intended to introduce Mr. Strickland, of Yorkshire in England, to your civilities and attention. His merits, independent of the recommendation of Sir Jno. Sinclair, will entitle
him to them.
    From Monticello, Mr. Strickland intends crossing the ridge for Win-
chester; and to return to this city either by Frederick town, or through
the Valley. With great truth & regard I am Dear Sir Your Affectionate
                                                        GO: WASHINGTON

RC (DLC); at foot of text: "Thos. Jefferson Esqr."; endorsed by TJ as received 14
May 1795 and so recorded in SJL.

On 2 April 1795 George Hammond, the
British minister to the United States, wrote
a letter to TJ introducing William STRICK-
LAND as "an extremely respectable En-

glish Gentleman, for whom I have a particular regard," and assuring him that "I shall
consider any kindness and attention shewn
to him as personal favors conferred upon
myself" (RC in ViU; at foot of text:
"Thomas Jefferson Esqre"; endorsed by TJ
as received 14 May 1795 and so recorded in
SJL).

From James Lyle

DEAR SIR   Manchester March 31. 1795
    I was favour'd with yours of the 14th. of Decemr. last by Mr. Ran-
dolph, who paid me £114.4.8 for which I gave my receipt. I had received from Mr. Clark on the 20th. of October £48.13.10. and yesterday received £49. further from him. He is just now here and says he
expects to send about £100 more soon. Below you have a note of the

payments which are regularly enterd on our Companys Books. I am with much esteem Dear Sir Your Mo hue St   JAMES LYLE

Thomas Jefferson Esqr. Cr.
1794
Octr. 20.   By Cash of Mr. Christor. Clark   £48.13.10
1795
Janry 5.   By Cash paid by T M Randolph Esqr.   114. 4. 8
March 30.   By Cash of Ch: Clark   49 —   —
                                                   _____
                                                   £211.18. 6

RC (MHi); endorsed by TJ as received 14 Apr. 1795 and so recorded in SJL.

To Richard Hanson

DEAR SIR   Monticello Apr. 2. 95.

Your favor of Mar. 14. is now before me: and I am glad you can make it convenient to receive Dr. Taylor's money in Philadelphia if he can raise it there on the mortgaged lands. I have no fear of risking the patents there, as our security rests on the mortgage deed, and I think it possible in the present land-gambling state of things, he may raise the money on them. As to the expences of the negociation, I do not know what may be either their nature or amount; but I do not see that they ought to fall either on Mr. Warre or myself. We are both entitled to receive our money here, and if we consent to recieve it elsewhere for the accomodation of the mortgagers, they should pay any reasonable and necessary expence attending it. I have written to Doctr. Taylor to settle this point with you, which being done, it will be necessary for you to furnish me with the name of your reciever, perhaps with a letter to him. Then it will remain how I shall find a conveyance for these patents to Philadelphia, for by post they would cost at least 30. dollars, which I would not take on myself.—I am sincerely desirous and anxious that Mr. Warre should recieve the money due on the bonds delivered you, with as little delay as possible, and would chearfully do any thing in my power to expedite it. I will use my best endeavors with Mr. Ronald's executors to get as speedy an issue to their debt as any thing I can do will procure. I would thank you from time to time to inform me of the sums and dates of your receipts on my account. I am with great esteem Dear Sir your most obedt. servt   TH: JEFFERSON

PrC (MHi); at foot of text: "Mr. Hanson"; endorsed in ink by TJ.

Hanson's FAVOR OF MAR. 14, recorded in SJL as received 25 Mch. 1795, has not been found. SJL records an additional 14 missing letters exchanged with Hanson between 9 May 1795 and 17 Apr. 1801.

To Henry Remsen

DEAR SIR   Monticello April 2. 95.

I wrote to you two or three posts ago, since which, the applications of my customers for 4d. nails have convinced me that I must make them, and experience of doing it on the anvil shews some other method must be tried. I have also recollected that at either Troy or some other little town up the Hudson I saw a man cutting the 4d. nails and that the implements were of very small cost, and not under a patent, and I suppose this to be the method of cutting to which your letter refers. I therefore have concluded to ask the favor of you to send me immediately all the implements (if they be few and of little cost as I suppose) and noting to me their cost I will order repaiment to you in Philadelphia, by return of post. If they cost more than a few dollars (say 10. or 20.) be so good as to inform me and I will decide on your information and write to you in pursuance.

Can you also be so good as to procure me answers to these questions?

What number of 4. pennies will a man cut in a day?

What number will a man head in a day?

Are they headed cold, or re-heated?

What is the proportion between the market price of cut and hammered nails?

Having given the merchants here expectations that in a few weeks I may be able to furnish them, I will take the liberty of asking as soon as convenient to you, as well the forwarding the implements, as the information on the above particulars, and any advice as to the manner of working which would not be too troublesome to you. My experience of your friendly offices, is the only apology I can make for the trouble I give you. I remain always Dear Sir your affectionate friend & servt

TH: JEFFERSON

RC (ICU); at foot of text: "Mr. Remsen"; endorsed by Remsen as received 14 Apr. 1795. Remsen's 15 Apr. 1795 reply, recorded in SJL as received 29 Apr. 1795, has not been found.

To Thomas A. Taylor

SIR   Monticello Apr. 2. 1795.

I have received your favor of Mar. 25. and one from Mr. Hanson consenting to appoint a person to recieve the money due to me on your bond and mortgage in Philadelphia, on condition I will pay the expence of the negociation. I know not what is the nature of the expence alluded to. I know the banks would recieve and repay the money without any charge. However, whatever be the nature or amount of the expence, it cannot concern me, as I am entitled to recieve and pay the money here. I presume that Mr. Banks and yourself, for whom the accomodation is proposed, will not hesitate to bear the expence of it, if a reasonable one, on which subject you can obtain explanations from Mr. Hanson. I am sincerely desirous to do every thing in my power to facilitate to you the paiment of this debt, and will therefore readily consent to lodge the patents in Philadelphia, with a certificate that on paiment of the debt and interest, costs of suit, and expences of negotiation as shall be settled between yourself and Mr. Hanson, I will discharge the lands of the debt. The only difficulty then remaining will be how to convey the patents there, for they weigh better than 2. ℔. which at the legal postage of 80. cents the ounce, would render their transmission by post too expensive. I write to Mr. Hanson to name to me his receiver, and to inform me when he and you shall have agreed about the expences of the negociation, and on receiving his answer, and yours, I will proceed in consequence. I am Sir your most obedt. humble servt   TH: JEFFERSON

PrC (MHi); at foot of text: "Dr. Taylor"; endorsed in ink by TJ.

Taylor's FAVOR OF MAR. 25, recorded in SJL as received from "Osborne's" on 31 Mch. 1795, has not been found.

From John Carey

SIR   London, April 6, 1795.

I do myself the honor of transmitting you two volumes of those official documents, which, through your favor and indulgence, I was enabled to transcribe. I would have published two or three volumes more, had not a chasm in the commander-in-chief's correspondence, and the want of many of the inclosures, stopped my progress. On this subject, I take the liberty of writing to Mr. Madison, Mr. Page, and Mr. Beckley, hoping, by their interposition on the spot, to have the deficiencies supplied. If successful, I shall immediately proceed, and finish the work as soon as possible.

Here I beg leave to observe, that, recollecting your caution respecting the premature publication of certain passages, I have endeavoured to pursue the path you had marked out, and to keep clear of every thing which might, at the present day, have an unpleasing tendency. Had I published in Philadelphia, I should have been less scrupulous: there, any unlucky slips could have been attributed only to inadvertence; whereas, now that I live under a government radically hostile to the Union, they might, by the American reader, be attributed to sinister motives on my part, and possibly give rise to some invective against even You, Sir, for having, though with the most laudable intentions, countenanced the publication. And, though perfectly convinced that such declamation[1] were incapable of disturbing a mind like yours, yet I was unwilling that my conduct should furnish the theme; and preferred injuring the sale of the book by the omission of many passages which would have been read with avidity on this side the Atlantic. If however, through excessive caution, I have erred on the other side, the error can be repaired in a second edition or an Appendix, where it will be easy to supply any passage unnecessarily omitted in my first publication.[2] With very sincere respect, I have the honor to be, Sir, your much obliged, & most obedient humble servant, JOHN CAREY

[The books I have taken the liberty of sending to the care of Mr. Madison.][3]

RC (DLC: Rare Book and Special Collections Division); pasted onto the flyleaf of the first volume of the enclosure; with clipped postscript supplied from Dupl. Dupl (DLC); dated 7 Apr. 1795; with variations, only the most important being noted below; at head of text: "*Duplicate*"; endorsed by TJ as a 25 Apr. 1795 letter received 30 June 1795 and so recorded in SJL. Enclosure: John Carey, ed., *Official Letters to the Honorable American Congress* (see note to Carey to TJ, 30 June 1792).

Carey's 31 Mch. 1795 letter informing James MADISON that the Philadelphia bookseller Henry Rice had been instructed to provide him and TJ with one set each of this work is in Madison, *Papers*, xv, 503-4.

[1] Dupl: "obloquy."
[2] Preceding sentence omitted in Dupl.
[3] Postscript supplied from Dupl.

From Edmund Randolph

DEAR SIR   Philadelphia, April 11th. 1795.

Knowing, that the President intended to answer your letter, relative to the shares in the two rivers, I did [not][1] think it necessary to trouble you with an assurance, that I would remind him of it. He tells me, that he has stated to you fully the arrangements, which he meditates.

Mr. Short mentioned to me in his last dispatches, that he had proposed to you some time before your resignation a plan for our diplomatic establishment. You will oblige me greatly by the perusal of it; as something must be done in this respect as soon as possible. I am dear Sir, with true regard Your friend and servant   EDM: RANDOLPH

FC (Lb in DNA: RG 59, DL); at head of text: "Thos. Jefferson esqr. Monticello." Recorded in SJL as received 21 Apr. 1795.

YOUR LETTER: TJ to George Washington, 23 Feb. 1795. STATED TO YOU: Washington to TJ, 15 Mch. 1795.

[1] Word supplied.

From William Champe Carter

DEAR SIR   Milton [on or before 13 Apr. 1795]

In consequence of what has passed between us relative to your purchasing a part of my land, I have judged it proper to acquaint you with my arrival in the county. If the terms proposed in my letter from Williamsburgh be such as will meet your acceptance I should wish that our contract might be immediately executed. With respectfull compts. I remain Dr Sir yr. ob Servt   WILLIAM C. CARTER

RC (DLC: William Short Papers); undated; endorsed by TJ as received 13 Apr. 1795 and so recorded in SJL.

MY LETTER FROM WILLIAMSBURGH: Carter to TJ, 19 Mch. 1795.

To John Taylor

TH: JEFFERSON TO J. TAYLOR   Monticello Apr. 13. 95.

This is not the long letter I intend to write in answer to yours of the 5th. Ult. That must await a rainy day, perhaps a rainy season. But as the sowing the succory will not await, I write a line for the present, merely to cover a little seed which I have procured from a neighbor for you. It must be sown immediately, in drills which will admit the plough, and very thin in the drill as the plant is a very tall and large one. It requires strong land, is perennial, and unquestionably valuable.—The mouldboard cannot come by post. I have with very great satisfaction and saving tried the seed box described in the New York agricultural transactions for sowing clover. If you have not the pamphlet, the box is simply of half inch poplar (for lightness) 7. feet long, 6 Inches broad 4 Inches deep, divided by partitions into seven equal compartments, or cells, a diagonal drawn in the bottom of each cell and 2 holes of $\frac{1}{2}$ I. diameter bored through the bottom on the diagonal equally distant from each other and from the corners: then a bit of strong paper is pasted over the holes, and a hole burnt thro' that with a wire of such size as on trial will be found to shed the seed exactly fast enough. A neighbor of mine, Colo. Lewis, the evennest seedsman we know came to try the box, in comparison of his own sowing, and pronounced that the evenness of the work with the box exceeded any thing possible from the human hand. I have sowed an hundred acres of red clover with it within this fortnight, at 11. gills to the acre. To have sowed it equally thick every where by hand would have taken 16. gills, and consequently $\frac{5}{16}$ of the space would have been too thick. Consequently I have saved 13. gallons of seed, or 13. dollars. I should have mentioned that 2 straps are nailed round the box for the seedsman to hold and shake it by as he would a sifter. He will sow a 9 [foot?] land at a time.—I have recieved the drill. Several of it's parts got lost on the journey. I can supply them all however, except the bands and buckets for the seeds. Your letter mentions three of these for seed of different kinds, and there came only one, which I judge to be the one for turnep seed. That for peas I shall particularly want. If you could forward the two deficient sizes to Colo. Gamble at Richmond I shall soon get them; and if before pea-sowing so much the better. We were to have tried the drill to-day on a piece of Lucerne ground; but a glorious rain the last night has agreeably disappointed us. Could it not be made for drilling wheat in the broad-cast? That is to say, sow 8 rows, 9 I. apart at a time. The Jersey drill, (described in the N.Y. Agricl. transactions) sows in 13 I. rows, 4 rows at a time. I have tried the Jersey drill with small seeds, and it will not answer without some additional apparatus. We should save much seed and sow evenner by sowing with machines in the broadcast. Such a machine will be very desireable to me when I get my vetch. Let me recommend to you to read Millar's gardener's dict. article Vicia. In my circle of crops I can have 2. or 3. fields of this every winter for either winter forage or spring green dressings, without their costing me a single ploughing more than I am to give without the vetch.—But I forgot I promised that this should not be a long letter. Adieu affectionately.

PrC (DLC).

No article mentioning the SEED BOX described by TJ has been found in the NEW YORK AGRICULTURAL TRANSACTIONS, but this journal did print a piece on the JERSEY DRILL (Walter Rutherford, "Observations on the Drilling of Wheat," Society, Instituted in the State of New-York, for the Promotion of Agriculture, Arts, and Manufactures, *Transactions*, I [1792], 121-2). See Sowerby, No. 661.

To William Champe Carter

DEAR SIR   Monticello Apr. 15. 95.

I recieved the day before yesterday your favor from Milton and am happy on your return to the neighborhood, and in the hopes of a neighborly sociability with Mrs. Carter and myself. With respect to the land, were it my own case, the difference of 6d. or 1/ an acre should not have given you the trouble of a reply. But I am acting for Mr. Short, and under uncertainty how he may like the situation price and other circumstances. I therefore proposed to secure myself from error or censure by adhering to the price Monroe gave. On his two purchases the neighbors seem to have decided that the first was a good one, the second hard. I cannot therefore go beyond what he gave you. It would seem by your letter to have been sixpence more than I had supposed, to wit 23/6 instead of 23/. I will give whatever he gave. If you think proper, I will meet you on the land any day and hour you will name, in order to go over it, and see that I was not misdirected when I went over it before, and to conclude the contract &c. Any day after tomorrow will suit me. With my respects to Mrs. Carter I am Dr. Sir with great esteem Your most obedt. servt   TH: JEFFERSON

PrC (DLC: William Short Papers); at foot of text: "W. C. Carter esq."

To John Taylor

TH:J. TO J. TAYLOR   Monticello Apr. 15. 95.

We have tried the drill with Lucerne seed, and found it shed a great deal too much, so that we were obliged to lay it aside. I presume therefore I was mistaken in saying the band and buckets which came were for turnep seed. We rather guess they were for peas or corn. I must correct therefore my petition for the two larger sizes, and in the uncertainty in which I am, I must rather pray for a complete set.—The French in Amsterdam, and Van Staphorst President of the revolutionary committee! Bravo! Adieu!

PrC (DLC).

To John Barnes

SIR   Monticello April 16. 1795.

Your favor of the 3d. inst. is duly received, containing a statement of the sale of the two certificates of the property of Mr. Short formerly transmitted you, and of the paiment of Mr. Pollard's draughts: all of which gives entire satisfaction. I expect tomorrow to conclude a purchase of some lands for Mr. Short, in consequence whereof I shall probably draw on you at three days sight[1] for the money remaining in your hands or part of it; and for the same object I now inclose you two other certificates, to wit, a three per cent one, for 2356.D. 01c. and a deferred one, for 2150. Dollars, to be sold to answer my draughts on you, which will be made at six weeks after sight. These draughts will probably go on by the next weeks post, and I have thought it best to send on the certificates and a power of attorney by the present as it will give you a week more for the sale.

I have also received your favor of the 5th. inst. covering triplicates of exchange George Meade on George Barclay in favor of V. Staphorsts & Hubbard for Philip Mazzei for £70–8–6 sterl. by order of Judge Blair which shall be duly forwarded.

Be pleased to favor me with information by return of post of the sum which I may with safety draw for on the two certificates now inclosed, as I will keep back a part of it so as to be within certain bounds till I hear from you. I am with esteem Sir Your most obedt. servt

TH: JEFFERSON

PrC (MHi); at foot of text: "Mr. John Barnes"; endorsed in ink by TJ on verso. Enclosures not found.

Barnes's letters of the 3D. INST. and the 5TH. INST., recorded in SJL as received 14 Apr. 1795, have not been found.

[1] Preceding four words interlined.

From William Branch Giles

SIR   Richmond April 16th 1795

After the date of my last letter to you from Philadelphia, I inclosed to Mr. Shippen the statement of your demand against him as representative of Mr. Banister. I also submitted to his inspection your letter to me relatively to that subject, and informed him that I was authorised to receive the amount, and close the transaction. Mr. Shippen acknowledged himself the proper person to receive the application and said the claim should be paid; but the time when, was always left indefinite, and he seemed to discover an indifference in the business which, I thought, not justifyed by the peculiar circumstances attending the original transaction.

I have lately been informed that you are about engageing in a scheme for converting the lime stone on the upper parts of James river, into lime, for the supply of the country adjacent to that river between the limestone and Richmond. I propose this summer to commence the building of a dwelling. Now my preferince is for Brick; and the only objection to that material consists in the difficulty of procureing lime. The place proposed for erecting the house is about 14 or 15 miles from a safe and convenient landing place on James river about 40 miles above richmond. Will you be so obligeing as to make an estimate of the price of lime delivered at the place described?

I had anticipated the pleasure of a visit to you at Monticello in the course of the last summer, but was prevented from reallizeing it, by a most distressing catastrophe in our family, (the death of my Father) and the consequent increase of domestic obligations; I now hope, in company with Mr. J. W. Eppes, to execute that intention in the course of the next month; and I indulge myself in the pleasing expectation of returning highly improved both in the Theoretical and Practical parts of farming.

Although you have forsworn Politicks, I cannot close this letter, without congratulateing you upon the literal verification of the old saying, *'The Dutch have taken Holland.'* The Tyranny of the Stadholder & Co. is no more; and a third republic is emerged therefrom; I hope, by this time in actual organization. A third Republic predicated upon, *the rights of men*, in opposition to *the monopoly of Priviliges* I consider as the certain harbinger of a general revolution of the human character and government. The magnitude of this event in the history of the World will furnish my apology for intrudeing it upon your notice. Be pleased to excuse me for writeing you so long a letter, and accept my most cordial wishes for your personal happines &c   WM B. GILES

RC (DLC); at foot of text: "Mr Jefferson"; endorsed by TJ as received 21 Apr. 1795 and so recorded in SJL.

MY LAST LETTER: Giles to TJ, 4 Jan. 1795. TJ's LETTER to Giles was that of 17 Dec. 1794. A THIRD REPUBLIC: the French conquest of the Netherlands led in January 1795 to the fall from power of William V, the last Stadholder in Dutch history, and to the establishment of the Batavian Republic (Simon Schama, *Patriots and Liberators: Revolution in the Netherlands, 1780-1813* [New York, 1977], 178-94, 212).

To James Brown

DEAR SIR   Monticello Apr. 18. 95.

I recieved a few days ago your kind favor of Mar. 14. The object of my letter had been, not at all a retardation of the paiment I had promised you during the present and ensuing month, but, as my crop of tobacco was much short of what was usual, it was merely to see how far my next best article of produce, to wit, nails, could take it's place with you. I have had 9 hammers at work for you for some time past. We have of nails on hand, and credits to go to your benefit about £80. and some time in the next month shall have enough for the balance. If I cannot sell them for cash here, I will send them to Richmond to be converted into cash there so as to be in time for my engagement.

1382.   In the margin are the weights of my tobacco (only 12 hhds)
1362   now in Richmond, averaging 1313℔. I am offered here 4/
1138   above the present market price. But you shall certainly have a

1196 preference on equal terms to any other purchaser. As I shall not
1360 go to Richmond myself, I must ask you by letter your highest
1426 price. You know I have an established privilege of being con-
1240 siderably above the market. I must tell you at the same time
1294 that the quality of the last year's crop is inferior, but still mine
1386 preserving it's comparative superiority stands on it's usual
1348 ground with respect to others. Let me have your ultimatum, if
1280 you please, by the post after next, say that which leaves Rich-
1345 mond the 3d. of May, till which time I will reserve myself here.
15757

I am with great esteem Dear Sir Your friend & servt

TH: JEFFERSON

RC (Mrs. Henry M. Sage, Albany, New York 1954); addressed: "Mr. James Brown Merchant Richmond"; stamped; endorsed by Brown as answered "3 May."

Brown's FAVOR OF MAR. 14., recorded in

SJL as received 2 Apr. 1795, has not been found. SJL also records a letter from Brown of 15 Nov. 1794, received from Richmond four days later, and a LETTER from TJ to Brown of 4 Feb. 1795, both of which are missing.

To Archibald Stuart

DEAR SIR   Monticello Apr. 18. 95.

I did not recieve your favor of the 7th. till the 17th. inst. Consequently you had then passed on to New London. I could not learn that
your brother was in the neighborhood. I inclose you a copy of an advertisement I had thought some time ago of putting in the public papers,
but did not do it. You will see by that the books I have to dispose of. The
last two or three lines of it are not for you, for you may take such of the
books as you chuse, and what time of paiment you please. If yet with any
body who will take the whole of the residue I shall be glad of it. I have
stated that at the price I offer them, the whole would be at about 4. Doll.
average a volume. But if they are separated, being of very unequal values, their respective prices can be proportioned to that sum total by
Worral's catalogue. Hargrave's Coke Littleton for instance cost as much
as any 3. or 4. of the other volumes.—When I spoke of meeting you on
your way to the Bedford court, I did not know that our own district
court was exactly at the same time, at which I was obliged to attend.
This put it out of my power to be in Bedford this month.—With respect
to the gentleman whom we expected to see there, satisfy him if you
please that there is no remain of disagreeable sentiment towards him on
my part. I was once sincerely affectioned towards him and it accords

with my philosophy to encorage the tranquilizing passions. Adieu.
Your's affectionately   TH: JEFFERSON

RC (ViHi); addressed: "Archibald Stuart esquire Atty at law New London." PrC
(MHi); endorsed in ink by TJ on verso. Enclosure not found.

SJL records TJ's receipt of Stuart's
FAVOR of 7 Apr. 1795, not found, on 13
Apr., not the 17TH. INST.
WORRAL'S CATALOGUE: John Worrall,
Bibliotheca Legum: or, A Compleat List of all

the Common and Statute Law Books of this
Realm . . . (London, 1765). See Sowerby,
No. 4732. HARGRAVE'S COKE LITTLETON:
Sir Edward Coke, *The First Part of the Insti-
tutes of the Laws of England. Or, A Commentary upon Littleton*, 13th ed., Francis Hargrave and Charles Butler, eds. (London,
1775-88).
THE GENTLEMAN: Patrick Henry (see TJ
to James Madison, 27 Apr. 1795).

To George Wythe

TH: JEFFERSON TO G: WYTHE   Monticello Apr. 18. 95.

I thank you sincerely for your book. I shall read it with great pleasure
and profit, and I needed something the reading of which would refresh
my law-memory.

My collection of acts of assembly are in a very chaotic state, insomuch
that I have not had the courage to attempt to arrange them since my
return home. As soon as this is done, I shall send the printed acts to be
bound in Richmond after which it will be more easy to consult them,
and probably I may be able to engage some young man in Charlottesville to copy acts for those who need them, for hire. I have no body
living with me who could do it, and I am become too lazy, with the pen,
and too much attached to the plough to do it myself. I live on my horse
from an early breakfast to a late dinner, and very often after that till
dark. This occasions me to be in great arrears in my pen-work. Adieu
with sincere affection.

PrC (DLC).

YOUR BOOK: Wythe's *Decisions of Cases in
Virginia, By The High Court of Chancery,*

*With Remarks upon Decrees By The Court of
Appeals, Reversing some of those Decisions*
(Richmond, 1795). See Sowerby, No.
1759.

Articles of Agreement with
William Champe Carter

Articles of agreement concluded between Wm. Champe Carter on the
one part and Thomas Jefferson as Attorney for William Short on the
other.

The said Wm. Champe covenants to convey to the said Wm. Short a fee simple estate in a certain tract of land known by the name of the Indian camp quarter, part of a tract of land devised to him by his father, and lying between the lands of James Monroe and the Blenheim lands, which part has been lately surveyed by Robert Lewis and found to contain thirteen hundred and thirty four acres, to hold the same clear of all incumbrances and charges by mortgage, dower or otherwise, and to recieve possession thereof immediately, and that he will as soon as may be execute sufficient instruments of conveyance for the same.

And the said Thomas as attorney for the said William Short covenants that in consideration of the said conveyance the said William Short shall pay to the said William Champe twenty three shillings and sixpence per acre, whereof three hundred dollars shall be paid by draught on Philadelphia at three days sight, six hundred dollars by a like draught at six weeks sight, and two thousand dollars shall be paid to Mr. Wilson Cary Nicholas for the said Wm. Champe by like draught at six weeks sight. And whereas at the running of the Southern boundary of the said land, where it adjoins the Blenheim tract no person attended on the part of Mrs. Carter mother of the said William Champe and tenant for life thereof, nor has her agreement to the said line been obtained, it is therefore agreed between the said parties that the said Mr. Champe will obtain a sufficient act of agreement on her part to the said line, whereupon the balance shall become payable in like manner by draughts on Philadelphia, or if her agreement cannot be obtained to the said line, then that her agreement shall be obtained to some other line as the boundary of her life estate, and a rateable deduction shall be made from the sum total of the purchase money, according to the quantity which such other line shall take away from that total, surveyed and marked by the said Robert Lewis.

Saving to the tenants now in the occupation of any part of the said lands their several rights thereto according to contracts heretofore made according to law.

In witness whereof the said parties have hereto set their hands and seals this 20th. day of April 1795.

Signed sealed and delivered   WILLIAM C. CARTER   (L.S.)
in the presence of
NICHOLAS LEWIS

                                 TH: JEFFERSON   (L.S.)

MS (DLC: William Short Papers); in TJ's hand, signed by Carter, Nicholas Lewis, and TJ; with remnants of seals.

SURVEYED BY ROBERT LEWIS: a reference to Lewis's 18 Apr. 1795 survey of Indian Camp Quarter (MS in same, at foot of survey by Lewis: "This is a plot of 1334 Acres of Land in the County of Albemarle lying on the South East side of the South West Mountains and on the waters of Buck-Island Creek. Surveied for Wm Short April 18th 1795 by Robt W Lewis," with notation on verso by TJ: "Carter to Short} the original survey made by Robert Lewis, according to which the quantity & price was fixed, and the conveyance made"; Tr in ViW, consisting of survey and Lewis's note in TJ's hand; enclosed in TJ to William Short, 13 Apr. 1800). DRAUGHT ON PHILADELPHIA: on 20 Apr. 1795 TJ made two drafts on Philadelphia merchant John Barnes in favor of Carter for the amounts of money specified above (PrCs in DLC: Short Papers; letterpressed on the same page). On 22 Apr. 1795 TJ made a draft on Barnes for $2,000 in favor of Wilson Cary Nicholas (Tr in same; in TJ's hand; undated, but see the following two documents).

From Wilson Cary Nicholas

DEAR SIR   Warren Apl. 20th. 1795

I saw Mr. Carter on my return who promised that he wou'd leave in your hands a sum of money for me. Be pleased to send me bills upon Philadelphia for whatever sum he intends for me, Mr. Staples receipt will be a sufficient voucher of the payment. I am with great respect Dear Sir your hum. Serv.   W C NICHOLAS

RC (DLC: William Short Papers); addressed: "Thomas Jefferson Esqr."; endorsed by TJ; with receipt of John Staples in TJ's hand on verso, dated 22 Apr. 1795 and signed by Staples on behalf of Nicholas, acknowledging TJ's draft on John Barnes for $2,000 payable to Nicholas or his order, "which paiment when made is to be placed to the credit of William Champe Carter."

To John Barnes

SIR   Monticello Apr. 23. 1795.

On the 16th. inst. I inclosed you a deferred certificate of 2150. Dollars, and one at 3. percent of 2356.01 D. to be sold to answer my draughts for paiment of a purchase of lands I was about to make for Mr. Short. This being concluded I have made on you the draughts stated below, of which this serves to advise you. The quantity of land having been found on survey to be half as much again as had been expected, I shall forward you a further supply of paper as soon as certain formalities in the conveyance are executed. In the mean time it will be important that I should receive from you information of the proceeds of the paper forwarded in my last as soon as you shall have disposed of it; and a conjecture of it's probable proceeds would be acceptable beforehand for my government so that I may approach somewhat to the limits without exceeding them. I am with esteem Sir Your most obedt. servt

TH: JEFFERSON

			D	dates.
Draughts payable *At 3. days sight.*	Joseph Mussi.		89.09	Apr. 23.
	Muir & Hyde.		130.	Apr. 23.
	Wm. Champe Carter		300.	Apr. 20.
			519.09	
At 6. weeks sight.	Wm. Champe Carter		600.	Apr. 20.
	Wilson Cary Nicholas		2000.	Apr. 22
			2600.	

PrC (MHi); at foot of text: "Mr. John Barnes"; endorsed in ink by TJ on verso.

To William Temple

SIR   Monticello Apr. 26. 95.

I wrote some time ago to Colo. Gamble asking a copy of my account with him that I might have it paid. In a letter which he wrote as he was setting out for Philadelphia he informed me you would be so good as to furnish it on application, which favor I now ask of you.

He mentioned in the same letter that he was resigning his retail business to you, and meant to add to it the branch of groceries if I should have occasion for any. My course as to groceries has hitherto been to send quarterly to a merchant in Philadelphia an invoice of what I wanted in that line for the next quarter, whereon he shipped them to Richmond, sent me his bill by post, and within two or three posts afterwards I procured and remitted him a bill for the amount. Tho' I get my groceries thus on good terms, yet I find the procuring of a bill on Philadelphia in this part of the country troublesome and difficult. If therefore I could retain the advantages of reasonable prices, and supplies of good quality, and obtain greater facility in the form of paiment, I should adopt it. My groceries come to between 4. and 500 Dollars a year, taken and paid for quarterly. The best resource of quarterly paiment in my power is Nails, of which I make enough every fortnight to pay a quarter's bill, and I would willingly send them to Richmond by the first boat or waggon after the receipt of the bill, and require there only the *wholesale price* at the time of their being recieved there. If such a form of paiment would suit you, and the quality and prices of your supplies be found to suit me, I should be willing to change my dealings from Philadelphia to Richmond. On this subject be so good as to write to me fully and frankly, stating what your convenience and the course of your commerce requires, as no dealings could be desireable to either you or myself unless founded in mutual convenience, and reasonable advantages to both parties. Below I sketch the articles for which I should have occasion that you may have a certain knolege of their nature. I am Sir Your very humble servt   TH: JEFFERSON

Coffee ⎫
Chocolate
tea.
white sugar   ⎬ called for quarterly.
brown sugar
Molasses
rice,
rum or French brandy ⎭
The following articles are called for occasionally.
Wine vinegar.
mustard
spices.
oil
sago
Cod's tongues and sounds
biscuit
candles[1]

PrC (MHi); with last words in list added by TJ in ink (see note below); at foot of first page: "Mr. William Temple"; endorsed in ink by TJ on verso: "Gamble & Temple."

William Temple operated a store in Richmond with wholesale merchant Robert Gamble that sold dry goods, hardware, groceries, and other merchandise. TJ purchased groceries and nailrod from Gamble & Temple in 1795 and 1796, using nails in partial payment, and settled accounts with the firm on 31 July 1796. The partnership was dissolved in 1799 (Richmond *Virginia Gazette, and General Advertiser*, 15 July 1795, 6 Dec. 1797, 2 May 1800; MB, 26 Nov. 1795, 3, 22 May, 31 July 1796; ViU: Accounts of the Nailery, entries for 18 July

and 7 Aug. 1795, Nov. 1795, and Apr. 1796).

COPY OF MY ACCOUNT: SJL indicates that TJ wrote Robert Gamble on 11 Mch. 1795 and that Gamble's LETTER to TJ of 20 Mch. was received 15 Apr. 1795; neither letter has been found. WRITE TO ME FULLY: according to SJL, Temple replied on 1 June 1795, a missive TJ received from Richmond four days later. SJL also records letters from TJ to Temple of 11 June and 1 July 1795 and 31 Jan. 1796, all of which are missing.

[1] Preceding two words added in ink by TJ. Above them TJ wrote in ink and then canceled "spirits."

To William Branch Giles

DEAR SIR   Monticello Apr. 27. 95.

Your favor of the 16th. came to hand by the last post. I have to thank you for the trouble you were so kind as to take in my demand on Mr. Bannister's estate. Mr. Shippen by letter promised me paiment out of

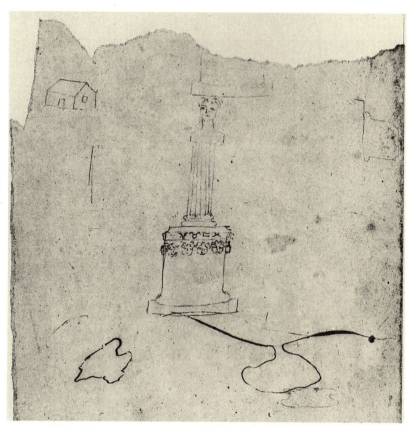

Giuseppe Ceracchi's Bust of Jefferson

James Madison

Dolley Payne Madison

François D'Ivernois

Christoph Daniel Ebeling

Thomas Mann Randolph was born Octob. 1. 1768. died June 1828
he intermarried with Martha Jefferson Feb. 23. 1790.

Anne Cary Randolph was born 1791. Jan. 23. died Feb. 11. 1826

Thomas Jefferson Randolph was born 1792. Sep. 12. died Oct 7th 1875

Ellen Wayles Randolph was born 1794. Aug. 30.
died 1795. July 26.

Ellen Wayles Randolph was born 1796. Oct. 13.
died 1876 April 21st

Cornelia Randolph was born 1799. July 26.
at Alexandria died 1871 Feb 24. 11-10 pm

Virginia Randolph was born 1801. Aug. 22.
at Alexandria died 1882 april 26 6.5 am

Mary Jefferson Randolph was born 1803. Nov. 2.
at Alexandria died 1876 March 29

James Randolph was born . . . 1806. Jan. 17. died Jan. 23. 1834

Benjamin Randolph was born 1808. July 16.
died 1871 Feb 15

Lewis Randolph was born 1810. Jan. 3. Sept. 24.
died 1837 Sep 24. died 1837

Septimia Randolph was born 1814. Jan. 3. Sep 14. 1887
died 1887 Sep 14

George Wythe Randolph was born 1818. Mar. 10.
at Edgehill died 1867 April 3

Thomas Mann Randolph died at Monticello
June 20th 1828

Martha J. Randolph died at Edgehill Va.
October 10th 1836 at Edgehill

Lewis Randolph died in Clark County
Arkansas. September 24th 1837.

Births all written in Thomas Jefferson's
hand.

Thomas Mann Randolph's death recorded by
his wife Martha Jefferson Randolph

Page of Jefferson's Prayer Book

This indenture made at Monticello in the county of Albemarle & commonwealth of Virginia on the fifth day of February one thousand seven hundred and ninety six witnesseth that I Thomas Jefferson of Monticello aforesaid do emancipate manumit & make free James Hemings, son of Betty Hemings, which said James is now of the age of thirty years so that in future he shall be free and of free condition, & discharged of all duties & claims of servitude whatsoever, & shall have all the rights and privileges of a freedman. In witness whereof I have hereto set my hand & seal on the day & year above written, and have made these presents double of the same date, tenor & indenture one whereof is lodged in the court of Albemarle aforesaid to be recorded, & the other is delivered by me to the said James Hemings to be produced when & where it may be necessary.

Signed, sealed & delivered
in presence of

John Carr

Francis Anderson

Th: Jefferson

Deed of Manumission for James Hemings

Inventory of Kitchen Utensils

19 Copper Stew pans — 19 Covers
6 Small Sauce pans
3 Copper Baking Moulds
2 Small Preserving pans
2 Large — — Ditto
2 Copper Fish kettles
2 Copper Brazing pans
2 Round Large — Ditto
2 Iron Stew pans
2 Large Boiling kettles tin'd inside
1 Large Brass — Ditto
12 pewter water Dishes
12 — — plates
3 Tin Coffie pots
8 Tin Dish Covers
2 frying pans of Iron & one of Copper
4 Round Baking Copper sheets tin'd
4 Square Copper Ditto untin'd
1 Copper Boiler
1 Copper teakettle 1 Iron Ditto

First Page of James Hemings's Inventory of Kitchen Utensils

1793. Dec. 5.   pa. 99 President's message to Congress...
1794.
  apr. 16.   73. instructions to Monroe.
  19.   100. Pres's message to Senate nominating Je...
  aug. 5.   58. E.R. to the Pres. letter.
                  100. do
1795. Oct. 31.
1795. man 7.   6. Fauchet's intercepted lre No. 10.
      June 29.   28. treaty arrives.
                   29. R's first conversn with Hammond
  July 2.   30. R. to Monroe.
  12.   30. R's opinion to the Pres.
  13.   31. 40. R's 2d conversn with Hammond
  14.   32. R's 3d conversn with Hammond.
  39.   39. R. to Monroe & the other ministers
  15.   32. 39. Pres. goes to Mt Vernon.
  18.   33. Pres. writes to E.R. from Ball. on Br...
                   33. R's memorial to Hammond.
  22.   34. Pres. to R.
  29.   35. do
  31.   36. do
  aug. 11.   39. Pres. returns to Phila.
  10–14   39. 39. Hamilton writes to Pres.
  19.   1. R. called before cabinet.
                   8. R. to Pres.
  20.   9. Pres. to R.
  21.   9. R. goes to Rho. isl.
  31.   10.   arrives there.
  Sep. 1.   11. R. to Fauchet. & answer.
  2.   12. Gardner's certif.
  21.   19. R. to Pres.
  27.   20. Pres. to R.
                  13. Fauchet's certif.
                  17. No. 3.
                  18. No. 6.
  Oct. 2   21. R. to Wolcot & answer.
  6.   25. Taylor to R.
  8.   22.3. R. to Wolcott & answer.
                  23. R. to Pres.
  21.   25. Pres. to R.
  24.   26. R. to Pres.
                  49. R's general lre to Pres.

Jefferson's Notes on Edmund Randolph's *Vindication*

the first proceeds of a sale then making at Hatcher's run on a twelve-month's credit. I sincerely congratulate you on the great prosperities of our two first allies, the French and Dutch. If I could but see them now at peace with the rest of their continent, I should have little doubt of dining with Pichegru in London next autumn; for I believe I should be almost tempted to leave my clover for a while to go and hail the dawn of liberty and republicanism in that island.—I shall be rendered very happy by the visit you promise me. The only thing wanting to make me completely so is a more frequent society with my friends. It is the more wanting as I am become more firmly fixt to the glebe. If you visit me as a farmer, it must be as a condisciple: for I am but a learner; an eager one indeed but yet desperate, being too old now to learn a new art. However I am as much delighted and occupied with it as if I was the greatest adept. I shall talk with you about it from morning till night, and put you on very short allowance as to political aliment. Now and then a pious speculation for the French and Dutch republicans, returning with due dispatch to clover, potatoes, wheat &c. That I may not lose the pleasure promised me, let it not be till the middle of May, by which time I shall be returned from a trip I meditate to Bedford. Adieu. Yours affection-ately   TH: JEFFERSON

PrC (DLC); at foot of text: "Mr. Giles."

Jean Charles PICHEGRU was the French general in command of the Army of the North, whose recent conquest of the Netherlands had set the stage for the proclamation of the Batavian Republic (Scott and Rothaus, *Historical Dictionary*, II, 759-60).

To John Harvie, Jr.

DEAR SIR   Monticello Apr. 27. 95.

When I visited Richmond the last year I took with me the papers relating to the lands in question between us, with a view to propose a settlement by arbitration as had been agreed between us: but your departure to Goochland the second day after my getting to Richmond prevented my mentioning it to you. The happiness we had of seeing you here some time after, was of too short duration to be interrupted by business; and since that I have procrastinated writing to you according to what is commonly observed that what may be done at any time is done at no time. No doubt it appears equally desirable to you as to me, since we have different opinions of our rights, that they should be settled without delay, for which reason I take the liberty of proposing to you the naming arbitrators from among the judges of our higher courts as we had agreed. In this description I should comprehend our federal court, as Mr. Blair is too distinguished, for all the properties which should recommend him, to be excluded from the nomination. I suppose three will be enough. The letters which have passed between us will sufficiently explain the grounds of our claims to the arbitrators, but perhaps a statement of facts from each party may be necessary, and where either is not satisfied of any fact alledged by the other, he may point it out that proof may be produced. If these ideas meet your approbation, on signifying the same in a line by post I will make a short statement of the case, and send it to you for your examination. I make no apology for bringing this matter before you at present, because the readiness with which we have agreed to submit it to the umpirage of reason shews that neither wishes what is not right. I am with sincere esteem Dear Sir your friend & servt   TH: JEFFERSON

PrC (MHi); at foot of text: "Colo. John Harvie"; endorsed in ink by TJ on verso. Tr (MHi); entirely in TJ's hand.

To James Madison

DEAR SIR   Monticello Apr. 27. 1795.

Your letter of Mar. 23. came to hand the 7th. of April, and notwithstanding the urgent reasons for answering a part of it immediately, yet as it mentioned that you would leave Philadelphia within a few days, I feared that the answer might pass you on the road. A letter from Philadelphia by the last post having announced to me your leaving that place the day preceding it's date, I am in hopes this will find you in Orange. In mine, to which yours of Mar. 23. was an answer I expressed my hope of the only change of position I ever wished to see you make, and I expressed it with entire sincerity, because there is not another person in the US. who being placed at the helm of our affairs, my mind would be so completely at rest for the fortune of our political bark. The wish too was pure and unmixed with any thing respecting myself personally. For as to myself the subject had been thoroughly weighed and decided on, and my retirement from office had been meant from all office high or low, without exception. I can say too with truth that the subject had not been presented to my mind by any vanity of my own. I knew myself and my fellow citizens too well to have ever thought of it. But the idea was forced upon me by continual insinuations in the public papers, while I was in office. As all these came from a hostile quarter, I knew that their object was to poison the public mind as to my motives, when they were not able to charge me with facts. But the idea being once presented to me, my own quiet required that I should face it and examine it. I did so thoroughly and had no difficulty to see that every reason which had determined me to retire from the office I then held, operated more strongly against that which was insinuated to be my object. I decided then on those general grounds which could alone be present to my mind at that time, that is to say, reputation, tranquillity, labor: for as to public duty, it could not be a topic of consideration in my case. If these general considerations were sufficient to ground a firm resolution never to permit myself to think of the office or be thought of for it, the special ones which have supervened on my retirement still more insuperably bar the door to it. My health is entirely broken down within the last eight months; my age requires that I should place my affairs in a clear state; these are sound if taken care of, but capable of considerable dangers if longer neglected; and above all things the delights I feel in the society of my family, and the agricultural pursuits in which I am so eagerly engaged. The little spice of ambition, which I had in my younger days, has long since evaporated, and I set still less store by a posthumous than present name. In stating to you the heads of reasons which have produced my determination, I do not mean an opening for future discussion, or that I may be reasoned out of it. The question is for ever closed with me; my sole object is to avail myself of the first opening ever given me from a friendly quarter (and I could not with decency do it before) of preventing any division or loss of votes, which might be fatal to the Southern[1] interest. If that has any chance of prevailing, it must be by avoiding the loss of a single vote, and by concentrating all it's strength on one object. Who this should be is a question I can more freely discuss with any body than yourself. In this I painfully feel the loss of Monroe. Had he been here I should have been at no loss for a channel thro which to make myself understood, if I have been misunderstood by any body through the instrumentality of Mr. Fenno and his abettors.—I long to see you. I am proceeding in my agricultural plans with a slow but sure step. To get under full way will require 4. or 5. years. But patience and perseverance will accomplish it. My little essay in red clover the last year has had the most encouraging success. I sowed then about 40. acres. I have sowed this year about 120. which the rain now falling comes very opportunely on. From 160. to 200. acres will be my yearly sowing. The seed-box described in the agricultural transactions of New York reduces the expence of seeding from 6/ to 2/3 the acre, and does the business better than is possible to be done by the human hand. May we hope a visit from you? If we may, let it be after the middle of May, by which time I hope to be returned from Bedford. I had had a proposition to meet Mr. Henry there this month to confer on the subject of a convention to the calling of which he is now become a convert. The session of our district court furnished me a just excuse for the time; but the impropriety of my entering into consultation on a measure in which I would take no part, is a permanent one. Present my most respectful compliments to Mrs. Madison and be assured of the warm attachment of dear Sir Your's affectionately   Th: Jefferson

RC (DLC: Madison Papers); at foot of first page: "Mr. Madison." PrC (DLC); with one alteration by TJ recorded in note below.

LETTER FROM PHILADELPHIA: probably Joseph Mussi to TJ, 8 Apr. 1795, recorded in SJL as received 21 Apr. 1795, but not found. IN MINE: TJ to Madison, 28 Dec. 1794. SOUTHERN INTEREST: see note 1

below. SEED-BOX: see TJ to John Taylor, 13 Apr. 1795.

[1] In PrC TJ canceled this word and interlined "Republican" above it in ink. For an analysis of this alteration and its significance, see James Roger Sharp, "Unraveling the Mystery of Jefferson's Letter of April 27, 1795," *Journal of the Early Republic*, VI (1986), 411-18.

To Jean Nicolas Démeunier

DEAR SIR   Monticello. Virginia Apr. 29. 95

Your favor of Mar. 30. from Philadelphia came to my hands a few days ago. That which you mention to have written from London has never been received; nor had I been able to discover what had been your fortune during the troubles of France after the death of the king. Being thoroughly persuaded that under all circumstances your conduct had been entirely innocent and friendly to the freedom of your country, I had hopes that you had not been obliged to quit your own country. Being myself a warm zealot for the attainment and enjoiment by all mankind of as much liberty as each may exercise without injury to the equal liberty of his fellow citizens, I have lamented that in France the endeavors to obtain this should have been attended with the effusion of so much blood. I was intimate with the leading characters of the year 1789. So I was with those of the Brissotine party who succeeded them: and have always been persuaded that their views were upright. Those who have followed have been less known to me: but I have been willing to hope that they also meant the establishment of a free government in their country, excepting perhaps the party which has lately been suppressed. The government of those now at the head of affairs appears to hold out many indications of good sense, moderation and virtue; and I cannot but presume from their character as well as your own that you would find a perfect safety in the bosom of your own country. I think it fortunate for the United States to have become the asylum for so many virtuous patriots of different denominations: but their circumstances, with which you were so well acquainted before, enable them to be but a bare asylum, and to offer nothing for their [aid] but an entire freedom to use their own means and faculties as they please. There is no such thing in this country as what would be called wealth in Europe. The richest are but a little at ease, and obliged to pay the most rigorous attention to their affairs to keep them together. I do not mean to speak here of the Beaujons of America. For we have some of these, tho' happily they are but ephemeral. Our public oeconomy also is such as to offer drudgery and subsistence only to those entrusted with it's administration, a wise and necessary precaution against the degeneracy of the public servants. In our private pursuits it is a great advantage that every honest employment is deemed honorable. I am myself a nail-maker. On returning home, after an absence of ten years, I found my farms so much deranged, that I saw evidently they would be a burthen to me instead of a support till I could regenerate them; and consequently that it was necessary for me to find some other resource in the mean time. I thought for a while of taking up the manufacture of pot-ash, which requires but small advances of money. I concluded at length however to begin a manufacture of nails, which needs little or no capital, and I now employ a dozen little boys from 10. to 16. years of age, overlooking all the details of their business myself, and drawing from it a profit on which I can get along till I can put my farms into a course of yeilding profit. My new trade of nail-making is to me in this country what an additional title of nobility, or the ensigns of a new order are in Europe.—In the commercial line, the grocer's business is that which requires the least capital in this country. The grocer generally obtains a credit of three months, and sells for ready money so as to be able to make his paiments and obtain a new supply. But I think I have observed that your countrymen who have been obliged to work out their own fortunes here, have succeeded best with a small farm. Labour indeed is dear here, but rents are low, and on the whole a reasonable profit and comfortable subsistance results. It is at the same time the most tranquil, healthy, and independant. And since you have been pleased to ask my opinion as to the best way of employing yourself till you can draw funds from France or return there yourself, I do presume that this is the business which would yeild the most happiness and contentment to one of your philosophic turn. But at the distance I am from New York, where you seem disposed to fix yourself, and little acquainted with the circumstances of that place I am much less qualified than disposed to suggest to you emploiments analogous to your turn of mind and at the same time to the circumstance of your present situation. Be assured that it will always give me lively pleasure to learn that your pursuits, whatever they may be, may lead you to contentment and success, being with very sincere esteem & respect Dear Sir your most obedt. servt   TH: JEFFERSON

PrC (DLC); faded in part; at foot of first page in ink: "M. Demeunier."

From Eli Alexander

SIR   April – 95.

The scantling for the harow I would wish to be 4 inches wide and 3 inches thick about 31 feet in shuch lengths as will cut six pieses five feet long 25 teeth a 11 inches long the size of the pattren if the irons is done. For the small plough I would be oblige to you if you would send Davy over in order to assist me to make the plough amediatlly. I am Sir your Humble Svt.   ELI ALEXANDER

RC (DLC); unaddressed.

From Robert Pollard

SIR   Richmond May 1st: 1795

I enclose you the Deed from David Ross to William Short for the Twenty shares in the James River Company, I purchased by your directions, which was drawn agreeably to a form obtained from Mr. John Marshall the Companys Counsel.

My Charge for Commission amounts to Ten pounds Sixteen shillings at One ℔ Cent which is at your Debit. I am Sir Yr Most Obd
                                                       ROBERT POLLARD

RC (DLC: William Short Papers); unaddressed, but internal evidence points to TJ as the recipient (see Pollard to TJ, 22 Feb. 1795, and note). Enclosure not found.

To James Monroe

DEAR SIR   Monticello May 5. 1795.

Mr. Nathaniel Anderson, formerly of Richmond, but now of our county, informs me that he has a son settled or about to settle in Havre, in the mercantile line, whom he wishes to be made known to you, and to have the benefit of your countenance in his new establishment. Tho' myself personally unacquainted with the son, I have long been much acquainted with the father whose merit affords a presumption of that of the son, and a sufficient inducement to recommend him to you. I take the liberty therefore of solliciting for him your acquaintance and patronage, that he may have the benefit of being known and noticed by you, which to a young man just entering into business, and in that country particularly will be of avail to him, and will be acknowleged by his family and friends here. I am with great esteem & attachment Dear Sir Your's sincerely   TH: JEFFERSON

PrC (DLC); at foot of text: "James Monroe. M.P. of the U.S."

A 21 Jan. 1795 letter from TJ to NATHANIEL ANDERSON and 27 Mch. 1794 and 13 Mch. 1795 letters from Anderson, recorded in SJL as received 2 Apr. 1794 and 18 Mch. 1795, have not been found. Four letters exchanged by TJ and Anderson between 29 Feb. and 31 May 1796 are also missing.

According to SJL, TJ this day also wrote a missing but related letter to Delamotte, the American vice-consul at Le Havre.

From Madame de Chastellux

DEAR SIR   Paris May the 6th. 1795.

Your generous good heart, and the friendship that existed between you, and my ever lamented husband embolden me to ask you a favour, with the firm confidence it will be granted shou'd my demand be seasonable, as I flatter myself you will find it is.

You was an inhabitant of Paris my dear Sir at the time of my first settlement in that large City: I was then the Wife of a man I loved and esteemed, the sharer of his fortune which tho' not considerable was sufficient, and the friend of a woman whose virtues are universally acknowledged, and whose wealth seemed to ensure my future welfare. I am now the Widow of that Man (your friend) the pention I received in that quality is no longer paid, I have no jointer or provision whatsoever, and my patroness in whose misfortunes I have been, and am still a constant partner, beeing entirely divested of her large property, has it not in her power to fulfill what her feeling and affectionate heart had intended for me. Tho' cruel this change in my situation appear's, I shou'd continue to bear it with fortitude as I have for these two year's past was I not a mother, but my heart bleeds when I look at my Boy whose misfortunes began before his birth and who is not only totaly unprovided for, but for the present deprived even of that education his age begins to call for, and which is in some measure still more necessary to one who according to every probability must work out his own fortune. My Alfred is past six and as yet has received no instruction but from his mother. Now my dear Sir shou'd your opinion induce you to think that his father's services, and affection to your Country, entitle him to put in a claim to your nations generosity, I hope, nay I am convinced that you will be so good as to make yourself my poor Boy's advocate and intercessor. I shou'd (independently of the relief it wou'd be to my mind) look upon any thing that was granted to him, either a yearly allowance or a portion of lands as most honourable to M. de Chastellux's memory, and an encouragement to his Son to deserve the protection of that country toward's which my heart and wishes are often directed, as I look upon it as my son's second home and flatter myself he will find there hereafter those advantages I am afraid he can no longer expect in france. Enclosed my dear Sir is a letter for general Washington, your Worthy President, I refer him to you for particular's as it realy hurts me to repeat what concerns my melancholy situation, nothing render's it supportable but the consciousness, that I have acted up to what I owed my husband's memory, my duty to my son, and my own honour. Trial's ever so severe leave after them pleasing feelings, I mean when their remembrance is exempt of every kind of reproach or repentance, and this I can say, thank god, is my case.

I am just upon the point of going down to the roche-guyon for a few days; your name will be often mentioned in that noble mansion, by Madame d'anville, a Woman who unites all the virtues of her Sex, but who alass is in a declining State of health. What a pity such beeing's shou'd ever dye! I shou'd think I injured you my dear Sir was I to make you any apology for the liberty I take, I am certain it will be agreable to you, except you shou'd think my demand indiscreet, if so my dear Sir look upon it only as a strong proof of my regard and confidence. Assure yourself that no circumstance whatsoever can alter the Sentiments of esteem and friendship I shall ever retain for you and believe me as Ever your affectionate humble Servant   PLUNKETT CHASTELLUX

RC (DLC); endorsed by TJ as received 8 Sep. 1795 and so recorded in SJL. Enclosure: Madame de Chastellux to George Washington, 6 May 1795, asking him to support, in honor of her husband's memory, the request for relief she has made to TJ, who will doubtless inform him of it (RC in MHi: Timothy Pickering Papers; endorsed by Washington).

Marie Joséphine Charlotte Brigitte Plunkett, Marquise de Chastellux (1759-1815), born in Louvain to an Irish father in Austrian military service, was the widow of TJ's friend, the Marquis de Chastellux, who died in October 1788, a year after their wedding and four months before the birth of their son, Alfred, Comte de Chastellux, who received no assistance from the federal government despite his mother's plea (Howard C. Rice, ed. and trans., *Travels in North America in the Years 1780, 1781 and 1782 by the Marquis de Chastellux*, 2 vols. [Chapel Hill, 1963], I, 20-3, 240n, II, 578n).

MY PATRONESS: the Duchesse d'Orléans, whom Madame de Chastellux served as a lady in waiting (same, I, 20-3).

To James Brown

DEAR SIR   Monticello May 7. 95.

Your favor by post came duly to hand: and I accept the offer of 30/.
tho it is but what I had been offered a week before I wrote to you, and
was the first offer made by the person, who I dare say would have bid
higher if I had given him an opening. But having recieved satisfactory
prices heretofore from yourself and the house you were connected with,
I prefer continuing in the same line, and the rather as I have been really
concerned that a previous express agreement to pay my store account
with the produce of the year, and the total loss of my wheat which was
the produce I had destined for it, threw the obligation on my tobacco[1]
which I had meant for the paiment of my balance to you. Nor was it in
my power to obtain any indu[lgence] in time. Mr. Fleming, to whom I
had to pay the money, [. . .][2] 3 days till I could get my answer from you,
his [. . .][3] Philadelphia, where he will employ the money. I gave him
therefore yesterday an order on you at 4. days sight for £196–14–3. I
now inclose you the manifests the whole weight being 15,758 ℔. My
overseer when he inclosed them to me, omitted to tell me where the
tobacco laid in Richmond. Tho' I presume you will have no difficulty in
finding it. I give Mr. Washington an order of this date on you for £5. a
fee in a case he has for me. I shall in the course of the month make up
your balance and am with great esteem Dr. Sir Your friend & servt

TH: JEFFERSON

RC (ViHi); parts of three lines torn away;
addressed: "Mr. James Brown Mercht.
Richmond"; stamped; endorsed by Brown.
Enclosures not found, but see TJ to Brown,
18 Apr. 1795.

Brown's missing FAVOR BY POST is recorded in SJL as written and received on 5
May, but his endorsement on TJ's letter to
him of 18 Apr. 1795 suggests that it was
probably dated 3 May 1795. See also MB, 5
May 1795.

With his payment to MR. FLEMING, TJ
began the settlement of his account with
John Fleming & James McClenahan, merchants who operated a business in Milton

from 1794 to 1798. In 1796 the firm became the sole distributor of Monticello nails
in that place (MB, 1 Nov. 1794, and note, 6,
27, 29 May 1795, and 5 May 1796, and
note). According to SJL, TJ exchanged
nine letters with Fleming & McClenahan
between 18 July 1794 and 9 Feb. 1798,
none of which has been found.

The FEE IN A CASE was for Bushrod
Washington's work in Baylor v. Lewis (MB,
7 May 1795).

[1] Remainder of sentence interlined.
[2] Two or three words torn away.
[3] Two or three words torn away.

To William O. Callis

DEAR SIR   Monticello May 8. 95.

The acquaintance which I had the pleasure of having with you formerly, would scarcely, after such a length of time, justify the trouble I am about to give you. I must therefore rely for it on the circumstances of the case, and your own goodness. Mr. Marks, on his intermarriage with my sister, received among other slaves, a woman of the name of Nance, a weaver by trade. She was then 24. years of age, had a son 5. years old and a daughter 2. or 3. The woman and her two children were delivered to him in 1785 at £95. He is now disposed to sell the woman, of which my sister has given me notice, knowing that, on resuming the business of domestic manufacture, I am in want of a weaver. She is now 34. years of age, and I believe has ceased to breed. Being too far distant from Mr. Marks to treat on this subject myself, and knowing nobody in his neighborhood, I have presumed to sollicit you to negociate the matter for me and to purchase her at whatever price you shall think her really worth. As the information has come to me after I had disposed of my last year's crop, and like other farmers I draw my resources from the earth, I could not engage any paiment but from the proceeds of the present year, say by a year after purchase, which of course will be considered in the price. If you will be so good as to take this trouble for me, and can agree for the woman, I bind myself to whatever you shall agree to, and will give my bond accordingly. She wishes me to buy her children. But I would not purchase the boy; [. . .] as to her youngest child, if she insists on it, and my sister desires it, I would take it. Pardon the liberty which my distant location has obliged me to take with you and accept assurances of the esteem with which I am Dear Sir Your most obedt. servt   TH: JEFFERSON

RC (ViU: photostat); addressed: "Colo. Callis Louisa."

William Overton Callis (1756-1814), a planter with extensive acreage who resided at Cuckoo in Louisa county, Virginia, had served as a Revolutionary War militia officer and as a captain in the Continental line. Besides holding local county offices, Callis became a state political leader, serving as a member of the Virginia convention for the ratification of the federal Constitution in 1788 and as a Louisa county representative in the House of Delegates for all but three years between 1788 and 1800, where he voted with the Republicans (Richard R. Beeman, *The Old Dominion and the New Nation, 1788-1801* [Lexington, Kentucky, 1972], 46, 249, 264; Harris, *Louisa County*, 22-3, 63, 130-31, 171, 183, 225, 442, 445; Swem and Williams, *Register*, 28-53; Heitman, *Register*, 113; Heinrich Gerlach to TJ, 27 Mch. 1781, and note; George Weedon to TJ, 29 Mch. 1781, and note). During his earlier ACQUAINTANCE with Callis, TJ put him in charge of his nephews, Peter and Dabney Carr, when he left for France in 1784. While Peter Carr soon left for school in Williamsburg, Dabney Carr remained under his care for a time (Callis to James Madison, 9 Aug. 1784, in Madison, *Papers*, VIII, 97-8; Madison to TJ, 20 Aug. 1784).

TJ purchased NANCE, a daughter of

Betty Hemings, from his brother-in-law Hastings Marks for £60 and Thomas M. Randolph acquired Nance's YOUNGEST CHILD, Critta, for £70 (MB, 1 Apr., 20 Sep. 1797, 17 Dec. 1798).

Callis's letter to TJ of 15 May 1795, which according to SJL was received by TJ nine days later, has not been found.

From John Harvie, Jr.

DR SIR   Richmond May 9th 1795

I am favour'd with your Letter of april the 27th. and have kept it up a few days, to search for your first Letters Stateing your Claim to the Land referr'd to, but have Mislaid them, your Letter from philadelphia relinquishing any Right to the Moiety of the Survey which I purchas'd of Colo. Randolph being the only one I can now find, you will therefore be pleas'd to send me your propos'd Statement of the Facts, which I will Consider and return you an Answer, for I really am much a Stranger to Mr. Marks's transactions in this Business, and do not know either the date or the precision of his Entry. If upon a View of the Case it appears to me you have the better Right, and I can Safely do it without destroying my Recourse upon Marks, I shall relinquish to you the Moiety I purchas'd of him without Hesitation. If the Right appears to me Doubtful, or such as ought to be Submitted as it relates to Marks to Arbitration, I will in that Case chearfully lay it before any three Gentlemen of your Nomination, and wish you to transmit me their Names that the Subject may in any way you think proper be brought before them. Be assur'd Sir that I have the Utmost Confidence that in bringing forward this Claim, you only Assert what appears to you to be your just Rights, and that I feel for you and I am sure ever shall the highest Esteem and personal regard being Dr Sir Your much Oblidg'd friend & Sevt

JNO HARVIE

RC (MHi); addressed: "Thomas Jefferson Esqr. Monticello in Albemarle"; stamped and postmarked; endorsed by TJ as received 19 May 1795 and so recorded in SJL.

FIRST LETTERS: see Memorandum on Land Dispute with John Harvie, Jr., [after 12 Feb. 1790], and note, in Vol. 27: 773-6. YOUR LETTER FROM PHILADELPHIA: TJ to Harvie, 7 Apr. 1791.

From Giuseppe Ceracchi

DEAR SIR   Philadelphia 11 May 1795

By the infamous manner with which I have been treated about the plan of suscription (of which by this time you must be well informed) I find my self very much hurted in every respects.

The President suscribed generousely but his act was not apprecieted, I then withdrow his suscription and consigned to the care of Mr. Randolph from which I had recceived it. Some of the Manegers have been indifferent and other openly against it. Mr. Wollcot told me that I had been scandalousely decceived by every one that show to take part in this business. This testimony Sir cast a very gloomy spot on the National Caracter, and show that concerted immorality is practised by the Gentilmen in high station. Hunder such evidence you may imagine Sir that a lion would suffer mortification, ther fore I shall fly from this Country as quick as possible in order to forgate all the discitfull gaemes plaed ageins my sincerity.

The sommes spended for to influence this project it amount to towenty five tousend Dollars. Consider that five hear since I left Rome with this project on my head, I abbandoned all other business, upon my arrival recollect the fatigues I vent thru'. I modeled towenty seven busts of your Filosopher, Heros, and graet men, the Magnifent model for the intended National Monument, in new York another scketch of it. Tho. al this hended to nothing but by the lamentations and regard that was payd by Gentilmen of sentiments from which hopes where given for the success for a second attempt.

The afferes of Europe and the accident of my axile from Rome simed to contribut to inforse in me this favorable idea, and for to proive how the Glory of America was ingraved in my heart, I emploied all my time, tho under the persecution, by deply studing a general plan upon the subject of Liberty in America, besides I executed some marbre and alabasters, for to indulge my feeling by the attachements I felt to some respectable individuals, and at last That immortal idea expressed in a Model of Liberty which it as been provued by every one that as seen it a Sublime one. All that been done hunder the dengeor of been confined and [chastized] which situation incrized my expenses behond any imagination.

But what as been the product of all this exercions *Ingratitude* I received for my rewards, the sacrifis of my mony, of time, and performances, and even the last of that honor which I was luking for In order to this dismal, and other, consideration, I think necessary, and my duty hereafter, to be watcfull to the interest of my family.

Therfor I hope you will find just, and of wright that I should call for the valeu of my work upon which you will be pleased to accept a bill of mine and in favour of Mr. George Meade ammounting the somme of *one tousend five hundred Dollars*, for the price of your marble Bust Originaly executed by me, which by this time you most have recceived from Mr. *Gamble* Marchant in Richemond to which it was directed about three month ago. While with graetfull consideration I am Sir Your most Obbt. and Hmble Serv   Jo CERACCHI

RC (DLC); addressed: "The Hnorbl Thom Jefferson Esqre Monticello in Virginia"; stamped and postmarked; endorsed by TJ as received 19 May 1795 and so recorded in SJL.

With the receipt of this letter TJ discovered that the MARBLE BUST Ceracchi had earlier hoped to present "as a patern of my cisel and a little mark of my estime" would cost $1,500. When he first acknowledged the artist's "flattering" proposal, TJ had expressed the hope of making "a just indemnification to the author" (see Ceracchi to TJ, 27 Mch. 1793; TJ to Ceracchi, 14 Nov. 1793), but he now evidently declined to pay the sum requested, though he eventually offered 3,000 livres tournois, if agreeable to Ceracchi, and finally, in 1800, drew on John Barnes for an equivalent payment of $550 for the likeness (TJ to Joseph Marx, 4 June 1796; MB, 10 June 1797, 14 Jan. 1800).

To James Steptoe

DEAR SIR   Monticello May 17. 95.

This will be handed you by Mr. Strickland, a very respectable English gentleman who is travelling through our country to see what is remarkeable in it. He proposes to go through New London, by the Peaks of Otter, to the Natural bridge. As I am unable to give him information of the rout and accomodations of it, which he is anxious to obtain, I take the liberty of referring him to you for that information which I have no doubt you can give him fully. He is a gentleman of worth and great information and will merit and justify any attentions and civilities which you may be pleased to shew him, and all that sort of information which a traveller has need of.

I have been in weekly expectation of setting out for Bedford where I should have the pleasure of seeing you. It will still however be some little time before I can leave home. I am with great esteem Dear Sir Your most obedt. servt   TH: JEFFERSON

PrC (DLC); at foot of text: "Mr. Steptoe."

To Archibald Stuart

DEAR SIR   Monticello May 17. 1795.

The bearer hereof is Mr. Strickland, an English gentleman who is passing through our country to make himself acquainted with it. As he means to take Staunton in his way from the Natural bridge to Winchester, he may have occasion there for information as to his route, the accomodations of it &c. I therefore take the liberty of introducing him to you, and the rather as his great worth, information and respectability will make it agreeable to you to have had an opportunity of rendering him those little attentions and services which smooth the way of the traveller. I am with constant affection Dear Sir Your friend & servt

TH: JEFFERSON

RC (ViU: McGregor Library); addressed: "Archibald Stewart esq. Staunton by mr Strickland." PrC (DLC).

To Isaac Zane

DEAR SIR   Monticello May 17. 1795.

This will be handed you by a Mr. Strickland, an English gentleman who is passing through our country to see what is remarkeable in it. He is a person of great information, worth and respectability, and merits and will justify all the civilities and attentions we can shew him in his passage through it. As his object will be best answered by a communication with gentlemen of the best information in the country, and ours cannot but be furthered by his knowing those most worthy of being known, I take the liberty of presenting him to you, and of giving you the previous assurance that you will be well satisfied with having had an opportunity of shewing him the attentions and civilities which you are willing to shew to others, and of giving him those informations which he as a traveller may need. I am the happier in performing this office as it gives me an opportunity of recalling myself to your recollection and of assuring you of the undiminished affection and respect of Dear Sir Your friend & servt   TH: JEFFERSON

PrC (DLC); at foot of text: "Mr. Zane."

To Archibald Stuart

DEAR SIR   Monticello May 23. 1795.

Your favor of the 3d. inst. has been recieved and I have this day packed all the books which were at home in 2. boxes and lodged them with Colo. Bell to be forwarded by the first careful waggon to Staunton. Those not now sent had been lent to my nephew Dabney Carr in Louisa, and I have to send a small cart for them, which shall be done soon, and they shall be packed and lodged with Colo. Bell in like manner. I have been able to put in a set of the statutes in 6. vols., instead of that in 3. vols., so as to bring them much lower down.—I think you have a watch and clock mender in Staunton. Does he ever pass this way? If he does, I should be glad he would call upon me to do a little work. I have a large clock for the top of my house which needs to be cleaned only and fixed up: also a small chamber or table clock which requires a small article of repair. It might employ him three or four days in the whole. We could furnish here all the tools and implements necessary for the work. On the back hereof you will find a catalogue of the books now sent. I am with great esteem Dear Sir Your sincere friend & servt

TH: JEFFERSON

Hargrave's Coke Littleton	The following remain yet
Barrington on the Statutes.	to be sent.
Hawkins's Pleas of the crown.	Fitzherbert's N.B.
Lilly's entries.	Atkyns 3. v.
Modern entries.	Burrows 3. v.
Sullivan's lectures.	Kelynge
Andrews reports.	P. Williams.
Barnardiston's	Ld. Raymond
Comyns.	1st. Salkeld
Croke	Strange.
Dyer	Vernon.
Davies	
Finch	
Foster	
Levintz.	
Modern rep. 11. vols.	
Plowden	
Precedents in Chancery	
2d. vol. of Salkeld.	
Shower	
Vezey	
Ventris	
Yelverton	
Year books.	
Tables to the reports	
Statutes at large.	

RC (ViU: McGregor Library); with list of books on verso; addressed: "Archibald Stuart esq Attorney at law Staunton"; stamped. PrC (MHi); lacks list of books. Dupl (ViHi); at head of text: "Duplicate"; with list subjoined, crosses being added in a different ink next to all books in left column; at foot of text: "turn over"; on verso of RC of TJ to Stuart, 11 June 1795.

YOUR FAVOR OF THE 3D. INST.: SJL records a letter from Stuart to TJ of 3 May 1795, received 7 May 1795, which has not been found. 6. VOLS., INSTEAD OF THAT IN 3:

TJ evidently sent a six-volume edition of *The Statutes at Large, from Magna Charta, to the Thirtieth Year of King George the Second* (London, 1758), rather than an earlier three-volume set, *The Statutes at Large . . .* *to March 14, 1704* (London, 1706). See Sowerby, No. 1815. In July TJ received two hundred dollars from Stuart "in part paiment for books" (MB, 25 July 1795).

To Robert Brooke

Sir   Monticello May 24. 1795.

A Subpoena in Chancery at the suit of Henry Banks agent and representative of Hunter, Banks, & Co. issued against myself and others was served on me two days ago, as *former governor of Virginia*. Who the other defendants are I know not, nor yet the foundation of the complaint; but I presume they are the members of the then executive council, and that it is for some of our acts or engagements on behalf of the public. No doubt the plaintiff, before this measure, had applied for satisfaction to the present public authorities, and that they have found his claim unjust. I have thought it my duty to give your Excellency this early notice of the suit, as it may be interesting for the public to take the defence into their own hands from the beginning. Possessed of whatever materials may be proper for defence, the Executive will be much more able to have it conducted properly than I should be, who have neither a scrip of a pen, nor trace in my memory relative to the subject: and it would be particularly agreeable to my great desire of being no further implicated in matters which do not concern me. Whether the defence is to be conducted by the public, or by myself, I should propose, if the counsel employed should think it maintainable, to plead that whatever I may have done in it, I did as the servant of the public and pray to be discharged, leaving the plaintiff to seek his redress from the Commonwealth, against whom the laws allow him a suit, unless they have been changed in that particular since my acquaintance with them. The favor of a line of information as to the necessity of my further attention to this suit will be thankfully received. I avail myself of this occasion of rendering my personal homage to the first magistrat of my country, and of assuring you of the sentiments of high respect and esteem with which I have the honor to be Your Excellency's Most obedt. & most humble servt   Th: Jefferson

RC (PHi: Dreer Collection); addressed: "Robert Brooke Governor of Virginia"; endorsed.

Robert Brooke (1761?-1800), an attorney and former member of the House of Delegates from Spotsylvania County, served as governor of Virginia from 1794 to 1796 and as state attorney general from 1796 to 1800 (St. George Tucker Brooke, "The Brooke Family," VMHB, XIX [1911], 100-4; Swem and Williams, *Register*, ix, 36, 38, 40, 42).

Henry Banks's SUIT sought compensation for vessels owned by the Richmond trading firm of Hunter, Banks & Company that had been captured or destroyed in April 1781 after being impressed by Virginia for service against invading British forces. In 1787 the state's Executive Council rejected Banks's application for settlement of the claim. Banks considered petitioning Congress, but instead determined, "as the evil flowed from the instrumentality of the State officers," to bring suit against TJ and other officials responsible for the impressment. TJ evidently succeeded in having himself discharged from the action. In District Court at Richmond in April 1796, Banks won a judgment of £9,681.15.6 against the commonwealth, which was overturned by the Court of Appeals on 3 May 1799 on the grounds that Hunter, Banks & Company had not pursued its claim in county court within the time prescribed by a 1781 statute of limitations (CVSP, IV, 371-2, VIII, 252; H. R. McIlwaine, ed., *Journals of the Council of the State of Virginia*, 5 vols. [Richmond, 1931-82], IV, 190; Call, *Reports*, IV, 338-46; Marshall, *Papers*, III, 30n; TJ to the Speaker of the House of Delegates, 3 Mch. 1781; note to James Maxwell to TJ, 26 Apr. 1781; Brooke to TJ, 4 Sep. 1795; TJ to Bushrod Washington, 1 Oct. 1795).

To William Short

DEAR SIR   Monticello May 25. 1795.

My last to you was of Dec. 23. 1793. Since that I have recieved yours of Nov. 7. 11. 13. 1794. May 22. 1795. Jan. 29. My not having written to you so long a time is to be ascribed with truth to the eagerness and activity with which I am pursuing my agricultural reformations, to the habit which this has induced of procrastinating every thing which will bear procrastination, and to the circumstance that my communications to you would bear it, as there was no change in the state of your affairs till lately. To the reasons to which it may be ascribed let me add one to which it is not nor ever can be ascribable, a want of affection and attention to whatever can interest either your fortune or fame.—Now to business.—I informed you in my last that I had employed a broker in Philadelphia to see if ground rents could be purchased for you there. His information, after long attention to the commission, was that they are scarcely ever at market, and in such small sums as not to be worth attention. The James river canal is now within a year of it's completion. The navigation at this time is practised to within three quarters of a mile of the city of Richmond, for which half toll is taken. It has been difficult to make purchases of shares in it. But an accidental circumstance lately enabled me to purchase 20. shares in a lump for you @ 18/ in the pound. For which I had stock sold for you in Philadelphia which fetched 19/4 in the pound. So that after brokerage on the shares in Richmond, and on the stock in Philadelphia you gain about 5. percent. I shall continue to purchase such smaller quantities as may occur. An opportunity also lately occurred of making an advantageous purchase of lands for you. It is now become next to impossible to purchase an acre of land in this neighborhood on the S.E. side of the mountain, and those on the N.W. side are much less agreeable and valuable in point of climate. Young Mr. Carter having lately purchased Fry's land on Hardware, offered for sale his tract called Indian camp between Colo. Monroe's and Blenheim. As the lands are good, lie tolerably well, and are adjacent to others (Blenheim) which may perhaps be bought by and by, I bought them for you @ 23/6 the acre. The survey which was made yielded 1334 acres. A great part of the money was paid, taking only six weeks to sell stock for the purpose, and the rest will be paid as soon as Mrs. Carter's acquiescence in the line is known. In the margin I give you a general idea of the tract. I propose the ensuing year, if you do not return or countermand it, to hire hands to cut down the whole of the 400. and 300 acres of arable lands not yet cleared, supposed about 450. acres, that you may at once lay it out into it's ultimate division of fields, and by a proper rotation of crops keep them always fine, instead of wearing out one half while you are clearing the other by piecemeal which has been our ruin here. It will cost probably £100. which will be paid by the rents of this and the next year: for most of the open lands are rented. To wit.

top of mountain

400. acres from the top to the foot of the mountain, too steep for culture, but abundantly timbered, and proper for Woodland pasture.

. . . .

about 400. as. of good land lying well, comprehending Cornelius's and Haden's tenements

. . . .

. about 100. as. being a very high .
. and beautiful ridge, all in timber, .
. not rich enough for culture, of a .
. grey colour. . . . .

about 300 as. of good land lying well, comprehending Lively's tenement.

. . . .

suppose 134 as. comprehending Price's tenement of 70. as. The rest poor but well timbered with pine.

Lively about 20. acres at will £6. Haden at will £12. Cornelius for 3. years to come about 20 or 24£. Price, 70 acres *for 2 lives* £8.[1] The last is the only tenant who seems to have precise bounds. Being for life it is fortunate he is a fine English farmer[2] is on the lower line, and out of your way. I should suppose a proper division of the 700. acres of arable would be into 5. fields, to be cultivated in this rotation, to wit. 1. wheat. 2 corn and potatoes. 3. rye. 4. red clover. 5. red clover. My own farms being more exhausted than yours, I am pursuing a milder course. I divide them into 7. fields, for this rotation. 1. wheat. 2. peas and potatoes. 3. corn and potatoes. 4. peas and potatoes till I can get the vetch from England. 5. rye. 6. clover. 7. clover. I began last year with sowing 40. acres of clover. It is now superb. I have sowed 120. acres this year, shall sow 160. acres the next year, and 200 acres every year thereafter.

No land in the world seems so congenial to red clover as our red mountain land. Yours has a noble brook on each side of it, which may be carried over a great part of it. I never saw a more fortunate position than there is on it for a house, and the land being grey, and not rich enough for culture (according to the common idea) but good for grass, covered entirely with the largest forest trees, and overlooking the whole farm on both sides, will permit you to make what you please of it. Monroe owns the part of Carter's tract between Colle and Indian camp, and will build and settle on it. You will be $2\frac{3}{4}$ miles from me, $1\frac{3}{4}$ miles from Colle, $\frac{3}{4}$ from Monroe and about 3 miles or $3\frac{1}{2}$ from Blenheim. Colle has been lately bought at £375. by a Mr. Catlet, whom I do not know. I bought the Indian camp for you because you have expressed some partiality for our neighborhood and climate, because there are no lands in this state of equal fertility and equal advantages as cheap as ours, and you can always get them off your hands for the same money and it's interest, should you not like the purchase. I would not have bought them had not the price been so low as to ensure this; and if the purchase should be inconsistent with your plans, I will immediately on your saying so undertake to reconvert it without loss. I shall do nothing further with them than to clear them, till you come or direct me what to do. In the mean time in continuing the tenants who are at will, I shall insist on such a course of culture as will preserve the lands in their tenure from being exhausted. There is not as yet a gulley in the whole tract. There will be 3. shares out of 7. (of 500. as. each) of Mr. Carter's land over the mountain for sale soon. It is not yet known which they will be, as the partition is not yet made. Should either of them be the plantation directly over the mountain from Indian camp and adjoining it, I shall be extremely tempted to add it to your purchase, because of it's extreme convenience to the Indian camp. It's cheapness will decide me. The purchase already made will employ about 15. laborers and 20 horses. I shall be anxious to receive your directions what to do, and offer myself to have executed any thing you desire. I received information some months ago from Mr. Skipwith that Dr. Griffin (now bankrupt) owed you about 600.£ military certificates, and that Mr. R. Adams knew of some property of his in Baltimore which might be got at. I immediately took measures to get information, of the nature of your demand (for this was the first I had ever heard of it) and where this property was. Before I could obtain the information I received another letter from Mr. Skipwith that James Brown had secured the debt. The interest which arises on your stock I take care to render immediately productive. Having no cypher with you I am at a loss to convey to you a particular idea. I must desire you to look at the 6th. line from the bottom of the last page of your letter of Jan. 29. That is the first I ever heard of it. Conclude it in great jeopardy for that gulph is without bottom. Nor can I help you in it, circumstances not permitting me to even to make an enquiry. All you have written to me in cypher since I left my office is lost to me, not having now your cypher.

I am an utter stranger to the foreign missions since my retirement. I never learnt the super-mission to Madrid till a few days before I received your letter. I had declined it myself. I never suspected Monroe's till he wrote me of the actual appointment. I can assure you that that was not the impediment to your having it; but a regular complaint made against you by the French government in the time of Le Brun, and which I supposed to proceed originally from Maulde. This was given in formally by their minister here.—At the desire of the Secretary of state, I am sending him your private letter to me of Sep. 15. 92. on the subject of the diplomatic arrangement, as he says he is referred to it by you. I have first erased the last two or three lines of it. I thank you for Don Quixot which came to hand yesterday. But I hear nothing of Cortez's letters. God bless you. Adieu. You know my hand without subscription.

P.S. I inclose you a letter which from it's appearance and some other circumstances I suspect has been very long on the way.

RC (ViW); unsigned; at foot of first page: "Mr. Short"; at foot of text: "turn over for P.S.," although postscript is lengthwise in margin of last page; endorsed by Short as received 1 Sep. 1795 and bears his marginal notations (see note 1 below). PrC (DLC: Short Papers); endorsed by TJ in ink; lacks TJ's notation as to postscript and Short's marginal notations. Enclosure not found. Probably enclosed in TJ to Joseph Yznardi, Jr., 27 May 1795, recorded in SJL but not found. A Dupl and a Tripl, referred to in Short to TJ, 30 Sep. 1795, and probably enclosed in TJ's letters of 30 May 1795 to Alexander Donald and 1 June 1795 to Edmund Randolph, have not been found.

LETTER FROM MR. SKIPWITH: Henry Skipwith to TJ, 11 Dec. 1794 (see TJ to Richard Adams, 18 Dec. 1794, and note). The 6TH. LINE FROM THE BOTTOM of Short's 29 Jan. 1795 letter concerned Secretary of State Edmund Randolph's arrangement to invest Short's official salary. For the two sentences that TJ ERASED to conceal Short's disgruntled comments about George Washington, see Short to TJ, 15 Sep. 1792, which the Editors there incorrectly surmised was sent to Randolph early in 1794.

A letter from Short of 14 Aug. 1794, recorded in SJL as received from Madrid "by Vilmont" on 16 Dec. 1794, has not been found.

[1] In the fold between the second and third pages, adjacent to TJ's description of his purchase of Indian Camp and his discussion of the income from its tenants, Short made the following notations:

		"acres
Lively –	20–	£6
Haden –	. . . . .	12
Cornelius	. . . . .	20
Price –	70–	8
		£46

20. acres at £6. are 6/. p. acre
70. acres at 8 are 2/3. p. acre

Purchase of 1334 acres at 23/6.
—make £1567.9."

[2] Preceding five words interlined.

To Froullé

Monticello in Virginia May 26. 95.

Having too far forgot my French to write a letter of any length in that
language, I must address you in English which you will readily get
translated. Your letter of Dec. 17. 1792. having been put into the box
of books which you sent me, did not get to my hands till Feb. 3. 1794.
the box having been sent from port to port in America by various mistakes, before it reached me. It happened unfortunately that being
shipped from Havre in the winter, the books, as always happens in a
winter passage, had been much wetted, and lying wet in America for a
twelvemonth before they were opened, were some of them completely
rotted. In this way the volumes of plates to the Encyclopedie suffered
more than any others, because being larger that the rest, they were laid
in the top of the box, and received the first and greatest effect of the salt
water. To guard against this in future I must desire any books I receive
from you to be packed in a good trunk, covered with leather, or rather
with sealskin: and to repair the loss I sustained on the last occasion I
note in the catalogue now sent 4. volumes of plates of the Encyclopedie
which were so entirely rotten that the leaves, on attempting to open
them, fell into powder. I must pray you to procure these 4. volumes
anew, or my edition of the work will be incomplete and of little value.
I hope that an original subscriber who has taken the work from the
beginning, and means to do it to the end, will be indulged in this. Your
last envoie was from the 39th. jusques et compris the 52d. livraison. I
am now to desire you to send what has been published since, that is to
say the 53d. and subsequent livraisons, with the other books I shall
note. Among these I beg you to distinguish the Greek edition of
Pilpay's fables published at Berlin, the Geoponica[1] and the sequel of
Aeschylus published at Hale and to spare no trouble in getting them.
Mr. Monroe our minister plenipotentiary at Paris will receive the books
and pay you for them. I shall be happy always to hear from you, to learn
that you preserve your health, and that you have not suffered by the civil
storms which have been blowing over your head, being with great and
sincere esteem and attachment Dear Sir Your friend & servt.

Th: Jefferson

Books which Mr. Froullé is desired to send me.
XLIVe. livraison. Encyclopedie. Planches de la botanique. Premiere
    livraison. This volume contained 200. pages of Discours and
    from the 1st. to the 100th. plate.
the next volume of Planches de la Botanique (the label being rotted off,

cannot be copied.) It contained Discours page 201. to 352. and
Plate 101. to 200.

another volume of which the label was rotted. The title page Ornitholo-
gie printed in 1790. It contained the Introduction lxxx. pages.
plate 178. to 230. of birds, and plate 1. to 48. of Quadrupeds.

LIe. livraison. Encyclopedie. Planche d'hist. natur. XIIe. partie. In-
sectes. It contained Discours page. 193. to 320. and plate 66. to
165. of Insects.

The above is a description of the 4. volumes wanting to be replaced in the former part of the work.

————

Encyclopedie methodique. Whatever has come out since the 52d. livraison, to-wit the 53d. and subsequent livraisons.

Cepede. Whatever has come out since his four first volumes 12mo. of
Ovipares.

Schütz Aeschylus. Halae. I have the Prometheus vinctus. Agamemnon.
Septem adversus Thebas. and Persae which came out in
1782.3.4. and I want what has come out since.

Diodorus Siculus. The 4to. edition Gr. Lat. if to be had. Send no other.

Denys d'Halicarnasse en François.

Eutropius. cum metaphrasi Graeca Paeanii. 8vo.

Histoire du bas empire par Le Beau. 22. v. 12mo.

Iornandes, Isidoris, Warnefridus &c. ex editione Gronovii. Amstal-
odami. 1655. 8vo.

Histoire du grand Genghiscan par Petit de la Croix. 12mo. Paris 1710.

la vie ou Memoires de Timour Beg par Petit de la Croix. 4. v. 12mo.
Paris 1722.

les institutions de Timour Beg par Langlés. Paris 1787.

Histoire de la revolution par Rabaud de St. Etienne.

Istoria del Peru dal Molina. Monsr. Molini bookseller at Paris promised
to get this work for me from Italy. Apply to him for it.

Lettres d'Abelard. Lat. Fr. 1723. 2. vols. 12mo.	par Dom Gervaise. voyez Dictionnaire de L'Avocat.
la vie d'Abelard. 1720. 2. vol. 12mo.	Abaillard.

Moralistes Anciens. par L'evesque. 14. vols. petit format.

Zimmerman de la Solitude par Mercier.

Droit des gens moderne de l'Europe par Martens. 12mo. 2. vols. in 1.

Pilpay's fables in Greek by Simeon Seth. Starck. Berlin. 1697. 12mo.

Geoponica Constantine. Gr. Lat. Niclas. Lipsiae. 1781. 2. v. 8vo.

Oeconomie rurale de Saboureux. 6. v. 8vo.

Deipnosophistes d'Athenée par Marolles. 4to.

Morelli Lexicon Graeco–Latino–Gallicum. petit in 8vo.

Elemens de l'art de la teinture par Bertholet. 2. v. 8vo. Didot.
l'art de bien faire les glaces d'office, par Emy. Paris. Le Clerc. 1768.
lettre d'Helvetius sur Montesquieu. brochure qui a paru 1789.
Connoissance des tems for 1795. and as much later as has been published

all to be bound except the Encyclopedie.

RC (NNGr); addressed: "Monsieur Froullé libraire Quai des Augustins à Paris." Enclosed in TJ to James Monroe, 26 May 1795.

Froullé's LETTER OF DEC. 17. 1792, re-corded in SJL as received 3 Feb. 1794, has not been found. The letter printed above is the last one they are known to have exchanged.

[1] Preceding two words interlined.

To James Monroe

DEAR SIR   Monticello May 26. 1795.

I have recieved your favor of Sep. 7. from Paris, which gave us the only news we have had from you since your arrival there. On my part it would be difficult to say why this is the first time I have written to you. Revising the case myself, I am sensible it has proceeded from that sort of procrastination which so often takes place when no circumstance fixes a business to a particular time. I have never thought it possible through the whole time that I should be ten days longer without writing to you, and thus more than a year has run off.

I am too much withdrawn from the scene of politics to give you any thing in that line worth your notice. The servile copyist of Mr. Pitt, thought he too must have his alarms, his insurrections and plots against the Constitution. Hence the incredible fact that the freedom of association, of conversation, and of the press, should in the 5th. year of our government have been attacked under the form of a denunciation of the democratic societies, a measure which even England, as boldly as she is advancing to the establishment of an absolute monarchy, has not yet been bold enough to attempt. Hence too the example of employing military force for civil purposes, when it has been impossible to produce a single fact of insurrection, unless that term be entirely confounded with occasional riots, and when the ordinary process of law had been resisted indeed in a few special cases, but by no means generally, nor had it's effect been duly tried. But it answered the favorite purposes of strengthening government and increasing the public debt; and therefore an insurrection was announced and proclaimed and armed against, and marched against, but could never be found. And all this under the sanction of a name which has done too much good not to be sufficient to cover harm also. And what is equally astonishing is that by the pomp of reports, proclamations, armies &c. the mind of the legislature itself was so fascinated as never to have asked where, when, and by whom has this insurrection been produced? The original of this scene in another country was calculated to excite the indignation of those whom it could not impose on: the mimicry of it here is too humiliating to excite any feeling but shame. Our comfort is that the public sense is coming right on the general principles of republicanism, and that it's success in France puts it out of danger here. We are still uninformed what is Mr. Jay's treaty: but we see that the British piracies have multiplied upon us lately more than ever. They had at one time been suspended.—We will quit these subjects for our own business.

The valuation by Mr. Lewis and Mr. Divers, which had been set on foot before your departure, took place Sep. 19. 1794. It was £173. currency and exchange being then at 40. per cent, it was equivalent to £125–11–5 sterling. On the 19th. of Nov. I drew on James Maury for £37–10 sterl. in favor of Wm. B. Giles, and shall now immediately draw for the balance. Mr. Madison and myself examined your different situations for a house. We did not think it admitted any sort of question but that that on the East side of the road, in the wood, was the best. There is a valley not far from it to the South West and on the Western side of the road which would be a fine situation for an orchard. Mr. Jones having purchased in Loudon we shall hardly see him here, and indeed have hardly seen him. If I can get proper orders from him I will have the ground abovementioned planted in fruit trees from my own nursery, where I have made an extra provision on your account. Indeed I wish you would determine to save 500. or 1000 £ a year from your present salary, which you ought to do as a compensation for your time, and send us a plan of a house and let us be building it, drawing on you for a fixed sum annually till it be done. I would undertake to employ people in the most economical way, to superintend them and the work, and have the place in a comfortable state for your reception. If you think proper to authorize me to do this I will begin immediately on receiving your permission. I am so confident you ought to do it and will do it that I have ventured to send a small claim or two to you, as explained in the two inclosed letters to La Motte and Froullé, with an expectation that you will give me an opportunity of replacing it here to those who shall be employed for you. Should you however not conclude to let us do any thing for you here, I would wish you to suppress both these letters. While speaking of Froullé, libraire, au quai des Augustins, I can assure you that after having run a severe guantlet under the Paris book-sellers, I rested at last on this old gentleman, whom I found in a long and inti-

mate course of after dealings to be one of the most conscientiously honest men I ever had dealings with. I recommend him to you strongly,
should you purchase books. I think La Motte at Havre, a very good and
friendly man, and worth your forming more than an official intimacy
with. Should you have occasion for wines from Burgundy, apply to
Monsr. Parent tonnelier à Beaune, who will furnish you with the genuine wines you may call for, and at honest prices. I found him indeed very
faithful in a long course of employment. He can particularly send you of
the best crops of Meursault, and Goutte d'or. For fine Champagne non
mousseux apply to Monsr. Dorsai, or to his homme d'affaires Monsr.
Louis, if still in place at his Chateau at Aij near Epernay in Champagne.
While recommending good subjects to you I must ask you to see for me
the following persons, present my affectionate remembrance to them,
and let me hear how they have weathered the storm. These are l'Abbé
Arnoux place Vendome, chez M. de Ville an excellent Mentor and
much affectioned to the Americans. Monsr. le Vieillard of Passy whom
Dr. Franklin presented to me as the honestest man in France, and a very
honest and friendly one I found him. Monsr. and Madame Grand at
Passy vastly good and friendly people also. Dr. Gem an old English
Physician in the fauxbourgs St. Germains, who practised only for his
friends and would take nothing, one of the most sensible and worthy
men I have ever known. But I reckon he is gone to England. Many
others I could name of great worth, but they would be too many, and
have perhaps changed their scene. If Mr. Balbatre the musical precep-
tor of my daughters of the fauxbourg St. Honore or it's neighborhood
can be found, be so good as to deliver him the affectionate compliments
of my family, and if he can send them any thing new and good in the
musical line, I will ask you to pay him for it, and let it be packed with
the books from Froullé. These, if they come at all, must come before the
winter, as a winter passage is inevitable ruin to books. I have bought for
Mr. Short the lands between yours and Blenheim 1334. acres @ 23/6
ready money. Three out of seven shares (of 500 as. each) of Carter's
land over the mountain will be for sale soon. It is not known where these
shares will lie as the partition is not yet made. Should ere a one join you
on the mountain, it would be worth your purchase. Collé is lately sold
for £375. to a Mr. Catlet, a farmer, whom I do not know. It is very
possible it will be for sale again. Should you conclude to build a house,
you must decide whether of brick or stone. The latter costs about one
half of the former, to wit about 8/ a perch of 25. cubic feet. I hope Mr.
Jones will change the system of corn and wheat alternately on your land
till the fields are entirely worn out, abandoned, and the new ones treated
in the same manner. This is the way my lands have been ruined. Yours

are yet in a saveable state. But a very little time will put some of them beyond recovery. The best plan would be to divide the open grounds into 5. feilds, and tend them in this order. 1. wheat. 2 corn and potatoes. 3. rye. 4. clover. 5. clover. and then begin wheat &c. over again. By this means they would go into corn but once in 5. years. It would be still better to hire 4. or 5. men for a twelve month to clear the whole body of your tendable lands at once, that you may at once come into the use of the whole, and allow more relief to the old, and an easier service to all of it in general, instead of wearing out one half while clearing the other by little and little as we have generally done in this neighborhood. I am going to have Short's all cleared in this way. [1] But of all this there can be no better judge than Mr. Jones. I have divided my farms into seven fields on this rotation. 1. wheat. 2. pease and potatoes. 3. corn and potatoes. 4. peas and potatoes till I can get the vetch from Europe. 5. rye. 6. clover. 7. clover. My lands were so worn that they require this gentle treatment to recover them. Some of yours are as far gone.—There are two or three objects which you should endeavor to enrich our country with. 1. the Alpine strawberry. 2. the skylark. 3. the *red*-legged partridge. I despair too much of the Nightingale to add that. We should associate Mrs. Monroe to you in these concerns. Present to her our most affectionate esteem, not forgetting Eliza. We are all well except Mr. Randolph, whose health is very frail indeed. It is the more discouraging as there seems to have been no founded conjecture what is the matter with him. Your brother is well, but Mrs. Monroe rather sickly. The death of Dr. Walker is the only event of that kind which has taken place in our neighborhood since you left us. Dr. Gilmer still lives. His eldest daughter is to be married to a Mr. Wurt the day after tomorrow. Frank Walker has succeeded to the whole of Dr. Walker's estate, said to be worth £20,000. Sam Carr married to a daughter of Overton Carr in Maryland, and probably will remove there. His mother (my sister) living at his place a little above Dr. Gilmers.—My budget is out. Adieu. God almighty bless you all.

P.S. If you can send us with Froullé's books[2] a supply of 20. or 30. ℔ of Maccaroni, they will be an agreeable addition to his bill.

RC (DLC: Monroe Papers); unsigned. PrC (DLC); at foot of text in ink: "James Monroe"; with one revision in ink (see note 2 below). Enclosures: (1) TJ to Delamotte, 26 May 1795 (recorded in SJL, but not found). (2) TJ to Froullé, 26 May 1795.

SERVILE COPYIST OF MR. PITT: Alexander Hamilton. DREW ON JAMES MAURY: see TJ to Maury, 20 Nov. 1794. A letter from TJ to Maury of 27 May 1795, recorded in SJL, has not been found.

[1] Sentence interlined.
[2] Word interlined in place of "bill," a revision TJ made in ink on PrC.

To John Adams

DEAR SIR   Monticello May 27. 95.

I inclose you a letter from our friend D'Ivernois according to his request expressed in it. Our geographical distance is insensible still to foreigners. They consider America of the size of a garden of which Massachusets is one square and Virginia another. I know not what may have been your sentiments or measures respecting the transplantation of the science of Geneva to this country. If not more successful than mine, the mission of their commissaries will make a bad matter worse. In our state we are already too wise to want instruction either foreign or domestic. And the worst circumstance is that the more ignorant we become the less value we set on science, and the less inclination we shall have to seek it.—We have had a hard winter and backward spring. This injured our wheat so much that it cannot be made a good crop by all the showers of heaven which are now falling down on us exactly as we want them. Our first cutting of clover is not yet begun. Strawberries not ripe till within this fortnight, and every thing backward in proportion. What with my farming and my nail manufactory I have my hands full. I am on horseback half the day, and counting and measuring nails the other half. I am trying potatoes on a large scale as a substitute for Indian corn for feeding animals. This is new in this country. But in this culture we cannot rival you. Present my sincere respects to Mrs. Adams and accept assurances of the respect and attachment of Dear Sir Your most obedt & most humble servt   TH: JEFFERSON

PrC (DLC); at foot of text: "The Vice President of the US." Enclosure: François D'Ivernois to TJ, 21 Mch. 1795.

From Rodolph Vall-Travers

SIR   London, Maÿ 29th. 1795;

Having left mÿ Papers in Holland, when I was called over, to settle my deceased Spouse's Succession; I cannot commemorate the several Letters, I had the Honor to address to your truely-venerable President, to your worthy self, and laudable philosophical Society, to Mr. Adams, your respectable Vice Presidt. and to my good Friend and Relation, Conrad Zollikofer, Merchant at Baltimore; at sundry Times, on various Occasions, both of a political and mercantile, and sometimes literary and scientific Nature; some of which had the Misfortune, of being captured by English Privateers. Which may likewise have happened in Regard to their Answers; none of which having ever come to Hand; neither by Mess. Adams, Dumas, Stophorst, Willinck, Havard & Plemp, the several dutch Correspondents of Adrian Valcks, at Baltimore and Philadelphia. This, I hope, will sufficiently apologize for mÿ long Silence, and unwillingly suspended Continuance of Service.

This present Letter, kindly forwarded by Mr. Pinckney's Secretary along with a Liste of the new improved philosophical Instruments; a Catalogue of the Leverian Musœum, daily enriched by its present worthy Proprietor, Mr. Parkinson; and Mr. Cavallo's new Treatise on Magnetism is to beg the Favor of your imparting the Contents to our honorable american Society, for promoting useful knowledge. Mr. Jn. Churchman, who has also lately published a magnetical Atlas, (last Year,) with 3. Variation Maps of the Needle, constructed after his Theory, has I make no Doubt, forwarded his Work himself and submitted it to the Judgment and Trial of his own learned Countrymen. But for Fear it might have been intercepted at Sea, I subjoin my Copy of his ingenious Conjectures, to be compared with those of Mr. Cavallo.

To facilitate and to promote the Study of Nature, your Society has been diligent, I presume, to collect the choicest Productions thereof, in your hemisphere.

The rich additions Mr. Parkinson makes to his Treasures in the mineral and Zoological Line, collected from all Parts of our Globe, with Specimens of the Progress of Arts of its known Inhabitants, enables him to furnish your american Musœums, out of his Duplicates, with very considerable and extensive Stocks, towards similar universal Collections of natural Curiosities; lending the human Mind to a rational and delightful Contemplation and Admiration of the Works of Creation. His Terms will be very reasonable; as Means only to pursue his incessant Endeavors, to complete his Repository as far as possible, by his extensive Correspondence. Well chosen and preserved objects of american Minerals and Zoology, not described in his Catalogue, will be recieved in Exchange, or for a reasonable Compensation in Money.

Any commands of ÿours, literary or political, shall be faithfully and punctually obeÿed, in anÿ Part of Europe, as often as honored with, by Sir! Your most devoted and respectfull Servant:

RODH. VALL-TRAVERS

P.S.

The printed Catalogue of the Leverian Musœum, published five Years ago, in 2. Vols. 4to. being very incomplete, not containing the 10th. Part of it's Minerals and Quadrupeds, The numerous objects of Fishes, marine Productions in Shells and Corals, Birds, Insects, Reptiles filling twelve Rooms; not being described as yet: Mr. Paterson has delaÿed sending his too imperfect Catalogue, till brought more forward.

But shou'd your Society incline to form a Collection of the above mentioned Description; and point out the Nature of their Wishes, with the Extent of the Summ to be appropriated to the Acquisition in View: Care wou'd be taken, to give every possible Satisfaction.   R.Vs.

All Letters directed to me in England, will come safe to Hand, under Cover to Sir John Thorold, Baronet, M.P. as knight of the County of Lincoln.

Or, under Cover to Mess. Havard & Plemp, Merchants at Rotterdam, whom I hope to see soon.

RC (PPAmP: Manuscript Communications, Trade); beneath dateline in John Vaughan's hand: "Read May 19. 1797 R. Valtravers to Mr. Jefferson. *Donations*."

MR. PINCKNEY'S SECRETARY: William A. Deas, who remained in London as interim chargé d'affaires when Pinckney departed for Spain on 11 May 1795 (Frances Leigh Williams, *A Founding Family: The Pinckneys of South Carolina* [New York, 1978], 305). CATALOGUE: *A Companion to the Museum, Late Sir Ashton Lever's*, 2 vols. (London, 1790), described items in the LEVERIAN MUSŒUM, a natural history collection

in London begun by Sir Ashton Lever and subsequently acquired in a lottery by James PARKINSON, whom Vall-Travers also refers to as "Paterson" (DNB, XI, 1016, XV, 313-14). NEW TREATISE: Tiberius Cavallo, *A Treatise on Magnetism, in Theory and Practice, with Original Experiments*, 2d ed. (London, 1795). MAGNETICAL ATLAS: John Churchman, *The Magnetic Atlas, or Variation Charts of the Whole Terraqueous Globe* (London, 1794). TJ presented the works by Cavallo and Churchman to the American Philosophical Society on 19 May 1797 (APS, *Proceedings*, XXII, pt. 3 [1885], 257).

To James Brown

DEAR SIR   Monticello May 30. 1795.

I have this day delivered to Mr. Snelson two barrels of nails, which with those delivered him before for himself and Mr. Reeves, and some other credits completes as I expect the balance I owed you. I shall endeavor to see Mr. Snelson if possible before our post-day, in order to be able to state to you the sums placed in his hands, which I cannot do of my own knolege with accuracy, tho' I know them within a small matter. In the mean time, as I had received no statement of interest from you, I have made out one myself on the justest principles I could, meaning it merely for my government in conjecturing when my balance should be completed, but su[bject to] your correction.—As soon as I get Mr. Snels[on's accoun]t, I will make a statement of the credits making [. . .] £154–4–9. I have to ask the favor of you to send the inclosed letter to

Mr. Donald through some safe channel. I am with great esteem Dear Sir Your friend & servt   TH: JEFFERSON

RC (ViHi); parts of three lines torn away; addressed: "James Brown esquire Mercht. Richmond"; stamped; endorsed by Brown. Enclosure: TJ to Alexander Donald, 30 May 1795.

A letter from TJ to Brown of 20 May 1795 is recorded in SJL but has not been found. According to SJL, Robert SNELSON and TJ exchanged five letters between 7 Mch. 1795 and 18 Feb. 1797, all of which are missing.

To Alexander Donald

MY DEAR SIR   Monticello May 30. 95.

When I left public office I expected to be so much at leisure that I should keep up a very animated correspondence with my friends. On my return home I found my farms in a ruinous condition, which made it necessary for me to undertake their recovery and culture myself. Forced to make myself acquainted both with the theory and practice, I at length became so fascinated with the occupation that I am now the most ardent farmer in the state. I live on my horse nearly the whole day, and when in the house it is in a state of fatigue which admits neither thought nor action. I rarely take up a book, and never a pen if I can help it. Hence instead of the animated correspondence I had calculated on, I have kept no correspondence but where pressing business called for it. The proof is that I have not written a line to Monroe since he left this country nor to Short or yourself since I came home to live. Yet certainly my affection for you all is not abated. And the truth is that thro the whole time I have constantly believed I should write to you within 10. days or a fortnight, till more than a year has slipped off. I have at length cut short the procrastination and am writing to you all, and take the liberty of putting Mr. Short's letter under your cover. Monroe's I must send otherwise, your country having undertaken the Quixotical task of forcing mankind by war to govern themselves *reasonably*, assuming her own notions too to be the true measure and standard of reason. But if she would bestow the same care and expence on her own island she would make her own people happier; and I doubt whether France is sensible of the felicities forced upon her. The money spent by Great Britain to force France to take care of herself, if applied to the improvement of her own soil and advantages, would have opened every stream for navigation to it's source, would have conducted every drop of running water in the kingdom over every farm it was capable of irrigating, and would have carried a market road to every arable acre of the mountains of Scotland and Wales. This would probably have added one fourth to the means of subsistence in that country, and consequently to it's population. However to provide for an increased population by new means of subsistence is more troublesome than to cut their throats, and especially when by the same operation you can oblige a neighbor in the same way by cutting the throats of a million or two for them. Your government seemed very desirous of administering to us also, and certainly at one time had ordered their surgeons to commence work upon us. By the help of a little quakerism on our part, and a turn of fortune on theirs, we are permitted to go on cultivating our fields in peace, and still feeding and employing their weavers and mechanics. Oh! shame on such a government!

The crop of tobacco which I had destined for you was put in to Mr. Brown's hands to be shipped to D. & B. I do not now recollect what accident detained it here longer than it should have been, but before it was shipped the misfortune of that house was known. Mr. Brown then shipped it to some other house, I know not to whom. The prices he got were unusually high, to wit for one parcel £16 sterl. a hhd, and £12–7– 6 for another. Yet when we consider the weight of the tobacco, about 1300 ℔. each hogshead, the former comes to 32/7 and the latter 25/4 pr. hundred currency. Tobacco is now here at 33/ which price is not more uncommon than £16. a hogshead to the shipper. With respect to myself I have a constant offer of 5. dollars at Philadelphia, and the top of the market if higher. I should always be a loser then when I should get less than £15. sterl. a hogshead, a price which no experience would justify any body in expecting for their shipments. Hence it is that I never was a shipper of tobacco, and the crop I had ordered to you was the only one I ever shipped in my life. Certainly were I to ship, and should I ever ship, it should be to you, since the maxim of 'no favor in trade' which is a true and just one, ensuring *equal* favor in the hands of a friend, leaves us free to indulge our friendship with a preference. At this place I make no tobacco. I still pursue it in Bedford, but am not sure how long I may find it my interest to do so. The town of Lynchburg in that neighborhood ensures a good market for wheat there, as that of Milton two miles below me does here. It is lately only that I have recieved my account from Mr. Brown, and was sorry to see that some of the items of the London account were not in it. Particularly the telescope and orrery, and you have never mentioned to me what they cost. Pray do this in your next that I may either make remittance for it or payment to Mr. Strange. Perhaps I may ere long send a bill of exchange for some books so as to include it with them.—Public news you do not expect from us.

Of private there is not much. Your old friend Dr. Walker is dead, and Frank is universal legatee, which was contrary to the expectations of the rest of the family. Our friend Mr. Madison of Orange is married.

In one of your letters you flatter us with the idea that you may one day visit us at Monticello. I love to believe whatever I ardently wish. You even talk of laying your bones in America, and I, like other people, am so much the dupe of the fondness for the natale solum as to believe seriously there is no quarter of the globe so desireable as America, no state in America so desireable as Virginia, no county in Virginia equal to Albemarle, and no spot in Albemarle to compare to Monticello. Come then, since you cannot have Monticello, and fix yourself along side of it, and let us take our soupe and wine together every day, and talk over the stories of our youth, and the tales of other times. We shall never see better. Only do not be too long in thinking yourself rich enough for retirement; otherwise we may both first make our great retirement to where there is neither soupe nor wine, and where we are told that neither moth nor rust doth corrupt. From this the lord preserve us both for many good years, and have us always in his holy keeping. Adieu. Your's affectionately   TH: JEFFERSON

PrC (MHi); at foot of first page: "A. Donald esqr"; endorsed by TJ in ink on verso. Enclosure: Dupl, now missing, of TJ to William Short, 25 May 1795 (acknowledged in Short to Donald, 30 Sep. 1795, in DLC: Short Papers). Enclosed in TJ to James Brown, 30 May 1795.

TJ had requested Donald to market his Bedford CROP OF TOBACCO in London in a letter of 11 Oct. 1792. D. & B.: the London mercantile firm of Donald & Burton, whose

MISFORTUNE is described in Donald to TJ, 10 Mch. 1793. TJ's ACCOUNT FROM MR. BROWN has not been found, but see TJ to Brown, 7 May 1795, and note. For the TELESCOPE AND ORRERY, see TJ to John Jones, 26 Dec. 1792, and note to Donald to TJ, 10 Mch. 1793. NATALE SOLUM: "native country." Donald closed his correspondence with TJ with a letter of 22 Feb. 1796, recorded in SJL as received from London 14 May 1796, but not found.

To Philip Mazzei

DEAR SIR   Monticello May 30. 1795.

It is long since I ought to have acknoleged your two last favors of May 19. and Nov. 18. 93. and could I have foreseen that waiting for little circumstances would have delayed my answer from week to week and month to month, I should have cut them short. The letters came very late to my hands, a little before I left my office, when every thing of course was hurry. After I returned home, in January of the last year, and got my papers, I found much to do previous to my looking into them. As soon as I could do this however, I took up yours and wrote to

Mr. Blair, stating your situation and recommending the sale of your property in the funds. It happened that just before my letter reached his residence, he had set out on a judiciary tour to the Northern states, and when he returned, the price of stocks was under a depression, which, as it was judged to be temporary, we thought it best to await the event of. In the mean time came a letter from Messrs. Van Staphorst & Hubbard which gave reason to believe you had a sure resource in them. It is not till lately I have been able to procure the information necessary for their perfect satisfaction; because Mr. Madison, to whom I applied for it last summer, had left the papers respecting Dohrman in Philadelphia and they could not be got at till he went there to the late session of Congress. I have now given them the best view I could get of your property here, and I will recapitulate it to you, that you may correct any thing in it which is wrong.

	D C.
1. Your money in the hands of the US. of 6. percents	1048.50
of 3. percents	786.37
of deferred debt	524.25
Total.	2359.12

Interest is due on this from about April 94. except what was received by Mr. Blair and laid out in two bills, to wit, N. Anderson on Wm. Anderson of London for £39–17–10½ and George Meade on George Barclay of London for £70.8–6 sterl. both payable to Van Staphorsts & Hubbard, forwarded to me, and now inclosed to them by triplicates, to be placed to your credit. Should you wish to sell out this property, it is at 19/to 19/6 in the pound.

2. Your claim against Dohrman for £2000. bearing interest from Nov. 1788. at 7. percent. This is New York money @ 8/ to the Dollar, and secured as you know by the mortgage of a complete township of about 20,000 acres of land given Dohrman by a resolution of Congress of Oct. 1. 1787. (which see in their journals) and is probably of the best land North of the Ohio. Mr. Madison has I believe instituted a suit to foreclose the mortgage some time ago as I strongly pressed him to do.

3. Your house and lot in Richmond. The ground in that quarter is rising slowly from the depression of price into which it had fallen: but the house is going to decay rapidly, and I believe there is no person who is authorized to pay any attention to it, to lease or to sell it. I doubt if more than £200. could be got for it.

4. The purchase money of Colle £250. I got a judgment lately for it, but by the present execution laws, the money will hardly be got till next spring. It shall be remitted to Messrs. Van Staphorst & Hubbard, deducting only my small balance.

5. Some balances of debts due you, of which I have no information, except that of Nicholas, certainly desperate, and that of Hylton probably so.

I have had an arbitration with Anthony Giannini on his claim of clothing and a passage to Italy. The arbitrators decided he had no claim to cloathing but that you were still liable, and myself also as your security, to pay his passage whenever he chuses to go to Italy, and can find a conveyance. Anthony not content with this, has brought a suit, which will be determined this summer. I shall do the best for you I can. If his right to a passage is still confirmed, I will buy it up if I can do it reasonably, that you may be clear of him.

I send herein a few seeds of our cymlin (with running vines) and some of the squash (with upright stems) the last I got at New York, and are the best ever yet known. I thank you for your kind offers of service. I know of nothing particular in your quarter which I would trouble you about. Were a ship coming from Leghorn direct to Richmond, and the Captain would bring, as a venture of his own, some good Verdeè wine, or good oil, and receive his pay here (you having previously fixed that with him, which otherwise he would be exorbitant in on his arrival) I should always like it. But such direct occasions never happen, and indirect ones through any other port of America, occasion more trouble and expence than the gratification will counterbalance.

Mr. and Mrs. Bellini are both become paralytic. He less so than she is. Indeed he is able to go on with his school. They are very poor. Our friend Madison (of Orange) is married. J. Blair has lost his wife and son. His daughters are both married to professors of the college. Andrews one of them. E. Randolph succeeded me as Secretary of state. G. Mason dead. I recollect nothing else to be noted concerning those whom you esteemed. I am returned home with an inflexible determination to leave it no more. My eldest daughter (married to the eldest son of Colo. T. M. Randolph deceased) her husband and three children are living with me. The youngest is well. So that we have a considerable domestic society. I am become the most ardent and active farmer in the state. I live constantly on horse back, rarely take up a book, and never a pen if I can avoid it. This has had it's share in the tardiness of the present letter. For if I am ever in the house, it is in such a state of fatigue as prevents both thought and action. I am just resuming my buildings. Derieux as you know had a present of 500. Louis from Me. Bellanger. He had afterwards a legacy of 15,000 livres from an uncle. Both are gone. He is removed to Payne's ordinary in Goochland, where he has set up a wet store, some of us having procured him a credit to begin with. I think he will succeed in this line. Me. Bellanger is sending him

[370]

6000. livres more, announcing it however as the dernier sous. I shall endeavor to prevail on him to preserve this sum as a capital to animate his commerce. He has a house full of children.—I shall always be happy to hear from you, and ready to do any thing requisite for you here. The remittance for Collé will be made to V. Staph. & Hub. unless otherwise ordered. I am with great affection and respect Dear Sir Your sincere friend & servt   TH: JEFFERSON

Dupl (DLC: Mazzei Papers); at head of text: "Duplicate"; at foot of first page: "Mr Mazzei"; endorsed by Mazzei:
"Jefferson, 30 Maggio ⎫ 1795
    rispta: 26. 8bre ⎭
℞ Amst., Londra, e Livorno.

e 24 Marzo 96
in nave Veneziana da Liv. ℞ Fil. in una a Madison, e quella a Ed. R. ambedue ante." The Editors supply the following translation:
"Jefferson, 30 May ⎫ 1795
    answered 26. October ⎭
℞ Amsterdam, London, and Livorno.

and 24 March 96
in the ship Veneziana from Livorno ℞ Philadelphia in one to Madison, and that to Edmund Randolph both before." Enclosed in TJ to Mazzei, 8 Sep. 1795.

Neither Mazzei's letter of 19 MAY 1793 nor the one that TJ WROTE TO MR. BLAIR has been found (see note to Mazzei to TJ, 18 Nov. 1793; John Blair to TJ, 13 June 1795, and note). A LETTER FROM MESSRS. VAN STAPHORST & HUBBARD to TJ of 14 Jan. 1794, recorded in SJL as received from Amsterdam on 10 June 1794, is also missing. TJ gave the firm THE BEST VIEW I COULD GET OF YOUR PROPERTY HERE in a letter of 28 May 1795, and sent the bills of exchange INCLOSED TO THEM BY TRIPLICATES in a letter of 27 May 1795, both recorded in SJL but not found (see two letters from Van Staphorst & Hubbard to TJ, 10 Oct. 1795).

Notes on Conversations with William Strickland

Turkey.
May. 1795. William Strickland esq. son of Sr. George Strickland of York in England informs me that about 3. years ago he found in the herald's office in London papers vouching the following facts.

That Sebastian Cabot, having grown old, and become poor, petitioned the crown for some recompence in consideration of his voyages and discoveries in America, and was allowed a pension.

That a   Strickland, an ancestor of his, had been one of Cabot's captains in those voyages, and petitioned also for a reward. But not being in necessitous circumstances, as Cabot was, he prayed that he might be permitted either to assume the newly discovered American bird, the turkey, for his crest, or to change the crest of his arms for that (I do not recollect which) as a token of his services. That the permission was accordingly given him by grant from the crown in the 1st. year of E.6. which he read in the herald's office: and that the crest of his family's arms has ever since been a turkey.—He mentioned that the circumstance which occasioned the propagation of the round potatoe in Ireland so long before England was that one or some of Sr. Walter Raleigh's ships touched in Ireland on their return from America, and the roots being still sound, were left there.

MS (DLC); entirely in TJ's hand, with title inserted afterward in the same ink; endorsed by TJ: "Turkey."

William Strickland (1753-1834), from whom TJ received this information, was the eldest son of Sir George Strickland, a Yorkshire agriculturist who introduced new methods of crop rotation and new types of farm machinery. A naturalist and honorary member of the British Board of Agriculture, Strickland established his own farm at Welburn in York before succeeding his father as the sixth baron of Boynton in 1808. He toured the United States in 1794 and 1795 collecting information on American farming practices for the Board that he later used as the basis for a critical assessment in *Observations on the Agriculture of the United States of America* (London, 1801). See Sowerby, No. 819. During Strickland's visit to Monticello from 14 to 16 May 1795, TJ gave him drawings and a small model of his moldboard plow, which the Englishman praised as an invention "formed upon the truest and most mechanical principle of any I had seen." Strickland's 1798 paper "On the Use of the Thermometer in Navigation" was read by Jonathan Williams at a meeting of the American Philosophical Society in 1800 and published in the Society's *Transactions* two years later. TJ's subsequent correspondence with Strickland—marked by exchanges of publications, seeds, and information on agriculture and natural history—continued until 1805 (William Strickland, *Journal of a Tour in the United States of America, 1794-1795*, ed. James E. Strickland [New York, 1971], xi-xii, 22-3n; Cokayne, *Baronetage*, ii, 115-16; TJ to James Steptoe, 17 May 1795; Strickland to TJ, 20, 28 May 1796, 16 July 1798; TJ to Strickland, 12 Mch. 1797, 23 Mch. 1798). For the dates of Strickland's visit to Monticello, see his journal, with a printed

format for recording weather, flora, and fauna, which he kept from 19 July 1794 to 1 Sep. 1795 while traveling in the United States (photocopy on deposit NHi: Strickland Papers).

To prepare for his trips to various locations in the United States, Strickland kept two notebooks, one arranged by state and the other by sites he planned to visit, in which he copied passages from various published sources, including the writings of the Marquis de Chastellux and John Bartram. In both notebooks, Strickland quoted extensively from the Stockdale edition of TJ's *Notes on the State of Virginia* (London, 1787). In his entry for "Monticello" in the second notebook, Strickland departed from his usual practice of simply excerpting sources and set down questions and topics he planned to discuss with TJ as follows: "to enquire of Mr: Jefferson concerning the oil nut; which grows three miles on this side Greenbriar town at the foot of the hill, and again on this side near the River. Bartram.

Enquire after the Pea Vine in all this country
Buffalo clover, and Seneca scent-Grass.

At least 50 caves are worked on the Greenbriar for Making nitre—Are they continued?

Silk grass and wild hemp. Round horned Elk. Indian tumuli are spheroidical about 40 feet diam: and 12 feet high, round the base an excavation out of which the earth had been taken to form the hillock—Jeff: P: 158—

Why hemp is not cultivated in Virginia—

Mr: Jefferson has a Park containing some American deer. Chast: V: II. P: 51.

In Virginia is a native hemp called silk grass the thread of which is stronger than hemp, beside which they have *3 or 4 sorts* of native hemp which thrive in the poorest lands. Amer. Husb: VI. P275.

Cassia Chamdæcrista—

After a long N:E: storm, rain will sometimes penetrate through walls of well burnt brick and good mortar: therefore brick and stone Houses are not accounted wholesome in Virginia. Jeff: P: 227" (unpaginated notebook in NHi: William Strickland Papers).

For the PENSION granted by Edward VI to Sebastian Cabot in 1548, see George P. Winship, *Cabot Bibliography* . . . (New York, 1900), 46.

Concerning the TURKEY crest that the same monarch granted to the Strickland family in 1550, see G. Bernard Wood, *Historic Homes of Yorkshire* (Edinburgh, 1957), 119-20. TJ had an ongoing interest in the history of the introduction of the North American turkey to England (TJ to Hugh Williamson, 10 Jan. 1801). He made the following note on the subject:

"Turkies
"Modus for the tithe of any thing of late introduction into England as turkies, hops, and whatever is in the same predicament, cannot be a valid modus for want of a sufficient duration [for a modus can only be founded on prescription from time immemorial] 2. Wooddeson. 106. and quotis. Watson 408. (edn. 1701) Bunb. 308." (MS in DLC: TJ Papers, 98: 16867; undated; written entirely in TJ's hand at the top of a narrow scrap; brackets in original).

To Tench Coxe

DEAR SIR   Monticello June 1. 1795.

I received a few days ago only your favor of Mar. 20. accompanied by the Collection of your papers lately printed, for which I cordially thank you. It will enable me to turn with more convenience to pieces which I consult with pleasure and instruction.

I congratulate you on the successes of our two allies. Those of the Hollanders are new, and therefore pleasing. It proves there is a god in heaven, and that he will not slumber without end on the iniquities of tyrants, or would-be tyrants, as their Stadtholder. This ball of liberty, I believe most piously, is now so well in motion that it will roll round the globe. At least the enlightened part of it, for light and liberty go together. It is our glory that we first put it into motion, and our happiness that being foremost we had no bad examples to follow. What a tremendous obstacle to the future attempts at liberty will be the atrocities of Robespierre!—We are enjoying a most seasonable sowing after a winter which had greatly injured our small grain. Nothing can give us a great crop. I doubt if it can be made even a good one. Our first hay-cutting (clover) begins to-day, this may mark to you the difference of your seasons and ours. My clover in common upland fields which were never manured will yeild 1500. ℔ to the acre at this cutting, which I consider as an encouraging beginning.—I take the liberty of asking your care of two letters, both of them of importance. I have not inclosed Monroe's either to our office of foreign affairs or the Minister of France, because I thought you might possibly find a safer channel than either. It requires safety and secrecy. But adopt either of those channels, if you think them the best. I am with much affection Dear Sir Your friend & servt

TH: JEFFERSON

PrC (DLC); at foot of text: "Tenche Coxe esq." Enclosures: (1) TJ to James Monroe, 26 May 1795, and enclosures. (2) TJ to Van Staphorst & Hubbard, 27 and 28 May 1795 (not found, but see TJ to Philip Mazzei, 30 May 1795, and note).

To Henry Knox

DEAR GENERAL   Monticello June 1. 1795.

I recollect you were so kind as to undertake to give me an account of the success of an experiment made at Boston with a mill on the construction which was invented and contested by three different persons. Clarke of this state was one. A Physician of one of the Eastern states, whose name I do not recollect, was another. He had brought forward some other inventions. The third claimant was of New York. The mill was to go with either wind or water. The axis was vertical. The sails were in frames like doors, vertical also. They opened and shut on the side next the axis, and their hinges were at the extremity of the arm. This description is meant merely to bring into your mind the kind of machine, and perhaps the wretched diagram in the margin may assist. I hear there is one constructed at Boston which succeeds. I want much to erect something which may work a saw mill, or work a smith's smiting hammer in a place where I can have no agent but wind. I wish to know if this machine has answered in experience, and in that case the dimensions of the sails will be important, and of what substance made. I think the Eastern inventor had a convenient method of stopping the machine when he chose by cords. I would not trouble you with other particulars, because I presume we can contrive them. Have you become a farmer? Is it not pleasanter than to be shut up within 4. walls and delving eternally with the pen? I am become the most ardent farmer in the state. I live on my horse from morning to night almost. Intervals are filled up with attentions to a nailery I carry on. I rarely look into a book, and more rarely take up a pen. I have proscribed newspapers, not taking a single one, nor scarcely ever looking into one. My next reformation will be to allow neither pen, ink, nor paper to be kept on the farm. When I have accomplished this I shall be in a fair way of indemnifying myself for the drudgery in which I have passed my life. If you are half as much delighted with the farm as I am, you bless your stars at your riddance from

public cares. Present my best respects to Mrs. Knox, and accept assurances of esteem and regard from Dear General Your most obedt. & most humble servt
Th: Jefferson

RC (Gilder Lehrman Collection: Knox Papers, on deposit NNPM); endorsed by Knox. PrC (DLC); at foot of first page in ink: "Genl. Knox."

The THREE DIFFERENT PERSONS who competed for a patent were John Clarke, Apollos Kinsley, and Daniel Stansbury, but the contending applications were for a "machine to work in a current of water" (*List of Patents*, 8).

From Robert Morris

Dear Sir   Philada June 1. 1795

I am much at a loss for an Apology to you but if the truth will form one you shall have it. When I received your letter of the 19th. of Febry. I determined not to answer untill I should go out to the Hills and enquire of Mr. Crouch about the Sheep. Your letter was laid by untill this could be done. My Constant Avocations put off the Walk to the Hills untill from Continual Employment the thing slipt out of my mind. At length I came across your letter again and then, ashamed of the neglect, away I went to the Hills; Crouch was not at home and nobody there that could give me a satisfactory Account, I mentioned the subject to Mrs. Morris who reminded me frequently and every time she did so, a second visit to the Hills was determined on. At length I saw Crouch who did not give me that satisfactory account which I expect. He says the Original imported Ram is dead but he has left a Successor which the Old Man thinks came from the imported Spanish Yew, but his memory being treacherous he cannot say positively that it is so. He firmly beleives it and from the appearance of the Animal I beleive so too. The Original imported Yew is alive but he thinks she is past breeding, there is one or two others which he beleives to be of the genuine Breed from the Spanish Ram and Yew but he cannot be positive. This Account of the spanish Family of Sheep mortified me on your Account exceedingly and cooled the Ardour I had felt in the desire of complying with your Wishes by assisting to give Virginia the opportunity of raising fine Wool—however the matter now stands as I have stated and if you think the pursuit still worthy of your Attention I will send round to Richmond any order of those above mentioned—that is, the Ram and Old Yew with the Young that are supposed to be genuine. Tell me to whose Care I shall address them at Richmond, or if you prefer to send for them they shall be delivered at once to whoever brings your Order. My time and attention has been and is too much engrossed by other Objects, or what you formerly said respecting these Sheep would have induced me to preserve and raise the Breed. As to trusting to others there is no getting proper attention to be paid without the Masters Eye or Interference, as you will observe in the case of Crouch whom I urged on the Subject. As I think my apology for neglecting to answer your letter in due time makes but an awkard figure, and as I feel, so I think it best to plead Guilty, and throw myself upon Mercy for forgiveness and to entitle myself to merciful Consideration I can truly say that the Crime has arisen not from intention or want of Respect, but from too much employment and engagement, beside, I suffer severe punishment every time the Recollection occurs. My Regard and friendship for you is your Avenger, therefore you must forgive as I cannot.

I have no doubt of the enjoyments you find in Retirement. You are a philosopher as well as a practicall Planter. These pursuits will occupy body and mind and when that is the case happiness is generally attendant. With respect to yourself, to retire was to act wisely, but as your Retirement regards the United States, the Public have to lament the loss of Abilities and Talents which have been eminently useful and which no doubt would have Continued to be so as the prime and vigour of life still remains. I think however that it is not improbable that you will again be drawn forth into public life. I have Retired from Public service and will never resume it, and I am trying to clear myself of a vast load of private business, in Order to enjoy if I can what will remain of life when my Work is accomplished in quiet and Calm. Mr. Jay is just arrived from England at New York and I suppose we shall soon know the sense of our Government upon the Treaty he has made with Britain. The Continuance of Neutrality and preservation of peace are great Objects and the most desirable to this Country which I hope will never be engaged in War. With my best Wishes for the Continuance of that Tranquility which you now enjoy I Remain in the utmost Sincerity and Truth Dear Sir Yr friend & obt hb St   RM

FC (Lb in DLC: Morris Papers); at head of text: "Thomas Jefferson Esqre Monticello—Virga." Recorded in SJL as received 23 June 1795. Enclosed in TJ to Archibald Stuart, 30 June 1795.

To Edmund Randolph

DEAR SIR   Monticello June 1. 95.

I have to acknolege the receipt of your favor of Apr. 11. and I now inclose the letter of Mr. Short on the diplomatic arrangement which you desire. It is marked *private*, as you see, having been a part of his private correspondence with me, which was the reason I did not leave it in the office. I take the liberty of inclosing to you a letter for him which I will thank you to forward by the safest conveyance, as it is on the subject of his private affairs and interesting to him to answer. He mentions to me that Mr. Blake would bring for me a copy of Don Quixote, and the Cortez's letters I had been so anxious to get. The former I have received but the latter were not with it. I imagine Mr. Blake has come without them.—We have been for two months past enjoying the most seasonable weather possible. It will improve our crop of wheat, but nothing can make it a good one, the winter had been so hard on it. We this day begin our first hay-cutting, which may mark to you by comparison the difference between our season and that where you are. I sowed three different fields the last spring (94.) on small grain after corn. It is thought none of it will yield less than 150. ℔ to the acre this cutting. I give you this scrap of our delights merely as a bon-bouche. My affectionate respects to the Presidt. and Mrs. Washington, as also to Mrs. Randolph. Adieu. Yours affectionately   TH: JEFFERSON

PrC (DLC); at foot of text: "The Secry. of State." Enclosures: (1) William Short to TJ, 15 Sep. 1792. (2) Tripl, not found, of TJ to Short, 25 May 1795.

To Benjamin Franklin Bache

DR. SIR   Monticello June 2. 1795.

The season being now arrived when all danger of the sea vanishes, I have had Mr. Franklin's gong packed and shall send it immediately to Richmond with instructions to forward it by some safe and known master of a vessel to Philadelphia. As there is rarely a week without some vessel going from thence to Philadelphia, I hope it will arrive soon and safe.

If you can make me up a set of your papers for the year 1794. I should be obliged to you. On delivering them to Mr. Crosby keeper of the Secretary of state's office, and dropping me a line of the cost by post I will return by post an order for the money payable in Philadelphia.— Whenever any copies of Dr. Franklin's works, 8vo. edition, come over I should be happy to know of it that I may take measures for procuring a set. I am with much esteem Dear Sir Your most obedt. servt

TH: JEFFERSON

RC (NN); unaddressed, recipient being identified in SJL.

William Temple Franklin's edition of his grandfather Benjamin FRANKLIN'S WORKS did not appear until 1817-18 (note to TJ to William T. Franklin, 27 Nov. 1790).

To John Barnes

DEAR SIR   Monticello June 3. 1795.

I received last night your favor of May 12. noting the sale of the stock last sent, and that a balance of 267.D. 43c. will remain on hand after deducting the draughts already paid or accepted. I now inclose another Certificate to be disposed of for Mr. Short, being 7504 Doll. 42. cents of deferred debt with a power of attorney to transfer the same, and also to receive the interest due on his stock of all description amounting as I calculate to 314.55 D., for the 1st. day of July next. In consequence of this I make on you the draughts below stated. It is rather doubtful whether I shall push the investments in land &c. for Mr. Short to the whole amount of the paper now sent. Should I not, it will be necessary to reconvert the balance which shall remain into stock. But of this I shall advise you in time. I am with great esteem Dear Sir Your most obedt. servt   TH: JEFFERSON

Draughts on Mr. Barnes above alluded to.

				D	c
at 3. days sight.	June 3.	James Bringhurst junr. & co.		46.74	
		Muir & Hyde		59.37	
		Robert Pollard		36.	
			142.11		
at 6. weeks sight.	June 3.	William Champe Carter		600.	
	4.	do.		600.	
	5.	do.		600.	
			1800.		

PrC (MHi); at foot of text: "Mr. Barnes." Enclosures not found.

Barnes's FAVOR OF MAY 12, recorded in SJL as received 2 June 1795, has not been found. Also not found is a letter from Barnes to TJ of 25 Apr. 1795, recorded in SJL as received 5 May 1795.

According to SJL, TJ on 3 June also wrote letters to the Philadelphia ironmonger JAMES BRINGHURST JUNR., the Philadelphia bookbinders MUIR & HYDE, and ROBERT POLLARD (all missing). A 9 May 1795 letter from Bringhurst, recorded in SJL as received 2 June 1795, and a 14 June 1795 letter from Pollard, recorded in SJL as received 16 June 1795, have not been found. SJL also records letters (now missing) to Muir & Hyde of 4 Feb. and 23 Apr. 1795. The second of these letters evidently concerned a draft of $130 on Barnes in favor of Muir & Hyde (MB, 23 Apr. 1795).

To John Barnes

June 3. 95.

Th: Jefferson owes Mr. Sampson Crosby, keeper of the Secretary of state's office 1.67 D., which not being worth the draught and postage of a letter express, he will thank Mr. Barnes to have it paid him, and to let him know that he may call on him for the little sums he may have occasion for in execution of a request of Th: J. to forward him some newspapers. These will amount to three or four dollars perhaps, and I would wish to have paid without the ceremony of asking my previous approbation.

PrC (MHi); endorsed in ink by TJ.

To William Champe Carter

DEAR SIR   Monticello June 3. 1795.

On a view of the plat of the lands purchased of you for Mr. Short, and taking the Eastern point of one of the Blenheim old fields as uncontrovertibly fixed, because met by a clearing of the Indian Camp, I conjecture that no jury could extend dividing lines from thence so as to leave to the Indian Camp less than 1200. acres. I therefore inclose you three draughts for 600. Doll. each which completes the paiment for that quantity. The balance shall be paid as soon as we can get Mrs. Cartar's agreement to our lines.

Rating the lands over the mountains at 3. dollars, I have thought it possible I might conclude to purchase your two shares at the deduction of a third as you proposed. I will take a little time for further consideration, but would be glad to know from you in the mean time if you would concur in the value I set on them. I am with great esteem Dear Sir Your most obedt. servt   TH: JEFFERSON

	Doll.
1200. acres @ 23/6 = 4700	
Draughts formerly	300.
	600
	2000
	2900
Draughts now inclosd.	1800
	4700

PrC (DLC: William Short Papers); at foot of text: "William Champe Carter esq." Enclosures: TJ's orders on John Barnes, 3, 4, and 5 June 1795, each in Carter's favor for $600 at six weeks' sight (RC of 4 June order in same, with TJ's signature canceled and "Mr. John Barnes Mercht Philadelphia South 3d. street" at foot of text; PrCs of all three orders in same, with 4 and 5 June orders letterpressed on one sheet, that of 4 June being canceled).

To Sarah Champe Carter

MADAM   Monticello June 4. 1795

I have lately made a purchase from Mr. Champe Carter of the plantation called the Indian camp adjoining Blenheim on the side on behalf of Mr. Short. Colo. Carter by his will having devised his lands by plantations, without fixing exact boundaries, it has been understood that the lines were to divide the woodlands between the plantations as equally as might be. I attended at the running of the dividing line between Blenheim and the Indian camp, and it was so conducted as to leave to each the whole of the cleared lands which had belonged to them, and to divide the intermediate woodlands equally as nearly as could be judged. There being no clearings on the mountain the line there was run directly up it. In running between the plantations I recollect that Stepney's plantation particularly was left as belonging to Blenheim. Tho the lines appeared to me to be fairly run, yet as nobody attended on your behalf, I have thought it my duty, not to close the transaction finally till you shall be pleased to express your acquiescence in the line, as it was to be the boundary of the plantation occupied by you. I have therefore taken the liberty of stating the matter to you, in hopes that you will be so good as to signify your wish on the subject, or to name some person who may examine for you whether the line is run consistently with your rights, and enable me to have the transaction finally completed. I avail myself with pleasure of this occasion of expressing to you the sentiments of respect with which I have the honor to be Madam your most obedient & most humble servt.   TH: JEFFERSON

PrC (DLC: William Short Papers); at foot of text: "Mrs. Carter of Blenheim"; endorsed in ink by TJ.

Sarah Champe Carter, the widow of Edward Carter, was the proprietress of Blenheim, a plantation in Albemarle she had inherited upon the death of her husband in 1792 (VMHB, XLIV, [1936], 352-3; Woods, *Albemarle*, 163-4).

From William Champe Carter

DEAR SIR   [ca. 4 June 1795]

I have received your favour containing three drafts each of 600 dollars. With respect to the land over the mountain I do not think they should be rated at less than 20/ per acre and from this would deduct a third, shou'd I think of selling at a lower price I will acquaint you with that determination. With great esteem I am Dear Sir Yr Ob Sert

WILLIAM C. CARTER

RC (DLC: William Short Papers); undated, but endorsed by TJ as received 4 June and so recorded in SJL.

From William Champe Carter

DEAR SIR   June 5th. [1795]

Having occasion to negotiate a draft of yours immediately I have found a difficulty in the business proceeding from the large amount of each bill. I have therefore sent the enclosed which (shou'd it equally suit your convenience) I will thank you to divide into six equal parts. With the greatest respect I am Dear Sir yr Ob Sert

WILLIAM CHAMPE CARTER

RC (DLC: William Short Papers); partially dated; endorsed by TJ as received 7 June 1795 and so recorded in SJL. Enclosure: second draft on John Barnes listed at TJ to Carter, 3 June 1795.

TJ wrote a brief note to Carter on 7 June 1795 enclosing six drafts in his favor on John Barnes for $100 each dated 6, 7, 8, 9, 10, and 11 June 1795 and payable at six weeks' sight, in exchange for the enclosed draft described above (PrC in DLC: William Short Papers, endorsed in ink by TJ; with PrCs of the enclosed drafts in same).

From James Blake

SIR   Phila June 6th, 1795.

I do myself the honor to inclose you a letter I received from Mr. Short the 6th. of January last—and a copy of an introduction Mr. Carmichael gave me to Richard Harrison Esquire of this city. Tho' I am no longer accountable to you for the discharge of the commission you were pleased to give me, still I should be happy my conduct would meet with your approbation.

Cortes's letters, (which you mention in your letter to Mr. George Meade) I am extremely sorry I had not the good fortune to bring with me, owing to the following circumstance. About the middle of last August Mr. Carmichael received permission to return to America, and expecting to leave Madrid in a few weeks after, sent his baggage to Cadiz—and with it C. letters packt up among his other books—but the winter season arrived, before he had made the arrangements necessary for his intended voyage—and I came away without him. For some days previous to my departure from Madrid, the copy of an Order to the Custom-house Officer at Cadiz, authorizing me to open a trunk and to take C. letters out—was prepared, but such was the state of Mr. Carmichael's nerves, that he was unable to write his name. This occasioned a disappointment, which indeed made me very unhappy—as it deprived me of the only occasion, that, perhaps, may ever present itself of rendering you any kind of service. I hope, however, on the arrival of Mr. Carmichael here, which I expect will be in a few days, to have the pleasure of sending you those letters, together with a manuscript respecting the Istmus of Darien, which Mr. Carmichael also intended for you. Cortes's letters are become so rare in Spain, that it cost even the Archbishop of Toledo (at whose expence they were published) a great deal of trouble to procure the copy of them which you are to have.

Mr. Short has probably mentioned to you the name of *Malespino*—a celebrated Naturalist, who has lately returned to Madrid, after having spent seven or eight years in Spanish North and South America, in making observations, drawing charts &c. This gentleman already knows you by Character, and expressed to Mr. Carmichael a great desire of having the pleasure of your correspondence—he speaks and writes the English language tolerably well. With sentiments of great respect I have the honor to be, Sir, Your most obedient & most humble servt.   JAMES BLAKE

RC (DLC); at foot of text: "Thos. Jefferson Esquire"; endorsed by TJ as received 21 July 1795 and so recorded in SJL. Enclosures: (1) William Short to TJ, 4 Nov. 1794. (2) William Carmichael to Richard Harrison, 2 Dec. 1794, Madrid, praising Blake for serving as his secretary for about a year and for having given "many proofs of his attention, secrecy and discretion in that character, and of his conduct in private life, which has always been that of a gentleman, and in every respect agreeable to my wishes," and urging Harrison to treat him "as my friend" (Tr in MHi; at head of text: "Copy"; endorsed by TJ).

THE COMMISSION: see TJ to Blake, 12 July 1793. CORTES'S LETTERS: see note to TJ to David Humphreys, 11 Apr. 1791. A letter (now missing) from TJ to GEORGE MEADE of Philadelphia is recorded in SJL under 22 May 1795, and no doubt was a reply to an undated letter from Meade, not found, that is recorded in SJL as received 19 May 1795. Meade's letter to TJ of 8 June 1795, recorded in SJL as received 23 June 1795, is also missing.

The MANUSCRIPT on the Isthmus of DARIEN, a commentary by the Spanish scientist and naval officer Antonio de Ulloa on a proposal to build a canal through Panama, has not been found (see William Carmichael to TJ, 24 July 1788, 26 Jan. 1789).

MALESPINO: TJ never corresponded with

Alejandro Malaspina, the Spanish naturalist, explorer, and naval officer who in the previous year had completed a five-year circumnavigation of the world in the course of which he explored, among other places, South and Central America, the Philippines, Australia, and New Zealand (Bleiberg, *Diccionario*, II, 860-2). But in April 1789 he did receive from William Carmichael a copy of a memorial to the Spanish government proposing such an expedition that was apparently composed by the Comte de Fleurieu ("Plan de un Viage centifico, y Politico à el rededor del Mundo," Tr in DLC: TJ Papers, 234: 42244; undated and unsigned; enclosed in Carmichael to TJ, 26 Jan. 1789, the note to which mistakenly describes the enclosure as unfound).

To John Barnes

SIR   Monticello June 8. 1795

In my letter of the 3d. instant inclosing some stock for sale I informed you of several bills I had drawn on you, and among others I mentioned three of the 3d. 4th. and 5th. of June for 600. Dollars each in favor of Mr. Wm. Champe Carter. Since that date, I have for the convenience of Mr. Carter, *taken back* the draught of June 4. for 600. D. and in exchange for it I have given him six draughts for 100. Doll. each payable to himself or order at six weeks sight, and dated June 6. 7. 8. 9. 10. 11. of which change this serves to advise you. I am Sir Your very humble servt   TH: JEFFERSON

P.S. I shall authorize Henry Remsen of New York to draw on you for a sum of from 50. Doll. to 100. D. the amount not being exactly known. Be pleased to honor it. Should it go beyond that amount, still honor it, as Mr. Remsen can be entirely relied on.

PrC (CSmH); at foot of text: "Mr. John Barnes"; endorsed in ink by TJ.

To John Taylor

TH:J. TO CITIZEN TAYLOR   Monticello. June 8. 95.

I inclose you a few seed of the Rutabaga, or Swedish winter turnep. This is the plant which the English government thought of value enough to be procured at public expence from Sweden, cultivated and dispersed. A Mr. Strickland, an English gentleman from Yorkshire, lately here, left a few seeds with me, of which I impart to you. He tells me it has such advantages over the common turnep that it is spreading rapidly over England, and will become their chief turnep. It's principal excellence is it's remaining in the field unhurt even by the severities of a Swedish winter. He suspects that in the seed he gave me, there is an accidental mixture of common turnep. It may be easily distinguished when it comes up, as the leaf of the Rutabaga resembles that of rape or cabbage, and not at all that of turnep.—My friendly respects to Mr. Pendleton. Adieu affectionately.

PrC (DLC).   A letter from Taylor to TJ of 26 May 1795, recorded in SJL as received 19 June 1795, has not been found.

To Archibald Stuart

DEAR SIR   Monticello June 11. 1795.

By a letter of yours, communicated to me by Colo. Bell, I am apprehensive mine of May 23d. did not get to you. I do not recollect whether I sent it by post or with the books. I now send a copy on the preceding page. Within a week from this time I think I shall be able to send for the other books, and they shall be immediately deposited with Colo. Bell.   I take the liberty of inclosing some nail cards which I will thank you to put into the hands of such of your merchants as you think substantial and punctual. Mr. Stuart, Mr. Sinclair, Gamble &   have been named to me as such. And probably others. I deliver the nails at Charlottesville, or Milton at the *wholesale* Richmond price at the time being. This is certified to me monthly by Mr. Robert Pollard of Richmond. Payment is expected in 3. months after they go out of my hands. I am now executing an order for Dr. Johnson of your town which will give them a sample of my nails. Our harvest commencing now within a few days, will suspend our work probably a month from this time. Any orders may be executed after that time at the rate of about 80. ℔ a day. I sell by the pound altogether, and the merchants here retail by the pound at about 25 percent on my prices. My barrels contain from about 125. to 175 ℔. according to the size of the nail. I note the present prices below. I am Dear Sir Your's affectionately   TH: JEFFERSON

RC (ViHi); written on verso of Dupl of TJ to Stuart, 23 May 1795; addressed: "Archibald Stuart esq. Staunton"; stamped. PrC (MHi). Attached price list and enclosures not found.

From John Blair

Extract of a letter from J. Blair to Th: Jefferson dated Wms.burg June 13. 1795.

'Three days ago I sold to Mr. Robert Andrews Mr. Mazzei's 6. per cent stock, viz 1048.D. 50c. @ 19/10 the market rate at Philadelphia according to the latest and very recent price-current, and have received for the same 1039.D. 84c. I am also willing to take to myself the residue of his stock at the rates mentioned in the same price current, viz. the 3. per cent @ 11/7 and the deferred at 14/1. The quantity of the former species is 786.D. 37c. and of the latter 524.D. 25c., and the two together, according to the respective rates abovementioned are worth 824.D. 60c. The whole amount for which the stock thus sells is 1864.D. 44c. and to this sum may be added 43.D. 25c. being interest which on the 26th. of Nov. last I drew for Mr. Mazzei for two quarters to the 30th. of Sep. last. The sum will then be 1907.D. 69c: interest for 2. more quarters (viz. 43.D. 25c.) is due to the 31st. of March last, and as the above sales reserve to Mr. Mazzei the interest for the current quarter, 21.D. 62c. more will be due the 30th. inst. amounting to 64.D. 87c.; so that the whole sum for which you may value yourself—for the use of Mr. Mazzei will be 1972.D. 56c. Altho' the stock is funded at the office in Richmond, where it generally sells something lower than that at the Public treasury in Philadelphia, yet you will observe Mr. Mazzei gets the price of stock at Philadelphia.'

Tr (Gilder Lehrman Collection, on deposit NNPM); entirely in TJ's hand. Recorded in SJL as received 23 June 1795. Enclosed in TJ to Philip Mazzei, 8 Sep. 1795.

SJL records letters from TJ to Blair of 11 Mch., 18 June, 30 Oct. 1794, and 24 June 1795, and from Blair to TJ of 10 Apr. 1794 from Williamsburg, 21 July 1794 from Richmond, and 6 Dec. 1794, received respectively on 8 May, 28 July, and 9 Dec. 1794, none of which has been found. SJL also records a letter (now missing) from Blair to TJ of 25 June 1800, received from Williamsburg on 3 July 1800.

From John Barnes

Sir   Philadelphia 14th June 1795.

I hasten to Acknowledge your esteemed favor dated the 3d. Inst. received by yesterdays post, covering Certife. No. 1464. for 7504.42 dollars deferr'ed Stock (the Honble: Wm. Shorts Esqr.) with power for my disposal, as well, to receive, the further Interest due, the insuing 1st. July, said to be 314.55 and with their proceeds, to honor your several drafts, of the 3d: 4th. and 5 Inst: viz. 142.11 dolls. a 3 days sight, and 1800. do. a 6 weeks. All which be assured, shall be duly attended to, and hope to meet a riseing market, between this and the middle next Month.

And for your goverment—in Case you should decline to invest the residue, or Ballance in Lands—I have annexed the present Current prices of different Stocks—not from the daily papers—which too frequently quote them from varied prices. I am Sir mst respectfully yr obedt huml servt.   JOHN BARNES

PS. I purpose waiting on Mr. S. Crosby to morrow to adjust with him your 1.67 dolls. and in future to settle, whatever small sums he may, Occasionaly have, to charge you with, for News papers &c. ℔ Account.

price Current Stocks — Philada. 15th. June

6 ℔Ct	20/1 –	
3 ℔ct	11/10 – 11d.	
Deferred	14/3 – 4d.	
B. US.	44 – 45	℔Ct
penna.	41	do.
No. Ama.	46 – 47	do.

RC (DLC: William Short Papers); at foot of first page: "Thomas Jefferson Esqr: Virginia"; endorsed by TJ as received 23 June 1795 and so recorded in SJL.

A letter of this date from TJ to Barnes is recorded in SJL but has not been found.

From James Madison

DEAR SIR   Orange June 14. 1795

I am almost ashamed to be so late in acknowledging your favor of april 27: but, saying nothing of some unknown cause of its not getting to hand till two weaks or more after its date, I have been in constant expectation and intention of paying my respects in person to Monticello within two or three days, and consequently of explaining and justifying my purposes better than it could be done by letter. A succession of incidents has as constantly delayed any visit, till the time has arrived for fulfilling a promised one to a particular relation of Mrs. M. in Hanover about 50 Miles distant. I am the more anxious to have this over, as the season will soon be unsafe in that quarter, and the harvest will require my presence. As soon after my return as possible I will indulge myself with the pleasure of seeing you. I have lately received a letter from Monroe of Feby. 25. which he wishes you to see and I shall bring with me. A prior one also of very interesting contents will be also worth your perusal. I have heard nothing yet from Philada. relating to the tenor of the Treaty with G.B.[1] Just about the close of the Session I wrote a coercive letter to Dohrman on the subject of his debt to Mazzei. He answered that he was, just on the receipt of it, about to let me know that the success of some of his efforts would soon enable him to close the business. My departure obliged me to put it into the hands of Beckley who was going to N.Y. from whom I learn that D. suspends the payment till a liquidation of the debt can be made, but with an apparent ability and purpose to avoid any delay beyond that. It seems that D. has receipts for past payments to Mazzei subsequent to his deed of Trust to me, and alledges with some probable reason that the sum in the deed was not the real amount of the debt but a round one fully covering and securing the maximum. There are some points also relating to the rate of damages and interest on the protested bills, on which there may be room for negociation. As well as I recollect both were to be settled according to the laws of N.Y. not of Virginia,[2] whether binding in the case or not, in consideration of the indulgence shewn him. I have urged a payment immediately of as much as may be due according to his own shewing, but have received no answer.[3] I have several little things for you as your seal &c. with a few pamphlets. Among the latter is a fugitive publication answering the misrepresentations of the Session prior to the last. It was extorted by the intreaties of some friends, just at the close of the Session, under a surfiet of politics, and contains about half what was sketched and meant for the press; the nausea of the subject and other circumstances have left the remainder unfinished. I shall bring these articles with me when I pay my visit. Yrs. always & affecy.

JS. MADISON JR

RC (DLC: Madison Papers); addressed: "Thomas Jefferson Monticello"; endorsed by TJ as received 23 June 1795 and so recorded in SJL. Tr (Facsimile in Gary Hendershott Catalogue, March 1992, Lot 10); extract entirely in TJ's hand, consisting of seven sentences containing variations in spelling and punctuation and one change (see notes below); at head of text: "Extract of a letter from James Madison to Th: Jefferson dated June 14. 1795. Orange"; enclosed in TJ to Philip Mazzei, 8 Sep. 1795. Tr (DLC: Nicholas P. Trist Papers); extract made by Trist in January 1828, consisting of three sentences (see note 3 below); conjoined to extracts of Madison to TJ, 23 Mch. 1795 and 5 Dec. 1796.

Both the LETTER FROM MONROE to Madison of 25 Feb. 1795 and A PRIOR ONE of 18 Feb. 1795 enclosed a copy of James Monroe's letter to Edmund Randolph, 12 Feb. 1795, which Monroe expressly desired Madison to show to TJ (Madison, *Papers*, xv, 477, 482). His letter to Randolph was a response to the Secretary of State's letter of 2 Dec. 1794 in which he severely criticized Monroe's conduct upon arrival in France (ASP, *Foreign Relations*, I, 689-90, 694-5).

Madison's COERCIVE LETTER to Arnold Henry Dohrman of 20 Mch. 1795 has not been found. HE ANSWERED: Dohrman to Madison, 24 Mch. 1795 (Madison, *Papers*, xv, 494-5). For the progress of the case in THE HANDS OF BECKLEY, see John Beckley to Madison, 25 May 1795 (same, xvi, 9-10).

FUGITIVE PUBLICATION: Madison's *Political Observations*, a pamphlet dated 20 Apr. 1795 and published anonymously, probably in New York (TJ's copy is in DLC: Rare Book and Special Collections Division; with "by James Madison" written by TJ below the title; contains corrections in an unidentified hand; printed in Madison, *Papers*, xv, 511-34). See Sowerby, No. 3177;

Madison, *Papers*, XVI, 10, 12. TJ received another copy of the pamphlet from Madison in 1823 after sharing his correspondence with William Johnson, a justice of the United States Supreme Court who had been appointed by TJ and who contemplated writing a history of political parties, a work TJ encouraged as a corrective to the Federalist views of Chief Justice John Marshall. "It had the advantage of being written with the subject full and fresh in my mind" Madison recalled of his tract, "and the disadvantage of being hurried, at the close of a fatiguing Session of Congress by an impa-

tience to return home, from which I was detained by that Job only. The temper of the pamphlet is explained if not excused by the excitements of the period" (TJ to Johnson, 4 Mch., 12 June 1823; TJ to Madison, 13 June 1823; Madison to TJ, 27 June 1823).

[1] Tr in TJ's hand begins with the next sentence.
[2] In his Tr, TJ inserted an asterisk above the first letter of this word.
[3] Tr in TJ's hand ends here. The Trist extract consists of the next three sentences.

To Henry Remsen

DEAR SIR   Monticello June 18. 95.

I have to acknolege the receipt of your favor of April 30th. By that I observed you expected Mr. Burral to be shortly in New York and to give you further information on the subject of the machine for cutting nails. Without waiting for the further information, (as I am much pressed for nails) I am disposed to accept his offer of making a machine for 40. Dollars. The difference of a few dollars is of little account in adopting a thing which is to be of long continuance. So that unless you shall have received information which in your own judgment renders some other more eligible, I will pray you to get one of Mr. Burral's very complete, and to forward it to Colo. Gamble in Richmond, with 500. ℔ of the proper iron for cutting 4 pennies, and a few (say 100.) 4 pennies, 6 pennies and 8 pennies, of the cut nails, by way of sample. Draw for the amount of the whole on Mr. John Barnes merchant South 3d. street Philadelphia who is enabled and instructed to honour your draughts at sight. Finding the nail making profitable and convenient, I am getting more and more into it. I have a dozen hands employed now, and shall increase them. I will by no means trouble you with giving me a price current of any extent. But whenever you are kind enough to favor me with a line, the price of bar iron, nail rod, and wheat will be acceptable. I have been anxious to hear that the French should have established a general peace with their continental enemies: but the hope, at least of a general one, lessens. I am with very cordial esteem Dear Sir Your sincere friend & servt   TH: JEFFERSON

P.S. The inclosed containing some bills of exchange I will thank you to send them by some safe conveyance.

RC (Mrs. Alice Ragland, Daytona Beach, Florida, 1964); at foot of text: "Mr. Remsen." Enclosure not found.

Remsen's FAVOR OF APRIL 30TH, recorded in SJL as received 19 May 1795, has not been found. He also wrote a letter to TJ (now missing) of 30 June 1795, recorded in SJL as received 21 July 1795.

From Henry Knox

MY DEAR SIR   Boston June 20. 1795.

I received your kind favor of the 1st. instant two days ago. Mr. Joseph Pope of this Town the inventor of the improvements in the horizontal Mills, and the proprietor of the Patent has lately still further improved them, so as to carry four pairs of stones. He is my particular acquaintance, and he will immediately have accurate drawings made and transmitted to you by which, with the descriptions, you will be enabled without further difficulty to erect one by your own workmen. Those which have been erected here answer well for small work.

I feel highly satisfied that I have quitted public Life. I propose to be a farmer principally of the grazing kind. I am therefore looking about for the best stock of horses, Cows bulls, and sheep, and I think I have made some acquisitions. My estate is at Penobscot bay and River. I shall reside at Thomaston St Georges River where, had it not been for your sad determination of renouncing pen ink and paper I should have been happy to have received a line from you at leisure. I must be at Philadelphia Next Winter upon business and shall of course carry my family there. We embark today for St Georges River about 200 Miles distant.

I sincerely wish you all possible happiness, for be assured my dear Sir there are few persons for whom I have so real an esteem and affection as for yourself.   H KNOX

RC (Me: Knox Papers); at foot of text: "Thomas Jefferson Esq Monticello"; endorsed by TJ as received 7 July 1795 and so recorded in SJL.

On 26 Jan. 1793, JOSEPH POPE received a

patent for his improvement in windmills (*List of Patents*, 7). His letters to TJ of 10 July 1795 and 11 Mch. 1800, recorded in SJL as received on 11 Aug. 1795 and 20 Mch. 1800, respectively, have not been found.

From Robert Pollard

SIR   Richmond June 21st. 1795

Your favor of the 18th is at hand. I have contracted with Mr. James Heron for Six shares in the James River Company at fifty four pounds the share, which with my Commission amounts to Three hundred twenty Seven pounds 4/4, for which you will please forward a draft on Mr. Barnes.

I hold one share only in the Company which you may take if you please on the same terms. The amount will then be £381.15. as stated at foot. I am Sir Yr Obd: H. servt   ROBERT POLLARD

6 Shares bought of J. Heron a £54	£324. 0.0	
Commission at 1 ℔ Ct	3. 4.4	£327 4.4
1 Share RP's	£54. 0 0	
Com:	10.8	54 10.8
		£381.15 [1]

RC (DLC: William Short Papers); with notation by TJ; endorsed by TJ as received 23 June 1795 and so recorded in SJL.

TJ's FAVOR OF THE 18TH, recorded in SJL, has not been found.

[1] TJ here added "= 1272.5."

To John Barnes

SIR   Monticello June 24. 1795.

Having made another purchase of James river canal shares for Mr. Short, I have this day drawn on you in favor of Mr. Robert Pollard for twelve hundred and seventy two dollars and a half at 30. days sight which be pleased to honor.

Your favor of June 14. came to hand last night. I am with esteem Sir Your most obedt. servt   TH: JEFFERSON

PrC (MHi); at foot of text: "Mr. John Barnes"; endorsed in ink by TJ.

From James Monroe

DEAR SIR   Paris June 27. 1795.

Of the above hasty view I have sent a copy to one or two other friends. Since it was written the committee have reported a plan of government as suggested of 2. branches, the one to be called a council of 500. consisting of so many members, the other of 250. called the council of antients. The age of the 1st. to be 30. and of the 2d. 40. They are to be chosen each for 2. years but to be supplied annually by halves. The Executive to be composed of 5. members to be elected for 5. years, but so arranged that only one withdraws annually. Each member is to have a salary of about £5000 sterg. per annum, the object whereof to receive and entertain foreign ministers &c. The Council of antients cannot originate a bill. If possible I will procure and send you a copy of the plan.

The British have recommenc'd the seizure of our vessels as formerly under the order of the 6th. of Novr. 1793. near 40. being carried in under by our last and which were the first accounts. This has produc'd an extreme ferment here, and it will be difficult under the irritation existing in consequence of Jay's treaty, to prevent a revival of the same practice on the part of France, and if we do nothing when it is known in America but abuse the English and drink toasts to the success of the French revolution, I do not know what step they will take in regard to us. My situation since the report of Mr. Jay's treaty has been painful beyond any thing ever experienc'd before, and for reasons you can readily conceive. I have however done every thing in my power to keep things where they should be, but how long this will be practicable under existing circumstances I know not. Denmark and Sweden will I think be active.

I have just received a letter from Mr. Derieux with one for his aunt. If possible I will now answer it; but in case I cannot, I beg you to tell him that I waited on her last fall with Mrs. Monroe, having previously written her repeatedly in his behalf, and after a long and earnest solicitation in his favor and returned without obtaining any thing for him. She had promised some thing before I went, and the dinner she gave us, was to pave the way for retracting and which she did. The old lady has about her (as I suspect) some persons who are poor, and who prefer their own welfare to his. By the law of France the property cannot be devised from her relatives, but tis probable these people will help to consume the annual profits; which latter however she says in consequence of the depreciation are nothing.

We wish most sincerely to get back and shall certainly do it, as soon as a decent respect for appearances will permit, especially if the present system of policy continues. I wish much to hear from you having written you several times but received not a line since my appointment here. Is there any thing in this quarter you wish to command of books or any other article; or can I serve you in any respect whatever? You will of course command me if I can be serviceable.

I have requested Mr. Madison to shew you some letters of mine to him. I wish to know much in what state my farms are. We are well: our child speaks French well and her and Mrs. M. desire to be affectionately rememberd to yourself and daughters, to whom as well as to Mr. R. and

Mr. C. as likewise to my brother and neighbours be so kind as remember me. With great respect & esteem I am Dear [Sir]¹ yr. Affectionate friend   JAS. MONROE

RC (DLC); on verso of last sheet by Monroe: "Mr. Jefferson"; endorsed by TJ as received 8 Sep. 1795 and so recorded in SJL.

The PLAN OF GOVERNMENT described by Monroe was presented to the National Convention on 23 June 1795 and included in the Constitution of the Year III adopted by France in September 1795 (Lefebvre, *Thermidorians*, 176-86; Stewart, *French Revolution*, 571, 580-8). THE BRITISH HAVE RECOMMENC'D THE SEIZURE OF OUR VESSELS: a secret order in council of 25 Apr. 1795 authorized British naval commanders to intercept neutral vessels carrying contraband provisions to French ports. Americans regarded this "provision order" as a renewal of the "additional instructions" of 8 June 1793, which had allowed British commanders to interdict cargoes of grain, flour, and meal bound for France and had been protested by TJ in his letter to Thomas Pinckney of 7 Sep. 1793. It was perceived also as a revival of a secretly promulgated order in council of 6 Nov. 1793 that had sanctioned the seizure of ships carrying the products of French colonies or provisions or supplies to those colonies. By raising the issue of foodstuffs as contraband the April 1795 order became an important point in the debate on Jay's Treaty and caused President Washington to hesitate before approving the pact (Combs, *Jay Treaty*, 164-70; Ritcheson, *Aftermath of Revolution*, 299, 354). In a 13 June 1795 letter Monroe had REQUESTED MR. MADISON "to shew my communications always to Mr. Jefferson, who I suspect declines intentionally a correspondence from a desire to enjoy free from interruption the comforts of private life" (Madison, *Papers*, XVI, 18; see also James Madison to TJ, 14 June 1795, and note). MR. R. AND MR. C.: Thomas Mann Randolph and perhaps Peter Carr.

¹ Word supplied.

E N C L O S U R E

Sketch of the State of Affairs in France

DEAR SIR   Paris 23. June 1795.

Your first enquiry will be, upon what basis does the revolution rest? Has it yet weathered the storms that have beaten against it, and taking all circumstances into view that merit consideration, is there ground for a well founded hope that it will terminate happily for France and of course for mankind? I will give you concisely the actual state of things, by comparing which with those great events which have preceeded and are known every where, you will be enabled to form as correct a judgment upon that point as can now be formed upon it.

To say that the Convention maintains its authority over the whole interior of the republick, notwithstanding its late difficulties, would give you but a superficial view of the subject, without developing in some degree the nature and probable consequences of those difficulties. Internal convulsions where they happen try the strength of parties, and demonstrate what their real object is, as well as that of the society in general, in regard to the points in controversy. Fortunately such have happened here, and of a character to furnish respectable data whereon to calculate not only the strength of parties, but likewise the probable issue of the revolution itself. Fortunately, permit me to say, for as political truths depend upon experiment, so we have reason to rejoice in those experiments which prove what it is the wish and the interest of mankind to see proven.

Within less than two months past I have seen the Convention twice assailed by a considerable force and which was in the latter instance armed, and upon both those occasions, have seen that force foiled, in the first without the effusion of blood, and in the second by the death of one man (Ferrand a deputy) only. Many circumstances too were combined to make those mov'ments formidable and to create a belief that they would shake the revolution, if there existed in the society a force able and willing to shake it: for the first took place at the moment when the city was agitated by a twofold crisis of famine, and the trial of Billaud de Varennes, Collot d'herbois and Barrere, leading members of the mountain party: and the second, when the famine was at the height and the distress of the people beyond what was ever seen on our side of the Atlantick. For several hours on both days, the proceedings of the Convention were interrupted, and on the last the rioters were in absolute possession of the hall and in a great measure of the government itself: so that in truth the superiority of active force was on their side, and danger only on the side of the members and the friends of the government. At such a moment as this, when the functions of the government were suspended, or exercised by the insurgents only, there was surely a fair opportunity for those who were in favor of a change, to pronounce themselves on that side: and the presumption is reasonable that all those who were in favor of it, or at least who were willing to hazard any thing in support of it, did pronounce themselves on that side. It was the epoch upon which foreign powers and the royalists had fixed their attention and upon which it was understood they would unite their efforts to bring about a counter-revolution nor was there any army at hand or other force to oppose the enterprize than the citizens of Paris itself. Upon a fair appeal therefore to the interest and the wishes of the inhabitants of this city, the issue was put, and the experiment in both cases and particularly the last proved what the strength of those who were for a counter revolution was, comparatively with that of those against it, like that of an infant against Hercules. Upon the first occasion the commotion was crushed, before the movers in it got the ascendancy, but upon the second it was otherwise, so that their force was fairly ascertained and shewn to be nothing.

Nor was the issue more unfavorable to royalty, if we may judge from what appeared, than the success of the party would have been if it had succeeded: for the principle upon which the mov'ment was undertaken by the great mass of those who acted in it, was not to favor royalty but to oppose it, being impressed with an opinion that the prevailing party were disposed to reestablish that species of government, and against which they declared themselves affirming that their object was, liberty to the patriots (the members of the mountain party who were under prosecution) and the establishment of the constitution of 1793, and which certainly has in it, none of the attributes of royalty.

In the course of these commotions the royalists did not display themselves to advantage: they shewed neither enterprize nor decision. In the commenc'ment they were active by intrigue only, fomenting, by all the means in their power, the discontents of the laborious poor, and which proceeded from the famine which oppressed them, contrasting their present distress with the abundant ease of former times &c &c, but when the moment of danger arrived, they took no part so as to make themselves responsible in case the effort failed. And upon the latter occasion, when the party got possession of the Convention and began for a while to rule, and were about to reestablish terrorism and not royalty, the royalists shifted their ground in a moment and became very vociferous against popular commotions, and equally pathetic in suport of the Convention and of the law, which a few hours before they disdained and endeavoured to subvert. In truth they saw that their own safety was involved in that of the Convention, and in consequence became interested in the welfare of that body from the strongest of all possible motives, a regard for themselves.

Upon the whole therefore I am of opinion that these mov'ments have tended rather to strengthen than to weaken the foundation of the revolution, for they have shewn that the mountain party which so long governed France, altho' it has latterly lost its influence, has not abandoned its principles, and that if it had recovered its authority it would not have introduced royalty but on the contrary a greater degree of rigor against the royalists than humanity allows, or the present preponderating party is disposed to exercise. Of this truth even the avowed royalists are already admonished; is it not therefore reasonable to conclude that those who were before wavering what part to take will for the future, cease to hesitate.

But you will ask is there not a party in the Convention itself favorable to monarchy, are not some of the leading members in the preponderating party inclined to that system of government? If the fact were so, these late mov'ments would have a tendency to check that bias: but I have no reason to think that the fact is so, with many I am personally acquainted, and from what I have seen of their conduct, for sometime past, in publick and in private life, I can assure you that whilst I have nothing to say against any of these members, I consider many of them as among the most enthusiastic admirers and advocates of the publick liberty that I have ever known. I have seen them too in situations where it was impossible to dissemble. Time and circumstances, it is true, may produce changes, and against which I do not pretend to reason: I only argue from data within my view, and deduce those consequences from them which according to the ordinary course of events are probable. So much then upon the state of parties and their respective views, and by which it appears that the publick liberty will not be endangered under the auspices of either.

In other respects the prospect has become more favorable to a happy termination of the revolution than was heretofore promised. The people of France may conquer their liberties and merit to be free, but without a good government it will be impossible to preserve them. This truth has latterly been more deeply impressed upon the Convention than it formerly was, and in consequence the attention of that body seems now to be principally turned to that object, a committee consisting of 11. members having been appointed for more than six weeks past, to report what changes it will be necessary in their judgment to make in the existing one of 1793 and whose report is daily expected. It is believed that this committee will propose some important changes in that constitution and that the Convention will adopt them, such as a division of the legislature into two branches &c. after the model of the American constitutions. I have heard many deputies confer on this subject and who were unanimous in favor of this change, and which is certainly of greater importance to the preservation of their liberty than any other that has been spoken of. As soon as this report is presented I will transmit it to you.

The external view is still more favorable. The atchievements of the last campaign surpassed everything that the modern world has witnessed: in every quarter their arms were tryumphant, but where the greatest danger pressed there the grandeur of their exploits was most conspicuous. Spain and Holland bear testimony in favor of this assertion, for the close of the campaign left the republick in possession of extensive territories belonging to the former, and of the whole of the latter. The armies of the Emperor too were often beaten and finally forced to abandon the field. Those of Prussia experienced upon several occasions the like fate; and as for the British, they retreated, till they came back upon sea, where hurrying on board the ships that were prepared to receive them they took their flight upon that element upon which alone they could hope for safety. From these successes you have already seen that France has gained the most solid and durable advantages. From an enemy Holland has become a friend and ally. In that country the government only was conquered, and by whose conquest the people became free: for upon the ruins of the miserable oligarchal tyranny which reigned there, we find a sister republick reared, marshalled by the side of France, and preparing to fight with her for the common liberty of the two people. Prussia has withdrawn from the war and is now in the closest amity with France. Spain is negotiating and will probably soon have peace. Austria is known to wish it, and England has absolutely made overtures secretly thro' the medium of Sr. Fk. Eden, whilst the ostensible object of his mission was an exchange of prisoners only. Exploits like these become a free people, nor are any but a free people able to perform them.

Such was the actual state of things when the campaign was lately opened on the part of France by the atchiev'ment of Luxembourg, one of the best fortified and strongest posts in the world. The siege was closely continued for more than six months, and finally suceeded after the provision was exhausted, and it was seen that the coalised powers could not raise it. At this post 12.000 men were taken with great amount in cannon and other warlike stores. Upon Mayence the whole pressure now is, nor is it probable that that garrison will long be able to sustain itself. Upon Spain also some recent advantage has been gained: indeed it is well-known that the troops of this republick can make what impression they please in that quarter.

Under these circumstances it is not probable that the war will be long continued upon the continent. The coalised powers have latterly placed their only hope, in the possibility of a counter-revolution here, upon account of the dissentions in the publick councils, and the scarcity of bread: but the late events and which I have already communicated, will shew how unproductive a resource the former has been and promises to be; and the revolution of a few weeks only, within which space the harvest will ripen, will I think likewise demonstrate that the latter was not less so. The war then will soon be narrowed to a contest between this republick and England, I mean such is the present prospect, and this will of course be a maritime one only, unless the former succeeds and in which case, the government of England will be conquered as that of Holland was. Among the maritime powers there is not one (unless Russia forms an exception and which is not absolutely certain) which does not wish to see the naval force of England broken or at least greatly diminished: whereas on the side of France there is Holland already embarked and Denmark and Sweden are unquestionably in the same interest; nor is it improbable that past and present injuries may force them to declare in support of it, for latterly the orders of the 6th. of Novr. have been revived by the Ct. of St. James, for seizing all neutral vessels laden with provision for France and under which many have been seized of theirs as well as ours. It is likewise probable that Spain will eventually be on the same side, for as she wishes not only to get rid of the war, but to revive with France her antient connection, and which contains on the part of France a guarantee of the Spanish possessions in So. America, and which it will otherwise be difficult to accomplish, I cannot well perceive how Spain will be able to avoid declaring herself on the side of France. Such is the external and internal state of things, and upon which you will be able to form your own conjecture, of the probable issue.

But you demand what ground does America occupy upon this great and interesting scene of affairs? How does she stand in the estimation of her generous and victorious Ally? As we were never called on to bear a part in the controversy upon the issue of which ours as well as her liberty was dependant, but were left to enjoy in peace the abundant fruits of our industry, whilst she defied the storm alone, I am not surprized that you should feel solicitous upon this point. A few lines will give the sketch you wish. Preceding unfavorable impressions, and which were known to exist, were erased by the declarations of the present Minister when he was introduced into the Convention, supported by the documents which he presented, and upon which basis the antient and close amity which had formerly subsisted was rapidly reviving and growing up. Some changes of importance were accomplished in our commercial affairs with this republick, and in particular the treaty of amity and commerce, which in pursuit of the policy of England had been violated, was put in activity, and whereby our trade is not only free in every article (strict contraband excepted) and to every country even to England herself, altho' it furnishes her with the most productive means for the support of the war, but likewise the trade of England is protected under our flag, and whilst it yields no protection to that of France. Such was the actual state of things when the report of Mr. Jay's treaty with the English government transpired and by which it was circulated that a new connection was formed between the United States and that power, beneficial to the latter and probably hurtful to France. This report operated like a stroke of thunder and produced upon all France amazement. What the treaty really is, is not yet known, but most certainly the bias in our favor has been greatly diminished, nor is it possible that the cordiality should be great under such circumstances. If the treaty is rejected, or contains in it nothing strictly objectionable, in either case we shall stand well here: but if it is adopted and does contain any thing which a just criticism can censure, be assured we shall hear from this government in terms of reproach. By this time you know what the treaty is, and therefore know according to its fate in what light we shall be considered here. If the treaty is not precisely what we wished it to be, most certainly the most favorable opportunity that was ever offered to make a good one, has been thrown away: for as France was successful, and a good understanding subsisted between us and France, it was really in our power to dictate what terms we pleased, provided we could make the English government believe that in any event we would take part against it. Accomplishing that point, every thing would have been accomplished; for of all possible calamities with which they are threatened, a war with us is that which they most dread: not so much indeed from the fear of our maritime force, as the effect it would produce upon their commerce, by which alone they are enabled to support a war. Such was the actual state of things at the time this treaty was formed, but a new scene has since been opened and which will shew how little confidence we ought to place in treaties with that power. For latterly and as I presume in violation of that treaty the same system of depredation and of plunder has been recommenced.

By the above hasty but true picture of affairs here you will perceive that this republick is rapidly rising or rather has already obtained a decided preponderance not only in the scale of Europe but indeed in that of human affairs. Having combatted alone and with success all the great powers of Europe, the superiority of her strength over theirs, at least whilst that of the latter is weilded by the heavy and expensive governments which exist there, is well established. Nor is it probable that this superiority will be soon diminished especially when it is considered that the revolution of the one is approaching fast to a happy close, under a government founded upon principles which when completed and resting firm, must cause a similar revolution every where. To stand well with this republick is therefore now the interest of all nations, nor indeed do any of them seem at the present moment to entertain a contrary opinion: for they have all made approaches and shewn their solicitude for peace, notwithstanding they know the danger that will probably overwhelm them in that event and especially if France gets a good government, since they deem that danger more remote and less terrible than the one which immediately threatens under the pressure of the French arms. Upon every principle therefore it were greatly to be regretted, if America should lose in any degree the ground upon which she hath heretofore stood in the estimation of her ally.

MS (DLC); in a clerk's hand, unsigned, with a correction by Monroe; being one version of a paper Monroe prepared for transmittal to several correspondents and for newspaper publication (see below); endorsed by TJ as received 8 Sep. 1795 and so recorded in SJL.

Although the version of this sketch received by TJ is the one printed in Monroe, *Writings*, II, 292-304, TJ seems not to have been the primary recipient Monroe had in mind when he composed it. In fact a copy sent to Pennsylvania farmer and physician George Logan took on the greatest significance, although not in any way that Monroe intended. According to a clerk's note on a fragmentary draft in Monroe's hand (DLC: Monroe Papers), copies of this paper were to go to Logan, Aaron Burr, John Beckley, Robert R. Livingston, and TJ. The canceled name "Randolph" in the same notation implies that Monroe considered sending one to Edmund Randolph, and although he is not on this list George Clinton, as indicated below, may also have been one of the initial recipients. When in 1798 Monroe sent a manuscript of the sketch, in his own hand, to John Taylor, he called the document "the original of my letter to Beckley of

which that to Dr. Logan was a copy" (retained copy of sketch and Monroe to Taylor, 8 Jan. 1798, both in MHi: Washburn Collection; letter printed in Massachusetts Historical Society, *Proceedings*, XLII [1909], 322-5). When Monroe sent his "short sketch of the actual state of things here" to Logan, covered by a letter of 24 June 1795, he noted that he was also dispatching copies to others, including Beckley. Monroe authorized Logan and Beckley to have the sketch inserted in the Philadelphia *Aurora*, and he expected to send additional reports for anonymous publication (MHi: Pickering Papers). The piece appeared in the *Aurora* on 31 Aug. 1795 as an "extract of a letter from an American gentleman in France." If Beckley was the conduit by which Monroe's circular reached the *Aurora* (he once played a similar role for James Madison), he did not betray the fact in a letter to Monroe of 23 Sep. 1795 (DLC: Monroe Papers; Edmund Berkeley and Dorothy Smith Berkeley, *John Beckley: Zealous Partisan in a Nation Divided* [Philadelphia, 1973], 108-9).

According to notations on copies in the papers of Timothy Pickering at MHi, Monroe's letter to Logan of 24 June 1795 and its enclosure ostensibly landed in the "Dead letter" section of the Post Office. The copies that Pickering, the former Postmaster General, directed to be made were probably faithful transcriptions of the now-missing originals addressed to Logan, since they reproduce minor emendations that appear in both the copy received by Livingston (see below) and the manuscript Monroe sent to Taylor in 1798. Early in July 1796 Pickering, then Secretary of State, sent the President a copy of Monroe's cover letter to Logan, cited it as evidence of its author's "political opinions and conduct," and successfully advocated Monroe's recall from Paris (copy in DLC: Washington Papers, in Pickering's hand, incorrectly dated 24 June 1796, printed in Monroe, *Writings*, III, 6-7; George Gibbs, *Memoirs of the Administrations of Washington and John Adams, Edited from the Papers of Oliver Wolcott, Secretary of the Treasury*, 2 vols. [New York, 1846], I, 367).

The *Aurora* professedly received Monroe's sketch from someone identified as "A.B." This was not Burr, who because he was traveling read it in the newspapers before he received the manuscript that Monroe sent to him. Burr's copy has not been found, but according to him it was dated 18 June 1795. Clinton may also have received one bearing that date (*Burr Papers*, I, 227, 228n, 229; Clinton to Monroe, 14 Apr. 1796, in DLC: Monroe Papers). An emendation to the copy received by Livingston, which is unsigned and in a clerk's hand, altered the date from 18 to 23 June (NHi: Livingston Papers). Changes in date were also made to the manuscript that Taylor received and the copy in Pickering's papers, each of which is dated 23 June in place of a canceled and illegible day. The MS that Monroe sent to TJ is dated 23 June without alteration, and as it silently incorporates emendations common to the other three manuscript versions it probably came late rather than early in the sequence of copies. The MS printed above lacks an introductory paragraph that appears in variant form in the "original" sent by Monroe to Taylor, Livingston's copy, and Logan's (represented by the Pickering copy). In a few places the wording as printed in the *Aurora* differs from all known manuscript copies, probably reflecting changes made at the newspaper.

For another instance in which Monroe's observations appeared in the *Aurora*, see Monroe to TJ, 18 Nov. 1795.

THE CONVENTION TWICE ASSAILED: the 1 Apr. and 20 May 1795 assaults on the National Convention by Parisian mobs are described in Georges Lefebvre, *The French Revolution*, trans. Elizabeth M. Evanson and others, 2 vols. (London, 1962-64), II, 144-5.

From Sarah Champe Carter

SIR   Fredericksburg June 30th 95—

I had the pleasure of receiving your letter of the 4th. instant and should have answered it some-time since, but have been for several weeks a good deal indisposed by the small pox, a circumstance, which, I hope, will apologize for the delay. I have no objection to the establishment of the line by which my son Champe had devided the lands sold you and there held by me as I am fully perswaided that he would do nothing to affect my interest. I must beg that you will accept my acknowledgements for your polite communication and beleive me to be With respect yr. Most Obt   SALLY CARTER

RC (DLC: William Short Papers); addressed: "Thomas Jefferson Esqr. Monticello"; endorsed by TJ as received 7 July 1795 and so recorded in SJL.

To Archibald Stuart

Dear Sir   Monticello June 30. 95.

It was not till lately I could send a cart into Louisa for the books I had lent my nephew Dabney Carr. I have now recieved them, and tomorrow shall lodge with Colo. Bell a box for you containing Fitzherbert's N.B. Atkyns 3. vols. Burrows 3. vols. P. Williams 3. v. Ld. Raymond 2. v. Salkeld 2 v. in one. Strange 2. vols. Vernon 2. vols. This completes the list except Kelynge not yet recovered.

I have lately recieved an answer from Robert Morris relative to the sheep. As the delay requires an apology from me to you, I inclose you his letter containing his apology to me, and stating the present situation of the subject. Should you send for them, give me previous notice, and I will send you a letter for Mr. Morris to authorize the application of it's bearer. I am with great esteem Dr. Sir Your affectionate friend & servt

Th: Jefferson

P.S. Be so good as to return the inclosed.
P.P.S. Kelynge is found, and put with the rest.

RC (ViHi); at foot of text: "Mr. Stuart." PrC (MHi); lacks first postscript, the second being added by TJ in ink; endorsed by TJ in ink. Enclosure: Robert Morris to TJ, 1 June 1795.

From Henry Tazewell

Dear Sir   Philadelphia 1. July 1795.

The Treaty between the U States and Gt. Britain having found its way to the press, I am enabled this Morning to transmit you a Copy.

If your anxiety has been excited in the same degree with others to see this famous Negotiation, it is not unlikely that the perusal of it, will give rise to some of those Sentiments which have been produced here.

It was consented to by the Senate 20 to 10, upon condition that the 12th Article should be suspended. The form in which this Consent was given, you will perceive by the inclosed paper. This conditional ratification has produced some embarrassment in the Executive. The result is yet unknown. Both the French and Spanish Ministers have spoken pretty freely to the Secretary of State, on the subject of this Treaty. I am with sentiments of respect your mo. obt   Henry Tazewell

RC (DLC); endorsed by TJ as received 21 July 1795 and so recorded in SJL. Enclosures: (1) *[Authentic.] Treaty of Amity,* *Commerce, and Navigation, between His Britannick Majesty, and the United States of America. By their President, with the advice and consent of their Senate* (Philadelphia, [1795]). See Evans, No. 29743. (2) Resolution of the Senate, [24 June 1795], ratifying the Jay Treaty "on condition that there be added to the said Treaty an Article whereby it shall be agreed to suspend the operation of so much of the 12th. Article as respects the Trade which his said Majesty thereby consents may be carried on between the U. States and his Islands in the West Indies in the manner and on the terms and conditions therein specified," and recommending that the President without delay enter into negotiations with the British for this purpose (Tr in MoSHi: Jefferson Collection; in Tazewell's hand; undated). See also JEP, I, 186.

The Jay TREATY, long delayed in its passage from London, was first received by President Washington on 7 Mch. 1795—four days after the close of the third Congress and after the President, doubtlessly anticipating its arrival, summoned a special session of the Senate to meet on 8 June to consider it—but it was not until 1 July 1795 that the text of the document FOUND ITS WAY TO THE PRESS. Washington submitted the treaty and related documents to the Senate when it convened on the appointed day. In order to prevent Republicans from mobilizing popular opposition to this controversial agreement, the Federalist majority immediately passed an order enjoining Senators to keep secret the contents of the treaty, printed copies of which were made available to them, and the accompanying documents. Four days later, on 12 June, Tazewell, a Republican who had been elected to fill the unexpired term of Senator John Taylor of Virginia in 1794 and had been president pro tempore since February 1795, introduced a motion to rescind the order, but the Senate rejected it on 13 June by a vote of 20 to 9. On 26 June, two days after conditionally ratifying the treaty—with Tazewell voting against ratification—the Senate rescinded the secrecy order by a vote of 18 to 9 after voting to enjoin members from making copies of the treaty or any of its articles. On that day, in an effort to portray Federalists as defenders of vital American national interests, the *Gazette of the United States* published the substance of Article 12 of the treaty and Enclosure No. 2 listed above. On 29 June, the fiercely Republican *Aurora* printed an abstract of the treaty supplied by the new French minister, Pierre A. Adet, who wanted to mobilize opposition to the agreement in order to deter the President from agreeing to it. At this point Senator Stevens Thomson Mason of Virginia, concerned about inaccuracies in the abstract and also eager to prevent ratification, provided Benjamin Franklin Bache, the *Aurora's* publisher, with a full text of the treaty, which Bache printed in the form of the pamphlet listed above as Enclosure No. 1 and first advertised for sale in his newspaper on 1 July (JEP, I, 178, 179, 181, 191-2; Madison, *Papers*, XVI, 15, 25-9, 32n; Turner, *CFM*, 738, 742; *Gazette of the United States*, 26 June 1795; Philadelphia *Aurora*, 29 June, 1 July 1795; Freeman, *Washington*, VII, 237-9, 249-57; Combs, *Jay Treaty*, 160-2). In addition, between 12 and 26 June Senator Pierce Butler of South Carolina had sent James Madison in installments a full transcript of the treaty as printed for the Senate, granting him permission to show it to TJ but cautioning him to advise TJ "not to Communicate it" (Madison, *Papers*, XVI, 15, 23, 24). There is no evidence that TJ ever saw this particular text.

The 12TH. ARTICLE of the Jay Treaty aroused intense opposition in the United States because it restricted American participation in the trade with the British West Indies to vessels of 70 tons or less and forbade the United States to re-export British West Indian molasses, sugar, coffee, cocoa, or cotton. The President ratified the treaty on 14 Aug. 1795 on condition that the British agree to the insertion of an additional article incorporating the senatorial reservation in Enclosure No. 2 listed above, a condition the British readily accepted (Miller, *Treaties*, II, 254-5, 266-7, 271-2).

From James Monroe

DEAR SIR   Paris July 3. 1795.

   Having written you very fully three days since I have nothing to add
at present to the details then given except that in an unexpected ren-
counter the other day the French have lost 3. ships and by the shameful
misconduct of the officers commanding them or some of them. They
have in consequence dismissed the Comy. of Marine which I think converts the loss of the ships into a signal victory, in such regard do I estimate his merits.

   By Mr. De Rieux I learn that poor Gilmer declines and that Bell has
been sick, that Mrs. Marks is dead—that Miss Gilmer is about to be
married—that Wardlow and Robt. Jouett are. This short note from
Goochland which opens the interior of a place extremely dear to me
contains every thing that I have heard from that quarter since my arrival
here. Be so kind as forward the enclosed to him and assure my neighbours I have not forgotten them, altho' they may have forgotten me. Is
there any thing here you wish me to procure for you. I beg you to give
me a note of it if there is. Our best respects to Mr. and Mrs. R. and both
yours and his families. Very sincerely I am Yr. affectionate friend &
servt   JAS. MONROE

RC (DLC); endorsed by TJ as received
15 Oct. 1795 and so recorded in SJL. Enclosure not found.

The letter written THREE DAYS SINCE was
actually Monroe's 30 June 1795 letter to
James Madison (Madison, *Papers*, XVI, 32-
4). His previous letter to TJ was dated 27
June 1795.

From James Ogilvie

SIR   Fredericksburg Academy [before 3 July 1795]
   I consider it as one of the characteristic blessings of Republicanism
that it disentangles man from that labyrinth of ceremonial and those
entrenchments of rank that inoculate and dissever society in countrys
where monarchy prevails and opens a free channel to that stream of
intercourse and communion from which so much of the improvement
and felicity of mankind springs: Tis on this account that tho' personally
unknown to you and without introduction I feel little of that embarassment which I should painfully feel in addressing myself in similar circumstances to a person bearing the same rank in Europe. Without farther preamble I am Proffessor of Humanity and the Belles Lettrs in the
Fredericksburg Academy and have occupy'd this department nearly

two years. Education from my childhood hath formed a fav'rite subject of my meditation and research, and since my residence here hath wholly engrossed my attention. I had long suspected that whilst Religion Philosophy and the fine Arts were so deeply infected with the maladys which the injustice and oppression of Europe diffused so widely, education could hardly be so fortunate as to have escaped untainted. My suspicions have now grown into convictions. Many capital defects in the Prescriptive system of education as well with regard to the manner of instructing as to the matter of instruction have suggested themselves to my mind and I have adventured some very material and fundamental alterations. Considering experiment as the basis of all sound science, except that which flows from intuition I have instituted a regular course of experiments upon the minds of my pupils, by the result of which I have authenticated and adjusted my deviations whether of practice or opinion from the established modes and sources [of]¹ instruction. Two public examinations have already been held when the proficiency of the youth under my care offerd I believe very general satisfaction nor were my deviations from the usual modes regarded with disapprobation. These deviations are daily growing more numerous and important and on a subject of such general and momentous concern I can by no means be persuaded to rest satisfied with my own judgment. That the community may be enabled to approbate the merits of my plan and that I may enjoy the benefits of advice from my enlightened fellow citizens I have determined to hold annually two examinations and to imp[ress] in occasional addresses and observations during these examinations the reasons that have induced me to deviate from the established modes. Our next public examination will take place on the first week of August and will continue throughout the week. On that occasion the higher classes will be examined in Government Morals Logic Rhetoric Criticism Elocution; Philology English Grammar Natural History, Latin and Greek. A more minute detail of particulars will appear in the Fredericksburg print previous to the examination. On the importance of Education 'twere impertinent to descant. The present imperfection is the theme of universal lamentation a lamentation in which the Philosopher and Philanthropist are the deepest mourners. From whom can we expect the amendment and reformation of education? This I imagine can only be expected from the exertions of individuals justly and generally encouraged and diffused. From what class of individuals from Theoretical and merely speculative Philosophers? This may well be doubted when we recollect the unsuccessful attempts of three illustrious minds Locke Helvetius and Rousseau. From prescriptive and Technical Teachers, from men whose minds are philtered by the Classic charm and darkened by the dogmas of Antiquity. For such in my mind is the condition of the most approved and celebrated teachers of modern times. Alas—could reformation come from this quarter education had been long since reformed. But there is sufficient reason to believe that from such men we can only expect new reinforcement to ancient errour. Deeply impressed with these convictions I have endeavored to blend Theory and Practice speculation and experiment and utterly incompetent as I am to complete the reformation of education I flatter myself that I am in the right road. I have made some progress and having determined to dedicate the greater part of my life to the prosecution of this design I entertain hopes of rendering my future exertions of some utility to my country and therefore of proportional felicity to myself. The design I am prosecuting is not so much a matter of private as of public concern and I look for the countenance and cooperation of my enlightend and patriotic fellow-citizens. Tis my most earnest desire to submit the plan I am pursuing to the scrutiny of those to whom their country looks up for judgment and decision on matters of general moment. Such Sir being my views the public voice admonishes me to turn to you and in compliance with this admonition I take the liberty to solicit the honour of your presence during our next examination. A stranger as I am to your person and acquaintance it would ill become me to solicit without introduction or recommendation A private favour, and altho the request I now make is addressed rather to your patriotism and Philanthropy than to your friendship and politeness yet I hope I may be permitted to add without impropriety that your compliance will confer distinguished honour on this Academy, gratify the wishes of the Trustees and afford unfeigned delight to Sir Your most obedient & respectful humble

JAMES OGILVIE

RC (DLC: TJ Papers, 99: 17001-2); undated, but assigned on the basis of Mann Page to TJ, 3 July 1795; torn in part; addressed: "Thomas Jefferson Esqr"; above address in Mann Page's hand: "This Letter was written previous to the Publication, which accounts for the difference in the Time of Exn." (see below); endorsed by TJ as a letter of "probably 95" received 14 July 1795 and recorded under that date in SJL. Enclosed in Mann Page to TJ, 3 July 1795.

When he wrote this letter, James Ogilvie (ca. 1775-1820), a teacher originally from Scotland, was beginning a controversial career as a promoter of oratory. Subsequent to his work at Fredericksburg Academy he went on to teach at various locales in Virginia, and from 1805 to 1807 he directed an academy at Milton. His pedagogical philosophy emphasized elocution and semiannual public examinations, and he favored the opinions of the radical British writer William Godwin, decried by some Federalist critics as permissive and skeptical. Although Ogilvie influenced such writers and speakers as Francis Walker Gilmer, William Cabell Rives, and William Wirt, he did so as a teacher and literary or oratorical model rather than as an original thinker. His orations were largely derivative, but delivered with impressive flair. A satirical attack in 1809 alluded to his affinity for laudanum, and he later admitted his "excessive use of opium." TJ nevertheless developed a cordial relationship with him. While at Milton, Ogilvie taught TJ's grandson, Thomas Jefferson Randolph. TJ also praised lectures Ogilvie delivered at Charlottesville, gave him a set of Cicero's works, granted him access to the library at Monticello, and entrusted the schoolmaster with a highly confidential letter to Thomas Mann Randolph. In 1808 Ogilvie began tours of American cities to lecture and promote a system of instruction in rhetoric. Despite some initial acclaim, he failed to establish himself as a philosopher, returned to Great Britain in 1816 or 1817, and died by his own hand in Scotland (DAB; Richard Beale Davis, *Intellectual Life in Jefferson's Virginia* [Chapel Hill, 1964], 40-2, 281-2, 368-70; Richard Beale Davis, "James Ogilvie and Washington Irving," *Americana*, xxxv [1941], 435-48; Burton R. Pollin, "Godwin's Letter to Ogilvie, Friend of Jefferson, and the Federalist Propaganda," *Journal of the History of Ideas*, xxviii [1967], 432-44; James Ogilvie, *Philosophical Essays; to Which are Subjoined, Copious Notes, Critical and Explanatory, and a Supplementary Narrative; with an Appendix* [Philadelphia, 1816], "Supplementary Narrative," i-x; TJ to Ogilvie, 31 Jan., 23 June 1806; Ogilvie to TJ, 12 Aug. 1807; TJ to John Glendy, 21 June 1808).

FIRST WEEK OF AUGUST: as indicated above by the note Mann Page added to this letter, by the time published notice appeared the examination had been moved to the second week of August. For the notice in THE FREDERICKSBURG PRINT, see Enclosure No. 2 to Mann Page to TJ, 3 July 1795.

[1] Word supplied.

From Mann Page

MY DEAR SIR   Mann'sfield. July 3rd. 1795

I have been requested to forward to you the enclosed Letter, which, as it relates to a subject, that I know, has long engaged your Attention, will, I am sure, be favourably received by you. I also send you a Publication in the Paper of this Day on the same Subject by the same Gentleman. If any thing can draw you from your Retirement, I am confidint that the Solicitation now made will not be ineffectual. The Importance of the Subject demands your Attention. A public Seminary requests your Sentiments on the Mode of Education which is pursued in it. And your Friends, who are the Trustees of the Academy, solicit your Advice on this important Occasion. You will not, I hope, refuse the Call of Mankind, of your Country and of your Friends but that you will come over. I shall feel myself happy to be honoured with your Company during the Time of the Examination. I am, dear sir, most sincerely your's affecately.

MANN PAGE

RC (DLC); endorsed by TJ as received 14 July 1795 and so recorded in SJL. Enclosures: (1) James Ogilvie to TJ, [before 3 July 1795]. (2) Ogilvie to "Fellow-Citizens," a long discourse on educational philosophy, presenting principles to improve the system of education, justifying his departure from prescriptive modes of education, and announcing a public examination to be held at Fredericksburg Academy during the second week of August (*Virginia Herald, and Fredericksburg Advertiser*, 3 July 1795).

Page was president of the TRUSTEES of Fredericksburg Academy (*Virginia Herald*, and *Fredericksburg Advertiser*, 31 July 1795). "Monitor" later called Ogilvie's published notice for the examination at Fredericksburg Academy "a piece of florid plagiarism" by "a vain and presumptuous pedant." Ogilvie in reply branded Monitor "a malignant defamer" whose criticism gave "singular proof of mental imbecility" (same, 14, 21, 31 July 1795).

A letter from Page to TJ of 7 Jan. 1795, recorded in SJL as received 12 Feb. 1795, has not been found.

From John Jay

SIR   New York 7 July 1795

Two days ago I received from Sir John Sinclair the Book herewith enclosed, which he presents to you and requests me to forward.

As its Size forbids its being sent by the post, and there is little Probability of my soon meeting with other opportunities to Virginia, I think it best to forward it to Pha. and beg the favor of Mr. Randolph to convey it to You. I have the Honor to be with great Respect Sir your most obt. & h'ble Servt   JOHN JAY

RC (NNPM); endorsed by TJ as received 21 July 1795 and so recorded in SJL. Dft (NNC: Jay Papers); contains minor emendations; with draft of Jay to Edmund Randolph, 7 July 1795, subjoined.

Enclosure: presumably Sir John Sinclair, *General View of the Agriculture of the Northern Counties and Islands of Scotland ...* (London, 1795). See Sowerby, No. 753.

To James Lyle

DEAR SIR   Monticello July 10. 1795.

I expected that Kinsolving's money would by this time have been brought in to remit to you. He confessed judgment on both bonds with a stay of execution, and in the spring brought me his tobacco notes to sell for him and receive the money. Not liking to do this I left it to himself to sell them and bring the order for the money. I have not heard from him since, tho' those who know him assure me I may rely on him. I still hope therefore that that money will soon get to your hands.

The paiments made and the bonds under collection pretty exactly complete the paiments of 1790. 1791. 1792. 1793. That of 1794. should have been paid with the crop of that year, had it not been for the total loss of that by the rust at this place, which threw the maintenance of my family entirely on the profits of my Bedford estate, which happened also to be uncommonly short. A nailery which I have established with my own negro boys now provides completely for the maintenance of my family, as we make from 8. to 10,000 nails a day and it is on the increase. My crops here and in Bedford therefore will be entirely free. That of this place for the present year, now in the house, with what is usually produced from Bedford enable me to be certain of paying the bond of 1794. the ensuing spring. That which is to become due this year will probably require the two ensuing crops to accomplish. I have pushed the business of sales as far as I can without entirely breaking up my plantations, and I am satisfied I can now from annual crops pay off the remnant of your debt as fast as it would be by a sale on the usual credits, and delay of collection. I am taught by the past to rely on your future indulgence, by the benefit of which I can get thro' this business, and be left at my ease, when rigorous exactions in point of time would have torn up my affairs. On my part no remissness shall take place, nor shall the matter be out of my mind till it be completely accomplished. My fidelity in doing this shall entirely justify the quiet with which you have left me to pursue my own means of paiment. I am with great esteem Dear Sir your affectionate friend & servt   TH: JEFFERSON

PrC (MHi); at foot of first page: "Mr. Lyle."

James KINSOLVING'S MONEY had been given to TJ in the form of bonds totaling £139.15 for slaves purchased in January 1793. TJ intended to apply the proceeds against his debt to Henderson, McCaul & Company, the firm represented by Lyle, but had to institute legal action in Albemarle County Court to secure payment from Kinsolving. On 14 Aug. 1794 and 2 Mch.

1795, Kinsolving CONFESSED JUDGMENT on the debt, with TJ agreeing to stays of execution. Kinsolving made a first payment of £3.12 in March 1795 and evidently discharged the remainder by 1 Sep. 1800 (MB, 7 Mch. 1795, and note, 1 Sep. 1800; Albemarle County Order Book, 1793-95, Albemarle County Circuit Court Clerk's Office, Charlottesville, p. 210, 306; Thomas Mann Randolph to TJ, 24 Jan. 1793; TJ to Lyle, 15 Apr. 1793, 8 Nov. 1795).

From John Craig Millar

SIR   Philadelp[. . .] of the Departt. of State July 10th. 1795

I have perhaps to solicit your forgiveness for the freedom I have used in not having immediately transmitted the inclosed, upon my arrival in the United States. My apology is—that I received it in circumstances which were inconsistent with the supposition of dispatch being requisite. Entertaining likewise not a distant hope of having it in my power to be the Bearer of the letter to Virginia, I was extremely unwilling to relinquish so probable a means of procuring the honour of a personal Interview with you.

I very much regret that the kindness of my friends in providing employment for me in this office, has at the same time, by rendering me stationary for some time in Philadelphia, deprived me of the Satisfaction

I should have felt in being permitted to wait on you. Mean time, as I do not know *the whole* of the Nature of the inclosed letter, I cannot any longer detain it. I have the honor to be Sir with high respect Your obedient Servant   JOHN CRAIG MILLAR

RC (ViW); torn; at foot of text: "Thos. Jefferson Esqre."; endorsed by TJ as received 21 July 1795 and so recorded in SJL. Enclosure: Dugald Stewart to TJ, 1 Mch. 1795.

John Craig Millar (1760-96), son of the noted law professor John Millar, was a Scottish attorney and author of *Elements of the Law Relating to Insurances* (Edinburgh, 1787). Ill health and Whiggish political beliefs led him to immigrate to America in 1795, where he served as a clerk in the Department of State and died of sunstroke in the Pennsylvania backcountry (DNB, s.v. "Millar, John"; William C. Lehmann, *John Millar of Glasgow, 1735-1801: His Life and Thought and his Contributions to Sociological Analysis* [Cambridge, 1960], 26, 411, 412).

From William Branch Giles

DEAR SIR   Richmond July 13th. *1795*

I have been several days in this place engaged in inquireing amongst the money changers, as to the present, and the probable future, prices of wheat and tobacco.

The market for wheat seems not yet to be fixed. I think there are but few purchasers at this time in the market. They speak however of from eight to ten shillings Per Bushel, and it is supposed by some that two dollars may be had in the course of two or three months. This supposition appears to me to be justifyed by the present prices at Baltimore, it is said that wheat commands two dollars there at this time. From this state of things I have concluded not to make sale of my crop for the present. A prime crop of upland Tobacco of twenty six *HHds*. sold for thirty three shillings on saturday last, although the current price seems not so high. Mr. Brown informed me that thirty six shillings had been demanded for large quantities of choise tobacco in the hands of the merchants, but I believe that no sale has as yet taken place at that price. The price seems to vary from twenty six to thirty three shillings, depending on the quantity, quality and weights. There does not appear to me to be any great anxiety for purchaseing this article, I have had a small parcel for sale, and have not been able to effect it upon advantageous terms. Presumeing that Mrs. Randolph is on her route to the Springs, Be pleased to make my best respects to Miss Maria, and consider me as your sincere friend &c   WM B. GILES

RC (DLC); at foot of text: "Thomas Jefferson Esquire"; endorsed by TJ as received 21 July 1795 and so recorded in SJL.

To James Madison

TH:J. TO J.M.   Monticello July 13. 95.

I send you the inclosed as you may perhaps not have seen it. Return it if you please. I have not yet seen the treaty, but suppose tomorrow's post may perhaps bring it. Mr. and Mrs. Randolph set out the day after tomorrow for the springs, to see if any of them can restore the nearly hopeless state of his health. Nil mihi rescribas. Attamen ipse veni. Vale.

RC (DLC: Madison Papers). PrC (DLC). Enclosure not found.

On the trips for Randolph's HEALTH, see note to TJ to Thomas Mann Randolph, 14 July 1794.

NIL MIHI RESCRIBAS. ATTAMEN IPSE VENI: "writing back is pointless. Come yourself!" See Ovid, *Heroides*, 1.2 (Grant Showerman, ed. and trans., *Heroides and Amores*, 2d ed. rev. by G. P. Goold [Cambridge, Mass., 1977], 10-11).

To Archibald Stuart

DEAR SIR   Monticello July 14. 1795.

Having lately had an opportunity of examining our tax law in the new volume of laws lately published, I find lands whereof the taxes have not been paid for three years are liable to have a warrant located on them by any person whatever, without notice to the owner. I am therefore become really uneasy about my Natural bridge tract, and the more so as I have no information from the Commissioner to whom I wrote on the subject. My letter may be the means of setting somebody on the attempt to locate the lands. I must therefore my dear Sir trouble you to get some friend to tender the last three years taxes to the proper person, or to do it for me yourself, and to take a reciept or if refused, an acknolegement of the tender in writing, and also to see that the Commissioners have placed the lands in the land roll if they had got off of it. Surely my letter will be considered as an enlistment of the land. I am with sincere affection Dear Sir Your friend & servt   TH: JEFFERSON

PrC (MHi); at foot of text: "Archibd. Stuart esq."; endorsed by TJ in ink.

TAX LAW IN THE NEW VOLUME: "An Act prescribing the Mode of ascertaining the Taxable Property within the Commonwealth, and of collecting the Public Revenue," passed 13 Dec. 1792 and printed in the 1794 edition of *A Collection of All Such*

Acts of the General Assembly of Virginia, of a Public and Permanent Nature, as are Now in Force; With a Table of the Principal Matters. [To] Which are Prefixed the Declaration of Rights, and Constitution, or Form of Government. Published Pursuant to an Act of the General Assembly . . . Passed on [28 Dec. 1792] (Richmond, 1794), 141. See Sowerby, No. 1862.

From Sir John Sinclair

DEAR SIR   Whitehall 15th. July 1795.

I take the Liberty of inclosing the Plan of an Agreement which I am anxious should be entered into by the Powers of Europe and the United States of America for the purpose of rewarding those who make any discovery of general benefit to Society. Having endeavoured in the inclosed paper to deliniate the nature and importance of such a measure, it is unnecessary for me to trouble you with attempting to enter into any further Detail. I can not however hesitate to express my hopes that such a measure will be acceptable to those who wish well to the interests of humanity, and can not fail therefore of meeting with your approbation.

Being extremely desirous that it should be taken up by the United States of America, I hope that you will recommend it to your government as a measure In the Success of which America is deeply interested. With great regard I have the Honor to be Dear Sir Your most obedient humble Servant.   JOHN SINCLAIR

PS. I have also sent you the outlines of our 15th. chapter of the intended General Report of The Board of Agriculture which relates to that important branch of Husbandry Manures. As it is but a Sketch I shall be greatly obliged by your Communications and remarks on this very interesting Subject.

RC (DLC); endorsed by TJ as received on 10 May 1796 and so recorded in SJL. Enclosures: (1) Sir John Sinclair, *Plan of an Agreement among the Powers in Europe, and the United States of America, for the Purpose of Rewarding Discoveries of General Benefit to Society* (London, 1795). See Sow- erby, No. 748. (2) Robert Somerville, *Outlines of the Fifteenth Chapter of the Proposed General Report from the Board of Agriculture, on the Subject of Manures. Drawn Up for the Consideration of the Board of Agriculture and Internal Improvement* (London, 1795). See Sowerby, No. 751.

To James Brown

DEAR SIR   Monticello July 16. 1795.

Mr. Snelson's business has prevented his rendering me an account till this day. I now inclose you his note for the balance due me £102–8–11¾. arising on nails delivered him before the 30th. May. I also inclose an order of Ro. Rives & Co. on you for £9–5–3. Below is a statement of our account as nearly as I can make it. By this there will be still about £10. due from me to you, occasioned by my balance with Mr. Snelson being that much less than I had counted. If you think proper to settle the balance exactly and transfer it to that store it shall be speedily satisfied,

or if you chuse it, it shall be paid in Richmond. I am with great esteem
Dr. Sir Your friend & servt   TH: JEFFERSON

RC (ViHi: Lewis L. Strauss Papers); clipped below signature, resulting in loss of subjoined statement of account.

To Archibald Stuart

DEAR SIR   Monticello July 20. 95.

I have recieved your favor of the 9th. It happened fortunately that I
had preserved the original rough paper on which I had estimated the
books separately which I had to dispose of. On that I find that the Modern entries, Burrows, Peere Williams, Salkeld and Strange were estimated at fifty dollars and twenty two cents. The same books cost me in
England £18–5. sterling which is 81.D. 11c. besides the charges of
importation. So that your brother I hope will have room to be content
with his purchase.—Since my last to you, a further progress in looking
over the new code has taught me that my land could not be lost for non
paiment of taxes without notice to me, by a law of the last session. So
that unless it had been taken before it is still safe. But as it is my wish not
to avoid the contribution of taxes which it owes to the public, I will still
thank you to pursue what I requested in my last. I am with great esteem
Dear Sir Your affectte. friend & servt   TH: JEFFERSON

PrC (MHi); at foot of text: "Mr. Stuart."

Stuart's FAVOR of 9 July 1795, recorded in SJL as received 16 July 1795, has not been found. A LAW OF THE LAST SESSION: an amending act, passed 25 Dec. 1794, which clarified the statute TJ mentioned in his letter to Stuart of 14 July 1795 (Shepherd, *Statutes*, I, 305-6).

To John Barnes

SIR   Monticello July 21. 95.

I drew on you about the 10th. or 11th. inst. in favor of William
Wardlaw or order for 40. Dollars, of which this serves to advise you, if
I did not write a letter of advice at the time. If I did, I omitted to keep
a copy of it and it has escaped my memory. I am with esteem Dear Sir
Your most obedt. servt   TH: JEFFERSON

PrC (MHi); at foot of text: "Mr. John Barnes."

TJ's draft in favor of Dr. WILLIAM WARDLAW of Charlottesville is recorded in MB, 11 July 1795. There is no record in SJL of an earlier letter to Barnes on this subject. A letter from Barnes to TJ of 22 June 1795, recorded in SJL as received 30 June 1795, has not been found.

Notes on Infractions of Neutral Rights by France and Great Britain

[after 21 July 1795]

Infractions of neutral rights by the French and English. Their dates.

1792. Nov. 15. British proclamation prohibiting exportation of grain &c. There were then sundry *neutral* vessels in British ports with flour &c. ready to sail.

This was previous to the decree of fraternity and to the opening of the Scheld.

Dec. Neutral vessels laden with *foreign* grain for *France* were stopt in the English ports by order of the government. About the middle of Dec. the French minister remonstrates against this.

1793. Jan. 8. Ld. Grenville replies that they were founded in the jealousies and uneasiness prevailing in the English government towards the French. This shewed the French that in the event of war Gr. Brit. meditated this means of distressing her, even against neutral rights.

Feb. 1. French declaration of war.

Mar. 25. Gr. Br. forms convention with Russia for cutting off supplies of provisions for France and for distressing her commerce even by preventing neutral powers from giving any protection whatever directly or indirectly in consequence of their neutrality, to the commerce or property of the French on the sea or in the ports of France.

The negociations for this Convention must have been begun in 1792.

The *first* orders of Gr. Br. were probably given at this date for seising provisions bound to France.[1] Mr. Pinckney's letter of July 5. 1793. to the Secy. of State gives Ld. Grenville's explanation of the intention of this convention, as *coextensive with the order of June 8.* and that Spain was to do the same. A similar convention with Spain Germany Prussia[2] afterwards appeared.[3]

Apr. 5. Ld. Auckland (see below).[4]

May 9. The French under apprehensions of famine in consequence of this combination give orders to seize and carry in provision vessels. They take the combination of the other powers to stop provisions as a ground.

June.[5] 8. British *additional* orders for seizing all provision vessels going to France.

Observations. The British minister in his conference with Pinckney does not pretend to found the order of June 8. on the French decree of May 9. but on the convention of Mar. 25. Hammond in his letter to the Secy. of state, does not take that ground, but says it was right under the Law of nations. Grenville adhered to the right under the law of nations both with Pinckney and Jay, and inserts it in our treaty.

July. Empress of Russia informs Sweden of her arrangements with Britain to stop all neutral ships bound to France.

Apr. 5. Ld. Auckland (knowing of the starving convention) holds up in his memorial to the Dutch government, famine as likely to afflict France.

MS (DLC: TJ Papers, 96: 16483); consists of one page entirely in TJ's hand; undated, but see below; important emendations noted below; endorsed by TJ on verso: "Neutrality, rights of it invaded. Notes."

TJ could have made this compilation no earlier than 21 July 1795, when he received Henry Tazewell's letter of 1 July and first saw the contents of the Jay Treaty. He may actually have penned these notes in 1798, when Tench Coxe wrote articles as "An American Merchant" discussing the same events (see *Philadelphia Gazette*, 3, 5, 16 Feb. 1798; Notes on Newspaper Articles, 21 Feb. 1798).

DECREE OF FRATERNITY: the first propagandist decree of the National Convention, dated 19 Nov. 1792 (see Gouverneur Morris to TJ, 1 Jan. 1793, and note). For the OPENING OF THE SCHELD, see William Short to TJ, 30 Nov. 1792 (first letter), and note. A SIMILAR CONVENTION WITH SPAIN GERMANY PRUSSIA: in 1793 Great Britain nego-

tiated conventions with Russia, Spain, Austria, Prussia, Sardinia, and the Two Sicilies (Ehrman, *Pitt*, 274-6, 278; Thomas Pinckney to TJ, 5 July 1793). HAMMOND IN HIS LETTER TO THE SECY. OF STATE: George Hammond to TJ, 12 Sep. 1793. In a MEMORIAL TO THE DUTCH GOVERNMENT on 5 Apr. 1793 Lord Auckland addressed the States General about French officials whom the Austrian army was holding prisoner in the Netherlands (*The Journal and Correspondence of William, Lord Auckland*, 4 vols. [London, 1861-62], III, 10; Rodolph Vall-Travers to TJ, 9 Apr. 1793).

[1] Sentence interlined.
[2] Preceding two words written over illegible text.
[3] Preceding seventeen words probably inserted.
[4] Line inserted.
[5] Word written over partially erased text, probably "July 5."

Notes on the Account with Richard Harvie & Company

Notes on the account of R. Harvie & Co. against me, and the bond given on it.

My dealings with Kippen & Co. commenced in 1762. but I had never had a single account from them when Mr. Harvie and myself settled, which was Apr. 18. 1775. Consequently I had no means of correcting any errors in his account which related to transactions with Kippen & Co. or Henderson McCaul & Co. It is only on recieving the accounts of those companies that I am able to rectify what was wrong in Mr. Harvie's.

At the time of my settlement with Mr. Harvie, interest was calculated on the different balances from year to year at the moment they became due, down to the date of the settlement Apr. 18. 1775. and these sums of interest were added to the principal and a bond given, converting the whole into principal, to wit, for £198–12–2$\frac{3}{4}$. Wherever therefore any improper debets are inserted, or credits omitted, in the account, interest must be calculated on them from their date, and a deduction made accordingly from the amount of the bond.

In Kippen & Co.'s account against me is the following debet. '1768. Aug. 31. To cash in account with Richd. Harvie & Co. on your order in May 1766. £25–0–0.' Mr. Harvie has given me no credit for this article. Consequently we are to deduct from the bond as follows.

		£		
1768. Aug. 31. Omission of credit for my order on Kippen & Co.		25– 0– 0		
	Y M D			
Interest on do. till Apr. 18. 1775.	6– 7 –18	8– 5–10		

In Henderson McCaul & Co.'s account is the following debet against me.

'1772. July 20. To cash in account with R. Harvie & Co.	£	s	d
to Walter Mousley	19–	4–	4$\frac{3}{4}$
to Henry Mullins	12–	5–	0
to Julius Shard	10–	0–	0
to Bartlet Ford	6–	10–	11$\frac{1}{2}$
to Stephen Willis	14–	8–	7
	62–	8–	11$\frac{1}{4}$'[1]

This matter is entered in my pocket memorandum book in these words.

'1772. May 15. received of N. Campbell by R. Harvie £42–15–11$\frac{1}{2}$
paid R. Harvie for B. Ford £6–10–11$\frac{1}{2}$
paid do. for Julius Shard £5.
paid do. for Henry Mullins £12–5.'

[413]

Mr. Harvie's entries are thus.

Dr.			Cr.		£ s d
1771. Dec. 14.	To Bartlet Ford £6–4–2		1772. Dec. 31.	By N. Campbell	19– 8–7
1772. Apr. 24.	To cash. 19–0–0		1773. Oct. 4.	By Bartlet Ford	6–11–0½
	To N. Campbell 19–8–7				

This is a perplexed transaction, nor does my memory serve at all in setting it to rights. However, a knowlege of the course of business between us, and these different entries, with more time to consider and examine into it, than when I sketched out the notes formerly given to Mr. Lyle, enable me to present a more probable view of it, and to reconcile all our entires by supposing only one instead of two erroneous charges in Mr. Harvie's statement.—I sold my crops habitually to Kippen & Co. and drew on them for money. Mr. Harvie having a store here connected with them, I sometimes got small articles of goods from him, but never drew money from him. My overseers and workmen usually had little debts with him of which I became paymaster, and did it by orders on Kippen & Co. I had to pay Mr. Harvie in 1772

		£
for	Bartlet Ford	6–10–11½
	Julius Shard, one of my workmen	10– 0– 0
	Stephen Willis, another of do.	14– 8– 7
	Henry Mullins	12– 5– 0
	Walter Mousley, one of my overseers	19– 4– 4¾
		62– 8–11¼

I gave orders in Mr. Harvie's favor for these sums on Kippen & Co. Neill Campbell being then their factor.

Mr. Campbell, Mr. Harvie and myself were at the next meeting of the merchants at the April General court. On the 15th. of May he received and brought me from Neill Campbell £42–15–11½ in part of the orders. It seems from my entry that[2] we agreed he should stop

	Ford's	£6–10–11½
	Mullins's	12– 5– 0
and half of Julius Shard's, towit		5.
		23–15–11½
and he paid me the balance		19– 0– 0
		42–15–11½

cash, concluding between us I suppose that the £19–4–4¾ destined for Mousley, we would settle with him each of us separately, as we afterwards did. Still there remained the other half of Shard's money £5–0–0

and Stephen Willis's	14–8–7
making together	19–8–7

and this is the very sum he afterwards drew or settled with N. Campbell, and both debited and credited by him in my account. Thus Kippen & Co.'s entries become fully justified. Mine are fully justified, for not being a party in[3] the settlement afterwards of the £19–8–7 it was not entered in my memorandum book. It enables us too to understand Mr. Harvie's entries, with respect to which I should before have observed that on a blank page of his account, but not in the account, were these words in his own handwriting.

'Henry Mullins   12– 5– 0 '
'Julius Shard   10–   '   a mere memorandum that they
'Bar. Ford   6–10–11½ '   were settled.
'Stephen Willis 14– 8– 7 '

Let us see now how Mr. Harvie made his entries.

He both debits and credits me with Ford's money. This was right.

He neither debits nor credits me with Mullins's and the half of Shard's first received. This too was right. He both debits and credits me with the other half of Shard's money £5. and Willis's £14–8–7 when he makes the entry 'To Neill Campbell £19–8–7, and By Neill Campbell £19–8–7.' But as to the £19. cash he debits me with it, and does not credit me. This is wrong. He ought either to have entered it to both Dr. and Cr. or to neither, as he did the other articles. It is clear he was only the bearer of the money from Neill Campbell to me, and he ought to have given me credit on the receipt of it, if he meant to charge me with his delivery of it.—My accounts settled with Ford, Shard, Willis and Mousley prove this exposition of facts. In the three former they allow me exactly these sums paid to Mr. Harvie. In Mousley's account there is no such allowance, which shews I paid him otherwise as before mentioned. Some of these accounts were shewn to Mr. Lyle. The others shall be produced. I had no account with Mullins, the transaction with him being single.

The bond then must be corrected as follows.

		£	s	d
1775. Apr. 18. Th:J. to R. Harvie & Co. Dr. by bond		198–12–	7¾	

	£	s	d
Cr.	£	s	d
1768. Aug.31. By omission of credit for my order on Kippen & Co.	25– 0–	0	
By interest on do. from Aug. 31. 1768. to Apr. 18. 1775	8– 5–10		
1772. Apr. 24. By wrong debet of cash	19– 0–	0	
By interest on do. from Apr. 24. 72. to Apr. 18. 75.	2–16– 8		
	55– 2– 6		
balance for which the bond ought to have been given	143–10– 1¾		

This exposition of facts reconciles all our entries, shews all are true in fact, and that only one in Mr. Harvies is erroneous in principle, because the entry is not double, or because the £19. cash should only have been noted on the blank page of the account with the other articles of the same paiment.

1775. Sep. 24. I gave Mr. Harvie an order on H. Mullins, which was assumed by Richd. Anderson for £70.

To enable Mr. Harvie to recollect this, I will state the transaction. Richard Anderson owed money to H. Mullins for tobacco in his hands. H. Mullins owed to Mr. Skipwith by bond £170. for negroes. Mr. Skipwith owed me by bond a greater sum for land. Skipwith gave me an order on Mullins for the £170. I gave orders on Mullins as follows. for Doctr. Walker £30.

R. Harvie £70.
Richd. Anderson £70.
170.

I credited the whole sum on Skipwith's bond.

Richard Anderson assumed the whole. I presume there were accounts running between his store and Mr. Harvie's, both being in Charlottesville, and perhaps they have failed to make the entry at that time. I suspect it from the following note now in my hands, and shewn to Mr. Lyle. 'Sir, I was to have paid £170. for Henry Mullins in Octob. 1775. so that if you will give him credit on his bond for that sum, I will be answerable to Mr. Harvie and Dr. Walker for your orders in favor of them, paiable at the same time. I am Sir your most obedt. servt. Richard Anderson. 28. Apr. 1777. to Thos. Jefferson esq.'—However these gentlemen may settle the matter between themselves does not concern me. I gave the order Sep. 24. 1775. The money was in R. Anderson's hands: Mr. Harvie keeping off the demand makes any loss by depreciation, if any occurred, his loss, not mine. It was gold and silver when I gave him the order.

Finally my account corrected with Mr. Harvie stands thus.

Th:J. to R. Harvie Dr. 1775. Apr. 18. to true balance for which the

bond should have been 143–10–1¾

Sep. 24. to interest from Apr. 18. to
this day 3– 2–2¼
146–12–4

Cr. By order on R. Anderson

that day 70–
Balance then remaining due 76–12–4

Mr. Harvie sent me a written notification that he had assigned this bond in 1775. to Kippen & Co. I shewed this notification to Mr. Lyle. On examining the bond, such an endorsement is still legible tho' defaced with the pen, and a subsequent assignment written to Mr. Lyle. This can not affect me; and the sum really due on the bond must be on interest only from the close of the war, according to agreement as to whatever I owed to Kippen & Co.

Th: Jefferson

July 22. 1795.

MS (MHi); entirely in TJ's hand.

After returning from France, TJ had attempted to rectify accounts related to the amount of the bond he had given to Richard Harvie in April 1775. Harvie, who kept a store in Charlottesville, had ties to the Glasgow firm of Kippen & Company, and James Lyle, to whom TJ wrote on this subject on 25 Nov. 1795, acted as factor for a successor company, Henderson, McCaul & Company. Interest accumulated on this and other obligations to the firms, and TJ made only sporadic payments. The bond—which included, at least in part, a debt owed by his mother—was not paid off during his lifetime (MB, 18 Apr. 1775, 1 Aug. 1789, 4

Mch. 1790, 24 June 1811, 16 June 1821, and notes; TJ to Robert Lewis, 2 Mch. 1790; TJ to Nicholas Lewis, 7 Mch. 1790; TJ to James Lyle, 7 Mch. 1790, 17 Sep. 1803; TJ to James Strange, 7 Oct. 1791; Memorandum on Accounts of Richard Harvie & Company, [after 17 Sep. 1803]).

According to SJL, TJ exchanged four letters with Henry Mullins between 23 Oct. and 27 Nov. 1794, none of which has been found.

[1] Closing quotation mark supplied.
[2] Sentence to this point interlined.
[3] Preceding three words written over an illegible word.

From John Breckinridge

Dear Sir   Fayette 25th. July 1795.

Your note for the clover seed came to hand a week ago, and an opportunity which I think prefereable to that by post now offers by Colo. Quarles, of sending you a few seeds. It is not easily got in my neighbourhood, having almost intirely disappeared. Pray ought I not to send you a little of the *Soil* also? I fear the seed will not acknowledge that about Monticello. I sincerely wish 1000 of the tens of thousands of acres of our fertile uncultivated lands, could be spread around you. You might then really farm with both pleasure and profit.

The time however is fast approaching, when our rich lands will not lie uncultivated. Emigrations to this country for 18 Months past, have exceeded any hitherto known. It is supposed, that as many removed here last spring, as came during the whole of the preceeding year; and it is thought not less than 15, or 20,000 then emigrated. Some of the northern Dutch with long purses, have visited us, and given for good farms as high as 3 and 4 £ ℔ acre. Indeed I am inclined to beleive no agricultural part of Amera. is in a more rapid state of Improvement than this Country. The inhabitants where they have the means (and very many of them have it) are making valuable and lasting improvements. The common mechanic arts are beginning to flourish. The paper I now write on, is made and sold within 6 Miles of me at 18/ ℔ ream. Our only want, is the navigation of the Mississippi; at least we think so; and that without it, we will ultimately come to nothing.

Genl. Wayne has yet made nothing of the Indian treaty. I am fearful the indians are not hearty in the business. It would be of mighty importance to us, would they only conclude a treaty; altho' they might have no intentions of observing it.

Our crops are very promising, and will be as acceptable as a new crop ever was here; as that of the last year is more generally consumed than is usual. Corn is 10 and 12/ ℔ barrl., and other produce in proportion. With great respect & esteem I am dear Sir Your mo: Obt. Svt.

J. BRECKINRIDGE

RC (DLC); at foot of text: "Thos. Jefferson esqr."; endorsed by TJ as received 23 Aug. 1795 and so recorded in SJL.

Anthony WAYNE had begun negotiations with tribes in the Northwest Territory on 16 June, and concluded the TREATY of Greenville on 3 Aug. 1795 (ASP, *Indian Affairs*, I, 562-83).

From Robert Pollard

SIR   Richmond July 25th: 1795

Your favor of the 24th last month covering a Draft on Mr. John Barnes of Philadelphia for twelve hundred and seventy two dollars and half, came safe to hand.

Mr. Heron has executed a Deed for the Six shares in the James River Company for Mr. Short, and I have a Deed drawn and ready to execute for the share I sold you for the Same Gentleman, which shall be executed previous to the next meeting of the Directors, and both of them presented for admission to Record.

Mr. Benjamin Harrison has offered me Six shares at the same price of those purchased from Mr. Heron. If you wish them bought, please advise me.

I am requested by Mr. Heron to inform that the Fish You write to Mr. Pleasants for are in his care, ready to be sent by the first Boat going to Milton. I am Sir Yr most Obd servt   ROBERT POLLARD

RC (DLC: William Short Papers); endorsed by TJ as received 28 July 1795 and so recorded in SJL.

TJ's 24 June 1795 FAVOR to Pollard, recorded in SJL, has not been found.

To Thomas Mann Randolph

DEAR SIR   Monticello July 26. 95.

Mr. Stuart having thought it best to associate a careful person at Staunton with James, they arrived here this morning with their sorrowful charge. They found here my sisters Bolling Carr and Marks. It is great consolation to us that your stay at Staunton had been so long as to render it impossible that the journey could have had any effect on the accident which happened. Anne and Jefferson are in high health. Mrs. Bolling is still afflicted with her rheumatism and her daughter and both servants are laid up with the fever and ague the consequence of their stay in Goochland. We all join in love to you both and trust you are looking forward with hope to the restoration of your own health and as early a return to us as is consistent with that. God bless you both. Yours affectionately   TH: JEFFERSON

RC (DLC); at foot of text: "Mr. Randolph"; endorsed by Randolph.

SORROWFUL CHARGE: TJ's young granddaughter Ellen Wayles Randolph died at Staunton while traveling with her parents to Sweet Springs. A death date of 26 July 1795 is recorded among the memoranda about the family of Martha Jefferson Randolph and Thomas Mann Randolph that TJ entered in the family prayer book in 1803 or later (see illustration), but that was more likely the date she was buried at Monticello, being the same day TJ paid local schoolteacher Benjamin Snead two dollars for the reading of a service for her (MB, 1 Apr. 1769, 26 July 1795, 24 Sep. 1806, and notes).

A letter from Randolph to TJ of 23 July 1795, recorded in SJL as received from Staunton two days later, has not been found.

To Archibald Stuart

MY DEAR SIR   Monticello July 26. 95.

I am very thankful to you for your kind attention to our lost infant. The person you sent arrived here safely with James and their charge, and will be properly rewarded. Knowing the disposition of James, I readily conceive his conduct, and would have wished that to have been properly rewarded too, were it not that it would have added new pain to the parents of the child. I write this line by the bearer merely to assure you that he has performed his office carefully and that it is gratefully recieved by Dear Sir Your friend & servt   TH: JEFFERSON

PrC (MHi); at foot of text: "Mr. Stuart"; endorsed in ink by TJ.

PROPERLY REWARDED: TJ paid the unidentified man sent by Stuart six dollars (MB, 26 July 1795).

Letters from Stuart to TJ of 23 and 26 July 1795, recorded in SJL as received on 25 and 26 July 1795, respectively, have not been found.

From John Barnes

Sir Philadelphia 28th: July 1795.

My last to you, was of the 6th: Instant. Since when, I am without any of your favors—nor has this Market varied the least, in point of a rise, but rather dull and stationary from 14/2 – 3 and 4 the most. Wether or not, the uncertain effects of the suspended treaty has contributed thereto, I am at a loss to determine but so it is—very few Orders indeed have of late Arrived from Europe. Till of late, I deferred selling in hopes of Obtaining 14/6. Fearing a fall, I was advised to Accept of the very best Offer say 14/5, and with which I thought it prudent to close the sale. Herewith have Annexed a sketch of the account for your better government. Apparent ballance in your favor 2470.24 dolls.—about 2500: said proceeds I do not expect, to be in Cash for, untill the latter End of Next Month. You will please therefore to regulate your future drafts, so, as to become due and payable, the Middle and latter end of Sepr:—when be Assured—they shall meet, with the Honor due, from Sir your Obedt: & very H servt: **JOHN BARNES**

RC (DLC: William Short Papers); addressed: "Thomas Jefferson Esquire Monticello Virginia"; with notation in Barnes's hand: "single *sheet*"; stamped and postmarked; endorsed by TJ as received 18 Aug. 1795 and so recorded in SJL.

Barnes's 6TH. July 1795 letter to ⟨J, recorded in SJL as received 21 July 1795, has not been found.

Account with John Barnes

Thomas Jefferson Esqr. of Virga: In a/c with John Barnes
By Clement Biddle for
William Shorts Certificate dated. 13th Decr. 1793

No. 1464 deferred Assumed debt, 7504.42 dolls. 14/5			5409.42.
for Int recd 1st July ℔ a/			314.55.
			5723.97.

Charges viz.

paid postage of 4 letters		1.28.	
My Commissn. on Sale, transfer ⎫	$\frac{1}{2}$ ℔ Ct	28.61.	29.89.
Accepting & paying drafts &ca. ⎭			5694.08.

from whence deduct the following drafts viz.

	⎧ " James Bringhurst	46.74.		
June 3d: 3 days st. ⎨ " Muir & Hyde		59.37.		
	⎩ " Robert Pollard	36	142.11.	
do: 6 weeks st.	" Wm: C. Carter	600.		
4th 6 do.	" do. do.	600.		
6th–11th 6 do.	" do: 6 of 100 each	600.	1800.	
June 14 paye. 2d July	" Caleb Lownes		240.67.	
" 24 a 30 days	" Robert Pollard		1272.50.	
pd. 16 July	" Sampson Crosby a/c ℔ recpt.		20.83.	3476.11.
			Dolls.	2217.97.
E. E. Philada: 28th July 1795		former Balce.		252.27.
JOHN BARNES				2470.24

MS (DLC: William Short Papers); in Barnes's hand.

From Tench Coxe

DEAR SIR   Philada. July 30. 1795.

I have postponed to answer the letter you did me the honor to write last untill I should have found a good opportunity to forward your pacquets to Mr. Monroe, and M. Van Staphorsts & Co. They went, about two weeks ago, in an American Ship, and were committed to the care of a Mr. Murgatroyd of Philadelphia. He is a young [man][1] of good connexions here, and I doubt not will place them in the hands of the gentlemen for whom they are directed.

We have no British News later than the 8th. of June, or French later than the 31st. May and 1st. June. It appears probable, that the want of provisions in G. Britain and Ireland, and their apprehensions from tumults raised for that and other causes with the hope of producing disorders in France have occasioned a renewal of the orders to Capture neutral Vessels, with provisions, bound to France. There are *some* reasons to suppose a similar measure in regard to french colonial productions for Amsterdam and Hamburg has been adopted. Either will be seriously taken by our countrymen—the latter will be attended with extreme dissatisfaction. Together they will be ill preparatives of the public mind for a sanction our pending treaty with Great Britain.[2]

I have read that important instrument with considerable attention, and cannot go further, as to the part countenanced by the Senate, than to say I am willing and desirous, that it also should be further amicably negociated and amended. It is made so as not only to hold us bound for what we were originally bound, while they are in part exonerated, but to make us responsible in damages for events arising from their conduct. The candor and the honest fame of our most important functionaries, and of the very respectable men who filled those places and our national honor are soiled by the fraudulent author of the first clear infraction of the old Treaty.

Powers are exercised in regard to *the tenure of lands* and *the law of Descents*, not invested in the general government.

The West India Article is not more exceptionable as to tonnage and exportation of commodities of the kinds raised in the Islands, than in regard to the objects of interchange in the direct intercourse between our ports and the W. Indies. We can fetch and carry about *twenty* articles of their and our *produce*, while they can fetch and carry, by a statute they can make in a week, all the productions and manufactures of these states or of their colonies.

While Britain has given to France, whom she terms her natural enemy the freedom of enemies goods in her ships, and the most equitable concession as to articles of contraband of war, the nature of that Amity in which she has made this treaty has permitted her to refuse an acquiescence in either of those Arrangements with us. Our Virgin crop of wood, and naval stores are made contraband of war. We have covenanted to relinquish those favorable principles of the Armed neutrality.

We have agreed not to seize the private property (funds, stocks and Debts) within our reach, but left them open the opportunity to seize our private property, no less sacred, on the Sea.

The spirit of this treaty, commercial and political, is as rigidly selfish as the navigation act of Great Britain—for tho some things are granted they are mere Indian presents, for which a greater value was to be placed within their reach at the Moment of Donation.

I do not know what are the prospects of the Business or even the present state of it. But I think the President is yet uncommitted—and waiting for information and argument. These few hasty remarks, in which I have expressed, but part of my mind, I make in some degree of confidence. I have the honor to be with great Respect, dear sir, Yr. mo. obt. hble Servt.   TENCH COXE

RC (DLC); endorsed by TJ as received 18 Aug. 1795 and so recorded in SJL. FC (PHi: Coxe Papers); with minor variations. FC (Lb in same); with one important variation (see note 1 below).

TJ's LETTER to Coxe was dated 1 June 1795. RENEWAL OF THE ORDERS: see note to James Monroe to TJ, 27 June 1795. THE TENURE OF LANDS AND THE LAW OF DESCENTS: a reference to Article 9 of the Jay Treaty, which concerned the possession, sale, and bequeathal of land held by British subjects in the United States and American citizens in British dominions (Miller, *Treaties*, II, 253-4). WEST INDIA ARTICLE: see

note to Henry Tazewell to TJ, 1 July 1795. BRITAIN HAS GIVEN TO FRANCE: for the relevant article of the 1786 commercial treaty between Great Britain and France, see note to TJ to Edmond Charles Genet, 24 July 1793. In contrast to the Jay Treaty, the 1780 League of ARMED NEUTRALITY excluded ship timber and naval stores from its definition of contraband (Miller, *Treaties*, II, 259; James B. Scott, ed., *The Armed Neutralities of 1780 and 1800* [New York, 1918], 274, 329).

¹ Word inadvertently omitted here and in FC supplied from second FC.
² Thus in all three texts.

From Christoph Daniel Ebeling

SIR   Hamburgh, Lower Saxony July 30th 1795

I should begin my letter with many excuses, that I, unknown and stranger to You, make bold, to address You; but a man of Your celebrity, of such patriotism and public spirit, as You have shewn the world, is certainly a benevolent man. So I confidently hope, You will pardon me the liberty I take. Your worthy Country men Mr. J. Belknap and president Stiles of Yale College have exhorted me, to beg Your kind advice in an arduous task I have undertaken. I begun to publish a general History, Geography and Topographical description of America, whereto I have collected Materials as far as my situation would admit, since about twenty Years. I have been happy beyond expectation and enjoy the very valuable friendship of the above mentioned Gentleman, as also Dr. Morse, Rev. President Willard, Mr. Noah Webster at New York, Dr. Smith Barton and Mr. Carey at Philadelphia, Dr. David Ramsay S.C. and others.¹ Mr. Barlow, Your celebrated bard, who lived more than a Year in my neighbourhood and has furnished me with excellent materials, also assisted me very much with his advice and instructive conversation. Our unhappy Europe is exceedingly desirous to be acquainted with Your free and happy country. This made the undertaking very acceptable and a large edition of the first Volumes of my Book was rapidly exhausted. My Book is on a far more larger plan than

Mr. Morse's. Two Volumes are published containing only New England inclusive Vermont, and New York. I should have the honour to send You a Copy if I knew that you read our language, but as a french translation is now preparing with large additions and corrections, I shall defer till this appears, wishing to offer You a less defective production. The third Volume of the German Work is now printing and will comprehend N. Jersey, Pensylvania, Delaware and Maryland.

The fourth is intended to complete the Work. As it will contain Virginia it would be impardonable, if I would not make use of Your excellent Notes of Virginia. We have allready a German Abridgment thereof published by Professor Sprengel at Halle, and very well made, but rather to short. You will kindly allow that I may avail myself of Your instructive Work, quoting it allways with gratefull acknowledgment of my debt to You. I have the London edition of 1787.

Since that time naturally there were many alterations made in Your state. Though I am well provided with the several Magazines, three or four complete Setts of American News papers especially Fenno's U. St. Gazette, Webster's Minerva, Columbian Centinell etc. Yet I suppose there may be other sources of information about Virginia, that escaped my notice. I wish allso to be made acquainted with a Bookseller in Your State who could furnish me with the Laws, and with one of the most instructive News papers of Virginia. I endeavoured to get these by way of Philadelphia, or Baltimore, but did not succeed.

I hope, not to be troublesome to You, Sir, when I ask You the favour, to make me acquainted with a Gentleman, who would charge himself with the care, to procure me, as soon as possible, those Books etc. I have marked on the inclosed Note. You would very much oblige me, when You would be pleased to add such, as may be usefull to me. All what would be intended for me, would savely come to hand, when directed to *Charles Ghequiere Esq. Merchant at Baltimore* who will also immediately return payment for all what is sent him on my account. By this way I hope to be not molestious to You.

Besides Your Notes, which will be my surest guide, I shall get from Dr. Morse the new Edition of his Geography, now printing; and wherein I hope to find the *newest* state of population, finances, trade of Virginia; besides what is to be found of the latter in the Reports made to congress and the Journals of Congress, which I have.

Of old Books I have Smith, Steith, Beverley, Keith, Jones and Hutchins's Observations with the Map of 1778. Hazard's Collection I make use of likewise.

My plan is the following

1) Authorities, Books, Maps, etc. inditing, which I principally followed and quoting them besides shortly at the proper places.

2) Situation and Extent. 3) Climate. Diseases etc. Currie, Rush and others I consulted.[2] 4) Soil, considered in what we call physical way (we take that word for natural philosophy) and history. Mountains, promontories. 5) Rivers, Lakes, Bays etc.

6) Produces of the three Kingdoms of Nature. Medicinal Springs
     a) the Mineralogy of each State. This, you know, is still the most defective part of American Natural History.
     b) Plants, herbs trees etc. I have Bartram and many other authors, Clayton, et. c) Agriculture, rural oconomy.
     d. animal Kingdom. Your Sketch will be my model. Catesby etc. I shall not neglect to consult. e) Rearing of tame Animals Cattle etc. Fishery. Insects etc.

7) Inhabitants. The last Census of Congress is in my hands. Negroes. Indians. Caracter and manners of the Inhabitants, as far as a general Description thereof *can* be made.

8. Government. Legislative etc. powers according to the last Constitution. Courts of Justice. Sketch of the principal laws in force, especially those on inheritances, policy, criminal Laws, and punishments.[3]
     Government before the Revolution compared.

9 Finances. Standing Revenue, Expences. Debts.

10. Militia. Fortifications. 11. Religious state. 12. State of Schools and Learning. Publ. Libraries. Academies. Learned Societies. Arts. Principal Authors living and deceased. (Of these I know only a few)

13. State of Manufactures and Trades.

14. Commerce. a) Institutions on its behalf. Highways Canals. Postoffices. b) Internal commerce. c.) Coins, measures etc. d) paper money, or state papers (Paper money before the revolution and the Assumtion of State debts) Banks. Laws of Trade. e) Staple commodities f) Navigation g) Coasting Trade. h) westindia Trade. i) African Trade. k) Trade with Europe. Exports Imports; Lists thereof.

15. Topography according to the Counties. The situation of the New Counties (Campbell, Franklin, Harrison, Hardy, Randolph Russel, Pendleton, Kanhawa), puzzle me much, as I am not well informed thereof, and find nothing in the Maps. The collection of Laws may shew me their Boundaries.

History. Especially with regard to the Aborigines, their Emigration or Extirpation by the Settling of Europeans. The first planting and its difficulties. The formation of Laws, growth of Trade. Such intestine dissentions as had influence on the Liberty condition and Laws. Wars. Struggles against Despotism. Commotions on Account of the Stamp Act etc. Part each State took in promoting the Revolution. The principal events of the revolution-war, as for as each State was the Scene thereof are only related in a chronological List in a Note, as they have allready been related by abler pens. Consequences of the Revolution after the peace. New Constitution, and Laws. Increase of Cultivation, population, new Counties, Trade.

For This latter part, viz the last 8 Years my materials and information concerning Virginia[4] is very incomplete, particularly for want of a Collection of Your Laws.

I must end my long and egoistical Letter, for I fear I have tired your patience. Was it not for my ardent desire to promote human happiness in my country, by a faithfull picture of Your constitutions, Laws and Government, I should not have entered into such detail of my plan. I wish it may be honoured by Your approbation, and what is even more welcome to me, by Your remarks on its defects.

The closing of my Letter has been delayed a few days and this enables me to atone in some way for the trouble I gave You, by communicating to You the very happy and certain news, that peace has been concluded at Basil on the 23d of July, between Spain and France, by Mssrs. Barthelemy and Yriarte. The preliminaries already arrived at Paris, and by several expresses, were sent to Hamburgh. The Conditions are unknown. An Armistice is to begin immediately, and France to remain previously in possession of what her Armies occupy in Spain; this only transpires. Peace with Germany is likewise considered as concluded by the intercession of the King of Prussia. The Armies are inactive every where in Germany. The Emperor wishes for peace, but is retained by the british Subsidies; which help him recover from the entire ruin of his finances. Internal Commotions in Hungary, and Vienna itself are discovered and suppressed by severe executions. Even some of the nobility were engaged therein. Bigottry lifts her head anew. In the northern Ports of Germany all is quiet, but there is a great agitation of minds. All Governments are anxious. Some take perverse measures. The liberty of the press in Danemarc, and the prussian country is very little restricted. There appear excellent Works and pamphlets, particularly about France and the Affairs of poland. We have more than six monthly Magazines destined *only* for the history of the french revolution, which are read with eagerness, even in the roman catholick parts of Germany, tho' forbidden in all the Emperors dominions.

The total defeat of the Emigrant Army landed at Quiberon and the capture of most of them, will be known to you allready. It was on the 21 of July. In England the Consternation is very great, and troops have been ordered to approach London out of fear of a tumult. The Emigrants, who are still (several Corps of them amounting to about 4000) in our neighbourhood, in the Hanoveren country, behave very badly. The weak Hannoverian Government begins to awaken, but cannot get rid of them, as their own Army is melted down to 3000. (The poor people fought against their inclination, by command only of the english King.) The Emigrants came over in great Numbers to Hambourg; as they behaved peaceably and were unarmed, our Senate connived at it, but they began to recruit. Whereupon the Mob collected against them, and were allready to pull down a House wherein the Emigrant recruiting Officer lived. Tho' it was found, he had escaped, and the others were immediately ordered out of town, the tumult could not be quelled without bloodshed. Foreign Sailors were to many amongst the mob. Four innocent Persons were Killed, and about ten wounded. Now all is quiet. This is the only disturbance occasioned during this war in our fortunate little Republic; whose constitution is as free as one in Europe, tho' we are surrounded by mighty Neighbours.

I finish my long letter with the repeated assurance of my great respect and sincere esteem, due to Your universally acknowledged merits, and have the Honor to be Sir Your most obedient Humble Servant

CHR. DANIEL EBELING
Professor of History and the greek
Language at the College of Hamburgh
and second Director of the Commercial
Academy.

RC (DLC); with marginal notes recorded below; endorsed by TJ as received 15 Oct. 1795 and so recorded in SJL.

Christoph Daniel Ebeling (1741-1817), a noted scholar, educator, and translator, was the foremost German authority of his time on America. While studying theology at the University of Göttingen from 1763 to 1767 in order to qualify himself for the ministry, Ebeling developed a strong interest in history, geography, and literature, with a special emphasis on America. Casting aside his ministerial aspirations, he became a teacher at the Hamburg Commercial Academy in 1769 and its co-director in the following year, a post he held for more than two decades. Appointed professor of history and Greek at the Hamburg Academic Gymnasium in 1784, he became noteworthy for his public course of lectures on the conditions necessary for the survival of free governments. Fifteen years later he also began a tenure as Hamburg's city librarian that lasted until his death. Beginning as early as 1765 Ebeling produced a stream of articles and translated works on American

affairs culminating in his greatest achievement, the GENERAL HISTORY of America for which he sought TJ's assistance, *Erdbeschreibung und Geschichte von Amerika. Die vereinten Staaten von Nordamerika*, 7 vols. (Hamburg, 1793-1816). This magisterial work, which praised the United States as an example of republican liberty, dealt with ten states from New Hampshire to Virginia. Ebeling's reliance on the *Notes on the State of Virginia* led him to consider dedicating the Virginia volume (the last one published) to TJ, but in the end he dedicated it to William Bentley, Samuel Miller, Samuel Latham Mitchill, and Henry St. George Tucker. Although not recorded in Sowerby, a copy of the Virginia volume—inscribed by Ebeling "To His Excellency Thomas Jefferson most respectfully offered by the Author" and bearing the initials by which TJ according to custom marked his books—was once part of TJ's library (PPL). The immensely valuable collection of American books, newspapers, and maps that Ebeling obtained from correspondents in the United States in connection with the preparation of his history was acquired after his death by Harvard University (*Allegemeine Deutsche Biographie*, 56 vols. [Leipzig, 1875-1912], v, 524-5; *Neue Deutsche Biographie*, 18 vols. [Berlin, 1952-], iv, 219-20; William C. Lane, ed., "Letters of Christoph Daniel Ebeling to Rev. Dr. William Bentley of Salem, Mass. and to other American Correspondents," American Antiquarian Society, *Proceedings*, n.s., xxxv [1925], 272-9; John L. Riordan, ed. and trans., "Albemarle in 1815: Notes of Christopher Daniel Ebeling," *Magazine of Albemarle County History*, xii [1952], 39-45; Horst Dippel, *Germany and the American Revolution*, trans. Bernhard A. Uhlendorf [Chapel Hill, 1977], 53-6).

For MR. MORSE's book, see note to Jedidiah Morse to TJ, 25 June 1793. GERMAN ABRIDGMENT: *Jeffersons Beschreibung von Virginien*, trans. Johann Reinhold Forster and Matthias Christian Sprengel, in *Beiträge zur Völker und Länderkunde*, viii (1788), 171-277, ix (1789), 1-130, an abridged translation of the 1787 edition of the *Notes* (Horst Dippel, comp., *Americana Germanica, 1770-1800: Bibliographie deutscher Amerikaliteratur* [Stuttgart, 1976], No. 461). HUTCHINS'S OBSERVATIONS: see note to Thomas Hutchins to TJ, 11 Feb. 1784. HAZARD'S COLLECTION: see note to TJ to Ebenezer Hazard, 18 Feb. 1791.

[1] Next to this sentence Ebeling wrote in the margin: "This very moment Dr. Morse makes me acquainted with the decease of the worthy President Stiles. I owe a Mst of 12 sheets concerning the history of Connecticut to his kindness. He collected it from the public records."

[2] Preceding sentence written in the margin and keyed for insertion here.

[3] Next to this paragraph Ebeling wrote in the margin: "I have the Continental Register published at Philadelphia 1795."

[4] Preceding two words interlined.

ENCLOSURE

Note on Sources

Books etc. I wish to get.

1) The Laws of the Common wealth of Virginia, as complete as possible. I suppose that they are collected in one Body. But as this may be printed some years ago; I want also the subsequent Laws.

2) Any *complete* set of Richmond, Alexandria or an other Gazette which gives the best account on the affairs of Virginia, its Assembly etc. for the year 1794. and 1795. To be continued in 1796, by divers remittances.

3) Journal of the Virginia Assembly if printed. At least from the latest years, 1793 sq.

4) Iredells, Laws of North Carolina printed at Edenton 1791. for Hodge and Wills.

5) Tatham's Large and Small Map of Virginia. Two Copies. With his Analyses of Virginia. Two Copies. I find them announced in the Virginia Gazette 1791. No. 255. but no American Bookseller can procure them.

6) Acts of the General Assembly of the then Province of Virginia. I have them complete down to 11. Geo. III. 1771 and 1772. but should wish occasionally to have them complete untill to the revolution if those sessions are to be got separately which are missing in my Copy.

7) Any Almanac of Virginia wherein the Names of the Officers of this State may be found; for 1795 or 1796.

Hamburgh
August 1st 1795

C. D. EBELING
professor

These Books etc. are to be sent to *Charles Ghequiere* Esq. Merchant at Baltimore who will kindly charge himself with the forwarding me them, as also pay the amount to the Purchaser.

* *

Should there be occasion to get the Laws of *Kentucky* likewise, they would be very acceptable.

MS (DLC); entirely in Ebeling's hand.

To Martha Jefferson Randolph

DEAR MARTHA   Monticello July 31. 95.

We have had no letter from you since your arrival at the Warmsprings, but are told you are gone on to the sweet springs. Not knowing how to write to you by post, I take the opportunity of sending this by Dr. Currie.—He has mentioned to me the home-less situation of Nancy Randolph. She is now with Mrs. Carrington. I do not know whether she is on such a footing with Mr. Randolph and yourself[1] as that her company would be desireable or otherwise to you. If the former, invite her here freely to stay with you. But if disagreeable, do not do it; my object in mentioning it being to place you both at your perfect ease on that subject.—Our own family is all well; the children remarkeably so. But the house has been a mere hospital of sick friends. Mrs. Bolling and Polly, and their servants sick. So also Mrs. Marks. Several others on their way to the springs; so that every corner of every room has been occupied. J. Eppes has been for some time gone to Champe Carter's and that neighborhood with P. Carr. Mrs. Dunbar is just gone there also. Our weather has been very seasonable. But I hear an unfavorable account of a field of corn of Mr. Randolph's on the road, as being yellow and ill-looking, supposed to be too thick planted. We are very anxious to hear what effect the springs have on his health. My best esteem to him. Adieu. Yours affectionately   TH: JEFFERSON

RC (NNPM).

NANCY RANDOLPH: see note to TJ to Martha Jefferson Randolph, 28 April 1793. There is no indication that Thomas

Mann Randolph's sister came to stay at Monticello.

[1] Preceding two words interlined.

To William Champe Carter

DEAR SIR   Monticello Aug. 3. 95.

I sometime ago received a letter from Mrs. Carter, in answer to mine, on the subject of the boundary between her and Mr. Short, wherein she says 'I have no objection to the establishment of the line by which my son Champe has divided the land sold you, and those held by me, as I am fully persuaded that he would do nothing to affect my interest.'— Considering the boundary therefore as settled, I inclose you a draught on Philadelphia and letter of advice for 524.83 D. the balance due for the lands as you will percieve by the inclosed account. I will now prepare a deed of conveyance and ask the favor of you to have it executed by Mrs. Carter (your lady) and yourself and returned to me. I have for some time been on the lookout for an opportunity of notifying this to you, and even now I write the present without knowing how I shall convey it. Messrs. Eppes and Carr went from here to your neighborhood, but I did not know it till they were gone. I am with great esteem Dear Sir Your most obedt. servt   TH: JEFFERSON

PrC (DLC: William Short Papers); at foot of text: "W. Champe Carter. esq." Enclosures: (1) TJ's draft on John Barnes, 3 Aug. 1795, requesting him to pay $524.83 to Carter at six weeks' sight (PrC in MHi; at foot of text: "Mr. John Barnes Mercht. Philadelphia. South 3d. street"). (2) TJ's letter of advice to Barnes of the same date, informing him of the draft (PrC in same). (3) William Champe Carter in Account with William Short, containing entries for 20 Apr.-3 Aug. 1795 showing TJ's drafts on Barnes totaling $5224.83 in favor of Carter and Wilson Cary Nicholas for the purchase of 1,334 acres of land for Short at 23/6 Virginia currency (PrC in DLC: Short Papers; entirely in TJ's hand; endorsed in ink by TJ).

LETTER FROM MRS. CARTER: Sarah Champe Carter to TJ, 30 June 1795.

A letter from TJ to William Champe Carter of 20 Nov. 1795 is recorded in SJL but has not been found.

To James Madison

TH:J. TO J.M.   Aug. 3. 95.

You will percieve by the inclosed that Hamilton has taken up his pen in support of the treaty. [Return it to me.] He spoke on it's behalf in the meeting at New York, and his party carried a decision in favor of it by a small majority. But the Livingstonians appealed to stones and clubs and beat him and his party off the ground. This from a gentleman just from Philadelphia. Adieu.

P.S. Richmond has decided against the treaty. It is said that not even Carrington undertakes to defend it.

RC (DLC: Madison Papers); brackets in original. Not recorded in SJL. Enclosure not identified, but see note below.

HAMILTON HAS TAKEN UP HIS PEN: "The Defence" No. I, the first of 38 essays by "Camillus" defending the Jay Treaty, appeared in the New York *Argus, or Greenleaf's New Daily Advertiser*, 22 July 1795. Alexander Hamilton and Rufus King collaborated in the series, but Hamilton wrote the first 22 installments published through

11 Nov. 1795 and 6 others of later dates. The final essay appeared 9 Jan. 1796 (Syrett, *Hamilton*, XVIII, 475-7).

The source of TJ's description of the MEETING AT NEW YORK on Saturday 18 July has not been identified, but an account from Philadelphia on 21 July "By a gentleman who left New York on Sunday evening" was printed in the "Postscript" to the 29 July 1795 issue of the Richmond *Virginia Gazette, and General Advertiser*. For the sequel, see Madison to TJ, 6 Aug. 1795, and note.

To Robert Pollard

SIR   Monticello Aug. 3. 95.

I have duly recieved your favor of July 25. wherein you say that Mr. B. Harrison has offered you six shares in the James river canal at the price paid Heron, to wit 18/ in the pound, if I chuse to buy them.—I am disposed still to extend Mr. Short's purchase of shares, at a price not exceeding that: but if they can be bought cheaper, I of course wish to get them cheaper. I must leave Mr. Harrison's offer therefore altogether to yourself. If you find it as cheap as they can be bought, I will take them, and by return of the post announcing the purchase I will inclose you a draught for the money on Mr. Barnes at 30. days sight.—The Milton boats being now down, I am in hopes Mr. Heron will have sent my fish by them. I am Sir Your very humble servt   TH: JEFFERSON

PrC (DLC: William Short Papers); faded; at foot of text: "Mr. R. Pollard."

List of Groceries for Gamble & Temple

[6 Aug. 1795?]

75. ℔ of coffee, as old as you can. (not green)[1]
125. ℔ brown sugar. clean and dry.
50. ℔ white sugar. single refined.
[10.] ℔ chocolate
50. ℔ rice.
25 ℔[2] of water biscuit. what they call crackers.
[10.] ℔ of raisins
10. ℔ of bitter almonds
3. ℔ black pepper
1. ℔ allspice

$\frac{1}{4}$ ℔ nutmeg
$\frac{1}{4}$ ℔ cloves
$\frac{1}{4}$ ℔ cinnamon
$\frac{1}{4}$ ℔ ginger
5. ℔ sago
a keg of cod's tongues and sounds.
50. ℔ myrtle wax candles, moulded. (no other kind)
15. gallons good French brandy.[3]
    Molasses.
    dried figs.
    do. dates.
    cheese
    tea
    vinegar.
1. ℔ blacking
50. bush. salt
    cranberries
    lamp oil

PrC (MHi); entirely in TJ's hand; undated, but assigned on the basis of SJL (see note below); two sets of digits altered and blurred; insertions in ink by TJ as recorded in notes below; endorsed in ink by TJ on verso: "Gamble & Temple."

According to SJL, TJ exchanged 29 letters with Gamble & Temple, all between 24 June 1795 and 24 Aug. 1796, none of which has been found. Since the entries for

TJ's letters to the firm of 6 Aug. and 1 Dec. 1795 refer to "groceries," the Editors have conjecturally assigned the list to the first of these dates.

[1] Preceding two words and parentheses added in ink.
[2] Digits and unit of measure inserted in ink in place of "a keg."
[3] TJ added the remainder of the list in ink.

From James Madison

DEAR SIR   Augst. 6. 95.
I return the paper covered by your favor of the third, which was handed me by a gentleman who picked it up in Charlottesville. I find that the meeting in N. York was not exactly as represented to you. The Republicans were never outnumbered; and the vote of a very full meeting was finally unanimous in remonstrating against the Treaty. The Chamber of Commerce has had a separate meeting and has passed some counteracting Resolutions. In Portsmouth, Boston and Philada. *unanimous* Remonstrances have also issued from Town Meetings and been sent by express to the P. The silence of the disaffected minorities is easily explained. I understand that Mr. Wythe presided at the Rich-

mond Meeting, a circumstance which will not be without its weight; especially as he presided at the former Meeting in support of the Proclamation. A gentleman who was present says he was told two individuals only in the City, (Hopkins and one of the Marshalls) openly espoused the Treaty. Even Andrews joins in the general denunciation of it. I have a letter from the Bishop which is a Philippic on the subject. In short from all quarters the public voice seems to proclaim the same detestation; except from Alexandria and its neighbourhood where there is some division. Docr. Stuart and the Lees take the side of the Treaty. I have a letter from Chancellor Livingston which tells me he has taken the liberty of writing a free letter to the P. with a view to impress on him the public sentiment and the consequences of ratifying an act so hostile to the opinions and interests of the people, and to the good understanding with France. The inclosed papers contain some remarks on the Treaty from a hand which will claim attention. They are borrowed, and you may therefore return them by Mr. Jones or any other convenient opportunity. Yrs. affecly.

Js. M. Jr.

RC (DLC: Madison Papers); with several slips of the pen silently corrected; endorsed by TJ as received 8 Aug. 1795 and so recorded in SJL, where TJ mistakenly listed it as a letter of 8 Aug. 1795. Enclosures not found.

The VERY FULL MEETING at New York occurred on 20 July 1795 and that of the CHAMBER OF COMMERCE took place the following day. Both sets of resolutions were sent to the President (Syrett, *Hamilton*, XVIII, 485-8n; Young, *Democratic Republicans*, 449-54). REMONSTRANCES . . . SENT BY EXPRESS TO THE P.: Washington received resolutions against the Jay Treaty from Boston, Portsmouth, New Hampshire, and Philadelphia dated 13, 17, and 26 July, 1795, respectively (Selectmen of the Town of Boston to Washington, 13 July 1795, Jonathan Warren to Washington, 17 July 1795, and William Shippen, Jr., to Washington, 26 July 1795, all in DLC: Washington Papers). Madison applauded George Wythe's role as chair of the RICHMOND MEETING held on 29 and 30 July, which resulted in resolutions and an address against the Jay Treaty that were sent to the President by Andrew Dunscomb, mayor of Richmond, because two years earlier Wythe had chaired an extensively publicized meeting organized by

Federalists to defend Washington's Proclamation of Neutrality and indirectly criticize Edmond Charles Genet (Dunscomb to Washington, 31 July 1795, in same; George Wythe to TJ and Edmund Randolph, 17 Aug. 1793, and note; Madison to TJ, 27 Aug. 1793, and note). LETTER FROM THE BISHOP: the Reverend James Madison to Madison, 25 July 1795, in Madison, *Papers*, XVI, 40-41. LETTER FROM CHANCELLOR LIVINGSTON: Robert R. Livingston to Madison, 6 July 1795, in which—with respect to TJ's letter to George Hammond of 5 Sep. 1793, annexed to the Jay treaty to clarify Article 7—he lamented: "You see my apprehentions on the score of Mr. Jeffersons sentiments relative to the rights of neutral vessels fully verified they have as I predicted furnished arguments to our enemies and are here considered as the most powerful appology for Mr. Jay" (same, 34-5). Livingston tried to counteract the use of TJ's letter by supporters of the treaty in the fifteenth of the sixteen anti-treaty essays he penned under the pseudonym of "Cato," a series first published in the New York *Argus, or Greenleaf's New Daily Advertiser* between 15 July and 30 Sep. 1795 (*The American Remembrancer; Or, an Impartial Collection of Essays, Resolves, Speeches, &c. Relative, or Having Affinity, to the Treaty with Great Britain*, 3 vols. [Philadelphia, 1795-96], II, 8-10; George Dangerfield, *Chancellor Robert R. Livingston of New York, 1746-1813* [New York, 1960], 272, 495n). LETTER TO THE P.: Livingston to Washington, 8 July 1795, urging the President to place the national interest above party conflict and reject the Jay treaty—a decision that would "procure to yourself a second time, by the common consent of America the endearing appallation of the savior of your country"—and expressing dread that ratification of the treaty would provoke "an immediate rupture with France," an event that he feared would be "the signal for a civil war at home" (DLC: Washington Papers).

From Robert Pollard

SIR   Richmond August 9th. 1795

Your favor of the 3d was brought by the post that arrived here yesterday.

The price Mr. Harrison asks for his shares in the James River Company is considered as the current price. Perhaps a single share might be purchased something lower, if money was kept in hand ready to pay down when the share was offered, but I am fully satisfied that it would be difficult to purchase any number of shares at the price Mr. Harrisons are offered, if the money was in hand. Should you wish to procure any more shares for Mr. Short I do not think you can calculate of having them purchased under the present price, for they have risen considerably since the last year and will probably continue to do so, as the Canal approaches its junction with tide water. I am Sir Yr. Most Obd

ROBERT POLLARD

6 Shares a £54.   £324.0.0
  Commission 1 ℔ Ct   3.4.6
                         £327:4:6[1] $1090: 75 Cents

RC (DLC: William Short Papers); with additions by TJ (see note 1 below); endorsed by TJ as received 11 Aug. 1795 and so recorded in SJL.

[1] TJ here added "or." Before this figure he added "1090.75 =."

To Thomas Mann Randolph

DEAR SIR   Monticello Aug. 11. 95.

I wrote to you by Doctr. Currie. We have no letter from you since that from Staunton: but we have heard by travellers of your having soon left the warm springs. Those who were sick here have recovered. The children are well, as is the rest of the family except Maria. A slight dysentery which has pervaded the neighborhood has attacked her. She is now in the 5th. day of it. We cannot see any symptom of radical amendment, but there is nothing as yet which threatens that the disorder will be severe. I was yesterday at Edgehill. Scilla was in her 4th. day of the same disorder, and also her youngest child, without our knowing any thing of it. I immediately sent her a dose of physic, and shall have her properly attended to. We have had a terrible storm which has thrown our corn generally prostrate. We shall be greatly at a loss in sowing wheat among it. Robertson set up as much of his as enabled him to sow 18. bushels of wheat. In general we shall be obliged to put in our wheat with the houghs. It will also much lessen the crop of corn. Robertson has got out between 3. and 400 bushels of your wheat, and has about 260. to get out. He judges by having measured the produce of one stack, 20. bushels, and has 13. stacks still to get out. He goes on constantly with 4. horses: but we have had such a quantity of wet weather as has greatly obstructed treading. The weavil is very generally apprehended.—The result of my trial of the acre of wheat and rye was 4.8 cubic yards of each in the stack, and 14. pecks of rye and 15. of wheat, when cleaned. This gives a cubic foot of wheat from every cubic yard of the stack, and of rye $\frac{1}{30}$ part of the stack. The ground having been of the weakest kind, for it yielded but $3\frac{1}{2}$ bushels to the acre, the experiment is decisively against the common opinion that it is better to put weak land into rye than wheat, and will change my rye after corn into wheat after corn.—Yesterday, the 10th. of August, was kept as a feast in Charlottesville. To-day the county meets there to express their opinion of the treaty. They propose after doing this, to invite the other counties of the Congressional district (Amherst, Fluvanna and Goochld.) to do the same, and to appoint 2. members from each to meet in a central committee to prepare an address to the President expressing the sentiments in which they shall have concurred. From North to South this monument of folly or venality is universally execrated. The chamber of commerce of New York, made up of English merchants, is the only body which has yet expressed a sentiment approving it.—Fleming wishes not to recieve our wheat till the latter end of next month. I shall urge it a little sooner. He has called for a waggon load of yours. We are very anxious to hear from you both. My love to my dear Martha. Adieu. Yours affectionately   TH:J.

RC (DLC: TJ Papers, 91: 15702); at foot of first page: "Mr. Randolph"; endorsed by Randolph.

WROTE TO YOU BY DOCTR. CURRIE: probably TJ to Martha Jefferson Randolph, 31 July 1795.

A letter from Randolph to TJ of 6 Aug. 1795, recorded in SJL as received from "Sulpher springs" on 14 Sep. 1795, has not been found.

To John Barnes

Sir   Monticello Aug. 12 1795.

This serves to advise you that I have this day drawn on you in favor of Robert Pollard or order for one thousand and ninety dollars seventy five cents at 30. days sight, which be pleased to honour.

I will thank you to send me 6. ℔. of best young Hyson tea, also 100. panes of crown glass 12. inches square, to be addressed to the care of Colo. Gamble, Richmond, well packed in a single package. I take the liberty of asking your care of the inclosed letter because I do not know the address of the person, but you can learn it of Mr. John Bringhurst. I observe at the same time that he can probably furnish the glass above desired of better quality than the crown glass, to wit, of Bohemian glass in which he deals. His price used to be 20. cents per square foot. I am Sir Your very humble servt   Th: Jefferson

PrC (CSmH); at foot of text: "Mr. John Barnes"; endorsed in ink by TJ. Enclosure: TJ to Joseph Donath, 12 Aug. 1795.

To Joseph Donath

Sir   Monticello in Virginia Aug. 12. 95.

I shall have occasion about midsummer of the next year for 250. panes of Bohemian glass of 18. inches square, of the middle of the three qualities as to thickness which you noted to me as costing in Philadelphia 20. cents per square foot. If you have constantly by you of that size and quality sufficient to supply me, when called for, it will be unnecessary for you to import it on purpose. Otherwise I must desire you to import it expressly for me, that I may not be disappointed. I shall have the sashes made and glazed in Philadelphia, to be forwarded here; so that it is there I shall have occasion to have the glass delivered. Be pleased to write me a line by post, directed as above, to inform me if I may rely on being supplied. I am Sir Your humble servt

Th: Jefferson

RC (ViU); addressed: "Mr. [Donath] Philadelphia" (recipient's name being clipped); note on address cover in John Barnes's hand: "28th. So. Front"; endorsed by Donath as answered 27 Aug. 1795. Enclosed in TJ to John Barnes, 12 Aug. 1795.

Notes for Account with John Barnes

Note of Mr. Barnes's Dr. & Cr.		Dr.	Cr.
1795.			
Apr. 14. Nett proceeds of 2800 ⎱ 6. pr. cents			
1093.89 ⎰			
int. to Apr. 1. 390.62		4132.22[1]	
By Pollard's draughts			3600.
Nett proceeds 2356.01 three pr. cents ⎱		2854.30[2]	
2150. deferred ⎰			
20. By W. C. Carter	300		
do.	600		
22. W. C. Nicholas	2000		2900.
23. Mussi 89.09			
Muir & Hyde 130.			219.09
June. 3. Nett proceeds 7504.42 deferred.		5379.53	
3. W. C. Carter	600		
5. do.	600		
6.7.8.9.10.11. six of 100. each	600		1800.[3]
June. 3. Pollard			36.
Bringhurst 46.74			
Muir & Hyde 59.37			106.11
14. Lownes			240.67
24. Pollard			1272.50
July. 1. interest to this day		314.55[4]	
July 11. Wardlow			40.
16. Crosby			20.83[5]
Aug. 3. W. C. Carter			524.83
12. Pollard			1090.75
tea & glass			32.[6]
		12680.60	11882.78

MS (DLC: William Short Papers); entirely in TJ's hand, with several figures added in pencil (see note 6 below); endorsed by TJ: "Barnes. John. Notes for acct."

[1] Written over partially erased digits "3600."

[2] Partially erased digits "28" appear on this line in the "Cr." column.

[3] Partially erased digit "1" appears on this line in the "Dr." column.

[4] Line inserted.

[5] Line inserted.

[6] This amount, the rule, and the totals are written in pencil.

To Robert Pollard

SIR   Monticello Aug. 12. 95.

I have recieved your favor of the 9th. inst. and now inclose you a draught on Mr. Barnes for 1090.D. 75c. at 30. days sight for the purchase of Mr. Harrison's six shares in the James river canal. You will be pleased to have the conveyance made to Mr. William Short. I think I shall stop here in the purchases of James river shares, unless you should know of any person who from particular circumstances would be disposed to sell so much cheaper as to make the purchase an object. I am with esteem Dear Sir Your most obedt servt   TH: JEFFERSON

P.S. The price of nails always desireable lest I should over charge and disoblige my customers.

PrC (DLC: William Short Papers); endorsed by TJ in ink on verso; with enclosure letterpressed at foot of text. Enclosure: TJ's draft on John Barnes, 12 Aug. 1795, requesting him to pay Pollard as specified above (PrC in same; faded; at foot of text: "Mr. John Barnes [. . .] Philadelphia").

To Thomas Mann Randolph

DEAR SIR   Monticello Aug. 18. 95.

I recieved by the last post your favor from Doctr. Le Mayeur's. Your horse also came safe, and the one you desired will be delivered to the post tomorrow morning: but in very bad plight, having been surfieted treading wheat. Zachary sends a saddle and mail [pelon],[1] but says there is neither bridle nor straps.—We are all well. Maria comes down stairs to-day for the first time. The children in perfect health. Colo. N. Lewis lies dangerously and almost desperately ill. I mentioned in my last the ravages committed by the rains. Since that we have had still worse. I imagine we never lost more soil than this summer. It is moderately estimated at a year's rent. Our crops of corn will be much shortened by the prostrate and drowned condition of the plants, particularly of the tossil which can perform it's office of impregnation but partially and imperfectly.—Our peaches are getting into perfection. They are fine in quality, and abundant.—Tobacco has fired excessively. Many have cut their crops green. I fear to hear from Bedford.—Dr. Gilmer is on his last legs. Yet has undertaken a trip to Rockingham. The sick at Edgehill mentioned in my last are doing well. Our love to our dear Martha, and am Dear Sir Yours affectionately   TH: JEFFERSON

RC (DLC); at foot of text: "Mr. Randolph"; endorsed by Randolph. PrC (MHi); endorsed in ink by TJ.

Randolph's FAVOR of 11 Aug. 1795, recorded in SJL as received from "Le Mayeur's" on 15 Aug. 1795, has not been found.

¹ Evidently "pillion."

To Thomas Mann Randolph

DEAR SIR   Monticello Aug. 20. 95.

Mr. Watkins arrived here yesterday evening, and besides the 120. Dollars (which were perfectly in time for my purpose) he lodged with me £20–8–4 to be forwarded to you. I have accordingly been to Charlottesville this morning and deposited the money with Colo. Bell, to be forwarded to the sweet springs if any direct and trusty conveyance occurs; if not, to be sent to Gamble & Grattan in Staunton with a notification to you that you may draw on them for it, or otherwise dispose of it.—Robertson has got out all your wheat to 100. bushels which he keeps for sowing.—Mr. Lewis is getting better.—We thought the storms and floods here very great till we heard from other quarters. It seems now they have been less with us than any where else. To the Northward as far as Pennsylva. we learn there has been an almost universal destruction of mills and forges. Lownes writes me word that the supply of bar iron will be cut off in consequence of it. Below great damage done. The stone dam which pent up the Belvidere branch is entirely broke down and all Arthur's distillery swept off. The canal also very much injured. The mills upon Appamattox are swept clean. We have heard of but two remaining. One of them is one of Mr. Skipwith's.—Here we have lost nothing in that way.—Mr. J. Rutledge is appointed Chief justice in the room of Mr. Jay.—Wheat at Richmond 9/. Maria on the recovery, but not quite well. My love to my dear Martha. The children (in good health) send their kisses to you both. I am Dear Sir Yours affectionately   TH: JEFFERSON

PrC (MHi); at foot of text: "Mr. Randolph"; endorsed in ink by TJ.

LOWNES WRITES ME: see note to TJ to Caleb Lownes, 9 Sep. 1795.
Letters from Thomas Mann Randolph to TJ of 14 and 24 Aug. 1795, recorded in SJL as received from Sweet Springs on 27 Aug. and 1 Sep. 1795, respectively,

have not been found. The Randolphs returned from Sweet Springs, in present day Monroe County, West Virginia, by the end of September (TJ to Eliza House Trist, 23 Sep. 1795). At some point TJ received the following diary recording the weather at Sweet Springs that Randolph had written on both sides of a small sheet:

"Sweet springs. 1795.

aug.	1. p. ins. Sol.	2. P.M.
16	65. f	75. f.
17	63. f	78. f.
18	64. f	81. f.
19	68. f	86. f.
20	70. f.	84. f.
21	. rain.	. rain.
22	. rain.	. rain.
23	74. cloudy.	
24	74. cloudy.	81. f.
25	70. do.	79. f.
26	..	..
27	..	..
28	70. f.	82. f.
29	69. f	81. f. after a shower
30	71. rain	78. flying clouds
31	..	..

Sept.

1	..		..	
2	.. slight showers		.. slight showers	
3	..	f.	..	f
4	50.	f	..	f
5	..	f.		f
6	...	rain	..	rain
7	...	cloudy	..	cloudy
8	...	f		f.
9	...	f		f. very hot
10.	66	f	76	f.
11.	63	f.	80	f.
12.	69	cloudy	78.	f.
13.	72	rain	76.	f.
14	..	f.	82.	f."

(MS in DLC: TJ Papers, 99: 17000; endorsed by TJ: "Meteorological").

To Mann Page

TH: JEFFERSON TO M. PAGE   Monticello Aug. 30. 95.

It was not in my power to attend at Fredericksburg according to the kind invitation in your letter and in that of Mr. Ogilvie. The heat of the weather, the business of the farm to which I have made myself necessary, forbade it; and to give one round reason for all, maturé sanus, I have laid up my Rosinante in his stall, before his unfitness for the road shall expose him faultering to the world. But why did not I answer you in time? Because in truth I am encouraging myself to grow lazy, and I was sure you would ascribe the delay to any thing sooner than a want of affection or respect to you, for this was not among the possible causes. In truth if any thing could ever induce me to sleep another night out of my own house, it would have been your friendly invitation and my sollicitude for the subject of it, the education of our youth. I do most anxiously wish to see the highest degrees of education given to the higher degrees of genius, and to all degrees of it so much as may enable them to read and understand what is going on in the world, and to keep their part of it going on right: for nothing can keep it right but their own vigilant and distrustful superintendance. I do not believe, with the Rochefoucaults and Montaignes, that fourteen out of fifteen men are rogues: I believe a great abatement from that proportion may be made in favor of general honesty. But I have always found that rogues would be uppermost, and I do not know that the proportion is too strong for the higher orders, and for those who, rising above the swinish multitude, always contrive to nestle themselves into the places of power and profit. These rogues set out with stealing the people's good opinion, and then steal from them the right of withdrawing it, by contriving laws and associations against the power of the people themselves. Our part of the country is in considerable fermentation on what they suspect to be a recent roguery of this kind. They say that while all hands were below deck mending sails, splicing ropes, and every one at his own business, and the captain in the cabbin attending to his log-book and chart, a rogue of a pilot has run them into an enemy's port.—But metaphor apart, there is much dissatisfaction with Mr. Jay and his treaty. For my part I consider myself now but as a passenger, leaving the world and it's government to those who are likely to live longer in it. That you may be among the longest of these is my sincere prayer. After begging you to be the bearer of my compliments and apologies to Mr. Ogilvie I bid you an affectionate farewell, always wishing to hear from you.

PrC (DLC); faded.

KIND INVITATION: see James Ogilvie to TJ, [before 3 July 1795], and Page to TJ,

3 July 1795. MATURÉ SANUS: "completely healthy," or, "about as healthy as one can expect."

From Anthony Gerna

SIR   Dublin, Septr. 2d. 1795

The reccollection of the kind reception, that you were pleased to give me, when in Paris, affords me a pleasure equal to any other; and inspires me with a hope, that I may be still so fortunate as to remain in your remembrance and favour. I therefore take the liberty of addressing you these few lines, accompanied with a small bundle of Books, which will be presented to you by Mr. Isaac Weld, a young Gentleman, whose gentle manners, and other excellent qualities, may entitle him to your notice. The abovemention'd little bundle contains in particular, a Sett of Fenn's Euclid and Arithmetic, of which I have sent *581* setts to America; and consigned to Messrs. James & Clibborn, merchants in Philadelphia in order to be disposed, at so low a price as to make it worth the attention of the public: And on such an Occasion, I humbly sollicit your Countenance.

The present awfull State of the World has induced me to retire from Business; and had I found the terms of passing to America, more moderate (being now here at twentyfive guineas per Person) I would perhaps have brought thither my Family in order to cultivate with their own hands, a small spot of ground of *your sacred* Continent. May Heaven preserve you for a long time, that you may contribute to whatever may tend to the advantage of Mankind. And may The Omnipotent infuse into the mind of men a Love of Truth and Justice, and keep them from the three infernal monsters, Ambition, Voluptuosness, and *Avarice*; that they may finally look upon each other as belonging to the same great Family, as they really are. I remain with great Sincerity and respect, Sir, your very humble most Obedient and Obliged Servant

ANTHONY GERNA

RC (DLC); endorsed by TJ as received 8 May 1796 and so recorded in SJL.

ISAAC WELD was the Irish topographer whose 1795-97 journey to America was the subject of his *Travels through the States of North America and the Provinces of Upper and Lower Canada, during the Years 1795, 1796, and 1797* (London, 1799). An excerpt from this work describing Weld's

May 1796 visit to Monticello is in Merrill D. Peterson, ed., *Visitors to Monticello* (Charlottesville, 1989), 18-20.

FENN'S EUCLID AND ARITHMETIC: Joseph Fenn, who also compiled and wrote separate works on geometry and algebra, surveyed both subjects in his *Instructions Given in the Drawing School Established by the Dublin-Society . . .*, 2 vols. (Dublin, 1769-72).

From William Short

DEAR SIR   St. Yldefonso Sep. 2. 1795

I had last night the inexpressible[1] pleasure of once more recieving a letter from you. It is the first you have written me since your retreat to Monticello. I am really happy in the extreme to see that your long silence has proceeded from the constant occupation of your agricultural pursuits. Accept my dear Sir my sincerest thanks for the moments you have abstracted therefrom to give to me. Your letter (of May 25th.) came here last night after having been sent from England to Mr. Yznardi who returned it to me from Cadiz. I lose not a moment to let you know it has come to my hands and to touch on such parts as admit of least delay. I shall answer it more fully immediately on my return to Madrid as I will be in a few days. The present letter will be sent to Mr. Yznardi that he may inclose it to[2] his friend in America. If I knew the name of the broker you employ there I should send it to him. You will at once see my reasons for not making use of the ordinary chanel.

I have recurred to my letter of Jan. 29. as you desire. I have never been more astonished. This circumstance like every other which has proceeded from the agents of Government for some time past towards me has seemed formed on purpose to embitter and perplex the rest of my life. I thank my God that a few weeks more and the curtain will be dropped for ever between them and me. This will not cure the wounds already recieved—but it will save me from recieving others.

I mentioned to you in what manner my years salary and outfit was detained in America. The Sec. of State paid it into the hands of M. de

Jaudenes and took his bill for the amount 9000. dollars which I was to recieve of M. de Gardoqui—viz in a depreciated paper-money. I refused this and desired the Sec. of State to recover the money paid to M. de Jaudenes, and either enable me to draw as the other agents, on Amsterdam, or appropriate to me in America the 9000, dollars thus recovered. In this latter case I desired him either to pay the money to you—or to vest it for me in the public funds bearing interest. He answered me in his letter of the 9th. of Nov. 94. that M. de Jaudenes had returned him the 9000 dollars—that he had already invested 3000 thereof for me in the 6. per cents—and should proceed to invest the remainder and give me a general account as soon as it was accomplished. In his succeeding letters he said nothing more on this subject until that of the 25th. of Febry. 95—and then in these words. "The 9000 dollars have been applied as you have directed and have been already informed." This is every tittle I have received on the subject—and indeed I was not surprized at this irregular and incomplete kind of information on a private subject, as it was precisely in the manner of his correspondence with me on public subjects. I can no longer however allow it to remain in this state—because at least it is probable that the interest arising on these funds will remain in the moneyed state, and will not be rendered productive by new investments as is my wish. I know no other way of having it otherwise placed but by desiring him to transfer the stock to you together with the interest which has accrued. I shall ground this on your having my general power of attorney and my wish to have this stock realized by you. He cannot I think decline immediately complying with this—and I hope you will have no aversion to recieve it in that way though I observe from your letter, your unwillingness to act in this case. I shall in writing to him on this subject inclose an open letter for you. I hope and trust it will get soon and safely to your hands and that the business will be thus arranged—but if that letter should not get to your hands as soon as I could wish, could not you without difficulty simply write to him, that I had requested you to recieve this stock and realize it and that as you had already made a purchase, this will have the appearance only of taking trouble from his hands. I mention this hoping you will have no reluctance—but if you should I can't expect or desire it of you and must run my chance—which will at least subject me to a continuation of the loss of the interest's remaining dead and unproductive. [3]

I beg you to accept a thousand and a thousand thanks my dear Sir, for the trouble you take for me in this respect, and particularly in having the interest arising on my stock rendered immediately productive as you mention. I thank you also for the purchase you have been so good as to make in the canal—and in land. I value this operation most highly because I know how real your friendship must be for me to induce you to act in such cases. I like the operation also on its own account because it contributes to[4] vary the grounds on which my little all rests. I mentioned to you in my long letter of Oct. 7. 93. that I could not judge of particulars from this distance and I therefore begged you to exercise your judgment. In whatever way it should have been exercised I can assure you I should have been satisfied—really satisfied. After this assurance I will proceed to give you my opinion on the subject as it presents itself to me here.

Notwithstanding I like both the vestments you have made—of the two I like best that in the canal shares—because I concieve at any given time from hence say three or four[5] years for instance, that vestment will produce more and be more easily converted into money than the other. I must observe however that I am quite ignorant of the constitution of the canal company—know not how much each share amounts to—nor what rate of interest on the sum placed in the shares, the half toll at present received produces—nor what rate the whole toll is likely to produce.

The reasons you give for the purchase of Indian camp are extremely inviting also—and particularly the probability of disposing of it hereafter for the cost with the interest. Whether I shall wish to dispose of it will of course depend on contingencies. The price paid is certainly low—and the position of the land extremely agreeable to me. As you say you shall be anxious to know my wishes as to what should be done, I will express them, merely as my wishes leaving you still free to add the plantation—and to hire the hands for cutting down the timber as you mention. I concieve the more freely I express my wishes, the more you will be at your ease. I should then rather chuse not to add to the purchase, the land over the mountain. But if you should suppose their junction would render Indian camp more easily saleable—and if there should be such a part of this lot rented out as that the rents of the whole should bear a nearer proportion to the whole purchase, than the rent of Indian camp does to the purchase money of it—this might change my idea—however as the ridge of the mountain separates this lot from Indian camp, I imagine their junction would not render Indian camp more saleable nor more convenient to hold. I should prefer also not to go to the expense of cutting down the lands for the present—unless there were a certainty of leasing them out immediately, so as that the rents should come nearer to the purchase money than at present. If the tract could be leased out to such people as Price then the placement of the purchase money would be more advantageous. I am agreeably surprized at the statement you make of the rate of rents. If these rents be well paid it would seem to me an advantageous mode—for I observe that although a small part of the land is rented, the annual rent you mention being 46 or 50 pound, is about 3. per cent per annum on the purchase money—now if tenants could be found for double the quantity, it would be 6. per cent [per]⁶ annum on the purchase money. This indeed if it be 6. per cent net, would be a fine placement, and be much better than having slaves or any thing else.

If more canal shares are to be purchased would it not be well to have some in the Potowmac also? I can illy judge from hence but it seems to me, this river has one advantage, inasmuch as legislative interference is less to be feared hereafter, as to do this the legislatures of two States must combine.

I have thus just galoped over your letter. Before this shall get to your hands I shall certainly have left this Country and the public service. I do not foresee any possibility of Mr. Pinckney's having any occasion for me beyond the beginning of the next month and I shall then set out for Paris. I beg you not to let this prevent your writing to me. Send your letters under cover to M. Monroe or Mr. Skipwith there—or if you find it more convenient, to our Minister or Chargé des affaires in London—or to Mr. Donald—there. The time and direction of my future movements will not be ultimately settled until I get to Paris, where I expect to spend the winter.⁷

I mentioned to you that I had asked a permission of temporary absence from hence before I knew of M. Pinckney's appointment—the President granted it, leaving the departure to my discretion, and authorized me to leave a *locum tenens*. This was more than I had a right to expect from him, considering the manner in which he has heretofore treated me. I mentioned to you also I should wait Mr. Pinckney's arrival here in order to resign. He did not get here until the last of June. My patience was exhausted before his arrival and I gave therefore notice to the Sec. of State of my intention to resign—and since his arrival have sent in my resignation. I shall leave Mr. Rutledge (Mr. Pinckney's secretary) as my locum tenens, until my successor shall arrive. He has agreed to wait, even if Mr. Pinckney should leave this place before that time. I am my dear Sir, most sincerely & affectionately your friend & servant   W Short

Dft (DLC: Short Papers); at foot of first page: "Mr. Jefferson"; with many emendations, only the most important being noted below. Recorded in SJL as received 27 Feb. 1796.

OPEN LETTER FOR YOU: Short to TJ, 3 Sep. 1795.

¹ Word interlined in place of "extreme."
² Remainder of sentence interlined in place of "his friend in Philadelphia."
³ Short here canceled "I repent extremely having not directed positively that these 9000 dollars should be paid to you— ⟨as they might have⟩ I conceived that the."
⁴ Remainder of sentence interlined in

place of "withdraw a part of my little all out of the funds."

⁵ Preceding three words interlined in place of "five."

⁶ Word supplied.

⁷ Short here canceled "After waiting an inconcievable time for Mr. Pinckney."

To John Wayles Eppes

DEAR SIR   Monticello Sep. 3. 95.

I find on recurring to the papers that the name of the person for whose tobacco I am charged was Thomas Cobbs. The year does not appear: but it must have been 1785. or 1786. Nor does the warehouse appear.—Mr. Giles joined us, the day after you left us, and after a stay of a week or 10 days he went on to the springs, from whence he will return with Mr. Randolph. A letter from Mr. Randolph 2 days ago comforts us with the information that he is so much mended as to give him strong hopes of an entire restoration of his health. He does not say when he shall be back. I suppose the first frosts will drive them home. I shall count strongly on having the pleasure of recieving the Eppington family this season. From Mr. Eppes's known industry I apprehend it will not be till he has done seeding his ground. But be it when it will it will give us all great pleasure. You promised to be of the party.   I do not hear from you about the horse. Compliments to the Eppingtons and Adieu. Yours affectionately   TH: JEFFERSON

PrC (CSmH); at foot of text: "Citizen J. W. Eppes."

For the origins of the lawsuit brought against TJ by THOMAS COBBS over two lost hogsheads of tobacco, see TJ to Nicholas Lewis, 11 Oct. 1791. LETTER FROM MR. RANDOLPH: see note to TJ to Thomas Mann Randolph, 20 Aug. 1795.

From William Short

DEAR SIR   St. Yldefonso Sep. 3. 1795

The present will be forwarded to you by the Sec. of State, to whom I inclose it in a letter I have just written to him, and in which I inform him of my desire that he should be relieved from the trouble he has been so kind as to take as to the converting into public funds the sum of 9000 dollars assigned me. The hour of the post is so near at hand that I can only write you now as to this subject—and to beg you to recieve and apply these funds as you may find most proper for me, or as may be required by my circumstances. Should you be not under the necessity of immediately disposing of them, I would thank you to have them enregistered in my name, unless that should have been already done by the Sec. of State—of which I am not informed by his letters. As long as these funds remain I hope you will be so good as to have the interest as it arises quarterly converted into more funds—as the means of rendering it productive. I know not whether the Sec. of State has followed this mode with the interest that has hitherto successively arisen—and indeed in the midst of his public and important occupations it can hardly be expected that he should have had time to have attended in this manner to my private concerns. I will thank you immediately on the reciept of this letter to concert with him the speediest mode of recieving and fructifying these funds if you do not dispose of them. I have asked the favor of him to write you on their subject in forwarding this letter. With much real haste I can only add assurances of the unalterable sentiments with which I remain Dear Sir, your friend & servt   W Short

Dft (DLC: Short Papers); at foot of text: "Mr. Jefferson—Monticello." Recorded in SJL as received 18 Nov. 1795. Enclosed in Short to the Secretary of State, 3 Sep. 1795 (same).

From Robert Brooke

Sir   Richmond September 4th. 1795.

I should have done myself the honor of acknowledging the receipt of your letter of the   of   last, at a much earlier period, but wished in my reply to be able to give you perfect information respecting the objects of the suit to which it related, as this would be most satisfactorily obtained from the Complainants Bill (which he promised should be filed in a very short time) I waited under an expectation that it would be done in which I am disappointed as it is not yet exhibited.

To avoid however the imputation of inattention (which be assured my respect for you will never Suffer me to deserve)[1] I beg leave now to communicate the limited information on the subject I have been able to obtain.

In a conversation with Mr. Banks I discovered that the principal object of the suit is to obtain a compensation for some Vessels the property of the late House of Hunter, Banks and Co. said to have been impressed for public service whilst you was at the head of the Executive department of the State, under which Circumstance you can certainly be considered only as a nominal defendant and ought to be exonerated by the public from every expence attendant on the defence. This I shall direct to be defrayed and I wish you could also be totally withdrawn from the suit that you might experience no further trouble respecting it; but as

[447]

the Executive have no power to effect a Change of parties I am apprehensive that in this respect our wishes cannot be gratified. I am Sir with the most perfect respect &c.   ROBERT BROOKE

FC (Vi: Executive Letterbook); at head of text: "Thomas Jefferson Esquire." Recorded in SJL as received 8 Sep. 1795, but erroneously listed there as a letter of 24 Sep. 1795.

YOUR LETTER: TJ to Brooke, 24 May 1795.

[1] Opening parenthesis supplied.

To James Monroe

DEAR SIR   Monticello Sep. 6. 95

I wrote you on the 26th. of May last. Since that Mr. Jones has been here and Mr. Madison, and have communicated to me some of your letters. Mr. Jones is taking good measures for saving and improving your land, but of all this he will inform you. I inclose you a letter for Mde. Bellanger, which I leave open for your perusal as it's contents may suggest to you some service to Derieux. I also inclose you a letter from him, and a draught on his uncle's executors for 4000ᵗᵗ. which we must trouble you to remit in some way or other without loss if possible: and if it cannot be recieved without too sensible a loss, I think it had better lie. Observe that the money is not to be remitted to Derieux, as he has conveyed it to Colo. Gamble and Colo. Bell to satisfy debts. I think it had better be sent to Colo. Bell, who will pay to Gamble his part of it. If you recieve it, it may be a convenience and safety to all parties for you to apply a part of it to answer the little commissions I gave you for Froullé and La Motte, and to order me to pay their amount to Colo. Bell which I will do on sight of your order[1] but name the sum I am to pay in dollars to avoid all questions of depreciation. In this case I would be willing to extend my commission to the procuring me some wines from Bordeaux to be purchased and shipped for me by Mr. Fenwick[2] to Richmond, consigned to Colo. Gamble. I will note the wines at the foot of my letter. When you shall have read the letter to Madame Bellanger, be so good as to seal and send it to her.—I trouble you also with a letter to Madame de Tessé, whom I suppose to be in Switzerland. Pray find a safe conveyance, and recieve for me any letters she may send for me. She is a person for whom I have great friendship. Mr. Gautier, banker, successor of Grand, to whom I inclose another letter, can probably inform you how to address and forward that to Madame de Tessé.—Nothing has happened in our neighborhood worth communication to you. Mr. Randolph's health was at the lowest ebb, and he determined to go to the

Sweet springs, where he still is. His last letter informs me that his amendment is so great as to give him hopes of an entire recovery.—In political matters there is always something new. Yet at such a distance and with such uncertain conveyances it is best to say little of them. It may be necessary however to observe to you that in all countries where parties are strongly marked, as the monocrats and republicans here, there will always be desertions from the one side to the other: and to caution you therefore in your correspondencies with *Dawson*[3] who is now closely connected in speculations as we are told with *Harry Lee* with *Steel* become a consummate tory, and even *Innes* who has changed backwards and forwards two or three times lately.—Mr. Jay's treaty has at length been made public. So general a burst of dissatisfaction never before appeared against any transaction. Those who understand the particular articles of it, condemn these articles, those who do not understand them minutely, condemn it generally as wearing a hostile face to France. This last is the most numerous class, comprehending the whole body of the people, who have taken a greater interest in this transaction than they were ever known to do in any other. It has, in my opinion, completely demolished the monarchical party here. The chamber of commerce in New York, against the body of the town, the merchants in Philadelphia, against the body of their town, also, and our town of Alexandria have come forward in it's support. Some individual champions also appear. *Marshal, Carington, Harvy, Bushrod Washington, Doctor Stewart*. A more powerful one is *Hamilton* under the signature of *Camillus*. *Adams* holds his tongue with an address above his character. We do not know whether the President has signed it or not. If he has, it is much believed the H. of representatives will oppose it as constitutionally void, and thus bring on an embarrassing and critical state in our government.—If you should recieve Derieux' money and order the wines, Mr. Fenwick ought to ship them in the winter months. Present my affectionate respects to Mrs. Monroe, and accept them yourself. No signature is necessary.

Wines to be procured and shipped by Mr. Fenwick from Bordeaux if it should be found advantageous to remit Mr. Derieux's money in that way. They will come at my risk.

250. bottles of the best vin rouge ordinaire used at the good tables of Bordeaux, such as Mr. Fenwick sent me before.
125. bottles of Sauterne. Old and ready for use.
 60. bottles of Frontignan.
 60. bottles of White Hermitage of the first quality, old and ready for use.

P.S. The day after writing the preceding letter, yours of June 23. and 27. came to hand. I open this, therefore to acknolege the receipt, and thank you for the information given. Soon after that date you will have received mine of May 26. and percieve, by that and this, that I had taken the liberty of asking some services from you.—Yes, the treaty is now known here, by a bold act of duty in one of our Senators, and what the sentiments upon it are, our public papers will tell you, for I take for granted they are forwarded to you from the Secretary of State's office. The same post which brought your letter, brought also advice of the death of Bradford, Atty. Genl. the resignation of E. Randolph (retiring perhaps from the storm he saw gathering) and of the resolutions of the chamber of commerce of Boston in opposition to those of the town of Boston in General. P. Marks is dead within these 24. hours. His wife had died some months before. I omitted in my letter to mention that J. Rutledge was appointed Chief Justice in the room of Mr. Jay, and that he, Govr. Pinckney and others of that Southern constellation had pronounced themselves more desperately than any others against the treaty.—Still deliver the letters to Made. Bellanger. A true state of the case, soothing and flattering terms may perhaps produce the execution of her last promise.

RC (DLC: Monroe Papers); unsigned; written partly in code (see note 3 below); at foot of first page: "M. Monroe." PrC (DLC). Enclosures: (1) TJ to Madame Plumard de Bellanger, 6 Sep. 1795 (recorded in SJL, but not found). (2) TJ to Madame de Tessé, 6 Sep. 1795. (3) TJ to Jean Antoine Gautier, 7 Sep. 1795. Other enclosures not found. Enclosed in TJ to Tench Coxe, 10 Sep. 1795.

ONE OF OUR SENATORS: Stevens Thomson Mason (see note to Henry Tazewell to TJ, 1 July 1795).

The RESIGNATION OF E. RANDOLPH as Secretary of State occurred on 19 Aug. 1795 after President Washington confronted him with French minister Jean Antoine Joseph Fauchet's dispatch No. 10 to his government of 31 Oct. 1794, the contents of which could be interpreted to mean that Randolph had provided Fauchet with secret information ("précieuses confessions") about political machinations surrounding the Whiskey Rebellion and had solicited a bribe to ensure the defeat of British intrigues in the West. Feeling betrayed by the President, who appeared to assume he was guilty, Randolph immediately submitted his resignation but requested that he be given a copy of the letter and that the affair be kept secret until he had a chance to prove his innocence. He spent the next ten weeks collecting and preparing for the press the evidence for his public vindication before removing to Richmond and resuming the practice of law. Meanwhile, the episode prompted the President to sign the Jay Treaty previously ratified by the Senate, on which Randolph had counseled delay, and to appoint Timothy Pickering, one of his two accusers in the Cabinet, to succeed him (Reardon, *Randolph*, 307-31; Stanley Elkins and Eric McKitrick, *The Age of Federalism* [New York, 1993], 422-31, 836-9n; Turner, *CFM*, 444-55; James Madison to TJ, 18 Oct. 1795; note to TJ to Madison, 26 Nov. 1795; Randolph to Madison, 1 Nov. 1795, in Madison, *Papers*, XVI, 117-8).

Rumors swirling around Randolph's resignation reportedly implicated Madison and TJ in charges of bribery and conspiracy. Senator Pierce Butler of South Carolina promptly warned Madison that he was a target in the "vile underhand game playing, with a View of injuring unspotted Characters." In November, Robert R. Livingston complained to Madison from New York that Fauchet's dispatch No. 10 "is made to speak any thing they think proper & the name of every man they wish to hunt down is inserted with the specific sum given to purchase him. I suppose I need not tell you that neither you nor Mr. Jefferson have esscaped." Randolph (who said he had not contacted Madison and other friends in order to avoid implicating them in the charges he levied against Washington in his *Vindication*) advised Madison that "the President and his party" intended "to destroy the republican force in the U.S." through a conspiracy "deeply laid and systematically pursued" (Butler to Madison, 21 Aug., Randolph to Madison, 1 Nov., and Livingston to Madison, 16 Nov. 1795, Madison, *Papers*, XVI, 54, 117, 126; Phila-

delphia *Aurora*, 21 Dec. 1795). See also Madison to TJ, 8 Nov. 1795. In addition to the comments on Fauchet's dispatch, TJ had also been indirectly brought into the episode by Randolph's denial of British minister George Hammond's accusation that he had been part of a conspiracy "to destroy the popularity of the President, and to thrust Mr. Jefferson into his chair" (Randolph, *Vindication*, 54). TJ did not comment on his purported involvement in the episode.

HER LAST PROMISE: see note to TJ to Madame Plumard de Bellanger, 24 Apr. 1794.

[1] Remainder of sentence interlined.
[2] Preceding three words interlined.
[3] This and subsequent words in italics are written in code, the decipherment being supplied by the Editors using Code No. 9.

To Madame de Tessé

Monticello Sep. 6. 1795.

When I parted with you, my dear Madam, in Paris, I little expected we should have been so long without seeing or hearing from each other. My return to that country was prevented by overpersuasions to undertake an office in our new government, which I did, much against my inclination. The disturbances which afterwards prevailed in France have given me reason to be satisfied that I did not return there: and I have at length been able to withdraw from public office with marks of having given as general satisfaction to my fellow-citizens as I could expect. I am now enjoying at home peace, peaches, and poplars, all of which I know you sufficiently prize. I am become the most industrious and ardent farmer of the canton and have so much to do to recover my farms from the desolated state in which I found them after a ten years absence, that I have no fear of ennui from want of emploiment in that way during my life, be it ever so long.—I heard that the state of your health, which was never such as your friends wished, had obliged you to go to Switzerland soon after I left you. Your relation in Philadelphia gave me more certain information afterwards of your being there and situated in comfort; and lately I have recieved through Mr. Gautier further information of you. I wish my next news may be that your country is placed in peace and freedom, and yourself returned to it and treated with that justice which I know to be due to your free and patriotic principles. We know little of what is passing in that country, for I would not call *knowlege* the misinformation we get thro' the English papers. We know from our own experience that they say of their enemies, not what is true, or what they believe to be true, but what they would wish the world to believe of them. Your repugnance to the sea forbids all hope in us that you may ever come to repose under the shade of our Magnolias. The state of society here, farther removed from that of France than it is in Switzerland, and, above all, the want of our language and little use here of yours, are further discoragements. Yet there are circumstances which would please you. A genial climate, a grateful soil, gardens planted by nature, liberty, safety, tranquility and a very secure and profitable revenue from whatever property we possess. Promise us therefore that when you can be safely wafted in a baloon, so as to avoid the nausea of sea sickness, you will come over. We will teach you to speak our language, and you will teach yourself to be contented with a more flegmatic society than that of Paris. But I beseech you let me hear from yourself, as there is no one in whose happiness I take a more lively interest. I join in this Madame de Tott and Monsieur de Tesse, whom I consider as parts of yourself. The difficulty of getting letters safely thro' wars by sea, and wars by land, have prevented my attempting it sooner; and even now I hardly know how this is to go. Mr. Monroe, our Minister Plenipotentiary at Paris, one of the worthiest characters on earth, and of whom it will be some recommendation to you that he is an elève of mine, will form a common center for our letters. I shall desire him to find the safest way of sending this, in which I purposely avoid every other object but that of conveying to yourself, Made. de Tott, and Monsr. de Tessé my fervent prayers for your happiness, and effusions of the sincere and unalterable attachment with which I am, Dear Madam, your affectionate friend & humble servt   TH: JEFFERSON

PrC (DLC); at foot of first page: "Madame de Tessé." Enclosed in TJ to James Monroe, 6 Sep. 1795.

YOUR RELATION IN PHILADELPHIA: Louis

Marie, Vicomte de Noailles, whom TJ saw in Philadelphia in 1793 (see notes to TJ's first letter to George Washington, 5 May 1793; and Madame de Tessé to TJ, 20 July [1786]).

To Jean Antoine Gautier

DEAR SIR   Monticello in Virginia Sep. 7. 95.

I received about three weeks ago your private favor of Mar. 24. 95. and also the letters of your house of the same date. Tho' the present is intended as an answer to your private letter, yet I will observe with respect to the accounts mentioned in those of your house, that I had no private account with Mr. Grand. That we began indeed by having one, but after one or two quarters it was found unnecessary and difficult, and it was therefore concluded to throw back the articles of it into the public account, so that Mr. Grand's accounts were only with Congress and the State of Virginia: and my private account was kept only between Congress and myself.—The deficiency sometimes of their fund, sometimes of that of Virginia having rendered mutual accomodations of money necessary, I passed a day, if you remember, at your office, revising my orders and endorsing on each of them for whose use the money was drawn. This was intended to enable the parties to settle justly between themselves, if any accident should happen to me before a settlement. A little before I left Philadelphia in 1793. I settled for the Auditor of the U.S. the account between Congress and Virginia, as far as the papers I then had, would enable me. But he had before that written to Mr. Grand for copies of my orders and the endorsements on them. These are since recieved, and will, I expect, enable me to settle the accounts fully as far as I had any thing to do with them. (My own private account I had before settled and balanced.) As soon as I can resume and complete the settlement between the U.S. and Virginia I will forward a copy of them to your house. With respect to the money deposited with you for the Algerine negociation, it was under the direction of Mr. Short, who will of course attend to the settlement of it.

The death of Mr. and Mrs. Grand, which I first learnt from your letter, has given me sincere regret, as their worth had inspired me with great esteem for them. I am very sensible also of Mr. Grand the son's recollection of me. I inclose to Mr. Monroe our M.P. at Paris a letter for Mde. de Tessé and have taken the liberty of referring him to you to enquire how it may be conveyed safely. I will thank you to convey my respects also to Madame Helvetius, M. de Vieillard and the Abbé Arnoud, all of whom I think of with great sensibility and affection. I had before charged Mr. Monroe with presenting me to their recollection.

I long to hear that France has established peace and a fixed form of government, and to see it get under way. I am persuaded that the extent of the country is favorable to the maintenance of good republican government. Montesquieu has accredited the contrary opinion, but experience has shewn and is shewing that small republics are governed with less justice, freedom, and safety, than large. In the former, local passions and interests, eternally silence justice: in the latter they are silenced by the general views of the great body to which these local passions do not extend. That France may be free and happy is my sincere prayer, as also that you may participate your full share of it. Accept assurances of the great attachment and esteem of Dear Sir Your most obedt. humble servt.   TH: JEFFERSON

PrC (DLC); at foot of first page: "Mr. Gautier"; endorsed in ink by TJ. Enclosed in TJ to James Monroe, 6 Sep. 1795.

SETTLED FOR THE AUDITOR: see Editorial Note and group of documents on the settlement of Jefferson's accounts as minister plenipotentiary in France, at 8 July 1792.

To Angelica Schuyler Church

DEAR MADAM   Monticello Sep. 8. 1795.

I know not how our letter account stands, but I am willing enough to suppose myself in debt that under that pretext I may recall myself to your memory. Your kind enquiries after our situation during the rage of the yellow fever in Philadelphia, by some delay on the way, did not get to me till 6. months after it's date. It found me in a safe asylum from all the cares and dangers of that metropolis. Nor has any thing arisen in our political field which has excited a wish that I had kept it a moment longer, or ever to return to it. I am now in that tranquil situation which is my delight, with all my family living with me, and forming a delicious society. I could only wish to be more within the reach of the friendships I have formed. I had hoped as Mr. Church grew older he would lose his relish for the bustle of a crouded country, and retire to ours. Still I could not however expect that you should prefer any other to your native state. Be this as it may, and wherever you be, I shall always pray for your happiness, and be glad to hear from you. Your esteem is among the foremost of those which I would wish to preserve in my retirement. We wish much too to hear of our friend Catharine. She will not be forgotten by us. Maria desires to preserve her place in her friendship. My daughter Randolph is absent, or I should be charged with her affections also to you both. I take the liberty of putting a letter to Mrs. Cosway under your cover. I hear nothing from Made. de Corny. God bless you, my dear Madam, and preserve you among his choicest favorites. Your affectionate friend & humble servt.   TH: JEFFERSON

RC (ViU); at foot of text: "Mrs. Angelica Church." PrC (DLC). Enclosure: TJ to Maria Cosway, 8 Sep. 1795. Enclosed in TJ to Thomas Pinckney, 8 Sep. 1795.

YOUR KIND ENQUIRIES: Church to TJ, 5 Nov. 1793.

To Maria Cosway

MY DEAR MADAM   Monticello Sep. 8. 179[5]

Your two favors, sent thro' Mr. Trumbul, found me retired to my home, in the full enjoiment of my farm, my family, and my books, having bidden an eternal Adieu to public life which I always hated, and was drawn into and kept in by one of those great events which happened only once in a millenium as I thought, but another country has shewn us they can happen twice in a life. While my countrymen are making a great buz about Mr. Jay and his treaty with your adoptive country, I am eating the peaches, grapes and figs of my own garden and only wish I could taste them in your native country, gathered on the spot and in your good company. I think you, Mrs. Church and myself must take a trip together to Italy, not forgetting Made. de Corny, tho she seems to have forgotten us, or some of us, for I have not had de pas nouvelles since I left France. Having revisited Italy, I wonder you could leave it again for the smoke and rains of London. However you have the privilege of making fair weather wherever you go. I suppose that in our way to Italy it will be hardly worth our while to go through France. Our acquaintance there must be entirely dissipated. I think however we may venture by the route of Languedoc, and Nice. We shall have the pleasure of climbing the Cornice of the Riviera di Genoa together, and of seeing many romantic scenes to which your pencil and imagination would do justice. (The chateau di Saorgio, by the bye, is on the Col de Tende road.) But I wish to see Genoa again and bespoke some charming rooms there against my return.—We will leave the rest of the journey to imagination, and return to what is real.—I am become, for instance, a real farmer, measuring fields, following my ploughs, helping the haymakers, and never knowing a day which has not done something for futurity. How much better this than to be shut up in the four walls of an office, the sun of[1] heaven excluded, the balmy breeze never felt, the evening closed with the barren consolation that the drudgery of the day is got through, the morning opening with the fable renewed of the Augean stable, a new load of labour in place of the old, and thus day after day worn through, with no prospect before us but of more days to wear through in the same way.—From such a life, good lord deliver me, and to such an one consign me only when the measure of thy wrath shall be completely filled! But it shall never be filled towards me as long as I am permitted, from the innocence of the scenes around me, to learn and to practice innocence towards all, hurt to none, help to as many as I am able—but I am rambling again, my dear friend, and must recall myself to order. In truth whenever I think of you, I am hurried off on the wings of imagination into regions where fancy submits all things to our will. I had better therefore seat you soberly before a London coal-fire, walk out into the sun myself, tell him he does not shine on a being whose happiness I wish more than yours; pray him devoutly to bind his beams together with tenfold force, to penetrate if possible the mass of smoke and fog under which you are buried, and to gild with his rays[2] the room you inhabit, and the road you travel: then tell you I have a most sincere and cordial friendship for you,[3] that I regret the distance which separates us, and will not permit myself to believe we are no more to meet till you meet[4] where time and distance are nothing. Your affectionate friend   TH: JEFFERSON

PrC (DLC: TJ Papers, 98: 16914, 232: 41488); badly faded, with first page partly overwritten in pencil in a later hand; at foot of first page: "Mrs. Maria Cosway." Enclosed in TJ to Angelica Schuyler Church, 8 Sep. 1795.

YOUR TWO FAVORS: Cosway to TJ, 13 and 24 Nov. 1794.

[1] Preceding three words interlined.
[2] Word interlined in ink in place of "beams."
[3] Here TJ canceled "and will not permit myself to believe."
[4] Thus in PrC.

To Philip Mazzei

DEAR SIR   Monticello Sep. 8. 95

The first copy of my letter of May 30. went soon after that date. A second copy accompanies this. Soon after that date I received letters from Mr. Blair and Mr. Madison, extracts from which I now inclose you. By that from Mr. Madison you will percieve that Dohrman alledges some deductions from the sum claimed. If he accedes to Mr. Madison's proposition of paying up what he acknoleges due, the money shall be immediately remitted to Messrs. Van Staphorsts: if he does not, it will afford a presumption that delay is his object, and the whole sum must be demanded by legal process, leaving to him to prove his discounts.

Considering your situation as stated by yourself, and that such feeble remittances only could be made from your other resources, Mr. Blair and myself concluded it better that your stock in the funds should be sold. You will percieve by the inclosed extract from him that the 2359.D. 12c. of all descriptions mentioned in my letter of May 30. have sold for 1972.D. 56c. including interest. Mr. Blair has now delivered me Wm. Hodgson's bill of exchange on Messrs. Robinson, Saunderson & Rumney of Whitehaven for £300. pounds sterling payable in London to Ichabod Hunter or order who has endorsed it to Messrs. Van Staphorsts for your account[1] and I this day inclose to them the 1st. of exchange, the 2d. and 3d. being to follow by other conveyances. This bill expresses to be for £420. Virginia currency (1400.D.) recieved. But Mr. Blair tells me there is to be in fact a deduction of a few dollars in your favor. He will invest the balance of the 1972.D. 56c. as soon as he can find a good bill, and it shall be immediately transmitted to the Van Staphorsts.

Giannini's law suit is not yet come to trial.

We have no small news interesting to you since the date of my last. A treaty which has been concluded with England[2] by the federal executive through the agency of Mr. Jay has excited a more general disgust than any public transaction since the days of our independance. It is thought to have stipulated some things beyond the power of the President and Senate, and that this will place us in an embarrassing situation. Preferring now tranquility to every other object, I determine to take no part in the passions of the day, but to pursue my farm and my nailery, pay my taxes, and leave public measures to those who have longer to live under them. I wish your Italy lay only on the other side of Chesapeak bay, that I might go and see it: if I were to take another voyage on this side the Styx, it would certainly be to see that. Be this as it may, I am and always shall be with great and sincere esteem Dear Sir Your affectionate friend & servt   TH: JEFFERSON

RC (NhD); at foot of first page: "Philip Mazzei." Enclosures: (1) Dupl of TJ to Mazzei, 30 May 1795. (2) Extract of John Blair to TJ, 13 June 1795. (3) Extract of James Madison to TJ, 14 June 1795, relating to Arnold Henry Dohrman's debt to Mazzei. Enclosed in TJ to Thomas Pinckney, 8 Sep. 1795.

INCLOSE TO THEM: SJL records a letter of this date from TJ to Van Staphorst & Hubbard that has not been found, but see their reply of 5 Jan. 1796.

[1] Preceding three words interlined.
[2] Preceding two words interlined.

To Thomas Pinckney

DEAR SIR   Monticello Sep. 8. 95.

I take the liberty of putting under your cover two letters, the one for Mrs. Church, the other for Mr. Mazzei, now settled at Pisa. I will sollicit you to put the latter into a safe channel as it is of considerable private interest. If the Grand Duke of Tuscany has any diplomatic or consular character at London, I presume it would be a safe conveyance.—The beginning of our year promised great crops. That of wheat has been good. But those of corn and tobacco are much injured, indeed almost ruined, by such continual floods of rain as were never before known. This circumstance too, preventing our treading out our wheat, which is generally done in the open air, exposes that much at this moment to the weavil. It has determined me, before another harvest, to prepare a threshing machine on the model you sent me, which the variety of other things wanting in my farms on my return to them, has as yet prevented my making.—The noise of the day in the political field, is Mr. Jay's treaty. But no body is so little able as myself to say what the public opinion is. I take no newspaper and by that device keep myself in a much loved ignorance of what people say at a distance. And I never go from home, so that my knolege does not even extend to the neighborhood. I am entirely a farmer, soul and body, never scarcely admitting a sentiment on any other subject, except when I have occasion to communicate with my friends, and to convey to them expressions, as I now take the liberty of doing to you, of the sentiments of esteem & respect with which I have the honor to be Dear Sir Your friend & servt

TH: JEFFERSON

PrC (DLC); at foot of text: "Mr. Pinckney. M.P. of the U.S. at London." Enclosures: (1) TJ to Angelica Schuyler Church, 8 Sep. 1795. (2) TJ to Philip Mazzei, 8 Sep. 1795. Enclosed in TJ to Tench Coxe, 10 Sep. 1795.

From Pierre Auguste Adet

MONSIEUR

Philadelphie Le 23 fructidor L'an 3eme de la République française (9 7bre 1795.)

J'esperois avoir L'honneur de vous Remettre moi-même La lettre que vous trouverés ci-jointe, et dont le professeur Pictet de genêve m'avoit Chargé avant Son départ de paris. Mais les affaires dont je Suis accablé ne me laissent pas de Relache, et Semblent s'accroitre pour m'enlever le Seul bonheur dont je fusse jaloux, celui d'offrir mes hommages au premier philosophe du nouveau monde.

J'ose Esperer que Sous les auspices du professeur pictet, vous voudrés bien m'accorder une portion de la bienveillance que vous lui avés temoignée. Entrainé par un penchant irrésistible vers l'étude des Sciences morales et physiques, je ne connois de plaisir que dans leur Étude. En parler avec Les philosophes qui S'en occupent aussi glorieusement que vous, profiter de leurs Leçons, Est ma plus douce occupation. Je ne puis donc vous Cacher combien je desire d'obtenir la permission de vous consulter quelquefois sur des questions relatives à L'histoire morale ou naturelle de ce pays. Si vous m'accordés cette demande je Serai au comble de mes vœux. Si elle est indiscrete daignés oublier que je vous l'ai faite pour ne vous Rappeller que des Sentiments d'Estime et de Respect que vous a voués.

P. A. ADET
ministre de la République française

RC (DLC); at foot of first page: "M. Jefferson"; endorsed by TJ as received 22 Sep. 1795 and so recorded in SJL. Enclosure: Marc Auguste Pictet to TJ, 1 Jan. 1795.

Pierre Auguste Adet (1763-1834), a French physician, chemist, diplomat, and government official, was secretary to the first commission sent by France to Saint-Domingue, chief of colonial administration, a member of the council of marine, and minister to Geneva, before serving as minister to the United States, 1795-96. In an effort to reverse the rapid deterioration in relations between France and the United States in the wake of the Jay Treaty, Adet took the unprecedented step, evidently by order of the Directory, of openly supporting TJ's presidential candidacy during the election of 1796. In the aftermath of the election he composed a shrewd analysis of TJ's attitude toward France for his superior in Paris: "Je ne scais si, comme on me l'assûre nous trouverons toujours en lui un homme entière-ment dévoué à nos intérêts. Mr. Jefferson nous aime, parcequ'il déteste l'Angleterre; il cherche à se rapprocher de nous, parcequ'il nous redoute moins que la Grande Bretagne; mais il changerait peut être demain de Sentiment à notre égard, si demain la Grande Bretagne cessait de lui inspirer des craintes. Jefferson quoiqu'ami de la liberté et des Sciences, quoiqu'admirateur des efforts que nous avons faits pour rompre nos fers et dissiper le nuage de l'ignorance qui pèse sur l'espèce humaine, Jefferson, dis-je, est Américaine et, à ce titre, il ne peut pas être sincèrement notre ami. Un Américain est l'ennemi né de tous les Peuples Européens." After returning to France, Adet served the Napoleonic regime as a member of the Tribunate, a prefect of Nièvre, and in the Senate, while continuing to pursue his interests in chemistry (*Dictionnaire*, I, 573-5; DeConde, *Entangling Alliance*, 456-8, 472-6; Adet to the Minister of Foreign Relations, 31 Dec. 1796, Turner, *CFM*, 983).

To Caleb Lownes

DEAR SIR   Monticello Sep. 9. 1795

I am to acknolege the receipt of your favor of Aug. 5. I have not yet heard from Mr. Swan of the arrival of the three ton of rods, but being very nearly out of rods, I have sent off a waggon for a load in confidence of the arrival. As three ton but barely suffice for a quarter, and it is necessary I should have some stock on hand to guard me against accidents of delay, I must pray you to send me another ton immediately. I inclose you an order on Mr. Barnes for 470. Dollars to pay for the three ton before ordered, the ton now desired, and the stove expected. I shall hope to have your opinion on the kitchen stove before you send it. I am with great esteem Dear Sir Your friend & servt   TH: JEFFERSON

RC (NjMoHP: Lloyd W. Smith Collection); at foot of text: "Mr. Caleb Lownes." Enclosure not found.

Lownes's letter of AUG. 5., recorded in SJL as received 18 Aug. 1795, has not been found. SJL also records missing letters from Lownes to TJ of 3 Dec. 1794, 23 Feb., 7 May, 6 Nov., 14 Dec. 1795, and 2 Feb. 1796, as well as from TJ to Lownes of 20 Nov., 18 Dec. 1794, 26 Mch., 6 May, 14 June, 20 July, 22 Oct., 25 Nov. 1795, and 17 Jan., 27 Mch. 1796. Letters from TJ to Samuel & John Swann of 4 Sep. 1795, and to John Swann of 24 Sep. 1795, both recorded in SJL, also have not been found.

This day TJ wrote a brief note to John BARNES advising that he was drawing on him in Lownes's favor for $470 at six days' sight and requesting him to honor the draft (PrC in CSmH; presumably the letter to Barnes recorded in SJL under 10 Sep. 1795).

Notes on St. George Tucker's Measurements of the Natural Bridge

Mr. Tucker's measures of the Natural bridge.
Sep. 9. 1795.

	f I
height from top of bridge to[1] bottom of water	196–9
the water 2. I. deep.	
conjectural thickness of the arch near middle	56–10
from abutment to abutment across the stream	
under upper side of bridge	70–9
under lower side of do.	54–2
narrowest part (a little below middle)[2]	48–8

MS (DLC); written entirely in TJ's hand on one side of a small parallelogram-shaped sheet; endorsed on verso: "Natural bridge."

Tucker's computations, like his observations of the heights of mountain peaks, are evidence of the jurist's avocational interest in the measurement of natural features during this period, testifying to his bent for scientific investigation epitomized by the years of effort he devoted to the astronomical problem of the precession of the equinoxes (TJ to Jonathan Williams, 3 July 1796; Hans C. von Baeyer, "The Universe According to St. George Tucker," *Eighteenth Century Life*, vi [1980], 67-79; Mary Haldane Coleman, *St. George Tucker: Citizen of No Mean City* [Richmond, 1938], 124-6).

[1] TJ here canceled "surf."
[2] Closing parenthesis supplied.

To Tench Coxe

DEAR SIR   Monticello Sep. 10. 95.

I have to acknolege the receipt of your favor of July 30. The sentiments therein expressed on the subject of the treaty coincide perfectly with those of this country, which I believe were never more unanimous. 4. or 5. individuals of Richmond, distinguished however by their talents as by their devotion to all the sacred acts of the government, and the town of Alexandria constitute the whole support of that instrument here. Camillus may according to his custom write an Encyclopedie on the subject, but it is too obstinate to be twisted by all his sophisms into a tolerable shape. Having interdicted to myself the reading of newspapers, and thinking or saying any thing on public matters beyond what the conversation of my neighbors draws me into, I leave such delights to those who, more rational than myself, prefer them to their tranquility, and to those whose stations keep them in that vortex, and make them better judges of what is passing around them.—My situation putting it out of my power to find good conveyances for my foreign letters, in these times of obstruction by sea and by land, I avail myself of your friendship to get them on: and now take the liberty of inclosing some. Our foreign ministers being entitled to charge their postages, and the risque of separating the 3d. letter, dispenses with apology on the subject of postage. That to Van Staphorsts covers bills of exchange, the property of Mr. Mazzei which I am remitting as it is collected. I am, with sincere esteem Dear Sir Your friend & servt   TH: JEFFERSON

PrC (DLC); at foot of text: "Tenche Coxe esq." Enclosures: (1) TJ to James Monroe, 6 Sep. 1795, and enclosures. (2) TJ to Thomas Pinckney, 8 Sep. 1795, and enclosures. (3) TJ to Van Staphorst & Hubbard, 8 Sep. 1795 (see note to TJ to Philip Mazzei, 8 Sep. 1795).

From Grand & Cie.

MONSIEUR   Paris le 11. 7bre. 1795.

Nous avons l'honneur de vous addresser Sous cette Enveloppe la Copie des Lettres que nous eûmes l'avantage de vous écrire les 25. Mai 1793 et 24. Mars 1795. Nous ésperons cependant quelles vous Seront parvenües, vû quelles vous ont été addressées par Triplicata.

Continuant, Monsieur, à être privés de l'honneur de vos Lettres et des ordres de la Trésorerie des Etats unis au Sujet du Solde de £48339.15 Tournois laissé entre nos mains en Billes de la Caisse d'Escompte forcés et depuis échangés Suivant les Décrêts contre assignats, Nous avons crû, Monsieur, après avoir si longtems attendû, dévoir Constater l'éspèce et les Numéros des assignats qui réprésentent le dit Solde de £48339.15 resté entre nos mains au Compte des Etats unis Sous votre Direction.

C'est ce que nous avons fait par l'acte Notarial dont nous avons lhonneur de joindre ici une Expédition légalisée, non Sans régretter que cet objet ait été laissé en france, tandis que les Changes continuoient Successivement a Se degrader.

Permettés, Monsieur, que nous prenions la Liberté de nous réferer au Contenu de cet acte, et veuillés agréer L'assurance du parfait respect avec lequel nous avons lhonneur d'étre, Monsieur Vôs tres humbles & obéïssants Serviteurs   GRAND & CO.

Indépendamment de quelques prêts considerables faits par notre Maison à quelques Citoyens des Etats unis dans des momens où ils étoient pressés par leurs Créanciers et qui ont été perdus pour nous, Il y en avoit un de £50000 Tournois que nous fimes a Mr. Thomas Barclay chargé d'aller faire un Traitté avec l'Empereur de Maroc, Mission qu'il auroit été Sans ce Sécours hors d'Etat de Remplir, vû l'embarras où le mettoient alors Ses Créanciers en france. Cette avance à aussi été perdue pour nous par la Situation ou Se Sons trouvées les affaires de Mr. Barclay et par l'evénement de la Mort. Vous avés eû, Monsieur, la bonté de nous permettre de vous remettre a votre depars de Paris une notte rélative a cette affaire. Nous dévons présumer qu'il n'aura pas été possible de nous accorder une indemnité pour cette Somme, quoique definitivement elle ait été employée pour le service des Etats unis.

LES DITS

RC (DLC); in a clerk's hand, signed for the firm by Jean Antoine Gautier, who wrote at foot of first page: "Monsieur Thomas Jefferson à Mounticelli Etat de Virginie"; endorsed by TJ as received 16 Jan. 1796 and so recorded in SJL. Enclosures: (1) Grand & Cie. to TJ, 26 Sep. 1789 (Tr in DLC: TJ Papers, 99: 16925; consisting of a variant extract in a clerk's hand of a letter summarized under the conjectured date of 9 May 1789 in Vol. 15: 109 [see note below]; at head of text: "Copie de la Lettre écrite à Monsieur Jefferson à Paris en datte du 26. 7bre. 1789"). (2) Grand & Cie. to TJ, 25 May 1793 (second letter). (3) Grand & Cie. to TJ, 24 Mch. 1795. (4) Notarial Declaration by Gautier on behalf of Grand & Cie., 31 Aug. 1795, verifying the series and numbers of assignats of the Republic totaling £48,339.15 livres tournois, to which discount bank notes remitted to the firm by TJ in August 1789 had been converted by successive arrêts and decrees, representing a balance that, despite the firm's entreaties to TJ and Alexander Hamilton for instructions, remains at the disposal of the United States in the hands of the firm formerly known as Grand & Cie., as ascertained by accounts by the firm, particularly that of 25 May 1793, the risk for which is now entirely the responsibility of the United States, this declaration being intended to establish that the firm is only the depository for the funds (MS in DLC: TJ Papers, 99: 16924, in a clerk's hand, bearing notarial stamp at head of text and with subjoined attestations of 1, 9, and 10 Sep. 1795 by notaries and officials of the French government; Tr in DNA: RG 53, Register's Estimates and Statements, in English, with attestation by James Cole Mountflorence of the American consulate in Paris, 18 Sep. 1795, all in a clerk's hand). For the account of 25 May 1793, see Enclosure No. 1 listed at Grand & Cie. to TJ, 25 May 1793 (first letter).

For the depreciation of the ASSIGNATS, see Jean Antoine Gautier to TJ, 7 June 1796.

The NOTTE dated "Samedi" that Grand & Cie. had given to TJ upon his departure for the United States on 26 Sep. 1789 relative to the AFFAIRE of the firm's loan to Thomas Barclay was enclosed in their undated letter to TJ and summarized with it by the Editors under the conjectured date of 9 May 1789 (Vol. 15: 109). Both 9 May and 26 Sep. 1789 fell on Saturday, but the letter printed here and the date of Enclosure No. 1 listed above establish that both the letter and the enclosed memorandum were sent to TJ on 26 Sep. 1789.

To Charles Lilburne Lewis

DEAR SIR   Monticello Sep. 11. 95.

All I know about the lands directed to be sold by my father's executors is that in an account settled between Dr. Walker and myself I am allowed a credit of £15. at the date of May 23. 1771. being for three eighths of my father's share of the lead mine, to wit my own eighth part, and those of my sisters Jane and Elizabeth @ £5. each. Consequently your share would be £5. with interest from that time to this, if it has never been settled between Dr. Walker and yourself.

I do not recollect when Catlet's paiment was to be made. The paper was I think left in Mr. Monroe's hands; you may rest assured that yours shall be of the first monies he pays. I am sent back again to you by Mr. Edward Moore for the amount of the smith's work entered in my books in the name of Isham Lewis, but done in fact as he says for the plantation at Buckisland of which Isham had then the direction. The amount is £3–9–9 with interest from the year 1785. If you can settle between yourselves who is to pay it I shall be satisfied so that somebody does it.

On the subject of the money due from Dr. Walker I omitted to observe that Mr. Frank Walker is the person to be applied to, as it was money received by his father for the loyal company. I believe none others of the lands referred to in my father's will were saved. I am Dear Sir Your affectionate humble servt   TH: JEFFERSON

RC (Mrs. Charles W. Biggs, Lewisburg, West Virginia, 1950); at foot of text: "Colo. Charles Lilburne Lewis."

TJ evidently was replying to a missing letter from Lewis of 11 Sep. 1795, recorded in SJL as received the same day.

TJ had previously expressed disinterest in the claim he and his siblings had to their father's share of a grant the Council of Virginia made in 1749 to the LOYAL COMPANY,

whose agent was Dr. Thomas Walker (TJ to James Madison, 11 Nov. 1784, and note; DAB, s.v. "Walker, Thomas"). A missing letter of 6 July 1795 recorded in SJL as written by TJ to "Moore (ironworks)" was doubtless addressed to Edward Moore.

SJL records fifteen other letters exchanged by TJ and Lewis between 24 Jan. 1794 and 18 Feb. 1797, none of which has been found.

To George Washington

DEAR SIR   Monticello Sep. 12. 1795.

The last post brought me a letter from Madame de Chastellux, covering the inclosed, which she informs me is on the same subject with hers to me, and that she refers you to me for particulars. I had very little acquaintance with her personally in Paris. I understood she was the daughter of an English general Plunket in the Austrian service, entirely without fortune. Chastellux is said to have been intrigued into the marriage at Spa, where he met with and married her. The prudence of her conduct however reconciled his friends.[1] He was himself without fortune, being a younger son, and therefore depended on his military pay and some pension. On his death, a small pension was continued to his widow by the crown, but her chief dependance was the Dutchess of Orleans who had taken an affection to her, gave her apartments, a place at her table, and some pension. The Orleans fortune being confiscated, all these dependancies are gone, and Madame de Chastellux with her infant son is, I dare say, entirely destitute of provision. These are the only particulars I know which, in compliance with her reference to me, are worthy noting to you. Her application should undoubtedly be to Congress, if to any member of the Federal government. Whether they ought to give relief, is one question, and not obviously in her favor, considering that every individual of the French army which was here would have equal right to provision. But another question would be whether any article in the constitution has authorised Congress to grant the public money in this way? I think the pensions or other aids heretofore given have been to persons employed by the former Congress, whose powers were larger, whose debts the present government was expressly authorised to pay, and who were understood to be under engagements to those persons.

I must say a word to you about the Succory you received from Mr. Young, and were so kind as to give me some of the seed. I sowed about $\frac{1}{4}$ or $\frac{1}{3}$ of an acre last year. It cut little figure that year. But this year it's growth has been most luxuriant indeed. I have not cut it, but kept the whole for seed, and to furnish young plants for transplanting which it does in very great abundance. From what I see of it, and what Mr. Strickland told me (that he had known it cut 5. times a year in England) I consider it as one of the greatest acquisitions a farmer can have. I sowed at the same time 2. acres of Lucerne, in exactly an equal soil, which in both instances had been originally rich, but was considerably exhausted. I gave the Lucerne this last year a good coat of dung, and due tillage; yet it is such poor dwindling stuff that I have abandoned it, while the Succory without dung or tillage is fine. I propose to sow and plant the next spring 2. acres at each of my farms, for the maintenance of 8. ploughhorses (4. to the acre) and I count on it's feeding them thro' the whole summer without any thing else. My plough horses have this summer (from April) had nothing but clover, and have gone through the summer's work as well as when they were crammed with corn. It is a great step towards recruiting our lands to abate the culture of corn. Never had any reformer so barbarous a state of things to encounter as I have. It will be the work of years before the eye will find any satisfaction in my fields. However nearly the whole of my grain is sowing now on fallow, and after the present season I shall never sow another acre after corn. The weavil is completely possessed of all the wheat in this neighborhood which is not yet got out, or which is got out *and cleaned*. I have avoided loss by keeping mine in the chaff. But I will never meet another harvest without a threshing-machine. The field pea of Europe and their winter vetch I find to be great desiderata in the farm. The former to cultivate in such of our fallows as will not yeild clover; as while we are keeping our ground clean for the next wheat sowing, the pea will shade it, and give us as valuable crop both of grain and fodder. The winter vetch sown on our fall fallows for corn, will give a fine crop of green[2] fodder in the spring, which may be cut in time to prepare the ground for corn. This will cost us not a single ploughing. I have taken two or three chances of getting these things from Europe, in time as I hope to try them the next season. I expect to take both these articles into the regular course of my husbandry thus. 1. wheat. followed by winter vetch. 2. corn followed by winter vetch. 3. a fallow of peas. 4. wheat. 5. 6. 7. three years of clover. A very decisive experiment has banished rye from my rotation. I mix potatoes with my corn, on your plan. You shall know the result of my trials of the European pea and vetch, and be furnished with seed, if they prove worth your notice.—We have had this year such rains as never came I believe since Noah's flood. Our clear profits will not repay the damage done our lands. Begging leave to place here my respects to Mrs. Washington, I ask you to accept assurances of the great & sincere esteem & respect with which I am Dear Sir your affectionate friend & humble servt   TH: JEFFERSON

RC (DLC: Washington Papers); at foot of first page: "The President of the US."; endorsed by Washington. PrC (DLC). Enclosure: see enclosure listed at Madame de Chastellux to TJ, 6 May 1795.

[1] Preceding sentence interlined.
[2] Word interlined.

To John Craig Millar

SIR   Monticello in Virginia Sep. 13. 1795.

I was sometime ago honored with your favor of July 10. covering that of Mr. Stewart of Mar. 1. whose letters and friends are always to me objects of great respect. It is flattering to our country to become an object of preference to men of science, whom any circumstances invite to a change of their soil. But it were to be wished it could hold out to them at the same time better prospects of rendering their science of more solid advantage to themselves. A perfect freedom in the use of our own faculties unrestrained by monopolies, or arbitratry disqualifications are the chief encoragements. Whatever line of pursuit you may think proper to propose to yourself, it would give me pleasure to be useful to you should it be in my power. But this I can hardly expect, in the state of retirement from all things and persons political to which I have resorted from an inclination which has been constant, and from a rigorous calculation of the sum of happiness offered by public and by private life. Should any circumstances lead you into this part of our continent, I shall be very happy to recieve you here, and to give you every proof of my respect to Dr. Stewart, as well as of my sense of that which the distinguished science of your family and connections is entitled to command, being with much regard, Sir Your most obedt. & most humble servt   TH: JEFFERSON

PrC (DLC); at foot of text: "Mr. John Craig Millar."

To Henry Tazewell

DEAR SIR   Monticello Sep. 13. 95.

I ought much sooner to have acknoleged your obliging attention in sending me a copy of the treaty. It was the first we recieved in this part of the country. Tho I have interdicted myself all serious attention to political matters, yet a very slight notice of that in question sufficed to[1] decide my mind against it. I am not satisfied we should not be better without treaties with any nation. But I am satisfied we should be better without such as this. The public dissatisfaction too and dissension it is likely to produce, are serious evils. I am not without hopes that the operations on the 12th. article may render a recurrence to the Senate yet necessary and so give to the majority an opportunity of correcting the error into which their exclusion of public light has led them. I hope also that the recent insults of the English will at length awaken in our Executive that sense of public honor and spirit which they have not lost sight of in their proceedings with other nations, and will establish the eternal truth that acquiescence under insult is not the way to escape war. I am with great esteem Dr. Sir Your most obedt. humble servt

TH: JEFFERSON

RC (NhD); at foot of text: "H. Tazewell   [1] TJ here canceled "satisfy me."
[esq.]." PrC (DLC).

To John Barnes

DEAR SIR   Monticello Sep. 14. 95.

The bearer hereof, Mr. Peyton, is a young gentleman who has lately entered into commerce at Milton, a small town near me. Proposing to establish a correspondence for his supplies at Philadelphia, and being an entire stranger there he has asked me to introduce him to some person who may be able to advise him to good characters for his dealings. I am personally but little acquainted with him, but he has a very good character in our neighborhood. I know still less of his capital, but as to that he is no doubt prepared to satisfy those to whom he shall address himself. I take the liberty of introducing him to you, as being acquainted with the mercantile characters of the place, and will thank you to introduce him to good men, as, I repeat again, that this is the sole object of the present letter.

Should Mr. Peyton get a supply of goods at Philadelphia, he proposes to come himself round with them by water, and would be a good conveyance for the tea and box of glass formerly desired of you. To these I will thank you to add a small box of tin plates, a proper quantity of solder for them, and 4. ℔ of pure tin in the lump. This last article is intended for tinning the inside of copper vessels, and is much better pure, than when mixed as is common. Mr. J. Bringhurst formerly advised me where it was to be had in Philadelphia, and will be obliging enough to advise you. I am with great esteem Dear Sir Your most obedt. servt   TH: JEFFERSON

PrC (ViU: Edgehill-Randolph Papers); at foot of text: "Mr. John Barnes."

MR. PEYTON: SJL records a letter of 14 Sep. 1795 from TJ to an unidentified "Peyton," probably Craven Peyton, which has not been found.

On 23 Sep. 1795 TJ wrote a brief note to Barnes advising that he was drawing on him for $96 at three days' sight in favor of Robert Pollard (PrC in MHi; filed with PrC

of draft). In regard to this draft, TJ elsewhere noted: "This being for my own purposes, credit Wm. Short for it" (MB, 23 Sep. 1795).

SJL records missing letters from Barnes to TJ of 22 and 27 Aug. 1795, both received on 16 Sep. 1795, and of 28 Sep. and 3 Oct. 1795, which were received on 9 and 20 Oct. 1795, respectively. SJL also records a letter from TJ to Barnes of 20 Oct. 1795, not found.

To Sampson Crosby

SIR   Monticello Sep. 15. 1795.

Your favor of July 28. came duly to hand, and since that I have recieved the box containing Dunlap's and Bache's volumes for 1794. and the two volumes of Genl. Washington's letters. As I am anxious to continue to recieve those newspapers at the end of the year, bound up, perhaps it would be better to bespeak them now for the present year, to be laid by till the close of the year in the printer's shops and then bound up.

With respect to the Venetian blinds, that you may get clear of them, I will ask the favor of you to put them into proper hands to be repaired and altered as below directed. Mr. Ingles named to me some person who would do it reasonably. Let the person who does it, pack them in a box, and I will thank you to have them forwarded. Mr. Barnes, on shewing him this letter will pay the expence, if it be done while he has money in his hands, for which reason I wish it to be done immediately.—What is become of Mr. Petit? I never hear from him nor of him. I am with esteem Dear Sir Your friend & servt.   TH: JEFFERSON

NB. there are of the Venetian blinds
1st. 5 large coarse ones painted white. These I would have new mounted, and painted green, and left of their present size.
2. There are some others painted green, and some not painted at all, made for windows 3. f. 3 I. wide and 6. f. 6 I. high. These I would have altered for windows 3. f. 3 I. wide and 9 f. 9 I. high. Of course three of them will make two. They will require new ferrit and cord, and to be painted green.

RC (PHi); endorsed by Crosby as received 26 Sep. 1795.

Sampson Crosby of Massachusetts had been "Office-keeper" and messenger for the Department of State since at least 1791, in which position he arranged for supplies and services. He subsequently became an innkeeper in Philadelphia (Vol. 17: 356, 372, 375-6; TJ to the Speaker of the House of Representatives, 2 Jan. 1793; Cornelius William Stafford, *The Philadelphia Directory, for 1800* . . . [Philadelphia, 1800], 36; TJ to Crosby, [26] Dec. 1795).
Crosby's FAVOR OF JULY 28, received on 18 Aug. 1795, his letter to TJ of 6 May 1795 received from Philadelphia on 19 May 1795, and TJ's reply of 2 June 1795 to the earlier letter, all recorded in SJL, have not been found. SJL also records missing letters from TJ to the Philadelphia cabinetmaker Henry Ingle of 1 Oct. 1794 and 11 Sep. and 2 Oct. 1796 as well as Ingle's replies of 18 Oct. 1794 and 15 Oct. 1796, received respectively on 26 Nov. 1794 and 28 Oct. 1796. See also TJ to John Barnes, 11 Sep. 1796.
GENL. WASHINGTON'S LETTERS: see note to John Carey to TJ, 30 June 1792.

To St. George Tucker

TH:J. TO CITIZEN TUCKER   Sep. 15. 95.

Come and take your nap with us to-night. I have not the pleasure of being acquainted with Mr. Carrington but if he will accompany you, I shall therefore be the more obliged to him. It will relieve you from the heats and drunken noise of Charlottesville and you will return in better tone to the functions of justice in the morning and more philanthropically disposed[1] to gloss over the follies which are to be brought before you.—To put in my claim in time, I set up a prescriptive right to dine the judges on the Sunday of their session.

RC (ViW); addressed: "Judge Tucker"; endorsed by Tucker. Not recorded in SJL.

[1] Word interlined.

To Joseph Donath

SIR   Monticello Sep. 16. 95.

I have this day recieved your favor of Aug. 27. Having imagined that you always had a stock of glass on hand of assorted sizes, so that I might at any time make up a deficiency, I sent you but a rough guess of the quantity I should want. Finding now that it is necessary to be more exact, I have estimated my wants with more care, and find they will be the quantity stated below, which therefore I must ask you to bring for me to Philadelphia where I shall have my sashes made. You will of course consider this order as *instead* of the former one and not *additional* to it. I am Sir Your humble servt   TH: JEFFERSON

350. panes of Bohemian[1] glass 18. inches square.
 25. panes of do. 18. by 24. inches.
    to be of $1\frac{1}{2}$ thickness.

RC (Robert G. Hopkins, Cincinnati, 1946); at foot of text: "Mr. Josiah Donath. No. 28. South Front street. Philadelphia."

Donath's FAVOR of 27 Aug. 1795, recorded in SJL as received 16 Sep. 1795, has not been found. SJL also records a letter from TJ to Donath of 20 Oct. 1795 and one from Donath to TJ of 31 Oct. 1795, received from Philadelphia on 10 Nov. 1795, neither of which has been found.

[1] Word interlined.

From Rodolph Vall-Travers

SIR   Altona, near Hamburg, Septr. 16th. 1795.

The Secretary of Mr. Jaÿ, your Plenipotentiary in England, having obligingly taken Charge, after his Patron's Departure for America, of mÿ last Packet to your Honor, as President of your philosophical illustrious Society, dated the 1t. of June last from London: I hope, it came safe and officially to Hand in due Time. It contained, (besides Mr. Cavallho's Theory of magnetic Fluids and their Effects on the Needle, laid before the roÿal Societÿ, when I was present at its Meeting) a Hint, given me by Mr. Patterson, the present liberal Proprietor and Improver of the celebrated Leverian Museum, of his Readiness to treat with your Society, about a Cession of all the numerous Duplicate Specimens of his rich Collections in most Branches of natural History, in best Preservation, to serve as a considerable Foundation for a similar american instructive Museum. He wou'd willingly recieve, in Exchange, an equal Number of Specimens, of american natural Curiosities, not contained as yet in his own Collections. The overplus, on either Side, to be ballanced by an equitable Compensation. This Negociation, if attended to by your Society, can be carried on by a direct Correspondence with Mr. Patterson and his Son.

The chief Improvements I found to be made in England, in mathematical and philosophical Instruments, since the Departure of my late Friend, Dr. Benjn. Franklin, and mine, being contained in the inclosed Catalogue of Messs. haas and Hurter, of great Marlborough-Street London, I herewith beg Leave to inclose it for the Society's Information, and occasional Demands.

My Health and far advanced Age requiring a milder Climate, under a well regulated republican Government, propitious to Arts, Sciences, and every Branch of useful Knowledge and Industry I cou'd wish to repair, the Sooner the better, to Venice, or its Vicinity: and shou'd rejoice very much, if my Abode in that, or any other Part of Italy, cou'd, by your Means, be made Subservient to some beneficial Objects of your Congress, and its confederate States, Societies and Individuals; either in the mercantile Line, as Consul; or in the literary Line, by instructive and interesting Communications of the most important literarÿ Productions in every learned academy in Italy; and lastly in the political Line, in Objects of defensive and commercial Treaties and Alliances, of Finances, of Improvements in Agriculture, Horticulture, and Manufactures, in Proportion to the Scale of Power, and the Tenor of Instructions, I might be entrusted with and enabled to act, with Diligence, and Energy.

Shou'd these my humble Offers meet with your kind Notice and Approbation, so as to be laid before your venerable and illustrious President, for his mature Consideration and possible Sanction: I wou'd strain every Exertion, to render myself not totally unworthy of both your Confidence and Protection; being with never ceasing Admiration of your eminent Merits, and fervent Prayers for your mutual Preservation and Prosperity Sir! Your Honors Most sincerily devoted humble Servant:

RODOLF VALLTRAVERS

RC (PPAmP: Archives); beneath dateline: "recommended to Messs. Lotz & Solltau, Merchants, on the Herren-Graben, at Hamborough"; at foot of text: "To T. Jefferson; Philadelfia"; endorsed by TJ as received 27 May 1796 and so recorded in SJL; notation by John Vaughan on verso of last page: "Recd at Philos: Society Communicated by directions of Mr Jefferson Read: 19 Augst 1796 Parkinson (of Levin Musœum) proposal for Exchanges." Enclosed in TJ to David Rittenhouse, 3 July 1796.

Vall-Travers's LAST PACKET . . . DATED THE 1T. OF JUNE LAST is printed under 29 May 1795. From 1791 until January 1795, TJ was one of three vice presidents of the American Philosophical Society, but he did not become its PRESIDENT until 1797 (APS, Proceedings, XXII, pt. 3 [1885], 187, 201, 211, 217, 227, 235, 246). MR. PATTERSON: that is, James Parkinson.

THE INCLOSED CATALOGUE may have been A Catalogue of Mathematical and Philosophical Instruments Made and Sold by J. B. Haas, No 4, Silver-Street, Golden-Square

(London, 1790?). MESSS. HAAS AND HURTER, who were possibly of Swiss origin, made barometers, thermometers, and other scientific instruments (E. G. R. Taylor, *The Mathematical Practitioners of Hanoverian England 1714-1840* [Cambridge, 1966], 313, 314; Maurice Daumas, *Scientific Instruments of the Seventeenth and Eighteenth Centuries*, trans. Mary Holbrook [New York, 1972], 219, 245).

After considering Vall-Travers's letter to TJ at a meeting of 19 Aug. 1796, the American Philosophical Society—whose published minutes erroneously describe it as a communication of 1796—ordered that the "draft of an answer" be prepared. At its 7 Oct. 1796 meeting the Society approved the reply presented by its corresponding secretaries and the publication in American newspapers of the Leverian Museum's request for exchanges of specimens (APS, *Proceedings*, XXII, pt. 3 [1885], 241, 242).

Inquest on Shadwell Mill

Albemarle county to wit. An Inquest taken at Shadwell in the parish of Fredericksville and county aforesaid on the 18th. day of September 1795. by virtue of a writ of Ad quod damnum issued from the court of the said county on the 12th. day of the same month before Francis Taliaferro deputy sheriff of the said county and by the oaths of Thomas Bell, William Chapman, Thomas W. Lewis, Henry Gambell, Robert Snelson, Bennett Henderson, Benjamin Sneed, John Sneed, Robert Sharp, Richard Price, Joel Shifflit and John Gamble good and lawful men of the same county, who being charged and sworn upon their oaths do say that they have met on the lands of Thomas Jefferson in the writ named on the North river at the place called Shadwell aforesaid where the said Thomas Jefferson petitioned the court of the said county for leave to erect a water grist mill, and have examined the lands above and below of the property of others, and find that Peter Jefferson formerly, and afterwards the said Thomas had at the said place a water grist mill which was destroyed by a flood in 1771. that he proposes now to rebuild the said mill either in the same spot at the mouth of a Spring branch, or in such other spot as shall be thought best between that and the foot of the Sandy falls about 28. poles above: that the lands next below on the North side the river belong to Thomas Mann Randolph, whose upper line is about 129. poles below the former mill, and those next below on the South side of the said river did belong to Bennet Henderson from whom they have descended in parcenary on John, William, Sally, James, Charles, Isham, Bennet Hilsboro', Eliza, Frances, Lucy, and Nancy Crawford, children and heirs of the said Bennet whose upper line is about 51. poles below the said former mill of the said Thomas Jefferson; that no part of those lands were overflowed or injured by the waters of the said former mill, or can be by those of the one now proposed: that they have examined also the place where the said Thomas Jefferson has taken his present canal out of the river and the lands above and they find that it is at a natural ridge of rocks about 244. poles above the place proposed for his mill, that it is still water nearly at present from thence up to the Secretary's ford about 462 poles above, and that the said Thomas Jefferson holds the lands on both sides of the river through the whole distance to about 10. or 12. poles above the said ford on the South side where the lands of Nicholas Lewis junr. join his, and more than a mile above the same on the North side where the lands of James Key join his: that the said Thomas Jefferson does not propose to raise a dam on the said natural ridge of rocks at the beginning of his said canal, but only to stop the sluices in the same; that neither that nor even any dam which he can build can overflow any lands either of his own or any other person above, nor throw backwater above his own lines, and therefore that it will not be to any damage of any of the proprietors of the lands above or below; that no Mansion house, office, curtilage, garden or orchard of any person above or below will be overflowed by either the back or tail-water of the said mill; that the health of the neighbors will not in their opinion be annoyed by any stagnation of the waters, nor any inconvenience be produced to any individuals in consequence of erecting the said mill, but on the contrary that it will be a convenience to the neighbors for the grinding their grain: that no navigation is at present practised through this part of the said river, the natural obstructions preventing the same, but that if the river be opened for navigation hereafter, the interests of the said Thomas ought to be postponed to that object, and those authorized to open the river should be free to make their opening in any part they think best, either of the said natural ridge of rocks, or of any stoppage which the said Thomas may have made: that since the erection of a mill dam in the year 1780. extending across the river from the lands beforementioned of the said Bennet Henderson deceased to those of Thomas Mann Randolph on the opposite side, few or no fish of passage have been taken above[1] the said dam, except at times when it has been out of repair: that so long as the said dam is continued at it's original height, no provision need be made by the said Thomas Jefferson for the passage of fish through or over the stoppages he proposes; but that if the said dam should be discontinued, or made so that fish may pass it, then the said Thomas Jefferson ought either to leave ten feet of the river unstopped at the South West side of the same, or, if the whole breadth of the river be stopped, then, as the water above the said natural ridge of rocks is not more than about 4 feet above the surface of the still water below the same, a slope made at some sufficient sluice thereof, of at least ten feet width, and of a length at least three times it's height, agreeable to the requisitions of the act of assembly of 1769. intituled 'an act to oblige the owners of mills, hedges or stops, on the rivers therein mentioned to make openings or slopes therein for the passage of fish' ought in that case to be made by the said Thomas Jefferson in a good and sufficient manner.

In witness whereof the said Jurors to this inquisition have severally put their seals the day, year and place first beforementioned.

THO. BELL	ROBT. SHARP
WM. CHAPMAN	BENJAMIN SNEAD
ROBERT SNELSON	RICHD. PRICE
JOHN GAMBIL	TW LEWIS
JOEL SHIFLETT	BENN HENDERSON
JNO. SNEED	HENRY GAMBIL

MS (Albemarle County Circuit Court Clerk's Office, Charlottesville); in TJ's hand, signed and sealed by members of the jury; originally containing blanks in body of text, later completed by TJ, for names of the deputy sheriff, jurors, and the first name of James Key, and for measurements in poles and feet; signed attestation by county clerk John Nicholas on verso of last page: "At Albemarle October Court 1795 This writ together with the Inquest of the Jury taken by virtue thereof were returned to Court & ordered to be recorded"; with other endorsements by unidentified clerks. Tr (Albemarle County Deed Book No. 11, same). Tr (ViU: Carr Papers); 19th-century transcript, being part of record of TJ v. Michie in the hand of George Carr. Enclosed in Bill in Chancery on the Henderson Milldam, [24 Sep. 1795].

This is one of a series of documents, extending over more than two decades, that relates to TJ's project to build a water-driven gristmill, in a slightly different location and with a long feeder canal, to replace a mill on the Rivanna River at Shadwell that had been built by his father around 1757 and destroyed by a flood in 1771. By the mid-1790s, grain had supplanted tobacco as the primary crop of the region around Monticello, with most farmers alternating their fields between wheat and corn from year to year. TJ recognized the new importance of grain farming, especially for overseas export, which more than tobacco planting also appealed to his evolving notions of political economy. On his own lands, as the Duc de La Rochefoucauld-Liancourt ob-

served in 1796, TJ developed a seven-year rotation plan utilizing restorative crops as well as grains, a system that promised to allow grain production without the long years of fallow eventually required by the simple wheat-corn rotation employed by his neighbors. He also believed that Albemarle County lagged behind other areas, such as the Shenandoah Valley, in building gristmills, and replacement of his father's mill was the first step in what became an ambitious program to produce flour (Betts, *Farm Book*, 201-2, 341-4; La Rochefoucauld-Liancourt, *Voyage*, v, 18-20; Robert Gamble to TJ, 10 May, TJ to Gamble, 19 May 1793; Malone, *Jefferson*, III, 200-1, 204; Robert D. Mitchell, *Commercialism and Frontier: Perspectives on the Early Shenandoah Valley* [Charlottesville, 1977], 172-8).

A partial record of TJ's actions on the Shadwell mill survives in two venues: in the Albemarle County Court, where he sought formal permission for construction; and in Virginia's High Court of Chancery in Richmond, where he filed suit to halt interference caused by a neighboring milldam on the Rivanna. TJ had begun the difficult work of excavating the new canal—three-quarters of a mile long, much of it through solid rock—in 1776, and two years later obtained permission from the county court to build a mill (see Enclosure No. 1 listed at John Carr to TJ, 22 Sep. 1795). Work on the canal continued intermittently until TJ's departure for France brought it to a halt in 1784. No construction had begun on the mill itself, and nothing came of TJ's sporadic efforts to revive the millsite during his service as Secretary of State (TJ to Thomas

Mann Randolph, Jr., 24 July 1791; John Clarke to TJ, 15 June 1793; Notice for Rental of Mill Seat, 18 June 1793; TJ to John Spurrier, 18 June 1793). The present initiative, doubtless sparked by TJ's concerns about a mill being built downstream (see below), began in September 1795 when he again petitioned the county court for permission to construct a mill. His petition, not found, resulted in an on-site investigation by a jury which signed the inquest printed above and had been convened AD QUOD DAMNUM—an ancient English writ commanding the sheriff to investigate the potential damages of an act—under a 1785 statute that was based on a draft, probably written by TJ, included in the revisal of the laws of Virginia (Hening, XII, 187-90; above in this series, Vol. 2: 320, 464-7; for the writ, see Enclosure No. 2 listed at John Carr to TJ, 22 Sep. 1795). On 5 Oct. 1795 the county court again granted TJ permission to erect a mill (Albemarle County Order Book, 1793-95, Albemarle County Circuit Court Clerk's Office, Charlottesville). The following year he revived the work on the canal in earnest, hiring laborers specifically for that task, which was not finally completed until 1805 (Betts, *Farm Book*, 343, 363-5).

In September 1795, as he sought renewed authority from the county for his mill project, TJ also instituted proceedings in the High Court of Chancery to stop work on a milldam that was located downstream from his millsite and was owned by the heirs of Bennett Henderson, who had died intestate in 1793. Henderson, one of whose collateral relatives was evidently on the jury that returned the county inquest, had acquired 1,200 acres of land at the falls of the Rivanna, where he built a tobacco inspection warehouse, a storehouse, a flour mill, and other facilities. His wife was TJ's first cousin Elizabeth Lewis, a sister of Charles Lilburne Lewis, who was both cousin and brother-in-law to TJ and who joined with Henderson in 1789 to develop the town of Milton (Merrill, *Jefferson's Nephews*, 58-9). Henderson's enterprises languished after his death, but by September 1795 his heirs' improvement of their dam, which threatened to elevate the water level at the Shadwell millsite, led TJ to retain Bushrod

Washington as attorney to file his complaint in chancery. On 10 Oct. 1795, George Wythe, the chancery court's judge, ordered the Hendersons to stop raising their dam (TJ to Washington, 23 Sep. 1795; Bill in Chancery on the Henderson Milldam, [24 Sep. 1795], and note). Since the level of the Rivanna at TJ's millsite—and consequently the precise location of his proposed mill—was affected by the Henderson dam, TJ postponed construction of his mill until the chancery case was resolved. In 1799 Daniel Call succeeded Washington, who had become an associate justice of the United States Supreme Court, as TJ's counsel in the suit. On 1 October of that year Wythe issued the court's decree ordering that the Henderson milldam be torn down sufficiently to return the water to its level before Peter Jefferson built his mill (TJ to Daniel Call, 15 Aug. 1799; Call to TJ, 13 Oct. 1799, and enclosure).

TJ did not have the Henderson dam destroyed until his own mill was completed in 1803. By then he had begun to build a second, larger mill nearby to manufacture flour on a commercial basis, and was covertly buying the Henderson heirs' parcels of land along the Rivanna River. TJ's acquisition of most of Bennett Henderson's original holdings, a complex process that lasted until 1817, generated new legal disputes over land titles and renewed efforts by members of the Henderson family to develop their own mill (TJ to Craven Peyton, 2 May 1803; Betts, *Farm Book*, 342-3; Craven Peyton's Bill in Chancery, 5 May 1804, ViU: Carr Papers, 19th-century transcript, being part of record of TJ v. Michie in the hand of George Carr; Merrill, *Jefferson's Nephews*, 58-70; MB, 14 July 1801, 8 May, 10 Sep. 1804, 31 July 1812, 7 Feb., 20 July 1817, and notes; Steven H. Hochman, "Thomas Jefferson: A Personal Financial Biography" [Ph.D. diss., University of Virginia, 1987], 230-40; Malone, *Jefferson*, VI, 254, 505-7).

The 1769 ACT OF ASSEMBLY required any milldam on the Rivanna River to have a passageway for fish open from March to May of each year (Hening, VIII, 361-2).

[1] Preceding three words interlined in place of "crossed."

To James Madison

I recieved about three weeks ago a box containing 6. doz. volumes of 283. pages 12mo. with a letter from Lambert, Beckley's clerk, that they came from Mr. Beckley and were to be divided between yourself, J. Walker, and myself. I have sent 2 doz. to J. Walker, and shall be glad of a conveyance for yours. In the mean time I send you by post the title page, table of contents, and one of the pieces, Curtius, lest it should not have come to you otherwise. It is evidently written by Hamilton, giving a first and general view of the subject that the public mind might be kept a little in check till he could resume the subject more at large, from the beginning, under his second signature of Camillus. The piece called 'the Features of the treaty' I do not send because you have seen it in the newspapers. It is said to be written by Coxe, but I should rather suspect by Beckley. The antidote is certainly not strong enough for the poison of Curtius. If I had not been informed the present came from Beckly, I should have suspected it from Jay or Hamilton. I gave a copy or two by way of experiment to honest sound hearted men of common under-standing, and they were not able to parry the sophistry of Curtius. I have ceased therefore to give them. Hamilton is really a colossus to the antirepublican party. Without numbers, he is an host within himself. They have got themselves into a defile, where they might be finished; but too much security on the Republican part, will give time to his talents and indefatigableness to extricate them. We have had only mid-ling performances to oppose to him. In truth, when he comes forward, there is nobody but yourself who can meet him. His adversaries having begun the attack, he has the advantage of answering them, and remains unanswered himself. A solid reply might yet completely demolish what was too feebly attacked, and has gathered strength from the weakness of the attack. The merchants were certainly (except those of them who are English) as open-mouthed at first[1] against the treaty as any. But the general expression of indignation has alarmed them for the strength of the government. They have feared the shock would be too great, and have chosen to tack about and support both treaty and government, rather than risk the government: thus it is that Hamilton, Jay &c. in the boldest act they ever ventured on to undermine the constitution[2] have the address to screen themselves and direct the hue and cry against those who wished to drag them into light. A bolder party-stroke was never struck. For it certainly is an attempt of a party which finds they have lost their majority in one branch of the legislature to make a law by the aid of the other branch, and of the executive, under color of a treaty, which shall bind up the hands of the adverse branch from ever restraining the commerce of their patron-nation. There appears a pause at present in the public sentiment, which may be followed by a revulsion. This is the effect [3] of the desertion of the merchants, of the President's chiding answer to Boston and Richmond, of the writings of Curtius and Camillus, and of the quietism into which the people naturally fall, after first sensations are over. For god's sake take up your pen, and give a fundamental reply to Curtius and Camillus.

Mr. Randolph and my daughter will be back from the springs in the ensuing week. He is almost entirely recovered by the use of the sweet springs. I expect the execution of your promise to bring Mrs. Madison to see us, with whom we should all be glad to get acquainted. I would have been with you before this, but that I have had almost constant threats of rheumatism so obstinately fixed in it's seat as to render it imprudent for me to move much. Adieu affectionately.

RC (DLC: Madison Papers); addressed: "James Madison junr. near Orange court house"; stamped; with several emendations, only the most important being noted below. PrC (DLC); lacks one emendation (see note 2 below).

The BOX TJ received with the LETTER FROM LAMBERT—probably William Lambert to TJ of 31 Aug. 1795, recorded in SJL as received from Richmond on 11 Sep. 1795 but not found—contained copies of *Treaty of Amity, Commerce, and Navigation, Between His Britannic Majesty and the United States of America, Conditionally Ratified by the Senate of the United States, at Philadelphia, June 24, 1795. To Which Is Annexed, a Copious Appendix*, published by Mathew Carey in Philadelphia on 12 Aug. 1795 (Sowerby, No. 505). Along with the pieces cited by TJ, the TABLE OF CONTENTS includes addresses, resolutions, and memorials against the treaty from Portsmouth, New Hampshire, Boston, New York, Philadelphia, and several other cities; the pro-treaty address of the merchants of New York and the resolutions of the New York Chamber of Commerce; prior treaties of the United States with France and Great Britain; and various executive and congressional documents, including Madison's resolutions on commercial discrimination of 3 Jan. 1794. The twelve essays by CURTIUS, included in the pamphlet as "Vindication of the Treaty of Amity, Commerce, and Navi-

gation, with Great Britain," were written by Noah Webster in collaboration with James Kent, not by Alexander HAMILTON as TJ conjectured, and first appeared in Webster's New York *American Minerva* between 18 July and 5 Aug. 1795. At several points, "Curtius" cited documents written by TJ to indicate that his ideas had been incorporated into the treaty. In his eighth essay, for example, "Curtius" reprinted TJ's letter to Edmond Charles Genet of 24 July 1793—which had declared that "by the general law of nations, the goods of a friend found in the vessel of an enemy are free, and the goods of an enemy found in the vessel of a friend are lawful prize"—and argued that Article 17 of the treaty, by making enemy goods on a friendly vessel lawful prize, reiterated the same concept. Quoting in his eleventh article from TJ's Report on Commerce of 16 Dec. 1793, which had stated that American trade with British dominions in Europe rested upon an uncertain annual proclamation, "Curtius" contended that the treaty changed the "precarious privilege" into a right (*American Minerva*, 29 July, 4 Aug. 1795; Young, *Democratic Republicans*, 455-6n). FEATURES OF THE TREATY: the essays originally published in *Dunlap & Claypoole's American Daily Advertiser* between 18 July and 7 Aug. 1795 as "Features of Mr. Jay's Treaty," which were written by Alexander J. Dallas, not Tench COXE or John BECKLEY as TJ assumed, and subsequently published in various pamphlets (see Evans, Nos. 28527, 29757, 31172). PRESIDENT'S CHIDING ANSWER TO BOSTON AND RICHMOND: Washington to the Selectmen of Boston, [28 July 1795], stating that the Constitution gave the President, with the advice and consent of the Senate, the power to make treaties, doubtless under the supposition that they would not "substitute for their own conviction the opinions of others," but rather would seek the truth only through "a temperate and well-informed investigation." The letter served as a prototype for Washington's replies to other protests against the treaty, including that of Richmond (Fitzpatrick, *Writings*, XXXIV, 252-4n).

[1] Preceding two words interlined.
[2] Preceding word interlined in place of "government." PrC lacks emendation.
[3] TJ here canceled "partly."

From John Carr

SIR   Sepr. 22d. 1795

When I informed you there were several orders for rebuilding your mill, I was under a mistake. Having occasion to examine the Books in other cases, the order now sent must frequently have presented itself, and not attending to the date or Language of the order, I was inducd to think thier were more; the Copy of the writ and inquest are under Cover also. I am Sir yours. &C   JOHN CARR

RC (MHi); addressed: "Mr. Thomas Jefferson. Albemarle"; endorsed by TJ as received 22 Sep. 1795. Enclosures were probably: (1) Order of Albemarle County Court, 8 Oct. 1778, granting TJ permission to construct a mill on the Rivanna River near the site of his former mill (Tr in ViU: Carr Papers, 19th-century transcript, being part of record of TJ v. Michie in the hand of George Carr). (2) Writ of Albemarle County Court, 12 Sep. 1795, ordering the county sheriff to summon 12 men to appear on 18 Sep. at the place where TJ seeks permission to erect a water grist mill, in order to examine the lands above and below it that might suffer damage to buildings or gardens, or an obstruction to ordinary navigation or the passage of fish, or a threat to the health of the neighbors from the stagnation of waters, the inquest to be returned on the first Monday in October (MS in Albemarle County Circuit Court Clerk's Office, Charlottesville, in hand of and signed by county clerk John Nicholas, attached to Inquest on Shadwell Mill, 18 Sep. 1795; Tr in Albemarle County Deed Book No. 11, same, in a clerk's hand; Tr in Albemarle County Order Book, 1793-95, same, consisting of abstract; Tr in ViU: Carr Papers, 19th-century transcript being part of record of TJ v. Michie in the hand of George Carr). (3) Certificate of John Carr, 14 Sep. 1795, attesting that he has searched the records of the Albemarle County Court from September 1773 to December 1782, finding no evidence that Bennett Henderson or John Harvie, Jr., had petitioned to build a mill at Mountain Falls on the Rivanna River, nor any order from the court granting permission for a mill on the Henderson site (Tr in ViU: Carr Papers, 19th-century transcript, being part of record of TJ v. Michie in the hand of George Carr). (4) Inquest on Shadwell Mill, 18 Sep. 1795.

John Carr (b. 1753), a younger brother of TJ's brother-in-law Dabney Carr, was a deputy clerk for Albemarle County. He later served as clerk of the county's first circuit court, 1809-19, and also clerk of the district court of Charlottesville (Edson I. Carr, *The Carr Family Records* [Rockton, Ill., 1894], 73, 111; Woods, *Albemarle*, 159; Johnston, *Memorials*, 26, 32).

To Eliza House Trist

Dear Madam   Monticello Sep. 23. 1795.

I recieved by our last post but one your favor from Alexandria. Mr. Giles had before informed us you intended a visit to that city this summer, and as I flattered myself with the hope of seeing you here also, and knew that Patsy would be a material object in your visit I was only waiting to know when she would return, in order to express to you our general wish to see you, and that I would send my Phaeton to meet you at Fredericksburg at any time. From thence here is but about 75. miles. The very day I recieved your letter announcing our disappointment, I received one from Mr. Randolph letting me know they would be here by the last of the month. We are sincerely concerned that you have but one blessing and have given that to Jacob: but hope that a new shoot will grow from the old stock another year and be given to us. But, scripture and metaphor apart we should have been happy to see you during this visit to Virginia, and shall be equally so the next. Another part of your letter gave more satisfaction. We had heard that Browse had purchased a poor tract of land with a great house on it in Gloucester. By your letter it seems not so.[1] No circumstances known to me could have rendered this a prudent purchase: and I wish he would not fix himself at all till he sees more of our country. Great misconceptions are entertained of what are in truth the most fertile, healthy, and pleasant parts of this state. I hope he will advise with some of his friends who know the whole country. Mr. Giles told me he had promised this. I shall be very happy to see him here, and am sure I can be useful to him in counsel on this subject. We are made happy by Mr. Randolph's almost perfect recovery of his health by the use of the Sweet springs. The warm springs had been of no service to him.—I am become the most industrious farmer in the world: and never had reformer greater obstacles to surmount from the barbarous mode of culture and management which had been carried on. I read but little. Take no newspapers, that I may not have the tranquility of my mind disturbed by their falsehoods and follies, and I have it in contemplation next to banish pen, ink, and paper from my farm. When I pay the sheriff my taxes it is his business to furnish the reciept, and I wish to have no necessity for any other paper. The society of my family and friends is becoming more and more the sole object of my delight, and among my best friends I have ever taken the freedom of counting yourself, assuring you in return of the sincerest sentiments of esteem and respect from Dear Madam Your affectionate friend & servt   Th: Jefferson

RC (G. G. Imbert, Paris, 1950); addressed: "Mrs. Elizabeth Trist Philadelphia"; stamped. PrC (DLC).

YOUR FAVOR FROM ALEXANDRIA: Mrs.

Trist to TJ of 1 Sep. 1795, recorded in SJL as received from Alexandria on 16 Sep. 1795, but not found.

[1] Preceding sentence interlined.

To Bushrod Washington

DEAR SIR   Monticello Sep. 23. 1795.

I presume I am not mistaken in supposing that an injunction is the proper and most effectual mode of preventing a person from drowning a millseat of mine by raising his dam below it. With this view I have prepared the inclosed bill and documents, and trouble you with them to procure and send me an injunction. The defendant being very actively employed at present in raising his dam, the case was too urging for me to wait till our next court (Monday sennight) to compleat my order, on which there will be no dispute. Besides asking you to obtain the writ, there are two difficulties to be foreseen. The one that it will be disobeyed, and he will go on raising his dam. What is to be done most speedy and effectual in that case? 2. The family being absolutely pennyless, tho' they can get work done to raise their mill by hypothecating it's profits, cannot raise a shilling to pull down what they build up. What is to be done here again? That it may not be supposed I take advantage of their poverty to suppress any right they may have, I give them notice that I will advance money for them to any counsel they may think proper to employ to defend it. But if I am to furnish the expence of pulling down what they have built up and are building, it will be considerable. I pray you to send me the writ with your instructions without a moment's delay which may be avoided. I write by the post of the 25th. to Mr. Pollard to pay your fee and tax. I do not know whether this letter will go by post or by a private hand. If the latter he who delivers it will call for the answer. If by post, be pleased to send the answer by post, which leaves Richmond for Charlottesville on Monday mornings. I am with esteem Dr. Sir Your most obedt. servt   TH: JEFFERSON

PrC (MHi); at foot of text: "Bushrod Washington esq." Enclosure: Bill in Chancery on the Henderson Milldam, [24 Sep. 1795]. Other enclosures not identified, but see note below.

Bushrod Washington (1762-1829), a nephew of George Washington, was a grad-uate of the College of William and Mary and had studied law with James Wilson in Philadelphia. He practiced in Westmoreland County, Virginia, won election to the House of Delegates in 1787, and the next year sat in the convention that ratified the federal Constitution. He moved his legal practice to Alexandria in 1788 and to Richmond two years later. In 1798, John Adams appointed him an associate justice of the Supreme Court, where he served until his death (DAB; DHSC, I, pt. 1, p. 124-6).

For the INJUNCTION obtained by Washington, see note to the following document. The other DOCUMENTS sent to Washington were likely the enclosures listed at John Carr to TJ, 22 Sep. 1795. TO COMPLEAT MY ORDER: for the steps taken by TJ to obtain the permission of the Albemarle County Court, see note to Inquest on Shadwell Mill, 18 Sep. 1795.

TJ's missing letter to Robert POLLARD was probably that recorded in SJL under the date of 23 Sep. 1795 with reference to TJ's order on John Barnes for $96 "for

Mulfd. & Washingt," from which Pollard was to pay £5 to Washington for his legal FEE and £23.3.9. to one Mulford in payment of a debt of J. P. P. Derieux for which TJ was security (MB, 23 Sep. 1795; note to TJ to John Barnes, 14 Sep. 1795).

According to a law passed in 1786, an attorney representing a client in a Virginia court had to pay a TAX equal to a tenth of his fee (Hening, XII, 285).

SJL records letters from TJ to Washington of 25 Feb., 11 Mch., 7 May, and 9 July 1795, and letters from Washington to TJ of 5 Apr. and 20 July 1795, received respectively on 14 Apr. and 28 July 1795, none of which has been found.

Bill in Chancery on the Henderson Milldam

[24 Sep. 1795]

To George Wythe Judge of the High Court of Chancery of Virginia humbly complaining Sheweth your orator Thomas Jefferson of the County of Albemarle, that he is and upwards of thirty years[1] has been seized[2] by devise from Peter Jefferson his father of a tract of land in the said County on both sides of Rivanna river and including the bed thereof on the north side of which river and on the said lands was a water grist mill erected by his said father under Authority from the Court of the County And standing when your Orator succeeded to the Estate: That the said mill together with the dam on which it depended for water after remaining 16 or 17 years was carried away by the extraordinnary flood which happened in the year 1771[3] and your Orator believing that by extending his Canal about $\frac{3}{4}$ of a mile above the mill[4] he Could draw his supply of water from above a natural ridge of rocks which would render a dam unnessary, accordingly undertook the said work, but it proving a very heavy one, the public troubles which soon and long afterwards prevailed, and the public Calls on your Orator to be absent from the state and from home, interrupted and prevented the progress of the work, so that though your Orator obtained due Authority from the Court for rebuilding the said mill and the work was repeatedly resumed dureing the short intervals of his return to and stay at home,[5] it has never yet been entirely finished, but in the Course of these several renewals of labour, the new part of the Canal of about 1100 yards in length has been dug to about $\frac{3}{4}$th of its sufficient depth as he Conjectures, and that, as nearly as he Can now estimate partly from his own recollection and partly from that of others about 6000 single days labour have been employed on it; exclusive of the raising by gun powder about 12000 Cubical feet of a rock too hard to be removed by any other agent and too vainy to be removed by that but to uncommon disadvantage: that having lately determined to go on with and Complete the said work, he has applied to the County Court of Albemarle for a renewal of his authority to do so, and the said Court having ordered a Jury as directed by law in Cases where, as in the present one the petitioner holds the lands on both sides of the stream through the whole Course of the works proposed and of the reflux of the water, and for some distance above and below them the jury have found the inquest a Copy of which is annexed as an exhibit to this bill.[6]

And your Orator further sheweth that dureing the time of his absences aforesaid towit in the year 1780 when he was Confined by public duty to a [residence in Williamsburg] after he had done the greater part of the work aforesaid and while the order of Court hereto annexed as an exhibit for rebuilding the said mill, was in full force[7] a Certain Bennett Henderson holding the lands next below him on the South side of the said river, undertook to erect a mill on the lands of the said Bennett and to make a dam across the river at a place Called the mountain falls, abuting on the opposite side on the lands of Thomas M Randolph, which he accordingly did of his own authority, without having obtained from the Court their permission according to law, as appears[8] by the Certificate of the Clerk of the said Court hereto annexed, and without notice given to your Orator, or any one authorised to act for him, as required by law, which would have enabled him to have shewn the injury he should sustain thereby and to Contest before the Court the building of said mill, in the manner it is built; And so little regardful was the said Bennett of law or justice that he entered on the lands of your Orator in his absence without his knowledge or permission or that of any person having authority from him and carried from the bank opposite to your Orators mill site the stone destined and reserved by your Orator for building his own mill house, and with the said stone the said Bennett erected his dam—that tho the said mountain falls afforded between the upper and lower land lines of the said Bennett and within the extent of a few perch a fall of water sufficient to have worked a better mill, yet the said Bennett so placed his mill as to avail himself as your Orator has been informed and believes of little more than half his fall and then erected a dam of such height that the back water which had not formerly approached within 20 poles of your Orators mill below, (its level being just so much lower than the bottom of his wheel as to leave it clear in its motion, except[9] in Considerable swells in the river) was raised about 18 inches or two feet above its former level, and was made to flow about 28 poles[10] above his said mill so that it would have drowned his wheel at Ordinary times if rebuilt of the same diamiter, or have obliged him to[11] lessen its diamiter and lose so much of the benefit of his fall of water, and moreover it drowned and rendered impassible a ford at your Orators mill, at which his Customers from the south side of the river usally passed over to his said mill: that floods and other accidents had since sensibly worn down the said dam of the Defendants and lessoned in a small degree the injury to your Orator: that the said Bennett Henderson has departed this life without will leaving the Defendants John, William, Sally, James, Charles, Isham, Bennett, Hilsborough, Eliza, Frances, Lucy and Nancy Crawford Henderson his children heirs and parceners of his said lands and the said Jno. hath taken out administration of his estate: That your Orator from an unwillingness to have any Contest with neighbours had hitherto taken no steps to obtain redress of the injuries done him but the said John has been lately not only repairing the said dam with a view to grind for Country Custom as heretofore, but as your Orator is informed and believes proposes to raise it two or three feet above its former level in order to fit her the better for the manufacture of flour, a degree of injury to which your Orator Can no longer forbear opposition for he expressly[12] Charges that every inch which the water of the said river has been or shall be raised above what was its ancient level, at the joint boundary of your Orator and the Defendants before the erection of either mill[13] is and will be so much taken from him, and is, and will be so much to the detriment of his mill seat, and takes and will take from him so much of the fall of water which taking place entirely within the lands of your Orator, and where the bed of the river is his by the purchase of his ancestors and the public grant to them, is as much a part of his right as the lands within which the falls happens and is and was a valuable part of the purchase and grant; that the right to the said fall of water has been further fixed in your Orator and his ancestors by prior use and occupation, and tho an interruption of the use has taken place for some time thro' the accidents of floods, of Civil troubles of wars and other unavoidable necessities, yet it has never been abandoned by your Orator, but on the Contrary hath been kept up by efforts renewed from time to time by your Orator with great expence and labour[14] evidenceing your Orators Continual Claim and determination to preserve and to use for himself the whole benefit of his own water fall; that the same Could not be justly taken from him nor encroached on, nor have the Defendants any right in law or equity to take or to keep them, but the Continuance of their said dam above the ancient level of the [water] at the joint boundary between your Orator and the Defendants, and the raising it still higher as has been proposed and begun by them or some of them is Contrary to equity and right.

And your Orator further sets forth that there is now living a Certain Thomas Morgan who was employed as miller for your Orator at his said mill from about the 1766 or 1767 till her destruction in 1771[15] and has Continued to live ever since on the lands adjoining to the said mill who is better acquainted than any other person living with the ancient level of the water at or about the said mill, and at the joint boundary of your Orator and the Defendants and with the highest point below the said mill to which the water reflowed before the erecting of the defendants dam, that the said Morgan is near or about ninety years of age as he himself stated, and as your Orator believes from strong Circumstances[16] and is extremely weak and infirm and not likely to live to the trial of any issue whatsoever which may be thought necessary for the final settlement of your Orators right, and that the benefit of his evidence which might be lost to your Orator by his death before his examination Could not be fully supplied as he believes by that of any other person living.

In Tender Consideration whereof and for as much as your Orator is most properly and effectually relieveable in the premises in this Court, within whose province it pecularly is to Cause a discontinuance of the injuries now existing, to prevent a renewal and aggravation of them, and to preserve to him the benefit of the testimony before mentioned: And to the end that the said Defendants may on their Corporal oaths true and perfect answer make to all and singular the premises as specifically and fully as [if] the same were here again repeated by way of interrogatory and more especially that they may declare whether the mill of your Orator was not erected prior to theirs? whether a great part of your Orators new Canal was not dug before the erection of their mill?[17] whether this mill was not erected without legal authority and especially without any notice given to your Orator as aforesaid as required by law to enable him to establish a true state of his rights, whether the back water before the erection of this dam approached within a Considerable and what distance of your Orators mill tail and wheel, whether their dam as it has stood heretofore did not raise the water Considerably and how much at the mill tail of your Orator and for some and what distance[18] above it? Whether it has not rendered it necessary for your Orator to raise the bottom of his wheel in rebuilding and Consequently to loose so much of his fall? whether the whole of the fall so to be taken from your Orator does not take place entirely and far within the lands of your Orator? And not the smallest part of it adjacent to their lands? whether it has not also drowned and rendered too deep for use the ford at your Orators mill? whether they or some and what of them have not begun to repair their said mill dam, and do not propose to raise it still higher than it was and to overflow still more the mill site of your Orator? whether the facts set forth with respect to the said Thomas Morgan are not true? for these purposes your Orator prays that you will be pleased to grant to him the writs of this Court of Subpoena and Injunction to be directed to the said John, Wm., Sally, James, Charles, Isham, Bennett Hilsborough, Eliza, Frances, Lucy and Nancy Crawford Henderson, children heirs and parceners of the said Bennett Henderson deceased and to each of them their agents and others Concerned in the premises Commanding them to be and appear in this Court on a Certain day and under a Certain penalty therein to be named then and there to answer the premises and to abide such decree as shall be therein made, and in the mean time enjoining them immediately and perpetually to desist from further proceedings to raise and reflow their back water on the said mill seat of your Orator and Commanding them to abate and draw down so much of their dam already erected as raises the water above its antient and natural level as it stood before the erection of either mill, at the joint boundary of your Orator and the Defendants And to authorise your Orator to take in due form and de bene esse the deposition of the said Thomas Morgan and to preserve the same of record in this Court in perpetuam rei memoriam and granting to your Orator such further and other relief as to this Court shall seem agreeable to equity and Your Orator as in duty bound will ever pray &c.

Th Jefferson

Tr (ViU: Carr Papers); 19th-century transcript, part of record of TJ v. Michie in the hand of George Carr, with several words omitted by copyist supplied in brackets from Dft; undated, but assigned on the basis of subjoined attestation in Carr's hand, dated 24 Sep. 1795, of Thomas Bell as justice of the peace, who attests that TJ appeared before him and swore that the allegations in the bill of complaint were true to the best of his knowledge; at head of text: "Exhibit No. 2." Dft (MHi); undated, but begun before 22 Sep. 1795 (see note 8 below); consists of heavily emended text entirely in TJ's hand; significant variations from Tr are recorded in notes below; endorsed by TJ: "Henderson John & al. in Chancery"; note below endorsement by TJ:

"Saml. McGehee ⎱ were the persons who took stone from my George Thomas ⎰ seat, with Henderson's people."

Enclosures: (1) Inquest on Shadwell Mill, 18 Sep. 1795. (2) Enclosures Nos. 1 and 3 listed at John Carr to TJ, 22 Sep. 1795. Enclosed in TJ to Bushrod Washington, 23 Sep. 1795.

In response to TJ's bill of complaint—which noted that Bennett Henderson was required by a 1748 act to have OBTAINED FROM THE COURT THEIR PERMISSION before building his mill (Hening, VI, 55-60)—George Wythe, judge of the High Court of Chancery, issued WRITS . . . OF SUBPOENA AND INJUNCTION to the Henderson heirs.

First, on 10 Oct. 1795 the Court granted an injunction "To restrain the defendants their agent and attorney and all other persons from further proceeding to raise and reflow their backwater on the mill seat of the plaintiff on the Rivanna until the further order of this court" (PrC of Tr in MHi; entirely in TJ's hand, including certification by clerk of the court Peter Tinsley; letterpressed perpendicularly on verso of subpoena described below). As TJ had requested, on 10 Oct. 1795 the Court also authorized "the examination of Thomas Morgan de bene esse" (Tr in ViU: Carr Papers; 19th-century transcript, part of record of TJ v. Michie in the hand of George Carr); for Morgan's DEPOSITION, see TJ to the Heirs of Bennett Henderson, 7 Nov. 1795. On 12 Oct. 1795 the Court issued a subpoena to the sheriff of Albemarle County ordering him to summon the children and heirs to appear in the High Court of Chancery in Richmond on the first day of the next court to answer the bill brought against them by TJ (PrC of Tr in MHi; entirely in TJ's hand, including Tinsley's certification).

¹ Preceding four words interlined in Dft in place of "a long time."
² Dft here adds "in fee simple."
³ Digit reworked from "2" in Dft.
⁴ In Dft TJ first wrote "by digging a new canal $\frac{3}{4}$ of a mile in length" and then altered it to read as above.
⁵ In Dft TJ here canceled "since that time, and was in the course of them about three fourths completed."
⁶ In Dft TJ here canceled "and made a part of it. The said court granted your orator a renewal of his authority to rebuild his mill as will appear by the [their] order of the said court a copy whereof is likewise annexed to this bill."
⁷ Passage "after he had" to this point lacking in Dft.
⁸ Dft here reads "is proved," which is interlined with the remainder of the clause in place of "your Orator has understood and believes (tho' he does not undertake to affirm the fact particularly having no other authority for the same but the common fame of the neighborhood)." TJ made this revision on the basis of John Carr's letter to him of 22 Sep. 1795.
⁹ In Dft TJ interlined the passage from "just so much" to this point in place of "his backwater flowed up to the which formerly did not reach within a considerable distance of your orator's mill, nor reach the bottom of his wheel but."
¹⁰ Preceding word and figures interlined in Dft in place of "an hundred yards."
¹¹ Next to this word in margin of Dft TJ wrote "safe use."
¹² Preceding sixteen words interlined in Dft in place of "and, as your orator is informed and believes [. . .] to repair the same, whereas your orator expressly."
¹³ Preceding eighteen words interlined in Dft in place of "natural level at the joint boundary of the plaintiff and defendant."
¹⁴ Preceding two words lacking in Dft.
¹⁵ Digit reworked from "2" in Dft.
¹⁶ Preceding three words lacking in Dft.
¹⁷ Dft lacks this question.
¹⁸ Preceding four words interlined in Dft in place of "a hundred yards."

From Richard Harrison

SIR   Treasury Department Auditors Office Sept. 28. 1795

Having lately received and examined the Accounts of Mr. Grand, Banker at Paris, I have extracted from them such Charges as appear proper against you; a Statement of which I now do myself the honor to transmit for your Inspection; and on which I should be glad to receive any observations you may find necessary.

Besides the Amount of this statement Mr. Grand charges the United States with Livrs. 18,392.^{tt}5.6, being, as he says, the Balance of your private Account; but as this sum is not noticed in the Account furnished by you I do not conceive myself authorized to pass it either to your debit or to his credit without your approbation. You will therefore be pleased to say how it is to be disposed of.

The Charges against you being once adjusted, I see no obstacle to a final settlement of your Accounts, except what may arise on the following points.

1st. The *Outfit* which you claim. However reasonable and just this may be in itself, as it was not sanctioned by any existing Law at the time, I much doubt the Competency of the Treasury officers to allow it.

2d. The *Period* to which your salary is continued. Besides the three Months for returning home, you extend it to the day on which you entered on the duties of Secretary of State. Under the *Old* Resolutions of Congress a Minister was entitled to Salary only to the time of receiving Notice of his Recal, and for three Months after. Some particular Circumstances, however, may attend your case of which I am ignorant; and if so, you will be good enough to inform me of them.

3d. House Rent. This was allowed under the old Regulations, but as the Law now stands it is understood, I believe, to be covered by the Outfit.

My view, Sir, in mentioning these difficulties is that Measures (if found ultimately necessary) may be taken for their Removal by an Act of the Legislature; and in case you address any particular Gentleman of that body on the subject, it might, perhaps, be of use for him to see me before the business is brought forward.

The Accounts of Mr. Adams are nearly in the same situation of yours. I have the honor to be, with sentiments of great Respect, Sir Your obedient and very hble Servant   R. HARRISON

P.S. By the Notes among your papers I observe you are possessed of some Vouchers for the purchase of Medals. These would be of use to me in the adjustment of some Accounts now in hand.

RC (DLC); at foot of text: "Thomas Jefferson Esq"; endorsed by TJ as received 6 Oct. 1795 and so recorded in SJL. Enclosure not found.

FINAL SETTLEMENT OF YOUR ACCOUNTS: see Editorial Note on the settlement of Jefferson's accounts as minister plenipotentiary in France, at 8 July 1792.

To William Alexander

SIR   Monticello Sep. 29. 95

According to the desire expressed in your note by Dr. Currie I have now lodged at Colo. Bell's in Charlottesville 3. casks of nails to be forwarded to Staunton to the care of Gamble & Grattan by any waggon which may be passing, or to be delivered or otherwise disposed of at your order. The contents of the casks, and cost carried to your debet are noted below. As it is impossible to make casks to hold exactly a given quantity, and it is necessary they should be exactly full, to bear transportation, we were obliged to put into the cask of Xs. more than you had ordered. Observe that we endeavor to make our VIIIs. 10. ℔ to the M̅. Xs. 13 ℔. XVI. 20. ℔. XXs. 25. ℔. as nearly as we can. You did not mention the size of the brads; but I took for granted they were for flooring, and made them XVIs. which when flatpointed we find better than the sharppointed XXd. brad, and they come cheaper. I am with esteem Sir Your most obedt. servt   TH: JEFFERSON

	℔			£ s d
1. cask	208	VIIId. nails @	11½ d	9–19–4
1 do.	60.	Xs.	11d.	2–15–0
1. do.	⎰ 40.	XVI.	10d.	1–13–4
	⎱ 50.	XX	9½ d	1–19–7
	3. casks @ 1/			– 3–
				16–10–3

PrC (ViHi); at foot of text: "Mr. Alexander. calf pasture"; endorsed in ink by TJ on verso.

Alexander's NOTE BY DR. CURRIE has not been found. SJL records a letter, not found, from TJ to Alexander of 8 Sep. 1795.

From William Short

DEAR SIR   Madrid Sept. 30. 1795

I wrote you two letters from St. Yldefonso under the dates of the 2d. and 3d. of this month—the first was sent to Mr. Yznardi to be forwarded directly to you—the second was sent by duplicate under cover to the Sec. of State. My stay at St. Yldefonso was prolonged until within these few days contrary to my expectation when I last wrote to you. During this time I have recieved the duplicate and triplicate of your friendly letter of May 25th. last—the original of which came to my hands as I informed you, on the 1st. inst. I am additionally obliged by the trouble you were so good as to take of sending several copies of this letter. I will for greater security send the present also both by Lisbon and Cadiz, with directions for it to be put into the post office at the port where it may arrive in the U.S.

I have written to the Sec. of State in several of my late letters and particularly in that of Sep. 3. covering mine of the same date to you, on the subject of my funds in his hands and requesting him to turn them over to you, in order to relieve him from the trouble in the midst of his public occupations and that they might be employed by you under the general power of attorney I had formerly sent You. I hope before this gets to you you will have heard from the Sec. of State on the subject and particularly in forwarding to you the letter I sent under his cover. I am extremely desirous that you should have these funds at your disposition. It has been already an extreme inconvenience and loss to me that they should have been kept for me in America instead of being deposited at Amsterdam as were the funds of the other foreign agents—but it would have been still worse if I had been forced to recieve them here in depreciated paper money according to the first plan of the Sec. of State with M. de Jaudenes. The Sec. of State wrote me that his plan was to accomodate Colo. Humphreys—and therefore he took the arrangement with Jaudenes—this is not the first instance in which both my interest and my reputation have been sacrificed by the Government in order to accomodate others—and I am really every day more and more at a loss to concieve why I should be treated in the unjust and partial manner that I have been by a Government that is supposed to have no affection or favoritism for its guide. At the time that I am treated in this manner the letters which I have recieved as well from the department of State as the Treasury inform me of the President's extreme satisfaction with my conduct &c. &c. &c.—and these compliments have been followed invariably wherever an opportunity has offered, by such measures towards me on the part of the Government as tended directly to humiliate and dishonor a public agent in my position. But why do I trouble you on this subject—it is more proper for our personal and unreserved conferences, in which I shall surprize you in renumerating some of the acts of the Government towards me. If the object has been to force me out of this place in order to make way for a favorite, whom they will clothe with a more honorable character and greater emoluments, as I do not doubt, they have perfectly succeeded. Would to Heaven they had been so kind as to have put me into their secret—they would have gained time and have saved me a duration of my anxiety—and avoided the odious measure of disgracing an agent, whom they have been constantly flattering for the punctuality and ability of his conduct. The measure of sending

Mr. Pinckney could not but be disgraceful to me and of this the Sec. of State was so much aware that he has practised with me, to call things by their true names, a degree of *duplicity and deception* that I am at a loss to account for. Would you suppose it possible that until Mr. Pinckney's arrival here, I never knew or suspected the true cause of his being sent, notwithstanding the letters I had recieved from the Sec. of State *ex officio* on the subject. I shall keep his correspondence with me as a monument of what I will not characterize. His first letter to me on the subject was dated Nov. 9. 94. He pays me a great many compliments and says the President has taken this determination in order to mark in a solemn way the sensations excited in him by the delay of this Court, and to satisfy the People of Kentuckey—&c. Under this idea I remained until Mr. Pinckney arrived—he then shewed me the letter of the Sec. of State to him in which he says expressly, the cause of the business being taken out of my hands is the letter which he incloses him and the conference thereon. This letter was from Jaudenes to the Sec. of State dated Aug. 16. 94.—in which he says he is ordered by the King to complain of Mr. Carmichael, and states my conduct also as not *muy circonspecta*, and desires another person to be sent to terminate the negotiation. On this letter the Sec. of State had a conference with Jaudenes who said that he did not know the cause of the dissatisfaction with me, but conjectured I was disagreeable as being the author of a memorial whilst Chargé des affaires at Paris, which had displeased this court. (This memorial was my letter to Montmorin on the navigation of the Misisipi written by your order whilst Sec. of State and couched in the terms that Montmorin desired and approved.) Thus the Sec. of State gives me one reason for Pinckney's being sent here—and to Pinckney a different one. Jaudenes's letter to him was the 16th. of Aug.—he wrote to me fully on the 18th. of Aug.—and did not say a single word of Jaudenes's denunciation—and was silent respecting it until he wrote to Pinckney in Nov. last. Whilst he thus concealed this denunciation from me instead of communicating it to me that I might clear it up, he sends it to Pinckney to shew to me, and so far from keeping it to himself and Pinckney, he has the letter of Jaudenes copied by one of his clerks and the conference thereon by another—so that he, two of his clerks, Jaudenes and all his confidents know of this denunciation against me, and another person being sent here by the President to supplant me, that is to say that I am disgraced and dishonored in the knowlege and opinion of these people, without the Sec. of State, even communicating to me this false denunciation. Whilst my reputation is thus wantonly committed by the Sec. of State to the discretion of his clerks and of Jaudenes he is informing me how tender he is of my feelings and that the Presidents message in nominating Mr. Pinckney shall leave no doubt of the approbation of my conduct. He mentions in a subsequent letter that he will send me that message—but this according to custom he forgot—and the two Philadelphia newspapers of Nov. and Dec. which have come here shew that it was not printed. It remains probably buried and unnoticed in the archives of the Senate, whilst Mr. Pinckney's supermission is public and proclames my disgrace, as those who do not know of the President's message, will probably not suspect that if my conduct was approved of, the President would deprive the U.S. at a critical and distressing moment of the services of their Minister at London and subject them to the heavy expense of sending and supporting him and his suite here. But this is not all the inconvenience—the whole of the last winter has been lost by this means to the U.S. Mr. Pinckney arrived here the 28th. of June—and circumstances were more favorable to the U.S. during the last winter than they are now or ever can be again. At that time this Court thought our treaty with England, an advantageous one to the U.S. and a final settlement of all differences with that country—they now know the contrary. They were then at war with France—they are now at peace—and at this moment the Env. Extr. is willing to accept and probably will accept such an arrangement with this Country, as it would seem to me the U.S. would certainly not have accepted during the last winter—and which I certainly as their agent would not accept even now. So much for the conduct of our wise administration in the arrangement of this business. Advantages have been lost for the U.S.— and this Government have trifled and fooled with them as long as they could and will end by settling the business in their own way—they will agree to the limits—promise the navigation which they will keep or not according to circumstances and adjourn any satisfaction for spoliations to the *Calendrier Grec*. I had almost forgotten to mention to you that on seeing the copy of the letter of Jaudenes denouncing my conduct, I had an explanation with the First Minister. He assured me in presence of Mr. Pinckney that he had recieved no such directions as to me, but as to Mr. Carmichael—he said on the contrary that he was ready and willing to continue and complete the negotiation with me &c. &c. I sent him a copy of Jaudenes's letter—and he has informed me in the name of the King by letter, their satisfaction with me and my conduct. Thus you see I have been dishonored—the U.S. put to a considerable expence— the whole of the last winter, and consequently the advantages it presented for this negotiation, lost on the vague, unauthorized, and calumnious denunciation, of an unknown, ignorant and impertinent puppy, who has probably been taught by M. de Gardoqui, this means of taking revenge—for the complaint made against him by your order of June

93.—and for this business having been to M. de Gardoqui's mortification, transferred from his hands to those of the Duke de la Alcudia.

But to quit this subject and proceed to the subjects of your letter—most of which I touched on in mine of the 2 and 3d inst. As to the laying out more money in the augmentation of the Indian camp tract—or in clearing that already purchased, I should according to my judgment prefer a suspension thereof, unless the annual income thereby should become a greater rate per cent on the money laid out—viz. if by clearing, tenants sure and solid could be got to take it. Indeed I did not suppose before recieving your letter that tenants could be got at all—but I see there are four on my land and one of them good—if such as he could be got, so as to yield say 5. per cent per annum sure and clear, on the purchase money I should like even a larger sum to be placed—but I suppose it difficult if not impossible to find many such tenants in that part of the country. As to canal shares I concieved them a safe and advantageous placement and particularly by having some shares in different well-chosen canals. I find from M. Pinckney that he does not concieve this will be a productive revenue to the *actionnaires*, though he considers it very advantageous to the public—and as the James River shares were selling at 18/. in the pound, or 10. per cent below par, it would seem that the productiveness was questionable there. Yet I am well pleased with having some of the shares—you mention having purchased 20. and an intention to purchase more—I know not the quantum of each share—and of course know not how much has been placed in that way—but unless you should be of an opposite opinion, I shall be satisfied not to add to those shares which shall have been already purchased. Should more canal purchases be made, I should prefer some in the Potowmac—and some in the Norfolk canal—I observe this mentioned in Coxe's review of the U.S.—I suppose it advanced towards its completion at present. However under present circumstances I should be as willing to postpone any further vestments until I shall return to America unless in something that produced already an annual rent equal to that of the funds sold. As the interest of the funds is paid quarterly and regularly—if it be immediately vested in more funds also productive, it is a kind of compound interest that must increase the capital rapidly—the only objection is my having too great a proportion of my all, in paper.

I am much obliged to Colo. Skipwith for having given you the information respecting Griffin's debt. I know not how I came to have a claim against Griffin—it must have been by some transaction between Colo. Skipwith and him. I must have been extremely and inconcievably negligent in my affairs on leaving America, as I am quite ignorant of many particulars. But I recollect having originally nothing in any way with Griffin. I left my affairs first in B. Harrison's hands—and from him Colo. Skipwith received them, and managed them until he turned them over to Donald. Colo. Skipwith has written to me at different times that he should send me a statement of his gestion—but this he has never done and for some years has not written to me at all. I left with B. Harrison the military certificates I had received from Harvie I think they amounted to £5140. There was cash also to be received from Harvie for my negroes—a small sum 100.£. I think to be received from J. Mayo for an horse sold—and about 40£ from R. Randolph of Curles. I have never known what part of these sums B. Harrison had recovered—nor what sum Colo. Skipwith recieved from him. Browne sent me an account of the certificates he received from Colo. Skipwith, but I think he mentioned there were more to be received from him, at the time he wrote me. It is probable there will never be any settlement of what passed previously to Browne's or Donald's being employed unless after my return to America. From that time as they are accustomed to account-keeping, and as the business became more simple the gestion will be clear, and indeed I suppose Browne's accounts state it fully. I did not understand from your letter of Dec. 23. 93. that this had been done at that time, as you mention there the doubts as to certain items. I hope you afterwards procured from Browne the explanation of these as it was then your intention to ask them. From your same letter I suppose also that Browne had not rendered you an account of the sums he had recieved from Colo. Skipwith for me or of his gestion up to that date—viz. in what manner the sums he turned over to you, were produced—but merely turned over the sums. Would it not be well to ask from him an account of his gestion? If so I will thank you to do it—and as he will certainly have this account on his books, it will be only giving him the trouble to transcribe it. You wrote me on your leaving Philadelphia the sum in certificates which you then had enregistered in my name, and that you should leave a broker to act as to the interest accruing, which you are so good as to render immediately productive, as your last letter informs me and for which I cannot too warmly and sincerely express to you my thanks. I beg you to continue the same with such funds as remain in the state of producing interest. As I mentioned above I am willing that what I now hold should remain in that state, from this consideration, as it must increase the capital considerably and rapidly and requires less trouble than any other kind of property and I am really ashamed of the trouble I give you at any rate—and I hope you will believe me when I assure you, that a great source of satisfaction which I derive from it is the proof which it is to me of your friendship. I regret much having not asked you to send me, the address of the broker you employ at Philadelphia, as it would have been very convenient to me to have had some person there to whom I could apply—on different occasions, such as sending me newspapers—the reports of the officers of State &c. &c. I should by this means have certainly had the possibility of procuring one way or another the message of the President nominating Mr. Pinckney here and the expressions of which the Sec. of State says will be so agreeable to me. I have never yet seen it, though the Sec. thinks he has sent it. It is the same as to newspapers—he sends huge packets of them by fits and starts, to London, where they are deposed and will remain forever, notwithstanding I have written to him that he might as well send them to Canton in China—but it would seem as if in his geography London and Madrid were two sea-ports near to each other. Although I shall have no occasion now for the broker in this way yet it will be useful to me to have such a person, in other respects as long as I remain in Europe—and at this moment I should be glad to know him in order to send to him my letters for you, as they would probably go surer in that way. I will thank you therefore to be so good as to send me his address, under cover either to our Minister or Consul at Paris— or our Minister or Mr. Donald in London. It will probably be a convenience to me also whilst at Paris to know the amount of funds at my disposition in Philadelphia, and I should be much obliged to you therefore to send me, or direct the broker to send me the statement thereof. I imagine he renders you quarterly accounts as his reciepts are quarterly. I will thank you to continue to give him your directions as usual, notwithstanding his sending me this statement, as I shall give him no directions for acting, but shall take the liberty of troubling you to ask your counsel in the case of wishing them to be disposed of in any other way. I observe by some late newspapers recieved from the ports that there is a bank at Philadelphia, which was the first established, and that it is more sought after than that of the U.S.—as the shares are more above par than the latter. I regret now having not asked the Sec. of State to place my 9000 dollars in this bank, as it has a quality which I like much, being as I suppose not connected with Government as the bank of the U.S. is. When I wrote to ask the Sec. of State to have this sum delivered to you, or placed by himself, one great object with me was that the placement might be made without a moment's longer delay so as that by beginning to produce an interest, it might indemnify me for the interest I was obliged to pay on the sums taken up for my purchases and expenses here. I fear however that this object was not attained, as the letter of the Sec. of State informed me in Nov. 94. that he had placed *3000* dollars—his letter of Feb. 25. 95. is the first which mentions the rest having been placed—he says there he had previously informed me of the completion of this placement—but in this he was mistaken, as his previous letter mentioned only the *3000* dollars—but the Sec.'s correspondence is full of these kinds of errors on public affairs as well as private, which have on several occasions given me much perplexity and embarassment, and I find I am not the only diplomatic correspondent who complains of him on this account. I shall be extremely happy to learn that he has turned over to you the funds he holds for me and I regret extremely having not desired him to deliver to you the 9000. dollars—but at that time I was uncertain what would be done on their subject, as the bill had been drawn by Jaudenes payable here. I shall at any rate be a considerable loser by the Sec. of State having undertaken to dispose of these funds instead of giving them to you, as in the latter case the interest accruing on the funds you would have had purchased, would have been rendered productive, whereas I cannot expect the Sec. of State will have taken that trouble.

So much for my cash affairs. There is another part of my business in which I have been also negligent. I was to recieve from Harvie certain Western Lands (viz. $\frac{2}{3}$ of 15,000 acres, $\frac{1}{3}$ was to go to Colo. J. Campbell—for locating)—and 1000 acres of Green sea land. I remember that Harvie and myself drew articles of agreement in Richmond—by which he was to convey to me the patents of these Western and Eastern lands—but I am ashamed to own that I know not what became of these articles of agreement. I suppose the copy belonging to me was left with B. Harrison, and was probably taken up from him by Colo. Skipwith—but whether he or my brother, or who has it I know not. I should esteem it a favor if you would be so good as to enquire about this of Colo. Skipwith or Harvie—it might not be proper perhaps to let the latter know my ignorance of what has become of the articles of agreement. I should be glad also to know whether these lands have been located or what has been done. As to the western I wrote to my brother a long time ago, but he probably never got my letter as in one he has since written to me, he makes no mention of the subject—he would be the best hand to manage this business of the western lands, and I should write to him if I did not despair of my letter getting to his hands as I find those I have written have miscarried—but if he should perchance come into Virginia, or chance should throw him in your way I will thank you to repeat to him my request already made that he should act and settle matters with Colo. Campbell as to our undivided interests in these lands, as he shall judge proper. It would be necessary they should be looked after in some way.[1] As to the Eastern lands I know not how to come at any knowlege respecting them unless it should be from Harvie himself, from whom I imagine it is proper to know whether he is ready and able to convey the patent. (At the time I purchased it was not patented).

I would thank you to inform me, if you know, and if not, to enquire whether Harvie is satisfied with the land &c. I sold him and whether he has kept it or sold it again.

Some two or three years after its date a letter from Mazzei found its way to me here—it with several others had been detained for me at the Hague by poor old doting Dumas more than two years before he thought of giving them to Mr. Adams a long time after his arrival at the Hague. Mazzei's was principally to cover one for you—as it was old and bulky I at first hesitated whether I ought to subject you to the postage—but on the whole I have determined to inclose it to the Sec. of State, who will forward it to you from Phila.

You have no doubt heard of Malaspina the Spanish circumnavigator. He is now preparing the account of his late voyage—it will be some time I fear before it will be printed and published. He is a great admirer of your principles and writings—your notes on Virginia are he tells me his *vade mecum*. As a tribute of his attachment he gave me for you a great variety of highland rice properly and securely done up in different parcels in a tin cannister and with a short memorial on the subject of this grain. I sent it to the Sec. of State last winter in the cannister to be forwarded to you. I hope you will have received it—but on further enquiry on this business since M. Pinckney's arrival here, I fear this species will not answer in our climate from the want of the constant rains which support it in Asia. I observe however that Coxe in his view of the U.S. says the highland rice has been used on the Ohio. It would be more precious than gold if it should succeed in the U.S.

Cortez's letters were as I informed you sent by Mr. Carmichael with his books to Cadiz. As you have not received them, Blake probably did not carry them from thence. The widow who went to Cadiz to embark promised me, in that case to carry this book and send it to you as she knew her husband destined it for you. If you should not have received it yet, you would do well to write to Blake who will certainly be acquainted with Mrs. Carmichael and easily procure it for you. I have found it absolutely impossible to procure another edition here—and indeed this was obtained as I mentioned to you by the meerest accident—there is certainly not another to be had in all Spain.

I mentioned to you in my last having sent my resignation to the President—how happy would it have been for me if I had never accepted this fatal mission—the result of which is that after spending the best years of my life, after having literally grown grey in the service of my country,

I return there with the stigma arising from the conduct of the President towards me in this last instance more particularly, though in other instances also—and with a sense of injustice on the part of a man I was disposed to admire as being just and free from favoritism and prejudice (for nobody wished to believe this more than I did)—and dis-gusted with the ungenerous uncandid and deceptive double conduct of an administration under which I am to pass the rest of my life—how different would have been my feelings—how different my satisfaction with myself—my country—and its Government if meer bare justice and impartiality had been exercised towards me, instead of compliments on one hand followed by injustice and disgrace on the other. Would to Heaven I were the only sufferer—but this double, delaying, and I may say inattentive and ignorant conduct of administration in the negotiation with Spain has lost the advantages of a crisis which will never recur to so great a degree—and which if properly employed would have put us in the way of securing an admission to commerce with the Floridas and Spanish islands—and would have enabled the U.S. in being the mediator between France and Spain, to have operated perhaps a great change in the colonial-commercial system of both, so far as concerns their respective W. India islands—and have given the U.S. a joint admission with them therein as to commerce.

You state in your letter of May 25. the cause of my not having the mission at Paris. The cause you mention would give rise to a great many reflexions on my part, which I suppress—but if that were really the cause I may add it is a strong proof of the avidity with which the President caught at what might exclude me, and if that had not presented itself, he would certainly have found out or made some other. Certainly none could be weaker or less valid than that you mention—viz. a regular complaint against me by Le Brun. Before the late nomination for France, Le Brun had been executed as an enemy to his Country, and all his friends executed or driven into exile by those who then held the reins of Government. Can it be reasonably supposed that[2] any complaint made by Le Brun, would have been an objection in the eyes of those to whom the President sent the late minister Plenipo:—can it be supposed for a moment that the President would have considered this circumstance an objection if he had wished to appoint me? On the contrary if Morris had been in my situation the President would have thought Le Brun's complaint, a favorable circumstance in the eyes of those who then governed. Besides he had time to communicate to me, and justice required that he should have done it Le Brun's complaint—that I might have justified myself. Pardon so long a letter. It is the last I shall write you from hence. Mr. Pinckney expects to terminate his business in a few days—and we shall go to Paris together. I leave Mr. Rutledge, his Secretary, as my *locum tenens* until my successor shall arrive. I beg you my dear Sir to let me hear from you as soon as you recieve this—and believe me unalterably your friend & servant   W: SHORT

RC (DLC); at foot of first page: "Mr. Jefferson. Monticello"; endorsed by TJ and recorded in SJL as received 27 Feb. 1796. PrC (PHi).

THE LETTER WHICH HE INCLOSES HIM AND THE CONFERENCE THEREON: see the enclosures printed at Edmund Randolph to TJ, 28 Aug. 1794. The PRESIDENTS MESSAGE to the Senate of 21 Nov. 1794 nominating Thomas Pinckney as envoy extraordinary to Spain expressed "full confidence" in Short as minister resident in Madrid (Fitzpatrick, *Writings*, XXXIV, 39). FIRST MINISTER: Manuel Godoy, Duque de la Alcudia, the Spanish first secretary. YOUR ORDER OF JUNE 93: TJ to William Carmichael and William Short, 30 June 1793.

COXE'S REVIEW: see enclosure listed at Tench Coxe to TJ, 20 Mch. 1795. THE BROKER YOU EMPLOY: John Barnes. BANK AT PHILADELPHIA: the Bank of North America. The LETTER FROM MAZZEI was presumably his missive to TJ of 11 Feb. 1793 (see TJ to Philip Mazzei, 31 Jan. 1796, and note). Because of a loss of official favor after his return to Spain, Alejandro MALASPINA did not publish his account of his exploits (Donald C. Cutter, *Malaspina & Galiano: Spanish Voyages to the Northwest Coast, 1791 & 1792* [Seattle, 1991], 137-9). LATE NOMINATION FOR FRANCE: see note to James Monroe to TJ, 27 May 1794.

[1] Preceding sentence interlined.
[2] MS: "than."

To Bushrod Washington

DEAR SIR   Monticello Oct. 1. 1795.

Some months ago a subpoena in Chancery at the suit of Mr. Banks was served on me *as former governor of Virginia*, calling on me and others not named [but I suppose the Counsellors of that day] to appear &c. Presuming it was for some act done on behalf of the commonwealth I wrote to the governor to know whether I must defend, or whether the executive would not undertake it for the Commonwealth, as they were possessed of the records and materials of defence. In his answer he assures me it shall be defended by the executive. Still however, as I dislike being in court even as a nominal defendant, I wish to be withdrawn, if possible, and must get the favor of you to appear for me. As it is a case in which I am not personally responsible, I mean to take every possible advantage in defence. The following means occur. 1. dismiss his suit rigorously for want of a bill, for he had not filed one at the date of the Governor's letter. 2. plead the act of limitations, if the case admits it. 3. plead that I did the act in the name, on behalf, and *as the servant of the Commonwealth*, against which therefore and not against me his suit lies. 4. justify under *the acts of assembly*, if there were any which authorized it, for not knowing what wrong he complains of, I do not know whether there was a law authorizing it or indemnifying. 5. justify *by public neces-*

sity; I have no doubt that such a necessity existed. 6. plead former decisions of the executive or legislature or courts against him, for it is suggested to me that the object of his suit has been before decided against him. I mention these several matters to you from which you will be pleased to select such as may suit the case as soon as we know what it is. The most desireable thing to me is to be dismissed out of court with my costs as soon as possible, which is the chief object of my asking the favor of you to appear for me, personally, and whenever you can get me discharged, leaving the cause afterwards to the management of the commonwealth. Inclosed in this letter I send your fee, and am with great esteem Dr. Sir Your most obedt. servt.   TH: JEFFERSON

RC (ViU); brackets in original; addressed: "Bushrod Washington esq. Atty at law Richmond"; endorsed.

I WROTE TO THE GOVERNOR: TJ to Robert Brooke, 24 May 1795. HIS ANSWER: Brooke to TJ, 4 Sep. 1795. The enclosed FEE was £5.3.2½ (MB, 2 Oct. 1795).

SJL records letters (now missing) from Washington to TJ of 12 and 24 Oct. 1795, received respectively on 15 and 26 Oct. 1795, and from TJ to Washington of 29 Oct. 1795.

From George Washington

DEAR SIR   Mount Vernon 4th. Octr. 1795

Your letter of the 12th. Ulto., after travelling to Philadelphia and back again, was received by me, at this place, the 1st. instant.

The letter from Madame de Chastellux to me, is short—referring to the one she has written to you for particulars respecting herself and infant son. Her application to me is unquestionably misplaced, and to Congress it would certainly be unavailing, as the Chevalier Chastellux' pretensions (on which hers must be founded) to any allowance from this country, were no greater than that of any, and every other officer of the French Army, who served in America the last war. To grant to one therefore, would open a wide door to applications of a similar nature, and to consequent embarrassments. Probably, the sum granted at the last session of Congress to the daughters of the Count de Grasse, has given rise to this application. That it has done so in other instances, I have good reasons to believe.

I am much pleased with the account you have given of the Succory. This, like all other things of the sort with me, since my absence from home, have come to nothing; for neither my Overseers nor Manager, will attend properly to anything but the crops they have usually cultivated: and in spite of all I can say, if there is the smallest discretionary power allowed them, they will fill the land with Indian Corn;[1] altho' they have a demonstrable proof, at every step they take, of its destructive effects. I am resolved however, as soon as it shall be in my power to attend a little more closely to my own concerns, to make this crop yield, in a great degree to other grain; to pulses, and to grasses. I am beginning again with Chiccory from a handful of seed given to me by Mr. Strickland; which, though flourishing at present has no appearance of seeding this year. Lucern has not succeeded better with me than with you; but I will give it another, and a fairer trial before it is abandoned altogether. Clover, when I can dress lots well, succeeds with me to my full expectation; but not on the fields in rotation; although I have been at much cost in seeding them. This has greatly disconcerted the system of rotation on which I had decided. I wish you may succeed in getting good seed of the winter Vetch: I have often imported it, but the seed never vegitated; or in so small a proportion as to be destroyed by weeds. I believe it would be an acquisition if it was once introduced properly in our farms. The Albany Pea, which is the same as the field Pea of Europe, I have tried, and found it grew well; but it is subject to the same bug that perforates the garden pea, and eats out the kernal; so it will happen, I fear, with the pea you propose to import. I had great expectation from a green dressing with Buck Wheat, as a preparatory fallow for a crop of Wheat; but it has not answered my expectation yet. I asscribe this however, more to mismanagement in the times of seeding and ploughing in, than to any defect in the system. The first ought to be so ordered, in point of time, as to meet a convenient season for ploughing it in while the plant is in its most succulent state; but this has never been done on my farms, and consequently has drawn as much *from*, as it has given *to* the earth. It has always appeared to me that there were two modes in which Buck Wheat might be used advantageously as a manure. One, to sow early; and as soon as a sufficiency of seed ripened to stock the ground a second time, to turn the whole in; and when the succeeding growth is getting in full bloom to turn that in also (before the seed begins to ripen): and when the fermentation and putrifaction ceases, to sow the ground in that state, and plough in the Wheat. The other mode is, to sow the Buck Wheat so late as that it shall be generally, about a foot high at the usual seeding of Wheat; then turn it in, and sow thereon immediately, as on a clover lay; harrowing in the seed lightly, to avoid disturbing the buried Buck Wheat. The last method I have never tried, but see no reason why it should not succeed. The other as I have observed before, I have practiced but the Buck Wheat has always stood too long, and consequently had become too dry and sticky, to answer the end of a succulant plant. But of all the improving and ameliorating crops, none, in my opinion, is equal to Potatoes on stiff, and hard bound land (as mine is). From a variety of instances I am satisfied that on such land, a crop of Potatoes is equal to an ordinary dressing. In *no* instance have I failed of good Wheat—Oats—or clover that followed Potatoes. And I conceit they give the soil a darker hue.

I shall thank you for the result of your proposed experiments relatively to the winter vetch and Pea, when they are made.

I am sorry to hear of the depredation committed by the Weavil in your parts. It is a great calamity at all times, and this year, when the demand for wheat is so great, and the price so high, must be a mortifying one to the farmer. The Rains have been very general, and more abundant since the first of August than ever happened in a summer within the memory of man. Scarcely a mill dam, or bridge between this and Philada. was able to resist them; and some were carried away a second, and even a third time.

Mrs. Washington is thankful for your kind remembrance of her, and unites with me in best wishes for you. With very great esteem & regard I am—Dear Sir Your Obedt. & affectionate   Go: Washington

RC (DLC); at foot of text: "Thomas Jefferson Esqr."; endorsed by TJ as received 13 Oct. 1795 and so recorded in SJL. FC (Lb in DLC: Washington Papers); only the most important variation is recorded below.

On 27 Feb. 1795 the President had approved an act of Congress providing $4,000 for the daughters of the Comte DE GRASSE, the commander of the French fleet at Yorktown (JS, II, 174).

[1] Remainder of sentence in FC: "altho' even to themselves; there are the most obvious traces, of its baneful effects."

From Van Staphorst & Hubbard

SIR   Amsterdam 10 October 1795.

We have before us your very esteemed favor of 27 May remitting us

£ 39.17.10$\frac{1}{2}$ Stg. Nathl. Anderson's Bill on Wm. Anderson of London
" 70. 8. 6   "   Geo. Meade's Do. on Geo. Barclay & Co. of Do.
£110. 6. 4$\frac{1}{2}$ Stg. on account of Mr. Philip Mazzei whom We have
                            advised thereof.

These Bills have both been protested for non acceptance. But We have endorsed them to the Consul of the United States in London, to pay the expences of an American ship carried into England. By which means We hope He will easily obtain a Licence from the British Government, permitting the persons on whom they are drawn to discharge them: which they will then do, in case their refusal to accept, was solely owing to the British Act of Parliament relative to Dutch property.

Your own Bill on Jas. Maury of Liverpool £50.5.6 is accepted, and will in course be to your Credit. We are ever with great regard and esteem Sir! Your mo. ob. hb. servants.

N & J. VAN STAPHORST & HUBBARD

Dupl (DLC); in a clerk's hand, signed by the firm; at head of text: "*Duplicate. Orig. via Philada. pr. Ship Sally. Wickes*" and "Thos. Jefferson Esqr. Monticello. Virginia"; endorsed by TJ as received 16 Sep. 1796 and so recorded in SJL.

TJ's FAVOR OF 27 MAY 1795 has not been found, but see TJ to Philip Mazzei, 30 May 1795, and note.

In 1794 PARLIAMENT had placed severe restrictions on French-owned property in Britain and on payment of any financial in-

struments endorsed or sent from locales under French authority, and Dutch firms became subject to similar prohibitions in 1795 upon the establishment of the French-allied Batavian Republic (Sir Thomas Edlyne Tomlins and John Raithby, eds., *The Statutes at Large, of England and Great Britain*, 20 vols. [London, 1811], XVIII, 271-6, 444-56).

A letter from James MAURY to TJ of 30 July 1795, recorded in SJL as received 13 Oct. 1795, has not been found.

From Van Staphorst & Hubbard

SIR   Amsterdam 10 October 1795.

  With infinite pleasure did We peruse the letter You favored us with, under date of 28 May, for the friendly Contents of which We beg of you to accept our most sincere hearty Thanks.

Mr. Mazzei's affairs are full as good as We supposed them and if He went out to take care of them himself, They would furnish him a comfortable retreat in his old age. Your letter to him has been forwarded.

We are infinitely obliged indeed, by the very friendly and cordial assistance you so chearfully offered to our friend Sterett, to attain our wish of becoming Citizens of the United States, and sincerely regret the circumstances that disappointed your efforts to have our and Messrs. Willinks names enrolled among the Citizens of the State of Virginia. As it is still a great and darling object with us, to succeed in this point, We are emboldened by your new and repeated tender of service, to sollicit your kind and efficacious Counsel and aid to Mr. Samuel Sterett, who will apply to you for it, in the prosecution of the petition We have directed him to present to the Legislature of Virginia, And then, from what you write us, We have no doubt of its success.

Our Mr. Jacob van Staphorst has formed a personal and intimate acquaintance with Mr. Monroe your Minister Plenipotentiary at Paris, To whom We have ever been disposed to render the services or agreeable offices in our power, and you may rely that after what you have said of this friend of your's, there is nothing He can ask of us, and that our present Circumstances will admit our acquiescing in, that We would not chearfully comply with. Please believe us ever with the most sincere respect and esteem Sir! Your mo. ob. hb. Servants

N. & J. Van Staphorst & Hubbard

Dupl (DLC); in a clerk's hand, signed by the firm; at head of text: "*Duplicate. Orig. via Phila. pr. Ship Sally. Wickes*"; at foot of first page: "Thos. Jefferson Esqr. Monticello. Virginia"; endorsed by TJ as received 16 Sep. 1796 and so recorded in SJL.

TJ's 28 MAY 1795 letter to Van Staphorst & Hubbard has not been found, but see TJ to Philip Mazzei, 30 May 1795, and note,

the letter FORWARDED by Van Staphorst & Hubbard. OUR WISH: see TJ to Wilson Cary Nicholas, 12 Dec. 1794, and note.

At a later date Van Staphorst & Hubbard evidently sent TJ an undated text of his account with the firm containing entries for 2 Aug. 1788-13 Oct. 1795 (MS in DLC: TJ Papers, 79: 13693; in a clerk's hand, signed by the firm; endorsed by TJ: "Van Staphorsts & Hubbard their account").

From Edward Rutledge

MY DEAR FRIEND   Charleston Octr. 12th: 1795.

It is a long time since I wrote you, and a much longer since I have heard from you. Your last, was written on the Eve of your resignation: mine, was an acknowledgment of it; and conveying my best good Wishes for your Happiness in retirement. I hope they have been answered, by your enjoyments in domestic Life; but not that you are so perfectly pleased with the latter, as to abandon for ever all thoughts of your Country. The Experience of every day, evinces that the Service of our Country, like the practice of Virtue, must bring with it, its own reward: whoever expects that Gratitude, to be the Fruit of patriotism, expects a vain thing, and disappointment, or Mortification will be his Portion. We have had a great deal of Trouble about the Treaty which Mr. Jay, has unfortunately formed, for this Country. It is to be sure a most wretched Affair, and should the War continue, and that Treaty be brought into operation, its Evils will multiply daily. But I will say no more on the Subject; being fully satisfied that, if you take no share in Politics, I have said enough: if you do, your own Remarks will have been superior to any thing which I could add.

The Youth, who will put this Letter into your Hands, is my only Son. He is making the Tour of his own Country, preparitory to his going to Europe. He is in my Eye, every thing that I wish, as far as a good Understanding, a well cultivated Mind, and sound Principles of Honor, and Virtue, entitle me to say so. He purposes going into Virginia, and naturally expected that I should introduce him to you. He knows the value I have for you, and presuming upon the Rights of a Child, he thinks himself entitled to participate in my Friendships. I should be highly pleased, if he could come in for a share of yours. I mean him, for my own profession, the Law; but it is also my intention, [to] fit him for public Life. I know full well that, he [will] enjoy more real Happiness in Domestic Society; yet, [as] I consider the Service of our Country, a sacred Duty, I must place it in his power to discharge that Duty, if the Voice of his Fellow Citizens should call him into Action; if not, his Bosom does not glow so warmly with Ambition, as to obtrude him, into her Councils. I will be much obliged to you, to point out to him, whatever may be worthy of Observation in your part of the Continent. He knows full well, all that is contained in your Notes on Virginia; but as the Country is continually more, and more explored, new Objects are frequently arising, to excite and gratify Curiosity; Yet I beg you, my dear Sir, to believe that nothing new can arise, to lessen the Esteem, and Regard of your old, and affectionate Friend   ED: RUTLEDGE

RC (DLC); torn; endorsed by TJ as received 28 Nov. 1795 and so recorded in SJL.

Rutledge's ACKNOWLEDGMENT of TJ's letter of 30 Dec. 1793 is not recorded in SJL and has not been found.

To Pierre Auguste Adet

SIR   Monticello Octob. 14. 1795.

I recieved with pleasure your letter of the 9th. Ult. by post, but should with greater pleasure have recieved it from your own hand, that I might have had an opportunity of testifying to you in person the great respect I bear for your character which had come to us before you, and of expressing my obligations to professor Pictet, for procuring me the honor of your acquaintance. It would have been a circumstance of still higher satisfaction and advantage to me if fortune had timed the periods of our service together, so that the drudgery of public business, which I always hated, might have been relieved by conversations with you on subjects which I always loved, and particularly in learning from you the new advances of science on the other side the Atlantic. The interests of our two republics also could not but have been promoted by the harmony of their servants. Two people whose interests, whose principles, whose habits of attachment, founded on fellowship in war and mutual kindnesses, have so many points of union, cannot but be easily kept together. I hope you have accordingly been sensible, Sir, of the general interest which my countrymen take in all the successes of your republic. In this no one joins with more enthusiasm than myself, an enthusiasm kindled by my love of liberty, by my gratitude to your nation who helped us to acquire it, by my wishes to see it extended to all men, and first to those whom we love most. I am now a private man, free to express my feelings, and their expression will be estimated at neither more nor less than they weigh, to wit the expressions of a private man. Your struggles for liberty keep alive the only sparks of sensation which public affairs now excite in me. As to the concerns of my own country, I leave them willingly and safely to those who will have a longer interest in cherishing them. My books, my family, my friends, and my farm, furnish more than enough to occupy me the remainder of my life, and of that tranquil occupation most analogous to my physical and moral constitution. The correspondence you are pleased to invite me to on the natural history of my country, cannot but be profitable and acceptable to me. My long absence from it indeed has deprived me of the means of throwing any new lights on it; but I shall have the benefit of participating of your views of it, and occasions of expressing to you those sentiments of esteem and respect with which I have the honor to be Sir Your most obedient & most humble servt   TH: JEFFERSON

P.S. I take the liberty of making you the channel of the answer to Mr. Pictet, as you were pleased to be of his letter.

PrC (DLC); at foot of first page: "Monsr. Adet." Enclosure: TJ to Marc Auguste Pictet, 14 Oct. 1795.

From Antonia Carmichael

MONSIEUR   pres de chester town ce 14 octobre 1795

Etant arrivée depuis quelques semaines dans ce pais et ne sachant par quel moyen vous faire passer un livre intitulé la Conquête du Mexique que feu mon mari vous avoit destiné ainsi que quelques papiers a votre adresse. Si les lettres d'Hernand Cortes a Charles Quint ainsi que les gravures vous font plaisir je crois pouvoir vous les procurer. J'ai l'honneur d'Être Monsieur Votre tres humble   veuve CARMICHAEL

Je vous prie d'Adresser vos lettres a Mr. Nicholson chester-town.

RC (DLC); in an unidentified hand, signed by Mrs. Carmichael; at foot of text: "A Monsieur Monsieur Jeffersson en Virginie"; endorsed by TJ as received 10 Nov. 1795 and so recorded in SJL.

Antonia Reynon Carmichael (d. 1800), the Spanish-born second wife and widow of William Carmichael, the former American chargé d'affaires and commissioner to Spain, who left her without funds after his death earlier in 1795, lived for the rest of her life near Chestertown, Maryland, and collected over $9,600 from the federal government in connection with the settlement of her husband's accounts (Samuel G. Coe, *The Mission of William Carmichael to Spain* [Baltimore, 1928], 97-8).

SJL records a letter from TJ to "Mde. de" Carmichael of 9 Nov. 1795 which has not been found.

To Marc Auguste Pictet

DEAR SIR   Monticello in Virginia Oct. 14. 1795.

I have to thank you for the honor of being made known to Mr. Adet, who did me that of forwarding your letter of Jan. 1. my distance from the seat of government not admitting the pleasure of recieving it from his own hands. I flatter myself, from the character of this gentleman, that his mission will be fruitful in good to both countries. You will ere this have heard from your friend in London the result of my effort in this state to effect his proposition. It was too flattering to us, and too congenial with my habits of life, for me to rest contented with doing merely what he desired. I knew of another institution which was about to be formed, approaching more nearly to the circumstances he wished, and more suitable for recieving this great engraftment. I immediately made the necessary applications; but, unfortunately, their success was prevented by some arrangements which had already taken place, and which did not leave room for this. As this attempt was unknown to your friend in London, I did not think it material to communicate it's failure to him. But it rendered more pleasing to me the information recieved from yourself, that your own institution is likely to be placed again on a tolerable footing.   Our country offers to the lovers of science a rich field of the works of nature, but little explored, except in the department of botany. One would imagine indeed from the European writings that our animal history was tolerably known. But time will shew in it the grossest errors. Our geology is untouched, and would have been a precious mine for you, as your views of it would have been precious to us. I will not allow myself to conclude that the present state of things is final. Our country is but beginning to develope it's resources. Some of these may yet unfold circumstances more favorable to my wishes, and to the greater interests of science. I shall in such case consider the favor of your letter as a permission to communicate further with you, and to hope that the present, is not the last, occasion I may use of assuring you of those sentiments of esteem and respect with which I have the honor to be Dear Sir Your most obedt. & most humble servt

TH: JEFFERSON

RC (Dr. Frédéric Rilliet, Geneva, Switzerland, 1947); at foot of first page: "M. Pictet." PrC (DLC). Enclosed in TJ to Pierre Auguste Adet, 14 Oct. 1795.

YOUR FRIEND IN LONDON: François D'Ivernois.

Notes on the Letter of
Christoph Daniel Ebeling

[after 15 Oct. 1795]

Notes on Professor Ebeling's letter of July 30. 95.

Professor Ebeling mentioning the persons in America from whom he derives information for his work, it may be useful for him to know how far he may rely on their authority.

President Stiles. An excellent man, of very great learning, but remarkable for his credulity.

Dr. Willard.
Dr. Barton
Dr. Ramsay
Mr. Barlow } All these are men of[1] respectable characters, worthy of[2] confidence as to any facts they may state, and rendered, by their good sense, good judges of them.

Mr. Morse.
Mr. Webster. } Good authorities for whatever relates to the Eastern states, and perhaps as far South as the Delaware.

But South of that, their information is worse than none at all; except as far as they quote good authorities. They both I believe took a single journey through the Southern parts, merely to acquire the right of being considered as eye-witnesses. But to pass once along a public road thro' a country, and in one direction only, to put up at it's taverns, and get into conversation with the idle, drunken, individuals who pass their time lounging in these taverns, is not the way to know a country, it's inhabitants or manners. To generalise a whole nation from these specimens is not the sort of information which Professor Ebeling would wish to compose his work from.

Fenno's Gazette of the U.S.
Webster's Minerva.
Columbian centinel. } To form a just judgment of a country from it's newspapers, the character of these papers should be known, in order that proper allowances and corrections may be used. This will require a long explanation, without which, these particular papers would give a foreigner a very false view of American affairs.

The people of America, before the revolution-war, being attached to England, had taken up, without examination, the English ideas of the superiority of their constitution over every thing of the kind which ever had been or ever would be tried. The revolution forced them to consider the subject for themselves, and the result was an universal conversion to republicanism. Those who did not come over to this opinion, either left us, and were called Refugees, or staid with us under the name of tories; and some, preferring profit to principle took side with us and floated with the general tide. Our first federal constitution, or confederation as it was called, was framed in the first moments of our separation from England, in the highest point of our jealousies of independance as to her and as to each other. It formed therefore too weak a band to produce an union of action as to foreign nations. This appeared at once on the establishment of peace, when the pressure of a common enemy, which had[3] hooped us together during the war, was taken away. Congress was found to be quite unable to point the action of the several states to a common object. A general desire therefore took place of amending the federal constitution. This was opposed by some of those who wished for monarchy to wit, the Refugees now returned, the old Tories, and the timid whigs who prefer tranquility to freedom,[4] hoping monarchy might be the remedy if a state of complete anarchy could be brought on. A Convention however being decided on, some of the Monocrats got elected, with a hope of introducing an English constitution. When they found that the great body of the delegates were strongly for adhering to republicanism, and for giving due strength to their government under that form, they then directed their efforts to the assimilation of all the parts of the new government to the English constitution as nearly as was attainable. In this they were not altogether without success; insomuch that the monarchical features of the new constitution produced a violent opposition to it from the most zealous republicans in the several states. For this reason, and because they also thought it carried the principle of a consolidation of the states farther than was requisite for the purpose of producing an union of action as to foreign powers, it is still doubted by some whether a majority of the people of the US. were not against adopting it. However it was carried through all the assemblies of the states, tho' by very small majorities in the largest states. The inconveniences of an inefficient government, driving the people as is usual, into the opposite extreme, the elections to the first Congress run very much in favor of those who were known to favor a very strong government. Hence the anti-republicans appeared a considerable majority in both houses of Congress. They pressed forward the plan therefore of strengthening all the features of the government which gave it resemblance to an English constitution, of adopting the English forms and principles of administration, and of forming like them a monied interest, by means of a funding system, not calculated to pay the public debt, but to render it perpetual, and to make it an engine in the hands of the Executive branch of government which added to the great patronage it possessed in the disposal of public offices, might enable it to assume by degrees a kingly authority. The biennial period of Congress being too short to betray to the people, spread over this great continent, this train of things during the first Congress, little change was made in the members to the second. But in the mean time two very distinct parties had formed in Congress: and before the third election, the people in general became apprised of the game which was playing for drawing over them a kind of government which they never had in contemplation. At the 3d. election therefore a decided majority of Republicans were sent to the lower house of Congress; and as information spread still farther among the people after the 4th. election the anti-republicans have become a weak minority. But the members of the Senate being changed but once in 6. years, the complection of that body will be much slower in it's assimilation to that of the people. This will account for the differences which may appear in the proceedings and spirit of the two houses. Still however it is inevitable that the Senate will at length be formed to the republican model[5] of the people, and the two houses of[6] the legislature, once brought to act on the true principles of the Constitution, backed by the people, will be able to[7] defeat the plan of sliding us into monarchy, and to keep the Executive within republican bounds, notwithstanding the immense patronage it possesses in the disposal of public offices, notwithstanding it has been able to draw into this vortex the[8] judiciary branch of the government and by their expectancy of sharing the other offices in the Executive gift to make them auxiliary to the Executive in all it's views instead of forming a balance between that and the legislature as it was originally intended[9] and notwithstanding the funding phalanx which a respect for public faith must protect, tho it was engaged by false brethren. Two parties then do exist within the US. They embrace respectively the following descriptions of persons.

The Anti-republicans consist of

1. The old refugees and tories.
2. British merchants residing among us,[10] and composing the main body of our merchants
3. American merchants trading on British capital. Another great portion.[11]
4. Speculators and Holders in the banks and public funds.
5. Officers of the federal government with some exceptions.
6. Office-hunters, willing to give up principles for places. A numerous and noisy tribe.[12]
7. Nervous persons, whose languid fibres have more analogy with a passive than active state of things.

The Republican part of our Union comprehends

1. The entire body of landholders throughout the United States

2. The body of labourers, not being landholders, whether in husbandry or the arts

The latter is to the aggregate of the former party probably as 500 to one; but their wealth is not as disproportionate, tho' it is also greatly superior, and is in truth the foundation of that of their antagonists. Trifling as are the numbers of the Anti-republican party, there are circumstances which give them an appearance of strength and numbers. They all live in cities, together, and can act in a body readily and at all times; they give chief employment to the newspapers, and therefore have most of them under their command. The Agricultural interest is dispersed over a great extent of country, have little means of intercommunication with each other, and feeling their own strength and will, are conscious that a single exertion of these will at any time crush the machinations against their government. As in the commerce of human life, there are commodities adapted to every demand, so there are newspapers adapted to the Antirepublican palate, and others to the Republican. Of the former class are the Columbian Centinel, the Hartford newspaper, Webster's Minerva, Fenno's Gazette of the US. Davies's Richmond paper &c. Of the latter are Adams's Boston paper, Greenleaf's of New York, Freneau's of New Jersey, Bache's of Philadelphia, Pleasant's of Virginia &c. Pleasant's paper comes out twice a week, Greenleaf's and Freneau's once a week. Bache's daily. I do not know how often Adams's. I shall according to your desire endeavor to get Pleasant's for you, for 1794. and 95. and will have it forwarded through 96. from time to time to your correspondent at Baltimore.

While on the subject of authorities and information, the following works are recommended to Professor Ebeling.

Minot's history of the insurrection in Massachusets in 1786. 8vo.

Mazzei. Recherches historiques et politiques sur les E.U. de l'Amerique. 4. vol. 8vo. This is to be had from Paris. The author is an exact man.

The article 'Etats Unis de l'Amerique' in the Dictionnaire d'Economie politique et diplomatique, de l'Encyclopedie Methodique. This article occupies about 90. pages, is by De Meusnier, and his materials were worthy of confidence, except so far as they were taken from the Abbe Raynal. Against these effusions of an imagination in delirio it is presumed Professor Ebeling needs not to be put on his guard. The earlier editions of the Abbé Raynal's work were equally bad as to both South and North America. A gentleman however of perfect information as to South America, undertook to reform that part of the work, and his changes and additions were for the most part adopted by the Abbé in his latter editions. But the North-American part remains in it's original state of worthlessness.

MS (DLC: TJ Papers, 98: 16893-5); consists of six pages entirely in TJ's hand; undated, unsigned, and possibly unfinished; with emendations, the most important of which are noted below.

TJ initially may have intended these notes, with their revealing interpretation of the development of partisan alignments in the United States from the time of the American Revolution, to serve either as the basis for a reply to Christoph Daniel Ebeling's letter of 30 July 1795, which TJ had received on 15 Oct. 1795, or as an enclosure to a letter he intended to write to the German historian. Nevertheless, the Editors have found no evidence that TJ actually responded to Ebeling: no reply is recorded in SJL, no letter or memorandum has been located, and no press copy of either survives in TJ's papers. Moreover, Ebeling's published correspondence with Americans, particularly between 1812 and 1817 when he contemplated dedicating his volume on Virginia to TJ, makes no mention of a response by TJ to his queries, and in an 1815 exchange with William Bentley, one of Ebeling's principal correspondents in the United States, TJ stated only that he "understood" Ebeling had been at work on a study of Virginia (American Antiquarian Society, *Proceedings*, n.s., XXXV [1925], 415, 418, 425, 435; Bentley to TJ, 30 Oct. 1815; TJ to Bentley, 28 Dec. 1815).

YOUR CORRESPONDENT AT BALTIMORE: Charles Ghequiere.

For TJ's involvement with Démeunier's ARTICLE on the United States in the *Encyclopédie Méthodique*, see Vol. 10: 3-65. The GENTLEMAN who UNDERTOOK TO REFORM Raynal's *Histoire* was the Spanish diplomat Pedro Jiménez de Góngora y Luján, duque de Almodóvar del Río, whose unfinished five-volume Spanish translation and abridgment (Madrid, 1784-90)—published under the pseudonym of Eduardo Malo de Luque because the work had been proscribed in Spain—revised and corrected Raynal's descriptions of Spanish America (Hoefer, *Nouv. biog. générale*, II, 194, XLI, 765; Bleiberg, *Diccionario*, II, 815). TJ owned one of the numerous later editions of the *Histoire*, but he evidently did not acquire the Spanish imprint (see Sowerby, No. 466).

[1] Here TJ canceled "most."
[2] Here TJ canceled "entire."
[3] Preceding two words written over an illegible erasure.
[4] Preceding eighteen words interlined.
[5] Word interlined in place of "principles."
[6] TJ here canceled "Congress."
[7] TJ here canceled "prevent the."
[8] TJ here canceled "whole."
[9] Preceding fifteen words interlined.
[10] Remainder of clause probably inserted.
[11] Preceding three words inserted by TJ.
[12] Preceding five words inserted by TJ.

From James Madison

DEAR SIR   Orange Octr. 18. 1795

On opening the letter forwarded by Pickering, which I omitted at Monticello, because I took for granted that it merely covered, like yours, a copy of the French Constitution, I found a letter from Monroe, of the 30 June, from which the following is an extract. "You will be surprised to hear that the only *Americans* [1] whom I found here, were a *set of New Engld. men connected with Britain and who upon British capital were trading to this country, that they are hostile to the French revolu-*

tion is what you well know: but that they should be *thriving upon the credit which the efforts* of others in other quarters gain *the American name here you could not expect, that as such they should be in possession of the little confidence we had and give a tone to characters on our side of the Atlantic was still less* to be expected. *But* such was the fact. With a few exceptions the *other Merchants* are *new made citizens from scotland. Swan who is a corrupt unprincipled rascal* had by virtue of being the *agent of France* and as we had no *minister* and *he being tho* (of the latter description) *the only or* most creditable *resident American here had a monopoly of the trade of both countries.* Indeed it is believed that he was connected with *the agents* on one side, *and the minister on the other.* I *mention this as a trait worthy your* attention. You will confide this view to *Mr. J—ferson*[2] *only.* But good may come from it, and especially if *the allurement here will draw them off from the other side of the channel."* The remainder of the letter is little more than you have probably seen from him.

I have seen Philada. papers down to the 12 inst: one of them contains another letter from E.R. to the P. dated the 8th.[3] and sent to the press on the *10*th applying for a paper refused him by Pickering, intimating that the want of this alone delayed his final statement and notifying the P. that his consent would be expected to a publication of it. It appears that the State elections in Pena. will be very warm, and are hinged on the distinction of Treaty and anti Treaty candidates. In Delaware they are over, and have given a Triumph to the Anti Treaty party. The French Constitution has been *unanimously* concluded by the Convention. It is not yet authenticated that war has taken place between England and Spain, but reports and circumstances continue to point at it. Yrs. affectionately   Js. MADISON JR

RC (DLC: Madison Papers); with extract in first paragraph written partly in code, being transcribed by Madison from James Monroe's letter to him of 30 June 1795 (Madison, *Papers*, XVI, 32-4), but containing minor coding anomalies including those originally introduced by Monroe, ten words encoded by Monroe that Madison copied *en clair*, and one omission of code by Madison (see note 2 below), with interlinear decipherment by TJ incorporating his correction of encoding errors (see note 1 below); endorsed by TJ as received 20 Oct. 1795 and so recorded in SJL.

LETTER FROM E.R. TO THE P.: Andrew Brown's *Philadelphia Gazette* of 10 Oct.

1795 contained an extract of a letter from Edmund Randolph to George Washington, 8 Oct. 1795, stating that his vindication required "the discussion of many confidential and delicate points"; that he could with confidence immediately appeal to the American people, "who can be of no party," but that he would wait for the President to supply the one document that was preventing him from completing his "general letter" to the President (the document requested was Washington's letter to him of 22 July 1795, which Timothy Pickering, his successor as Secretary of State, had refused to turn over); and that he expected the President to communicate to him any factual errors in the general letter and to "consent to the whole of the affair, howsoever confidential and delicate, being exhibited to the world." Brown printed the extract at Randolph's request, along with a covering letter of 10 Oct. 1795 in which Randolph declared his intention only to show the public "what is the state of my vindication." The full text of Randolph's letter to the President is in DLC: Washington Papers. Washington agreed to make the document in question available to Randolph, and in a private letter of 21 Oct. 1795 informed him that he was "at full liberty to publish, without reserve, *any*, and *every* private and confidential letter I ever wrote you; nay more, every word I ever uttered to, or in your presence, from whence you can derive any advantage in your vindication," his only condition being that "this letter may be inserted in the compilation you are now making" (Fitzpatrick, *Writings*, XXXIV, 339-42; Reardon, *Randolph*, 321-2). For Randolph's resignation, see TJ to James Monroe, 6 Sep. 1795; on his *Vindication*, which included his general or open letter to Washington alluded to above, see TJ to Madison, 26 Nov. 1795, and note.

¹ This and subsequent italicized words in the present paragraph are written in code, the text being supplied from TJ's decipherment and verified by the Editors against Code No. 9.
² Deciphered thus by TJ, reflecting Madison's error in copying a code from Monroe's letter.
³ Passage from this point through "*10*th" interlined.

To Wilson Cary Nicholas

DEAR SIR   Monticello Oct. 19. 1795.

Mr. Jefferson the bearer hereof is not entirely unknown to you I believe. He asks of me however a line of introduction. He is a candidate for the office rendered vacant by the death of Mr. Hay, and he wishes me to say to you what I know of him. He has respectable talents, is well-read in the law, and is a good republican, and a very honest man. If no fitter person offers, I need not ask your aid to him; if a fitter offers, I would not ask it, but wish you to do, as I would myself, vote for the fittest. He mentions several candidates; of course you will have considerable choice.

Colo. Burr left this two or three days ago, after a stay of one day. We do not yet hear of Mr. Randolph's publication. I am with great esteem Dr. Sir Your friend & servt   TH: JEFFERSON

RC (MHi); addressed: "Wilson C. Nicholas Warren"; endorsed.

John Garland JEFFERSON, who according to SJL wrote a letter to TJ of 6 Oct. 1795, now missing, that was received on 14 Oct. 1795, hoped to succeed Charles HAY as clerk of the Virginia House of Delegates (Swem and Williams, *Register*, 41, 43).

From James Blake

Phila. Octr. 20. 1795

The widow of Mr. Carmichael is arrived in the United States—and resides near Chester-Town in Maryland. I made her acquainted with the disappointment I had respecting a copy of Cortes's letters, which her husband intended for you—and she informed me, she would send it to Baltimore, to any acquaintance of yours you would please to mention. Pray, Sir, will you be so good as to write her a line on the subject, and address it as below. With great respect I have the honor to be—Sir, Your most obedient & most humble servant   James Blake

Madame
    Madame Carmichael Near Chester-Town Maryland

RC (DLC); at foot of text: "Thomas Jefferson Esquire"; endorsed by TJ as received 3 Nov. 1795 and so recorded in SJL.

To James Brown

Dear Sir   Monticello Oct. 20. 95.

Your favor of the 11th. has come duly to hand. Before it's receipt I had carried the purchases of James river shares, for Mr. Short nearly to the extent intended, and had determined to go no further, as I learn that the company is aground and will not have funds to complete the canal, without raising a very large sum (£10,000 it is said) either on the old shares or by selling new ones, which will lessen so much the value of the old. This circumstance has entirely decided me to purchase no more for Mr. Short, or I should with pleasure have accomodated you and served him at the same time in taking some of your shares, at a proper price.

Can you inform me what is his chance of having his money recovered from Dr. J. Griffin and in what state it is? I am with very great esteem Dear Sir Your friend & servt   Th: Jefferson

RC (Mrs. Henry M. Sage, Albany, New York, 1954); addressed: "Mr. James Brown Mercht Richmond"; endorsed by Brown.

Brown's favor of the 11th, recorded in SJL as received on 17 Oct. 1795, and an earlier letter from Brown recorded in SJL as written 19 July and received 21 July 1795, have not been found.

From James Lyle

DEAR SIR Manchester Octr. 23d. 1795

The 5th. of this month I received by an order from Mr. Christopher Clark the Attorney in Bedford, on Mr. Hart of Richmond, the sum of one hundred and twenty pounds which is to your credit with our Company. I believe he received it from Mr. Milner, one of your debtors.

Pray if it be not too troublesome inform me where we can find the papers relative to the suit Harding had against Edwd. Carter Alexr. McCaul &c. about the land which E. Carter sold to Stamps and which Harding recovered. Is the mortgage that Stamps made to Mr. McCaul in your possession, or where shall I find it? I observe by original papers, depositions &c. in the General Court that Copies of them all have been had from thence, I suppose the mortgage may be with them. You will oblige me much as well as Mr. Chas. Carter, for what information you can give concerning them. I am asham'd of presuming to give you this trouble but I hope you will excuse it, as Mr. McCaul and I are both concernd in the final event of that suit. I am with great Regard Dear Sir Your Mo hu st   JAMES LYLE

RC (MHi); question mark supplied; endorsed by TJ as received 27 Oct. 1795 and so recorded in SJL.

In 1771, TJ had represented Alexander McCaul's claim to land involved in a chancery SUIT, Harding v. Carter (MB, 13 Apr. 1771, 7 Feb. 1774).

To James Lyle

DEAR SIR   Monticello Oct. 28. 95.

I recieved last night your favor of the 23d.—The fall before the death of Colo. E. Carter, he called on me for the papers which I had had in the suit of Harding v Carter, and I delivered to him the bundle. It consisted only of copies of the bill, answer &c. from the records. Mr. Charles Carter lately called on me on the subject, and I informed him I had delivered all the papers to his father, but that as they were only copies from the records, he could easily have them replaced by other copies. With respect to the mortgage from Stamps to Mr. McCaul, I suppose I had not even a copy of it: because the only point I had to support was the invalidity of the sale of the lands made by John Moore to Harding, for Mr. Carter and during his infancy. The court decreed the sale to have been valid, which was most unquestionably wrong. But I presume, as the lands lay in Goochland, the mortgage was recorded either in that court or the General court, and that a copy of it can easily be had. This is all the information I am able to give you on this subject.

I remark the sum recieved by you from Milner on my account. Kinsolving, who has unwisely kept his last year's tobacco on hand till now, waiting for a better price, promised me about three weeks ago that he would go directly to Richmond, sell it, and pay you the proceeds. By your silence as to him I fear he has not done it. I shall therefore urge him without delay. I am with great esteem Dear Sir Your friend & servt

TH: JEFFERSON

PrC (MHi); at foot of text: "Mr. James Lyle"; endorsed by TJ in ink.

SJL records a letter from TJ to James KINSOLVING of 19 Sep. 1795 that has not been found.

From William Branch Giles

SIR   Petersburg October 29th 1795

I arrived in this place last evening, and found the memorial contained in the inclosed paper in circulation here, although I heard nothing of it in Richmond where I have spent several of the last preceeding days. Upon inquiry I find it almost impossible to get any paper respecting the treaty into the press here without some pointed remarks upon its unconstitutional feature, which is considered by the observing people the most prominent, as well as the most odious. This memorial is printed in hand bills, as well as in the newspaper, one of which I should also inclose you, but in consequence of some errors in the first impressions, it will probably undergo a reprinting in the course of a few days. I am told it will probably be subscribed in the neighbouring counties of this place almost universally, if the time should not be too short, to give the people an opportunity of doing so.

I propose to make another visit to Monticello before I go into winter quarters.

Mr. Henning to whom this letter is intrusted is about to leave this place this moment for Charlottsville, and promises to attend particularly to its delivery.

Be pleased to make my best respects to the Ladies of your family to Mr. Randolph and Mr. Carr and accept my fervant wishes for your personal happiness &c.   WM. B. GILES

RC (DLC); at foot of text: "Mr Jefferson"; endorsed by TJ as received 3 Nov. 1795 and so recorded in SJL. Enclosure not found, but see note below.

The MEMORIAL . . . IN CIRCULATION for signatures was a 12 Oct. 1795 petition to the Virginia General Assembly against the

Jay Treaty, drafted by James Madison, which argued that the addition to the treaty of an article suspending Article 12 would require its resubmission to the "constituted authorities" for ratification, and criticized the treaty at length for failing to obtain compensation for British violations of the Treaty of Paris, making disadvantageous commercial concessions to the British, and failing to gain British recognition of basic American neutral rights, all of which made it "unworthy the voluntary acceptance of an independent people" (Madison, *Papers*, XVI, 95-104). Giles probably enclosed the first printing, now lost, that appeared in the *Virginia Gazette, and Petersburg Intelligencer*, sometime between 13 and 27 Oct.

1795, and TJ appears to have taken some interest in the additions Madison made to the petition (same, 66n, 68n; TJ to George Washington, 19 June 1796, and note). The origins of the petition and the evolution of the text in surviving manuscript and printed forms, as well as the General Assembly's response to it, are discussed in Madison, *Papers*, XVI, 62-9n.

From Tench Coxe

DEAR SIR   Philada. Octr. 30. 1795

Your letters for Mr. Pinckney, Mr. Monroe &ca. were all carefully forwarded. I should have given you this information before, but I wanted to send you the four papers (in the enclosed pamphlets) under the Signature of "*Juricola*." I have said to individuals, without reserve, in public and private life, that they were mine, as I have no more reserve in discussions thro the press, than in a speech in the legislature or a report from the executive Department. I considered it important to impress on the Presidents mind convictions of decorum, respect, moderation, information and reason in the mind and feelings of the writer, and I held it necessary to the preservation of the liberality of my own Character to attend to several of those points in speaking of the other party to the Treaty. When I had got far into the Negro Question (No. 3 being in the press) I first learned, that there was a remote probability of the Presidents giving some conditional Sanction to the Treaty, and just after the publication of No. 4, I found it certain that he had given his approbation to it. Tho a few More papers[1] relative to the question of the Debts, were prepared, I determined to stop, because I thought it might be supposed I wished to censure the Executive of which I was a part. I had satisfied myself that however perfect the right of the British *creditors* may have been and however they might be entitled to damages from one or other of the Nations[2] that the United States, as a political body, had done more than the non restora[tion] of Peace and the continuance of forcible possession of its territory entitled *G. Britain* to demand. I am sorry these papers were not published before the Executive measures in regard to the Treaty had been taken. With perfect respect, I am dear sir, Yr. mo. obedt. & hble Servant   TENCH COXE

RC (DLC); slightly torn; endorsed by TJ as received 10 Nov. 1795 and so recorded in SJL. Enclosures: "Juricola" [Tench Coxe], "An examination of the pending Treaty with Great Britain. To the President of the United States of America," in Mathew Carey, ed., *The American Remembrancer; or, an Impartial Collection of Essays, Re-*

solves, Speeches, &c. Relative, or Having Af-finity, to the Treaty with Great Britain, 3 vols. (Philadelphia, 1795-96), II, 14-17, 75-94, which urged the President to suspend ratification of the Jay Treaty until it had been amended to grant the United States more liberal terms of trade with the British West Indies and to provide compensation for American slaves taken by the British during the Revolutionary War (see Sowerby, No. 3520). The four articles were originally published in the *Philadelphia Gazette*, 31 July, 4, 8, and 12 Aug. 1795. See also Cooke, *Coxe*, 276-9.

EXECUTIVE OF WHICH I WAS A PART: Coxe was commissioner of the revenue in the Department of the Treasury.

[1] Remainder of clause interlined.
[2] Preceding seven words interlined.

From Louis of Parma

MONSIEUR   Escorial ce 2. Novbre. 1795.

Depuis bien longtemps je desirais ardemment de pouvoir établir une correspondance avec quelque personne des États Unis d'Amérique qui fût amateur, et intelligent en histoire Naturelle. Mon bût était d'enrichir ma collection par les productions de ce pays en tous les trois règnes, et pouvoir servir mon correspondant avec des échanges de toutes les productions d'Europe qu'il pût desirer. Je cherchais en même temps une instruction sur les moeurs, et le gouvernement de ce pays, ce que j'esperais pouvant y trouver une personne comme je la désirais. Mais comment faire? Comment trouver une personne comme je la cherchais, dans un pays ou je ne connais personne?

Dans le moment où je croyais en être le plus éloigné, j'espere d'en être voisin. J'ai eu le bonheur de connaître ici Mr. Pickney vôtre ministre extraordinaire auprès de cette cour; son amabilité, ses talents, (que j'ai entendu louer par tous ceux qui ont eu occasion de le traiter) et son merite, m'ont donné le courage de lui expliquer mon desir. Il m'a proposé, de me mettre en correspondance avec vous; et les éloges qu'il m'à fait de toutes vos qualités, ont augmenté le desir que j'avais déjà formé. Mais en même temps, j'ai reflechi à mon insolence: comment aller disturber un homme de tant de merite comme vous, avec une proposition qui ne peut que l'incommoder, et ne peut lui faire aucun plaisir? Comment demander un plaisir à une personne que je ne connais pas, quand je vois qu'on a de la peine à l'obtenir, de ceux que l'on traite tous les jours? Non; je remedierai en partie à ma faute, (si je puis) en vous priant de jetter ma lettre au feu, et de ne plus y penser, si ma proposition, et correspondance peut vous ennuyer la moindre chose; il peut se faire que vous vous soyéz donné entierement à l'agriculture abbandonnant toutes les autres occupations; il peut se faire que vous ne vouliéz plus vous incommoder de correspondances, ou aumoins que vous ne les vouliéz conserver qu'avec ceux qui peuvent vous être d'agrément comme des litterats, et savans, et non des butors comme je le suis. Enfin dans tous ces cas, je vous prie à ne pas vous prendre un moment d'ennui pour moi. Seulement si vous me jugiéz capable de vous être utile à quelque chose, pour vous procurer des productions Européennes, et que ma proposition ne vous génat pas; alors je vous prierais à me repondre, et établir le plan sur lequel nous pourrons commencer nôtre correspondance: de toute façon il ne s'effacera jamais de mon coeur les sentimens d'estime que j'ai pour vous, et avec lesquels je suis Monsieur Vôtre très attaché

LOUIS PE. DE PARME

RC (DLC); endorsed by TJ as received 3 June 1796 and so recorded in SJL. Enclosed in Thomas Pinckney to TJ, 16 Mch. 1796.

Louis (1773-1803) was prince and heir to the throne of the northern Italian duchy of Parma, which was ruled by a branch of the Spanish Bourbons. That dynastic connection was reinforced when Louis married his cousin, the Infanta María Luisa, a younger daughter of King Carlos IV of Spain, in August 1795. Little is known of Louis's education in Parma, but he evidently devoted himself to the study of the natural sciences, especially the flora and fauna of Parma, and was apparently interested in the development of resin and other plant derivatives. In Europe, Charles Willson Peale reported, Louis "was esteemed a man of Science, or at least an encourager of Sciences," and the French industrial chemist Jean Antoine Chaptal, while declining Louis's suggestion that they jointly build factories in Spain, noted

that the prince had a very good understanding of chemistry. By the treaties of San Ildefonso, Aranjuez, and Lunéville negotiated between Spain and France in 1800-01, Napoleon Bonaparte renamed Tuscany the kingdom of Etruria, removed its ruling archduke, and installed Louis as king in 1801; in exchange, Spain retroceded to France the territory of Louisiana that it had controlled since 1763. Louis's reign in Florence as Ludovico I was hampered by the continuing French military presence and by the worsening epilepsy and mental aberrations that led to his early death (*Enciclopedia Italiana di Scienze, Lettere ed Arti*, 36 vols. [Rome, 1929-39], XXI, 597; Paul Marmottan, *Le Royaume d'Étrurie (1801-1807)*, 2d ed. [Paris, 1896], 50-4, 107, 122-23, 305-6, 335-6; Prince Sixte de Bourbon, *La Reine d'Étrurie* [Paris, 1928], 3; Peale, *Papers*, II, pt. 2, p. 684; Jean Antoine Chaptal, *Mes Souvenirs sur Napoléon* [Paris, 1893], 39-40; DSB, s.v. "Chaptal, Jean Antoine").

From Bushrod Washington

DEAR SIR   Richmond Nov. 2. 95

I wish I could give you the satisfaction you wish as to the time when your case will be finally decided. We must proceed regularly and there is no rule by which to guess when the case will come on in its turn which it must do if defended with a view to delay.

I can only say that I shall use diligence in pushing it forward, and shall try by a motion out of turn to get it sooner decided. This is sometimes done and not often opposed. Of the steps I take you shall be immediately apprised.

I have given a rule for a Bill in Bank's suit against you and shall dismiss it at the next rule day if it be not filed.

Excuse this small piece of paper. I never discovered until I had set down to write, that I had no more, and have not time now to send for a supply as your messenger is impatient. I am very respectfully Dear Sir Yr mo ob. Serv 　　　　　　　　　　　　　　　BUSHD: WASHINGTON

RC (MHi); addressed: "Thos. Jefferson Esq Monticello"; endorsed by TJ as received 12 Oct. 1795, but correctly recorded in SJL as received 12 Nov. 1795.

YOUR CASE: see TJ to Washington, 23 Sep. 1795.

SJL records letters from TJ to Washington of 5 Nov. on "F. & J's suit," 13 Nov. on "Cary's exr.," 25 Nov. 1795 on "v. Henderson. Cary's exr.," and 13 Mch. 1796, as well as letters from Washington to TJ of 21 Nov. and 5 Dec. 1795, received on 24 Nov. and 9 Dec. 1795, respectively, none of which has been found.

From James Lyle

DEAR SIR 　　　　　　　　　　　　　　Manchester Nov. 3d. 1795

I am just now favoured with yours, by your servant, and thank you for the information relative the affair of Harding.

One Linsey Coleman of Amherst Co. informs me he deliverd to Wm. Mitchel our then Collector, (before the War) a note of yours and Mr. Skipwiths to him L Coleman for about £70 odd pounds, he has no credit, by you or Mr. Skipwith for any such sum, Pray can you throw any light on this. Coleman says he has Wm. Mitchells receipt for the order, although I have never seen it. At your leisure I will be glad to know, if you remember any thing of the Transaction. I have not seen the Gentleman you mention. I just now recollect, Kinsolving called on me but did not like our price for the Tobacco. He told me the money was to be paid to me for you. I desired him to sell his tobacco in Richmond and bring the money or leave it with Wm. Mitchell at Richmond for me, but heard nothing of him after. I am Dear Sir Your Mo humle servt.

　　　　　　　　　　　　　　　　　　　　　　JAMES LYLE

RC (MHi); endorsed by TJ as received 12 Oct. 1795, but correctly recorded in SJL as received 12 Nov. 1795.

FAVOURED WITH YOURS: TJ to Lyle, 28 Oct. 1795.

To the Heirs of Bennett Henderson

To John, William, Sally, James, Charles, Isham, Bennet Hilsborough, Eliza, Frances, Lucy and Nancy Crawford Henderson, children of Bennet Henderson deceased.

Be pleased to take notice that on the 24th of November at the dwelling house of Thomas Morgan between the hours of eleven and one in the day, I shall proceed to take the deposition of the said Thomas Morgan by virtue of a commission issued from the high court of Chancery in a suit instituted by me against you in the said court concerning the reflowing of backwater on my mill seat occasioned by your mill dam.

TH: JEFFERSON
November 7th 1795

MS (CtY); in TJ's hand, except for dates inserted by Deputy Sheriff Francis Taliaferro beneath TJ's signature and in blank left by TJ in body of text; with attestation on verso in Taliaferro's hand, signed and dated by Justice of the Peace Thomas Bell, 17 Nov. 1795, recording Taliaferro's oath that "he gave the within notice to John & William Henderson on Thursday the 12th of November & that John Henderson Acknolledg that he recd the within Notice for the Rest of the Children."

Bennett Henderson's children are evidently named above, and in other documents relating to TJ's suit against them, in their birth order. John, the only sibling of legal age at the time of their father's death in 1793, took the lead in opposing TJ in later lawsuits involving the Henderson family's lands and mill (Albemarle County Court Order of Guardianship, 9 Oct. 1794, and Craven Peyton's Bill in Chancery, 5 May 1804, both in ViU: Carr Papers, 19th-century transcript, being part of record of TJ v. Michie in the hand of George Carr; TQHGM, x [1928], 60).

On 24 Nov. 1795 Thomas Bell and Benjamin Brown took THE DEPOSITION OF THE SAID THOMAS MORGAN at Morgan's house,

the deponent declaring that he was "aged about ninety four years"; that he had come into TJ's employ in about April 1766 and worked as miller at TJ's mill at Shadwell until the mill "was carried away by the great Fresh" of 1771; that he had since that flood lived within half a mile of the mill site; that there had formerly been a shoal near TJ's mill that was only under water during "a full winter tide" and that a horse ford had crossed the river at the mill; that since the construction of the mill at Mountain Falls by the deceased Bennett Henderson the depth of the "dead water" upstream at TJ's mill had increased by about two feet, overflowing the shoal, rendering the ford unusable, and making it impossible, in times of high water, to operate a mill wheel on TJ's site; and that Henderson had built his mill in 1780, when TJ was away on public service, and took from TJ's property stone that Morgan understood TJ intended to use to rebuild his mill and which Henderson used to construct his own mill dam at Mountain Falls (ViU: Carr Papers, 19th-century transcript, being part of record of TJ v. Michie in the hand of George Carr).

BY VIRTUE OF A COMMISSION: see note to Bill in Chancery on the Henderson Milldam, [24 Sep. 1795].

To James Lyle

DEAR SIR   Monticello Nov. 8. 1795.

Mr. Kinsolving having paid me £20–10–2 I now enclose you Mr. Snelson's order on James Brown for that sum less 10/ by a mistake of addition at the time of taking it. Kinsolving still has some tobacco of his last crop, to which he will add some new, and let me have the proceeds. At least so he promised, and therefore I let my execution lie. It shall be forwarded to you as soon as recieved. I am with great esteem Dear Sir Your friend & servt   TH: JEFFERSON

PrC (MHi); at foot of text: "Mr. James Lyle"; endorsed in ink by TJ.

MR. SNELSON'S ORDER ON JAMES BROWN has not been found, but was recorded in MB under 7 Nov. 1795, representing payments made by James Kinsolving on 7 Mch. and 2 Nov. 1795.

From James Madison

DEAR SIR   Fredg. Novr. 8th 1795.

I am thus far on my way to Philada. and shall proceed on the journey this morning. I left with my Father subject to your order the packet of papers promised you. In case of his absence, the overseer will be charged with them. Should you send a special messenger, it will be well to provide against much roughness in the carriage, as the papers are in a state not unsusceptible of being injured by it. I hear nothing new at this place, except that Wheat is falling in Philada. and consequently so here. Two reasons are assigned—the bad quality of the crop—and the English harvest turning out better than was expected. The last cause is no doubt exaggerated, if not forged, but rather in England than here for the papers are full of such paragraphs copied from English papers or English letters. Mr. Randolph's publication is said to be in the press, but has not yet made its appearance. In the mean time Reports continue to circulate to his disadvantage; and I find that malice is busy in attempts to complicate others with his affair. I hope you will not forget to draw on our friend in N. Carolina, for his political anecdotes &c. He will at least in answer to your queries, give you a history of the particular points comprehended in your review. What passed in relation to the Seat of Govt. I know has been entered in his Diary. Yrs. truly

JS. M. JR.

RC (DLC: Madison Papers); endorsed by TJ as received 18 Nov. 1795 from Fredericksburg and so recorded in SJL.

The PACKET OF PAPERS included Madison's manuscript record of the debates in the Federal Convention of 1787 (Madison to

TJ, 4 Apr., 1 May 1796; TJ to Madison, 17 Apr. 1796). For TJ's earlier use of these records, see Editorial Note on the great collaborators, at 13 Mch. 1791; and Madison, *Papers*, x, 7-8n.

MALICE IS BUSY IN ATTEMPTS TO COMPLICATE OTHERS: see note to TJ to James Monroe, 6 Sep. 1795. OUR FRIEND IN N. CAROLINA: Benjamin Hawkins (see TJ to Hawkins, 22 Mch. 1796).

To Madame de Kersaint

MADAM   Monticello Virginia Nov. 9. 1795.

I am honored with your favor of Oct. 20. from Philadelphia. I left France at so early a period of it's revolution that I had not the advantage of being personally acquainted with many characters which afterwards distinguished themselves. The public papers have made known to us the talents and merit of Monsr. de Kersaint; but not having been personally known to him, nor honored with his correspondence, it is not in my power to inform you what connections he had in this country either of business or of acquaintance. Be pleased to accept my regrets that this small service is not within my reach, with assurances of the good wishes and respect with which I have the honor to be Madam Your most obedt. & most humble servt   TH: JEFFERSON

PrC (DLC); at foot of text: "Mde. de Kersaint"; endorsed in ink by TJ on verso.

Claire Louise Françoise de Paul d'Alesso d'Eragny, a native of Martinique, was the widow of Armand Guy Simon de Coetnempren, Comte de Kersaint, a French naval officer and Girondin member of the National Convention who had been executed in Paris in December 1793 for alleged counterrevolutionary activities, and the mother of Claire de Kersaint, later Duchesse de Durfort-Duras, who became an author of some note in Restoration France. Madame de Kersaint

and her daughter lived at 281 South Front Street in Philadelphia from 1794 to 1796, when they returned to Europe (*Dictionnaire*, XVIII, 1156-7; Hoefer, *Nouv. biog. générale*, XV, 464-5; A. Bardoux, *La Duchesse de Duras* [Paris, 1898], 38-44, 48-51, 86; Edmund Hogan, *The Prospect of Philadelphia, and Check on the Next Directory. Part I* [Philadelphia, 1795], 115; TJ to George Washington, 1 Apr. 1793, and note). Her FAVOR OF OCT. 20. recorded in SJL as received 3 Nov. 1795, has not been found.

To James Lyle

DEAR SIR   Monticello Nov. 12. 95.

I am this moment favored with yours of the 3 inst. My memory (as far as it can be trusted) assures me I never had a transaction of any kind with any body of the name of Coleman in my life. I have moreover searched my memorandum books which have been kept with exactness and are alphabeted. I do not find such a name on them for 22. years back, which is as far as I have examined them. I suspect the bond you speak of must have been from Mr. Skipwith and Mr. Eppes; or else that it is some affair of Mr. Skipwith's in which I may have been security, tho' I recollect none such, nor have any conception what it can have been. If my name be really to any such paper I shall be obliged to Mr. Coleman for an explanation of the time, subject &c., and certainly whatever is incumbent on me shall be done without difficulty.

I hope you have received by post the order for the money Mr. Kinsolving paid me. I am with great esteem Dear Sir Your friend & servt.

TH: JEFFERSON

PrC (MHi); at foot of text: "Mr. Lyle"; endorsed in ink by TJ.

To Richard Harrison

DEAR SIR   Monticello Nov. 13. 1795.

I have to acknolege the receipt of your favor of Sep. 28. on the subject of Mr. Grand's and my accounts with the US. I have also lately recieved some papers from Mr. Grand which I am in hopes will enable me to complete the statement which I began for your office, and continued as low down as you had then recieved Mr. Grand's accounts. That statement, as far as it comes, is perfect, and if there be any apparent variations between that and Mr. Grand's you will find them to be of form only and not of substance. Reserving myself to take up the whole subject, as soon as I have time I will just make some observations for the present.

As to the balance of eighteen thousand and odd livres on Mr. Grand's private account against me, transferred by him to the US. it results merely from the form in which he began to keep his accounts when I first went there, and which he discontinued soon after. I kept no private account with Mr. Grand, and therefore could in reality owe him no balance. According to my statements (which I still think the most simple) he was to debit to the US. all the monies he issued for their use, whether on my order or any other. Then as between myself and the US. I kept an exact account, debiting them my salary and other allowances and crediting them every sous I recieved from Mr. Grand or any body else for them. And I can affirm most safely that there never was a sous of their money paid to me or for me which is not credited to them in the statement I gave you as far as the date came. As to other monies paid by Mr. Grand for the US. on my orders, I gave you also an exact state of them, and an explanation of the purpose for which they were given, so that you might carry every article to the account of the proper person. From my mode of statement then it results that you are enabled to carry to the proper account every article of paiment made by Mr. Grand, and that as to those properly belonging to my own account, I formed them into an account myself and delivered you.

In what do Mr. Grand's accounts differ from mine? Only in form. He begun as I observed keeping a private account against me. That is, he debited to me privately all the sums he paid on the orders for my private use, and instead of making the same debits in detail again to the US. he charges them my orders for a quarter's salary at the end of the quarter. If he charged them the sums in detail, and also my order, that would be a double charge; but I am confident if you will look you will find that none of the details he has charged to me are also charged by him to the US. I presume you will find that during the period he pursued this private account, (which I believe was only for one or two quarters) his whole debets against the US for my private account, consist of two articles, to wit, my order or orders for salary; and the 18,000^{tt} balance over and above that order or orders. And if you will add those two articles together, and then add together all the articles of detail charged to me in my private account and not charged by him to the US. they will be found exactly equal. Upon the whole then as to the question whether you are to allow Mr. Grand what he calls my private balance of 18,000.^{tt} I think you must allow it in his account, just as you allow him my quarterly order or orders. (I forget whether there were one or two of these.)[1] If you do not allow him these two articles in the lump, to wit the order or orders, and the balance of 18,000.^{tt} then you ought to allow him to substitute the detail issues of money which he had put into my private account and not into his public one[2] and which are exactly equivalent. I repeat that if you will look into his private account against me, you will find exactly the articles of detail of which my quarterly order or orders and the 18,000^{tt} balance are the equivalent, and which he has not charged in detail in the general account of the US. If he has, he has done wrong: but this is an error I suppose him incapable of.— However I will ere long go through with the statement of all his issues of money, from the time where the one I made out for you ended, till I left France, so that there may not be a shilling paid by Mr. Grand and charged to the US. which you may not be able to debit to the proper person and purpose.

With respect to the other articles of your letter they shall be attended to at the same time, and I shall concur with Mr. Adams and yourself in making any reference you may think proper as to articles you think yourself not authorised to pass. In the mean time I am with great respect & esteem Dr Sir Your most obedt. servt   TH: JEFFERSON

PrC (DLC); at foot of first page: "Mr. Harrison"; endorsed by TJ in ink on verso.

LATELY RECIEVED SOME PAPERS FROM MR. GRAND: see Enclosure No. 1 listed at Grand & Cie. to TJ, 24 Mch. 1795. The STATEMENT WHICH I BEGAN FOR YOUR OFFICE was apparently the Explanations of Ferdinand Grand's Accounts, 21 Feb. 1792. TJ later found that he was mistaken

about MR. GRAND'S PRIVATE ACCOUNT AGAINST ME and advised the Auditor to disregard the present letter (see TJ to Harrison, 8 Mch. 1796). FORMED THEM INTO AN ACCOUNT MYSELF: see Accounts as Minister Plenipotentiary in France, 8 July 1792 (Vol. 24: 175-93).

[1] Closing parenthesis supplied.
[2] Preceding six words interlined.

From Volney, with Postscript by Thomas Lee Shippen

MONSIEUR   Farley 13 9bre 1795

Lorsque j'arrivai de france à Philadelphie, il y eût hier un Mois, Ma premiere pensée fut de Me prévaloir de l'avantage que j'ai eu de Vous Voir à Paris, pour Vous rendre les devoirs d'un Voyageur qui Vient Visiter Votre pays, et pour solliciter de Votre amour pour les arts les renseignemens et les avis nécessaires à bien diriger Mon plan de conduite et de travail: Mais sur les premieres informations que je pris pour Vous adresser une lettre, ce que l'on Me représenta de Votre retraite et presque de Votre Solitude absolue me fit craindre de devenir indiscret, et je contraignis, quoiqu'à regret, mon empressement à retablir avec Vous des relations dont j'ai connu tout le prix: Le Ministre de France en M'apprenant il y a quelques jours qu'il avait reçu de Vous une lettre detaillée avait ranimé Mon Espoir; aujourdhui Mr. Shippen qui a la complaisance de Me garder depuis trois jours à Son agreable Campagne, Me fait un reproche même de Ma timidité, il Me détermine d'autant plus aisément qu'il favorise Mon plus agréable penchant. C'est d'ailleurs un argument Victorieux que de penser qu'il faut tôt ou tard que j'aille en Virginie, et qu'il Vous Sera presqu'impossible d'eviter de Ma part une Visite, puisqu'enfin Vous n'êtes pas chartreux, et qu'au contraire Vous vivez environné d'une famille propre a augmenter Votre goût pour l'état social. Si j'eusse Suivi le plan de Mr. Monroe, j'aurais été d'emblée Me loger à Charlotte-Ville pour y reunir à la nécessité d'apprendre L'anglais, Les Secours et les agrémens de Votre Bibliothèque et de Vos entretiens, Sans Néantmoins Vous être importun: Mais deja des affaires m'ont lié à Philadelphie, et j'en subis le joug

[525]

d'autant plus Volontiers que peut-etre il me prépare un affranchisse-
ment futur, et une indéfinie liberté. Elle est precieuse, cette liberté,
quand on a passé dix mois en prison avec la perspective chaque jour du
supplice pour le lendemain. . . . Mais je suis en Amerique, il faut tout
oublier, excepté les souvenirs de l'Estime et de l'amitié. C'est Sous ces
auspices que j'ai L'honneur de Vous rappeler le Mien, et de Vous demander Si je pourrai Sans abuser de Votre honêteté Vous adresser
quelquefois des questions, particulierement Sur Votre agriculture,
objet principal de Mes gouts et de Mes interets. Je ne puis Mieux terminer cette lettre qu'en remettant La plume à Mr. Shippen qui va peut-
etre changer De langage Mais Non de Sentiment.　　　C: Volney

It is with the greatest diffidence I assure you Sir, that I take the pen from
my friend Mr. Volney's hand to use it instead of him; both because I feel
all the indiscretion of contrasting any thing I can write with what he has
written, and because I am sorry you should be so great a loser by the
change. What leads me to the commission of this error, is first of all, a
selfish motive—to call myself to your remembrance, and to be presented
to you in such good company—and next, a desire of adding the little
mite of my recommendation to the great mass which Mr. [V's] character and fame necessarily carry along with them. It is impossible in my
opinion to say too much of him, but as what I say must pass under his
eyes, I cannot permit myself to say any more, than that any thing you
can do for him, and I know nobody who can do half as much, will be
very flattering and gratifying to me, and that in serving him, you will be
continuing to me that line of services which is already so long and which
has made me long since, and now as much as ever, your faithful and
attached friend, and your much obliged and devoted servant

　　　　　　　　　　　　　　　　　　　Th. L[ee] Shippen

RC (DLC); in Volney's hand, with postscript by Shippen; slightly torn; ellipsis in
original; note by Volney below postscript:
"Volney, poste restante à Philadelphie"; addressed by Shippen: "Thomas Jefferson Esquire Monticello near Charlottesville Virginia"; stamped and postmarked; endorsed
by TJ as received 1 Dec. 1795 and so recorded in SJL.

TJ's letter to the MINISTRE DE FRANCE,
Pierre Auguste Adet, is dated 14 Oct. 1795.
DIX MOIS EN PRISON: see note to Volney to
TJ, 16 Nov. 1793.

To Thomas Mann Randolph

TH:J. TO MR. RANDOLPH   Monticello. Nov. 14. 95.

Biby's boats are arrived and have not brought my 4d. nail machine nor hoop iron. Gamble & Temple write me it was in the hands of a Mr. Ball, and sent somewhere up, perhaps to Westham. Will you be so good as to have it sought for, or it may lie months in some out of the way place, or perhaps never be found. It had better come up in some waggon to Colo. Bell, if it can be handily got aboard one, as there is no Milton boat down, and the article is important to be guarded against miscarriage. All well. Adieu.

RC (DLC); endorsed by Randolph. Not recorded in SJL.

GAMBLE & TEMPLE WRITE ME: the firm's letter to TJ of 4 Nov. 1795, recorded in SJL as received 12 Nov. 1795, has not been found.

From James Monroe

DEAR SIR   Paris Novr. 18. 1795.

Your favor of the 26. of May did not reach me till lately, owing as I presume to its having been committed to some private hand and by whom it was retained to be delivered personally till that prospect was abandoned. I was extremely gratified by it as it led me into a society which is very dear to me and often uppermost in my mind. I have indeed much to reproach myself for not having written you and others of our neighbours more frequently, but I have relied much on you not only to excuse me personally but to make my excuse to others, by assuring them how little of my time remains from publick and other duties, for those with whom by the strong claims of friendship I have a right to take liberties. Before this however you have doubtless received mine of June last and which gave a short sketch of affairs here, so that culpable as I am, still I am less so than I might have been.

I accept with great pleasure your proposal to forward my establishment on the tract adjoining you, in the expectation however that you will give yourself no further trouble in it than by employing for me a suitable undertaker who will receive from you the plan he is to execute, that you will draw on me for the money to pay him, and make my plantation one of the routs you take when you ride for exercise, at which time you may note how far the execution corresponds with the plan. With this view I shall look out for a model to be forwarded you as soon as possible, subjecting it to your correction, and give you full power to place my house orchards &ca. where you please, and to draw on me by way of commencement for the sum of 1.000. dolrs. to be paid where you please 3. months after it is presented. If to be paid without this republick tis probable the draft will be most easily disposed of in sterling money. This sum is all I can answer in the course of the ensuing year calculating always on the possible contingence of a recall and upon which I have always calculated from the moment of my introduction into the Convention, and still calculate depending on the course of events on your side of the Atlantick. With this sum a suitable number of hands may be hired and oxen bought to draw the stone, which with you I prefer, put the ground in order &ca. &ca. to be in readiness to proceed with greater activity the year following. These hands may plant the trees enclose and sew the ground in grass which is laid of and destined for the buildings, of which however you will best judge observing that Hogg be instruct[ed] to give occasional aids with the other hands when necessary. Believe me there is nothing about which I am more anxious than to hear that this plan is commenc'd and rapidly advancing, for be assured admitting my own discretion is my only guide much time will not intervene before I am planted there myself. I have mentioned the proposal you are so kind as [to]¹ make me to Mr. Jones, but as tis possible my letter may unfold that item in my private affairs not to him, but to some of my good friends in a neighbring country, as my official dispatches have those of a publick nature, I beg of you likewise to communicate it to him as of my wishes in that respect.

I have written La Motte and directed him to draw on me for what you owe him and have his answer saying he has drawn, for 3. or 4.00ᵗᵗ, but yet his bill is not presented. I likewise think him an honest man and deserving more than a mere official attention. I found him on my arrival under arrestation not because he had committed any positive crime but because the whole commercial class had drawn upon it, and oft not without cause, the suspicion of being unfriendly to the revolution, and which in his instance was increased by the circumstance of his having married an Engh. woman. He was however shortly afterwards set at liberty and since he has exercised his consular functions. I will also procure you the books and other articles mentioned but shall not forward them till the spring for the reason you mention. I will likewise seek out those of your friends who have survived the storm, remind them of your inquiry after their welfare and apprize you of the result. A terrible storm indeed it has been and great its havoc especially among those of a certain sphere of life, but still I doubt not I shall find many who have survived it among your friends.

I rejoice to hear that Short is to be our neighbour. By his last letter I am to expect him here in a week or two and with Mr. Pinckney, the latter having as I presume adjusted the affair of the Miss: and the boundaries. I suspect the relict of Mr. Rochf:ct. forms the attraction. If the Carters will take me for their paymaster for what lands they have for sale and fix a price which you approve I would most willingly purchase the whole. I have western lands in possession of Mr. Jones for a part of which only he has been offered £2000. Pensyla. currency and which I should be happy to vest near me: an idea equally applicable to the case of Collé.

You have I presume seen the new constitution and will I doubt not concur with me that altho defective when tested by those principles which the light of our hemisphere has furnished, yet it is infinitely superior to any thing ever seen before on this side of the Atlantick. The division of the legislature into two branches, one to consist of 500. and the other of half that number, will secure always in both due attention to the interest of the mass of the people, with adequate wisdom in each for all the subjects that may occur. The mode of election too and the frequency of it in both branches seems to render it impossible that the Executive should ever gain such an influence in the legislature, as by combination, corruption, or otherwise, to introduce a system whereby to endanger the publick liberty: whilst on the other hand the Executive by its numbers and permanence, one of 5. yeilding his place to a successor annually only, seems in regard to this theatre, where the danger is always great and suspicion of course always at the height, well calculated to unite energy and system in its measures with the publick confidence, at the same time that it furnishes within itself a substantial guarantee in favor of the publick liberty. The judiciary too is better organized than heretofore. About 10. days past the constitution was completely installed in all its branches and since each has been in the exercise of its respective functions. The effect which the change has produc'd is great indeed. The Council of Antients occupies the hall lately held by the Convention, and the contrast which a tranquil body, in whose presence no person is allowed to wear his hat, or speak loud, a body who have little to do, and who discuss that little with temper and manners, is so great when compared with the scene often exhibited by its predecessor, that the Spectators look on with amazement and pleasure. The other day a demand was made by the directoire on the 500. for a sum of money and which was immediately granted and the bill in consequence sent to the 250. who upon examination discovered there was no appropriation of it and for that reason rejected the bill. The directoire then accomodated its demand to the article in the constitution as did likewise the council of 500. and whereupon the other council passed the bill. I mention this circumstance to shew the change in legislative proceedings whereby calm deliberation has succeeded a system which was neither calm nor deliberative. Since the government was organized, not more than two or three laws have passed and those of no great importance, and the people go to rest of a night in tranquility consoling themselves with the grateful reflection, that now a strong impediment is opposed to the rage for legislation. They rejoice to find that their legislators have supplied the place of action by reflection. Under this government too the spirit of faction seems to be curbed. Formerly when a member of any note rose and denounc'd another, it put his life in hazard let his merit or demerit be what it might. But latterly some denunciations were threaten'd in the 500., and to which the parties menac'd rose and demanded that their accusers should put in writing the allegations and sign them that they might prepare for and appear in defence, but this silencd the others, and thus tranquility seems to be established and confidence daily increasing.

The paroxisms which preceded the final dissolution of the convention and particularly that of the attack upon it, on the 13. of Vendre. or   of Octr. you will have heard long before this reaches you. In a few words however I will give you a general idea of it: The change of the government or transmission of the powers of government from one system to the other was a great experiment in the present state of affairs and which would not be made without some danger to the revolution; but yet such was the general solicitude to get rid of the revolutionary system that a refusal to make the experiment would likewise be attended with danger. All France seemed to call out for a stable government and this call was finally answer'd by presenting before the nation the constitution in question. But experience had shewn that each succeeding assembly had persecuted the members of the preceding one: a constituent especially was an object not less attractive of the rage of Robt.spre. than a cidevant Bishop or even a chouan. And reasoning from experience it was to be feared, that the deputies of the late convention would be exposed in like manner to the resentment of those who took their places, and this created in them a desire to keep their places and which was attempted by two decrees whose object was to provide for the re election of $\frac{2}{3}$ds. of the legislature of the new government from among the members of the convention, according to a principle of the constitution which applies hereafter and requires an annual change of $\frac{1}{3}$d. only, and which decrees were submitted with the constitution for the sanction of the people. By some of the primary assemblies these decrees were adopted and by others rejected: the convention however reported and in my opinion with truth that the majority was for them and of course that they were obligatory on the Electoral assemblies. This was denied by the opponents to the decrees by whom a systematic effort was made to defeat them, first by news paper discussion, next by section: arrets which defied the authority of the convention, and finally by assembling in arms in great force to attack that body and which [was]² done on the day above mentioned.

I candidly think that this attack upon the convention as it failed was of great utility to the revolution. The system of terror was carried to such a height by Robertspiere and his associates, that in the vibration back which ensued, some danger seemed to threaten, not the overthrow of the revolution, but to put at a greater distance than there was otherwise reason to hope its happy termination: for when this vibration had gained its utmost point, it so happened that the government was to be transferrd into other hands. In this stage too the royalists who were formerly persecuted more than was upon any principle justifiable, and in whose favor and upon that account a general sympathy was excited, and which was of course due to humanity and had no connection with their political principles, had gained an attention which under other circumstances would not have been shewn them. The probability therefore is that if the election had come on unaided by that incident, more than a majority of that description of people would have been thrown into the legislature. But as the attack failed, it produc'd in a great measure the opposit effect, for in consequence the decrees were not only strictly executed, but the former censure against the royalists whose views were now completely unmasked, proportionally revived: many of whom and among those some who were candidates for the legislature and with good prospect of success, took refuge in the neighboring countries or the Vendee, according as circumstances favored their escape.

On the side of the convention there were 3000. foot and 600. horse of Pichegru's army and about 1000. or 1.200. of the citizens of Paris (the latter of whom were honored by their opponents with the title of terrorists) and on the opposit side there were perhaps in activity twice that number, whilst the other citizens of Paris were neutral. The battle was short for as soon as the assailants saw that opposition was made their numbers diminished, and continued to diminish by battallions, till finally none were left but those who were too marked in their characters to hope for concealment: and which latter party surrendered in a body on the next day at noon to the number of about 500. In the contest 4. or 500. on both sides were killed and wounded. It was extremely complained of on the part of the assailants that the convention accepted of

the service of the *terrorists*, and that it suffered cannon to be used in its
defense, since they the assailants had none or but few, and whence they
urged that the fight was not a fair one. You will observe that all Paris
was against the decrees, 2. or 3. sections only excepted, and because as
many of their own deputies were heretofore cut off they would be forc'd
to elect their members from among those of the Convention who be-
longd to other departments, and because they did not like to chose even
those of them who remained. This being the temper of the city in the
commencment the royalists took advantage of it first by opposing the
decrees and which they did with great address, contending for the un-
alienable right of suffrage which they said was thereby infringed, and
demanding wherefore had the good citizens of France fought and bled
so freely, and otherwise sufferd so much if they were now to be en-
slaved, a slavery too the more odious because it was imposed by those
who had assumed the mask of patriotism? One step led on to another till
finally recourse was had to arms.

Before this event I doubted whether foreign powers had much
agency in the interior movments and convulsions of this republick, but
by it I was satisfied they had, for it was known in Engld. Hamburg and
Balse before it happened that there would be a movment here at the
time it took place: at which time too the Ct. d'Artois approached the
coast from Engld. and between whom and the authors of that movment
in Paris and the Vendee there was obviously the utmost harmony of
measures. Something of the kind is to be trac'd in several preceding
events but not so strongly marked, at least not to my knowledge as in
the present case. Yet the ordeal thro' which France has passed and is
passing in the establishment of a republican system is called an experiment of that system, whose convulsions are contrasted with the gloomy
and sullen repose of the neighb'ring despotisms, by the enemies of republican government and to the disadvantage of this latter species of
government. So often does it happen by the decrees of a blind fatality,
that the authors of crimes not only succeed in exculpating themselves
from the reproach they justly merit, but even in fixing the imputation of
guilt upon the [innocent]. [3]

The French were lately checked on the other side of the Rhine and
which caused their retreat to the Rhine: but yet they hold the two posts
of Manheim and dusseldorph on the other side. Tis thought some serious rencounters will take place there soon and which may produce a
serious effect likewise upon the war with the Emperor and on the continent. The late organization of the directoire by which men of real talents
and integrity, and in the instances of Carnot and Barras men of great
military talents, are plac'd in it, the former of whom planned the last

campaign, and the latter commanded the national gds. in the great epoch of the 9th of Therr. when the tyranny of Robertpre. was broken, and on the last event of the 13th. of Vendre. is well calculated to secure a wise arrangment on the part of France.

In negotiation nothing has been lately done. If any negotiations were depending they were doubtless suspended to wait the issue of the late elections and the organization which ensued, in the hope on the part of the coalised powers, that something would turn up from the struggles that were then expected to favor their views. But now that that prospect seems to be over tis probable they will be commenc'd, and peace their early offspring. An event which will be greatly promoted if Pichegru succeeds against the Austrians, and still more so if his majesty of Engld. is again intimidated by the unfriendly greetings of his discontented and afflicted subjects. Unhappy old man, his reign has indeed been a reign of mourning and of sorrow to the world: for we trace upon its several stages in America, the East and in Europe no other vestiges but those which are marked by the blood of the inocent, who were slaughtered in all those various climes of the world and without regard to age sex or condition. And yet we are told by many that he is a mild, an amiable and a pious man, and that the government in which he presides, and by means whereof these atrocities were perpetrated, is that model of perfection of which, thro' all antiquity, Cicero and Tacitus had alone formed only a faint idea, but with which the world was never blessed before. But you know I must not speak irreverently of dignities and therefore I will add no more on this subject at least for the present.

I hear that the French have just gained a considerable advantage over the Austrians on this side of the Rhine near Manheim. The Austrians crossed the R. in its neighbourhood to make a diversion there, were met by a body of French defeated and driven back. Other particulars we have not. Mrs. M and our child join in affectionate wishes to yourself and whole family and pray you also to make them to my brother Joseph and all our neighbours and that you will believe me most affectionately yours

RC (DLC); unsigned; three words omitted by Monroe have been supplied, two from extract printed in Philadelphia *Aurora* (see below); endorsed by TJ as received 21 May 1796 and so recorded in SJL.

The Philadelphia *Aurora* published an extract of this letter on 20 Feb. 1796, before TJ received his copy. It is likely that Monroe, as he had with his letter OF JUNE LAST, sent copies of the letter to multiple correspondents (see Monroe to TJ, 27 June 1795, and enclosure).

RELICT OF MR. ROCHF:CT.: a reference to William Short's relationship with the Duchesse Alexandrine de La Rochefoucauld (see note to Short to TJ, 15 Jan. 1793). The PAROXISMS described by Monroe culminated on 5 Oct. 1795 in the attack by royalist sections of Paris on the expiring National Convention and the dispersal of those forces by Convention troops under

Napoleon Bonaparte. Later that month the Convention was replaced by the Directory under the new constitution (Lefebvre, *Thermidorians*, 187-204). CHOUAN: a supporter of the counterrevolutionary movement that flourished in Maine and Brittany from 1791 to 1800 (Jean Tulard and others, *Histoire et dictionnaire de la Révolution française, 1789-1799* [Paris, 1987], 648).

[1] Word supplied.
[2] Word supplied from *Aurora*.
[3] Word supplied from *Aurora*.

From James Lyle

DEAR SIR   Manchester Nov. 19th. 1795

I am this moment favored with your letter. Last night I received yours of the 8th. Instant enclosing Ro. Snelsons order on Mr. James Brown for £20.0.2 which I expect to receive tomorrow. I am obliged to you for mentioning so fully the affair of Coleman. If any thing of the kind be existing, I imagin it must be with Mr. Skipwith and Mr. Eppes. I expect to see Mr. Coleman, or to hear from him soon. When I get to the bottom of the business I will inform you. I am sorry to trouble you so much with our matters. I am with Esteem Dear Sir Your obliged and Mo hue servt.   JAMES LYLE

RC (MHi); endorsed by TJ as received 2 Dec. 1795 and so recorded in SJL.

YOUR LETTER: TJ to Lyle, 12 Nov. 1795.

From Thomas Mann Randolph

Extract of a letter dated Richmd. Nov. 22. 1795.

'Mann[1] Page's motion for a resolution approving the conduct of the minority in the national senate was warmly agitated three whole days, Wednesday, Thursd. and Friday. It was much less ably defended than opposed. John Marshal it was once apprehended would make a great number of converts by an argument which cannot be considered in any other light than an uncandid artifice to prevent what would be a virtual censure of the President's conduct. He maintained *that the treaty in all it's commercial parts was still under the power of the H. of R.* He contended that it was more in the spirit of the constitution for it to be rendered nugatory after it received the sanction of the P. and S. *by the H. of R. refusing it their support*, than for it's existence to be prevented, for it to be stifled in embryo by their declaring upon application from the P. to know their sentiments before he had given it his signature, that they would withhold that support. He compared the relation of the Executive to the Legislative department to that between the states and the

Congress under the old confederation. The old Congress might have given up the right of laying discriminating duties in favor of any nation by treaty: it would never have thought of taking before hand the assent of each state thereto. Yet no one would have pretended to deny the power of the states to lay such. This doctrine, I believe, is all that is original in his argument. The sophisms of Camillus, and the nice distinctions of the Examiner made up the rest. It is clear that it was brought forward for the purpose of gaining over the unwary and the wavering. It has never been admitted by the writers in favor of the treaty to the Northward. It's author was disappointed however. Upon a division the vote stood 100. to 50. After the question Charles Lee brought forward a motion of compliment to the P. It was of most uncommon length, which was undoubtedly intended to puzzle: and the word 'wisdom' in expressing the confidence of the house in the P. was so artfully introduced that if the fraudulent design had not been detected in time, the vote of the house, as to it's effect upon the P. would have been entirely done away. A resolution so worded as to acquit the P. of all evil intention, but at the same time silently censuring his error, was passed by a majority of 33. 89 to 56.

Some of the warmest of the victorious party talk of bringing forward a motion for a vote of applause to S. T. Mason. But the more moderate say their triumph is sufficient, and it is supposed this will be dropped.'

Tr (DLC: Rives Papers); consists of extract in TJ's hand from a letter acknowledged in TJ to Randolph, 25 Nov. 1795. PrC (DLC). The missing RC is recorded in SJL as received from Richmond on 24 Nov. 1795. Enclosed in TJ to James Madison, 26 Nov. 1795.

MANN PAGE'S MOTION FOR A RESOLUTION approving the votes of Senators Henry Tazewell and Stevens Thomson Mason against the ratification of the Jay Treaty was introduced in the House of Delegates on 17 Nov. 1795 and debated in the committee of the whole on the 18, 19, and 20 Nov. before being passed by a two-to-one margin. The opposition unsuccessfully sought to amend the resolution to state that, while the General Assembly had "full confidence in the public servants in each branch of the general government," the powers granted to "the continental government, and to the state governments, are and should remain separate and distinct, so that neither exercise what is granted to the other," and that "without a full discussion and investiga-

tion" of the treaty which is "unnecessary in the House of Delegates, and ought to be avoided," the state legislators "cannot be prepared to express any mature opinion upon the conduct of the Senators from Virginia touching that subject" (JHD, Nov.-Dec. 1795, p. 19, 23, 24, 27).

CAMILLUS: see note to TJ to Madison, 3 Aug. 1795. THE EXAMINER: Representative William Loughton Smith, who defended the Jay Treaty under the pseudonym of "A Citizen of South-Carolina" in *A Candid Examination of the Objections to the Treaty of Amity, Commerce, and Navigation, Between the United States and Great-Britain, as Stated in the Report of the Committee, Appointed by the Citizens of the United States, in Charleston, South-Carolina* (Charleston, 1795). TJ acquired a reprint that was published, shortly after Washington signed the treaty, under the title of *The Eyes Opened, or the Carolinians Convinced, by an Honourable and Eloquent Representative in the Congress of the United States, in the Following Well Received and Candid Examination of the Objections to His Excellency Governor*

Jay's Late Treaty with Great-Britain; and Which has been Ratified by President Washington, at the City of Philadelphia (New York, 1795), to which was appended the original title page and a postscript. TJ initially ascribed the work to William Cobbett (see Sowerby, No. 3181).

The MOTION OF COMPLIMENT TO THE P. proposed in the House of Delegates on 21 Nov. 1795 stated that "the motives which influenced the President of the United States to ratify the treaty lately negociated with Great-Britain, meet the entire approbation of this House; and that the President of the United States for his great abilities,

wisdom and integrity, merits and possesses the undiminished confidence of his country." It was amended to read: "That this House do entertain the highest sense of the integrity and patriotism of the President of the United States; and that while they approve the vote of the Senators of this state in the Congress of the United States, relative to the treaty with Great Britain, they in no wise mean to censure the motives which influenced him in his conduct thereupon" (JHD, Nov.-Dec. 1795, p. 28).

¹ Before this sentence, TJ first wrote and then canceled "The H. of Delegates."

To James Lyle

DEAR SIR   Monticello Nov. 25. 1795

Mr. Lindsay Coleman called on me yesterday on the transaction which has been the subject of our two last letters. He says it was a matter of Mr. Wayles's, and that the note in question was given by Mr. Eppes and myself as executors. I cannot recall to my mind one tittle of what he mentions, and the transaction not relating to my private affairs is the reason I made no entry in my books. I have written the inclosed letter to Mr. Eppes, which will explain to you that it is to be settled with him, and I wish you could write him a line, and inclose him a copy of the note, which may enable him to answer you on the subject.

Mr. R. Harvie and myself are endeavoring to unravel the disputed items which affect my bond to him. They are three.

1768. £25. cash from Kippen & Co. not credited by R.H.

1772. £19–4–4¾ entered in Walter Mousley's name.

1775. Sep. 24. an order on R. Anderson for Donald, Scot & Co. for £70. not credited on my bond.

It is probable that the £25. will appear to be chargeable to me. The other two articles we think will still be found in the hands of Mousley, and Donald Scott & Co. However it is not yet settled. I am with great esteem Dear Sir Your friend & servt   TH: JEFFERSON

PrC (MHi); at foot of text: "Mr. James Lyle"; endorsed in ink by TJ on verso. Enclosure: TJ to Francis Eppes, 25 Nov. 1795, recorded in SJL as written on the subject of "Coleman," but not found.

A letter from Francis EPPES to TJ of 25 Nov. 1795, which according to SJL was re-

ceived 2 Dec. 1795 and pertained to "Bevins' exr.," has not been found. SJL records eight other letters exchanged by TJ and Eppes between 25 Sep. 1794 and 6 Nov. 1795, all of which are missing. MY BOND TO HIM: see Notes on the Account with Richard Harvie & Company, 22 July 1795.

To Thomas Mann Randolph

Th:J. to Mr. Randolph   Monticello Nov. 25. 95

I recieved last night your favor of the 22d. and thank you for the intelligence it contained respecting the proceedings of the H. of Delegates. It was very interesting, and had not before reached us.

I am obliged to be very troublesome to you while in Richmond. B. Clarke was with me the other day, and to my great astonishment I find that 800. acres of my Poplar forest land is to this moment unpatented, and lies open to a Caveat. The Certificate which I now inclose was sent by the surveyor to Clarke, who sent it to Mr. Lewis just before he returned me all my papers, and being buried in the mass of them, never came to my knowlege till now. As there is danger of saying any thing about it, till they are secured, I have stated the case on a separate paper, without describing the lands, and must get you to consult on that paper with the Register of the land office. If he can recieve the Certificate, then deliver him the inclosed one, and do for me whatever is necessary. I presume there will be 13/4 per hundred to pay, which I must ask you to do for me. If the certificate cannot be recieved, I presume I must have a land warrant for 800 acres, at 12/ per hundred. In this case also I must get you to take out the warrants for me.

I have also 98. or 99. acres formerly in Bedford (now Campbell) I believe on Ivy creek, which I am not certain are patented. They were bought of Richard Stith by Mr. Wayles. If they are patented in Mr. Wayles's name, it will be between Jan. 1771. and the latter end of 1773. If in my name, it will have been since the last period. I must ask the favor of you to have the search made in the proper offices, and to inform me if the patent has issued, or the works been returned, because if not, I must take immediate and secret measures to obtain the Certificate and return it.

I must also trouble you to get me a copy of the collection of the Virginia laws published the last year.

All here are well. Adieu affectionately.

RC (DLC); at foot of first page: "Mr. Randolph"; endorsed by Randolph. PrC (MHi). Enclosure: Certificate from Richard Stith, 25 Oct. 1770, renewed 23 Dec. 1795, based on the 20 Mch. 1770 entry by John Wayles for "all the vacant Land adjoining the lines of his Poplar forest Tract," and consisting of 25 Oct. 1770 survey "for (John Wayles, Esqr.—now Patent for and in the name of) the honourable Thomas Jefferson—800 Acres of Land Situate in Bedford County including heads of branches of Buffalo Creek and dreaming Creek" (MS in ViU; entirely in Stith's hand and signed by him as surveyor, with his insertion above date of survey: "again Dec 23, 1795"; endorsed by Stith: "honourable Thomas Jefferson's Certificate for 800 Acres—Bedford"). Second enclosure printed below.

TJ had not previously secured patents for the two tracts discussed in this letter, which had been surveyed a quarter of a century earlier. A patent for the 800. ACRES OF MY POPLAR FOREST LAND was not issued until 23 May 1797, when Governor James Wood signed the grant, by virtue of land office treasury warrant No. 1722 issued 6 Dec. 1795 (FC in Vi: Land Patent Books, XXXIX, 312-13). TJ did not receive title to the 98. OR 99. ACRES FORMERLY IN BEDFORD (NOW CAMPBELL) until 22 May 1797, when Governor Wood, by virtue of land office treasury warrant No. 1724 issued 5 Dec. 1795, granted him a patent for a 100-acre tract located "on the South branches of Ivy Creek" (printed form at ViU, with blanks filled and description of land entered in a clerk's hand, signed and sealed by Wood, endorsed as recorded in "Book No. 39 page 303"; FC in Vi: Land Patent Books, XXXIX,

303-4). Stith certified the survey of this Ivy Creek tract "adjoining Wilkersons and Johnsons lines" on 23 Dec. 1795 (Tr in ViU, in an unknown hand, with Stith's signature incorrectly copied as "Smith," courses noted on plat in pencil in TJ's hand, with surveying notations in another hand on verso, endorsed in an unknown hand: "hnbl. Tho. Jeffersons certificate & plat for 100 acres Campbell," endorsed by TJ: "100 as. on Ivy creek. Campbell. Stith's"; Tr in ViU, in an unknown hand, including attestation by William P. Martin, Campbell County surveyor, endorsed: "Mr. Jeffersons Platt 100 Acres"). For TJ's instructions on surveys for these lands, see his letters to Bowling Clark and Stith, 12 Dec. 1795.

ENCLOSURE

State of the Case for the Virginia Land Office

[ca. 25 Nov. 1795]

State of case. A tract of land was entered for by John Wayles Mar. 20. 1770. and was surveyed the Octob. following, but the Certificate not sent to him. On his death in 1773. this land fell to Th: Jefferson according to a partition recorded in the General court. The war till 1783. and his absence from home from that time till 1794. prevented his looking to it, and the Surveyor in 1791. only sent the certificate to his overseer, but it never came to his knolege till within these few days. Can the certificate be now recieved at the Register's office? There is no caveat against it. From an examination of the laws in the Chancellor's revisal, and in the late edition, the following articles seem to be applicable to the case.

Act. 1779. c. 12. §. 1. All surveys made on any of the Eastern waters before the end of this session are valid.

§. 2. Provided they be returned to the land office within 12. months after the end of the session. Otherwise void.

1783. c. 39. §. 2. Plats and certificates having from accidents not been returned to the register's office within the time limited by law, the Register shall be obliged to recieve them: and the lands not liable to forfeiture for such failure before the 1st. day of June next, unless where a caveat is already entered.[1]

It is understood that by this last act the right to return the certificate is unlimited in point of time, tho' the protection against Caveats was limited to the 1st. of June then next following. This construction seems confirmed by the following paragraph from the act of

1792. c. 86. §. 36. 'And[2] whereas in some cases plats and certificates of survey have not been recorded in the Surveyor's office, nor returned to the Register's office within the times respectively limited by law, and it is doubtful whether the lands held under such surveys are not still liable to be caveated, Be it therefore enacted that where no Caveat shall be entered *before the said duties respectively shall be performed* such lands shall not thereafter be liable to forfeiture on account of such failure' Here it is implied that the Certificate may be returned, even after the time limited by law, if no Caveat is entered *before the return*.

However this I presume is a case well understood at the land office, and governed by an established practice.

If they cannot recieve the certificate, in what way am I to proceed to save the lands? Must a warrant be taken out and located on it with the Surveyor? If no location has been made by any other in the mean time, there is no inconvenience in this. But if any other has made a location which would fit the same lands, it would take place against my new location, altho' my old certificate would supersede it if that can be established.

MS (DLC: TJ Papers, 98: 16777); undated; written entirely in TJ's hand in two different inks, possibly at two sittings (see note 1 below).

CHANCELLOR'S REVISAL: *A Collection of All Such Public Acts of the General Assembly, and Ordinances of the Conventions of Virginia, Passed Since the Year 1768, as are*

Now in Force, With a Table of the Principal Matters (Richmond, 1785). See Sowerby, No. 1861. LATE EDITION: see TJ to Archibald Stuart, 14 July 1795.

[1] Remainder of text written in a different ink.

[2] Opening quotation mark supplied.

To James Madison

Nov. 26. 95.

Your favor from Fredericksburg came safe to hand. I inclose you the extract of a letter I recieved from Mr. R. now in Richmond. Tho you will have been informed of the facts before this reaches you, yet you will see more of the subject by having different views of it presented to you. Though Marshall will be able to embarras the Republican party in the assembly a good deal, yet upon the whole, his having gone into it will be of service. He has been hitherto able to do more mischief, acting under the mask of republicanism than he will be able to do after throwing it plainly off. His lax lounging manners have made him popular with the bulk of the people of Richmond, and a profound hypocrisy with many thinking men in our country. But having come forth in the plenitude of his English principles, the latter will see that it is high time to make him known. His doctrine that the whole commercial part of the treaty (and he might have added the whole unconstitutional part of it) rests in the power of the H. of R. is certainly the true doctrine; and as the articles which stipulate what requires the consent of the three branches of the legislature, must be referred to the H. of R. for their concurrence, so they, being free agents, may approve or reject them, either by a vote[1] declaring that, or by refusing to pass acts. I should think the former mode the most safe and honorable. The people in this part of the country continue very firmly disposed against the treaty. I imagine the 50 negative votes comprehend the whole force of the Alexandrian party and the bigots and passive obedience men of the whole state who have got themselves into the legislature. I observe an expression in Randolph's printed secret intimating that the President, tho' an honest man himself, may be circumvented by snares and artifices, and is in fact surrounded by men who wish to clothe the Executive with more than constitutional powers. This when public, will make great impression. It is not only a truth, but a truth levelled to every capacity, and will justify to themselves[2] the most zealous votaries, for ceasing to repose the unlimited confidence they have done in the measures which have been pursued.—Communicate the inclosed paper, if you please, to Mr. Giles.— Our autumn is fine. The weather mild, and intermixed with moderate rains at proper intervals. No ice yet, and not much frost. Adieu affectionately.

RC (DLC: Madison Papers, Rives Collection); unsigned. PrC (DLC). Enclosure: Thomas Mann Randolph to TJ, 22 Nov. 1795.

TJ's observations on Edmund RANDOLPH'S PRINTED SECRET indicate that he was one of several persons who saw, before its publication by Samuel H. Smith in mid-December, at least part of A Vindication of Mr. Randolph's Resignation (Philadelphia, 1795), the former Secretary of State's rebuttal of charges that he had made improper disclosures to and solicited money from Jean Antoine Joseph Fauchet (see Sowerby, No. 3180; for Randolph's resignation as Secretary of State, see note to TJ to James Monroe, 6 Sep. 1795). The pamphlet contained a "Statement of Facts," a narrative history of the events surrounding his resignation; pertinent letters and documents, including correspondence between Randolph and Washington and translations of excerpts from Fauchet's dispatches No. 3 (4 June 1794), No. 6 (5 Sep. 1794), and all of No. 10 (31 Oct. 1794); the certificate Randolph obtained from Fauchet before his return to France, which described the circumstances surrounding the dispatches and confirmed that Randolph had never divulged government secrets or sought bribes; and Randolph's open letter of 8 Oct.

1795 to the President in which he argued that Washington had prejudged his case and been taken in by a plot masterminded by British minister George Hammond to gain the President's signature on the Jay Treaty by estranging him from the only member of the Cabinet who discouraged him from signing the treaty until conditions were met by the British—a letter in which Randolph asserted that "the *immediate* ratification of the treaty with Great Britain can be traced to no other source, than a surrender of yourself to the first impressions" from Fauchet's dispatch No. 10 (Randolph, *Vindication*, 49-53).

The concept that the President, THO' AN HONEST MAN HIMSELF, was surrounded by SNARES AND ARTIFICES set by those WHO WISH TO CLOTHE THE EXECUTIVE WITH MORE THAN CONSTITUTIONAL POWERS, was the theme of a conversation between Randolph and Fauchet in April 1794 depicted in Dispatch No. 3, reiterated by Fauchet in his certificate in behalf of Randolph, and examined again by Randolph in his open letter to the President (same, 15, 17-18, 75-6).

After submitting his manuscript to the press in early November, Randolph left Philadelphia and settled in Richmond. It is likely that he received signatures from the press as they were produced (Reardon, *Randolph*, 331-2). TJ's reference to Randolph's revelations indicates that at this time he had access at least through page 15 (signature C) and probably through page 76 (signature K) of the pamphlet. William Branch Giles later informed TJ that he had been "favored with its perusal as far as page 84," or through signature L (Giles to TJ, 9 Dec. 1795). TJ received a copy of the published pamphlet ca. 29 Dec. 1795 and commented on it two days later (Giles to TJ, 15 Dec. 1795; TJ to Giles, 31 Dec. 1795). For TJ's notes on the pamphlet, see Notes on Edmund Randolph's *Vindication*, [after 29 Dec. 1795].

[1] Preceding two words interlined in place of an illegible cancellation.
[2] Preceding two words interlined.

From Richard Harrison

DEAR SIR   Treasury Department Auditors Office Novere. 28th. 1795.

I have had the honor to receive your Letter of the 13th Inst. in answer to mine of the 28th. September. On looking over the papers in my hands, I do not find among them what Mr. Grand calls your *private* account, nor do I recollect ever to have seen it. If you would be good enough to furnish a Copy of this, it might, with the other papers you propose to forward, enable me to remove all difficulties with respect to the receits, and payments of money. I have the honor to be with Sentiments of great respect Sir Your most obed Hble Servt.

R. HARRISON

RC (DLC); at foot of text: "Thomas Jefferson Esquire"; endorsed by TJ as received 9 Dec. 1795 and so recorded in SJL.

To Edward Rutledge

MY DEAR SIR   Monticello Nov. 30. 95.

I received your favor of Oct. 12. by your son, who has been kind enough to visit me here, and from whose visit I have recieved all that pleasure which I do from whatever comes from you, and especially from a subject so deservedly dear to you. He found me in a retirement I doat on, living like an Antediluvian patriarch among my children and grand children, and tilling my soil. As he had lately come from Philadelphia, Boston &c. he was able to give me a great deal of information of what is passing in the world, and I pestered him with questions pretty much as our friends Lynch, Nelson &c. will us when we step across the Styx, for they will wish to know what has been passing above ground since they left us. You hope I have not abandoned entirely the service of our country: after a five and twenty years continual employment in it, I trust it will be thought I have fulfilled my tour, like a punctual soldier, and may claim my discharge. But I am glad of the sentiment from you, my friend, because it gives a hope you will practice what you preach, and come forward in aid of the public vessel. I will not admit your old excuse, that you are in public service tho' at home. The campaigns which are fought in a man's own house are not to be counted. The present situation of the President, unable to get the offices filled, really calls with uncommon obligation on those whom nature has fitted for them. I join with you in thinking the treaty an execrable thing. But both negotiators must have understood that as there were articles in it which could not be carried into execution without the aid of the legislatures on both sides, that therefore it must be referred to them, and that these legislatures being free agents, would not give it their support if they disapproved of it. I trust the popular branch of our legislature will disapprove of it, and thus rid us of this infamous act, which is really nothing more than a treaty of alliance between England and the Anglomen of this country against the legislature and people of the United states.—I told your son I had long had it in contemplation to write to you for half a dozen *sour* orange trees, of a proper size for small boxes, as they abound with you. The only trouble they would give would be the putting them into boxes long enough before sending them for them to take root, and when rooted to put them into some vessel coming *direct to Richmond* to the care of Mr. Daniel Hylton there. Your son is kind enough to undertake the commission. With constant and unchanged affections I am my dear friend Your's affectionately   TH: JEFFERSON

RC (PHi); addressed: "Edward Rutledge esq. Charleston." PrC (DLC).

To James Madison

TH:J. TO J.M.   Dec. 3. 95.

The inclosed letter came under cover to me from Mde. de Chastellux. As I know not where the Duke de Liancourt is, and have no particular motive for making it the occasion of renewing a slight acquaintance, never valued, I will ask the favor of you to have it handed him. We have no news but the death of Doctr. Gilmer, which happened the night before last. I hear nothing from our assembly. A post or two more I hope will bring us the first movements of your campaign, which will be most interesting. Adieu affectionately.

RC (DLC: Madison Papers). PrC (DLC). Enclosure not found, but see note below.

The INCLOSED LETTER was probably included in a missive from Madame de Chastellux to TJ of 7 Sep. 1795, recorded in SJL as received 1 Dec. 1795, but not found.

From Maria Cosway

DEAR SIR   London 4 Decr: 1795

At last I have the long wished pleasure of receiving a letter from you? I cannot tell how much it has made me happy for I could not suspect you could forgit me, tho am sensible My not having sufficient Merit to engage your remembrance, but can only trust to the Sentiments known to me for so long a time and formed Upon So much Sure foundation. How glad am I to hear your detachment from the busling world, what is this world? Happy, very happy those who Make it a good passage to a better One, to an everlasting life, we can be very happy in this with these veiws of it for then we only think of the virtues we can practice, the vices we Can avoid, the end we are created for, the recompence is destind to us which no body can usurpe and when we act for the Omnipresent or Omnipotent who sees every thing how can we wish, or be disturb'd at the Momentary circumstances which pass like lightning to leave every thing in ashes.

You will soon have the pleasure of seeing the Charming Anjelica. I loose her with Much regret she is the woman I love Most, and feel Most happy with in this Country. Poor Madm. de Corney has met with a great Change in her life from what she was. I wanted Much to send a letter to you by My brother George Hadfield but the resolution of his going away without taking leave prevented My knowing of his departure till he was gone, however I know You will be kind to all and need Not Say any thing particular for him. I hope he will meet with encouragement, he has talents and an amiable Character, tho he is my brother I must be just.

You Mention Geneva in Your letter with satisfaction. Many thanks for I love it very Much as well as admire it. How happy I was there in those enchanting walls of the Most beautifull Situation. What a sound a Monastory is! If all thought it the heaven I do, the world would end and the gospel obliged to alter its prediction. What a differance in this town in this bustling situation, from that solitude? Those bells who put me in Mind Constantly of our Maker our duties and our end, who united My Mind with angels and heaven! Here indeed the Crowns must be treeple and so they will be if recompance is to be according to difficulty and pain. My duties however are here and here I make My Crowns, my happiness in the will of God, a will which Must be done, let us follow it with Love.

I will not attempt to enter into political news or insignificant things. Theathers and Masquerades, assemblies Concerts and Cards, Shops and shows make all the occupation of these good people. My little girl, my pencil and my home make mine, and endevor to make my time very short by making it useful.

What would I give to surprize you on your Monticello! I have Your picture by Troumbel on the side of my Chimney always before me, and always regret that perhaps never can I see the Original. At least if I could have oftner your letters t'would be some compensation, but to be deprived of both is too much.

Resolve and break this long intervals. Yours most affy:

M. Cosway

RC (MHi); endorsed by TJ as received 3 June 1796 and so recorded in SJL.

LETTER FROM YOU: TJ to Maria Cosway, 8 Sep. 1795.

TJ did not acknowledge or reply to this letter—according to SJL Mrs. Cosway's last until 20 July 1801—and waited until 31 Jan. 1803 before responding to that letter and another from her of 25 Feb. 1802. See also TJ to Angelica Schuyler Church, 24 May 1797.

From James Madison

DEAR SIR   Philada. Decr. 6. 1795.

The inclosed letter with a pamphlet under the same cover came to me a few days ago from the post office with a charge of a dollar postage. I have delayed to forward it till further expence could be avoided. The pamphlet I will send by the first good opportunity. I have your favor of the 26th. ult., corroborating the view I had before received of matters at Richmond. There is likely to be a Quorum of both Houses of Congress tomorrow. Muhlenberg and Dayton will probably be the candidates for the Chair in the H. of Reps. I can say nothing yet of the complexion of the body, more than has been known from general accounts long ago. With respect to the Cabinet, I am without the least information. It does not appear that any final step has been taken for filling the vacant Departments. The offer of the Secretaryship of State to P. Henry is a circumstance which I should not have believed without the most unquestionable testimony. Col. Coles tells me Mr. Henry read the letter to him on that subject. It appears that there have been some agitations in Paris produced by the *decree of two thirds*, tacked to the Constitution; but as the Jacobins united with the Convention in crushing them, the crisis was probably the expiring struggle of the Counter revolutionists. From the nature of the Decree, it is not wonderful that it should not have been swallowed without some resistance. Randolph's pamphlet is not yet out. I am told it will appear in a few days. As soon as I can send you a copy you shall have one. Yrs. affey.

Js. MADISON JR

RC (DLC: Madison Papers); endorsed by TJ as received 16 Dec. 1795 and so recorded in SJL. Enclosure not found.

George Washington offered the SECRETARYSHIP OF STATE to Patrick Henry in a letter dated 9 Oct. 1795. Henry responded a week later by declining the invitation to join the Cabinet. By the end of November, Timothy Pickering had agreed to leave the War Department and become Secretary of State, Charles Lee had accepted the Attorney Generalship, vacant since William Bradford's death in August 1795, and, in January 1796, James McHenry became Secretary of War (Fitzpatrick, *Writings*, XXXIV, 334-5; Freeman, *Washington*, VII, 299, 312-13, 322-6, 340). For TJ's comments on these appointments, see TJ to James Monroe, 2 Mch. 1796.

AGITATIONS IN PARIS PRODUCED BY THE DECREE OF TWO THIRDS: see James Monroe to TJ, 18 Nov. 1795, and note.

From James Blake

SIR   Phila. Dec. 8. 1795.

I beg leave to inform you that I have this morning put Cortes's letters into Mr. Crosby's hands to be forwarded to you as soon as possible. Mrs. Carmichael brought them with her here from Maryland—but forgot the manuscript. She assured me, however, she would not fail to send it by the first opportunity. With great respect I have the honor to be, Sir, Your most obedient & most humble servant   JAMES BLAKE

RC (DLC); facing complimentary close: "*No. 2. North 5th. street*"; at foot of text: "Thomas Jefferson Esquire"; endorsed by TJ as received 22 Dec. 1795 and so recorded in SJL.

From William Branch Giles

DEAR SIR   Philadelphia December 9th 1795

Having had no intelligence of importance to communicate, and presumeing upon your anxiety to see the President's speech to the present Congress, I have delayed writing until I could gratify you with its inclosure. It is accordingly contained in the accompanying Newspaper.

You will observe that the speech wears a conciliatory and not a dictatorial complexion; and in this respect, has not, I beleive, corresponded with the general expectation. The mild form of communication assumed by the President, clearly proves, that he is at length of opinion, that the public temper, as well as that of the house of Representatives, requires perswasives, and will not tolerate threats; and that his personal influence would be more impressive, by presenting to them the amiable solicitude of his heart for the promotion of the general welfare; than by relying on the wisdom of his head in the means which have been pursued for its attainment.

This course was certainly well calculated to effect its object; for the speech, from its perswasive quality alone, seems to have made a considerable impression upon the house of Representatives; but how far it may vary its ultimate measures I am not able to form any probable conjecture.

You will also observe a studied silence respecting France. The speech does not inform us, whether the former good humor of our sister Republic still continues towards us; nor whither she is in any degree sowared by our late unkind treatment. It does not contain one tittle of kind intelligence as to her own health, and the state of her own constitution. In the contrast drawn betwen the happy situation of the U.S., and the miseries of Europe in consequence of the existing war, it does indeed remind us of the misfortunes of the republic, without a compassionate[1] intimation of the glorious cause which produced them: nor is there a single sympathiseing sensation which the similitude of our late struggle with the present one of France, would naturally have suggested.

This is the more surpriseing, as it is known here by a few, and must have been known to the Executive, that the peace with Algiers was in some measure obtained through the good offices of France; nor would the same good offices have been withheld in securing to us the trade of the Missisippee in the late peace with Spain, if it had been intimated to the Republic that such a measure would have been desireable to the U.S. But Mr. Pinkney passed through Paris on his Spanish mission, without either discloseing the state of the negotiation with England, or intimateing the object of his mission to Spain.[2] Hence it was concluded that the interposition of the Republic was not desired, and the peace was concluded without it.

The manner in which the treaty with G. Brittain is mentioned in the speech, has embarrassed its opposers in decideing on the proper course to be taken in the answer.

If it be attempted to bring the treaty into view for the purpose of animadversion: it will be said by its favorers; that it is not *officially* before us; that the attempt evidences an officious and unjustifyable solicitude to disturb the harmony of the different branches of the government and of the house itself; that the thing is still incomplette; that the expression of the sence of the house may affect the ultimate determination of the Brittish Cabinet; to which will be added the old unmeaning clamor of disorganization, war &c &c.

If its opposers should not avail themselves of the opportunity afforded by the speech of testifying their disapprobation, and should wait until it be *officially* communicated; it will not only afford an opportunity of makeing proseletes to the treaty; but it will then be said, that it was uncandid not to notify the Executive of an intention of withholding the means for its execution at the earliest moment; that the proper time for opposition being past, it is now too late to commence it &c &c.

My own opinion is that an attempt should be made to manifest our disapprobation in the answer; and, if possible, in a manner which will be the most delicate and respectful to the other branches of the government, and which would not justify an inference that a due cooperation will not be afforded upon all justifyable occasions. This I think would be the most candid course, and would leave to the favorers of the treaty either the alternative of hazzarding a vote upon its merits, or repelling its discussion upon some collateral grounds; and if we should even be unsuccesful in the attempt, we should proceed to the attack with a better grace, when the treaty shall be *officially* laid before us.

From conversations with individual members I am induced to fear, that the present house of Representatives, from whose firmness and patriotism so much has been expected by the public, will not answer the pleasing anticipation.

A great majority of the house is opposed to the treaty intrinsically; but some whose firmness has been counted upon, will not resist the weight of the President and senate. The common language with persons of this description, is, the treaty is a bad thing; but it is the act of the constituted authorities: the house of Representatives can exercise no discression, but as to the most advisable means of effectuateing it: Disagreement amongst the different departments of the government should be avoided &c. &c. I therefore think that the majority will depend much upon the manner, in which the question is presented to the house. If a complimentory stricture should be reported in the answer, I have no doubt but that it would be stricken out upon motion; Because all the opposers to the treaty would unite in a negative vote: But I believe it would be impossible to unite them in any affirmative vote of disapprobation, which could be proposed.

The Eastern representation seems to act more in covert and concert, than at any former period; and the effect of calumny and misrepresentatives has been so complete, that the new members seem to nestle under the wings of the old; and to fly all communication with their Southern bretheren for fear of a disorganiseing infection. Strange as this may seem it is nevertheless true!

Mr. Randolph's vindication is not yet before the public at full length. I have by special indulgence been favored with its perusal as far as page 84. The first pages contain all the evidence, and part of his general letter (as he terms it) to the President. The publication will afford an infinite fund of matter for political parties; but its effects upon the public mind, as it respects the President, or the state of parties, I think extremely problematical. It will probably depend upon the management and the activity of the parties themselves. As to Mr. Randolph, there will be no doubt of its effect. He will be exculpated from the charge of corruption; but will be deemed the most indiscreet of ministers.

I will transmit you a copy as soon as it shall appear at full length.

Be pleased to present my most respectful regards to the ladies of your family; and accept my best wishes for your own uninterrupted happiness &c. &c.   WM. B. GILES

RC (DLC); at foot of text: "Thomas Jefferson *Esqr*"; only the most important emendations are recorded below; endorsed by TJ as received 25 Dec. 1795 and so recorded in SJL. Enclosure not identified, but see note below.

The PRESIDENT'S SPEECH to Congress of 8 Dec. 1795 touched on progress in relations with the Indians, Morocco, Algiers, Spain, and Great Britain, and presented a number of domestic issues for Congress to consider. Commenting on the pacification of the Whiskey Rebellion in this seventh annual address, Washington expressed the CONCILIATORY view that while it was his "sacred duty, to exercise with firmness and energy, the Constitutional powers with which I am vested, yet it appears to me no less consistent with the public good, than it is with my personal feelings, to mingle in the operations of government, every degree of moderation and tenderness, which the national justice, dignity and safety may permit" (Fitzpatrick, *Writings*, XXXIV, 386-93). Washington followed closely a draft by Alexander Hamilton and inserted a paragraph

on the Whiskey Rebellion written by John Jay and revised by Hamilton (Syrett, *Hamilton*, XIX, 460-7).

In his speech Washington also advised Congress that he had recently learned that a treaty for PEACE WITH ALGIERS was imminent (Fitzpatrick, *Writings*, XXXIV, 387; for the 5 Sep. 1795 treaty in question, see Miller, *Treaties*, II, 275-304). The LATE PEACE WITH SPAIN was the 22 July 1795 Treaty of Basle between France and Spain (Clive Parry, ed., *The Consolidated Treaty Series*, 231 vols. [Dobbs Ferry, N.Y., 1969-81], LII, 411-17). Washington's address also "officially disclosed" to the House of Representatives that he was awaiting the British response to the Senate's conditional ratification of the Jay TREATY, to which he had given his approval "after full and mature deliberation." Upon receipt, the President promised to lay it before Congress "without delay" (Fitzpatrick, *Writings*, XXXIV, 388).

[1] Word interlined in place of "solitary."
[2] Giles here canceled what appears to be "the other."

To Thomas Lee Shippen

DEAR SIR   Monticello Dec. 9. 95.

I recieved with great pleasure your favor at the foot of Mr. Volney's letter, and had learned with still greater from Mr. Rutledge, a few days before, your recovery from the situation in which I left you. I have the better opinion too of your felicity as I find you date from the country. I am myself so passionately devoted to a country life, that my mind rarely recurs to the scenes it has passed over. A visitor, like Mr. Rutledge, sometimes recalls them to me, and makes me feel in them a momentary flash of in[terest]. The vollies of questions I put to him, have given him an example of what he may expect when he shall cross the Styx from his friends gone there before him, and who will be anxious to learn what shall have passed above ground since their departure.—You once gave us a hope of seeing you in our neighborhood; nay more, of seeing you here. It would make us all extremely happy. Mrs. Shippen's friends in this vicinity are well. They have removed a few miles [farther] from us, which makes considerable odds in the pract[ice] of visiting. Be so good as to present me respectfully to her and to your father, and to accept assurances of the esteem with which I am Dear Sir Your sincere friend & servt   TH: J[EFFERS]ON

PrC (DLC); torn; at foot of text: "Mr. Shippen."

Shippen's FAVOR was written AT THE FOOT OF MR. VOLNEY'S LETTER of 13 Nov. 1795.

SJL records a letter from TJ to Shippen of 7 Feb. 1796, and one from Shippen to TJ of 25 Feb. that was received 12 Mch. 1796, neither of which has been found.

From Sir Peyton Skipwith

DEAR SIR   Prestwould 9th. Decr. 1795.

In the year 1782 I furnished our friend Mr. William Short with £92.10—soon after his Father paid me £20. in part of the cash lent which reduced the sum to £72.10. You will see by Mr. Shorts letters that in consequence of his ordering three or four suits in the General Court at my instance, he considered himself intitled to a credit for the service, supposing his friend Capt. Marshall would compleat the business that he had himself but barely began, and I beleive Mr. Marshalls views were friendly, but considering my business to be going on but slowly, and unwilling to be often troublesome to Capt. Marshall who had from me received no emolument for his services, I determined, and did pay him, I beleive much more than the legal fees; I therefore do not think my Nephew intitled to fees also, nor do I believe he wou'd accept or receive fees if he was here. I have made out the account with interest upon the sum lent from the time of his first letter acknowledging the loan. It is probable that if Mr. Short had not been fortunate in life, I should never have demanded principal, or interest, but as the case has been otherwise with him, and I have myself in consequence of an unfortunate securityship been lately more pushed in money matters than ever I was in my life, I think it just, and reasonable that I should be paid the sum I claim, indeed, circumstanced as I am, I doubt not but if my

Nephew was on the spot, he wou'd on loan if I desired it contribute in any reasonable degree that I might require. Upon this ground I take the liberty to address you, and will thank you, as I am told Mr. Short is honoured with your attention to his money matters in this Country to pay to the bearer the claim (you will see by his own letters) I have against Mr. Short; nor wou'd I now be troublesome with my demand, but that I am well assured that from my former readiness to aid him, it wou'd pain him to know I wanted it and could not obtain the payment of the loan I had made him.

I am told that you have a number of Negroes profitably employed in the business of making Nails, a business I have long wished to engage in myself. I have therefore taken the liberty of directing my Young Man, if agreeable to you, to view your Factory with attention, and care, for the purpose of directing the necessary Shop, or Shops &c. at his return. With every sentiment of esteem and respect I have the honor to be Dear Sir your Obedt. and very Hble. Servt,   PEYTON SKIPWITH

RC (DLC: William Short Papers); in a clerk's hand, signed by Skipwith; endorsed by TJ as received 24 Dec. 1795 and so recorded in SJL. Enclosure: William Short in account with Skipwith, n.d., commencing with the loan to Short on 28 Oct. 1782, less the credited payment by Short's father, plus £47.6 in interest to 14 Dec. 1795, for a balance due of £119.16 (MS in same; in the hand of and signed by John Hill, Skipwith's agent).

Virginia planter Sir Peyton Skipwith (1740-1805), a brother of William Short's mother, Elizabeth Skipwith Short, owed his title to a baronetcy created by James I in 1622, to which Skipwith succeeded in 1764 on the death of his father, Sir William Skipwith. In 1794 he had commenced construction of an elaborate house at Prestwould, his Mecklenburg County plantation

named after the family's seat in England, but his finances became hard pressed when he was forced to repay prewar debts to British merchants (Herbert A. Elliott, "Sir Peyton Skipwith and the Byrd Land," VMHB, LXXX [1972], 52-9; Shackelford, *Jefferson's Adoptive Son*, 2, 141; Cokayne, *Baronetage*, I, 214-15).

CAPT. MARSHALL WOULD COMPLEAT THE BUSINESS: initially Short had intended to repay the debt to his uncle by acting as Skipwith's attorney in several Byrd lawsuits, but on Short's departure for Europe in 1784 John Marshall took over the cases. The debt was resolved in 1802, when it was found that Skipwith had actually recovered the amount of the obligation by drawing heavily on Short's funds—then managed by Benjamin Harrison—while Short was in Europe (Shackelford, *Jefferson's Adoptive Son*, 141-2, 192n).

To Volney

DEAR SIR   Monticello Dec. 9. 95.

Two or three days before the reciept of your favor from Philadelphia I had learnt your arrival there from Mr. Rutledge who had done me the favor to call on me. Accept my sincere felicitations on your safe arrival among us. It had been very long that the public papers had ceased to inform us what had become of you. There are many others of my friends about whose fate I am in the dark. It would have given me great pleasure if you had executed Colo. Monroe's plan of making Charlottesville your school for our language, and tho' you appear to have fixed on Philadelphia as better accomodated to your views you leave me to hope that you propose a visit to this state, and that you will not pass me by. It will be peculiarly gratifying to me to possess you here, and to be your Mentor for whatever may regard this state. You will find me entirely absorbed in the regeneration of my farms, which will require a long time to be reclaimed from the state of barbarism in which I found them after an absence of ten years. My progress is the slower as my health is of late extremely impaired. Your enquiries respecting our agriculture shall be answered to the best of my abilities; and certainly you shall have no answers which shall not have been previously [approved by] those more versed in the practice of husband[ry than mys]elf. If you have views of fixing yourself [on a farm] in the [U]S. it will be wise in you to visit different parts of them. In some parts little can be done with a [greater capital], in others much with a small one. Soil, climate, price, the objects of culture, and state of society are all worthy attention. The multitude of enquiries I should have to make on the subject of my friends in France, were I to begin, forbids me to enter on them and tho' I have bewailed most sincerely the lot of some of them, yet I never can cease to wish that the severe revolution through which France has been passing, may issue in some form of government favorable to liberty and tranquility. On this will depend the aggravation of the chains of other nations, or their rescue from them. Nor shall we fail to feel the influence. Our citizens are divided into two political sects. One which fears the people most, the other the government. You will readily judge in which of these the people themselves are. For my part I have no fear of a people, well-informed, easy in their circumstances, dispersed over their *farms*, and occupied on them. I say *over their farms*, because these constitute the body of our citizens. The inhabitants of towns are but zero in the scale. But I leave all these things to those who will have a longer interest in them, and wish to hear nothing connected with politics. It will always give me pleasure to hear of my friends, and particularly to know from yourself that you can accomodate yourself to our country, our people and our manners, and to have occasions of renewing to you assurance of the esteem with which I am Dear Sir Your most obedt. & most humble servt   Th: JEFFERSON

PrC (DLC); torn; at foot of first page: "M. de Volney."

To John Barnes

Dʀ Sɪʀ   Monticello Dec. 11. 95.

I have this day drawn on you in favor of Messrs. Plumsted & McCaul for 50.D. 75 C. which please to honor. I have at the same time taken the liberty of telling them you would be kind enough to recieve, and forward to me, 2 Chinese gongs which they will deliver you. If they are not packed in a box I must trouble you to have that done. Send me also at the same time 6. ℔ of your best young Hyson and a small box of Spanish Segars. One of these articles will perhaps [. . .] in the box [with] the gong, to le[ssen pac]kages.[1] I wrote to Mr. Mussi to forward me another case of oil and call on you for paiment. If this be not sent off, I could wish it to come with the gongs, tea and segars, as Messrs. Gamble & Temple at Richmond, complain of the multitude of small and single parcels addressed to them for me.

I have to acknolege yours of Nov. 21. Since writing you on the subject of my tobacco I have seen my manager from the plantation where it is made; and he gives me so indifferent an account of the quality of his this year's tobacco owing to the immense deluges of rain we had in the season, that I determine not to send it to Philadelphia, at which market I wish to preserve the credit of my crop, so as to be entitled to the very highest price whenever it is sent there. To this it's quality will entitle it in common years: and the crop of the ensuing year I shall forward to you for that market. I am with much esteem Dr. Sir Your most obedt servt

                                                    Tʜ: Jᴇꜰꜰᴇʀꜱᴏɴ

PrC (MHi); mutilated at fold; at foot of text: "Mr. John Barnes"; endorsed in ink by TJ on verso.

SJL records a letter of this date from TJ to ᴘʟᴜᴍꜱᴛᴇᴅ & ᴍᴄᴄᴀᴜʟ concerning "50.75 on Barnes for gongs," as well as another to them of 5 Nov. 1795, and letters from Plumstead & McCaul to TJ of 9 Sep. 1793 and 15 Oct. and 17 Nov. 1795, none of which has been found.

Barnes's letter of ɴᴏᴠ. 21., recorded in SJL as received 1 Dec. 1795, and a letter from TJ to Barnes of 26 Nov. 1795 on "£66.67 to Gamble & Temple," have not been found. The latter concerned TJ's payment for "half a ton of nail rod" (ᴍʙ, 26 Nov.

1795). ᴍʏ ᴍᴀɴᴀɢᴇʀ: Bowling Clark, the overseer of Poplar Forest, where the bulk of TJ's tobacco was grown (Betts, *Farm Book*, 150, 255-6).

On 7 Nov. 1795 TJ wrote an order on Barnes in favor of the Milton merchants Fleming & McClenahan for $125 payable at sight (PrC in MHi, at foot of text: "Mr. John Barnes Mercht. Philadelphia"). TJ notified Barnes of the draft in a letter of advice of the same date (PrC in same). The payment was to settle TJ's account with Eli Alexander, his recently retired overseer at Shadwell (ᴍʙ, 1 Nov. 1794, 7 Nov. 1795).

[1] Sentence interlined.

To Bowling Clark

DEAR SIR   Monticello Dec. 12. 95.

I found it safest on the whole to take out new warrants and lay them on my 800. acres of land in Bedford, and 98. acres adjoining Tullas's. I now inclose you the warrants with a letter to Mr. Stith, which will explain itself to you, and I leave it open for your perusal. I imagine he will hardly resurvey it, but give you a certificate of new date copied from the old one, only correcting the error in that.

Having got from him the certificate for the 98. acres it will be necessary to go with that and the small warrant to the surveyor of Campbell, and get a new certificate. I suppose he will copy the old one, giving it a new date, for it will hardly be worth while to resurvey, and the less movement there is in the matter the better. It will be best to let both surveyors know at once that we will pay them new fees, and do not desire to give them the trouble of actually resurveying as they can certainly trust to the old surveys. The bearer comes express on this business, and I should be glad if you can send me the new certificates by the people who come with the beeves &c. as I shall be uneasy till I get my patent. I inclose Mr. Stith's certificate to facilitate to him the making out a new one. I am Dear Sir Your friend & servt   TH: JEFFERSON

PrC (MHi); at foot of text: "Mr. Bowling Clarke"; endorsed by TJ in ink. Enclosures: (1) TJ to Richard Stith, 12 Dec. 1795. (2) Richard Stith's Certificate, 25 Oct. 1770, renewed 23 Dec. 1795, listed at TJ to Thomas Mann Randolph, 25 Nov. 1795. Other enclosures not found.

SJL records 11 letters between TJ and Clark from 28 Dec. 1794 to 19 Oct. 1795, none of which has been found. An additional 69 letters exchanged between 20 Dec. 1795 and 25 Oct. 1801 are recorded in SJL but missing.

To Richard Stith

DEAR SIR   Monticello Dec. 12. 1795

I had been in hopes ere this to have taken a trip to the Poplar Forest and to have had the pleasure of seeing you there; but I have been so much afflicted with Rheumatism of late as to render it unsafe for me to attempt a journey.

You were kind enough to give to Mr. Clarke the certificate for my 800. acres of land adjoining Poplar forest, which he sent to Mr. Lewis just about the time he was resigning my business. He delivered my whole mass of papers to me without calling my attention to this certificate, and it has laid unnoticed in the bundles till lately. I have thought it safest now to lay new warrants on the land, and take a new certificate, for which Mr. Clarke will apply to you and pay the fees. Having twice carefully platted the lines, I find they run over one another, which makes me conclude there is an error in some of them: and I conjecture it to be in the line adjoining Murray N.65.E. for if that was lengthened a little it would bring the beginning and the ending together and disentangle the lines. If you can correct the error wherever it is I shall be glad to have it done.

I do not know whether you ever gave either to Mr. Wayles or myself the certificate for the 98. acres purchased of you on Ivy creek. I will thank you to furnish it to Mr. Clarke, and to give that aid which you have always done in so friendly a way for both Mr. Wayles and myself. I am with great esteem Dear Sir Your most obedt. servt

TH: JEFFERSON

PrC (MHi); at foot of text: "Mr. Richard Stith"; endorsed in ink by TJ. Enclosed in TJ to Bowling Clark, 12 Dec. 1795.

From James Madison

DEAR SIR   Philada. Decr. 13. 1795

I received yesterday your favor covering a letter to Monsr. Liancourt which I have put into the hands of Noailles who will attend to the delivery of it. I inclose a copy of the P's speech. The Senate have answered it, as was to be expected. You will see the first fruits of their open doors in the debates it produced. The answer of the House of Reps. will be reported tomorrow. It has been delayed by a disagreement of ideas in the Committee, which consisted of Sedgwick, Sitgreaves and myself. The two former are strongly for the Treaty, and wish to favor it, at the same time that they are afraid to hazard direct expressions to that effect. The policy of that party is to obtain it a quiet passage thro' the present Session, pretending that it is too soon now to meddle with it, as they will hereafter pretend that it is then too late. The means employed are to blazon the public prosperity, to confound the Treaty with the President, and to mouth over the stale topics of war and confusion. The answer as it stands to be reported contains a clause which will put the House of Reps. in a dilemma similar to that forced on the House of Delegates, and I believe will never be swallowed because it is in part notoriously untrue. It affirms the confidence of his fellow Citizens to be undiminished, which will be denied by many who sincerely wish it to be the case. It cannot yet be determined what course the business will take. It seems most probable at present that the answer will be neutralized; and the subject immediately after taken up in a Come. of the whole

[554]

on the State of the Union; which will have the advantage of disentangleing it from the P. and of accomodating the wishes of some individuals who will be much influenced by the mode. There is pretty certainly a great majority against the Treaty on its merits; but besides the ordinary difficulty of preventing scisms, there is a real obscurity in the constitutional part of the question, and a diversity of sincere opinions about it, which the other side will make the most of. Nothing very late from abroad. The provision order has been repealed, but the spoliations go on. The publication of E.R. is not yet out. It is said it will appear the latter end of the present week. Adieu. Yrs. affy.   Js M Jr.

Flour 14 dollrs. and tis thought will rise to 16. The purchases of British agents for the W. India armaments are no doubt one of the causes of this extraordinary rise.

RC (DLC: Madison Papers); endorsed by TJ as received 25 Dec. 1795 and so recorded in SJL. Enclosure not found, but see note below.

YOUR FAVOR: TJ to Madison, 3 Dec. 1795. The enclosed COPY OF THE P'S SPEECH was probably that printed in the Philadelphia *Aurora*, 9 Dec. 1795; the DEBATES in the Senate on 11 Dec. were printed in same, 12 Dec. 1795. The answer of the House of Representatives drafted by Madison as chairman of the Federalist-dominated committee assigned to prepare the reply ignored the issue of the Jay Treaty (Madison, *Papers*, XVI, 164-6). For THE ANSWER AS IT STANDS TO BE REPORTED by the committee with the CLAUSE Madison opposed, see William Branch Giles to TJ, 15 Dec. 1795, and note. The reply as it was approved with an additional amendment by the House on 16 Dec. 1795 merely made a passing reference to the treaty (JHR, II, 379-80). PROVISION ORDER: see note to James Monroe to TJ, 27 June 1795.

From William Branch Giles

DEAR SIR   Philadelphia December *15th. 1795*

I take pleasure in forwarding you the accompanying newspaper, because whilst it announces the arrival of the treaty after the exchange of ratifications; it also contains the antidote to its execution. The speech of the Brittish King will I think silence the war-hoop which has resounded through the U.S. for some time past; and if the treaty can once be brought before the house of Representatives upon its intrinsic contents, a great majority will probably appear against it. The only difficulty will be, to convince the house of its constitutional right to exercise its discression respecting the instrument itself.

I also send herewith the rough draft of the answer as reported by the select committee to the Presidents speech. It has been this day under discussion. A motion was made to strike out the words 'probably unequalled' in the 4th. page. This motion was opposed by the treaty party but after very few observations was carried 43 to 39. This motion was considered by some as unimportant and was not deemed any evidence of the real state of the majority. A motion was then made to strike out the word *undiminished* in the same section. The discussion was entered upon with great reluctance by the favorers of the motion, but was managed with peculiar calmness and moderation on their part. After a very short discussion it was found that a great majority would probably appear in favor of the motion for strikeing out. But the majority from a delicacy towards the President which I think much to their honor; consented that the committee of whole house should rise without takeing the question at all, and the answer should be recommitted to a select committee with the addition of two members for the purpose of modifying the whole clause. This course was pursued and the committee have agreed to a modification calculated to relieve the president's feelings as much as would consist with propriety, perhaps somewhat more: but it will probably be generally acquiesed in tomorrow without debate.

The select committee originally consisted of Mr. Madison, Mr. Sedgewick and Mr. Sitgreves. It can hardly be necessary therefore for me to inform you, that this whole Section was Theodore's last effort at the sublime and beautiful.

The Senate have this day negatived the nomination of Mr. Rutledge as chief justice of the U.S. I have written this letter in very great haste, the marks of which are very visible.

Be pleased to make my best respects to the ladies of your family and believe me to be your most affectionate friend &c.   Wm. B. Giles

Mr. Randolph's vindication is promised to us on friday next, on monday it shall be forwarded.

RC (DLC); above postscript: "Mr. Thomas Jefferson"; endorsed by TJ as received 29 Dec. 1795 and so recorded in SJL. Enclosure: [*Made the 14th of December, 1795.*] *Report From the Committee appointed to prepare and report an address to the President of the United States, in answer to his speech to both Houses of Congress* [Philadelphia, 1795]. See Evans, No. 31368. Other enclosure described below.

ACCOMPANYING NEWSPAPER: possibly the *Gazette of the United States*, 15 Dec. 1795, containing extracts of George III's 30 Oct. 1795 speech to Parliament briefly announcing royal ratification of the Jay Treaty but otherwise concentrating on the war with France.

On 14 Dec. 1795, in response to a motion offered by Giles, the House of Representatives agreed to print for the use of its members the draft ANSWER, submitted to the House that day by James Madison, to the President's 8 Dec. 1795 address to Congress. On this day the House debated the resultant publication (see enclosure listed above), deleting the first two words of a reference to the "probably unequalled spectacle of national happiness" the country currently enjoyed, but letting stand in the same paragraph a statement about the "undiminished confidence of your fellow citizens" enjoyed by the President. On the following day, however, having in the meantime referred the draft to another committee, the House approved a final version of its answer to the President's speech that omitted this language about popular confidence in him

(Madison, *Papers*, XVI, 166-7n; *Annals*, V, 134-5, 144-9).

The Senate this day rejected the President's nomination of John RUTLEDGE as chief justice of the Supreme Court, a vote based on Rutledge's public opposition to the Jay Treaty and rumors about his mental instability (DHSC, I, pt. 1, p. 17, 94-100). Rutledge had held an interim appointment to this office since July 1795.

RANDOLPH'S VINDICATION IS PROMISED: a notice in this day's Philadelphia *Aurora* announced that Randolph's pamphlet would be available at Samuel Smith's printing shop on FRIDAY, 18 Dec. 1795.

To Henry Remsen

Dear Sir   Monticello Dec. 17. 95.

Your favor of Nov. 23. came to hand yesterday. Three days after the date of mine of Oct. 16. yours of Sep. 11. came to hand, and very soon after I learnt the arrival of the nail machine at Richmond. I expect now every day to recieve it here, for such is the lax and careless mode of business in this state that both the time and insurance for getting any thing brought from Richmond here (70 miles) is more than from N. York to Richmond. The peas you are so kind as to send will be a considerable acquisition to me, and I shall be glad of the other 10. bushels. My object is to put them into the fields I fallow for wheat, consequently I shall drill them, that I may be able to continue my ploughings, for which I shall be paid by the crop of peas. I omitted to ask at what time they are gathered, tho I presume in good time for putting in wheat, which here is from the 20th Sep. to the last of Oct. How much do they bring *to the acre* in middling uplands? I have to thank you for Dr. Mitchell's pamphlet as also for newspapers from time to time, which are well worth the postage. I would propose on this subject that you should take for me Greenleaf's paper, and, after reading it yourself, forward it to me by post. I will pay the subscription money with the first draught sent you. I am anxious to learn how the French bear our treaty with England. I am afraid we have no favors[1] to expect from them to our commerce in future. They may be silent on the principle the Count de Vergennes once expressed to me 'great nations, Sir, said he, never complain'.—I sincerely rejoice that yourself and your connections have escaped the fatal fever, being always with very sincere esteem Dear Sir Your affectionate friend & servt   TH: JEFFERSON

RC (Gilder Lehrman Collection, on deposit NNPM); at foot of text: "Mr. Remsen."

Remsen's letters to TJ of NOV. 23 and SEP. 11, recorded in SJL as received 16 Dec. and 19 Oct. 1795, respectively, and

TJ's letter to Remsen of OCT. 16 have not been found. SJL also records missing letters from TJ to Remsen of 15, 28 Feb. 1796, and 11 Mch. 1797, and from Remsen to TJ of 7 Mch. 1796 and 6 Feb. 1797.

DR. MITCHELL'S PAMPHLET: Samuel L. Mitchill, *The Life*, *Exploits*, *and Precepts of*

From William Branch Giles

DEAR SIR   Philadelphia December 20th. *1795*

In the accompanying Newspaper you will observe the answer of the House of Representatives, to the Presidents speech; and by comparing the original report of the Committee with the answer in its matured state, you will easily discern the opinions of the House in the alterations made. Perhaps the motives of the house for agreeing to the answer in its present shape may not be equally discernable. The opposers of the treaty embarrassed by the dexterity employed by the President in notifying the House of the existance of the treaty, without *officially* communicateing it; still more embarrassed by the cautious policy of its favorers in avoiding a complimentory stricture either upon the contents of the instrument, or the act of ratification; and most of all, embarrassed by the irresistable personal influence of the President; deemed it advisable *in the answer* to speak of that subject hypothetically; and thus to neutralyse the treaty question as much as possible. For whilst they were determined not to submit to any implication in favor of the treaty, they could not venture at a bold declaration against it by way of answer. It was concluded that the declaration of the sense of the house upon the treaty should be a distinct, solemn and independant act; and for that purpose the subject ought to be taken up in a committee of the whole upon the state of the union, upon some general proposition which might seem best calculated to unite all its real opposers—a resolution for instance to the following effect, That the treaty &c. &c. is not calculated to promote the interest or the happiness of the U.S. This course of proceeding is attended with its conveniences and inconveniencies. On the one hand, a general declaration of this nature, would cement the opposition, almost as much as a negative vote against an approbatory remark would have done; because no room is afforded for flying off on account of form; whereas it was impossible to state *in the answer* any declaration against the treaty, without hazzarding objections to its form, as well as mingling personal sensations towards the president, with the merits of the question; and thus subject the proposition to an intire failure. On the other hand, every day of age, is a day of strength to the Treaty: not on account of the daily discovery of intrinsic merit; but on account of the astonishing exertions and artifices employed to give it efficacy. Pitt's system of alarm seems to be most servily copied by the administration, and its partizans. Foreign war—Internal disorganization—'nefarious and detestable conspiracies'—French influence—Disunion of states—Bribery &c. &c. have been sounded in the public ear, until the public mind seems to be distracted. If this be not the reign of terror, it is at least, the reign of alarm, and its effect hitherto has exceeded all rational calculation: but it is hoped that these terrific spectres will vanish into thin air in the course of the present Session of Congress. If a proposition of the nature before described could be carried by a respectable majority, I am of opinion that any direction may afterwards be given to the opposition, which would be deemed most effectual to prevent the execution of the treaty. This would probably consist either of resolutions containing the reasons of the declaration and a refusal to furnish the means for effectuateing the treaty, or in an address to the president to the same effect.

It was once hoped that Dayton would be the mover of the proposition, but it is now feared that he will not. He is unequivocal in his detestation of the treaty, but doubts have arisen as to the manner of acting upon it. A distinction founded upon the President's Speech, between the *real knowledge*, and the *official knowledge* of the House, and a thousand other absurdities are conjured up to perplex the mind and unfit it for action; so that in the midst of the confusion it is impossible to form any probable conjecture as to the majority or the ultimate course which will be pursued by the house. The treaty is not arrived as was suggested, and it is beleived that the President does not wish its arrival until after the riseing of Congress.

The Alarmists have commenced a most violent and unmerciful attack upon Mr. Randolph's vindication, and no doubt will keep it up, but no estimate can yet be formed of its effect upon the public mind. Be pleased to present my most respectful regards to the Ladies of Monticello and beleive me to be your affectionate friend &c.   Wм. B. Giles

RC (DLC); at foot of text: "Thomas Jefferson *Esqr*"; endorsed by TJ as received 29 Dec. 1795 and so recorded in SJL. Enclosure not found, but see note below.

ACCOMPANYING NEWSPAPER: many newspapers, including the Philadelphia *Aurora* of 18 Dec. 1795 and the *Gazette of the United States* of 17 Dec. 1795, printed the ANSWER OF THE HOUSE OF REPRESENTATIVES to the PRESIDENT'S SPEECH.

To Sir Peyton Skipwith

DEAR SIR   Monticello Dec. 24. 95.

I have just recieved your favor of the 9th. and am sorry it is not in my power to do any thing in the business mentioned in it. I have been authorised by Mr. Short only to have a part of his stock sold and invested in Canal-shares and some lands; but not at all to settle, pay or meddle with any debt. I retain your account however and will inclose a copy of it in my first letter and do whatever else he shall direct. Probably it will be from 6. to 9. months before I get an answer.

The person who delivered your letter has examined my little nailery in all it's parts, and received whatever information he desired. When I began the business, it was a fine one. But a fall in the price of nails and rise in the price of nail rod, have made it less profitable by 20. percent within this 12. month. This you know is a great thing to be struck off from clear profits. I am apprehensive the fall in the price of nails is permanent. The rise of iron, like the rise of price in every thing else we get from or thro' the great trading towns, proceeds chiefly from their immense circulation of bank-paper. Those towns are now in the state we were in about 1778. with this unfortunate difference that the bankers are able to sink the value of the precious metals with that of their paper; whereas our old paper left the metals at their former level. I am with great esteem Dear Sir Your most obedt. servt.

TH: JEFFERSON

RC (Mrs. J. Hall Pleasants, Baltimore, Maryland, 1944); addressed: "Sir Peyton Skipwith Prestwould." PrC (DLC: William Short Papers); badly faded; endorsed in ink by TJ on verso.

To Benjamin Franklin Bache

DEAR SIR   Monticello Dec. 26. 1795.

Mr. Crosby writes me he has bespoke from you a set of your papers for the present year to be bound up and forwarded to me after the end of the year as usual. Independant of this I shall be glad to become your subscriber from the 1st. day of this month for another set to be forwarded to me by post. As some of these will miscarry, I shall hope that on forwarding to you at the end of the next year a list of the papers wanting you will be so good as to furnish them at the pro ratâ price that I may have the whole year bound up here. I now inclose you an order on Mr. Barnes, 3d. street, South, for a year's subscription. The papers from the 1st. day of this month till you recieve this, to be forwarded by the first post.

I sent off your gong as early last spring as I thought the navigation safe; but the directions I gave from anxiety to get it safe to you were so particular that they have retarded it's passage. It got safely to Colo. Gamble's hands in Richmond some time ago, under a charge to send it by some Captain of a vessel *resident* in Philadelphia. I hope by this time you will have recieved it, tho' I have not heard of it's leaving Richmond. When are we to see the new edition of Dr. Franklin's works? The delay gives me apprehensions. I am with great esteem Dr. Sir Your most obedt. servt

TH: JEFFERSON

RC (PWacD: Feinstone Collection, on deposit PPAmP); addressed: "Mr. Benjamin Franklin Bache Philadelphia"; endorsed in unidentified hand: "Ths. Jefferson's orders for directing the Aurora to Monticello." Enclosure not found. Enclosed in TJ to Sampson Crosby, 26 Dec. 1795.

A 25 Jan. 1796 letter from Bache to TJ, recorded in SJL as received 27 Feb. 1796, has not been found.

According to SJL, on this date TJ also wrote letters to "Pleasants & son," printers of the *Virginia Gazette, and Richmond and Manchester Advertiser*, which in April 1795 had become the *Richmond and Manchester Advertiser*, Augustine Davis, printer of the Richmond *Virginia Gazette, and General Advertiser*, and Andrew Brown, printer of the *Philadelphia Gazette*, none of which has been found (Brigham, *American Newspapers*, II, 911, 1136, 1148; Sowerby, Nos. 540, 579, 584). A missing letter from Davis to TJ of 13 Jan. 1796 is recorded in SJL as received on 16 Jan. 1796.

To Sampson Crosby

DEAR SIR   Monticello Dec. 9. [i.e. 26] 1795.

I have safely recieved your favor of the 9th. and have no doubt the box of blinds will soon be at Richmond. I am in hopes the Captain has either been directed to deliver them to Gamble & Temple, my correspondents there, or that he will take the trouble to find by enquiry some one acquainted with me who will recieve them and pay his freight.

I now return you Mr. Randolph's certificate, and with pleasure add mine, tho' I regret that you have occasion for it, or may by possibility. I am afraid too you are looking towards a very vexatious kind of life, that of tavern keeping. Would not the taking private lodgers give you less trouble and more time for some other auxiliary business? But of this you are the best judge, and after all I am in hopes you will have no occasion for either.

I inclose a letter for Mr. Bache, open for your perusal, as you have been kind enough to transact these matters with him for me. Be pleased to stick a wafer in it and deliver it. I am with esteem Dear Sir Your friend & servt   TH: JEFFERSON

P.S. Mr. Petit did not write to me by the post. I am a little uneasy at his silence.

RC (NjGbS); misdated, but recorded in SJL as a 26 Dec. 1795 letter; at foot of text: "Mr: Sampson Crosby"; endorsed as received 23 Jan. 1796. Enclosure: TJ to Benjamin Franklin Bache, 26 Dec. 1795. Other enclosures not found.

Crosby's FAVOR OF THE 9TH., recorded in SJL as received 22 Dec. 1795, has not been found. A 26 Jan. 1796 letter from Adrien PETIT, recorded in SJL as received 1 Apr. 1796, and TJ's letters to Petit of 18 July 1794 and 10 July 1796 are also missing.

From James Madison

DEAR SIR   Philada. Decr. 27. 1795.

Mr. R's pamphlet is out and will be forwarded by the first opportunity. Altho' I have kept up an enquiry, I have not been able to collect the impression it makes. As it relates to the P. nothing seems to be said: and as it relates to parties in general very little. By Fenno's and Webster's papers, it appears that an effort will be used to run down Mr. R. and if necessary for the purpose to call in the incidents to which his pecuniary embarrassments here exposed him. The speech of the P. will have shewn you the guarded and perplexing shape, in which the Treaty was brought into view. The answer was the result of circumstances which my communications to you expl[ain in p]art. The silence of it as to the Treaty was an accomodation to t[he wishes] of a few who preferred taking it up by itself afterwards. These individuals have not shewn as much forwardness as was expected, and owing to that cause, and to the account of an exchange of Ratifications and the momently[1] expectation of the Treaty, nothing is yet done on the subject. The situation is truly perplexing. It is clear that a majority if brought to the merits of the Treaty are against it. But as the Treaty is not regularly before the House, and an application to the P. brings him personally into the question with some plausible objections to the measure, there is great danger that eno' will fly off, to leave the opponents of the Treaty in a minority. Enquiries are on foot to ascertain the true state of opinions and the probable turn of votes; and if there be found a firm majority on the right side, an attempt will be made to get at the subject.

There are accounts from Paris to the 5th. of Novr. The new Constitution was taking an auspicious commencement. Monroe's letters to me of Octr. 23 and 24. give a favorable prospect on that side; as well as with regard to French affairs in general. He confirms the late naval advantages, and speaks of the check on the Rhine as a bagatelle. He knew only from Report, the Ratification of the Treaty by the P. His language breathes equal mortification and apprehension from the event. He says that England would have refused us nothing, and we have yielded every thing; and he cannot but speak as reason dictates. A nation threatened with famine at home, and depending on the forlorn hope of West-India armaments which our market only can feed, was a nation to make rather than receive concessions. I am just told that 97 out of 98 of the Bermuda Judge's decrees against our vessels are announced to be reversed in England. This is another proof of Monroe's opinion. The reversal in such a lump must have resulted not from principle, but from policy, as the lumping condemnation proceeded from cupidity. Flour at 14 dolrs. at present. We have had no winter as yet. The weather is now as mild as October. I hope it will assist you against your Rheumatic com.[2]

RC (DLC: Madison Papers); possibly incomplete, with second paragraph written perpendicularly to the first (see note 2 below); bracketed words torn away at seal supplied interlinearly by Madison after TJ's death; with one later annotation made by Madison recorded in note 1 below; endorsed by TJ as received 23 Jan. 1796 and so recorded in SJL.

MONROE'S LETTERS TO ME: see Madison, *Papers*, XVI, 105-13.

[1] Madison here later interlined "momentary."
[2] Text ends thus with a hyphen or a period.

Notes on Edmund Randolph's *Vindication*

[after 29 Dec. 1795]

[. . .] [of dates.]

1793. Dec.	5.	pa. 99.	President's message to Congress.
1794.		73.	instructions to Monroe.
Apr.	16.	100.	Pres's message to Senate nominating Jay.
	19.	58.	E.R. to the Pres. letter.
Aug.	5.	100.	do.
Oct.	31.	6.	Fauchet's intercepted lre No. 10.
1795. Mar.	7	28	treaty arrives.[1]
1795. June	29.	29.	R's first conversn with Hammond.
July	2.	30.	R. to Monroe.
	12.	30.	R's opinion to the Pres.
	13.	31.40.	R's 2d. conversn with Hammond.
	14.	32.	R's 3d. conversn with Hammond.
		39.	R. to Monroe & the other ministers.

15.	32.39.	Pres. goes to Mt. Vernon.
18.	33.	Pres. writes to E.R. from Balt. on Boston add.
	33.	R's memorial to Hammond.
22.	34.	Pres. to R.
29.	35.	do.
31.	36.	do.
Aug. 11.	39.	Pres. returns to Philada.
10-14	40.	Hamilton writes to Pres.[2]
19.	1.	R. called before cabinet.
	8.	R. to Pres.
20.	9.	Pres. to R.
21.	9.	R. goes to Rho. isld.
31.	10.	arrives there.
Sep. 1.	11.	R. to Fauchet. & answer.
2.	12.	Gardner's certif.
21.	19.	R. to Pres.
27.	20.	Pres. to R.
	13.	Fauchet's certif.
	17.	No. 3.
	18.	No. 6.
Oct. 2.	21.	R. to Wolcot & answer.
6.	25.	Taylor to R.
8.	22.3.	R. to Wolcott & answer.
	23.	R. to Pres.
21.	25.	Pres. to R.
24.	26.	R. to Pres.
	49.	R's general lre to Pres.

N (DLC: Rare Book and Special Collections Division); written by TJ on verso of page 103 of his copy of [Edmund Randolph], *A Vindication of Mr. Randolph's Resignation* (Philadelphia, 1795), the signatures in this copy being bound out of order so that TJ's notes face page 41; date assigned on the basis of TJ's receipt of the pamphlet (see below); consisting of a chronological key to the *Vindication*, TJ's caption at head of text being partially clipped; significant emendations, and marginalia by TJ on another page of the pamphlet, are noted below. See Sowerby, No. 3180. Except for its scrambled signatures, TJ's copy matches Evans No. 29384, not 29385, which is another impression of the pamphlet.

Although by late November 1795 TJ had acquired an incomplete version of Randolph's *Vindication* (see TJ to James Madison, 26 Nov. 1795), he could not have inscribed this list—which contains late page references and appears on the verso of the final page of the pamphlet's text—before the last portions of the work were printed. William Branch Giles had expected to obtain the finished pamphlet on its advertised publication date of Friday, 18 Dec., and send it to TJ on Monday, 21 Dec. 1795 (see Giles to TJ, 15 Dec. 1795). In subsequent letters

Giles did not state when he actually sent the *Vindication*, but it is unlikely to have reached TJ earlier than 29 Dec., when he received Giles's letters of 15 and 20 Dec. 1795. TJ acknowledged receipt of the pamphlet in his reply to Giles of 31 Dec. 1795.

In the margin of page 97 of his copy of Randolph's *Vindication*, keyed between the fifth and sixth words of the sentence "You [i.e., Washington] will remember a remarkable phrase of your own upon this occasion," TJ wrote perpendicularly: "'that if he should not ratify the treaty he should lose the support of one party, and not gain the other, who would still continue to abuse him as much as ever, and so between two stools the breech will come to the ground.'" TJ may have learned of the President's remark during the meeting described in Notes of a Conversation with Edmund Randolph, [after 1795].

R. TO MONROE & THE OTHER MINISTERS: page 39 of the pamphlet includes extracts from letters written by Randolph to James Monroe on 14 July and to "all our foreign

ministers" on 21 July 1795. BOSTON ADD.: see TJ to James Madison, 21 Sep. 1795, and note, for Washington's reply to the address from Boston.

HAMILTON WRITES TO PRES.: this "very influential letter in the President's hands" is described but not printed in the *Vindication*, 40, where Randolph gave its date as "the 10th or 14th of July" and did not name its author. Alexander Hamilton's letter of 10 Aug. 1795 to Oliver Wolcott (printed in Syrett, *Hamilton*, XIX, 111-12) matches the description in Randolph's pamphlet.

R. CALLED BEFORE CABINET: TJ here mistakenly noted page 5, on which the pamphlet's text begins, as page 1. R's GENERAL LRE TO PRES., on pages 49-98 of the pamphlet, takes the form of an undated letter to Washington but is actually Randolph's public explanation of his own conduct.

[1] Line inserted.
[2] TJ wrote "Hamilton's lre" before altering it to read as above.

To William Branch Giles

DEAR SIR   Monticello Dec. 31. 95.

Your favors of Dec. 15. and 20. came to hand by the last post. I am well pleased with the manner in which your house has testified their sense of the treaty. While their refusal to pass the original clause of the reported answer proved their condemnation of it, the contrivance to let it disappear silently respected appearances in favor of the President, who errs as other men do, but errs with integrity. Randolph seems to have hit upon the true theory of our constitution, that when a treaty is made, involving matters confided by the constitution to the three branches of the legislature conjointly, the representatives are as free as the President and Senate were to consider whether the national interests requires or forbids their giving the forms and force of law to the articles over which they have a power.—I thank you much for the pamphlet. His narrative is so straight and plain, that even those who did not know him will acquit him of the charge of bribery: those who know him had done it from the first. Tho he mistakes his own political character in the aggregate, yet he gives it to you in the detail. Thus he supposes himself a man of no party (page 97.) that his opinions not containing

any systematic adherence to party, fall sometimes on one side and sometimes on the other. (pa. 58.) Yet he gives you these facts,[1] which shew
that they fall generally on both sides, and are complete inconsistencies.

1. He never gave an opinion in the Cabinet against the rights of the
   people (pa. 97.) yet he advised the denunciation of the popular societies. (67)

2. He would not neglect the overtures of a commercial treaty with
   France (79) yet he always opposed it while atty general, and never
   seems to have proposed it while Secretary of state.

3. He concurs in resorting to the militia to quell the pretended insurrection in the West (81.) and proposes an augmentation from
   12,500 to 15,000 to march against men at their ploughs, (pa. 80.)
   yet on the 5th. of Aug. he is against their marching (83. 101.) and
   on the 25th. of Aug. he is for it. (84.)

4. He concurs in the measure of a mission extraordinary to London
(as inferred from pa. 58.) but objects to the men, to wit Hamilton and
Jay (58.)

5. He was against granting commercial powers to Mr. Jay (58.) yet
he besieged the doors of the Senate to procure their advice to ratify.

6. He advises the President to a ratification on the merits of the
treaty (97.) but to a suspension till the provision order is repealed. (98.)
The fact is that he has generally given his principles to the one party and
his practice to the other; the oyster to one, the shell to the other. Unfortunately the shell was generally the lot of his friends the French and
republicans, and the oyster of their antagonists. Had he been firm to the
principles he professes in the year 1793. the President would have been
kept from a habitual concert with the British and Antirepublican party.
But at that time I do not know which R. feared most, a British fleet, or
French disorganisers. Whether his conduct is to be ascribed to a superior view of things, an adherence to right without regard to party, as he
pretends, or to an anxiety to trim between both, those who know his
character and capacity will decide. Were parties here divided merely by
a greediness for office, as in England, to take a part with either would be
unworthy of a reasonable or moral man. But where the principle of
difference is as substantial and as strongly pronounced as between the
republicans and the Monocrats of our country I hold it as honorable to
take a firm and decided part, and as immoral to pursue a middle line, as
between the parties of Honest men, and Rogues, into which every country is divided.

A copy of the pamphlet came by this post to Charlottesville. I suppose we shall be able to judge soon what kind of impression it is likely
to make. It has been a great treat to me, as it is a continuation of that

Cabinet history with the former part of which I was intimate. I remark in the reply of the President a small travestie of the sentiment contained in the answer of the Representatives. They[2] acknolege that he has *contributed* a great share[3] to the national happiness by his services. He thanks them for ascribing to his *agency* a great share of those benefits. The former keeps in view the co-operation of others towards the public good. The latter presents to view his sole-agency. At a time when there would have been less anxiety to publish to the people a strong approbation from your house, this strengthening of your expression would not have been noticed.

Our attentions have been so absorbed by the first manifestations of the sentiments of your house, that we have lost sight of our own legislature: insomuch that I do not know whether they are sitting or not. The rejection of Mr. Rutledge by the Senate is a bold thing, because they cannot pretend any objection to him but his disapprobation of the treaty. It is of course a declaration that they will recieve none but tories hereafter into any department of the government. I should not wonder if Monroe were to be recalled under the idea of his being of the partisans of France, whom the President considers as the partisans *of war and confusion* in his letter of July 31, and as disposed to excite them to hostile measures, or at least to unfriendly sentiments,[4] a most infatuated blindness to the true character of the sentiments entertained in favor of France.—The bottom of my page warns me that it is time to end my commentaries on the facts you have furnished me. You would of course however wish to know the sensations here on those facts. My friendly respects to Mr. Madison to whom the next week's dose will be directed. Adieu. Affectionately   TH: JEFFERSON

RC (NNPM); at foot of first page: "Mr. Giles"; endorsed. PrC (DLC).

ORIGINAL CLAUSE: see note to Giles to TJ, 15 Dec. 1795. THE PAMPHLET: Edmund Randolph's *Vindication*. For the PROVISION ORDER, see note to James Monroe to TJ, 27 June 1795.

In the 17 Dec. 1795 REPLY OF THE PRESIDENT to the answer the House of Representatives had made to his speech, Washington referred to the nation's "numerous blessings" and offered the House his "thanks for your declaration, that to my agency you ascribe the enjoyment of a great share of these benefits" (JHR, II, 381).

Washington's LETTER OF JULY 31 to Randolph (printed in *Vindication*, 36-8) stated, with respect to the possible impact of domestic opponents of the Jay Treaty on American relations with France and Great Britain: "If the Treaty is ratified the partisans of the French (or rather of War and confusion) will excite them to hostile measures, or at least to unfriendly Sentiments; if it is not, there is no foreseeing *all* the consequences which may follow, as it respts. G.B." (Fitzpatrick, *Writings*, XXXIV, 266).

[1] Remainder of sentence interlined.
[2] TJ here canceled "ascribe to him."
[3] Preceding three words interlined.
[4] Preceding fifteen words interlined.

Notes of a Conversation with Edmund Randolph

[after 1795]

Randolph's letter of Dec. 15. 94. to Jay approved by P. That treaty was against a party, viz. my Report on commerce

H's letter to R. execrating commercial part of treaty

Jay's 1st. authority merely to demand reparation

a fortnight afterwards H. proposed commercial

Jay considered 12th. article as equivalent for every thing

Presidt. said if he communicated all Jay's papers to Senate, every man would pronounce him bribed

papers communicated to Senate only shewed Jay's puerilities

those not communicated would have shewn his concealments of details

on the 6th. Nov. Jay wrote his reasons against the treaty

yet on the 19th. Nov. he signed it

my paper extorted by Jay and King from P. was on condition should not be used during P's life.

P. notified the Senators privately that their rejection of J. Rutlege would not be disagreeable. Rejected by silent vote.

they did not go upon his insanity, not then certainly known tho' some extravagances had been spoken of

the P. speaking with R. on the hypothesis of a separation of the Union into Northern and Southern said he had made up his mind to remove and be of the Northern[1]

MS (DLC: TJ Papers, 98: 16747); un-dated, but written after December 1795 (see below); written entirely in TJ's hand on a small scrap at two sittings (see note 1 below); with notation on verso written in same ink as recto: "heads of information given me by E. Randolph."

Internal evidence indicates that TJ wrote these notes on the basis of a conversation with Edmund Randolph that could have taken place in Virginia no earlier than 15 Dec. 1795, when the Senate rejected the President's nomination of John Rutledge as Chief Justice of the United States Supreme Court (William Branch Giles to TJ, 15 Dec. 1795, and note). Since Randolph had returned to Virginia for good about the third week of November 1795, three months after his resignation as Secretary of State and approximately three weeks before Washington submitted Rutledge's nomination to the Senate, his information about its defeat must have been secondhand. Rutledge's attempted suicide, which did not become public in Philadelphia until late in December, further suggests that TJ's retrospective comment about his derangement was written sometime after the new year (DHSC, I, pt. 2, p. 820-2).

Randolph's LETTER OF DEC. 15. 94. to John Jay is in ASP, Foreign Relations, I, 509-12. TJ's REPORT ON COMMERCE is dated 16 Dec. 1793. Alexander Hamilton's LETTER to Randolph, the substance of which Randolph incorporated into his aforementioned letter to Jay, was an undated series of observations on British proposals for a commercial treaty with the United States that Jay had received from Lord Grenville in September 1794 and forwarded to the Secretary of State (Syrett, *Hamilton*, XVII, 409-10). PAPERS COMMUNICATED TO SENATE: the official documents relating to the negotiation of the Jay Treaty that Washington submitted to the Senate on 8 June 1795 (ASP, *Foreign Relations*, I, 470-501, 503-4). MY PAPER: Memorandum of a Conversation with Edmund Charles Genet, 10 July 1793, of which in fact Washington provided Jay and Rufus KING with only a brief extract (see note to TJ to Randolph, 18 Dec. 1793).

[1] This paragraph written on verso in different ink.

From Martha Jefferson Randolph

Dunginess Jan 1rst 1796

Mr. Randolph having determined to spend some months at Varina I am under the necessity of troubling you my dearest Father with a memorandum of the articles we shall want from Monticello. We have spent the hollidays and indeed every day in such a perpetual round of visiting and recieving visits that I have not had a moment to my self since I came down and we shall leave this on our way to Richmond next sunday where I hope to recieve a letter from you. Give my love to Maria and the children and believe me dearest Father with unchangeable affection your's in great haste   M RANDOLPH

The waggon will be at Monticello the 5th or 6th of the month.

RC (ViU: Edgehill-Randolph Papers); endorsed by TJ as received 4 Jan. 1796 and so recorded in SJL. Enclosure not found.

From George Wythe

G WYTHE TO T JEFFERSON   Richmond, 1 of January, 1796.

The general assembly, at their late session, enacted that a collection of the laws, public and private, relative to lands, shall be printed. Those, who are appointed to perform the work, despair of doing it, without your aid. If you will permit your copies to be sent hither, I will be answerable for thear restitution in the same order as when they shall be received. Be so good as let me know, if the copies may be obtained, in what manner they may be forwarded, with least inconvenience. Farewell.

RC (DLC). Endorsed by TJ as received 11 Jan. 1796 and so recorded in SJL.

On 4 Dec. 1795, the Virginia Assembly passed legislation which called for the COLLECTION OF THE LAWS . . . RELATIVE TO LANDS. Those APPOINTED TO PERFORM THE WORK, along with Wythe, were John Brown, John Marshall, Bushrod Washington, and John Wickham (Shepherd, *Statutes*, I, 360). For the history of the publication of the collection of laws, see note to Wythe to TJ, 26 Mch. 1795.

From James Hopkins

HONOURABLE & DEAR SIR   Amherst County Jany. 2d. 1796

A short time since I receiv'd a Verbal Message from Mr. Joshua Fry, by his Brother requesting to know if I had any Papers in my Possession relating to the Title of a Tract of Land in Albemarle Call'd the Limestone-Quarry—of which his Father and mine with Other Gentlemen were the Joint proprietors—Informing at the same Time that Mr. Christo. Hudson had laid a Warrant on the said Land, Asserting That there was Neither Patent nor Deed for the same Nor had been any Taxes paid for it.

Being at some Distance from home when I received the Message—I told Mr. Fry that I perfectly Recollected having seen among my Fathers Papers some years ago a Deed from Col. Phillip Mayo to Col. Peter Jefferson and Others (including the Gentlemen he had named) and that I would on my return home Examine and Agreeable to his Brother's desire Transmit him a Copy of That as well as any Other Papers I should find respecting the said Lands. Mr. Fry's Message further Stated that he had Sold his proportion of the Land to (the late) Governor Lee—which was the Reason of his enquiry about the Title at this juncture, and that Mr. Lee wished to Purchase the other Shares if Agreeable to the Proprietors. Accordingly on my Return after an elaborate Search of some Days I found not only the Deed in question, but a Copy of the Courses of the said Land (which are not mentiond in the Deed) from the Record of the Patent in the late Secretarys Office—Copies of both which I inclosed to Mr. Joshua Fry, having requested that he would Communicate the same to the Other Gentlemen who were Co-Partners in the Land as Opportunity might Offer and particularly to you—Charging it on myself to do the same so soon as could be Convenient. Accordingly Sir I have herewith Inclosed you Copies of the same Papers—By which you will see that Mr. Hudson is quite Mistaken in his Notion respecting the Lands being Unpatented or Undeeded. As to Taxes I am sure ever Since the Permanent Revenue Act took place I have paid more Taxes in Albemarle than the other Lands I possess there should have Amounted to, and therefore had just reason to suppose my proportion of the Limestone Tract was included—tho' I cannot say I ever made particular enquiry into it. Yet I suppose the land could in no wise be forfeited on that Account, unless the Taxes had been Demanded and refused which Case I am Convinced does not Exist. I am more in Doubt however lest the Record of the Deed made in Albemarle Court should have been destroyd by the Brittish on their Irruption there—having unluckily forgot this, when I made search there some years ago for the Other Deeds wherein I was Interested—some of which I think were near the same Date with this and the Records for all which were preservd. Whether the Law for restoring or Renewing the Records destroyd then by the Brittish is still in Force or Expired I know not. However if Mr. Hudson is Serious and persists in his Resolution of endeavouring to take away our Land (which I can scarce imagine) I should think there ought to be a Meeting of the Proprietors to Consult and Conclude upon the proper Means of Defending it, in which Case we should all Assuredly look up to you Sir not only as the first Partner—but much more as the first in Capacity to Direct and Conduct us thro' the Difficulty—Not doubting in the Interim you will Cause the requisite Examinations to be made. I have only Now to beg your Pardon Honorable Sir for this Intrusion on that Repose which Assuredly you Meditated to enjoy on Retireing from the Weight of Publick Cares—Persuaded that in this Case you will more easily Excuse the Interruption of the Communication I have made, than you would my Negligence in Omitting it. With a Breast replete with Warmest Sentiments of Unceasing Gratitude for the long and Eminent Services which you have renderd our Common Country both at home and Abroad and praying that Heaven may render you its Choicest Benedictions both here and hereafter I am Honble. & Dear sir Your ever Obliged & most Respectful (tho' Unworthy)

JA HOPKINS

RC (MHi); endorsed by TJ as received 4 Jan. 1796 and so recorded in SJL. Enclosure: Description of the courses bounding Philip Mayo's patent for 400 acres on Hardware River in Albemarle County, n.d. (Tr in same; entirely in Hopkins's hand, including attestations by Robert Minge and Benjamin Waller). Other enclosure not found.

James Hopkins (d. 1803), son of Dr. Arthur Hopkins, who died by 1766, was an Amherst County physician. He later sought, through provisions in his will, to establish bounties and a hospital in Virginia to encourage advances in the treatment of consumption, hydrophobia, and other severe diseases (Lyman Chalkley, *Chronicles of the Scotch-Irish Settlement in Virginia: Extracted from the Original Court Records of Augusta County, 1745-1800*, 3 vols. [Rosslyn, Va., 1912-13], II, 258; VMHB, XXVI [1918], 318).

Hopkins's communications were with grandsons rather than sons of Peter Jefferson's old associate Joshua FRY—none of whose children was a namesake (Slaughter, *Fry*, 35-7).

TJ did not yet own his father's share in the limestone-bearing tract located twelve miles from Monticello (for his acquisition of it, see Agreement with Randolph Jefferson, 17 Apr. 1796). By 1819 Christopher HUDSON owned three or four of the six shares and opposed two adjoining landowners who claimed part of the tract based on long-term possession. TJ cooperated in Hudson's legal efforts at that time, but considered the land "worthless" because of its poor location and because he owned another quarry with better stone closer to Monticello (TJ to Robert Anderson, 13 June 1819).

PERMANENT REVENUE ACT: "An act for ascertaining certain taxes and duties, and for establishing a permanent revenue," passed in the November 1781 session of the Virginia General Assembly (Hening, X, 501-17). LAW FOR RESTORING OR RENEWING THE RECORDS: "An act for the relief of persons who have been or may be injured by the destruction of the records of county courts," which also passed in the November 1781 session. A similar act of December 1787 provided for replacement of county records "destroyed by fraud, accident, or otherwise." Each statute empowered county clerks to reenter documents into county records and provided for commissioners to take depositions concerning lost documents (same, x, 453-4, xi, 72, xii, 497-9).

SJL records six letters exchanged by TJ and Hopkins between 7 Apr. 1796 and 30 Nov. 1799, none of which has been found.

To J. P. P. Derieux

Dear Sir   Monticello Jan. 3. 1796.

I have recieved your favor on the subject of Mr. Payne's advertisement of the sale of your tenement. If his mortgage was prior to your lease, and was recorded, your lease cannot affect his right, because nothing done by Mr. Wood after the mortgage ought to derogate from his prior contracts. Mr. Payne however cannot take possession against your consent, but will be driven to a suit in Chancery against Wood and yourself to foreclose the equity of redemption, and I think the costs of the suit would fall on Wood, and it's determination would not be till after your lease is out, if you employ a lawyer to defend it. You will judge on this view of the thing whether best to defend it, or give up and have recourse against Wood for his breach of contract.—I find a man of the name of Patrick, whom I hire, has endeavored to swindle you out of 10/. He is a great rascal. He had no letter from me to you, for I did not know he would go by your house, nor would I have trusted him with a letter. With my respectful salutations to Mrs. Derieux I am Dear Sir, Your friend & servt   TH: JEFFERSON

RC (Dabney S. Lancaster, Richmond, 1945); at foot of text: "Mr. Derieux."

YOUR FAVOR: SJL records a letter from Derieux to TJ of 22 Dec. that was received 26 Dec. 1795, and 20 other letters exchanged by TJ and Derieux between 28 Mch. 1794 and 20 June 1796, none of which has been found.

During 1796-97 TJ hired the labor of William Wood's slave PATRICK for construction work at Monticello along with other slaves owned by members of Wood's family, who lived about seven miles from Monticello (MB, note to 22 Sep. 1795, 1, 4 Jan., 22 Oct. 1796, 3 Jan. 1797).

To Archibald Stuart

Dear Sir   Monticello Jan. 3. 96

I troubled you once before on the subject of my nails, and must trouble you once more, but hope my present plan will protect you from all further embarrasment with it. I sat out with refusing to retail, expecting the merchants of my neighborhood and the upper country would have given a preference to my supplies, because delivered *here* at the *Richmond whole sale prices*, and at hand to be called for in small parcels, so that they needed not to keep large sums invested in that article and lying dead on their hands. The importing merchants however decline taking them from a principle of suppressing every effort towards domestic manufacture, and the merchants who purchase here being much under the influence of the importers, take their nails from them with their other goods. I have determined therefore to establish deposits of my nails to be retailed at Milton, Charlottesville, Staunton, Wormester and Warren, but first at the three first places, because I presume my present works, which turn out a ton a month, will fully furnish them, and two additional fires which will be at work in a short time, will raise it to a ton and a half a month, and enable me to extend my supplies to Wormester and Warren. I shall retail at the Richmond *whole sale* prices, laying on 5. percent at Milton and Charlottesville for commission to the retailers, and 10. per cent at the other places for commission and transportation. My present retailing prices at Staunton would be Sixes $12\frac{1}{2}$d. per ℔ equal to $7/3\frac{1}{2}$ per ℳ

Eights	12d.	equal to 10/
Tens	$11\frac{1}{2}$d.	equal to $12/5\frac{1}{2}$
Twelves	11d.	equal to 14/8
Sixteens	$10\frac{1}{2}$d.	equal to 17/6
Twenties	10d.	equal to 20/10

It is tolerably certain that the moment my deposit opens, there will be an entire stoppage to the sale of all imported nails, for nobody can *retail* them in the upper country at the Richmond *wholesale* prices, advanced only 5. or 10. percent. And as I mean to employ only one person in each place to retail, it will be of some advantage to the merchant who will undertake it, to have the entire monopoly of the nail business, and so draw to his store every one who wants nails; besides the commission of 5. percent, which in an article to be sold for ready money only, and where he does not employ a farthing of his own capital, I am advised is a sufficient allowance for commission. I should expect them to send me a copy of their sales once a month, and to hold the proceeds ready for my draughts at stated periods, say monthly. I trouble you to engage some person whom you can recommend for punctuality, to retail for me. I have heard very favorable accounts of a Mr. Stuart, merchant of Staunton, and should not hesitate to prefer him if he will undertake it. If not, pray do me the favor to find some other. I have written you the details, not that you need trouble yourself with explaining them to any person but that you may put this letter into his hands. As soon as you will name

[573]

to me the person you engage I will send him an assortment of nails by the first waggons which will take them in.—Will you be so good as to procure for me a good bearskin, dressed with a soft skin and the hair on. Dr. Johnson will on your application be so good as to pay for it, and take credit in his account with me.—My respectful salutations to Mrs. Stuart, and assurances of attachment to yourself from Your's affectionately   Th: Jefferson

RC (ViHi); at foot of first page: "Mr. Stuart." Erroneously recorded in SJL as a letter to Alexander Stuart.

This letter was not immediately sent (see TJ to Stuart, 22 Feb. 1796).

TROUBLED YOU ONCE BEFORE: TJ to Stuart, 11 June 1795.

From Van Staphorst & Hubbard

SIR   Amsterdam 5 January 1796.

Confirming what We had the pleasure of writing you the 10th. October, We have to acknowledge receipt of your very esteemed favor of 8 September, remitting us Wm. Hodgdon's Bill at 90 days Sight on Robinson Sanderson & Rumney of Whitehaven payable in London, £300. Stg. which We shall in course place to the credit of Mr. Philip Mazzei, to whom We have communicated the receipt of this remittance on forwarding him the Duplicate of your letter that covered it. Wishing you sincerely the uninterrupted enjoyment of health and prosperity, during many successive returns of the season, We are with great esteem and regard Sir! Your mo. ob. hb. servants

N. & J. Van Staphorst & Hubbard

RC (DLC); in a clerk's hand, signed by the firm; at foot of text: "Thos. Jefferson Esq. Monticello. Virginia"; endorsed by TJ as received 14 May 1796 and so recorded in SJL. A Dupl recorded in SJL as received 16 Sep. 1796 has not been found.

DUPLICATE OF YOUR LETTER: see TJ to Philip Mazzei, 8 Sep. 1795, and note, for a description of TJ's missing letter of that date to Van Staphorst & Hubbard.

To Thomas Mann Randolph

DEAR SIR   Monticello Jan. 6. 96.

Colo. J. Nicholas not having been able to get two magistrats to attend, according to the former notice given Cobbs, to take the depositions of Messrs. Owen & Mosby, inspectors of Shockoe, I have given him (Cobbs) a second notice to attend for that purpose at Shockoe warehouse on Saturday the 30th. inst. at noon. I must trouble you to act for me, getting 2. magistrates to attend, their names to be inserted in the inclosed commission at the time of taking the depositions. When they have taken the depositions they are to annex them to this commission and seal them up and address them to the clerk of Albemarle. In this state be pleased to recieve the packet and send it by post under cover to me.

The following particulars will claim attention.

The 2. hhds. for which he has brought suit are supposed to have been delivered at Shockoe about the beginning of Oct. 1786 a day or two before the inspection opened. The day of delivery is material, and the marks, numbers, weights, and to whom delivered.

Had Thomas Cobbs any other tobaccoes carried to Shockoe in 1786. If he had, state the marks, Nos. weights and to whom delivered.

How many hhds. of tobacco did he carry to that warehouse for two or three years before and after 1786? The object of this is to shew that his annual crop was about 2. hhds., and that when we have accounted for two, he could not have two more.

When Colo. Bell took away the 2. hhds. in Dec. 1786. he says he found there 2 others, marked either like those he took, or very little different, which he did not take on some suspicion they might belong to another Thomas Cobbs, then of Buckingham. Did that other Thomas Cobbs carry his tobacco ever to Shockoe, or did he in the year 1786? If not, these must have been the very hogsheads for which suit is brought.

The particular marks of these 2. hhds. refused by Bell, may be useful.

Is there no mistake in the marks given in the former certificate of the inspectors for the 2. hhds. of 1786. viz. TNC. for TWC.

I had asked the favor of Mr. Carr, if the depositions could not be regularly taken while he was in Richmd. still to call on the Inspectors, and to state the facts as they would attest them. If this has been done, and he should have left the form of their depositions with them, you will have no other trouble than to get the magistrates to swear the deponents and put the deposition under cover.

I shall write to you separately on other subjects. Adieu. Yours affectionately   TH: JEFFERSON

RC (DLC); endorsed by Randolph: "Th. Jefferson. with a dedimus from Albemarle Court." Enclosure not found.

NOTICE GIVEN COBBS: for Thomas Cobbs's suit against TJ, see TJ to John

Wayles Eppes, 3 Sep. 1795, and note. A letter from TJ to Cobbs of 4 Jan. 1796, recorded in SJL but not found, may have been that in which TJ gave him a SECOND NOTICE.

Letters from Randolph to TJ of 26,

28 Nov. and 6 Dec. 1795, the first two from Richmond and the third regarding "Bedford lands," recorded in SJL as received 28 Nov. and 2, 9 Dec. 1795, respectively, have not been found.

From James Madison

DEAR SIR   Philadelphia, January 10, 1796.

The House of Representatives have been latterly occupied with a pretty curious affair. Certain Traders and others, of Detroit, entered into a contract with certain individuals of the United States, for obtaining the peninsula formed by Lakes Huron and Michigan, and containing 20 or 30 millions of acres of valuable land. The traders, by means of their influence over the Indians, were to extinguish the Indian Title; and the other party, by means of their influence, and that of their connexions, with Congress, to extinguish the title of the United States. The Country was to be divided into shares, of which the greater part was to be disposed of by the party who had to deal with Congress. The reason of this, obvious enough in itself, has been sufficiently established by proof. Ever since the session commenced, two of the partners deputed to work the project through Congress have been employed with great industry, opening themselves in different degrees and forms, to different members, according to circumstances. Some of the members, who scented the criminality of the object, waited for a full disclosure. Others, through an eagerness of some sort or other, ran with the tale *first* to the President, and then into the House of Representatives, without concerting or considering a single step that ought to follow. In consequence of the information to the President, and a representation to the District Judge *of the United States*, a warrant issued, and the offenders were taken into custody by the Marshal. The House could not be prevailed on to take a single day to consider the subject, and a warrant issued from the Speaker, also, by virtue of which the Prisoners were transferred to the Sergeant-at-arms. For the proceedings which have ensued, I must refer you to the newspapers. They ended in the discharge of one of the men, and in the reprimand of the other at the bar, and remanding him to Gaol, where he now lies. In the arguments of the Counsel, and in the debates in the House, the want of jurisdiction in such a case over persons not members of the body was insisted on, but was overruled by a very great majority. There cannot be the least doubt, either of the turpitude of the charge, or the guilt of the accused; but it will be difficult, I believe, to deduce the privilege from the Constitution, or to limit it in practice, or even to find a precedent for it in the arbitrary claims of the

British House of Commons. What an engine may such a privilege become, in the hands of a body once corrupted, for protecting its corruptions against public animadversion, under the pretext of maintaining its dignity and preserving the necessary confidence of the public! You will observe that a part of the charge consisted of the slanderous assertion that a majority of the Senate, and nearly a majority of the other House, had embarked in the job for turning a public measure to their private emolument. Apply the principle to other transactions, and the strictures which the press has made on them, and the extent of its mischief will be seen at once. There is much room to suspect that more important characters, both on the British and American sides of this affair, were behind the ostensible parties to it.

The Treaty has not yet been touched. I understand from Mr. Giles that the delay has been explained by him to you. A *copy* of the British ratification arrived lately, and it was hoped a communication of it would have followed. The Executive decided otherwise; and to appease the restlessness of the House of Representatives, Pickering laid the papers before the Speaker, to satisfy him, and enable him to explain the matter to others *individually*. This mode of proceeding does not augment the respect which a more direct and less reserved stile of conduct would inspire, especially as the papers were sufficiently authentic for any use the House of Representatives would be likely to make of them. It is now said that the original is arrived by a British Packet just announced from New York. Having been kept within doors by the badness of the day, I have not ascertained the truth of the account.

I have letters from Col. Monroe of the 23 and 24 of Octr. His picture of the affairs of France, particularly of the prospect exhibited in the approaching establishment of the Constitution, is very favorable. This, as far as we know, has had an easy birth, and wears a promising countenance. He had not learnt with certainty the ratification of the Treaty by the President, but wrote under the belief of it. His regrets, and his apprehensions, were as strong as might be expected. I have a letter from T. Paine, which breathes the same sentiments, and contains some keen observations on the administration of the Government here. It appears that the neglect to claim him as an American Citizen when confined by Robespierre, or even to interfere in any way whatever in his favor, has filled him with an indelible rancour against the President, to whom it appears he has written on the subject. His letter to me is in the stile of a dying one, and we hear that he is since dead, of the abscess in his side, brought on by his imprisonment. His letter desires that he may be remembered to you.

I inclose a copy of the proceedings relating to the presentation of the French flag. What think you of the President's Jacobinical speech to Adèt?

Randolph's vindication has just undergone the lash of the Author of the "Bone to gnaw." It is handled with much satirical scurrility, not without strictures of sufficient ingenuity and plausibility to aid the plan of running him down. By Mr. Carr, who is now here, we will endeavor to contrive you a copy.

MS not found; reprinted from Madison, *Letters*, II, 70-73. Recorded in SJL as received 23 Jan. 1796. Enclosure: see note below.

The CURIOUS AFFAIR which engaged the attention of the House of Representatives between 28 Dec. 1795 and 13 Jan. 1796 involved John Askin and six other Detroit residents, all British merchants, who entered into an agreement with Ebenezer Allen and Charles Whitney of Vermont, and Robert Randall of Philadelphia, to gain control of 18 to 20 million acres of land in what is now the lower PENINSULA of Michigan and northern Ohio, Indiana, and Illinois. The territory was to be divided into forty-one equal SHARES, five for the Detroit contingent, who would use their influence to extinguish the "right of the Native Indians," and thirty-six for the three Americans to gain preemption rights from the United States. Randall and Whitney, who were DEPUTED TO WORK THE PROJECT THROUGH CONGRESS, approached House members with offers of shares or money in return for support of the project. The South Carolina congressman William Loughton Smith RAN WITH THE TALE to the President on 24 Dec. 1795 and, with information provided by William Vans Murray of Maryland, William B. Giles of Virginia, and Daniel Buck of Vermont, the matter was brought INTO THE HOUSE OF REPRESENTATIVES on 28 Dec. 1795. The President had A WARRANT ISSUED for Randall's apprehension and the House issued the same for Whitney. Both were taken into custody and brought before the bar of the House on 29 Dec. 1795 on charges of contempt and breach of privileges. Whitney, who immediately pleaded "not guilty" and answered questions brought by the House, was held in custody until 7 Jan. 1796, when the House voted

52-30 to DISCHARGE him. Randall, meanwhile, requested time to prepare his answer and to obtain counsel for the trial, which began on 4 Jan. 1796, with the prominent Philadelphia attorneys Edward Tilghman, Jr., and William Lewis representing him. Two days later, by a vote of 78 to 17, the House found Randall guilty. He was given a REPRIMAND by the Speaker and continued to be held in custody until 13 Jan., when he was discharged upon payment of fees (Milo M. Quaife, ed., *The John Askin Papers*, 2 vols. [Detroit, 1928-31], I, 568-72; JHR, II, 389-94, 397-401, 405-7, 414; *Annals*, V, 166-70, 200-6; Madison, *Papers*, XVI, 175n).

LETTERS FROM COL. MONROE: James Monroe to Madison, 23 and 24 Oct. 1795, in Madison, *Papers*, XVI, 105-13. LETTER FROM T. PAINE: Thomas Paine to Madison, 24 Sep. 1795, which closed with the postscript "Remember me to Mr. Jefferson" (same, 89-93). Paine expressed his RANCOUR AGAINST THE PRESIDENT in letters to Washington of 22 Feb. and 20 Sep. 1795, the first of which was not sent. Both were included in the pamphlet containing Paine's letter to Washington of 30 July 1796, published by Benjamin Franklin Bache as *Letter to George Washington, President of the United States of America, on Affairs Public and Private. By Thomas Paine, Author of the Works Entitled, Common Sense, Rights of Man, Age of Reason, &c.* (Philadelphia, 1796). See Sowerby, No. 3189.

The COPY OF THE PROCEEDINGS enclosed by Madison—*In the House of Representatives of the United States, Monday, the 4th of January, 1796* (Philadelphia, 1796), Evans, No. 31365—included documents relating to the PRESENTATION OF THE FRENCH FLAG to Congress and was printed in a thousand copies by order of the House. The decorative silk flag had been sent to the

United States by the French government as a reciprocal gesture for the presentation of the American flag to the National Convention, where by order of that body it was displayed next to the French colors, in an emotional ceremony on 11 Sep. 1794 not long after James Monroe's arrival in Paris as minister to France. Pierre Auguste Adet, the French minister to the United States, presented the French republican standard to the President with an address during the celebrations of the New Year on 1 Jan. 1796. The PRESIDENT'S JACOBINICAL SPEECH, printed in the pamphlet, declared in reply: "I rejoice that liberty, which you have so long embraced with enthusiasm,—liberty, of which you have been the invincible defenders, now finds an asylum in the bosom of a regularly organized government;—a government, which, being formed to secure the happiness of the French people, corresponds with the ardent wishes of my heart, while it gratifies the pride of every citizen of the United States, by its resemblance to their own" (same, 6). To Adet's bitter disappointment, however,

Washington merely directed that the flag be deposited in the archives of the United States (Annals, v, 195-200; Ammon, Monroe, 119-21; Madison to Monroe, 26 Jan. 1796, Madison, Papers, XVI, 204; Bernard Mayo, "Joshua Barney and the French Revolution," Maryland Historical Magazine, XXXVI [1941], 359-60; for the politics behind this episode, see Freeman, Washington, VII, 337-8).

BONE TO GNAW: [William Cobbett], A Bone to Gnaw, for the Democrats; or, Observations on a Pamphlet, Entitled, "The Political Progress of Britain" (Philadelphia, 1795). See Evans, No. 28431. This pamphlet started as a counterattack on the initial publication in the United States of James T. Callender's anti-British work, as listed in Cobbett's title, but went on to denounce the "Crusade against Royalty" in America. Using his pen name "Peter Porcupine," Cobbett wrote another pamphlet entitled A New-Year's Gift to the Democrats; or Observations on a Pamphlet, Entitled, "A Vindication of Mr. Randolph's Resignation" (Philadelphia, 1796). See Evans, No. 30215.

To Thomas Mann Randolph

TH:J. TO T M RANDOLPH   Monticello Jan. 11. 96.

I expected this would have gone by your waggon before this. But several accidents have delayed her departure. On bringing her here to have some repairs of smiths' work they found she must have a new axle, and my carpenters being all at work at Shadwell, Nat took her back to Edgehill to make the axle. A fresh then prevented her coming over again till Friday evening. Saturday and this day will complete the smith's work, but now we have a snow 6. I. deep and it is raining and freezing. I therefore write by post which leaves this now for Richmond on Tuesdays, and comes in on Fridays.

I went on Saturday with Divers to see Mr. Meriwether's machine thresh. It gets out only 6. bushels an hour, but it is only double geered and worked by 2. horses. The drum wheel revolves 36. times for one of the horse wheel. My model is treble geered, requires 4. horses, perhaps 6. but the drum wheel revolves 100. times for once of the horse wheel, consequently makes 3. strokes for one of Meriwether's, and each stroke with 3. times the velocity. We are making out our bill of scantling for it. Both Divers and myself were however well satisfied with Mr. Meriwether's. He will build on the same model; but I am for trying the treble.—Mr. Hornsby talks of moving to Kentuckey. If he does, N. Lewis junr. goes also. They go to see the country and determine in the spring. If they move, N.L's land will be for sale. He talks wildly as to price, £3 an acre for 700. acres. I should think it a good bargain at £1200. and a hard one at £1600. His father thinks of buying or rather exchanging for it, as he has lands in Kentuckey adjoining Mr. Hornsby's. These lands would suit Mr. R. of Dungioness.—Mrs. Gilmer is decided against leaving Pen-park. I have been fortunate in getting 5. prime fellows @ £15. a year, and 3. sawyers @ £18. and £20. each, so that with Essex &c. I have a good force for my works.—Our nail business has changed it's appearance a good deal. A rise in the price of iron and fall in that of nails has struck off 20. per cent from the clear profits since the last winter. The two importing houses at Milton have also brought a deluge of British nails with a view as is said of putting down my work. I have hereupon been obliged to enter the lists with them, by establishing a deposit of nails for retail at Milton, another at Charlottesville, and shall send another to Staunton. I ask from the people no more than I did from the merchants with an advance only of 5. percent commission to the retailer. That is to say I *retail* at 5. per cent on the Richmond *wholesale* prices. This I presume will soon give me a clear field, and defeat in this particular this effort of the general system of Scotch policy to suppress every attempt at domestic manufacture.—I am in hopes my cutting machine, hoop iron and rope will be up soon. If this should find you in Richmond perhaps you can aid in getting them off, as also 3. or 4. tons of nail rod lodged for me at Gamble & Temple's.—Jefferson is and has been constantly well, as we all are. We shall write by Nat. again. Suck will not be able to go, as she is still confined. Little Critta will go. My love to my dear Martha. Adieu affectionately.

P.S. Corn @ 15/ here and rising. Very scarce. I am obliged to buy considerably.—I must trouble you for another land warrant for 25. acres of land.

RC (DLC); endorsed by Randolph. Not recorded in SJL.

MR. R. OF DUNGIONESS: probably Thomas Eston Randolph of Dungeness (see note to TJ to William Randolph, [ca. June] 1776; Monticello Association, *Collected Papers*, ed. George G. Shackelford, 2 vols. [Princeton and Charlottesville, 1965-84], I, 175).

GETTING 5. PRIME FELLOWS: TJ purchased the services of five slaves from Lucy, Jane, and William Wood, giving a bond of £16 for the first hired and bonds of £15 for each of the other men (MB, 1, 4 Jan. 1796).

To Thomas Mann Randolph

Th:J. to TMR.   Monticello Jan. 12. 96.

I wrote you by post. The weather having broke away we are trying
to get the waggon off before the river becomes impassable. I put on
board her a box for Mr. Wythe containing my whole and precious collection of the printed laws of Virginia, to be bound as noted to Mr.
Wythe who has occasion to keep them some time for his use. I have
taken the liberty of saying you would answer the charges of the binder
(Bran) for binding, and procure for him an unbound copy of the collection of 1794. which is to make the 8th. volume of the whole. Maria has
attended to the execution of Martha's memorandums, and has noted
what is done under each on the inclosed paper. Suck goes as well as
Critta. I have still a pipe of wine remaining at James Brown's. Being
entirely unacquainted with Billy's sobriety and honesty I must leave to
yourself to judge whether you think he may be relied on to bring it up
unadulterated, and if you think so, and he should be otherwise un-
loaded, I will thank you to give him an order to recieve it from Mr.
Brown. My love to my dear Martha, and Adieu affectionately.

RC (DLC); endorsed by Randolph; with
subjoined note in Randolph's hand: "March
21. 96. Deposited with Brend a copy of the
laws of 1794. Note. Brend says it must be a
considerable time before he can bind them."
Enclosure not found.

I WROTE YOU BY POST: see preceding letter. For MARTHA'S MEMORANDUMS, see
Martha Jefferson Randolph to TJ, 1 Jan.
1796. TJ paid Billy and Nat, two of Randolph's slaves, two dollars for delivering the
PIPE OF WINE (MB, 15 Feb. 1796).

To George Wythe

Th:J. to G: Wythe   Monticello Jan. 12. 96.

I recieved last night your letter on the subject of the laws, and certainly will trust you with any thing I have in the world. A waggon was
going off this morning from hence to Varina, and I have exerted myself
to send them by that. As I have always intended to have my copies
bound up so as to make as complete a set as I could, I thought it best to
do this now, before you begin to make use of them. I have therefore
arranged them into 7. volumes, and propose to make the revisal of
1794. the 8th. as you will see by the directions to the book binder. I
have ordered the box to be delivered to you, merely that you may open
it, see it's contents, and by delivering them to the book binder acquire
a right of pressing him to expedite his work. As to all the expences I
shall provide for them through the channel of Mr. Randolph. When

done, take the whole collection, and keep it till it has answered your purpose. I mean to write you a particular statement of the contents of my collection and it's deficiencies; but this requires more time than the departure of the waggon allows me. It shall follow by post because I am not without hopes you may have some duplicates from which you can spare copies to fill up the chasms of mine. Adieu affectionately.

P.S. Mr. Bran has formerly done a good deal of binding for me, and would take pains to serve an old customer well.

PrC (DLC).

The DIRECTIONS TO THE BOOK BINDER, Thomas Brend of Richmond, were probably enclosed in the box that left in the wagon on 12 Jan. 1796 with the printed laws TJ wished to have bound, but have not been found. For TJ's amendment to these directions, see the following letter. The binding of the volumes was not completed until 1799 (*Virginia Argus*, 19 Nov. 1796; Wythe to TJ, 1 Feb. 1797; TJ to Wythe, 29 May 1799).

STATEMENT OF THE CONTENTS OF MY COLLECTION: see enclosure to TJ to Wythe, 16 Jan. 1796 (second letter).

To George Wythe

TH:J. TO G. WYTHE   Monticello Jan. 16. 96.

I was so hurried to get ready my collection of printed laws before the departure of the waggon, that I did the work imperfectly. I have since found the laws of 1783. May and Octob. which I should be glad to have added to the end of my 6th. volume. If you can procure a copy of those of 1773. I will pray you to add it to the end of the 5th. volume, and in both cases to make corresponding changes in the middle one of the three printed labels proposed on these volumes. Indeed I would wish the middle label of the Vth. volume to be | Fugitive Sheets. 1734-1773 | and of the VIth. to be | Fugitive Sheets 1775-1783 |

I chuse to bring down the VIth. volume to 1783. that it may terminate at the same period with the Chancellors revisal.

I write you a separate letter which perhaps may lead to the preservation of these laws. Perhaps your friend Mr. Taylor, of whom I hear so many good and clever things, may think this business worthy his patronage. Adieu affectionately.

PrC (DLC).

LAWS OF 1783. MAY AND OCTOB.: see Sowerby, Nos. 1859-60.

To George Wythe

TH: JEFFERSON TO G. WYTHE   Monticello Jan. 16. 1796.

In my letter which accompanied the box containing my collection of
Printed laws, I promised to send you by post a statement of the contents
of the box. On taking up the subject I found it better to take a more
general review of the whole of the laws I possess, as well Manuscript as
Printed, as also of those which I do not possess, and suppose to be no
longer extant. This general view you will have in the inclosed paper,
whereof the articles stated to be Printed, constitute the contents of the
box I sent you. Those in MS. were not sent, because not supposed to
have been within your view, and because some of them will not bear
removal, being so rotten, that, on turning over a leaf, it sometimes falls
into powder. These I preserve by wrapping and sewing them up in
oiled cloth, so that neither air nor moisture can have access to them.
Very early in the course of my researches into the laws of Virginia, I
observed that many of them were already lost, and many more on the
point of being lost, as existing only in single copies in the hands of careful or curious individuals, on whose deaths they would probably be used
for waste paper. I set myself therefore to work to collect all which were
then existing, in order that when the day should come in which the
public should advert to the magnitude of their loss in these precious
monuments of our property and our history,[1] a part of their regret might
be spared by information that a portion has been saved from the wreck
which is worthy of their attention and preservation. In searching after
these remains, I spared neither time, trouble, nor expence; and am of
opinion that scarcely any law escaped me, which was in being as late as
the year 1770. in the middle or Southern parts of the state. In the
Northern parts perhaps something might still be found. In the clerks'
offices in the antient counties some of those MS. copies of the laws may
possibly still exist which used to be furnished at the public expence to
every county before the use of the Press was introduced; and in the same
places, and in the hands of antient magistrates, or of their families, some
of the fugitive sheets of the laws of separate sessions, which have been
usually distributed since the practice commenced of printing them. But,
recurring to what we actually possess, the Question is What means will
be the most effectual for preserving these remains from future loss? All
the care I can take of them will not preserve them from the worm, from
the natural decay of the paper, from the accident of fire, or those of
removal, when it is necessary for any public purpose, as in the case of
those now sent you. Our experience has proved to us that a single copy,
or a few, deposited in MS. in the public offices, cannot be relied on for

any great length of time. The ravages of fire and of ferocious enemies have had but too much part in producing the very loss we now deplore. How many of the precious works of antiquity were lost, while they existed[2] only in manuscript? Has there ever been one lost since the art of printing has rendered it practicable to multiply and disperse copies? This leads us then to the only means of preserving those remains of our laws now under consideration, that is, a multiplication of printed copies. I think therefore that there should be printed at the public expence, an edition of all the laws ever passed by our legislatures which can now be found; that a copy should be deposited in every public library in America, in the principal public offices within the state, and some perhaps in the most distinguished public libraries of Europe, and that the rest should be sold to individuals, towards reimbursing the expences of the edition. Nor do I think that this would be a voluminous work. The MSS. would probably furnish matter for one printed volume in folio, and would comprehend all the laws from 1624. to 1701. which period includes Pervis.—My collection of Fugitive sheets forms, as we know, two volumes, and comprehends all the extant laws from 1734. to 1783. and the laws which can be gleaned up, from the Revisals, to supply the chasm between 1701. and 1734. with those from 1783. to the close of the present century (by which term the work might be compleated) would not be more than the matter of another volume. So that four volumes in folio probably[3] would give every law ever passed which is now extant: whereas those who wish to possess as many of them as can be procured, must now buy the six folio volumes of Revisals, to wit, Pervis, and those of 1732. 1748. 1768. 1783. and 1794. and in all of them possess not one half of what they wish. What would be the expence of the edition, I cannot say; nor how much would be reimbursed by the sales; but I am sure it would be moderate compared with the rates which the public have hitherto paid for printing their laws, provided a sufficient latitude be given as to printers and places. The first step would be to make out a single copy from the MSS. which would employ a clerk about a year, or something more, to which expence about a fourth should be added for the collation of the MSS. which would employ three persons at a time about half a day, or a day, in every week. As I have already spent more time in making myself acquainted with the contents and arrangement of these MSS. than any other person probably ever will, and their condition does not admit their removal to a distance, I will chearfully undertake the direction and superintendance of this work, if it can be done in the neighboring towns of Charlottesville or Milton, farther than which I could not undertake to go from home. For the residue of the work, my printed volumes might be delivered to the Printer.

I have troubled you with these details, because you are in the place where they may be used for the public service, if they admit of such use, and because the order of assembly, which you mention, shews they are sensible of the necessity of preserving such of these laws as relate to our landed property, and a little further consideration will perhaps convince them that it is better to do the whole work once for all, than to be recurring to it by piece-meal, as particular parts of it shall be required, and that too perhaps when the materials shall be lost. You are the best judge of the weight of these observations, and of the mode of giving them any effect they may merit. Adieu affectionately.

PrC (DLC: TJ Papers, 99: 17025-7). Dft (DLC: James Madison Papers); entirely in TJ's hand; with several emendations, the most important being recorded below, and minor variations in capitalization and punctuation. PrC of Dft (DLC: TJ Papers, 99: 17021-3); lacks several emendations, the most important being noted below. Dft enclosed in TJ to Madison, 24 Jan. 1796 (recorded in SJL, but not found).

The present letter—excepting the final sentence and complimentary close and with minor variations in capitalization and punctuation—was published in broadside form later in the year by a committee of the Virginia House of Delegates. Subjoined to it were the "statement of the particular acts" contained in the enclosure printed below and a statement by the committee, consisting of Wythe, John Brown, John Marshall, Bushrod Washington, and John Wickham, dated "November, 1796" at Richmond: "The persons appointed, by an act of the last session, to superintend an edition of all legislative acts concerning lands, having pe-

rused the foregoing letter, written in answer to an application to the author for his copies of the acts, more compleat than any which can be elsewhere procured, and supposing that the General Assembly, upon reconsideration of the subject, might wish to enlarge the work, declined entering upon the business, until the sentiments of that honorable body shall be known" (DLC: Broadside Collection, Portfolio 180, No. 11; consists of four printed pages on two sheets; at head of text: "Extract of a Letter from Thomas Jefferson to George Wythe"; endorsed by TJ: "Virginia laws"). See Evans No. 30637. For the purpose and distribution of the broadside, see Wythe to TJ, 27 July 1796, 1 Feb. 1797; TJ to Wythe, 8 Aug. 1796.

[1] In Dft TJ here canceled an estimated nine illegible words.
[2] In Dft TJ interlined this word in place of "were preserved." Emendation not in PrC of Dft.
[3] Word interlined in Dft. Emendation not in PrC of Dft.

Statement of the Laws of Virginia

A statement of the Volumes of the Laws of Virginia, Manuscript and Printed in my possession

A M.S. marked A. given me by the late Peyton Randolph. It had belonged to his father Sr. John Randolph, who had collected papers with a view to write the history of Virginia. It is attested by R. Hickman, and contains the acts of 1623/4 Mar. 5. 35. acts

MS. marked ⟨43⟩ purchased of the executors of the late Peyton Randolph, having been among the collections of Sr. John Randolph. From the resemblance of the mark to some I have formerly [seen] in the Secretary's office, I suspect this to be an original volume of records, [probab]lly borrowed by Sr. John Randolph. It contains the laws from 1629. to 1633.

[MS.] marked F. purchased from the administrator of Colo. Richard Bland deceased. It contains laws from 1639 to 1667.

MS. marked D. purchased from the administrator of Colo. Richard Bland deceased. It contains laws from 1642/3 to 1661/2.

MS. copied by myself of the laws of 1660/1 Mar. 23.

MS. from the Charles City office, to which it belongs probably. I found it in Lorton's tavern, brought in to be used for waste paper. Much had already been cut off for thread papers and other uses. [1] Debnam, the then clerk, very readily gave it to me, as also another hereafter mentioned. It still contains from chap. 31. of the session of 1661/2 to 1702.

MS. marked B. purchased of the executors of the late Peyton Randolph, part of Sr. John Randolph's collection. It contains laws from 1662. to 1697.

MS. Appendix to a copy of Pervis's collection from the Westover library, given by the late Colo. W. Byrd to Mr. Wayles, whose library came to my hands.

MS. from the Charles City office, given to me by Debnam as abovementioned. It contains from c. 2. to c. 53. of the laws of 1705.

MS. given me by the present John Page of Rosewell. It had belonged to Matthew[2] Page his grandfather, who was one of the Committee of 1705. for revising the laws, and was probably furnished with this copy for that work.[3]

Printed laws.

Pervis's collection. This forms the 1st. vol. of my collection of the Printed laws of Virginia.

Revisal of 1732. This forms the 2d. vol.

Revisal of 1748. This is vol. the 3d.

Revisal of 1768. This is vol. the 4th.

Fugitive sheets of the laws[4] of particular sessions bound together from 1734. to 1772. Making vol. the 5th.

do. · from 1775. to 1783. Making vol. the 6th.

Revisal of 1783. by the Chancellors. Making vol. 7th.

Revisal of 1794. Making vol. the 8th.

Th: Jefferson
Jan. 13. 1796.

A statement of the particular acts of the assembly of Virginia in my possession either MS. or Printed, and of those not in my possession, and presumed to be lost.

1619. June.	The first session of assembly ever held in Virginia. Lost.
1620. May.	Lost.
1622.	Lost.
1623/4 Mar. 5.	I have in MS.
1626.	Lost.
1629. Oct. 16.[5]	I have in MS.
1629/30 Mar. 24.	I have in MS.
[1631]. Feb. 21.	I have in MS.

1632. Sep. 4.	60. acts. I have in MS.
1632/3 Feb. 1.	6. acts in MS
1633. Aug. 21.	16. acts in MS.
1639. Jan. 6.	in MS.
1642. Apr. 1.	the 21st. & 22d. acts in MS.
1642/3 Mar. 2.	a revisal.[6] I have in MS.
1644. Oct. 1.	in MS.
1644/5 Feb. 17.	in MS.
1645. Nov. 20.	in MS.
1646. Oct. 5.	in MS.
1647. Nov. 3.	in MS.
1648. Oct. 12.	in MS.
1649. Oct. 10.	in MS.
1652. Apr. 26.	in MS.
Nov. 25.	in MS.
1653. July 5.	in MS.
1654. Nov. 20.	in MS.
1655. Mar.	in MS.
1655/6 Mar. 10.	in MS.
1656. Dec. 1.	in MS.
1657/8 Mar. 13.	A revisal in MS.
1658/9 Mar. 1.	in MS.
1659/60 Mar. 13.	in MS.
1660. Oct. 11.	in MS.
1660/1 Mar. 23.	in MS.
1661/2 Mar. 23.	Chap. 1. to 138. inclusive. Printed.
1662. Dec. 2. or 23.	Chap. 1. 2. 3. 4. 5. 6. 7. 8. 9. 10. 11. 12. 13. 15. 17. 18. 21. 23. Printed. 14. 16. 19. 20. 22. in MS.
1663. Sep. 10.	Chap. 1. 2. 4. 7. 8. 9. 10. 11. 14. 16. 17. Printed. 3. 5. 6. 12. 13. 15. 18. in MS.
1664. Sep. 20.	9. Acts. Printed. [3. 9. Inserted.][7]
1665. Oct. 10.	Chap. 1. 2. 3. 5. 6. 7. 8. 9. Printed. 4. 10. in MS.
1666. June 5.	Chap. 2. 3. 4. Printed. 1. in M.S.
[Oct. 23].	Chap. 1. 2. 3. 5. 6. 7. 9. 10. 11. 12. 13. 15. 16. 17. 18. 19. 20. 21. 22. 23. 24. Printed 4. 8. 14. in M.S.
1667. Sep. 3.	Chap. 1. 2. 3. 4. Printed 5. 6. 7. in M.S.
1668. Sep. 17.	Chap. 1. 2. 3. 4. 5. 6. 7. 8. 9. Printed
1669. Oct. 20.	Chap. 1. 2. 3. 4. 5. 6. 7. Printed. 8. 9. in MS.
1670. Oct. 3.	Chap. 1. 2. 3. 4. 5. 6. 7. 8. 9. 10. 12. Printed 11. in MS.
1671. Sep. 20.	Chap. 1. 4. 5. 6. Printed. 2. 3. 7. in MS.
1672. Sep. 24.	Chap. 1. 2. 3. 4. 5. 7. 8. 9. 10. Printed. 6. 11. in MS.

1673. Oct. 20.	Chap. 1. 2. 3. 4. 5. Printed.
	6. 7. in MS.
1674. Sep. 21.	Chap. 1. 3. 4. 6. 7. Printed.
	2. 5. 8. 9. 10. in MS.
1675/6 Mar. 7.	Chap. 3. Printed.
	1. 2. 4. in MS.
1676. June 5.	Chap. 1. to 20. in MS.
1676/7 Feb. 20.	Chap. 4. 6. 7. 8. 9. 10. 11. 13. 14. 16. 17. 20. Printed.
	1. 2. 3. 5. 12. 15. 18. 19. in MS.
1677. Oct. 10.	Chap. 1. 2. 3. 4. 5. 8. 9. 10. 11. 12. Printed.
	6. 7. in MS.
1679. Apr. 25.	Chap. 1. 2. 3. 4. 5. 6. 7. 8. 9. Printed.
	10. 11. in MS.
1680. June 8.	Chap. 1. to 17. Printed.
1682. Nov. 10.	Chap. 1. to 13. Printed.
1684. Apr. 16.	Chap. 2. Printed.
	1. 3. 4. 5. 6. 7. 8. 9. 10 in MS.
1686. Oct. 20.	Chap. 1. to 11. in MS.
1691. Apr. 16.	Chap. 12. Printed.
	1. 2. 3. 4. 5. 6. 7. 8. 9. 10. 11. 13. 14. 15. 16. 17.
	18. [19. 20. 21.] in MS.
1692. Apr. 1.	Chap. 1. to 7. in MS.
1692/3 Mar. 2.	Chap. 1. to 7. in MS.
1693. Oct. 10.	Chap. 1. to 5. in MS.
1695. Apr. 18.	Chap. 1. to 6. in MS.
1696. Sep. 24.	Chap. 1. to 14. in MS.
1697. Oct. 21.	Chap. 1. in MS.
1698. Sep. 28.	no law past at this session.
1699. Apr. 27.	Chap. 1. to 16. in MS.
1700. Dec. 5.	Chap. 1. to 4. in MS.
1701. Aug. 6.	Chap. 1. to 6. in MS.
[1702. May] 30.	[Chap.] 1. 2. Lost.
[Aug. 14.	Chap. 1. a part of it i]n MS.
	2. 3. [4.] Lost.
[1702/3] Mar. 19.	[no act passed.]
[1704.] Apr. [20.	Chap. 1.] to 11. Lost.
[1705. Apr. 18.	Chap. 1. to] 4. Lost.
Oct. [25.	Chap. 2. 3. 5. 6.] 7. 8. 9. 10. 12. 13. 14. 15. 17. [19.] 20.
	22. 23. 25. 27. 28. 29. 30. 32. 33. [35. 38.] 39. 40. 41.
	43. 44. [45. 46. 47. 48. 49. 50. 52. 53. Printed.]
	4. 11. 16. 18. 21. 24. 26. 31. 34. 36. 37. 42. 51.
	55. in MS.
	1. 54. Lost.
1710. Oct. 25.	Chap. 3. 4. 5. 8. 11. 12. 13. 14. Printed.
	1. 2. 6. 7. 9. 10. 15. 16. 17. in MS.
1711. Nov. 7.	Chap. 2. 3. Printed.
	1. in MS. Here the MSS. end.
	4. 5. Lost.
1712. Oct. 22.	Chap. 4. 5. Printed.
	1. 2. 3. 6. 7. Lost.

1713. Nov. 5.	Chap. 3. 4. 6. 7. 8. Printed.
	1. 2. 5. 9. 10. 11. 12. Lost.
1714. Nov. 16.	Chap. 1. 2. 3. 5. Printed.
	4. Lost.
1715. Aug. 3.	Chap. 1. 2. 3. Lost.
1718. Apr. 23.	Chap. 1. 3. The substance Printed in Beverley's abridgment.
	2. 4. Lost.
Nov. 11.	Chap. 1. 2. Lost.
1720. Nov. 2.	Chap. 3. 4. 5. 6. 7. 8. Printed.
	1. 2. Substance in Beverl. abr.
	9. 10. 11. 12. 13. 14. 15. 16. 17. 18. Lost.
1722. May 9.	Chap. 1. 2. 3. 6. 7. 8. 9. Printed.
	4. 5. 10. 11. 12. 13. 14. 15. 16. Lost.
1723. May 9.	Chap. 2. 4. 8. 10. Printed.
	1. 3. 5. 6. 7. 9. 11. 12. 13. 14. 15. Lost.
1726. May 12.	Chap. 1. 2. 3. 4. 6. 7. 8. Printed.
	5. 9. 10. 11. 12. 13. 14. Lost.
1727/8 Feb. 1.	Chap. 3. 5. 6. 7. 8. 9. 10. 11. 12. 13. 14. Printed.
	1. 2. 4. 15. 16. 17. 18. 19. 20. 21. 22. Lost.
1730. May 21.	Chap. 1. to 19. Printed.
	20. to 29. Lost.
1732. May 18.	Chap. 1. to 20. Printed.
	21. to 35. Lost.
	Here begins my collection of the Fugitive sheets of Laws printed for each session.
1734. Aug. 22.	31. Acts. Printed.
1736. Aug. 5.	25. Acts Printed.
1738. Nov. 1.	25. Acts Printed.
1740. May. 22.	15. Acts. Printed.
Aug. 1.	1. Act. Printed.
[1742.] May. [6.	33. Acts. Printed.
1744. Sep. 4.	46. Acts. Printed.
1745/6] Feb. 20.	30. Acts. [Printed
1746. July 11.	2. Acts. Lost.
1747. Mar. 30.	5. Acts. Lost.
1748. Oct. 27.]	Chap. 1. to 55.[8] 57. 77. Printed.
	5[6. 58].[9] to 76. 78 to 89. Lost.[10]
[1752. Feb. 27.	53.] Acts. Printed.
[1753. No]v. 1.	28. Acts. Printed.
[1754. Feb. 14.]	3. Acts. Printed.
[Aug. 22.]	3. Acts. Printed.
Oct. 17.	7. Acts. Printed.
1755. May [1.	24]. Acts. Printed.
Aug. 5.	8. Acts. Printed.
Oct. 27.	6. Acts. Printed.
1756. Mar. 25.	13. Acts. Printed.
Sep. 20.	3. Acts. Printed
1757. Apr. 14.	[30]. Acts. Printed.

1758.	Mar. 30.	[2]. Acts. Printed.
	Sep. 14.	13. Acts. Printed
	Nov. 9.	1. Act. Printed.
1759.	Feb. 22.	34. Acts. Printed.
	Nov. 1.	6. Acts. Printed
1760.	Mar. 4.	3. Acts. Printed.
	May. 19.	Printed.
	Oct. 6.	4. Acts. Printed.
1761.	Mar. 5.	31. Acts. Printed.
	Nov. 3.	13. Acts. Printed.
1762.	Jan. 14.	3. Acts. Printed.
	Mar. 30.	7. Acts. Printed.
	Nov. 2.	44. Acts. Printed.
1763.	May 19	13. Acts. Printed
1764.	Jan. 12.	13. Acts. Printed.
	Oct. 30.	54. Acts. Printed.
1766.	Nov. 6.	61 Acts. Printed.
1768.	Mar. 31.	7. Acts. Printed.
1769.	May. 8.	a Convention. No act passed.
	Nov. 7.	89. Acts. Printed.
1771.	July 11.	4. Acts. Printed.
1772.	Feb. 10.	68. Acts. Printed.
1773.	Mar. 4.	16. Acts. Lost from my collection.
1774.	May. 5.	dissolved before any act passed.
1775.	June 1.	the last assembly under the Royal government. It was discontinued by not meeting on it's own adjournment, without having passed any Law.

Conventions.

1775	July 17.	Ordinances. Printed.
	Dec.	Ordinances. Printed.
1776.	May. 6.	Ordinances. Printed.

Assemblies.

	Oct. 7.	Acts. Printed.
1777.	May 5.	Acts. Printed.
	Oct. 20.	Acts. Printed.
1778.	May. 4.	Acts. Printed.
	Oct. 5.	Acts. Printed.
1779.	May. 3.	Acts. Printed.
	Oct. 4.	Acts. Printed.
1780.	May. 1.	Acts. Printed.
	Oct. 16.	Acts. Printed.
1781.	Mar. [11]	
	May. 7.	Acts. Printed.
	Nov. 5.	Acts. Printed.
1782.	May. 6.	Acts. Printed.
1783.	May. 5.	Acts. Printed
	Oct. 20.	Acts. Printed.

Note that the terms 'Printed' or 'in MS.' mean that I have the Laws Printed or in MS.

PrC (DLC: TJ Papers, 99: 17009, 17011-15); consists of six pages entirely in TJ's hand; badly faded in part and torn, with bracketed passages supplied from Dft except where noted. Dft (DLC: Madison Papers); with the "statement of the particular acts" beginning on verso of the "statement of the Volumes" and continuing on two additional sheets, cancellations in both sections (see notes 3 and 5 below) indicating that TJ compiled them as complementary inventories; the most important emendations and variations are noted below. PrC of Dft (DLC: TJ Papers, 99: 17010, 17016-20); badly faded in part; lacks several emendations, as noted below. A printed broadside (DLC: Broadside Collection, Portfolio 180, No. 11) containing the "statement of the particular acts" includes two variations (see notes 7 and 11 below) and minor variations in capitalization and punctuation (see note to covering letter). Dft enclosed in TJ to Madison, 24 Jan. 1796 (not found).

The manuscript and printed volumes of laws listed in the STATEMENT OF THE VOLUMES are described in Sowerby, Nos. 1822-30, 1832, 1837-62.

[1] Preceding sentence interlined.
[2] Word inserted by TJ in blank space in Dft. PrC of Dft has blank space.
[3] In Dft TJ here canceled: "The above is an exact statement of my M.S. collection, as I left it when I went to Europe. During my absence the whole were borrowed from my library. After being balloted about by land and by sea, and being some years under a pile of cordage on a warehouse at New York and supposed lost, they were returned to me at Philadelphia, without the volume marked ⟨43⟩ which therefore I suppose is lost. If so, the laws of the six sessions of 1629. 1630. to 1633. are gone forever, as they existed in no other book." Emendation not in PrC of Dft.
[4] Sentence to this point in Dft altered from "Acts." Emendation not in PrC of Dft.
[5] In Dft a brace begins here and extends through the entry for "1633," with "I had in M.S. in the vol. ⟨43⟩ qu. if now existing?" being written at the point of the brace. TJ amended the note to read "I have in M.S." Emendation not in PrC of Dft.
[6] In Dft a brace begins here and extends through the entry for "1660/1," with "I have in M.S." being written at the point of the brace.
[7] Word possibly "Inverted." Dft and broadside lack preceding two figures and word.
[8] In Dft remainder reads "Printed. also Chap. 57. 77."
[9] Supplied from broadside.
[10] In Dft this line reads: "56. to 89. Lost. (except Chap. 57. 77.)."
[11] Broadside: "Mar. 1. acts printed."

To John Barnes

DEAR SIR   Monticello Jan. 17. 1796.

This serves to advise you that I have this day drawn on you for [150]. Doll. at three days sight in favor of Mr. Charles Johnston & Co. of Richmond, which please to honor. Several little disbursements which you have made for me, of unknown amount, render it desireable to recieve a continuation of your last account.

Yesterday came to hand a box of Segars, which I presume is from you. I expected it would have been accompanied by the tea. I recieved some time ago, two pair of shoes from Mr. Starr. Mr. Peyton seems so positive that the boots and half boots were delivered to the same captain, that I am induced to trouble you with the enquiry. I am assured by

Gamble & Temple that the shoes only were delivered to them. Have I before desired you to pay Messrs. Bache and Brown a year's newspapers each? If I have not, be so good as to do it. I am with great esteem Dear Sir Your most obedt. servt   TH: JEFFERSON

PrC (CSmH); endorsed in ink on verso: "Barnes John."

SJL records 71 letters exchanged by TJ and the Richmond mercantile firm of

CHARLES JOHNSTON & CO. or Johnston himself between 26 Dec. 1795 and 16 Apr. 1800, as well as a letter of 14 Sep. 1795 from TJ to the shoemaker James STARR which are not found.

To Thomas Mann Randolph

TH:J. TO TMR.   Monticello. Monday Jan. 18. 96.

Your waggon with Suck and Critta set off from here on Wednesday the 13th. By the time they got to Pouncey's hill they found the roads so deep that they could not get along. They returned to Edgehill and carried the greatest part of their load to Milton to be sent down by water. Since that such floods of rain have fallen, and the river so risen that all communication has been cut off for some days. Every boat and batteau at Milton is carried off, one of them loaded. I hope your things were not yet aboard any boat, but do not know. The river was still rising last night. I have not heard from it this morning: and write the present under uncertainty whether we can get it to the post office by the evening.—Your favor of the 12th. is recieved. The letter to Mr. Millar shall go to him this evening, or as soon as Moore's creek is passable, and your order in his favor shall be paid. You have a right to draw freely, for the hire of the four men (not 5. as your letter seemed to suppose) will leave me still considerably in your debt. Essex sets off down to-day. The other three remain.—I am sorry for the sentiment expressed in the close of your letter. Your health is certainly bad. That is visible to the eye. No body has seen it with more anxiety than my self: but never with any apprehensions as to the issue. At your time of life the resources of nature are so powerful that, in a case which gives her time, they are infallible. In the whole course of my observations, I cannot recollect one instance of a chronic complaint in any person of your age not being surmounted, except in the case of consumption, which is not yours. One very disagreeable circumstance indeed is the effect of the disease on your spirits. But this is merely mechanical. It is not the result of reasoning on the known nature of your complaint. That I am satisfied is known to nobody. The wisest physicians agree in another fact, that there never was an instance of a chronic complaint relieved by medecine, even where the character of the disease is known. But where it is unknown, medecine is given at hap-hazard, and may do much mischief. Keep up your strength then, by such exercise as you find does not fatigue you, and by eating such things and in such quantities as you find you can digest. This will give time to the vis medicatrix naturae, which, if it be not thwarted in it's efforts by medecine, is infallible in it's resources at your time of life. It's efforts would indeed be immensely aided if you could, by the force of reason and confidence in her, counteract the mechanical effects of the disease on your spirits. But if you cannot do this, still exercise moderately, eat soberly but sufficiently, and take no medecine, and your friends will have nothing to fear. I think we may strongly conjecture that your complaint is a gout, because no other disease is so long in declaring itself, and because you have a hereditary expectation of that. However if the symptoms be permitted to develope themselves, they will in time unfold the disease, and bring on that crisis which is contrived by nature to relieve it. That this may be soon we all sincerely pray. My love to my dear Martha. I will write to her by the next post, and shall doubtless be able to tell her then as I am now that Jefferson is in high health. Adieu to both of you affectionately.

RC (DLC); endorsed by Randolph.

Randolph's FAVOR OF THE 12TH., not recorded in SJL and not found, may have been his missing letter of 9 Jan. 1796, recorded in SJL as received from Varina on 16 Jan. 1796. SJL also records a letter TJ wrote to Randolph on 14 Jan. 1796 (now missing). VIS MEDICATRIX NATURAE: "healing power of nature."

To John Barnes

DR. SIR   Monticello Jan. 24. 1796.

Your favor of Dec. 24. came to hand yesterday. The present serves to [advise] you that on the 22d. instant I drew on you for 10[0] Dollars in favor of David Jackson or order and this day for 86. Doll. 28½ Cents in favor of Isaac Millar or order, which be pleased to honor on account of Sir Your very humble servt   TH: JEFFERSON

PrC (MHi); faded in part; at foot of text: "Mr. John Barnes."

Barnes's FAVOR OF DEC. 24., recorded in SJL as received 23 Jan. 1796 and mistakenly noted there as a letter of the same date, has not been found.

TJ's draft of the 22D. INSTANT, not found, was in favor of Dr. David Jackson of Philadelphia for Dr. William Wardlaw of Charlottesville. TJ's draft of THIS DAY ordered Barnes to pay Isaac Miller as de-

scribed above at three days' sight (PrC in MHi; at foot of text: "Mr. John Barnes Mercht Philadelphia. S. 3d. street"). This draft was to pay Miller, the postmaster at Charlottesville, TJ's quarterly postage charge of $18.965, plus another $30.00 for Thomas Mann Randolph, TJ having received the remaining $37.32 in cash from Miller (MB, 22, 24 Jan. 1796). According to SJL, TJ advised Barnes of the first draft in a letter of 22 Jan. 1796 (now missing).

From Jonathan Williams

As you are now retired from public Business you will not, probably, consider a philosophical communication as an unpleasant Intrusion on your Leisure; If, however, I were to offer an Apology, it would be the Experience I have had of your Indulgence in many Conversations. In the Summer of 1791 I went with my Family to the Redsprings in Bottetourt, and took with me the best Thermometer and Barometer I could procure. With these Instruments I intended to estimate the Height of the Country as I passed, and if constant attention with repeated Observation give me any claim to confidence, I may make some pretence to it; but my calculations and conclusions must stand the test of examination. Wishing however to leave as little as possible to doubt and uncertainty, I determined to put this barometrical mode of Calculation to what appeared to me a proper Trial, and accordingly I placed two Barometers in Christ Church, one at the Pulpit below, the other in the steeple 166 feet above, and at many periods, during Winter and Summer, I examined their relative State, noting the Temperature of the Air by a Thermometer both above and below. The Results these gave by barometrical Calculation varied from 105 to 203 feet tho' the known Height was 166. This induced me to doubt either my own Accuracy or this mode of Calculation in general tho' the Memoirs of M. Du Luc and some others in the English Philosophical Transactions seem to justify much Dependence upon them. Under this Impression, I thought it better to be silent than to publish an Error, and my whole proceeding would have been unknown if in an accidental Conversation with Dr. Rittenhouse and Mr. Patterson they had not desired me to produce the Journal as it was, leaving it to others to comment upon it; assuring me at the same time that they thought these Trials in the lower part of the atmosphere, especially in a City filled with Smoke and various exhalations, by no means to be relied on as operating against the general principles of barometrical Calculation.

These Assurances produced a Communication to the Philosophical Society of which I inclose an Extract, with four Sections of some of the mountains, taking the Level of Richmond for the Basis. To this should be added the height of Richmond from the Sea, which I have not ascertained; but considering the current of James River, I suppose about 150 feet not far out of the way.

The English Barometer is graduated so as to show a Range of 3 Inches; and it seems to be allowed that the rise and fall in the course of a Year generally marks this difference in the height of the Mercury. In

Philadelphia the annual Range is not half of this, and it appears by your Notes that the Barometer varied at Williamsburg but $1.\frac{86}{100}$. in a Year and during 9 months at Monticello (about 500 feet higher) the difference between the two extremes was only $1.\frac{21}{100}$. While I was stationary behind the Mountains (11 days at staunton and 29 at the Redsprings) the Barometer varied at the former place $0.\frac{40}{100}$ and at the latter only $0.\frac{20}{100}$ although the Thermometer varied more than 30 degrees and we had the extremes of weather as to fair and dry or cloudy and heavy rain: In one day, after a very fine morning, we had the severest Gust I saw in that Country, which affected the Barometer only $\frac{43}{100}$, the Thermometer in the same time rising about 6 degrees. This was in the Calfpasture about 20 miles from Staunton, and before the Gust the Barometer was at its highest point.

To discover the cause of these differences on one and the other side of the Atlantic we must probably have recourse to some general Law, perhaps the more prevalent humidity on one side than on the other; But I confess I am inclined to suspect that mere elevation, if accurately ascertained, would afford an interesting Clue to a Discovery which might in its consequence be of more importance than appears at first sight. If we could collect accurate meteorological Journals during one and the same Year in the lower and higher parts of the Country, it would perhaps appear that the Barometer is proportionably less liable to variation in high than in low Countries, and perhaps a place might be found where it would be always stationary: I need not mention to you some interesting Conclusions such an Experiment would produce. Your extensive acquaintance and the weight of your reccommendation to Gentlemen living among the Mountains probably would effect this desireable Purpose. I wish also to obtain the height of Rockfish Gap above the Foot on each side by a spirit Level; If I were in that Country with such an Instrument I should think nothing of a Journey of 20 or 30 Miles on purpose. The Reasons I have given relative to the inaccuraces of the lower parts of the Atmosphere, induce me to wish for this Correction of my barometrical Measurement; I am not so Anxious as to the higher Country, where the steadiness of the Mercury justifies a Dependance on its accuracy. With a View to correct my mode of Calculation I have tried the Andes by Don Ulloa's state of the Barometer, and Mr. Charles Assent in the Balloon at Paris by the fall in the mercury noted by him, and my Results do not materially differ from those of these celebrated Men.

I shall take it as a Favour if you will kindly and candidly give me all the Information and advice that you think interesting on these Subjects, as I am desirous to have my Communication to the Society wholly suppressed at the Time of publishing the next Volume, unless the Opinion of able Men should justify its appearance among the Transactions. I am with great Respect Sir Your most obedient & most humble Servant

JONA WILLIAMS

RC (CSmH); at foot of text: "The Hon Th: Jefferson." Recorded in SJL as received on 10 May 1796.

Jonathan Williams (1750-1815), the son of a wealthy Boston merchant of the same name, received his education in that city and with the aid of Benjamin Franklin, his great uncle, gained further commercial experience in England, 1770-76, and France, 1776-85. He subsequently established himself as a merchant in Philadelphia, where he pursued an interest in science and was elected a secretary of the American Philosophical Society four times between 1791 and 1797, a councillor six times between 1798 and 1813, and a vice president in 1815. TJ appointed him superintendent of the U.S. Military Academy at West Point and inspector of fortifications, 1801-03 and 1805-12 (DAB; APS, *Proceedings*, XXII, pt. 3 [1885], 187, 201, 211, 216, 246, 266, 290, 330, 392, 419, 438, 451).

DU LUC: Genevan scientist Jean André Deluc (or De Luc) solved some of the problems that had made barometric observations since the seventeenth century inconsistent, including inaccurate instruments and the effects of temperature, and developed new methods and formulas for the measurement of elevations by barometer. His book, *Recherches sur les Modifications de l'Atmosphère*, 2 vols. (Geneva, 1772), fostered several papers in the PHILOSOPHICAL TRANSACTIONS of the Royal Society of London for 1774 and 1777-79. The South American barometric readings of Antonio de ULLOA and Jorge Juan y Santacilia of Spain appeared in their *Observaciones as-*

tronomicas, y phisicas; hechas de orden de S. Mag. en los reynos del Peru (Madrid, 1748), 102-31, which also described methods of calculating altitudes. Jacques Alexandre César CHARLES had taken barometric readings during an ascent to over 9,000 feet in a hydrogen BALLOON in France in 1783, as described in his *Représentation du globe aérostatique: qui s'est élévé de dessus l'un des bassins du Jardin Royal des Thuilleries. Le 1er. Décembre 1783* (Paris, 1783). See Abraham Wolf, *A History of Science, Technology, and Philosophy in the Eighteenth Century* (New York, 1939), 288-302, 578; and sketches of Charles and Ulloa in DSB, III, 207-8, XIII, 530-1.

COMMUNICATION TO THE SOCIETY: Williams had presented his findings, including "a journal of observations," at a meeting of the American Philosophical Society on 20 Nov. 1795. As printed in the TRANSACTIONS of the society for 1799, the report consisted of a letter from Williams to Robert Patterson, one of the society's secretaries, of 13 Nov. 1795, touching many of the points in Williams's letter to TJ above; the tabular "journal" (see Enclosure I below); a diagram (see Enclosure II below); and a "postscript" from Williams to Patterson, 18 Aug. 1796, containing an extract of TJ's 3 July 1796 letter to Williams and mentioning problems associated with optical measurement of heights of mountains ("Barometrical Measurement of the Blue-Ridge, Warm-Spring, and Alleghany Mountains, in Virginia, taken in the Summer of the year 1791," APS, *Transactions*, IV [1799], 216-23; APS, *Proceedings*, XXII, pt. 3 [1885], 234-5).

I

Extract from Jonathan Williams's Meteorological Journal

Meteorological Notes . . 1791

Places	Dates	Therr:	Barometer	Fall	Rise	Assent in Feet	Descent in feet	Height above Richmond.
Richmond	June 26.	70.	29.80					
Woods	29.	65.	29.70.	0.10		100[1]		100
Gap	"	76.	28.60.	1.10		1050[2]		1150
Top		79.	27.90.	0.70		672		1822
Foot	30th.	75.	28.90		1.00		959.	863.
Staunton		73.	28.70.	0.20		192		1055.
Wm. spring 1 Mountain Foot.	July 14.	63.	28.82		0.12		112.	943.
summit		82	27.80.	1.02		955.		1898
2d Mountain summit	"	77.	27:44	0.36		349		2247.
Warm springs		77.	28.03.		0.59		562	1685.
Morris		61.	28.67		0.64		614	1071
Browns	15th.	67.	28.80.		0.13		122.	949.
Red springs[3]		66.	28.20.	0.60		563		1512
Allegaheney in the Road	31st.	80.	27.64	0.56		525		2037
summit		76.	26.86.	0.78		723		2760.

MS (DLC); consists of one page entirely in Williams's hand; endorsed by TJ: "[Williams Jonathan Jan. 24.] 96. recd. May 10." As printed in APS, *Transactions*, IV (1799), 219-20, Williams's table, called "A Meteorological Journal, made with a View to discover the Height of the Country, at various Places, from Richmond, to the Alleghany Mountains in Bottetourt, Virginia.—1791," contains several variations in text as noted below, additional columns for time of day, weather, and distance from Richmond, as well as additional places, more complete names for some sites, and five notes adding details of some observations.

[1] Here and in next column APS, *Transactions*, reads "95."

[2] APS, *Transactions*: "1055."

[3] APS, *Transactions*, gives date of 16 July for this observation.

Height of Virginia Mountains by Barometrical Measurement

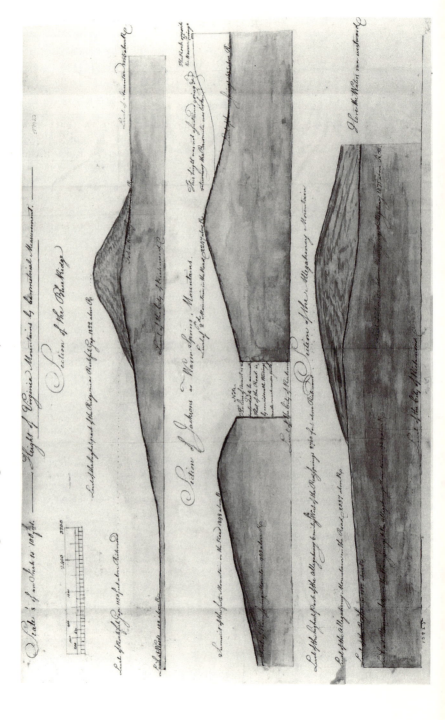

MS (DLC: TJ Papers, 80: 13925); entirely in Williams's hand; endorsed by TJ: "Mountains. height of. Jon. Williams." For the printed version of this diagram, see APS, *Transactions*, IV (1799), pl. facing p. 221.

To Martha Jefferson Randolph

MY DEAR MARTHA   Jan. 25. 1796.

After the departure of my last letter to Mr. Randolph I found the details I had given him respecting the waggon were erroneous. The rise of the river had cut off our communications for several days. I presume it arrived at Varina as soon as my letter.

We are all well here. Jefferson particularly so. He is become the finest boy possible. Always in good humor, always amusing himself, and very orderly. It appears that his continued fretfulness before was owing to his being teazed by his companions.—I hope Mr. Randolph received my letter covering the commission for taking the depositions of the Shockoe inspectors. The notice given is for Saturday next, at noon at the warehouse. The notice has been duly served, so that if the business can be then done, we shall have no further trouble with it.—We have had two or three days of extreme cold. The thermometer was down to 15°.—I hear that P. Carr is at Philadelphia. He was to form the depositions of the Inspectors so as to leave nothing further to be done but to swear to them. But as I did not hear from him I presume he did nothing. Maria and Virginia give their love to you. Jefferson is always talking of sending letters to you. Kiss Anne for me, and present my best esteem to Mr. Randolph. Adieu Your's affectionately   TH: JEFFERSON

RC (NNPM); at foot of text: "Mrs. Martha Randolph." PrC (ViU: Edgehill-Randolph Papers); endorsed by TJ in ink on verso. MY LETTER COVERING THE COMMISSION: TJ to Thomas Mann Randolph, 6 Jan. 1796.

From Van Staphorst & Hubbard

SIR   Amsterdam 27 January 1796

Being deprived of your very esteemed favors Since our last Respects of 5 Ultimo, We have but to return you inclosed with Protests for Non Acceptance and non payment, the Bill You remitted us
Nathl. Anderson of 11 June 1794 at 60 days Sight on Wm. Anderson of London for 39.17.10½ Stg. with our Endorsement of Same, to enable You to recover the principal, Costs, Interest and Damages, for the account of Mr. Philip Mazzei.

The costs of the protests Eleven Shillings Sterling, We shall charge to Mr. Mazzei. We are respectfully, Sir! Your mo: ob: hb: Servts.

N. & J. VAN STAPHORST & HUBBARD

RC (DLC); in a clerk's hand, signed by the firm; at head of text: "Thos. Jefferson Esqr. Monticello in Virginia"; endorsed by TJ as received 14 May 1796 and so recorded in SJL. A Dupl recorded in SJL as received 16 Sep. 1796 has not been found. Enclosures not found, but see TJ to Philip Mazzei, 30 May 1795.

From John Adams

DEAR SIR   Philadelphia January 31. 1796

I have received from our old Acquaintance D'Ivernois the inclosed Volume for you in the Course of the last Week.

I consider all Reasoning upon French affairs of little moment. The Fates must determine hereafter as they have done heretofore. Reasoning has been all lost—Passion, Prejudice, Interest, Necessity has governed and will govern; and a Century must roll away before any permanent and quiet System will be established. An Amelioration of human affairs I hope and believe will be the Result, but You and I must look down from the Battlements of Heaven if We ever have the Pleasure of Seeing it.

The Treaty is not arrived and Congress seems averse to engage in Business with spirit till that is considered.

I envy you the society of your Family but another Year and one Month may make me the Object of Envy. Mean time I am, with Esteem & Affection your   JOHN ADAMS

RC (DLC); at foot of text: "Mr Jefferson"; endorsed by TJ as received 20 Feb. 1796 and so recorded in SJL. Enclosure: François D'Ivernois, *La Révolution française à Genève; Tableau historique et po-* *litique de la conduite de la France envers les Genevois, depuis le mois d'octobre 1792, jusqu'au mois de juillet 1795*, 3d ed. (London, 1795); see enclosure listed at D'Ivernois to TJ, 11 Nov. 1794.

From James Madison

DEAR SIR   Philada. Jany. 31. 1796

I inclose a letter from Jno. Bringhurst explaining a claim on you for about £17. Pa. Currency, and requesting me to advance it. Taking him to be an honest man in distress, I shall probably venture a compliance with his solicitation, if it should be found that he cannot wait for your orders. In the mean time you can inform me whether the account be accurately stated: but if so, you need not forward the money, as it will be equally convenient to me to receive it in Virginia.

The original of the British Ratification of the Treaty is still to arrive, and we are not likely to be furnished with a copy. Some members are anxious to apply to the President for the communication, and some would take up the subject on its mere notoriety. It is pretty evident however, that either attempt would be defeated by the advantage which the rub against the P. in one case, and[1] the informality in the other,[2] would give to the friends of the Treaty, in the discussion, and the pretext they[3] would afford to the insincere or cautious opponents. The Treaty with Spain also is not yet [arri]ved, tho' there is reason for hourly expecting it. The same as to the [Treaty] with Algiers. You will see in the gazette inclosed a sketch of the debate on the proposition to employ Robinson of Petersburg as Stenographer to the House of Reps. The more the subject is opened, the more the objections are found to be insuperable. There is little doubt that the project will be rejected.

A committee of ways and means are employed in investigating our revenues and our wants. It is found that there are between six and seven millions of anticipations due to the Banks, that our ordinary income is barely at par with our ordinary expenditures, and that new taxes must be ready to meet near $1\frac{1}{2}$ millions which will accrue in 1801. The proposition of the Treasury is to fund the anticipations and the foreign debt due in instalments, with an absolute[4] irredeemability for such a period, say 20 or 30 years, as will sell the new Stock at par. This is treading as fast on the heels of G.B. as circumstances will permit. It is probable the House will not consent to such an abandonment of the sound[5] principles it has been latterly favoring; but loans at least in some form or other will be indispensable, in order to face the demands on the public until[6] new taxes can be brought into action. With respect to [this, t]he Committee are now in deliberation and embarrassments. The excise system is unproductive, and new excises that will be popular even in the Eastern States do not occur. On the other hand direct taxes have been so blackened in order to recom[mend] the fiscal policy of indirect ones, and to inspire hatred, and jealousies in the Eastern [against the Southern States, and particularly] Virginia, that it is doubtful whether the measure, now that it is become necessa[ry, will be born]e. Gallatin [is] a real Treasure in this department of legislation. He is sound in his principles, accurate in his calculations and indefatigable in his researches. Who could have supposed that Hamilton could have gone off in the triumph he assumed with such a condition of the finances behind him?

You will see that Govr. Adams has lanced a pretty bold attack against the Treaty. The Legislature have not yet answered his speech. Their unhandsome treatment of the Virga. amendments portends a counter-tone. Nothing could more than this treatment demonstrate the success with which party calumny has sown animosity and malignity in the State of Massts. against a State which feels no return of illwill, and towards Which there were formerly in that quarter the strongest habits of cordiality and cooperation. Yrs. always & affey.   Js. M. Jr

The navigation project of Genl. Smith waits for a favorable moment of discussion. The Treaty party would make war on it, as secretly levelled at that transaction, and thus endeavor to escape the consequences of sacrificing the obvious interests of the Eastern States.

RC (DLC: Madison Papers); with words torn away at seal and obscured by tape supplied in brackets from Madison, *Letters*, ii, 75-6; only the most important emendations are noted below; addressed: "Thomas Jefferson Charlottesville Virginia via. Richmond"; franked, stamped and postmarked; endorsed by TJ as received 20 Feb. 1796 and so recorded in SJL.

The enclosed LETTER, from John Bringhurst to Madison, has not been found. The GAZETTE INCLOSED was probably Andrew Brown's *Philadelphia Gazette* of 30 Jan. 1796, which carried the extensive debates in the House of Representatives on the previous day concerning the employment of David Robertson of Petersburg, Virginia, as STENOGRAPHER. On 28 Jan. 1796, William Loughton Smith, of South Carolina, had reported on Robertson's proposal to prepare accounts of House debates for the *Philadelphia Gazette* for $4,000 per session, with $1,100 to be paid by Brown and $2,900 by the government. On 2 Feb. 1796, the House agreed to discontinue further consideration of the matter (*Annals*, v, 271, 274-82, 286).

A standing COMMITTEE OF WAYS AND MEANS, of which Madison was a member, had been established by the House of Representatives on 21 Dec. 1795; it subsequently considered the estimates for 1796 previously submitted by Secretary of the Treasury Oliver Wolcott, Jr., as well as matters pertaining to the national debt. Madison apparently was also chairman of a subcommittee that took up the question of DIRECT TAXES. The Pennsylvania Republican Albert GALLATIN served on both of these committees (JHR, ii, 385; Patrick J. Furlong, "The Origins of the House Committee of

Ways and Means," WMQ, 3d ser., xxv [1968], 594-600).

In his address before the General Court on 19 Jan. 1796, Governor Samuel Adams delivered a BOLD ATTACK AGAINST THE TREATY, describing it as "pregnant with evil." He asserted that the Jay Treaty assumed "powers specially vested in Congress for the security of the people," and he feared "that it may restore to Great Britain such an influence over the government and people of this country as may not be consistent with the general welfare" (Philadelphia *Aurora*, 29 Jan. 1796). The Massachusetts legislature refused to endorse Adams's criticism of the treaty in their answers to HIS SPEECH (same, 3 Feb. 1796). On 19 Jan. the Massachusetts House and Senate refused to consider the AMENDMENTS to the Constitution proposed by the Virginia legislature on 15 Dec. 1795 and then forwarded to the other states. The four amendments called for both houses of Congress to approve any treaty affecting the commerce power; for removal of impeachment trials from the Senate; for reduction of the terms of Senators from six to three years; and for the prohibition of federal judges from holding any other office or appointment (same, 29 Jan. 1796; Thomas J. Farnham, "The Virginia Amendments of 1795: An Episode in the Opposition to Jay's Treaty," VMHB, LXXV [1967], 85-6; Shepherd, *Statutes*, i, 434).

NAVIGATION PROJECT OF GENL. SMITH: On 4 Jan. 1796, Congressman Samuel Smith of Maryland laid before the House of Representatives a resolution to make it unlawful "for any foreign ship or other vessel to land in the United States any goods, wares, or merchandise, except such as are of the produce, growth, or manufacture, of the nation to which such ship or other vessel may belong." After a debate on 15 Jan. 1796 over committal of the resolution, it was agreed to bring the measure before the whole House on 20 Jan. 1796, but the consideration was postponed and it was not brought forth again during the session (*Annals*, v, 195, 245-9; JHR, II, 425).

[1] Preceding ten words interlined.
[2] Preceding three words interlined.
[3] Reworked from "it."
[4] Preceding word interlined.
[5] Preceding word interlined.
[6] Remainder of text is written lengthwise in margin and then continues perpendicular to first part of the letter.

To Philip Mazzei

MY DEAR FRIEND   Monticello Jan. 31. 1796.

It is very long since I heard from you unless it be an exception that I received within these two or three days for the first time your letters of May 23. 1792. and Feb. 11. 1793. the contents of which shall be attended to. Nor have I for a long time heard from Messrs. Van Staphorsts & Hubbard. My letters to you of May and Sep. last will have informed you that at the same dates I remitted to them the following bills recieved from Mr. Blair.

	£ sterl.
May 27. 1795. Anderson's bill on Wm. Anderson of London, dated 1794. June 11. payable to V.S. & H.	39–17–10½
also Meade's bill on Barclay of London, payable to V.S. & H. dated Apr. 4. 95.	70– 8– 6
Sep. 8. Hodgson's bill on Robinson, Saunderson & Rumney of Whitehaven, payable to Hunter, endorsed to V.S. & H. & dated Aug. 17. 95.	300– 0– 0
on this day I remit them the same Hodgson's bill on the same Robinson &c. payable to Hunter, endorsed to V.S. & H. & dated Dec. 21. 95.	137–16– 6
which several remittances, amounting in the whole to the sum of	548– 2–10½

have been made in triplicates, and were expressed to be on your account.

I had counted with confidence on our recovering, this spring, the money for Colle. But one of the debtors being bankrupt, and the other so distressed as to use all possible shifts, our lawyer thought it best to accept the assumpsit of Mr. Charles Carter of Blenheim in discharge of our suit. Mr. Carter has failed in his promise, so we are at sea again. No time shall be lost however in getting the money. It is absolutely sure in the end. I give this information to the V.S. & H.—Recollecting no small news, but the marriage of Mr. Madison of Orange, the death of T.

Pleasants of 4. mile creek, and the resignation, say removal of E.R. from the Secretary of state's office, and in hopes of hearing from you soon, I shorten my letter because it is to be forwarded in triplicates. Adieu Yours affectionately   TH: JEFFERSON

RC (DLC); addressed: "Monsr. Philippe Mazzei à Pisa"; endorsed by Mazzei as received 5 Jan. 1797. Tr (NhD); 19th-century copy.

Mazzei's letter of FEB. 11. 1793., recorded in SJL as received 23 Jan. 1796, has not been found. I REMIT THEM: SJL records a letter of this date from TJ to Van Staphorst & Hubbard on "Hodgson's bill £137–16–6," missing except for this extract of the concluding paragraph: "I had confided that the sum of something upwards of £200. Virginia Currency for which Mr. Mazzei's lands called Colle were sold, would have been recovered this spring, but an ill judged tho' well intended step of our lawyer, accepting the assumpsit of a third person in discharge of our legal process, has placed that matter again out of our power, so that I cannot judge at what date this new measure may bring in the money" (quoted in Van Staphorst & Hubbard to Mazzei, 8 Apr. 1796, Archivio Filippo Mazzei, Pisa).

To Thomas Mann Randolph

TH:J. TO TMR.   Monticello Jan. 31. 96.

We are all well here. Jefferson was never in finer health. Tho' our winter has on the whole been a fine one, we have had some severe weather. This morning the thermometer was at $1°\frac{3}{4}$ above nought; I never before saw it below 6°. in this state. The wind has got Southwardly and promises a change. Corn is a very scarce article in our neighborhood. My crop of it fell vastly short of even moderate expectations, which added to much waste before I was aware of it promises me a year of greater difficulty than I have known.

I am a little uneasy at not having heard whether you recieved my letter covering the commission in my suit with Cobbs. If the deposition's are taken I should be glad to recieve them by post that we may see what may be made of them.—The death of T. Pleasants of 4. mile creek, announced in the papers, deranges my plan of being furnished with fish for my people: and my want of acquaintance in Richmond leaves me at a loss to whom to apply. I have been well supplied from Darmstads but the fish were previously examined by T. Pleasants. I should imagine that on being informed I would take from him every year, he would take pains to serve me well. Still I should be at his mercy for price and quality and I do not know his character. If Russell deals in that article, I might trust to him for my annual supply. I must ask your advice on this subject, which your knolege of these and other traders in that article, and opportunities of conferring with them will enable you to give me.

My love to my dear Martha, and to Anne also. I shall be happy to hear of your better health. Adieu affectionately.

RC (DLC); endorsed by Randolph as received 5 Feb. 1796.

MY LETTER COVERING THE COMMISSION: TJ to Randolph, 6 Jan. 1796.

Deed of Manumission for James Hemings

This indenture made at Monticello in the county of Albemarle and commonwealth of Virginia on the fifth day of February one thousand seven hundred and ninety six witnesseth that I Thomas Jefferson of Monticello aforesaid do emancipate, manumit and make free James Hemings, son of Betty Hemings, which said James is now of the age of thirty years so that in future he shall be free and of free condition, and discharged of all duties and claims of servitude whatsoever, and shall have all the rights and privileges of a freedman. In witness whereof I have hereto set my hand and seal on the day and year abovewritten, and have made these presents double of the same date, tenor and indenture one whereof is lodged in the court of Albemarle aforesaid to be recorded, and the other is delivered by me to the said James Hemings to be produced when and where it may be necessary.

Signed, sealed and delivered   TH: JEFFERSON
in presence of
John Carr
Francis Anderson

MS (ViU); in TJ's hand, except for signatures of Carr and Anderson; indented, with TJ's seal affixed; notation on verso: "At Albemarle April Court 1796. This Deed of Manumission was produced into Court and proved by the Oaths of John Carr and Francis Anderson witnesses thereto & ordered to be Recorded. teste Jno. Nicholas, CAC"; endorsed in several hands: "Jefferson to Hemings} Deed," "April 1796 proved and to be recorded," and "Recorded & exmd." Tr (Albemarle County Deed Book No. 12, Albemarle County Circuit Court Clerk's Office, Charlottesville); with Nicholas's attestation at foot of text; in left margin: "Jefferson to Hemings} Deed exd." Entered 5 Apr. 1796 in Albemarle County Court Order Book, 1795-98, in same.

For an earlier document setting forth the conditions of manumission, see Agreement with James Hemings, 15 Sep. 1793.

From James Madison

Philada. Feby. 7. 1796

Several mails preceding that of yesterday brought nothing more Southern than Baltimore. This will account for my not receiving your favor of the 24th. Ult., till yesterday. I will make the inquiries, and execute the commissions in it with pleasure, and without delay. I am afraid to make the same promise as to the weekly history of what passes in the Government behind the curtain; especially as the Cypher might be required for some parts of it. What I can I will do on the subject. I have already made a partial collection of the Tracts you wish. I know not what is meant by the correspondence of Jay and Jefferson; probably it is the correspondence not between them, but between each and others.

I thank you for the Copy of your statement and letter to Mr. Wythe. I value it not only as a gratification to myself; but as another security for the preservation of the document.

Dorhman maintains a silence, that justifies strong suspicions of aversion or inability to pay his debts. I feel no longer any other restraints from resorting to his deed of trust, but that which Mazzei's interest dictates. As yet the land would sell for considerably less than the sum due. The general rise of price which is going on will probably soon remove this difficulty, especially if the Treaty with Spain, should have done what is hoped, as to the navigation of the Mississippi.

You will see that the aspect of English affairs grows more and more lowering. The alarm of the Sedition Bills, the bounty on foreign Wheat *and flour*, the detention of the armament fitted up, for the forlorn experiment in the West Indies, are more portentous than any thing previous to these signs of a ripening crisis. The accounts from France are not of very late date, but continue to be auspicious. The Treaties with Algiers and Spain, loiter as that with England did. It is to be hoped this is the only instance in which the parallel holds.

An idea begins to shew itself that an unrestrained exportation of the Bread-articles, threatens a scarcity in our own Country. The[1] large towns will of course be the first seat of such an apprehensions. It is certain that the Crops of Grain in North Carolina failed to such a degree as to start the price of Corn at a dollr. a bushel, where it used to sell at $\frac{1}{3}$ of a dollar. In Virginia, if the present price be the measure of the quantity, there will be little corn to spare, and probably not a great deal more of Wheat. In this State it is turning out more and more in evidence that the crop of Wheat has been very scanty. The Eastern States always require large importations from the others. In N.J. and N.Y. alone, the crops of Wheat appear to have been good; and that is probably exaggeration on the favorable side. Flour at present in this place is rising under the information of the English bounty. All in the Market is said to be bought up, probably by English Agents. It sold a day or two ago, or rather there was offered for it, 14 dollrs. a barrel, and the best informed, speak with confidence of successive rises. In this attitude of things What a noble stroke would be an embargo? It would probably do as much good as harm at home; and would force peace, on the rest of the World, and perhaps liberty along with it. But you know the spell[2] within the Government, as well as the obstacles to such a measure in the clamors that would be raised among the Merchants, the Millers, and farmers, to say nothing of the Tories &c. who would make more noise than any of them.

I intreat you not to procrastinate, much less abandon your historical task. You owe it to yourself, to truth, to the world. Adieu always yours most affey

---

There is some reason to think that Jno. Rutledge is not right in his mind. Cushing has been put at the head of the Bench, but it is said will decline the pre-eminence. Chase in the place of Blair!!!! A vacancy remains to be filled. McHenry Secretary at War—Through what official interstice can a ray of republican truths now penetrate to the P.

You will see by the inclosed letter [from J.] B. that I have ad[vanced] him 25 drs. I have already told you that repayment in Virga. will [serve] for me as well as [here.]

RC (DLC: Madison Papers); unsigned; parts of last two lines torn away; with several emendations, only the most important being noted below; addressed: "Mr. Jefferson Charlottesville via Richmond"; franked, stamped, and postmarked; endorsed by TJ as received 20 Feb. 1796 and so recorded in SJL. Enclosure: probably John Bringhurst to TJ, 3 Feb. 1796 (recorded in SJL as received from Wilmington 20 Feb. 1796, but not found).

YOUR FAVOR: TJ to Madison, 24 Jan. 1796 (recorded in SJL, but not found).

STATEMENT AND LETTER TO MR. WYTHE: see TJ's second letter to George Wythe, 16 Jan. 1796, and enclosure.

[1] Remainder of text is written lengthwise in margin and then continues perpendicular to first part of the letter.

[2] Preceding four words interlined in place of two or three canceled and illegible words.

To Thomas Mann Randolph

TH:J. TO TMR.   [7 Feb. 1796]

Your two favors of Jan. 24. and Feb. 3. are both recieved. We have had a very fine winter a few days only excepted about the middle of January. This day sennight was the coldest morning ever known in this country as far as my observations have gone. The mercury was at $1\frac{3}{4}°$. I never before saw it lower than 6°. in Virginia.—From what I hear of the state of the three notched road I am sorry I proposed the bringing up my wine, as I am afraid Billy's team will either fail in it, or be extremely injured by it. I will pay all the attention I can to your affairs at Edgehill. I shall scarcely be able to go there, being so unable to ride, that I have not been to Shadwell for a month past. There is vast alarm here about corn. The price at present from 15/ to 18/. but not to be had indeed at any price. My situation on that subject is threatening beyond any thing I ever experienced. We shall starve literally if I cannot buy 200 barrels, and as yet I have been able to find but 60.— Mr. Divers shall recieve immediately the payment you desire, of 120.D. I trouble you to return my certificates for the 800. and 100. acres in Bedford, and to obtain the grants. I must also repeat my petition for the land warrant of 50. acres, as I have that quantity still to secure in Campbell county. The delay of my letter of the 6th. has been unfortunate. There would be time still, were I to send an express to Buckingham to give a 3d. notice to Cobbs, and then another to Richmond. But this is very troublesome, and if the Inspectors will give a certificate of the tobaccos past by Cobbs for 2. or 3 years before and after 1786. we will try to have it recieved as ev-idence.—Faris is gone down and promised me to call on Britton again for the machine. The difficulty has been to find him at home. Should he fail this time it would be well to have the machine carried back to Colo. Gamble's, from whence it can be got at any time. I am sorry you are to be plagued with forwarding a 2d. rope, but we can not proceed either to demolish our walls or dig our cellars till the columns are taken out of the way. We have had enough else to do hitherto in cutting coal wood so that we have not suffered for want of the roap as yet. While you are getting this I will thank you to get and forward also a cord for our kitchen jack, which has been unemployed 6. months for want of one. If you can put me on the trace of the 1st. rope you sent, if it was by any of our boatmen, perhaps I may be able to find it out, and at least make them pay for it. When on the subject of Cobbs I omitted to mention that I never recieved a sentence from P. Carr respecting it. If he wrote at all, his letter miscarried; but I imagine he only meant that he would write, and was too lazy to carry his intention into execution.—My nailrod is arrived safe. The hoop iron I presume is with the cutting machine as they came together.—Maria has found your succory seed, which shall be sent by the first safe opportunity. Jefferson is well as we all are. My love to my dear Martha, and kisses to Anne. Adieu affectionately.

RC (DLC); undated, but assigned on basis of SJL and PrC; endorsed by Ran- dolph as received 19 Feb. 1796. PrC (Thomas Jefferson Memorial Foundation, on deposit ViU); endorsed by TJ in ink on verso: "Randolph TM Feb. 7. 96."

Pasted to this letter in DLC, but perhaps unrelated to it, is a small scrap of paper with the following note in TJ's hand: "Is it possible to buy herring now, where and at what price? I want about 5000. to serve till the new fishing season comes."

Randolph's FAVORS of 24 Jan. and 3 Feb. 1796, recorded in SJL as received 1 and 6 Feb. 1796, respectively, the first from Varina, have not been found. For TJ's CERTIFICATES FOR THE 800. AND 100. ACRES, see note to TJ to Randolph, 25 Nov. 1795. MY LETTER OF THE 6TH: TJ to Randolph, 6 Jan. 1796.

To John Barnes

DEAR SIR   Monticello Feb. 14. 96.

As I imagine your river will be opening by the time you recieve this, I will ask the favor of you to send me by the first vessel to Richmond a hogshead (say 120 gallons) of molasses. It is material it should come immediately as it cannot be brought up from Richmond here but in the cold season. I am with great esteem Dear Sir Your friend & servt

TH: JEFFERSON

P.S. There are very often to be had at Philadelphia kegs of Cod's tongues and sounds. I should be very glad of a keg if to be had.

PrC (MHi); endorsed in ink by TJ on verso in part: "Barnes John."

To Martha Jefferson Randolph

Monticello Feb. 14. 96.

We are all well here, my dear daughter, and Jefferson particularly so. He often repeats that you told a story, 'that you did,' when you got into the carriage and said you would come back for him. His cheeks swell with emphasis as he asseverates this. We are just beginning our demolitions, and find they will be very troublesome. It was high time to do it, from the rotten state in which we found some of our timbers.—The first time Mr. Randolph goes to Richmond, I will ask the favor of him to call on Swan, the cabinet maker, who is agent for Mr. Lownes my iron merchant in Philadelphia. Lownes is in arrears with me twenty three hundred weight of nailrod, and informed me that Swan had standing directions from him to furnish at all times any quantities I should call for. I wrote to Mr. Swan a month ago to know if he could furnish me this 23. ℔ weight, but have no answer, and from his inattention to business, expect to get none, unless Mr. Randolph will be so good as to call on him, and write me his answer, and by no means trust to his doing

[609]

it himself. Adieu affectionately my dear Martha; kisses to Anne, and my best salutations to Mr. Randolph.

RC (NNPM); unsigned. PrC (MHi); endorsed in ink by TJ on verso.

I WROTE TO MR. SWAN: TJ to John Swann, 17 Jan. 1796, recorded in SJL but not found. A letter from TJ to Swann of 29 Feb. 1796, and the latter's reply of 25 Apr. 1796, received 3 May 1796, both recorded in SJL, are also missing.

James Hemings's Inventory of Kitchen Utensils at Monticello

[20 Feb. 1796]

Invetory of Kitchen Utincils
19 Copper Stew pans—19 Covers
 6 Small Sauce pans
 3 Copper Baking Moulds
 2 Small preserving pans
 2 Large ——— Ditto
 2 Copper Fish kettles
 2 Copper Brazing pans
 2 Round Large — Ditto
 2 Iron Stew pans
 2 Large Boiling kettles tin'd inside
 1 Large Brass —— Ditto
12 pewter water Dishes
12 —— —— plates
 3 Tin Coffie pots
 8 Tin Dish Covers
 2 frying pans of Iron & one of Copper
 4 Round Baking Copper Sheets tin'd
 4 Square Copper Ditto untin'd
 1 Copper Boiler
 1 Copper tea kettle 1 Iron Ditto
 2 Small Copper Baking pans
 1 Turkish Bonnet Baking mould
 3 Waffel Irons
 2 Grid Irons
 2 Spits—1 Jack—3 Cleavers—2 hold fasts
 3 Copper Laidles—4 Copper Spoons—1 Basing Spoon
 3 Copper Skimmers—2 Cast Iron Bakers
 2 pair Tongs—2 Shovels—1 poker—1 Bake Shovel

2 Large Iron pots—2 Dutch ovens
1 Iron Chaffing Dish,—21 Small Copper Baking moulds
2 Gelly moulds—2 Treising moulds
1 Butter Tin kettle—2 Culinders—1 tin 1 of pewter
1 Brass Culinder 2 Graters—1 old Copper fish kettle
9 wooden Spoons—3 past cuting moulds
1 Brass pistle & mortar—1 Marble Ditto
2 wooden paste Rolers—2 Chopping Knives
6 Iron Crevets—3 tin tart moulds—5 Kitchen apperns
1 old Brass Kettle—1 Iron Candle stick
2 Brass Chaffing Dishes

MS (DLC); undated; in the hand of James Hemings; endorsed by TJ: "Kitchen furniture. note of by James Hemings Feb. 20. 1796."

To John Barnes

DEAR SIR   Monticello Feb. 21. 1796.

I recieved yesterday your two favors of Jan. 30. and Feb. 8. the accidents of the season having delayed the former a week. I am mortified at my own inattention to the state of our accounts, which tho' till yesterday I could not know accurately, as the exact amount of some of the particulars had not been communicated, yet I could not have mistaken so as to have overdrawn as much as I have done. I am very thankful for the honor you have nevertheless done my bills, and lose not a moment in covering your advances by inclosing an authority to recieve 629.D. 10c. immediately and 314.D. 55c. at about [5 or] 6. weeks date, on which basis you can, if necessary, safely take the money from a bank, and debit me the discount. Be assured you shall never suffer by any confidence you are pleased to place in me. It is not necessary to forward the vouchers mentioned in your letter. I ought before now to have observed to you that in all cases of purchasing and forwarding articles to me I have expected and wish you to charge me your usual commission for business of that kind. I am with great esteem Dear Sir Your most obedt servt

TH: JEFFERSON

PrC (MHi); faded in part; at foot of text: "Mr. John Barnes."

Barnes's FAVORS OF JAN. 30. AND FEB. 8., recorded in SJL as received 20 Feb. 1796, have not been found.

Power of Attorney for John Barnes

Know all men by these presents that I Thomas Jefferson named in a certain letter of attorney from William Short of the state of Virginia and one of the ministers of the US. abroad to me bearing date the 2d. day of April 1793. and now lodged in the bank of the US. by virtue of the power and authority thereby given me, do substitute and appoint John Barnes of Philadelphia, as well my own as the true and lawful attorney and substitute of the said William Short named in the said letter of attorney to recieve from the treasury or bank of the US. the interest which became due on the stock of different descriptions of the said William Short registered in the proper office of the US. at the seat of Government in Philadelphia from the 1st. day of July to the 1st. day of October and from the said 1st. day of October to the 1st. day of January last past, amounting to six hundred and twenty nine dollars ten cents, to wit 314 Dollars 55. cents for each quarter, as also to recieve the interest on the said stock which shall become due from the said 1st. day of January last past to the 1st. day of April next ensuing and becoming payable on the said 1st. day of April amounting to three hundred and fourteen dollars fifty five cents, or to whatever other sum the said interest shall amount. Hereby ratifying and confirming the paiment of the said interest to the said John Barnes, and the discharge which he shall give for the same as done by virtue of the power of attorney aforesaid. In witness whereof I have hereunto set my hand and seal this 21st. day of February 1796.

TH: JEFFERSON

Sealed & delivered

in presence of

TH: BELL

MS (ViU: photocopy); in TJ's hand; with attestations on verso signed by Justice of the Peace Thomas Bell and Clerk of Court John Nicholas, in TJ's hand with blanks filled by Bell and Nicholas; endorsed in part as received 4 Mch. 1796.

To James Madison

TH:J. TO J.M.   Monticello Feb. 21. 96.

I propose to write you a longer letter in answer to your two favors of Jan. 31. and Feb. 7. which came by our last post. But as I may possibly not have time before it's departure, I inclose you a letter to J. Bringhurst, as the perusal of it will answer that article of your letters. When read, be pleased to seal and send it. I thank you as much for your advance to him as if I had really owed it, and if he does not repay it immediately, let me know it and I will do it. I have always considered paiments for my honor, as debts of honor, whether they were right or wrong. Adieu affectionately

RC (DLC: Madison Papers); addressed: "James Madison Congress Philadelphia"; franked. PrC (DLC); endorsed by TJ in ink on verso. Enclosure: TJ to John Bringhurst, 21 Feb. 1796 (recorded in SJL but not found).

From James Madison

DEAR SIR   Philada. Feby. 21. 1796

Since my last I have made enquiry as to Lownes. In general he is well spoken of, in every respect. Old Mr. Howell however, told me he was not a punctual man and was slow in his payments. I then mentioned my reasons for asking him. He proceeded to say that his son dealt in the same article with Lownes, and that if you chose to take your Iron rod here, he would be responsible for the most exact compliance of his son. I next brought Sharpless into view. He spoke of him as a man fully to be relied on, and as a man with whom his son had had some dealings. He said there was but one objection to taking your supplies at short hand from Sharpless, which was that there was very little direct intercourse from Wilmington to Southern ports: that almost every thing exported thence, came first to Philada. I asked whether vessels could not stop there and take in articles; not he said unless the freight of them was an object. As the order of my enquiries drew out the old gentleman's opinion of Lownes, before he could well feel the interest of his son in the case, his testimony is entitled to respect. I have written to Jno. Bringhurst who resides at Wilmington to get and send me a full account of Sharpless and of the terms on which he would supply you; but have not yet received an answer.

I find as I conjectured that the provision made for the daughters of Degrasse was not in the way of loan but of gift. It would be difficult perhaps to justify the act in either way, by the text of the Constitution. The precedent nevertheless is in favor of Made. de Chatelleux's son. Whether his claim will be viewed with the same indulgence on the score of his father's merits is more than I can venture to decide. The services of De Grasse were critical. Chatelleux you recollect was not a favorite here, tho' the cause may have been erroneous. Congress also were afraid of the Precedent at the time, and endeavored to interweave ingredients of peculiarity. I am really apprehensive that a compliance with the wishes of Made. de Chat: would entail on us a provision for the families of the whole French army that served[1] in this Country. Congs. are occupied with a Bill for selling the Western lands. Opinions are various and the result doubtful. The British Treaty not yet before us; nor The Spanish before the Senate, or even arrived as far as I know. The Algerine is come to hand and under the deliberation of the Senate. The history of it contains some curious features, which it is not possible for me to explain in time. In general it costs an immense sum, and the annual tribute is to be paid in *naval Stores*, infinitely *underated* in the Tariff. The friendly interference of France, tho' applied for and in train, was precluded by the Agent's precipitancy in closing the Treaty; for the hardness of which the apology is that it was the best that could be got. The letter from Paris in the inclosed paper, is Monroe's, and the latest in date that has been received from him. The federal Court has not yet given judgment in the case of payments into the Virga. Treasury. Marshal and Cambell were the Counsel on one side, and Lewis and Tilghman on the other. Marshal's argument is highly spoken of. Campbell and Ingersoll will appear vs. the Carrage tax. Hamilton is here and to join Lee on the other side.

RC (DLC: Madison Papers); unsigned; addressed: "Charlottesville via Richmond Virginia"; endorsed by TJ as received 4 Mch. 1796 and so recorded in SJL.

For the CLAIM on behalf of the late Marquis de Chastellux's son, see Madame de Chastellux to TJ, 6 May 1795, and note.
LETTER FROM PARIS IN THE INCLOSED PAPER: see James Monroe to TJ, 18 Nov. 1795.
CASE OF PAYMENTS INTO THE VIRGA. TREASURY: the Supreme Court delivered its judgment in the British debt case of Ware, Administrator of Jones v. Hylton on 7 Mch. 1796, ruling that payments to British creditors required under the Treaty of Paris of 1783 took precedence over the Virginia sequestration law of 1777 that allowed debtors to discharge these liabilities by making

payments into the state loan office (Marshall, *Papers*, III, 4-7, V, 295-9, 327-8). John Marshall's ARGUMENT before the Court on 9 Feb. 1796 is in same, V, 317-27.
The constitutionality of the carriage TAX was being decided in Hylton v. U.S., a case which began in the Circuit Court at Richmond, where opposition to the legislation imposing the tax was strong. The Supreme Court heard arguments in the case, the first to decide the constitutionality of a federal law, on 23-25 Feb. and on 8 Mar. 1796 rendered a unanimous decision upholding the legislation (Goebel and Smith, *Law Practice of Hamilton*, IV, 297-355).

[1] Remainder of text is written lengthwise in margin and then continues perpendicular to the first part of the letter.

To John Harvie, Jr.

DEAR SIR   Monticello Feb. 22. 1796.

I have been longer than I ought to have been without taking up the subject of our lands, but so it is that every day there is something which must be done and shoving off that which will bear delay. I expected when I came home to be quite at my leisure. On the contrary I never was so hard run with business. In looking over the papers which had been left here when I went to Europe, I have found a treasurer's receipt for the composition money of those lands dated in 1781. which appears to have been presented to you to obtain a warrant for surveying the land, and your advice is noted at the bottom to have the lands surveyed first, then to present the survey and receipt to the Auditors for their certificate after which the patent would issue from your office. All this I have no doubt you have forgotten, but still, as being previous to your purchase of the same lands, it removes all objection of want of notice, had there been room for such an objection. However I will make you a proposition which may perhaps save us further trouble. I am told you wish to buy my lands at Pouncey's hill. I am at this moment under a situation which makes me willing to sell that, and the tract in contest between us, to which I am as confident in my right as in that to the house I live in. A judgment went during the last year against Mr. Wayles's executors, as security for the late Richd. Randolph, my proportion of which is between 7. and 800.£. We are indulged with a little time to raise it, and my other resources having been previously engaged I am now on the ways and means of providing for this sum. I can give you your own time for paying the purchase money, because I can command the money if I will say when it shall be repaid, which the possession of your bond, without parting with it, would enable me to do. I have lately been over the land at Pouncey's and find it very far superior to what I had any idea of. It lies on the ridge between Pouncey's and Carrol's creeks, and is as level through the whole as the lands from the Tuckahoe house to the public road. The soil is gray, and of a fine farming quality. The growth large pine with an undergrowth of hiccory and oak. Sharpe, Huckstept and other farmers of the neighborhood declare to me they would rather have it acre for acre for farming than the best red land at the Mountains. Besides the value of the soil, the timber on it is of capital value. My father bought it 40. years ago for it's timber, but when he built at Shadwell he thought the trees had not yet got sufficient growth. It was the same case when I built here, so that it has escaped being plundered, and has now had 40. years more of growth. It is now in perfection, and such a growth of fine pine I think I never saw. There are very few acres on it which would not furnish 30. stocks, say 3000. f. of plank underreckoned. The lands are within a mile of the sawmill, and the timber of every acre would pay for it's own cutting and leave more than double the price of the land in hand. There are 400. acres of it, and my price for that and the tract on the mountain is £700. paiable when it suits you. The quality of that on the mountain you know. I never saw it, but am assured it is fine tobacco land heavily timbered with locust. I certainly never expected to have offered another acre of land for sale. For of all things it is that of which I am the most tenacious. However at this moment, while I am devising the means of facing a securityship which had not been prepared for, I am willing to part with these lands. If provision be otherwise made, as must be done within a few weeks, if these lands are not now sold, I speak with certainty that during my life they will never again be purchaseable, nor probably in the life which will follow mine. There never before was a moment in which I would have parted with them, and there never will be another. I will ask your answer if you please within a post or two, that I may in time make other provision. Should you not chuse to accede to my proposition, I will without delay send you the statement respecting the lands on the mountain, as you desired, that we may have it adjusted. I am with great esteem Dear Sir Your friend & servt   TH: JEFFERSON

Plat of the land at Pouncey's

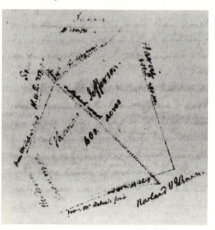

PrC (MHi); at foot of first page: "Colo. Harvie"; endorsed by TJ in ink on verso.

TJ did not sell the 400-acre POUNCEY'S tract, located about five miles from Monticello, until 1820 (MB, note to 15 July 1797,

13 July 1820). See also TJ to Benjamin Hawkins, 22 Mch. 1796.

JUDGMENT . . . AGAINST MR. WAYLES'S EXECUTORS: the Bivins suit (see List of Unretained Letters, [ca. 9 June 1794], and note).

To Thomas Mann Randolph

TH:J. TO TMR.   Monticello Feb. 22. 96.

The last post brought us your favor of the 17th. My nail machine with the hoop iron is safe arrived by Faris as also my wine by Billy. The roads were so bad that he was obliged to put out the rest of his load at Elisha Lake's about 20. miles above Richmond. I shall get Colo. Bell to engage some waggon to bring them up. Robertson has fallowed about

100 acres. He has done the rich nole, and is now breaking up the Chapel ridge. He can spare me 8. barrels of corn. The peas he has not threshed out but supposes there will be 20. or 30. bushels.—He has delivered all your wheat, at Milton, being 420 bushels. My letters of the 7th. inst. from Philada. inform me flour was then 14. D. and universally admitted it would still rise. I begin to expect 14 or 15/ for our crop of the last year.—We have generally had pretty good weather. The last night there fell about $2\frac{1}{2}$ I. of snow, which however will mostly go off to-day, and we may hope an early spring. The prospect of this will influence the price of corn. 15/ has hitherto been the common price, and 18/ has been given in a few instances. It is held up closely by those who have it for sale, and they are but few. The sending to Richmond Colo. C. Lewis's and Mr. Harvie's crops takes off about 500. barrels from our market.—Have you directed Robertson to take on himself a share of the Chapel ridge fence. He spoke to me the other day as having no idea that he was to do any more than his fence along the road, supposing we were to do the whole of the dividing fence. I have directed Page to do one half, the upper one, and told Robertson I thought he should do the lower half.—We are all well here. My warmest love to my dear Martha, kisses to Anne and an affectionate Adieu to yourself with wishes for your better health.

RC (DLC); endorsed by Randolph.

Randolph's FAVOR of 17 Feb. 1796, recorded in SJL as received from Varina three days later, and that of 8 Feb. 1796, received from Varina a week later, have not been found.

To Archibald Stuart

DEAR SIR   Monticello Feb. 22. 1796.

My letter of Jan. 3. was still in my hands, when the reciept of considerable orders for nails, immediately wanting, prevented my commencing a supply for Staunton. I therefore thought it better to hold up my letter till I could begin on a stock for Staunton. We are now at work on them, and in about 10. days shall have ready a supply of VIs. VIIIs. Xs. XIIs. XVIs. XXs. and of XVI. penny brads. Say 100. ℔ of each, which shall be followed by successive and timely supplies.

I percieve by the last Philadelphia prices current that there is a rise of 1d. to $1\frac{1}{2}$ d. per ℔ on nails. I wait to see if this is permanent or a casualty of the day; in the former case that addition will be made to the prices stated in the former letter. I will thank you to put me immediately into the hands of some good retailer, and I will promise to trouble you no more on this subject.—I have just recieved my cutting machine, and iron for 4. pennies, which I shall shortly begin to cut. I doubt whether the larger nails will be called for cut, as they are not fit for country work. Should they be desired however, I will provide proper iron and furnish them. Let me hear from you as soon as you can. Adieu Your's affectionately

TH: JEFFERSON

RC (ViHi); addressed: "Mr. Alexander Stuart Staunton," but correctly recorded in SJL as a letter to Archibald Stuart; stamped.

On 27 Feb. 1796 John Kelly, a Charlottesville merchant, wrote a brief note to TJ ordering twenty pounds of BRADS to sat- isfy the demand of the "generality of the people" (RC in DLC; unrelated notation by TJ on verso: "Short Wm. acct. on winding up my affairs at Paris").

A letter from Archibald Stuart to TJ of 28 Feb. 1796, recorded in SJL as received 7 Mch. 1796, has not been found.

To John Adams

Monticello Feb. 28. 96.

I am to thank you, my dear Sir, for forwarding M. D'Ivernois' book on the French revolution. I recieve every thing with respect which comes from him. But it is on politics, a subject I never loved, and now hate. I will not promise therefore to read it thoroughly. I fear the oligarchical executive of the French will not do. We have always seen a small council get into cabals and quarrels, the more bitter and relentless the fewer they are. We saw this in our committee of the states; and that they were from their bad passions, incapable of doing the business of their country. I think that for the prompt, clear and consistent action so necessary in an Executive, unity of person is necessary as with us. I am aware of the objection to this, that the office becoming more important may bring on serious discord in elections. [1] In our country I think it will be long first; not within our day; and we may safely trust to the wisdom of our Successors the remedies of the evil to arise in theirs. Both experiments however are now fairly committed, and the result will be seen. Never was a finer canvas presented to work on than our countrymen. All of them engaged in agriculture or the pursuits of honest industry, independant in their circumstances, enlightened as to their rights, and firm in their habits of order and obedience to the laws. This I hope will be the age of experiments in government, and [2] that their basis will be founded on principles of honesty, not of mere force. We have seen no instance of this since the days of the Roman republic, nor do we read of any before that. Either force or corruption has been the principle of every modern government, unless the Dutch perhaps be excepted, and

I am not well enough informed to except them absolutely. If ever the morals of a people could be made the basis of their own government, it is our case; and he who could propose to govern such a people by the corruption of their legislature, before he could have one night of quiet sleep, must convince himself that the human soul as well as body is mortal. I am glad to see that whatever grounds of apprehension may have appeared of a wish to govern us otherwise than on principles of reason and honesty, we are getting the better of them. I am sure, from the honesty of your heart, you join me in detestation of the corruption of the English government, and that no man on earth is more incapable than yourself of seeing that copied among us, willingly. I have been among those who have feared the design to introduce it here, and it has been a strong reason with me for wishing there was an ocean of fire between that island and us.—But away politics.

I owe a letter to the Auditor on the subject of my accounts while a foreign minister, and he informs me yours hang on the same difficulties with mine. Before the present government there was a usage either practised on or understood which regulated our charges. This government has directed the future by a law. But this is not retrospective, and I cannot conceive why the treasury cannot settle accounts under the old Congress on the principles that body acted on. I shall very shortly write to Mr. Harrison on this subject, and if we cannot have it settled otherwise I suppose we must apply to the legislature. In this I will act in concert with you if you approve of it. Present my very affectionate respects to Mrs. Adams, and be assured that no one more cordially esteems your virtues than Dear Sir Your sincere friend & servt

TH: JEFFERSON

RC (MHi: Adams Papers); addressed: "John Adams Vice-president of the US. Philadelphia"; franked; endorsed by Adams as answered 6 Apr. 1796. PrC (DLC).

OLIGARCHICAL EXECUTIVE: under the French constitution of 1795 executive authority was lodged in a Directory of five persons chosen by the legislature (Stewart, *French Revolution*, 588-9). For the ill-fated COMMITTEE OF THE STATES, which exercised limited congressional authority for a few months during an extended adjournment of the Confederation Congress in 1784, see Edmund C. Burnett, *The Continental Congress* (New York, 1941), 606-7, 609-12. THE AUDITOR: Richard Harrison. DIRECTED THE FUTURE BY A LAW: an act, first approved 1 July 1790 and continued by acts of 9 Feb. 1793 and 20 Mch. 1794, limited the expenses of a minister plenipotentiary, exclusive of outfit, to $9,000 per year and limited outfit to the amount of one year of the minister's salary (U.S. Statutes at Large, I, 128-9, 299-300, 345).

[1] Preceding two words interlined.
[2] TJ here canceled "first."

To John Barnes

DEAR SIR Monticello Feb. 28. 96.

Immediately after inclosing you the power of attorney for recieving interest, it occurred to me that there was a portion of principal reimburseable at the beginning of the present year, and which was announced to cease bearing interest. Inclosed I send you a power of attorney to recieve it, and shall draw for it as occasion presents in order to vest it here either in purchases for Mr. Short or in loans on landed security as has been done with the rest of his money drawn here in compliance with his desire to change the form of a part of his property, and let none of it remain unproductive. I am with great esteem Dear Sir Your most obedt. servt TH: JEFFERSON

PrC (MHi); endorsed in ink by TJ on verso in part: "Barnes John." Enclosure not found.

To Tobias Lear

DEAR SIR Monticello Feb. 28. 1796.

A friend of mine having desired me to invest some money for him in canal shares, I am desirous of getting information relative to the Patowmac canal as to the following particulars. What proportion of the work is done? What proportion remains to do? When will it probably be completed? What per cent profit will it probably yield, in the present state of population and produce? Can shares be bought? At what price? Is it known whether the proprietors will be safe against further contributions, or how far they will probably be called on? The erection of new shares is equivalent to new contributions. Having no person at Georgetown from whom I can obtain this information, I take the liberty of troubling you with the enquiry, on the footing of former acquaintance, and of the esteem I entertain for you: and I am obliged to ask it as soon as you can conveniently give the information, as I must decide without delay. The post will bring me your answer in 5. days from it's date. I trouble you the more willingly as it gives me an opportunity of recalling myself to your recollection, and of assuring you of the satisfaction it will give me to learn in what degree your new pursuit is likely to fulfill your wishes. I am with great and constant esteem Dear Sir Your friend & servt TH: JEFFERSON

RC (CSmH); at foot of text: "Mr. Lear"; endorsed by Lear as received 10 Mch. and answered 13 Mch. 1796.

FRIEND OF MINE: William Short. YOUR NEW PURSUIT: Lear had been president of the Potomac Canal Company since 1795

(DAB). His 13 Mch. 1796 reply to TJ, recorded in SJL as received from Washington on 25 Mch. 1796 and mistakenly described there as a letter of the latter date, has not been found.

To Van Staphorst & Hubbard

GENTLEMEN   Monticello in Virginia Feb. 28. 1796.

I have written to you in date May 27. Sep. 8. and Jan. 31. last past inclosing several remittances for Mr. Mazzei and one for myself by triplicates, to which I refer you.

If there be any indiscretion in the application I am now about to make to you, ascribe it to the sentiments of friendship and confidence with which your conduct has inspired me, and which I had wished to make reciprocal, and freely decline it if inconsistent with your convenience, assuring yourselves it will not [in] the least alter my dispositions to esteem and serve you. These can merit respect no longer than they are disinterested. I will be short in my explanation. After an absence of ten years from my estate, I found it much deteriorated, and requiring time and advances to bring it back again to the productive state of which it is very susceptible. But I am only a farmer and have no resource but the productions of the farms themselves to bring them into a state of profit. If their profits be small, their restoration will be slow in proportion. An advance of from one to two thousand dollars would produce a state of productiveness which, without it, will be tardy. My estate is a large one for this country, to wit, upwards of ten thousand acres of valuable land on the navigable parts of James river and two hundred negroes, and not a shilling's worth of it either is or ever was under any incumbrance for debt. I may be [. . .] in mentioning this as it is a proper ground whereon to ask you whether you would be willing to answer my draughts on you to any, and what amount within the bounds beforementioned? I ask it of nobody in this country because capitals here are small and employed in more active business than simple loans. I will send you my *bond* for the money payable at what time or times you please. This by the laws of this state, the same in this respect as those of England, will render my lands as well as my personalty responsible for the debt, in case of my death. The interest, say six per cent, shall be remitted annually, with perfect punctuality tho it would be more convenient to pay it to your agent here; as in my inland situation it is difficult to invest money in good bills. Perhaps it would be more convenient to you that your agent here should furnish the money. At any rate it would be advantageous in the sale of my bills that he should endorse them.—I repeat it again that I do not mean to lay you under any restraint by this application; but

shall be better pleased with your doing on it what best pleases yourselves, only making it known to me as soon as convenient. In every
event I shall preserve for you and your interest the sentiments of esteem
& respect with which I am Gentlemen Your friend & humble servt

TH: JEFFERSON

PrC (DLC); faded; at foot of first page: "Messrs. Nichs. & Jacob Van Staphorst & Hubbard"; endorsed in ink by TJ on verso. Enclosed in TJ to Tench Coxe, 28 Feb. 1796, presenting "his friendly compliments and esteem" and requesting him "to procure a safe conveyance" for it (PrC in DLC; endorsed in ink by TJ on verso).

To James Blake

DEAR SIR   Monticello Feb. 29. 1796.

I have to acknolege the receipt of your favor of Dec. 8. as also of
Cortez's letters which came safe to hand, and return you my thanks for
the great attention you have been so kind as to pay to this matter. Will
you add to the favor by presenting to Mrs. Carmichael the homage of
my thanks for this volume, which I value the more as a mark of the
friendly attentions of Mr. Carmichael. In the course of my correspondence with him I had asked him to turn his enquiries to the isthmus of
Darien, and I presume the manuscript you mention must contain information on this subject. My object was in some new edition of my Notes
on Virginia to have said something on the subject of that Isthmus. I
shall recieve it with great thankfulness if the possession of it be not
interesting to Mrs. Carmichael: to whom with a great deal of respect as
well as to yourself I am Dear Sir Your most obedt. humble servt

TH: JEFFERSON

PrC (DLC); at foot of text: "Mr James Blake No. 2. N. 5. street"; endorsed in ink by
TJ on verso.

To Sampson Crosby

DEAR SIR   Monticello Feb. 29. 96.

I did not answer your favor of Jan. 18. immediately on the reciept of
it because I had written just before it came, to inform you of the reciept
of your former letter. I have kept back the present one to be able to
acknolege to you the reciept of the blinds themselves which have come
safely to hand, and claim a repetition of those thanks which I have so
often cause to render you. Wishing you every success and happiness I
am affectionately Dear S[ir Y]our friend & servt   TH: JEFFERSON

RC (ViU); torn at seal; addressed: "Mr. Sampson Crosby at the Secy. of state's office Philadelphia"; stamped; endorsed by Crosby as received 10 Mch. 96.

Crosby's FAVOR OF JAN. 18., received on 2 Feb. 1796, and a subsequent letter of 3 Aug. 1796, received nine days later, are both recorded in SJL but have not been found.

From John Harvie, Jr.

Dr Sir   Feby 29th 1796

In Answer to your Letter of the 22nd. of this Month, I am Sorry it is not in my power to Accede to your proposals, in being the purchaser of your pounceys tract of Land, for although the four Acres that lyes between my line and the Louisa Road would be a desirable Acquisition to me on Account of Rail Timber, yet that Object must Yeild to my Inability of becomeing the proprietor of the whole tract many late disappointments in Money Matters makeing it Necessary for me to be very discreet how I Involve myself in further Engagements. The Moiety of the 490 Acres that I hold from James Marks, (the only Subject of Controversy now between us as you Relinquished any Claim to the part I purchased of Colo. Randolph) I think of much less Value than it has been Represented to you, and only Important to me as it lyes back of my line. I am at any Moment ready to have the Right determined between us in the way that shall be most agreeable to yourself. I propose being at Belmont in a week or two at furthest when I will do myself the pleasure of waiting on you. In the Mean time I beg leave to Subscribe myself with the most perfect Esteem Dr Sir Yr friend & most Obt Servt.

                                                              Jno Harvie

RC (MHi); endorsed by TJ as received 4 Mch. 1796 and so recorded in SJL.

From James Madison

Dear Sir   Philada. Feby. 29. 1796

The Treaty with Spain arrived on Tuesday last. It adjusts both the boundary and navigation in a very satisfactory manner. I have not yet been able to decide whether, on the latter point it clashes or not with the British Treaty; the article being differently represented by different members of the Senate. Nor am I able to say whether any of the articles come within the objections to the constitutionality of the British Treaty. In what relates to contraband and other points in the law of Nations, I understand it presents an honorable contrast to Jay's stipulations. The

Algerine Treaty has some curious features. Among other's, the sum of one Million paid for the ransom and the peace, does not appear before the Senate, as any part of the Treaty; but has been paid as a verbal part of the Contract, under the authority of the law of appropriation: So that the most material part of the Treaty has been made by the President and the Legislature, without the Treaty-Agency of the Senate. The British Treaty as finally ratified has been republished in the newspapers from foreign copies, but is Still not laid before Congress.

The President's birthday has been celebrated with unexampled splendor. The crisis explains the policy of this. It is remarkable however that the annual motion to adjourn for half an hour to pay the compliment of the day, was rejected this year by 50 vs. 38. altho' last year on the yeas and nays 13 only voted in the negative.

Nothing from abroad. Bringhurst is making enquiry as to Sharpless. Mr. Rittenhouse the same as to the Kitchen Stoves. Adieu

RC (DLC: Madison Papers); unsigned; endorsed by TJ as received 12 Mch. 1796 and so recorded in SJL.

On Monday, 22 Feb. 1796, the State Department received the TREATY WITH SPAIN signed by Thomas Pinckney at San Lorenzo on 27 Oct. 1795. The pact dealt with the navigation of the Mississippi and right of deposit at New Orleans, the boundary with Spanish Louisiana and the Floridas, and commercial arrangements between the two countries. President Washington submitted the treaty to the Senate four days after its arrival, and it was ratified on 3 Mch. 1796 (JEP, I, 200, 203; Miller, Treaties, II, 318-38).

To Robert Pollard

SIR   Monticello Feb. 29. 1796.

Being willing on behalf of Mr. Short to subscribe the thirty dollars a share required for carrying on the James river canal, I ask the favor of you to subscribe on his behalf to the amount of the shares he holds, hereby giving you authority for that purpose, and confirming the signature which shall be made by you.

I will remind you that the titles of the transfers of some of these shares remain still to be forwarded by due, which I suppose has escaped you, not doubting you have taken transfers in due form. I am with esteem Sir Your very humble servt   TH: JEFFERSON

P.S. I have this day drawn on Mr. Charles Johnston & Co. for £15. in favor of Horatio Turpin of which this serves for advice.

RC (Vi: James River Company Papers); addressed: "Mr. Robert Pollard Richmond"; endorsed. PrC (DLC: William Short Papers); addressee's name added in ink by TJ above postscript; with undated draft on Johnston & Co. in favor of Horatio Turpin letterpressed on same sheet.

SJL records a letter of this date to TJ's cousin, Dr. Philip Turpin, which has not been found. According to TJ's Memorandum Books, his draft on CHARLES JOHNSTON & CO. was a payment to Dr. Turpin for "debt & interest due him for attending my people at Elk hill after the departure of the British army" (MB, 31 [i.e., 29] Feb. 1796).

SJL records letters, now missing, from Pollard to TJ of 5 Sep. and 3 Oct. 1795, received on 8 Sep. and 6 Oct. 1795, and from TJ to Pollard of 3 Sep. 1795.

To Thomas Mann Randolph

TH:J. TO TMR.   Monticello Feb. 29. 96.

All are well here and at Edgehill. The most remarkeable fact in our neighborhood is the marriage of Capt. Allcock to Mrs. Walker, widow of Dr. Walker. I have no information of the last week's work at Edgehill. Mine was never more backward. Petit is entirely ruined by Milton. He is 40. or 50. acres behind Page in his ploughing. He is not more than half done the wheat fallowing; tho' we have had a fine winter for ploughing. We are engaged in our demolitions, but probably shall not begin our digging till April. Colo. Bell will have my groceries brought on from Leak's where your waggon was obliged to lighten. Robertson sowed his clover last week, we think it too early. I have been obliged to send to Collins to try to get 4. bushels of seed. I have recieved some of the Albany peas from N. York which I am told is the field pea of Europe. I have enough to try a whole field of them. Spring is now opening on us. The birds issuing from their state of torpor; Narcissuses putting up &c. My love to my dear Martha. Adieu affectionately

RC (DLC); endorsed by Randolph as received 5 Mch. 1796. PrC (ViU: Edgehill-Randolph Papers); endorsed in ink by TJ on verso.

SJL records a letter from TJ to Minton COLLINS of 28 Feb. 1796, which has not been found. According to SJL, TJ and Collins exchanged 14 other letters between 3 Oct. 1794 and 24 Mch. 1799, all of which are missing.

A letter from Randolph to TJ of 24 Feb. 1796, recorded in SJL as received from Varina three days later, has not been found.

INDEX

Abelard, Pierre: *Veritables Lettres d'Abeillard et d'Héloise*, 358

Abridgment of the Publick Laws of Virginia, in Force and Use, June 10. 1720 (William Beverley): and TJ's collection of Va. laws, 589

Adams, Abigail, 57, 363, 619

Adams, John: letters to, 57, 261-2, 363, 618-19; letters from, 50-1, 71-2, 207-8, 258-9, 600; and D'Ivernois, xxxviii, 124, 130, 133n, 144-5n, 164, 207-8, 258, 261-2, 275, 276, 307-8, 311, 313, 363, 600; envies TJ's retirement, 50, 71, 72; casts vote in Senate, 69; on Jay Treaty, 71-2, 449; opposes aristocratic government, 71; on written laws and political revolutions, 71; contrasts farming and politics, 208; political opinions of, 208; laments changes in Cabinet, 258; and Vall-Travers, 363-4; appoints B. Washington to Supreme Court, 480n; accounts with U.S., 486, 524, 619; on French Revolution, 600

Adams, John Quincy, 495

Adams, Richard: letter to, 219-20; letter from, 224; identified, 219-20n; letter from cited, 224n; and Short's financial affairs, 241, 355

Adams, Samuel: opposes Jay Treaty, 601; address of quoted, 602n; mentioned, 133n

Adams, Samuel G., 116n

Adams, Thomas: edits *Independent Chronicle*, 509

Adet, Pierre Auguste: letter to, 503-4; letter from, 458-9; identified, 459n; as diplomat to Geneva, 192, 194, 239; recruits Genevan scholars, 194; minister of France to U.S., 314; and Jay Treaty, 400n; regard for TJ as philosopher, 458, 503-4; assesses TJ's views, 459n; supports TJ for president, 459n; and Pictet, 503, 504, 505; and Volney, 525; presents French flag to Washington, 578-9

Aeneid (Virgil): quoted, 14, 163n

Aeschylus: writings of, 358

Aesop: fable of wolves and sheep, 219; mentioned, 185, 229

Agamemnon (Aeschylus): TJ owns, 358

agriculture: O. Bertrand sends information, prospectus on, 16-19, 74-5; in Belgium, 17; plan for state society of, 36;

Coxe's thoughts on, 89-90; and shortage of labor in U.S., 94, 294; importance of, in U.S., 277; cultivation of vetch in Europe, 291; and restoration of land, 299-301; TJ on small farms as sources of income, 341; Strickland's observations on, 372n; British Board of Agriculture, 409; Volney's interest in, 526, 551; honesty of Americans engaged in, 618

Aij, France. *See* Ay (Aij), France

Albemarle Co., Va.: crops and weather in, 56, 457-8; hiring of slaves in, 242; land prices, 305, 309, 327-8, 333, 354, 356n, 379, 381, 580; building costs in, 361; TJ praises, 368; plans address to President on Jay Treaty, 435; lack of gristmills in, 473n

Albemarle County Court: rumor of Genet's recall at, 21; TJ plans to attend, 331, 340; TJ sues in, 406n; approval for mills, 471-4, 477, 480-1; damage to records during War for Independence, 570-1

Alcock, Weston, 625

Alexander, Eli: letter from, 342; identified, 235n; engaged as overseer at Shadwell, 22; computes consumption of corn, 235; memorandums from, 235, 236, 243; buckwheat recipe, 236; compiles list of stock, 243; farm equipment, 342; TJ's account with, 552n

Alexander, William (Augusta Co.): letter to, 487; orders nails, 487; letter from cited, 487n; letter to cited, 487n

Alexandria, Va.: newspapers, 428; and Jay Treaty, 433, 449, 460, 540

Algiers: and British diplomacy, truce with Portugal, 25, 28n, 102; corsairs attack U.S. shipping, 27-8; relations with Denmark, 188; U.S. relations with, 546, 548n; U.S. treaty with, 601, 606, 613-14, 624

Algiers, American captives in: ransom of, 453

Algiers, Dey of. *See* Ali Hassan, Dey of Algiers

alien law: of New York, 153

Ali Hassan, Dey of Algiers, 102, 188

Allegheny Co., Pa.: and Whiskey Insurrection, 183n; state assembly expels legislators from, 222n

Allegheny mountains: height of measured, 597-8

[627]

celery: in inventory of seeds at Monticello, 257

Cellier, Charles E., 199

census: studied by Ebeling, 425

Central America: Ulloa's commentary on Panama, 382, 545, 622; explored by Malaspina, 383n

Cepede. *See* Lacépède, Bernard Germain Étienne de LaVille-sur-Illon, Comte de

Ceracchi, Giuseppe: letters from, 33-4, 200-1, 302-4, 347-9; bust of TJ, xxxvii, 33, 336 (illus.), 200, 235n, 302, 317n, 348-9; plan for national monument, xxxvii, 33-4, 302-4, 347-9; bust of Madison, 34; arrives at Boston with family, 155; letter from cited, 201n; letters to cited, 201n

Ceracchi, Therese Schlishan, 201

Cervantes, Miguel de: *Don Quixote*, 185-6, 255, 356, 377

Chalmers, George: *Collection of Treaties*, 211-13, 228

Champagne, France: wines of, 361

Chapman, William, 471-3

Chaptal, Jean Antoine, 518n

chariot: T. M. Randolph sends for, 225; wheels for, 249

Charleroi, Belgium: battles fought near, 146

Charles, Jacques Alexandre César: *Représentation du globe aérostatique*, 595, 596n

Charles IV, King of Spain: and negotiations with U.S., 119-20, 489, 490; father-in-law of Louis of Parma, 518n

Charles City Co., Va.: and TJ's collection of Va. laws, 586

Charleston, S.C.: protests British spoliations on U.S. commerce, 44-5; sends memorial to Congress, 44

Charlottesville, Va.: market for wheat at, 35; post from Richmond to, 58, 479; postmastership, 101, 104-5; and sales of TJ's nails, 384, 487, 573, 580, 618n; celebrates feast day, 435; holds public meeting on Jay Treaty, 435; courts held at, 468; TJ characterizes as hot and noisy, 468; Volney considers settling in, 525, 551

Chase, Samuel, 607

Chastellux, Alfred Louis Jean Philippe, Comte de: seeks compensation from U.S., 343-4, 613-14; mentioned, 464, 498

Chastellux, François Jean de Beauvoir, Marquis de: financial support for family

of, 343-4, 463, 498, 613; *Travels in North America*, 372n

Chastellux, Marie Joséphine Charlotte Brigitte Plunkett, Marquise de: letter from, 343-4; identified, 344n; applies for pension from U.S., 343-4, 463-4, 498, 613-14; transmits letter, 542; letter from cited, 542n

Chauvelin, François Bernard, 411

Chauvet, David: fled Geneva, 131, 133n, 158

Cherokee river: as site of Eldorado, 37-8

chicory: recommended by A. Young, 95-6; Washington grows, 499

children: of slave families, 100, 223n, 247, 346-7, 435; minor illnesses of, 111, 270, 293, 435; speech development, 111, 182; write, dictate letters, 112, 249; disposition, character of, 249, 251, 260, 599; pastimes, 249, 270; suffer from homesickness, 249, 609; death of TJ's infant granddaughter, 419. *See also* Randolph, Ellen Wayles, I (Eleonor, TJ's granddaughter); Randolph, Anne Cary (TJ's granddaughter); Randolph, Thomas Jefferson (TJ's grandson)

chocolate: on TJ's grocery lists, 336, 431

Christ Church (Philadelphia): site of barometric measurements, 594

Christian VII, King of Denmark, 23, 188

Christie, Gabriel: characterized by Madison, 267; seeks letter of introduction, 267, 292, 315; seeks vetch seed for TJ, 291

Church, Angelica Schuyler (Mrs. John Barker Church): letter to, 454; M. Cosway's friendship for, 201, 210, 455, 543; TJ's friendship for, 454; letter for sent care of T. Pinckney, 457

Church, Catherine (Kitty), 454

Church, Edward, 255

Church, John Barker, 454

Churchman, John: *Magnetic Atlas*, 364

Cicero, Marcus Tullius: mentioned by Ceracchi, 303; works of, 404n; Monroe alludes to, 533

cichorium intybus: sent to G. Washington, 232. *See also* succory

cigars: TJ orders, 552, 591

Cincinnati, Society of: and command of provisional army, 41; contrasted with democratic societies, 228-9; TJ's opinion of, 228-9

Cincinnatus: mentioned by Ceracchi, 303

ciphers: for Monroe, 96, 100; TJ has none

INDEX

INDEX

Hawkins, Robert: debt to TJ, 108, 223
Hawkins, William: cited by Hening, 105; *Treatise of the Pleas of the Crown*, 351
hay: and restoration of land, 296; at Monticello, 377
Hay, Charles, 512
Hay, George, 291n
Hazard, Ebenezer: *Historical Collections*, 424, 428n
Heath, Henry: and TJ's groceries, 98
Heath, William. *See* Heth, William
Hébert, Jacques René, 92
Helvétius, Anne Catherine de Ligneville, 317, 453
Helvétius, Claude Adrien: *Lettres*, 359; and reform of education, 402
Hemings, Critta (ca. 1783-1819): purchased by T. M. Randolph, 346-7; and trip to Varina, 580, 581, 592
Hemings, Dolly (Mrs. Robert Hemings), 247
Hemings, Elizabeth (Betty): family, 222-3, 347n, 605
Hemings, James: deed of manumission for, xxxix, 336 (illus.), 605; inventories kitchen utensils, xxxix, 610-11; brings articles from Varina to Monticello, 270; brings body of TJ's granddaughter to Monticello, 419
Hemings, Nance, 346-7
Hemings, Peter, xxxix
Hemings, Robert: identified, 222-3n; manumission of, xxxix, 222, 225-7; deed of manumission for, 222; letters from cited, 223n; letter to cited, 223n; valuation of, 225-7; child of, 247; relations with TJ, 247
Hemings, Thenia, 100
hemp, 19, 372-3n
Henderson, Mr., 87
Henderson, Bennett: on jury of inquest, 471-3
Henderson, Bennett (d. 1793): and TJ's books and furniture, 8; TJ's suit against heirs of, 471-4, 477, 479-80, 480-5, 518-19, 520; TJ buys property of, 474n; notice to heirs of, 520
Henderson, Bennett Hillsborough: TJ sues, 471, 479-80, 480-5, 518-19, 520
Henderson, Charles: TJ sues, 471, 479-80, 480-5, 518-19, 520
Henderson, Eliza (Elizabeth): TJ sues, 471, 479-80, 480-5, 518-19, 520
Henderson, Elizabeth Lewis (Mrs. Bennett Henderson), 474n

Henderson, Frances: TJ sues, 471, 479-80, 480-5, 518-19, 520
Henderson, Isham: TJ sues, 471, 479-80, 480-5, 518-19, 520
Henderson, James: TJ sues, 471, 479-80, 480-5, 518-19, 520
Henderson, Rev. James, 370
Henderson, Jane Blair, 370
Henderson, John: TJ sues, 471, 479-80, 480-5, 518-19, 520; administers father's estate, 482, 520n
Henderson, Lucy: TJ sues, 471, 479-80, 480-5, 518-19, 520
Henderson, McCaul & Co.: TJ indebted to, 51, 54, 406n, 413, 417n. *See also* Lyle, James
Henderson, Nancy Crawford: TJ sues, 471, 479-80, 480-5, 518-19, 520
Henderson, Richard, 64
Henderson, Sally (Sarah): TJ sues, 471, 479-80, 480-5, 518-19, 520
Henderson, William: TJ sues, 471, 479-80, 480-5, 518-19, 520
Hening, William Waller: letter from, 105-6; identified, 105-6n; *New Virginia Justice*, 105-6; *Statutes at Large*, 319; carries letters, 515
Henrico Co., Va.: and R. Randolph land conveyances, 285-91
Henry, John, 203
Henry, Patrick: asked to serve in Washington's administration, 119, 254, 544-5; TJ's relationship with, 331-2; supports call for convention to revise Va. constitution, 339-40
Herbois. *See* Collot d'Herbois, Jean Marie
Hercules, 393
Heroides (Ovid): TJ quotes from, 408n
Heron, James: shares in James River Co., 389, 418, 431
Heth, William, 288
Heysell, H. (Danish ship captain), 188
Hichborn, Benjamin, 103
Hickman, Richard, 585
hides: delivered to TJ, 243
Histoire de Timur-Bec (Yazdi Sharaf Ad-Din 'Ali): ordered by TJ, 358
Histoire du Bas-Empire (Charles Le Beau): ordered by TJ, 358
Histoire du Grand Genghizcan (François Petis de la Croix): ordered by TJ, 358
Histoire naturelle des quadrupèdes ovipares (Comte de Lacépède), 358
Histoire naturelle des serpents (Comte de Lacépède), 358

Jay Treaty (*cont.*)
reaction of France to, 391, 396, 557; and British orders in council, 392n; ratified conditionally and signed, 399-400, 422, 450n; TJ sent copy of, 399-400, 408, 466; Article 12, 400n, 422, 466; Grenville's negotiation of, 412; and TJ's notes on infractions of neutral rights, 412n; Article 9, 422-3; public opinion on, 430-1, 432-3, 441, 449; reactions of Va. to, 430, 432-3, 460, 515-16, 534-6, 539-40; Article 7, 433n; merchants' support for, 449; contents published, 450; TJ's views on, 457, 458, 475-6, 542; and party politics, state elections, 475-6, 511; various essays on, 475-6; Article 17, 476n; and Spain, 490; Rutledge criticizes, 502-3, 542; constitutionality of, 539; and House of Representatives, 554-5, 555-7, 558-9, 562, 565, 567, 577, 600, 601, 613, 624; Monroe's reaction to, 563; E. Randolph and, 566, 568-9; and TJ's Report on Commerce, 568; compared with Pinckney Treaty, 623. *See also* Washington, George: President
Jefferson, Elizabeth (TJ's sister), 462
Jefferson, George, Jr., 60-1
Jefferson, George (TJ's cousin), 60-2
Jefferson, Jane Randolph (Mrs. Peter Jefferson, TJ's mother), 417n, 462
Jefferson, John Garland: letters to, 60-2, 87-8; seeks to recover inherited land, 60-2, 87; letters from cited, 62n, 88n, 512n; seeks clerkship, 512
Jefferson, Mary (Maria, Polly, TJ's daughter): regards sent to, 101, 147, 189, 207, 208, 391, 401, 407, 515, 559; Ceracchi intends bust of TJ for, 200; sends regards to Blackdens, 216; at Monticello, 242, 541; relationship with sister, 247, 249, 270, 293, 569, 581, 599; reported well, 370; suffers from dysentery, 434-5, 438, 439; and C. Church, 454; finds succory seed, 608
Jefferson, Peter (TJ's father): share in Loyal Co., 462-3; built water mill, 471, 473-4n, 480; and limestone tract, 570-1; acquired Pouncey's tract, 615

JEFFERSON, THOMAS

Agriculture
and farm implements, 11-12, 68, 112, 226, 326-7, 328, 342, 579-80; grows potatoes, 11, 55, 67, 68, 75, 232-3, 354, 362; uses livestock for motive power, 12, 112-13, 235, 435, 438, 579; breeds livestock, 48, 227, 235; exchanges ideas with others, 55-6, 93-5, 230, 231, 330, 370, 498-500, 526, 551; orchards, 56; works to restore farms, 58, 551; inventories livestock, 65-6, 243; seeks information, 67, 259-60; and crop rotation, 68, 75, 231-3, 354, 361-2, 465, 473n, 557; on degradation of land, 68; feeding of livestock, 93, 231-2, 233, 235, 464; experiments with crops, 167, 232-3, 264, 265, 270, 291-2, 327, 339, 383-4, 435, 464-5; acquires livestock, 184, 214, 243-4, 251, 260, 264, 267-8, 271, 375-6, 399; enthusiasm for farming, 228, 332, 337, 363, 366, 374, 451, 455, 457, 478, 541; builds moldboard plow, 233-4; raises livestock for milk and meat, 233, 235, 243; on utilization of livestock manure, 233; grows radishes, 257, 293; may cease to grow tobacco, 367, 552n; reports on crops, 373, 457. *See also* clover; corn; Monticello; Taylor, John; tobacco; wheat

Architecture
TJ's advice sought on, 178-9

Business and Financial Affairs
on calculation of sterling debt, 15; keeps memorandum books, 20-2, 522, 536; payments to Henderson, McCaul & Co., 51, 54; collects bonds in Bedford Co., 108-9, 218, 223, 246, 514; pays taxes and fees, 168, 345, 593n; various accounts, 227-8, 247-8, 345, 365, 413-17; land transactions, 245-6, 272-3, 614-16; arrangements with R. Hanson, 246, 272-3, 322, 323-4; business relations with T. M. Randolph, 246-7, 592; and Ast's insurance plan, 257-8; payment to John Brown, 270; potash and pearl ash, 302; lime and limestone, 329, 570-1; boundary dispute, 337-8, 347, 614-16, 623; account with James Brown, 345, 365, 409-10; seeks information on windmills, 374, 389; describes his financial situation, 405-6; Kinsolving's indebtedness to, 405-6, 515, 519, 521; reliance on Poplar Forest income, 405-6; and Cobbs suit, 446, 574-5, 599, 604, 608; payments for Lewises, 463; advises Monroe, 527-8; land titles, 537-9, 553, 554, 580; ac-

INDEX

JEFFERSON, THOMAS (*cont.*)
explorations, 382-3n, 495, 545, 622; weather, 439-40n; Natural Bridge measured, 460; values news of advances in Europe, 503; and Louis of Parma, 517-18. *See also* American Philosophical Society; natural history; *Notes on the State of Virginia*

Secretary of State
resignation from office, 3, 4-5, 6, 7-8n, 36; and Report on Public Lands, 63, 64n; misrouted official letters returned, 74; and O. Bertrand's correspondence, 74; and relations with Spain, 120-2, 148, 490-1; and relations with Great Britain, 392n, 411-12; and support for Article 17 of Jay Treaty, 476n; and Short's memorandum to Montmorin, 489. *See also* Genet, Edmond Charles; Hammond, George

Slaveholder
manumits J. and R. Hemings, xxxix, 222-3, 605; sells T. Hemings, 100; hires slaves, 224, 225, 242, 251, 260, 572n, 580, 592; purchases Nance Hemings, 346-7; questions Billy's character, 581; gives number of slaves owned, 621-2; at Elk Hill after American Revolution, 625n

Travels
trip to Richmond, 54, 60, 97, 98, 337; plans trip to Poplar Forest, 113-14, 337, 349

Writings
Notes on the Letter of Christoph Daniel Ebeling, xxxviii, 506-10; Report on Commerce, 6-7, 22n, 26-8, 49, 476n, 568; Notes for Revising the Virginia Constitution, 236-9; Notes on Potash and Pearl Ash, 271-2; Notes on Conversations with William Strickland, 371-3; Notes on Infractions of Neutral Rights by France and Great Britain, 411-12; Notes of a Conversation with Edmund Randolph, 568-9; Statement of the Laws of Virginia, 585-91, 606. See also *Notes on the State of Virginia*

Jeffersons Beschreibung von Virginien (Johann Reinhold Forster and Matthias Christian Sprengel), 424, 428n

Jersey Chronicle (Mount Pleasant, N.J.), 509
Johnson, Mr., 538n
Johnson, Dr. (Staunton, Va.), 384, 574
Johnson, Joshua (U.S. consul in London), 500
Johnson, William, 388n
Johnston, Charles: payment to, 591; letters from cited, 592n; letters to cited, 592n
Johnston, Charles, & Co., 624-5
Jones, Hugh: *Present State of Virginia*, 424
Jones, Joseph: health of, 56; Monroe hopes to visit, 87; and Monroe's business affairs, property, 100, 114, 147, 361-2, 448, 528, 529; purchases land in Loudon Co., 360; forwards papers, 433
Jones, William, 116n
Jordanes: writings of ordered by TJ, 358
Jouett, Robert, 401
Jourdan, Jean Baptiste, Comte, 146
Joy, George: sends books to TJ, 211-13, 228; TJ's comments on letter by, 228
Juan y Santacilia, Jorge: *Observaciones astronomicas, y phisicas*, 596n
Jupiter (TJ's slave): blamed for mule's escape, 264
"Juricola": as signature for Coxe, 516

Kames, Henry Home, Lord, 75
Keith, Sir William: *History*, 424
Kelly, John: letter from quoted, 618n
Kelyng, Sir John: *Reports of Divers Cases*, 351, 399
Kent, James, 476n
Kent Academy (Maryland), 158n
Kentucky: democratic society of, 9-10; and French plan to liberate Louisiana, 9-10; and news from Philadelphia, 21-2; as destination for English emigrants, 24; boundaries, 63; and U.S. right to navigate Mississippi, 117-19, 254, 418; disunionist sentiments in, 118, 119n; settlement and economic development, 417-18; Ebeling seeks printed laws of, 429; and U.S. relations with Spain, 489-90
Kersaint, Armand Guy Simon de Coetnempren, Comte de, 522
Kersaint, Claire Louise Françoise de Paul d'Alesso d'Eragny: letter to, 522; TJ unable to assist, 522; letter from cited, 522n

Lownes, Caleb: letter to, 459; financial transactions with, 65, 169, 247-8, 304, 421, 437; power of attorney to, 148-50; letters to cited, 149-50n, 169n, 183n, 459n; letters from cited, 150n, 183n, 459n; and shipment of gongs, 183; supplies TJ with nailrod, 226-7, 439, 609; characterized, 613

Loyal Company, 462-3

lucerne (alfalfa): TJ cultivates, abandons, 67-8, 464; sowing of, 233, 327, 328; Washington reports on growing of, 499

Lud. Kusterus de vero usu Verborum Mediorum Eorumque Differentia A Verbis Activis & Passivis (Ludolf Kuster): praised by TJ, 181; returned to TJ, 184-5

Luque, Eduardo Malo de: pseudonym used by Almodóvar del Río, 510n

Luxembourg (city): siege of, 395

Lyle, James: letters to, 54, 218, 223, 405-6, 514-15, 521, 522-3, 536; letters from, 51, 321-2, 514, 519, 534; and TJ's debt to Henderson, McCaul & Co., 51, 54, 108-9, 218, 223, 226, 242, 249, 321-2, 405-6, 414-17, 514-15, 521, 522-3, 534; and Harding v. Carter, 514-15; and L. Coleman transaction, 519, 522-3, 534, 536

Lynch, Thomas, 541

Lynchburg, Va.: as market for wheat, 367

Lyons, France: and Genevan Revolution, 141, 142

Maastricht, Netherlands: and War of First Coalition, 146

Mably, Gabriel Bonnot de: *Observations sur l'histoire de France*, 186, 315

macaroni: for TJ, 362

Macarty, William, 5n

McCaul, Alexander: TJ's payments to, 51; Harding's legal case against, 514. *See also* Henderson, McCaul & Co.

McClenahan, James, 345n

McCullum, David, 115n

McGehee, Samuel, 484n

McHenry, James: appointed Secretary of War, 545n, 607

machines: on introduction into U.S., 273

Mackie, Thomas & Peter, 248

Madison, Dolley Payne Todd (Mrs. James Madison): invited to Monticello, xxxvii, 260, 476; marriage, xxxvii, 179; portrait of, xxxvii-xxxviii, 336 (illus.); TJ sends respects to, xxxvii, 182, 186, 230, 340;

sends respects to TJ, 203; visits family, 386

Madison, Bishop James: opposes Jay Treaty, 433

MADISON, JAMES: letters to, 21-2, 49-50, 75-6, 182-3, 186-7, 216, 217, 228-30, 259-60, 274, 291-3, 338-40, 408, 430-1, 475-7, 539-41, 542, 612-13; letters from, 26-8, 31-3, 35-6, 38, 43, 43-5, 45-6, 51-2, 62-3, 72-4, 84-5, 92-3, 178-9, 202-4, 211-14, 220-2, 244-5, 265-7, 284, 315-16, 386-8, 432-4, 510-12, 521-2, 544-5, 554-5, 562-3, 576-9, 600-3, 606-7, 613-14, 623-4; portrait of, xxxvii-xxxviii, 336 (illus.); characterized as pro-French, 26, 28n; letter from cited, 179n; targeted by Federalists, 450-1n; letter to cited, 607n

Congress

resolutions on TJ's Report on Commerce, 11, 21-2, 29, 34, 35-6, 38, 40-1, 44, 49; describes bills and political maneuvers in, 26-7, 35, 38, 43-4, 45-6, 51-2, 72-3, 84, 92-3, 244-5, 250-1, 266-7, 544, 576-8, 601-3; and House ways and means committee, 46n, 601-2; on influence of Washington's popularity, 84, 92; and answer to President's annual addresses in House, 212-13, 554-5, 562. *See also* Jay Treaty

Opinions

on carriage tax, 72-4, 92; on military, 92, 202, 266; on Whiskey Insurrection, 202, 221; on British relations with U.S., 203; on criticism of democratic societies, 211-13, 220-1; on Hamilton, 245, 265-6; on relationship of legislative and executive, 250; on public debt and taxes, 266, 601; on vacancies in Cabinet, 544-5; on jurisdiction of House of Representatives, 576-7; on relations between Mass. and Va., 601-2; on export of breadstuffs to West Indies, 606; on preservation of documents, 606; on embargo, 607; on constitutionality of congressional gifts to foreign Revolutionary War officers, 613

Personal Affairs

marriage, xxxvii, 179, 368, 370, 603; and Genet's future plans, 27-8; bust by Ceracchi, 34; as correspondent, 55, 228; relationship with Monroe,

letters from cited, 417n; letters to cited, 417n

Murgatroyd, Thomas, 421

Murray, Anthony, 554

Murray, William Vans, 578n

museums: American, gathering of objects for, 364, 469-70. *See also* Leverian Museum

Mussi, Joseph: letters to, 155, 206, 247-8; and TJ's Philadelphia purchases, 155, 179-80, 248, 552; letters from cited, 155n, 206n, 248n, 340n; letters to cited, 155n, 206n, 248n; finds stonecutter for TJ, 206; sends clover seed to TJ, 206, 242, 247; TJ's account with, 242, 247-8, 249; drafts in favor of, 335, 437

mustard: in inventory of seeds at Monticello, 257; on TJ's grocery list, 336

nailery, nailrod. *See* Jefferson, Thomas: Nailery

Nal, Mathieu, 199

Napoleon. *See* Bonaparte, Napoleon

Nat (T. M. Randolph's slave): and wagon for T. M. Randolph, 579-80; delivers wine to TJ, 581n

Natural Bridge, Va.: Strickland to visit, 349; TJ's land taxes on, 408, 410; measured by Tucker, 460

natural history: TJ orders books on, 357-8; collections of specimens in Leverian Museum, 364-5, 469-70; taught at Fredericksburg Academy, 402; of America, studied by Ebeling, 425; Adet and TJ share interest in, 458, 504; insufficiently studied in America, 505; Louis of Parma's interest in, 517-18

Natural History of Carolina, Florida, and the Bahama Islands (Mark Catesby), 425

Natural History of Fossils (Emanuel Mendes da Costa): loaned to E. Randolph, 187, 211-13

naturalization: and English alien laws, 30; and Gallatin, 30; under Articles of Confederation, 30, 31n; debates on naturalization bill, 241, 244-5, 250

naval stores: made contraband by Britain, 422; and Treaty with Algiers, 614

Naville, François Andre, 143

Nelson, Thomas, Jr., 289n, 541

Nelson, William, Jr.: letter to, 63-4; identified, 64n; and Va.-N.C. boundary, 63-4; letter from cited, 64n

Netherlands: and War of First Coalition,

23-4, 39, 91, 244, 310, 373, 395; loans to U.S., 78-9; colleges disrupted by French Revolution, 151; Auckland addresses States General of, 411-12; British restrictions on Dutch firms, 500-1; government of, 618. *See also* Batavian Republic; William V, Prince of Orange

neutrality: British expectations of U.S., 20; and ships of war in U.S. ports, 24; British violations of U.S., 28n; French respect for U.S., 32-3; and War of First Coalition, 90-1; neutrality act, ban on sale of prizes, 92-3; of Denmark and Sweden, 391, 412; and French and British decrees and orders, 411-12; League of Armed Neutrality, 422, 423n; Proclamation of Neutrality, 433n. *See also* France: Foreign Relations; Great Britain: U.S. Relations with

Nevison, John, 99n

New England: British seize ships from, 35, 44; fears standing army, 202; and congressional debate on democratic societies, 213; studied by Ebeling, 424; description of merchants in France from, 510-11

New Hampshire: congressional election in, 202-3; studied by Ebeling, 427n

New Jersey: Burr's support in, 86; congressional election in, 202, 221, 251; protests against high salaries in federal government, 221-2; studied by Ebeling, 424; wheat crop in, 606-7

New London, Va.: Strickland to visit, 349

New Natura Brevium (Sir Anthony Fitzherbert): TJ sells to A. Stuart, 351, 399

New Orleans: and French plan to liberate Louisiana, 9; and Pinckney Treaty, 624n

New Virginia Justice (William Waller Hening): submitted to TJ, 105-6

New-Year's Gift to the Democrats; or Observations on a Pamphlet, Entitled, "A Vindication of Mr. Randolph's Resignation" (William Cobbett), 578-9

New York: T. M. Randolph travels to, 104n, 112; and alien law, 153; congressional elections in, 202-3, 221, 265; gubernatorial election in, 265, 316; agriculture, 327, 339, 606-7; studied by Ebeling, 424

New York City: Republicans organize public meetings at, 26-8, 32; fortification of harbor at, 28n; democratic society of, 73-4; market at, 111-12; Van Staphorsts consider moving to, 217;

INDEX

Osmont, Louis, 5-6
osnaburgs (osnabrigs): in Philadelphia, 76, 84, 93; purchased by TJ, 155
Ostend, Austrian Netherlands: French occupy, 103
Ottoman Empire: and War of First Coalition, 92
Outlines of a Plan, for establishing a State Society of Agriculture in Pennsylvania: sent to TJ, 36
Outlines of the Fifteenth Chapter of the Proposed General Report (Robert Somerville), 409
Ovid: *Heroides*, 408n
Owen & Mosby (tobacco inspectors): and Cobbs suit, 574-5, 599, 608
oxen: corn consumption of, 235; at Shadwell, 243; and restoration of land, 298
Oxford University, 312

Paca, William, 86
Page, John: and J. Carey's publication of letters, 324; and TJ's collection of Va. laws, 586
Page, Mann: letter to, 440-1; letter from, 404-5; and Ogilvie, 403-4n, 440-1; and Fredericksburg Academy, 404-5; letter from cited, 405n
Page, Mann, Jr., 534-5
Page, Matthew, 586
Page, William, 617, 625
Paine, Elijah, 203
Paine, Thomas: on landed estates as luxury, 73; *Letter to George Washington*, 577-8
palmae christi: in inventory of seeds at Monticello, 257
Panama: Ulloa's manuscript on, 382, 545, 622; TJ's interest in Isthmus of, 622
Paradis de Raymondis, Jean Zacharie: *Traite elementaire de morale et du Bonheur*, 187
Parent, M., 361
Paris: threatened by Frederick William II, 90; Ceracchi prefers as work site, 303; anti-Convention mobs in, 393, 398n; and 13 Vendémiaire conflict, 531-2, 533-4n, 544-5; Charles's balloon ascent, 595, 596n
Parker, Richard, 231
Parkinson, Mr. (James Parkinson's son), 470
Parkinson, James: and Leverian museum, 364, 469-70

Parma, Prince of. *See* Louis of Parma
parsnips: in inventory of seeds at Monticello, 257
pastures: J. Taylor's views on, 94, 296; and TJ's crop-rotation plan, 233
patents: procedures for obtaining, 106; sought by Richard Morris, 106-7; for mills, 374-5, 389
Paterson, Mr., 12
Paterson, William, 86
Patrick (Randolph slave): hired by TJ, 224n, 251, 260, 580, 592; TJ criticizes, 572
Patrick (Wood slave): TJ hires, 580
Patten, John, 203
Patterson, James. *See* Parkinson, James
Patterson, Robert, 594, 596n
Paulus Diaconus: writings of ordered by TJ, 358
Payne, Mr., 572
Payne's ordinary: T. M. Randolphs at, 182; Derieux at, 370
Pays de Vaud, Switzerland: dominated by Bern, 57, 71, 72n; accepts refugees from Genevan Revolution, 143, 163n; and Genevan exiles, 191
Peace Treaty, Definitive (1783): and northwest posts, 25, 51; British infractions of, 28n; and Ware, Administrator of Jones v. Hylton, 614n
peaches: trees, used as boundary for fields, 231, 301; at Monticello, 438; TJ enjoys, 451, 455
Peale, Charles Willson, 273n, 518n
pearl ash: TJ's notes on, 271-2; plans for production of, 302
peas: grown in New York, 37; and TJ's crop-rotation plan, 68, 75, 232-3, 354, 362, 464-5; and J. Taylor's views, 95, 294-5; sowing of, 112, 233-4, 327, 328; in inventory of seeds at Monticello, 256-7; vines of, in Strickland's notes, 372n; Washington reports on growing of, 499-500; Albany, obtained by TJ from N.Y., 557, 625; as crop at Edgehill, 617
Peggy (ship), 175, 175n
Pendleton, Edmund: and P. Carr's inheritance, 226; TJ sends respects to, 234, 384; as Pollard's brother-in-law, 274n; on Va. Court of Appeals, 291n
Pennsylvania: Cooper, Priestley plan to settle in, 24; plans for agricultural society in, 36; democratic society of, 73-4; authority over Presque Isle, 85, 86n, 87; mobilizes militia, 85, 87; D'Ivernois addresses on Genevan Revolution, 123;

Presque Isle, Pa.: conflicting claims to, 85-6, 87

press, freedom of: threatened by attacks on democratic societies, 228, 359; and Va. Constitution, 238

Prestwould (Mecklenburg Co., Va.), 550n

Prevost, Pierre: and Academy of Geneva, 124, 190, 269, 276

Prevost-Cabanis, Jacob François, 141

Price, Joseph: Short's tenant, 354, 356n, 444

Price, Richard: on jury of inquest, 471-3

Price, William (register of Va. land office), 537

Priestley, Joseph: plans to emigrate to U.S., 24, 67, 92; says revolution inevitable in Britain, 102; TJ's admiration for, 279

Prince of Wales (ship): Bivins captain of, 98n

Prince of Wales case: J. Marshall's opinion on, 114-15; and Wayles estate, 289n

Prometheus Vinctus (Aeschylus): TJ owns, 358

Protestantism: and Academy of Geneva, 126

Prussia: and War of First Coalition, 23, 310; Diet of, 90; interferes in French internal politics, 90; and Poland, 147, 172; peace with France, 245, 395; convention with Great Britain, 411, 412n; freedom of press in, 426. *See also* Frederick William II, King of Prussia

public debt: in Europe, and impact on government, 102. *See also* United States: Public Finance

pumpkins: in inventory of seeds at Monticello, 257

Purport of a Letter on Sheep. Written in Maryland, March the 30th, 1789 (John Beale Bordley): TJ seeks copy of, 259-60, 315-16

Purvis (Pervis), John: *Complete Collection of all the Laws of Virginia now in force*, 584, 586

Putnam, Rufus, 30, 31n

Quakers, 32

Quarles, Robert, 417

Quiberon Bay, France: French royalist forces defeated at, 426

Quinz livres des Deipnosophistes (Athenaeus): ordered by TJ, 358

Rabaut Saint Étienne, Jean Paul: *Précis historique de la Révolution Françoise*, 358

radish seed: in inventory of seeds at Monticello, 257; scarlet, TJ orders, 293

Raleigh, Sir Walter, 372

Ramsay, David: signs memorial, 44; and Ebeling, 423; TJ characterizes, 506

Randall, Robert, 576-8

Randolph, Anne Cary (Nancy, sister of Thomas Mann Randolph), 429

Randolph, Anne Cary (TJ's granddaughter): health of, 111, 242, 270, 293, 419, 429, 434, 438; relationship with parents, 112, 247, 249, 260, 264, 439, 569; characterized by TJ, 249; receives gift, 270; TJ's affection for, 599, 605, 608, 610, 617; mentioned, 182, 370, 541

Randolph, Ann Meade, 287

Randolph, Beverley, 63, 64n

Randolph, Brett, 285-91

Randolph, David Meade: sued by Wayles executors, 114-15, 285-91

Randolph, Edmund: letters to, 15-16, 53, 74, 89, 148, 187, 275, 376-7; letters from, 117-19, 325; appointed, confirmed as Secretary of State, 4-5, 6, 78, 370; letter to Carmichael and Short quoted, 5n; forwards letters, 15, 100, 487, 495; letters from cited, 16n, 77n, 275n; and public opinion, 24, 521; resignation, 25n, 450-1, 563-5, 604; correspondence with Hammond, 27-8, 34, 84; as interpreter for Fauchet, 27; and appointments of ministers, envoys, 40, 70, 86-7, 117-19, 148; reports on Cabinet politics, 42; forwards book, 62, 405; TJ forwards letter to, 74; letter to L'Epine quoted, 77n; and Dombey's papers, 89; confers with Jaudenes, 120-2; borrows books from TJ, 186, 187, 202, 211, 315; sells property, 187; and American captives in Algiers, 188; and Mazzei's claim, 202; and D'Ivernois, 208n, 274, 275, 315; and Short, 252, 445; criticized by Short, 254, 488-90, 493-4; and Short's proposals for diplomatic establishment, 255, 325, 356, 376-7; and Short's salary, 256, 355-6, 442-3, 446-7, 488, 493-4; as attorney in Randolph heirs case, 289n, 291n; and Ceracchi's monument, 304n, 348; and Monroe, 387n, 397n; on Jay Treaty, 450n, 565; to forward rice to TJ, 495; certificate for Crosby, 561; relations with Washington, 563-5; TJ's opinion

INDEX

of, 565-7; notes of a conversation with, 568-9; mentioned, 50. See also *Vindication of Mr. Randolph's Resignation*

Randolph, Elizabeth Nicholas (Mrs. Edmund Randolph), 187, 377

Randolph, Ellen Wayles, I (Eleonor, TJ's granddaughter): buried at Monticello, xxxviii-xxxix, 419n; birth, 155-6; travels with parents, 182; at Monticello, 370; death, 419; mentioned, 284

Randolph, Henry, 289n

Randolph, Sir John: collects Va. laws, 585-6

Randolph, John (d. 1775), 116n

Randolph, John (d. 1784): case involving bond of, 115-17

Randolph, Maria Beverley, 287

Randolph, Martha Jefferson (Patsy, Mrs. Thomas Mann Randolph, TJ's daughter): letters to, 249-50, 260-1, 429, 599, 609-10; letters from, 246-7, 569; death of daughter, xxxviii-xxxix, 419; letter to quoted, 8n; regards sent to, 101, 147, 189, 207, 208, 391, 401, 407, 515, 559; health of, 115, 226; gives birth to daughter, 155; and Monticello, 166, 225, 370, 454, 541; praised by TJ for knowledge of French, 166; and separation from children, 182, 260; Ceracchi intends bust of TJ for, 200; sends regards to Blackdens, 216; letter from cited, 227n; at Varina, 241-2, 247, 260; TJ's affection for, 242, 250, 251, 252, 264, 419, 435, 438, 439, 580, 593, 605, 608, 617, 625; purchases wallpaper for TJ, 246; affection for TJ, 247; speaks with R. Hemings, 247; affectionate wishes from sister and TJ, 270, 293; marriage settlement, 283-4; travels with husband, 408, 439n, 476; fails to write, 429; relationship with sister-in-law after scandal, 429; and E. Trist's visit, 478; visits Dungeness, 569; requests articles from Monticello, 581

Randolph, Nancy. *See* Randolph, Anne Cary (Nancy, sister of Thomas Mann Randolph)

Randolph, Peyton, 585-6

Randolph, Richard (d. 1786): and Bivins bond, 98-100, 615; suit against heirs of, 114-15, 285-91; debt to Short, 492

Randolph, Richard (d. ca. 1799): sued by Wayles executors, 114-15, 285-91

Randolph, Ryland, 285-91

Randolph, Thomas Eston, 580

Randolph, Thomas Jefferson (TJ's grandson): characterized by TJ, 111, 249, 599; health of, 111, 242, 270, 293, 419, 429, 434, 438, 580, 604, 608; relationship with parents, 247, 264, 439, 569, 609; fears dogs, 251, 260; and toy gun, 270; education of, 404n; mentioned, xxxvii, 182, 370, 541

Randolph, Thomas Mann, Sr.: slaves hired from estate of, 224n, 225; and son's marriage settlement, 282-4; and disposition of R. Randolph's estate, 290n; and Edgehill boundary dispute, 347; death, 370; and J. Harvie's land title, 623

Randolph, Thomas Mann (TJ's son-in-law): letters to, 104, 111-12, 182, 225-7, 242, 251-2, 264, 270, 281-4, 293, 419, 434-5, 438-9, 439-40, 527, 537-8, 574-6, 579-80, 581, 592-3, 604-5, 607-9, 616-17, 625; letter from, 534-6; death of daughter, xxxviii-xxxix, 419; business at Richmond, 8-9, 246; memorandum to, 8-9; notations on TJ's queries, 8-9; Monroes send regards to, 101, 147, 391, 401; travels to restore health, 104, 111-12, 226, 408, 419, 429, 434, 439n, 446, 448-9, 476; letters from cited, 112n, 227n, 250n, 264n, 284n, 293n, 419n, 435n, 439n, 575-6n, 593n, 609n, 617n, 625n; health of, 115, 213, 250, 362, 478, 592-3; certifies power of attorney, 149; executes business for TJ, 168, 218, 223, 242, 246-7, 249, 270, 293, 321-2, 604, 609; and mares for TJ, 227, 251, 260; letters to cited, 227n, 593n; hires slaves for TJ, 251, 260, 592; purchases slave, 347n; at Monticello, 370, 541; and Ogilvie, 404n; relationship with sister after scandal, 429; weather diary, 439-40n; lands adjoining TJ's, 471, 472, 481; Giles sends respects to, 515; reports on proceedings in Va. House of Delegates, 534-6, 537, 539-40; and documents for TJ's lands, 537-9, 580, 608; TJ sends wagon to, 579-80; takes TJ's collection of Va. laws to bindery, 581-2; TJ makes payment for, 593n; and Cobbs suit, 599, 604, 608. *See also* Varina

Randolph, Virginia, 599

rape (plant): in inventory of seeds at Monticello, 257; sent by A. Stuart, 271; compared with rutabaga, 384

Raymond, Robert, Lord Raymond: *Reports of Cases Argued and Adjudged*, 351, 399

INDEX

Thornton, William: praises Ceracchi bust, xxxvii; as Federal District Commissioner, 207, 306-8; and plans for a university, 306-8

Thorold, Sir John, 365

Thouin, André, 16

threshing machines: model acquired by TJ, 11-12, 304, 457-8; Paterson's design, 12; TJ's notes on, 12; TJ's need for, 464; compared by TJ, 579-80

Tilghman, Edward, Jr., 576-8, 614

Timur (Timour Beg; Tamerlane): history by Sharaf Ad-Din 'Ali, 358; *Instituts Politiques et Militaires de Tamerlan*, 358

tin: TJ orders, 467; in inventory of kitchen at Monticello, 610-11

titles of nobility: as issue in debate on naturalization bill, 244-5, 250

tobacco: marketing of TJ's, 22, 65, 205, 330-1, 345, 367, 368n, 414, 552; excise tax on, 72, 244-5n; for payment of TJ's accounts, 112, 169, 405; as crop at Poplar Forest, 260, 552; prices of, 367; TJ to reduce production of, 367; damage to crop, 405, 438, 457, 552; Kinsolving's, 405, 515, 519, 521; loss of, 446, 574-5; declining primacy of in Va., 473n; land for, 615

Toledo, Archbishop of. *See* Lorenzana y Butron, Francisco Antonio

Topographical Analysis of the Commonwealth of Virginia, Compiled for the Year 1790-1 (William Tatham), 428

Topographical Description of Virginia, Pennsylvania, Maryland and North Carolina (Thomas Hutchins), 424, 428n

tory: as a political label, 245, 449, 506-9, 567, 607

To the President and Congress of the United States of America (Democratic Society of Kentucky): sent to TJ, 9-10

Tott, Sophie Ernestine, Mme de, 452

Toulon, France: British strength at, greater than expected, 23; recaptured by France, 25, 33, 37, 39-40, 63

toys: for TJ's grandchildren, 270

Traduction d'Anciens Ouvrages Latins relatifs à l'Agriculture et à la Médecine (Charles François Saboureux de La Bonnetrie): ordered by TJ, 358

Tragoediae (Aeschylus): ordered by TJ, 358

Traite elementaire de morale et du Bonheur (Jean Zacharie Paradis de Raymondis): loaned to E. Randolph, 187

Traités sur les coutumes Anglo-Normandes

(David Houard): loaned to J. Wilson, 186-7, 315-16

Transactions (N.Y. Society for the Promotion of Agriculture, Arts, and Manufactures): TJ consults, 326-7, 339-40

Travels, during The Years 1787, 1788, and 1789 (Arthur Young), 96n, 295-301

Travels in North America (François Jean de Beauvoir, Marquis de Chastellux), 372n

Travels through North and South Carolina, Georgia, East and West Florida (William Bartram), 425

Travels through the States of North America and the Provinces of Upper and Lower Canada, during the Years 1795, 1796, and 1797 (Isaac Weld), 441, 442n

Treasury, U.S. Department of the: congressional investigation of, 44, 52; role in fiscal legislation, 44, 45-6, 47, 72, 244-5; Coxe as commissioner of revenue in, 517n; condition of, after Hamilton's departure, 601; submits proposal for funding of public debt, 601. *See also* Hamilton, Alexander; United States: Public Finance

Treatise de la Morale et la bonheur. See *Traite elementaire de morale et du Bonheur* (Jean Zacharie Paradis de Raymondis)

Treatise of the Pleas of the Crown (William Hawkins): TJ sells to A. Stuart, 351

Treatise on Magnetism, in Theory and Practice (Tiberius Cavallo), 364, 469

Treaty of Amity, Commerce, and Navigation, between His Britannick Majesty, and the United States of America: TJ receives, 399-400; M. Carey publishes with "Copious Appendix," 475-6

trees: as field boundaries, 231, 301; and restoration of land, 296. *See also* fruit trees

Trent, Peterfield, 66

Trilingue dictionarium latinum, graecum, et gallicum (Fédéric Morel): ordered by TJ, 358

Trist, Eliza House: letters to, 155-6, 478-9; Monticello visit, 155, 478; as friend of Ceracchi, 200; letter from cited, 479n

Trist, Hore Browse, Jr.: TJ's friendship for, 478

Tronchin-Labat, Jean Armand, 191

Trumbull, John: letter from, 207; offers to forward correspondence, 201, 210, 455; reports conclusion of Jay Treaty, 207; portrait of Jefferson by, 544

Walker, Thomas, Jr.: letters to, 48, 227-8; identified, 48n; TJ's account with, 227-8; letters to cited, 228n

Waller, Benjamin Carter: letters to, 107, 180-1; letter from, 107-8; and Wayles estate debt, 107-8, 180-1; letter to cited, 181n

wallpaper: purchased for TJ, 246

Warden, John, 291n

Wardlaw, William: marriage of, 401; financial transactions, 410, 437, 593n

Ware, John: and settlement of TJ's account, 66

Warminster, Va.: market for TJ's nails at, 573

Warm Springs, Va.: barometric readings at, 597-8

Warnefridus. *See* Paulus Diaconus

Warre (Ware), John Tyndale: and case of J. Randolph's bond, 116n; TJ's account with, 322

Warsaw, Poland: Prussia lifts siege of, 172

Washington, Bushrod: letters to, 479-80, 497-8; letter from, 518-19; identified, 479-80n; praised by TJ, 283; as TJ's attorney, 345, 474n; supports Jay Treaty, 449; and suit against Henderson heirs, 479-80; and Banks's suit, 497-8, 518-19; letters from cited, 498n, 519n; letters to cited, 498n, 519n; and publication of Va. laws, 569, 585n

WASHINGTON, GEORGE: letters to, 74-5, 463-5; letters from, 3, 56-7, 275-8, 306-9, 321, 498-500; correspondence from Revolution published by J. Carey, 324

Agriculture
gives succory seed to TJ, 68-9; and O. Bertrand's agricultural prospectus, 74-5; attempts to grow the horse bean, 232; receives succory seed from A. Young, 232, 464; reports on crops at Mt. Vernon, 498-500

Opinions
on establishing a university, 275, 278, 306-8, 325; on republicanism and education, 308; attitude toward France, 567

Personal Affairs
receives figs from Gibraltar, 53; and Academy of Geneva, 124, 130, 133n, 208n, 269n, 274, 306-9, 315, 325; shares in canal companies, 275-8, 306-8, 325; and Ceracchi's monument, 304n, 348; introduces Strick-

land, 321; and Vall-Travers, 363-4; bound volumes of correspondence, 467; Bushrod Washington nephew of, 479n

President
and resignations, 3, 222n, 450-1n, 495-6; relations with E. Randolph, 4-5, 6, 450-1n, 511-12, 540, 547-8, 562, 563-5, 566; and relations with France, 22-3, 27, 70, 71n, 78-9, 80, 82, 83, 86-7, 578-9; sends correspondence and papers to Congress, 28n, 30, 31n, 47n, 84-5, 624n; and Indian treaties, 31n; and embargo powers, 38n, 44n; relations with Hamilton, 44, 52, 55, 564, 565n; and relations with Great Britain, 51, 566; appoints Jay envoy to Great Britain, 63n, 71, 563; popularity of, 73, 84, 92; and British in northwest, 84-6, 87; and standing army, 85, 202; and Republican politics, 86-7; and Monroe, 87, 100, 397-8n; offers TJ special envoyship to Spain, 117-19; sends agent to Ky., 117; 1794 annual address, 182-3, 202, 205, 212-13, 266-7; and Whiskey Insurrection, 182-3, 202-4, 548n; and American captives in Algiers, 188; and Jay Treaty, 205, 392n, 399-400, 422-3, 432-4, 435, 449, 450n, 457, 466, 476-7, 516-17, 545-8, 554-7, 558-9, 562, 564, 565, 567, 568-9, 601, 624; criticizes democratic societies, 212-13, 219, 359; reply to House of Representatives, 212-14; influence in Congress, 215, 250, 601; mentioned, 251; and Short's diplomatic career, 253-5, 445, 488-90, 493, 496, 497n; and Mme de Chastellux's application, 344, 498; Short's indiscreet comments about, 356n; ties to Federalists, 359-60, 607; and Proclamation of Neutrality, 433n; conduct evaluated, 534-6; and Cabinet vacancies, 542, 544-5; 1795 annual address, 545-8, 554-5, 562; influenced by northerners, 568; and case of Randall and Whitney, 576-8; and T. Paine, 577-8; celebration of birthday, 624

Relations with Jefferson
and TJ's retirement, 3; TJ's respect for, 148, 377, 565; TJ criticizes, 228-9, 466, 566-7; Rittenhouse forwards TJ's letter, 279; TJ quotes remark by, 565n

INDEX

A comprehensive index of Volumes 1-20 of the
First Series has been issued as Volume 21.
Each subsequent volume has its own index,
as does each volume or set of volumes
in the Second Series.